BOOKS BY RICHARD J. BARNET

The Rockets' Red Glare:
When America Goes to War
The Presidents and the People

The Alliance:
America-Europe-Japan
Makers of the Postwar World

Real Security:
Restoring American Power in a Dangerous Decade

The Lean Years:
Politics in the Age of Scarcity

The Giants:
Russia and America

Global Reach:
The Power of the Multinational Corporations
(with Ronald E. Müller)

Roots of War:
The Men and Institutions Behind U.S. Foreign Policy

The Economy of Death

Intervention and Revolution

After Twenty Years
(with Marcus Raskin)

Who Wants Disarmament?

RICHARD J. BARNET
JOHN CAVANAGH

SIMON & SCHUSTER

NEW YORK LONDON TORONTO SYDNEY TOKYO SINGAPORE

GLOBAL

IMPERIAL

CORPORATIONS

AND

THE NEW WORLD ORDER

DREAMS

SIMON & SCHUSTER
ROCKEFELLER CENTER
1230 AVENUE OF THE AMERICAS
NEW YORK, NEW YORK 10020

DESIGNED BY LEVAVI & LEVAVI
MANUFACTURED IN THE UNITED STATES OF AMERICA

10   9   8   7   6   5   4   3   2   1

LIBRARY OF CONGRESS CATALOGING-IN-PUBLICATION DATA

BARNET, RICHARD J.
    GLOBAL DREAMS : IMPERIAL CORPORATIONS AND THE NEW
WORLD ORDER /   RICHARD J. BARNET, JOHN CAVANAGH.
        P.   CM.
    INCLUDES BIBLIOGRAPHICAL REFERENCES AND INDEX.
    1. INTERNATIONAL BUSINESS ENTERPRISES—CASE
STUDIES. 2. ECONOMIC   HISTORY—1945–   I. CAVANAGH,
JOHN.   II. TITLE.
    HD2755.5.B378 1994   93-36362
    338.8'8—DC20   CIP

ISBN: 0-671-63377-5

FOR ANN AND ROBIN

ACKNOWLEDGMENTS

Many people in many different ways helped us with this book. We owe a special debt to Peter Andreas and Sarah Anderson, both energetic and able researchers who provided great help over the five years we have been working on this project. At various times we were also assisted by Karen Baker, Karan Capoor, Mark Chapman, David Douglass, Jason Duell, Diana Española, Christine Farrell, Anne Finn, Sandra Gross, Leanne Hong, Hsain Ilahiane, Farhana Khera, Neil Malik, Ruveni Pieris-Seneviratne, Philippa Rizopoulos, Shinjinee Sen, and Jeremy Weintraub. These interns at the Institute for Policy Studies came from many parts of the country and from a number of foreign countries, and their different perspectives were most helpful.

For setting up interviews and visits at Sony, we are particularly grateful to Jeannie Lo and Koh Shimizu. At Bertelsmann, Manfred Harnischfeger and Helmuth Runde were equally helpful as was Chris Vinyard at Ford.

Many individuals helped by sharing their files or supplying useful materials or opening new doors of inquiry: Marcos Arruda, Walden Bello, Patrick Bond, Corinne Canlas, Paul Carton, Fantu Cheru, Jeff Chester, Frederick Clairmonte, Suzanne Davis, Rob van Drimmelin, Richard Feinberg, Ping Ferry, Paul Garver, George Gerbner, Bill Goold, Robert Gottlieb, Pharis Harvey, Robert Herzstein, Michael Jacobsen, Morton Janklow, Josh Karliner, Martin Khor, Joyce and Gabriel Kolko, Jerome Levinson, David Londoner, Raul Madrid, Gisele Mills, Morton Mintz, Kathryn Montgomery, Richard O'Brien,

Michael Pertchuk, Clyde Prestowitz, Jeck Reyes, Joel Rocamora, Rustum Roy, Saskia Sassen, Herbert Schiller, Pam Sparr, Alberto Vitale, Peter Weiss, Phil Wilbur, and Richard Worthington.

A number of people have read all or parts of the manuscript and offered important suggestions: Ann Barnet, Steve Beckman, Edward Broad, Robin Broad, Nader Darehshori, Cam Duncan, Tom Engelhardt, Michael Gellert, Richard Healey, David Horowitz, Terry Kistler, David Korten, Saul Landau, Thea Lee, Michael diNovi, Dave Pedersen, Richard Pollay, Mark Ritchie, Jonathan Schell, Tom Schlesinger, Harley Shaiken, Michael Shuman, Robert Spero, and Howard Wachtel.

We wish also to thank Alice Mayhew, our editor, and Lynn Nesbit, our agent, for their support and guidance as well as our colleagues at the Institute for Policy Studies.

CONTENTS

Introduction: The Age of Globalization   13

PART ONE
GLOBAL IMAGES, GLOBAL BEAT   23

1. Global Dreams   25
2. The Technology of Pleasure   42
3. A Small Town Global Giant   68
4. Of the Making of Books   90
5. If Music Be the Food of Love   112
6. Global Entertainment and Local Taste   137

PART TWO
THE GLOBAL SHOPPING MALL   161

1. The Global Customer   163
2. Marlboro Country   184
3. The Global Grocer   208
4. A Matter of Taste   233

PART THREE

THE GLOBAL WORKPLACE 257

1. Mass Production in Postmodern Times 259
2. The New Division of Labor and the Global Job Crisis 283
3. The Transformed Workplace 310
4. Politics, Markets, and Jobs 339

PART FOUR

GLOBAL MONEY 359

1. Bankers in a World of Debt 361
2. Money Without a Home 385
3. Global Finance and America's Banking Crisis 403

Conclusion: Global Thinking in a Disorderly World 419
Notes 431
Selected Bibliography 459
Index 466

INTRODUCTION

THE AGE OF GLOBALIZATION

I.

A QUARTER CENTURY AGO, PICTURES TAKEN FROM SPACE OF a fragile blue ball swathed in a thin membrane of life-sustaining vapors altered forever the way we envision our planet. Spaceship Earth offered a unifying metaphor to awaken planetary consciousness. Today more and more human beings are in touch with one another than ever before. Billions more, without even knowing it, are becoming entangled across great distances in global webs that are transforming their lives.

The world is getting smaller, as people like to say, but it is not coming together. Indeed, as economies are drawn closer, nations, cities, and neighborhoods are being pulled apart. The processes of global economic integration are stimulating political and social disintegration. Family ties are severed, established authority is undermined, and the bonds of local community are strained. Like cells, nations are multiplying by dividing.

We are all participants in one way or another in an unprecedented political and economic happening, but we cannot make sense of it. We know that we are supposed to think globally, but it is hard to wrap the mind even around a city block, much less a planet. No wonder we are at the mercy of buzzwords and sound bites. "Globalization" is the most fashionable word of the 1990s, so portentous and wonderfully patient as to puzzle Alice in Wonderland and thrill the Red Queen because it means precisely whatever the user says it means. Just as poets and songwriters celebrated the rise of modern nationalism, so in our day corporate managers, environmental prophets, business philosophers, rock stars, and writers of advertising copy offer themselves as poet laureates of the global village. But much breathless talk about globalization we hear all around us is what the late Clare Boothe Luce used to call globaloney.

The emerging global order is spearheaded by a few hundred corporate giants, many of them bigger than most sovereign nations. Ford's economy is larger than Saudi Arabia's and Norway's. Philip Morris's annual sales exceed New Zealand's gross domestic product. The multinational corporation of twenty years ago carried on separate operations in many different countries and tailored its operations to local conditions. In the 1990s large business enterprises, even some smaller ones, have the technological means and strategic vision to burst old limits—of time, space, national boundaries, language, custom, and ideology. By acquiring earth-spanning technologies, by developing products that can be produced anywhere and sold everywhere, by spreading credit around the world, and by connecting global channels of communication that can penetrate any village or neighborhood, these institutions we normally think of as economic rather than political, private rather than public, are becoming the world empires of the twenty-first century. The architects and managers of these space-age business enterprises understand that the balance of power in world politics has shifted in recent years from territorially bound governments to companies that can roam the world. As the hopes and pretensions of government shrink almost everywhere, these imperial corporations are occupying public space and exerting a more profound influence over the lives of ever larger numbers of people.

II.

This book offers an angle of vision for viewing the transformed global economy. It is one way to think about what is happening to us. We focus on the struggles of some of the most dynamic corporations that are integrating the planet in the ordinary course of doing business. While hundreds of millions of people in the world are playing their part in creating the ties that bind across great distances, a few hundred business enterprises control the human energy, capital, and technology that are making it happen. They are the midwives of the new world economy.

Global corporations are the first secular institutions run by men (and a handful of women) who think and plan on a global scale. Things that managers of multinational companies dreamed of twenty years ago are becoming reality—Coca-Cola's ads that reach billions in the same instant, Citibank's credit cards for Asian yuppies, Nike's network for producing millions of sport shoes in factories others paid for. A relatively few companies with worldwide connections dominate the four intersecting webs of global commercial activity on which the new world economy largely rests: the Global Cultural Bazaar; the Global Shopping Mall; the Global Workplace; and the Global Financial Network.

These worldwide webs of economic activity have already achieved a degree of global integration never before achieved by any world empire or nation-state. The driving force behind each of them can be traced in large measure to the same few hundred corporate giants with headquarters in the United States, Japan, Germany, France, Switzerland, the Netherlands, and the United Kingdom. The combined assets of the top 300 firms now make up roughly a quarter of the productive assets in the world.[1]

The Global Cultural Bazaar is the newest of the global webs, and the most nearly universal in its reach. Films, television, radio, music, magazines, T-shirts, games, toys, and theme parks are the media for disseminating global images and spreading global dreams. Rock stars and Hollywood blockbusters are truly global products. All across the planet people are using the same electronic devices to watch or listen to the same commercially produced songs and stories. Thanks to satellite, cable, and tape recorders, even autocratic governments are losing the tight control they once had over the flow of information and their hold on the fantasy lives of their subjects.

Even in culturally conservative societies in what we still call the Third World the dinner hour is falling victim to television. In bars, teahouses, and cafés and in living quarters around the world the same absence of conversation and human interaction is noticeable as family members, singly or together, sit riveted in front of a cathode tube. As in the United States, Europe, and Japan, centuries-old ways of life are disappearing under the spell of advanced communication technologies. The cultural products most widely distributed around the world bear the stamp "Made in the U.S.A.," and almost any Hollywood film or video is bound to offend traditional values somewhere. Scenes depicting independent women, amorous couples, and kids talking back to parents upset all sorts of people across the globe as assaults on family, religion, and order. Because the steady streams of global commercial products in many places, including parts of the United States, are feared as barbarian intrusions, they are provoking local and nationalist backlashes, often carried out in the name of God.

Our look at the global communications and entertainment industry, orchestrators of a new world culture, focuses on two media giants, Bertelsmann, originally a German printer and publisher, and Sony, an innovative Japan-based electronics hardware company now at the center of the global film and music business. We explore how these firms navigated the shoals of global competition with Philips, Time Warner, Matsushita, and the other giants and how globally distributed commercial cultural products are changing the ways we see, hear, and think.

The Global Shopping Mall is a planetary supermarket with a dazzling spread of things to eat, drink, wear, and enjoy. We will explore the rise of global advertising, distribution, and marketing and examine their impacts. Dreams of affluent living are communicated to the farthest reaches of the globe, but only a minority of the people in the world can afford to shop at the Mall. Of the 5.4 billion people on earth, almost 3.6 billion have neither cash nor credit to buy much of anything. A majority of people on the planet are at most window-shoppers.

Our discussion of the marketing of global products focuses on the Philip Morris story for two reasons. First, the company produces Marlboros, the world's biggest-selling brand-name product, one so deadly that it is forcing the company into a global strategy of transformation. In the process, Philip Morris now challenges Nestlé and Unilever as the world's largest food company at a time when the globalization of food production, distribution, and marketing is changing eating habits all over the world and transforming national economies.

The Global Workplace is a network of factories, workshops, law offices, hospitals, restaurants, and all sorts of other places where goods are produced, information is processed, and services of every description are rendered. Everything from cigarettes to cars contains materials from dozens of countries pieced together in a globally integrated assembly line driven by the logic of the bottom line. Data processors, law offices, advertising agencies, and insurance companies have become global assembly lines of a different sort. A world-wide labor market for creative merchandising ideas, computer knowledge, patient fingers, managerial know-how, and every other marketable skill coexists with a global labor pool in which more and more of us, from the chief executive officer to the wastebasket emptier, are swimming. Hundreds of millions more of the world's uprooted and dispossessed are desperate to jump in.

The Ford Motor Company played an historic role in the development of mass production, and in many ways it is the American-based automaker that has most successfully adapted to the post-mass-production era, the most avid in trying to develop a car that can be sold anywhere in the world, and the most resourceful in making transnational alliances with its Japanese competitors. The pressures on Ford and its competitors to cut labor costs have had a profound effect on the world labor market. A look at a range of other industries, too, including clothing, information processing, and electronics, brings the true dimensions of the global job crisis into sharper focus. We examine evidence from around the world on the impact of population pressures, automation, and the global reorganization of work on job prospects everywhere. There is much data that point to a stark reality: A huge and increasing proportion of human beings are not needed and will never be needed to make goods or to provide services because too many people in the world are too poor to buy them.

The Global Financial Network is a constantly changing maze of currency transactions, global securities, MasterCards, euroyen, swaps, ruffs, and an ever more innovative array of speculative devices for repackaging and reselling money. This network is much closer to a chain of gambling casinos than to the dull gray banks of yesteryear. Twenty-four hours a day, trillions of dollars flow through the world's major foreign-exchange markets as bits of data traveling at split-second speed.[2] No more than 10 percent of this staggering sum has anything to do with trade in goods and services.[3] International traffic in money has become an end in itself, a highly profitable game. John Maynard Keynes, who had intimations of how technology might one day be harnessed in the service of nonrecreational gambling, predicted the rise of this "casino economy," as he called it. Yet as banking activities have become more global and more speculative, the credit needs of billions of people and millions of small businesses are not met.

We picked Citicorp, the largest bank based in the United States, as the window through which to explore the rapidly changing world of finance not only because Citi is a venerable institution that keeps reinventing itself as the global economy changes, but because it has been an innovator in overcoming the barriers to global banking. We explore the political and social implications of globalization of financial markets and the fierce competition among U.S. banks and their much larger competitors based in Japan and Europe.

Viewed together, these four webs offer a picture very different from that of a global village. The Global Cultural Bazaar is reaching the majority of households with its global dreams. Much smaller numbers are playing any role at all in the three networks that produce, market, and finance the world's goods and services. In the new world economy, there is a huge gulf between the beneficiaries and the excluded and, as world population grows, it is widening.

III.

We have made a point of picking innovative companies that are leaders in their industries. With the conspicuous exception of Philip Morris's cigarette business, which the company promotes with a disregard for health and truth, these companies are a positive social force in many ways. They make things millions of people want. They are more environmentally conscious than many, although by virtue of the scale of their operations they are significant polluters and gobblers of natural resources. They treat their employees decently and pay well in most cases. In interviews with top executives at Bertelsmann, Sony, and Ford—Philip Morris and Citicorp declined to cooperate in the project—we encountered executives of broad vision and understanding of global issues that affect their markets. Their capacity for global thinking struck us as far more developed than that exhibited by most officials of national governments. But they do not appear to dwell much on the long-term social or political consequences of what their companies make or what they do. The combined negative impact of corporate activities on the job market or the environment or education or family life is regarded as beyond their power to address and therefore not within their province.

This book is not an exposé of rapacious corporations, corporate greed, or corporate corruption. Had this been our aim, we would have picked any number of other companies to study. Rather, our objective was to look at some of the winners in the fight for global markets in order better to understand the global system that is being created and where it is going.

The most disturbing aspect of this system is that the formidable power and mobility of global corporations are undermining the effectiveness of national governments to carry out essential policies on behalf of their people. Leaders of nation-states are losing much of the control over their own territory they once had. More and more, they must conform to the demands of the outside world because the outsiders are already inside the gates. Business enterprises that routinely operate across borders are linking far-flung pieces of territory into a new world economy that bypasses all sorts of established political arrangements and conventions. Tax laws intended for another age, traditional ways to control capital flows and interest rates, full-employment policies, and old approaches to resource development and environmental protection are becoming obsolete, unenforceable, or irrelevant.

National leaders no longer have the ability to comprehend, much less control, these giants because they are mobile, and like the mythic Greek figure Proteus they are constantly changing appearances to suit different circumstances. The shifting relationships between the managers of global corporations and political authorities are creating a new political reality almost everywhere.

An extraordinary global machine has been developed to make, sell, and service commodities and to render all manner of services, but no political ideology or economic theory has yet evolved to take account of the tectonic shift that has occurred. The modern nation-state, that extraordinary legacy of Madison, Napoleon, Bolívar, Lincoln, Bismarck, Wilson, Roosevelt, Stalin, Mao, Nehru, Kenyatta, and the millions all over the world who have sacrificed and died for it, looks more and more like an institution of a bygone age. In much of Asia, Africa, and Latin America, the state is collapsing under the weight of debt, bloated bureaucracy, and corruption. Local peoples' movements and surprisingly sophisticated informal economic arrangements, many of them off the books and beyond the reach of government, are growing up to fill the vacuum. The United States, although still the largest national economy and by far the world's greatest military power, is increasingly subject to the vicissitudes of a world economy no nation can dominate. Foreign trade and investment have become much more important to the U.S. economy. A generation ago the sum of all U.S. exports and imports amounted to around 10 percent of the gross national product. Today it is more than 25 percent.[4] In the process, the economic health of the United States has become increasingly at the mercy of decisions of foreign corporations, banks, governments, and investors.

However, the nation-state is far from disappearing. On the contrary, the Cold War victory has unleashed a revival of nationalism, a bloody nightmare in the Balkans that is a prototype of the national-security crises of the 1990s. Every ethnic group and religious faction, it seems, wants its own national banner. National governments everywhere are getting bigger, but are neither more effective nor popular. In Ronald Reagan's America and Margaret Thatcher's Britain, the size and budget of the state expanded even as these leaders denounced government and preached "privatization." It is altogether obvious that what governments do or fail to do is still important. Politicians and generals determine when and where the dogs of war are unleashed, not corporate chairmen or commodity traders. National governments, acting either unilaterally or in concert, still set the rules under which the world economy functions, and national policies for economic development continue to exert a profound influence on the competitive positions of particular corporations. But the nation-state everywhere faces a crisis of redefinition without a practical ideology that confronts the realities of the emerging global order.

As the twentieth century draws to a close, much of the official truth that sustained and guided governments for fifty years or more has collapsed and new political visions are in short supply. The repudiation of socialism is of course the most spectacular ideological turnabout of the 1990s, but the inexorable intrusions of a world economy over which national governments exercise diminishing control have drained other established political orthodoxies of meaning and power. Like Leninism, Keynesianism was premised on the idea that national economies were real. Within the borders of a nation-state, at least within militarily powerful, advanced industrial nations, government could provide economic stability, development, and social progress. The Leninists believed they could accomplish these worthy objectives through state planning and a command economy. The Keynesians thought it could all be done more humanely by more modest government intervention in the marketplace, essentially by adjusting interest and tax rates and by well-targeted government spending.

What it takes to manage a successful national economy in the new global environment to achieve stability and growth without destroying people, crushing their spirit, or wrecking the environment is as yet unknown. Political programs can stimulate short-term booms, but all across the political spectrum long-term economic management has become a mystery since nothing quite works as theory predicts. Juggling interest rates and exchange rates, raising and lowering taxes, all produce unwelcome surprises. As politicians across the political spectrum are learning, staking one's reputation on promises of prosperity is not the best way to get your name emblazoned on a bridge. The same global economic changes that hastened the breakdown of the Cold War order are still straining nations everywhere.

The ideas for navigating the transition to the postnational order that beckons as the only apparent alternative to anarchic disorder and the breakup of nations are not likely to originate in corporate boardrooms. The interests and self-defined responsibilities of corporate leaders are global but parochial; their eyes are on the global market, but most of the world's people remain invisible. Hundreds of millions are now residents in the global village being created by the great corporations, but billions more are not and have no such prospects. "Going global" is a strategy for picking and choosing from a global menu. Vast areas of the world and the people who live there are written off. Contrast corporate globalism with past notions of world civilization. Even when they espoused a universal spirit, aspiring world cultures were rooted in particular places. Athens. Rome. Constantinople. But the ideology of the age of globalization celebrates the liberation from passionate attachments to any specific piece of territory. This is quite different from the universal consciousness of which poets, philosophers, and prophets have dreamed through the ages.

IV.

As the processes of globalization accelerate, the more conscious we become of the pull of localism in all its forms. For most people across the world, place and rootedness are as important as ever. Their very identity is tied to a place, and they cannot conceive of living anywhere else, for they are dependent on a piece of ground for their livelihood and on a particular culture and language for their sense of well-being. For them the forces of globalization are a threat. Hundreds of millions of people over the last generation have been up-rooted from the land because of the spread of export agriculture or industrial development, or they have been drawn to the city by the pull of urban life. But unlike peripatetic lawyers, executives, rock stars, and other jet-age nomads who see the world as a giant menu of personal and professional choices, most of these people have no better prospects than marginal employment in the capital city or a life of insecurity in a faraway land. As people migrate to the great cities of the world, largely in response to global economic and cultural integration in its various forms, old ways of life, family traditions, child-rearing practices, and local authority structures are swept away. All this is creating a crisis not just of politics but of culture.

Global integration has many positive aspects that we will explore throughout this book, but in the late twentieth century there is strong evidence that, as national economies become increasingly intertwined, nations are breaking up in many different ways, and no alternative community is yet on the horizon. For some regions and city blocks all around the world, globalization brings unparalleled prosperity. For others on another continent or just across town the consequence may be crushing poverty. The inhabitants of a penthouse apartment on the Upper East Side of Manhattan are drawn by taste, style, habit, and outlook into a closer relationship with similarly situated citizens of Brussels, Rio, or Tokyo and further and further away from poorer, less mobile residents who may live a block or two away.

As traditional communities disappear and ancient cultures are overwhelmed, billions of human beings are losing the sense of place and sense of self that give life meaning. The fundamental political conflict in the opening decades of the new century, we believe, will not be between nations or even between trading blocs but between the forces of globalization and the territorially based forces of local survival seeking to preserve and to redefine community.

PART ONE

GLOBAL IMAGES, GLOBAL BEAT

CHAPTER 1

GLOBAL DREAMS

I.

UNLIKE AMERICAN AUTOMOBILES, TELEVISION SETS, AND machine tools, American cultural products—movies, TV programs, videos, records, cassettes, and CDs—are sweeping the globe. Reruns of *Dallas* and the *Cosby* show fill TV screens on every continent. The 1990 fairy-tale hit *Pretty Woman* became the all-time best-selling film in Sweden and Israel within weeks of its release. Disneyland is now a global empire; its Japanese incarnation outside Tokyo draws 300,000 visitors a week, and Euro Disneyland, a theme park on the outskirts of Paris occupying space one-fifth the size of the city itself, eventually hopes to draw more tourists than the Eiffel Tower, Sistine Chapel, British Museum, and the Swiss Alps combined.

In 1989 packaged cultural products netted a U.S. trade surplus of some $8 billion, which made entertainment the third-largest surplus item that year, right after food and aerospace products.[1] Include such mythic amenities of American life and leisure as McDonald burgers (teriyaki burgers in Japan), Coke, Levis, Marlboros, and a variety of licensed spin-offs from films, TV, and sports—Teenage Mutant Ninja Turtle bubble bath was a planetary hit a few years back—and the conclusion is inescapable: The American dream is the nation's number-one export.

A new division of labor is taking place across the planet. Despite the revival of some U.S. hardware exports in the 1990s, what we once called "durables"—that old-fashioned word used to describe the washing machines, refrigerators, and electronic equipment on which the American economy rose to world preeminence—are mostly made elsewhere. The products of the global commercial-culture industry look, feel, and sound American. But dreams are evanescent, and the products that embody them usually have short lives. The turnover in Levis is more rapid than in automobiles, and a compact disc, though said to be more or less indestructible, soon sits on the shelf while the latest hit is being played. Meanwhile the refrigerator keeps running. The market for cultural products is totally dependent upon what economists call "discretionary income," but the term understates the compulsion teenagers feel as they are carried on waves of peer pressure into the local movie theater or music shop.

It is now obvious that you do not have to be American to sell American culture. Japanese corporations have bought major Hollywood studios and are looking for more. Only three of America's largest studios are still U.S. companies. Six global corporations dominate the popular-music industry, not only in the United States but across the world. These "six sovereign states of pop music," as one student of the industry puts it, supply almost every record in most stores in the United States, and "there is virtually no American pop singer or rock band of national stature that a major does not, in one way or another, have a piece of."[2] But only one of the six, Warner, is still a U.S. company. Bertelsmann, a German media company, owns among other labels RCA and Arista records in the United States. Sony owns Sony Music, formerly known as CBS Records. The other three are Thorn-EMI, a successful British electronics firm and defense contractor, PolyGram, a London-based division of Philips, the Dutch electronics giant, and MCA, now owned by the Japanese electronics giant Matsushita.[3]

Popular culture caught the imagination of investors in the boom years of the 1980s. In the last two years of the decade alone, according to the management-consulting firm McKinsey & Co., about $80 billion was spent on takeovers in the entertainment industry.[4] In 1989 the global entertainment industry generated about $150 billion in worldwide sales. Growth in global entertainment revenues slowed in the recession years all around the world, but even so about half the revenues earned by American films and records were generated outside the United States.[5]

The spectacular growth of global commercial entertainment has inspired a number of explanations. The role of technology has clearly been important. Consider the music industry. In the 1970s just as sales of vinyl records flattened, the market for the newly developed audiocassette exploded as portable boom boxes arrived on beaches, on inner-city streets, and in suburban teenagers' bedrooms, and people of all ages wired themselves up to their Walkmans. Then came the compact disc, and no lover of crackle-free sound could afford to be without it. Then the music video neatly inverted an older technology, and fans could now listen to songs with sight tracks. Much as in the shaving-products industry, the prices of the electronic machines to play tapes, CDs, and videos fell rapidly while the prices of the "blades"—even when discounted—stayed high.

The same pattern developed with respect to visual images. The wiring of the world through cable TV and fiber-optic technologies and the instantaneous global transmission of pictures, talk, and music by satellite greatly accelerated the spread of a global market for movies, videos, and TV programs. The VCR turned homes, bars, day-care centers, buses, waiting rooms, and nursing homes into a global chain of movie theaters. On the remote island of Siquijor in the Philippines, the inhabitants still gather at the "The Hangout" to eat halo-halo (chopped ice, corn flakes, fruit, and beans) and watch *Rambo* on videotape. In Colombia, long-distance buses keep their avid all-night movie fans on the edges of their seats (and the others grumpily awake) with *Robocop*. Hours once written off as commercially irrelevant were suddenly transformed into marketable time; insomniacs, housebound invalids, children with enough disposable income to rent a film, and couch potatoes of every variety could thrust a videocassette into their VCR at any time of the day or night. Old television programs and movies bounce off satellites or travel by cable into homes, schools, and prisons around the world, achieving a certain immortality previously denied to most cultural products. Not many dead poets, pundits, or even departed best-selling novelists last long on the shelf, but thanks to videotape and the near-universal hunger for American movies, music, and TV programs, dead rock stars and movie actors go on forever.

A second explanation for the global explosion in the entertainment business has to do with economies of scale. In its study *Globalization of the Media Industry*, McKinsey & Co. concludes that music companies can recover their costs for developing artists and purchasing the rights to songs only by extending the life of their products through space and time. Companies are driven to ever greater vertical and horizontal integration in the increasingly fierce fight over market shares, which McKinsey & Co. pronounces "the one and only game in town."[6] "Going global" is an economic imperative in the movie industry too. Since only 20 percent of films earn back their investment at theaters in the United States, profits for big, expensive productions increasingly depend on reaching worldwide audiences. A film that costs $30 million to make can expect to earn $13 million at the box office in the United States and more than $15 million from foreign box offices, cable, video, and prime-time network showings. As the potential audience expands, so do promotion costs, and so the drive to extend the life of cultural products becomes ever stronger. Whether a movie ever turns a profit—and only about four out of ten do—depends on the "ancillaries," as the industry terms these global opportunities to squeeze new life out of mostly forgettable films. The increasing dependence on a global market affects the content of films as well, especially the increasing use of the universal language of violence.

A third set of explanations for the bonanza in an industry built entirely on discretionary spending is based on cheery projections about spare time. Nonworking hours are increasing for all sorts of contradictory reasons all across the globe. Some people have stopped working a forty-hour week because they don't need to. They make enough money working less, or they have enough money to retire. Others are forced into retirement and still larger numbers have hours to fill because they cannot find steady work. To be sure, millions of others are working harder than ever. In *The Overworked American*, Juliet Schor documented the expansion of work time and the erosion of leisure hours in the United States over the past twenty years. More and more husbands and wives are forced to work harder to support the family, and many couples hold more than one job apiece to make ends meet. But the overworked are also entertainment consumers, collapsing with a beer or a snack in front of the tube at the end of a long day.

A fourth explanation for the bull market in entertainment is global demographic change. Paradoxically, commercially relevant segments of the world population are getting younger and older at the same time. In the United States, as in other advanced industrial countries with near-zero or negative birthrates, the population is aging. About one-eighth of Americans will be 65 or older by the year 2000.[7] In retirement many are looking for ways to enjoy the leisure hours for which they worked hard all their lives, and the entertainment and leisure industries offer a cornucopia of time-filling products. But thanks to continued high birth rates in less-developed countries and dramatically improved infant-survival rates over the last twenty years due to advances in public health, the world as a whole is getting younger. The "global teenager" and the "global preteenager" are also prime targets of the entertainment conglomerates. In the United States almost a quarter of the record-buying public is between the ages of 10 and 19.[8] About 78 percent of record buyers are below 35, and what they buy is pop in its various genres. In a good year Walt Disney sells $1.5 billion worth of watches, hats, and comic books in Japan alone.

II.

In 1990, according to the World Tourism Organization of the United Nations, 429 million people—almost 8 percent of the global population—traveled from one country to another as tourists.[9] The democratization of travel is a recent development. Seeing the world is no longer the exclusive prerogative of soldiers, sailors, traveling salesmen, a few professors, and a small leisure class. But even today most people in the world never leave their own countries. Indeed, it is still the case that hundreds of millions of people never venture beyond their own villages.

However, enough people with enough money are traveling abroad and within their own countries to make the global mass tourist industry—unknown before World War II when few but the rich could "tour"—the world's largest employer.[10] The global stock of lodging, restaurant, and transportation facilities is estimated to be worth about $3 trillion, and one out of every fifteen workers across the planet spends the day transporting, feeding, housing, herding, cosseting, or amusing tourists.[11]

In 1990, consumers in the world's industrial countries spent $232 billion on tourism. In the developed world traveling for fun is the third-largest household expense after food and housing. Americans spend most of their tourism dollars at home seeing America first and last. Just about 10 percent of the population have passports. But tourists from Europe and Japan are heading for international airports, international highways, and border-crossing trains in ever larger numbers.

For many nations across the world the major "export" never leaves the country; their prime source of foreign exchange is a variety of touristic experiences for foreign travelers. Tours of cathedrals and museums, trips to mountains and lakes, and visits to game parks are packaged and promoted to draw desperately needed dollars, marks, francs, and yen from an ever larger number of tourists. However, thanks to the global financial network and the development of local tourist facilities all around the world by global airlines and hotel chains, prepaid, all-expenses-included tours in which the dollars end up in London or New York rather than in the exotic vacationland itself are cutting into the foreign-exchange earnings of some under-developed countries.

One consequence of all this wanderlust is the degradation of the natural environment. Congestion has turned a visit to Yosemite National Park into something resembling a freeway experience. Famous wildlife preserves such as Amboselli National Park in Kenya have been torn up by safari vehicles and by elephants trying to get out of their way. Lake Como is polluted. The glorious prehistoric cave paintings at Lascaux were closed to the public many years ago to save them from tourist hordes whose breath was literally dissolving them.

As the enjoyment of natural public space—mountains, lakes, and forests—becomes more difficult, the market for leisure experiences in private space has grown. Entrepreneurs all over the world are creating climate-controlled alternatives to the natural environment where crowds are pampered and protected from inclement weather, panhandlers, and pickpockets. (In its ads Euro Disney promotes its hotels, furnished with homey fireplaces, as a refuge from the cold and drizzle of a Paris afternoon.) The contemporary theme park is a world's fair that is never over, an amusement park, a giant boutique, and a resort all wrapped up in one. These fragments of exotic cultures blended into a variety of safe, predictable experiences are popping up everywhere, local expressions of an idealized, fun-filled global village. Theme parks offer carefully packaged simulated experiences with the look and feel of a mythic past or a fabulous future, and they are luring travelers from every corner of the globe.

The ancestors of the contemporary theme park include the medieval carnival, the eighteenth-century English pleasure garden, and the elaborate European centers of family entertainment such as the Prater in Vienna and the Tivoli Gardens in Copenhagen. Disney World and its imitators can be thought of as direct descendants of the urban amusement parks that flourished all across the United States—there were between 1,500 and 2,000 of them in 1919—and the nineteenth-century international exposition. For more than a hundred years Americans have excelled in putting on extravaganzas to attract tourists. Coney Island in New York became a magnet for millions of tourists in the late nineteenth century. Between 1876 and 1916 almost 100 million people from all over the United States and Europe visited international expositions in Philadelphia, New Orleans, Buffalo, Seattle, and eight other American cities.[12] They came to get a feel for Americana and to see the new industrial technology on display, to let their imaginations soar at the prospect of a new civilization in the making, and, whether they were aware of it or not, to be instructed in what Henry Adams called "the religion of World's Fairs."[13]

Global entertainment centers for the twenty-first century have been constructed in the last few years in all sorts of surprising places. Outside Cairo a half-day's camel ride beyond the Sphinx, a watery oasis is rising from the desert. Crazy Water features fifty-foot water slides and body surfing in a special pool designed for desert conditions that even makes its own waves. Thousands of gallons of water are trucked in daily from the Nile. Nippon Steel Corporation built Space World on the site of a closed steel plant on the island of Kyushu; it features world-class scary rides and the chance to feel what it is like to walk in space. In Romania the tourist office is trying to turn Transylvania into a huge theme park by promoting a "Dracula tour." "I have read *Dracula*, and it is a stupid book, full of lies," a Romanian museum curator told the *Wall Street Journal*. "But let us be realistic. Why else would anyone visit Transylvania?"

Matsushita's MCA has made a theme park out of Universal Studios in Hollywood and, with expert directorial advice from Steven Spielberg, opened another Hollywood extravaganza in Orlando in direct competition with Disney. MCA plans to take on Disney in Tokyo and Europe as well using its heavy artillery, *E.T.* and *King Kong*. The city of Surajkund in India is planning "a whole integrated concept of a fun center" with a hall of science, a replica of an ethnic village, and a monorail. Heritage USA, once part of Jim Bakker's Praise the Lord television ministry, still operates a 2,200-acre "Christian theme park" just south of Charlotte, North Carolina. Lego has a theme park made entirely of its famous snap-together blocks right outside the company headquarters in Billund, Denmark. Maharishi Mahesh Yogi, the Indian guru who popularized transcendental meditation, is investing $1 billion in yet another park near Orlando; the guru promises that Maharishi Vedaland, which will feature the Garden of Illusions and the Forest of Knowledge, is to be the first of a chain.[14]

Theme parks attract a huge clientele because they combine the thrill of new experience with the convenience and safety of a mall. The climate is controlled. The nearby city may be polluted, but there are no noxious odors here. The security within the gates inspires more confidence than one has on the streets outside. Strange languages and unfamiliar customs pose no problem. The staff knows what to expect. Above all, the water in the drinking fountains is clean and gentle to the stomach and there are plenty of restrooms. Sightseeing can be interspersed with a swim at adjacent hotels. Inside the park, restaurants of every variety beckon. The rides offer a range of experiences—things to feel, touch, and smell as well as see and hear—and an immediacy that film, video, and music by themselves cannot match. The promotional message is clear: Wherever you are, you can visit the Old World or the New without the risk, inconvenience, or expense of actually going there.

The world leader in the business is Disney, which opened the original Disneyland in Anaheim, California, in 1955. Its theme song, "It's a Small World After All," promoted an idealized vision of America spiced with reassuring glimpses of exotic cultures all calculated to promote heartwarming feelings about living together as one happy family. There were dark tunnels and bumpy rides to scare the children a little but none of the terrors of the real world. You could take a Mark Twain riverboat to a Frontierland that never was, and feel safe, dazzled, and uplifted. The Disney characters that everyone knew from the cartoons and comic books were on hand to shepherd the guests and to direct them to the Mickey Mouse watches and Little Mermaid records.

Disney repeated its Southern California triumph in Florida in the 1970s. Disney World, a nostalgic recreation of Main Street combined with a futuristic Epcot Center featuring Spaceship Earth, rose amid the citrus groves outside Orlando, and soon this once-sleepy grapefruit depot became the greatest single tourist attraction in the United States. In 1990, 28.5 million visitors descended on it, more than all the visitors to Britain that year. Indeed, by one estimate, this one-park complex became the fourth-largest tourist attraction in the world after France, Spain, and the United States.[15]

In 1983 the company opened Tokyo Disneyland. More than 15 million visitors a year now visit the park, about a million more ticket buyers than at the original Disneyland at Anaheim, California, and the "economic ripple effect," according to the Mitsubishi Research Institute, approaches $6.3 billion, about the value of Japan's entire annual export of cameras. Plans are under way for another park next door.

In a sugar-beet field twenty miles to the east of Paris, Euro Disneyland opened in the spring of 1992. This $5-billion splash offers Main Street, Adventure Island, Mickey Mouse, and many other tried-and-true recreations of Americana packaged in the Disney style. Disney "imagineers," as they call themselves, replicated their time-tested exhibits with only the most trivial modifications to "Europeanize" the product. Snow White speaks in German. Discoveryland features a trip to the past and future with Jules Verne, a nod to French culture intended to make French families feel better about the American invaders. But the clean collegiate 1950s look of the "cast," to which everyone from the clowns to the popcorn vendors belongs, the stiff prices, and the no-alcohol rule Disney adheres to irrespective of local custom all served as red capes to enrage Parisian bulls. (There are millions of Frenchmen who still blame *le snackbar* for destroying lunch as a social institution.)

From the first, Disney and Paris seemed like an improbable match. When Robert Fitzpatrick, the head of the Euro Disneyland project, announced his plans in 1987 at a press conference in front of the Bourse, he was greeted by a volley of eggs and tomatoes. Parisian intellectuals attacked the transplantation of Disney's dream world as an assault on French culture; "a cultural Chernobyl," one prominent theater director called it.[16] The minister of culture boycotted the opening, proclaiming it to be an unwelcome symbol of "the America of clichés and a consumer society."[17]

"Why did they pick on France?" many asked. When the word was out that Disney was about to launch its most ambitious global attraction yet, officials from more than 200 localities all over the world descended on the company with pleas and cash inducements to work the Disney magic in their hometowns. But Paris was chosen because of demographics and subsidies. About 17 million Europeans live less than two hours away from Paris by car, and 310 million can fly there in the same time or less. The French government was so eager that Paris be Disney's European home that it made the company an offer it could not refuse. Jacques Chirac, the mayor of Paris who was also serving as prime minister at the time, came up with more than $1 billion in cash contributions, incentives, and long-term low-interest loans in the expectation that the project would create 30,000 French jobs.

In the summer of 1992, shortly after the park opened, French farmers drove their tractors up to the entrance to Euro Disneyland and blocked it. This globally televised act of protest was directed against the U.S. government for demanding that French agricultural subsidies be cut, but it focused world attention on the loveless marriage of Disneyland and Paris. The early crowds proved thinner than expected, and the local press could not conceal its delight that the French were resisting Disney's relentless cheer and market-tested thrills. Company officials had predicted a certain amount of Mickey Mouse bashing. The fear of "cultural penetration" was inevitable because the Disney culture is so uncompromisingly American.

But that is precisely its attraction. In its exhibits and merchandise Disney is selling a version of the American dream featuring universal themes of love and adventure seen through unmistakably American eyes. Disney officials knew that this is exactly the experience large numbers of non-Americans want. They are still betting that the disdain of the cultural arbiters who write columns or talk on television will sooner or later be rejected by the French public, who are as beguiled by the American dream as any people. For all the articles in *Le Monde* attacking American TV, French television and movie theaters are excellent customers of Hollywood products. Each month millions of French children read *Le Journal du Mickey*.[18]

Theme parks are educational experiences. Parents consider Disney creations "wholesome entertainment," a painless way to expose children to the larger world and a welcome alternative to television. In some parks the appeal is explicitly instructional. Japanese parents can take their children to a magic world of learning inspired by *Sesame Street*. Gold Rush City in California is a sprawling historical pageant. Disneyland and its progeny offer glimpses of science and nature. But what do people learn?

The forerunners of the theme park were, as Robert W. Rydell has shown in his history of early American expositions, explicitly intended to exert a "moral influence" on the millions of visitors who came. "Expositions are the timekeepers of progress," declared President William McKinley at the Pan-American Exposition at Buffalo in 1901 a few hours before he was shot.[19] The designers of the early world's fairs had lessons they wished to impart—views of empire, views of science, views of racial superiority, and views of what constitutes progress. Government played a major role in planning, designing, and financing world's fairs. They were selling the United States, the American way of life, and of course American products.

The lessons at Disneyland are different. To be sure, the patriotic, often idealized, picture of America's past is an indispensable part of the experience, but the blend of reality and fantasy is not overtly didactic. Theme parks are mood enhancers. The object is to have a good time. The customer buys forty-eight hours of diversion that require more active participation than watching television, but not too much more. Like the crowds at the great expositions in St. Louis and Buffalo a hundred years ago, Disney's customers come from all over the world to be astonished by virtuoso technology. But now, it can make the Wild West live again and bring the stars so close you can touch them. Theme parks offer illusions of connectedness while providing protected private space and canned dreams.

Hundreds of millions of people are popping in and out of these fantasy worlds at a moment in history when the traditional eighteenth- and nineteenth-century visions of human interconnectedness seemingly lie in tatters. Nation-states are coming apart because they cannot make good on social contracts, as Rousseau envisaged, and the confederation of nations into a world order of perpetual peace of which Kant dreamed still seems far away. A Hegelian world spirit to bind all humanity has yet to appear, and Marxist notions of class solidarity seem quaint. The global environmental movement is theoretically based on a powerful unifying theme, but as a practical matter it is badly divided. There are beginnings of new global citizens networks that are fighting rain-forest destruction, toxic waste trade, cigarette marketing, and unsustainable development models, but their numbers are still small. Little remains to explain, much less promote, global interconnectedness other than the great world religions, which, in their doctrines at least, offer a global vision. Perhaps archaeologists digging in the Florida swamps and in the marshes outside Paris and Tokyo a thousand years from now will conclude that they have found traces of another.

III.

In the small Philippine city of Balanga, a stopping point along the Bataan Death March in World War II, the local bakeshop features Teenage Mutant Ninja Turtles and Bugs Bunny birthday cakes. Why do so many millions of people around the world spend so much of their time and money on records, videos, T-shirts, and an infinite variety of other spin-offs from American dreams? What is it about the distinctive grammar of American pop culture that accounts for its extraordinary hold on the popular imagination all across the world?

Americans have been the pioneer exporters of commercial culture. The global distribution of mass entertainment was first developed by Hollywood studios and the U.S. record industry, and no other country has come close to matching the outpouring of cultural products from the United States that began in the early decades of this century. The Indian film industry is now by far the largest in the world, but it has no significant global market except among Indians abroad. The world standard has been defined and set by Americans, and nowhere else do writers, producers, and artists meet that standard so well. In the years of the American Century the power, wealth, luxury, and the sense of possibility and personal freedom symbolized by the United States and reflected in its music, video, and film products fascinated people all over the world—even where American culture was officially denounced as decadent, subversive, or silly. The efforts of authoritarian governments to erect walls against the penetration of American dreams and the American fun culture actually promoted their spread. Despite the worldwide publicity about violence, homelessness, and declining standards in the United States in the years since the Cold War ended, the American myth, projected across the world by a flow of Hollywood films, records, and television programs, continues to draw millions to American shores. Hundreds of millions more can make the trip vicariously in front of a VCR or boom box.

Ironically, the world power with the greatest investment in the status quo, the one that has been willing to spend its blood and treasure for almost fifty years battling revolutions and insurgencies around the world, is spreading messages of rebellion through its cultural products. As a leading arts critic in Japan puts it, "the image of America radiates unlimited freedom." Japanese are attracted to American movies because Hollywood formulas and film technique, more daring, more lavish, and less formalistic than movie-making conventions elsewhere, offer the illusion of escape from their regimented, workaholic society. Rebellion against parents, against nameless authority, old ways, humdrum lives, against old men who send young men to war are insistent themes in lyrics, video, and film. A pop song can carry an anxious 12-year-old from the slum streets of

Rio to a fantasy world of luxury and thrills. Alex Ayuli, a member of the English band Lush, calls the group's music "dream pop." "It's kind of a nihilistic thing, a way for kids to get away from this horrible English life; it allows you to lose yourself in music and get away from your factory job."[20] Or you can lie on a straw mat on the dirt floor of a Bangkok shanty listening to Michael Jackson and imagine yourself living another life. You can see yourself eating breakfast in the gadget-filled kitchen where Hollywood sitcoms are shot. The film director Milos Forman explains it this way: "People love fairy tales and there is no country that does them better than the United States. . . . Every child dreams to be a prince; every adult has a secret closet dream to be Rambo and kill your enemy. . . ." (One of the most famous and feared leaders of the death squads in Colombia called himself Rambo.)

John Micklethwait, writing in the *Economist,* concludes that "entertainment has replaced its most potent rival for human emotion, religion, as the opium of the masses."[21] But religion and entertainment have always had a complex relationship. In the 1960s the Beatles scandalized the faithful by announcing that they were more famous than Jesus Christ and thereby became even more famous. The religious movements that gained adherents in the United States in the 1980s did so in large measure by incorporating themes and techniques of the popular culture into their ritual. The success of showbiz religion in the 1980s—Jerry Falwell, Jimmy Swaggart, Pat Robertson's *700 Club*—and the strangely entrancing mix of the religious and the erotic that became the hallmark of Madonna's rock style suggest that entertainment is transforming popular religion rather than supplanting it. The rise of fundamentalism around the world is undoubtedly a reaction to the crisis of secular ideologies, but it has been aided by the growing reach of entertainment technologies. The principal weapons of the Iranian revolution of 1979 were smuggled audiotapes of Khomeini's message.

A more persuasive explanation for the huge audience for global entertainment is that it is filling the vacuum left by the collapse of traditional local-based institutions and reflects the radical changes in the ways human beings are interacting across the world. The decline of traditional family life almost everywhere, the atrophying of civic life, and the pervasive loss of faith in politics appear to be a worldwide trend. Popular culture acts as a sponge to soak up spare time and energy that in earlier times might well have been devoted to nurturing and instructing children or to participating in political, religious, civic, or community activities or in crafts, reading, and continuing self-education. But such pursuits sound a bit old-fashioned today, although political theory still rests on the assumption that these activities are central to the functioning of a democratic society. Yet increasingly, vicarious experience via film, video, and music is a substitute for civic life and community. As it becomes harder for young people in many parts of the world to carve out satisfying roles, the rush of commercial sounds and images offers escape.

Leaders of the entertainment industry argue exactly the opposite. American pop culture, they say, creates political consciousness. Jack Valenti, president of the Motion Picture Association of America, told *Time* magazine—itself a subsidiary of the giant Time Warner entertainment complex—that American TV, rock music, and films were "a primary catalyst in the collapse of communism in Eastern Europe and the Soviet Union." This is puffing surely, but there is something to it. As the Voice of America discovered early on, because jazz and rock were powerful symbols of freedom and self-expression for underground fans across the Soviet land mass, listening to forbidden music was a form of protest that was only slightly risky. Since they could not keep underground tapes out anyway, little by little Soviet authorities felt compelled even in the Brezhnev era to ease up. The results were exactly what they feared.

All through human history songs have served as expressions of discontent. In 2000 B.C. Chinese emperors were telling their subordinates to listen to the people's songs if they wanted to know what dangerous political thoughts they were harboring. Long before it became a nursery rhyme "Little Jack Horner" was a song of protest against Henry VIII's seizure of church property.[22] Much of American popular music is rooted in protest—the labor movement, the civil rights movement, and the countercultural movements of the 1960s. "The fact is that for many of us who've grown up since World War II," Jann Wenner, the editor of *Rolling Stone,* wrote in 1971, "rock 'n' roll provided the first revolutionary insight into who we are and where we are at in this country . . . behind that Eisenhower–Walt Disney–Doris Day facade was (damn!) a real America: funky, violent, deeply divided, despairing, exultant, rooted in rich historical tradition and ethnic variety. . . ."[23]

But songs of protest can be turned into consumer products and lose their bite. Protest itself becomes something to sell. According to one study of videos on MTV conducted in 1984, about 20 percent of the songs communicated some form of social protest—against nuclear war, prejudice, or the business establishment.[24] At the height of the counterculture craze and student militancy of the late 1960s, the leading record company in the United States marketed its product under the slogan "The Revolution Is on CBS."[25] In the end, the industrialization of protest music had most of the angry fist-shakers swaying.

As traditional family ties and the bonds of small-town life weaken almost everywhere, entertainment serves to build new forms of community, but more often it serves as a substitute for community. Ever since Roman times, politicians bent on defusing popular political demands for democracy and power-sharing have been attracted to the "bread and circus" strategy. Producing circuses can yield more of a payoff for princes or presidents than distributing bread, and it is usually cheaper, given the number of people to feed.

In democracies, candidates try to tap into popular culture by enlisting rock stars and film personalities in their cause. In 1992 the United States elected its first president who presented himself as an aficionado of commercial pop culture. By appearing on MTV and playing the saxophone on the *Arsenio Hall Show* during the campaign and at one of his inaugural balls, and by revealing that his daughter had been named after a romantic popular song, Bill Clinton established connections with millions of voters who would never listen to his speeches.

As individuals turn away from the public space to dream private dreams, films, records, and video serve as dream aids. In the 1930s and 1940s Aldous Huxley and George Orwell wrote chilling prophecies about the power of mass-entertainment technology to destroy democracy, to undermine human relationships, and to shrink the autonomy of the individual. Orwell emphasized the power of government to drum a totalitarian message into the public consciousness with the technology of domination. Huxley predicted that people would be more effectively manipulated by instruments of pleasure.[26]

In the age of Hitler and Stalin the promotion of official paranoid fantasies through state communications networks became a hideous art form, and throughout the world dictatorial leaders still exercise their hold on populations—by disseminating official truth over state radio and TV. What Orwell did not predict is that by 1984 decades of official truth would have created an appetite in mass society for private, personal messages that only individual artists could create and only large commercial enterprises could market on a global scale.

Nor did he have an intuition about the contradictory character of technology, how the transistor radio, audio- and videotape, fiber optics, and satellite technology would actually undermine the state monopoly of communications. First, propaganda organs of rival powers beamed competing official truth at the Soviet population and other target audiences—employing American hit music as teasers—through Voice of America and the BBC. Then rival political leaders began infiltrating tapes of subversive messages even into countries under tight control. Finally, the expanded reach of commercial-entertainment messages broke the state monopoly. Who would not rather listen to Michael Jackson than Leonid Brezhnev?

Commercial entertainment turns out to be a more effective opiate than either religion, which even when domesticated by the state can harbor a subversive message—God against Caesar—or official propaganda, which, except for brief highs like some of the Hitler spectaculars in Nuremberg, is inescapably boring. The power of commercial entertainment is in its sheer volume and in its technological virtuosity. It can blanket the airways. It has limitless resources to keep the hundreds of millions of home videos, Walkmans, and hi-fis on the planet fed around the clock—in short, the capability to preempt every waking hour.

Some critics attribute the entertainment explosion to the decline of the work ethic. Even in workaholic Japan a quarter of those surveyed in the late 1980s considered themselves to be "leisure-oriented," as compared with only 15 percent in a 1974 survey. As work weeks become shorter in some countries and part-time employment, job-sharing, and taking turns at home with the children become established patterns in the labor market in developed countries, more people have time on their hands. A high proportion of joggers in the park and diligent users of Exercycles and treadmills in the bedroom fight the boredom or ease the pain by wiring themselves up to the local rock station or to tapes of top-forty hits.

But changing fashions in the workplace also provide opportunities to consume "leisure" products, notably pop music. Whether on the four-hour daily commute on the freeway into Los Angeles or on the train from Westchester suburbs to downtown Manhattan offices or deep within the acres of carnation fields in the remote reaches of Kenya, more and more late-twentieth-century human beings are listening to packaged music all day long. Piped-in music increases the productivity of factory workers, or so it is believed, and light melodies punctuated by gentle rhythms mixed and processed for easy

listening make up the perpetual background noise for anyone working in shopping malls or supermarkets, or riding in state-of-the-art
elevators. Even a generation ago offices in large bureaucracies were
still emitting mostly paper-rustling noises or the murmurs of officially discouraged conversation; today many offices where information is processed and paper is pushed are alive with the sound of
music.

The globalization of mass culture of course has powerful political
effects. They cut in different directions and we will explore them
throughout this book. But surely no effect is greater than this: The
culture and entertainment industry has helped make politics a spectator sport. The pursuit of happiness now means amusement and
diversion, an understanding that is as profoundly private and apo-
litical as Thomas Jefferson's original definition was political and public.

CHAPTER TWO

THE TECHNOLOGY
OF PLEASURE

I.

IN THE FIRST HALF OF THE TWENTIETH CENTURY THE EXPLO-
sion in mass production took place in a variety of industries connected with transportation and household appliances. Manufacturers
appealed to the mass consumer market for automobiles, airplane
rides, vacuum cleaners, refrigerators, and electric toasters with irresistible promises to save people time and drudgery. But since the end
of World War II, with notable exceptions such as the microwave
oven, disposable diapers, and frostfree refrigerators, mass-market
consumer products are mostly designed to fill time rather than to
save it.

Akio Morita is one of the world's great innovators in the technology of filling time, and his influence on leisure habits around the
world is immense. Cofounder and guiding spirit of Sony for forty
years, he created a global electronics and entertainment giant by
dreaming about new entertainment hardware products and putting
his intuition to the test through aggressive marketing. Sony bears the
stamp of Morita's character—a blend of drive, chutzpah, and calculated playfulness.

If money alone had been his interest, the obvious road would have
been to follow tradition and to take over the family enterprise, a
leading brewery and distributor of sake and soy sauce. For fourteen
generations, beginning in the seventeenth century, the Moritas, a

wealthy samurai family, had been in the business, and it was a fore-
gone conclusion that Akio, the eldest son, would eventually take it
over. From the time he was in the third grade his father would take
him to the brewery to learn about balance sheets and market strategy. "You are the boss from the start," his father would tell the small
boy.

Morita grew up in one of the few Japanese families surrounded by
global products. The chauffeur-driven family car was a Buick and the
refrigerator was a Westinghouse from a distant land he knew only
from Hollywood films and his uncle's home movies of a visit to
Coney Island. His father bought one of the first Victor phonographs
in Japan, an electrical monster that cost about half the price of a car.
When his father put on Ravel's "Bolero," Morita recalls, the sound
"bowled me over."[1] He dreamed of making a phonograph himself.
By the early 1930s making radios was becoming a popular hobby in
Japan, and columns offering diagrams and advice for eager amateur
engineers appeared regularly in newspapers. The young Akio spent
every minute he could tinkering with wires and electrical components, and he managed to put together a crude electric phonograph
and radio receiver all by himself while still a schoolboy.

At Osaka University Morita became a protégé of a well-known
professor of physics. On the eve of World War II Japanese consumer
goods were considered junk in most places around the world, but
Japanese scientists were secretly at work on such advanced technologies as light-beam telephone transmission and heat-seeking weapons. Morita was given a navy commission to work on the latter
project all during the war. On the day Japan surrendered, he recalls
putting on his uniform, buckling on his sword, and standing at attention as the Son of Heaven spoke to his people for the first time.

The world had turned upside down, and Morita did not know
exactly what he would do. The one thing he knew he did not want to
do was to go into the sake business. For the first son in a Japanese
family not to go into his father's business was much more than a
career choice. It was, as Morita puts it, like "taking on another
family."[2] During his navy service Morita had met Masaru Ibuka, an
electrical engineer who had run a successful instrument company
before the war. Although Ibuka was thirteen years older, the two men
became friends. Morita was impressed with Ibuka's ingenuity and
audacious turn of mind. He liked the idea that Ibuka hired music
students with perfect pitch to determine whether his radar devices
oscillated at exactly the right number of cycles.

Morita and Ibuka decided to start a new company together. On May 7, 1946, the Tokyo Telecommunications Research Laboratories was incorporated. With $500 in capital, Morita and Ibuka opened for business in a small room on the third floor of a bombed-out blackened department store in a section of downtown Tokyo that had been subjected to massive fire-bombing all during the previous spring and summer. A few months later renovations of the department store began, and they were forced to move into a dilapidated wooden shack with gaping holes in the roof. "We literally had to open umbrellas over our desks sometimes," Morita recalls. The American occupation authorities who had oversight responsibility for the electronics industry were appalled by the makeshift little company and considered closing it down.

When Akio had asked his father for release from the family business, the elder Morita, though deeply skeptical about his son's decision to abandon sake and soy sauce, graciously advanced him money, taking stock as payment. In a few years he was one of Sony's largest stockholders. Today the Morita family owns about 10 percent of the stock. Ibuka, too, had useful family connections. His father-in-law had been the right-hand man of Prince Konoe, a former prime minister, and the old-boy network was helpful in persuading Japanese Broadcasting, National Railways, and other government agencies to buy the electronic testing equipment the fledgling company was producing. By the end of 1946 Morita had twenty employees at work producing thirty or so voltmeters a month.

II.

From the first Morita believed that the survival of the company could be assured only by inventing and marketing new products. To compete with Matsushita Electric in established products seemed out of the question. Matsushita, already a giant, had most of the Japanese consumer electronics market in its pocket. Japan's premier consumer-electronics company was founded in 1918 by a grade-school dropout, Konosuke Matsushita, who, legend has it, pawned his wife's kimonos to raise the capital to get started. He believed in planning ahead, and in May 1932 he announced his 250-year plan for the corporation. Although Matsushita died in 1989 leaving an estate of $1.5 billion, his spirit lives on in the company "creed," a mantra known as the "Seven Spirits of Matsushita," and the company song, "Love, Light, and a Dream." All are used in daily "spiritual training" at Matsushita's 110 plants in Japan and at many of their overseas operations.[3] Matsushita is still by far the world's largest producer of consumer electronics. In 1991 Matsushita had worldwide sales of $48.6 billion, nearly double Sony's. It employed 210,848 men and women; Sony had about 113,000.[4]

Matsushita was so formidable a company that Morita knew that his fledgling company could survive only by being innovative. His idea was to concentrate heavily on high-tech products for overseas markets. "We do not market a product that has been developed already," he explained years later, "but develop a market for the product we make."[5] Matsushita had built his empire on a humble piece of low technology for Japanese consumers—an adapter for plugging an electric appliance into a light-bulb socket. (He could undercut the competition by 30 percent, he discovered, if he used discarded light bulbs for the screw-in part.)

Morita was determined to dazzle foreigners with exciting new products and to make the point that "made in Japan" was a label of distinction, not a badge of shame. Today more than 70 percent of Sony's sales are outside Japan while Matsushita still makes 60 percent of its total sales in the Japanese islands. But Matsushita's volume is so immense that millions of Americans who have never heard of Matsushita have been buying its products for years under its various brand names—Panasonic, Quasar, Technics. Matsushita VCRs have also sold in the United States with General Electric, Magnavox, Sylvania, and JCPenney labels.

The new technology that opened the way for Sony to become a global company was the tape recorder. The first such device Morita and Ibuka ever laid their eyes on was at the headquarters of the American occupation authorities who watched over the electronics industry. The two engineers were fascinated by the technology. But it took almost four years to develop a machine they could sell. In 1950 Sony began marketing tape recorders that weighed a hundred pounds and sold for $400. Morita remembers selling the first one to the Tokyo Art Institute because, as he recalls, "a young voice student there saw the usefulness of it for music students. . . . But he criticized it a lot and told us many things that were wrong with it. So I hired him." Decades later Norio Ohga became president of Sony.

Morita's big breakthrough was a large order from the Ministry of

Justice, which, thanks to the intercession of Ibuka's father-in-law, agreed to try out the tape recorder as a substitute for court stenographers. The Supreme Court of Japan took twenty immediately, and the company was on its way. Morita became an aggressive salesman. He would bring the machine along to parties and record songs and patter to the delight of the guests. Someone in the company came across an American pamphlet entitled 999 Uses of the Tape Recorder in the offices of the U.S. Army occupation forces, and Morita had it translated as a promotion for the company. The pamphlet offered ingenious reasons why no one could go through life without a tape recorder; for example, astronomers who have to keep both hands on their telescopes could use the machine to record their observations even as they were staring into the heavens. The universal reaction was that the tape recorder was a wonderful toy but much too expensive. So Ibuka concentrated on making the device lighter and cheaper, and Morita began selling thousands of them to schools all over Japan.

From the outset the company was determined to make and sell both machines and everything that went into them—batteries, tapes, and later records and movies. Tape was a problem since there was no plastic in Japan at the time. So Ibuka and Morita decided to make tape out of paper sprayed with oxalic ferrite powder mixed with Japanese lacquer, all of which worked well enough to convince them that once plastic became available they would have a salable product.

Even in the earliest years Morita was fascinated with the possibilities of the U.S. market; the colossus of North America was the only industrial economy on earth that had not been ruined by the recent world war. Ibuka visited the United States in 1952, the year the American occupation ended, to see what the market for tape recorders might be. The trip turned out to be a turning point for the company because of a lucky tip. He learned that AT&T, which had invented the transistor at its Bell Laboratories in late 1947, was willing to license it. This electronic amplifying device made use of semiconductors, the tiny device that became the key to computer technology and made miniaturization possible. (Early computers, such as the one at the University of Pennsylvania that ran on 18,000 vacuum tubes, took up an entire room and turned it into a sauna when going full blast.[6])

Ibuka was itching to get his hands on transistor technology. He had more than a hundred engineers turning out successful tape recorders. The machines could always be improved, but he feared that his most creative employees were becoming bored turning out the same basic product day after day. In the original prospectus establishing Tokyo Telecommunications, Ibuka had promised "the establishment of an ideal factory—free, dynamic, and pleasant—where technical personnel of sincere motivation can exercise their technological skills to the highest levels."[7] He had no clear idea what could be made with the transistor. The engineers at AT&T thought they were good only for making hearing aids, but Ibuka had an intuition that the engineers back in Tokyo could come up with something more interesting.

Because AT&T was a regulated monopoly, it was required under U.S. antitrust law to license its inventions to all qualified applicants; foreign companies were as eligible to apply as American companies. Ibuka was astonished that the U.S. government was not more protective of a critical technology. Japan's own policy, as Japanese trade officials have put it, is to protect indigenous technology that is deemed to be "critical to the security of a nation's economy" because it enhances Japan's "autonomy and bargaining power."[8] The engineers at the Western Electric division of AT&T who held the patent on the transistor, on the other hand, were impressed that a small Japanese company had managed to make a tape recorder all by itself. The American giant saw no reason not to issue the license. The price was a $25,000 advance against royalties.

Morita arrived in New York in 1953 to conclude the deal. He took the occasion to gather up everything he could find in print on transistors and stick it in his suitcase. His first American trip convinced him that the company name, Tokyo Tsushin Kogyo Kabushiki Kasha, was not a winner, even in translation. He was led to the name Sony by the Latin word for sound, *sonus*. Although the word means nothing in any language, in Japanese Sony reminds people of the borrowed English words "sonny boy," which connote youth, cuteness, and intelligence. Sony is now among the top ten instantly recognizable global brands.

In 1954 Ibuka returned to America for three months during which he gathered detailed information at Bell, Westinghouse, Union Carbide, and other places. Every night he wrote seven- or eight-page airmail letters to Tokyo on thin airmail foolscap illustrated with meticulous diagrams. By the time Ibuka returned to Japan, the research team in Tokyo had already received enough detailed information on transistors to fill up four fat folders. Within six months they produced a transistor. In the course of the research one of the physicists, Leo Esaki, was struck by what has come to be known as the "diode tunneling effect"—subatomic particles moving in waves through apparently impenetrable barriers—and years later he was awarded the Nobel Prize. By early 1955 the team had produced a transistor radio, and by August it was on the market.

III.

"Miniaturization and compactness," Morita notes, "have always appealed to the Japanese. Our boxes have been made to nest; our fans fold, our art rolls into neat scrolls."[9] In Japan space has always been scarce, and this reality is reflected in almost every aspect of Japanese life—from short poems and dainty box lunches to small gestures with large meanings. (Japanese wrestlers are the obvious exception.) From the start Morita was intrigued by the idea of pocket-size products because of an intuitive sense that if Japanese delighted in small things that could be tucked away when not being used, other people would, too. He told his engineers that he wanted a radio that could fit into a shirt pocket. The goal was met; the tiny radios were demonstrated in specially designed shirts with enlarged pockets. The miniature radio was followed by the "babycorder," the "tummy television" (nine-inch, then five-inch, then four-inch television sets that could rest on your stomach), the Walkman, the "passport-size" camcorder, and many other diminutive electronic consumer products made possible by the transistor.

Sony innovators have had a feel for what will intrigue the public combined with supreme confidence in their intuition. "Our plan is to lead the public with new products," Morita kept saying, "rather than ask them what kind of products they want." While Sony's major competitor, Matsushita, runs an Institute of Human Electronics to "observe 'advanced consumers' and use the information to unearth new product needs," Sony prides itself on having no market-research facility. "We do not get involved in marketing studies to build products," one veteran Sony engineer puts it, but the company builds the products that appeal to the engineers themselves.[10] "The market research is all in my head! You see, we create markets," says Morita, who is plainly in awe of what he calls his own "sixth sense."[11]

All this fits Sony's carefully cultivated cocky reputation, but the image is somewhat clearer than the truth. Sony Corporation of America undertook six years of customer research before its ProMavica still-video system was put on the market. Not only did Sony employ a market-research firm in California but also mail surveys, customer interviews, telephone surveys, and focus groups.[12] Still, there is no doubt that Morita has encouraged a "whimsical, freewheeling corporate culture" where the ideas of the staff are taken seriously.[13]

Morita himself claims credit both for conceiving the idea of Walkman, the pocket-size tape player, and for anticipating its enthusiastic reception, despite the unanimous view of the company's marketing staff that nobody would buy it. The idea occurred to him when he saw Ibuka lugging around a heavy portable tape player with big headphones because he could not bear to be without music as he moved from room to room. Morita ordered a small, light machine, and Sony engineers produced exactly what he wanted.

Walkman is one of the world's most global products. Well over 100 million have been sold; more than a million a month are still coming off the lines. There are now a hundred varieties sold around the world—from a solar-powered, waterproof version for the beach to an ultralight model for tennis players to attach to a sweat band. Morita's original design called for two headsets so that a couple might share the sound; indeed, he thought it "rude" for people to retreat into their individual private worlds, but that is what the customers wanted. As with many Japanese consumer products, no basic new technology was involved, just painstaking adaptation of old ideas to new uses. "A minor thing, no technological breakthrough," Morita calls it.[14]

But it was a phenomenal marketing breakthrough. The name was coined "by some young people while I was away on a trip," Morita recalls, and initially he hated it because it was "ungrammatical."[15] The product was considered so unpromising that it had a low advertising budget. The skeptical marketing director launched Walkman by hiring schoolchildren to roller skate in Tokyo's Yoyogi Park with the little radios hitched to their belts. "The reporters got the idea," Morita recalls. "We were selling a lifestyle."[16] Sony still resorts to marketing spectaculars—an ever-changing electronic tableau outside Sony's main showroom on the Ginza in Tokyo featuring Japanese rice fields and bird songs one week, monkeys and jungle squawks the next.[17] In 1991 Sony hoisted a giant television above Times Square and offered free advertising to Walt Disney and Reebok as a way to promote its new line of TVs.

From the first Ibuka and Morita were determined to develop a global market for their products. In his autobiography *Made in Japan* Morita describes how he felt on his first visit abroad when a waiter in Düsseldorf served him ice cream with a little paper parasol on top. "This is from your country," he said with a condescending smile, pointing to the little decoration. Stung by Japan's world reputation for exporting only junk—despite his country's impressive industrial base and research capability developed in the early decades of the twentieth century—Morita has been at once admiring, proud, skillful, scolding, prickly, and awed in his dealings with Europe and America. In the early years Sony printed "Made in Japan" in the smallest type possible, so small in fact that U.S. Customs made them enlarge the label. In everything Morita says, whether in Tokyo or New York, he makes no effort to hide his deep ambivalence about the United States, the country that still sets the standards to surpass, still leads in scientific innovation that can be turned into consumer products—increasingly by non-American firms—and still offers the most critical (and most open) market for Sony's products. Morita told Clyde Prestowitz, then a senior trade official in the Reagan administration, that the company "had developed as rapidly as it had by being able to sell in the United States," which, in a rare bit of understatement, he described as "an easier market to penetrate than Japan."[18] The United States of America remains the key to Sony's global strategy.

Beginning in the mid-1950s Morita would spend months in the United States. At first he ate at the Automat and stayed in cheap hotels. But he was advised that Americans would have no confidence in him unless he adopted a suitable lifestyle. His English was poor, and he found the complex American market a daunting challenge. He began commuting from Tokyo to New York, and gradually he developed a circle of advisers, lawyers, and distributors to guide him. For Morita image was as important as technological excellence, perhaps even more so. When the Bulova Watch Company offered to take 100,000 radios, an order in excess of Sony's entire capital, provided only that they be sold under the Bulova name since Sony's was unknown, Morita refused. "Fifty years from now," he says he said, "I promise you that our name will be just as famous as your company name is today."[19]

By the end of the 1950s more than half of Sony's sales were outside Japan, and the U.S. market was now critical. In 1960, the year John F. Kennedy was elected president of the United States, Sony established its U.S. subsidiary and soon thereafter became the first Japanese company to offer its stock for sale in the United States. Morita was determined to have a showroom in the most elegant block of Fifth Avenue, near Tiffany's and Cartier, and to become the first company to fly the Japanese flag on the most famous boulevard in America. Once this was arranged, he moved his entire family to New York so that he could run the American operation himself.

Morita stayed a little over a year in the United States. In his sojourn in America Morita developed complex feelings about the society made up of his best customers. He loved the energy and excitement of New York and valued the friendships it was so astonishingly easy to make. His children were captivated by Disneyland, their first stop in America on the way to New York, and the older ones grew to like summer camp in Maine, that utterly strange environment into which they were dropped on arrival. In the twelve-room apartment the Moritas rented from the violin virtuoso Nathan Milstein they entertained the luminaries of the music world with the same meticulous attention to detail for which the company had already become famous. Morita's wife, Yoshika, though she knew almost no English, became expert at making celebrities from many different countries feel at home in a Japanese household. One technique, which she later described in a book published in Japan, was to keep lists of what guests ate and what they left on their plates. (Leonard Bernstein was a sushi enthusiast, but the pianist André Watts's mother did not eat fish.)

Morita saw many things in America he did not like. American schools were too permissive. There were too many lawyers, and they had too much to say about how business should operate. Americans were too individualistic, and their companies were too obsessed with quick profits. After he returned to Japan he would make monthly trips back across the Pacific to look after his fast-growing business, and soon he was receiving so much media exposure in the United States that his became the most famous Japanese face in America. As his company's fate became increasingly dependent upon American taste, fashion, and creativity over the years, the Sony chairman became increasingly vocal in telling Americans how he felt about their society even as he was demonstrating his video system on the *Tonight* show or his camcorders on *60 Minutes*.

Morita's early travels had confirmed his intuition about what Americans would buy if they had the chance. In a land of patios, houses with many rooms, joggers, and swimming pools there was a huge market for small color-television sets, portable tape recorders, and later portable CD players, but also for conventional-size products if they were demonstrably better than the competition's. Sony's Trinitron, a new picture tube using an electron gun with one large lens instead of several, produced a clearer, sharper picture, and this improvement in television technology won an "Emmy" in 1972, the first product ever to be so honored.

In the 1970s Sony began to establish overseas production facilities, first in the United States, then in Europe. Initially, the primary motivations were to be close to the market and to save transportation costs. It occurred to Morita that a TV picture tube was nothing more than "a glass envelope containing a vacuum," and that it didn't make sense to pay good money to ship vacuums across the Pacific.[20] So in 1971 Sony set up its first factory on American soil in a San Diego industrial park. Sony now makes a million television sets a year in the San Diego plant with all the components purchased in the United States with the exception of the electron gun and some special integrated circuits. The result, Morita rightly claims, is that "our sets are more completely American than some famous U.S. brand sets that are actually built in the Far East by American companies and their subcontractors and shipped to the United States. Any 'American' television set is about 80 percent Japanese inside."[21]

Morita then turned to Europe, opening a showroom on the Champs Élyśees. He was so taken with French high life that he installed an exact copy of the famous Paris restaurant Maxim's in the basement of Sony headquarters in Tokyo complete "with authentic decor, French chefs, and the same menu, wines, and style as in Paris." The first European plant was a television factory in Bridgend in South Wales; it opened in 1974 as "a screwdriver operation," but by the end of 1990 it was turning out 3,500 sets a day from parts that were more than 90 percent procured locally. By the early 1980s the production of that one plant represented about 30 percent of all British color-TV exports and Sony received the Queen's Award. The Prince of Wales had personally lobbied Morita to locate the plant in "my region." Morita, who is sensitive about the charges of the cozy government-business relationship in Japan, thinks the British and French give Japan Inc. more than a good race. He reminds American audiences how Prime Minister Margaret Thatcher lobbied Japanese companies to build factories in Britain while on a state visit to Japan, even interrupting her attendance at a Tokyo summit to make a pitch to the head of Nissan Motors.[22] He sounds shocked, but there is a twinkle in his eye.

IV.

All through the 1970s Sony kept growing at a startling rate as one new electronic gadget after another caught the imagination of people all around the world. The key to our success, Morita would lecture Americans, is our ability to generate profits for expansion, and the key to profits is production. "If you do not produce—add value to raw materials—you cannot make a reasonable profit."[23] Morita has always insisted that he has standing to criticize American business practices and economic philosophy because Sony is an American manufacturer with thousands of employees in the United States. American consumers of electronic entertainment equipment have been the mainstay of Sony's growth, and it is important to the company that they continue to feel rich enough to keep buying. Indeed, the United States is so critical to the health of the world economy and to the prosperity of non-American companies selling in that market that "America's lack of competitiveness is a global concern."[24]

Morita's lectures went unheeded. Instead, there occurred in the United States beginning in the late 1970s what Morita calls "the hollowing of American industry."[25] Forty years ago a third of all American jobs were in manufacturing; by the mid-1980s factory employment accounted for only 20 percent of the work force in the United States.[26] Major U.S. firms had relocated their factories to various spots around the globe where labor was cheap and unions no problem. GE became Singapore's largest employer outside of government, and more than 100,000 Singaporeans were signed up to work for other American-based companies. AT&T became one of Taiwan's major exporters. Whirlpool cut its work force in the United States 10 percent and spread its operations across forty-five countries. In 1987 the world's largest maker of washing machines closed the last of its four plants in Benton Harbor, Michigan, the company hometown, promising to build a marina, a mall, and a hotel on the site of its former production facilities. It then purchased a controlling interest in Philips's appliance business, the second largest in Europe.[27]

In 1980 corporations with headquarters in the United States still accounted for the same share of total world exports as they did in

1966.[28] But a sizable chunk of these exports no longer had any connection with the territory of the United States. The goods were not made there and they did not wind up there. U.S. corporations had outgrown their home country. Machine tools, robots, cameras, tires, and heavy machinery were imported from Asian factories and stamped with the name of once-great American manufacturers who manufactured no more. Companies like Nike and Schwinn began to see themselves as designers, merchandisers, and distributors rather than manufacturers. These "networks," a term they understandably preferred to "hollow corporation," could move rapidly around the world chasing cheap labor and responding quickly to shifts in consumer tastes.

Business-school professors celebrated the rise of the "postindustrial corporation" that had left manufacturing behind and had staked out a cleaner future based on information-processing, communications, marketing, and deal-making. The "service economy" furnished everything from hamburgers eaten on the run and crews to clean offices in the dead of night to insurance policies, letters of credit, African safaris, legal advice, and computerized data of all sorts— anything you can't drop on your foot, as the *Economist* puts it. A new division of labor was taking place in the world that would assure America's continuing preeminence in the global economy. Developing countries would have the smokestacks. The United States would control the software that made the whole global system work.

While American manufacturers were turning themselves into purchasing networks and banks, British, Dutch, and Japanese firms bought up factories in the United States. By 1991 foreign-owned firms controlled one-half of the U.S. consumer-electronics industry, one-third of the chemical industry, 20 percent of the automobile industry, 70 percent of the tire industry, and almost 50 percent of the film and recording industry.[29]

Morita believed that the United States was heading for a fall, and that this was not good for Sony or for Japan. Each year the United States was importing $40 billion to $50 billion more in goods and services from Japan than it was exporting to that country. This huge trade imbalance was a major economic problem for the United States and a source of growing tension between the two nations. Both the United States and Japan were counting on changes in the domestic economic policy and business practices of the other to avert a bruising trade war. In the Structural Impediment Initiative talks concluded in 1990, the United States admitted that the failures of its education system and its seemingly uncontrollable budget deficit bore some responsibility for America's trade problems with Japan. The U.S. trade representative promised that something would be done about it. In turn Japan promised to open its markets further and encourage Japanese to spend more. But neither nation's promises satisfied the other, especially since most of them were unlikely to be kept. Usually Morita's criticisms resonated with what such prominent Americans as Lester Thurow, the dean of the Sloan School of Management at MIT, and the financier Felix Rohatyn were saying. But in 1989 the one Japanese entrepreneur who worried most about his company's image in the United States committed a public-relations blunder. He contributed to a book by Shintaro Ishihara, a right-wing nationalist politician and agreed to be listed as a coauthor. *The Japan That Can Say No* set off a small firestorm in Washington after the Pentagon got hold of it, had the book hastily translated, and surreptitiously made it available to "opinion-makers" all over town. In his contribution, Ishihara pronounced the United States to be a nation mired in greed, arrogance, racism, and sloth. Morita dissociated himself from these views and refused to put his name on the authorized American edition the following year, but his disclaimer made him appear devious.

Then came Sony's purchase of Columbia Pictures, which *Newsweek* portrayed on its cover as Japan's "invasion" of Hollywood. To make matters worse, just as Ronald Reagan found himself under fire for accepting $2 million from Japanese companies for spending forty-eight hours in Japan, Sony made a contribution to the former president's library. Reagan reciprocated by expressing his delight that Morita's company would be restoring "decency" and "good taste" to the silver screen.

V.

In the 1970s, Sony had guessed wrong about the premier consumer-electronic product of the decade, the home video recorder. As usual, Sony was the pioneer. Its Betamax was a technically superior but expensive machine that could record for one hour. But Matsushita's JVC developed the video home system (VHS), which could record for two hours and cost less. In December 1974 Morita had demonstrated Betamax to the number-two man at JVC, who had been his superior officer in the navy during the war, and Sony's founder suggested that the two companies collaborate. They had, after all, worked together a few years earlier on Sony's U-Matic, the professional video system that had helped to revolutionize television broadcasting. But Sony's experience had been happier than JVC's. Sony did well with sales of the U-Matic in America where the professional video-recording industry was advanced, but in Japan the Matsushita subsidiary was reduced to sending its engineers out to try to sell the bulky sets door to door.

JVC engineers were envious of Sony's child-prodigy image. They resented being asked to sign on to a piece of technology without an opportunity to make their own adaptations or even to study it. Sony made it clear that it was ready to go into mass production. In a phrase borrowed from Soviet rhetoric of the day, JVC management gave the order to "overtake and pass Sony." Within two years of Sony's launching of Betamax, JVC had a cheaper, incompatible version on the market all over the world. At first movie and videocassette producers made their wares available in both sizes, but in the end nearly all went with Matsushita. "We didn't put enough effort into making a family," was Morita's pained explanation. "The other side, coming later, made a family."[30] In 1975 Sony had had the entire world VCR market to itself; by 1983 it was holding on to a bare 12 percent.

As Sony's net profits dropped from eight cents on a dollar of sales to two cents in the early 1980s, Morita was no longer being described in the world business press as "wizard," "electronics genius," and "miracle man." Now the word was "arrogant." Accompanying the stories were pictures of a troubled white-haired man who had stopped flashing his mischievous grin. In late 1983 *Forbes* reported, "Sony is producing premium products for a market where it can no longer charge a premium price. With most of its innovations, it simply doesn't have time."[31]

In the age of globalization both space and time are compressed. The compression of space had worked to Sony's advantage. It was a pioneer in discovering that neither oceans nor tariff walls were serious obstacles to global marketing, including the marketing of its own stock on twenty stock exchanges around the world. But the compression of time meant that even the most innovative ideas could be copied and put on the market at a cheaper price in an astonishingly short time, sometimes as little as four months. Korean companies like Samsung and Gold Star and a few other Asian producers—well supplied with cheaper labor and often skillfully guided and financed by highly interventionist, authoritarian governments—were undercutting Sony products. South Korea today is the fourth-largest producer of electronic equipment in the world and the third-largest producer of DRAM semiconductors. One out of every twenty personal computers in the world is manufactured in South Korea.[32] The pressures of globalization, which Sony had done so much to stimulate, had caught up with the company.

January 1984 was a low point in Sony's history. Professional hecklers came to Sony's stockholders' meeting and kept it going for thirteen hours screaming at management for Morita's disastrous "one-man show" and his failure to understand what was happening to the electronics industry. Even the good news earlier in the month had an ironic twist. After more than seven years defending against a lawsuit brought by Universal Pictures alleging that home recording of televised movies infringed the studio's copyright, Sony won a narrow victory in the U.S. Supreme Court. But Sony's competitors were for the moment at least the principal beneficiaries. Sony had begun making VHS recorders, but Betamax was fast disappearing from the world market.

Years before, Sony had helped to drive Motorola—along with every other American company except Zenith—out of the consumer-electronics business. But now the market was increasingly fickle and the competition harrowing. Morita saw the need to diversify, and he set 1990 as the target date by which half of Sony's business would be in something other than consumer electronics. But the professional Sony watchers on Wall Street wondered whether a company dominated by such a strong, supremely confident character could make the changes. Morita had always assumed that Sony could keep producing superior products and make a good profit if it spent enough on research and kept making the clever, small, inexpensive modifications that would keep opening up new market niches. In the depths of the recession of the early 1980s Morita was still insisting that the company should spend 10 percent of its sales revenue on research because that was "investment in the future." But one of his engineers took issue with him publicly. "Because we spend 10% doesn't guarantee we can come up with good products," Senri Miyaoka told a *Forbes* reporter. Matsushita, the archrival, was spending less than half that amount, and was making a tidy profit in the midst of a global recession. Sony was forced to reinvent itself.

In 1982 Norio Ohga had become president of Sony and took over day-to-day operations. "A new leader should have different ideas of how we get into a real technological age," a subdued Morita observed. "The world is turning digital, and maybe I'm still living analog."[33] By the mid-1980s the need for a new strategy had become even clearer. Profits bounded back with recovery from the recession. A parade of new products poured forth from Sony factories every few months—CDs, CD players, portable CD players, 8-mm video cameras. But thanks largely to the trade deficit, the value of the yen rose dramatically against the dollar. As Japanese currency soared, Sony products became too expensive in export markets, especially in the United States. By 1987 Morita was complaining that the falling dollar amounted to "a nearly 50% tax on us."[34] At the same time Sony dealers in the United States were baiting customers with the famous Sony name, and selling them competitors' products that were cheaper. Sony sent spies around to the stores and threatened to break off relations with dealers who violated their contracts to use "best efforts" to sell its products, but fighting dealers was not the road to success.[35]

The new president had had a long history with Sony. While he was still a music student, Ohga had volunteered blunt expert criticism of Sony's early effort to produce a tape recorder. Any singer would love to have a "vocal mirror" but yours is blurry, he told Morita, who was so taken with Ohga that he paid for his musical education. Morita then hired him as a consultant while the younger man pursued his career. While studying in Berlin in the 1950s, "Ohga was our spy," Morita laughingly recalls. The young singer would gain access to European electronics firms and report back to the chairman.[36] Later he sang with the symphony orchestra of the NHK radio and television network and gave recitals with his wife, who is a well-known concert pianist. With his square shoulders and barrel chest, he still cuts an operatic figure.

In 1959 Morita put the stocky baritone in charge of developing an instantly recognizable style that would create a Sony identity for every product. Later he was made head of a joint venture with CBS Records that became the biggest record company in Japan. As the years went by, Morita let go gradually. He continued as chairman, but in 1989 he stepped down as CEO to serve as "company philosopher" and to pursue his new hobbies. "I took up tennis at age fifty-five, downhill skiing at sixty, and at sixty-four I went back to waterskiing, but I find it very hard on the thighs." In his most active business years he had also found time to become a licensed helicopter pilot.[37] "Morita has so much of an outside role," says Ohga, "that he has given me ninety percent of the company."[38]

Though still regarded by conservative Japanese businessmen as a cocky upstart, Morita was elected vice-chairman of Keidanren, the association of Japan's most powerful corporations, in recognition of his unique access in the United States. He used the office as a platform to push *kyosei*, a new set of business principles for Japan to allay the anger of its American and European competitors and to forestall the inevitable retaliation. Morita fears that if Japanese companies continue to outcompete American and European companies, Japanese goods and investment will eventually be closed out of their most successful markets. Morita counsels Japanese companies to be less aggressive in the fight for market shares and to concentrate on selling smaller numbers of high-profit goods abroad. Japanese firms should reduce the work week, show greater generosity to stockholders, and greater support for local communities around the world where they operate. His colleagues in Keidanren subscribed to the idea of relaxing the single-minded pursuit of ever greater shares of foreign markets, but corporations and governments around the world remained skeptical that Japanese corporations would ever be ready to jettison the business culture that has worked so well for them.

VII.

Under Morita's leadership Sony had established a global image by appealing to local tastes, even local prejudices around the world. Morita himself fit American corporate style so well that he became one of the very few Japanese executives to be asked to join the boards of American-based companies. He has been a board member at Pan Am and IBM World Trade and has sat on the Morgan Guarantee Trust International Council. In Europe too he paid careful attention to local sensibilities, personally insisting that the plans for a new factory in Alsace be revised to make sure that only Alsatian-looking stones were used. The vineyard that came with the land was kept in production, and the modest Reisling that resulted was relabeled Chateau Sony.

Morita had used his time in the United States to persuade the business press how un-Japanese his company really is. As early as 1969 the *Wall Street Journal* was celebrating the reassuring "radical internal changes" inside Sony under the "cosmopolitan" Mr. Morita. The name Sony sounds so un-Japanese to American ears that, according to a survey by *Fortune* magazine, "a high percentage of retailers who carried Sony products claimed they had never sold anything made in Japan, and never would."[39] In his interviews all over the world outside Japan Morita always emphasized how different Sony's practices are from those of other Japanese corporations. Most Japanese firms pay great attention to school grades in their hiring; Sony does not look at them. Morita wrote a book decrying the custom of judging people by their academic credentials. Most Japanese companies recruit reliable look-alikes; Sony seeks out bright eccentrics. Sony has no problem hiring people away from competitors, a practice considered a breach of corporate etiquette by most firms in Japan. Morita proscribed the customary company song because no one, he says, could imagine anyone so "introspective" as Ibuka singing in public.

Morita talks incessantly about Sony's dependence on the global market. But in seeking both a global identity and a local look for the company everywhere it operates, the founder does not attempt to distance his company from its country of origin in the way some American corporations do. He talks about "company patriotism" but he proudly notes, "All our Sony factories today fly the Japanese flag, the Sony flag, and the flag of the host country. Like Olympic athletes, we are, after all, in a concrete way representing Japan and should wear the symbol of our country proudly."[40] One of the original purposes of incorporation, according to a 1950 prospectus, was to promote "dynamic activities in technology and production for the reconstruction of Japan and the elevation of the nation's culture."[41]

Indeed, in a number of respects Sony is a quintessentially Japanese corporation. In Japan every employee must recite Ibuka's poem "Sony Spirit" every day. At three o'clock in the afternoon knee bends and other limbering exercises at the work station are prescribed for all, another ritual that binds the "family," as Morita calls his workers. (In the United States, Sony workers are at liberty to skip the calisthenics in their afternoon break.) At Sony operations in Japan it is not unusual to work sixty hours or more a week. The composition of the work force is typical—male, highly educated, and well compensated at the professional levels and mostly young, female, and underpaid as the jobs become more menial. Men do the inventing. The "office ladies" serve tea. As in most Japanese companies, everyone from the chairman to the janitor must don the company uniform on entering the premises, a mandatory show of egalitarian sensibility and company bonding. Sony's tan jackets with detachable sleeves were created by one of Japan's most famous designers. Morita boasts that anyone appearing at a local store in the sleeveless Sony outfit doesn't need a credit card.

Ironically, in the years when Sony, thanks to its breezy chairman, was cultivating its American look, it was in one critical respect behaving in a most un-American way. Sony management worried little about producing quick profits. Morita and the other physicists and engineers who ran the company were so fascinated with technology and so confident that scientific fun could always be translated eventually into profitable projects that money was no object. "At Sony, the financial review comes last, not first," Michael P. Schulhof, vice-chairman of Sony USA and a member of Sony's board, notes. "When we launched CDs, we did no market surveys and hired no consultants. We invested $100 million developing the technology and building a factory before the first CD player was put on the market. . . . This runs very counter to an American company, where the chief financial officer does the final review, calculates the return on investment, and knows nothing about the technology."[42]

Although the company has always prided itself on being a successful upstart in the world of Japanese business, a brainy fish swimming against the tide in a sea of conformity, Morita and Ibuka's creation has always been an exceedingly well-connected upstart that has benefited greatly from the Japanese business culture. In Japan intense competition is tempered by custom, clubbiness, and shared understandings about what can and cannot be attempted to advance the fortunes of individual firms and entrepreneurs. Driving a competitor out of business is simply not done. In Sony's dark time in the early 1980s a member of the board of Sony's archcompetitor, Matsushita, who made no secret of what he thought of Sony's arrogance was asked how long it would be before Morita's company went belly-up. "Look, we'd never let Sony go under. It represents the good name of Japanese electronics for too many people abroad."[43] Nor is there any opportunity for hostile takeovers. Corporations are relatively unaffected by short-term fluctuations in profits or stock values.

The world of Japanese business is dominated by the six *keiretsu*, the modern version of the old family-held giant trading companies known before World War II as *zaibatsu*. These loose associations of interconnected corporations held together by interlocking stock ownership and a fierce group loyalty can generate enormous financial and market power. Thus Mitsubishi Electric (number three in Japan) is part of a group, that also includes Kirin Brewery, Japan's largest, and no worker in Mitsubishi Heavy Industries, Japan's largest, or at Mitsubishi Bank, or in Mitsubishi Trading Company, or in Mitsubishi Steel, or in Nikon cameras (another Mitsubishi firm and the second-largest camera producer in Japan) would be caught drinking any beer but Kirin. Mitsubishi also runs a matchmaking operation called the Diamond Family Club that has arranged 1,600 marriages for the employees of its network of companies in the last twenty years. The presidents of the top two dozen or so Mitsubishi companies lunch together on the second Friday of every month ostensibly to talk "about politics and social problems."[44]

Sony is not part of this world, and it cannot match the financial strength or market power of the *keiretsu* giants. However, as Morita himself recounts, the company knows how to make good use of the old-boy network. Junshiro Mandai—one of Japan's great bankers, Morita calls him—had been head of Mitsui Bank before the war. He was removed from Mitsui by the occupation authorities. By 1953 the Americans were no longer in control, and Mandai became chairman of Sony. Mitsui Bank had helped Sony from the beginning, but it was getting harder for Morita to persuade the bank to expand its line of credit. "One day Mandai took Ibuka and me to the bank . . . and told everyone in authoritative tones, 'My company has decided to increase shares, and I just might be able to arrange for you to buy some.' It was almost a command, coming from such a great figure." Several bank executives later told Morita that they felt they had to scrape together cash to buy the shares "because Mandai had virtually ordered it."[45] In the early years Sony's board also included Morita's father, Ibuka's father-in-law, a former cabinet minister, and Michiji Tajima, who became director-general of the Imperial Household Agency. From the first the company could draw on money, power, and impressive connections.

Perhaps Matsushita might look more Japanese than Sony, what with its songs, mantras, and spiritual training, but Konosuke Matsushita was as passionate about cost-cutting as any American-style entrepreneur. Matsushita was one of the first Japanese companies to hire cheap Asian labor. About half of its seventy factories outside Japan are in the Far East. Matsushita was much influenced by Henry Ford. Make a simple product, keep it cheap, and don't keep changing it. Matsushita was a pioneer in the use of robots. As late as 1983 Masaaki Morita, the chairman's brother who was then Sony's chief of production, was complaining how hard it was to use robots effectively because "we have to come up with something new every half year or so."[46] But that would soon change.

VIII.

Under Ohga's leadership Sony has evolved a four-part strategy. The first leg of Sony's recovery plan was product diversification. In 1980 the company had developed the 3.5-inch floppy disk for personal computers and now has a leading share of the world market. Swallowing its pride, Sony now produces components for other companies to market under their own labels in large quantities. Thus the Apple notebook computer is mostly a Sony, and the company sells semiconductors in volume to its competitors.

Second, Sony began consciously locating its production abroad in the interest of cost-cutting. About a third of its products are now made outside Japan, and Ohga's plans are to increase this proportion in the 1990s. In the Morita era labor costs were not a major consideration in Sony's global strategy. While Sony mastered global marketing, it did not follow its major competitors on the global chase for cheap labor. The lure of Southern California, Alabama, Wales, and other overseas locations selected for Sony factories in the 1970s had to do with access to markets, gaining understanding of foreign customers, worries about trade restrictions, and political sensibilities. These localities were hardly the bargain basement of the world labor market. Moreover, as late as 1988 Sony kept 90 percent of its engineers in Japan. In large part this was a conscious strategy to protect the innovative technology on which Sony's success depended. All Walkmans were made in Japan, and even though more than 60 percent of videocassette recorders were made in Europe, the spinning tape head that is the critical component was made exclusively in Japan. The same was true for the electron gun, the celebrated feature of Sony's Trinitron. But concentrating the engineering talent in Japan was also cost-effective. Japan produces more engineers per capita than any other country, and most are paid no more than twice what a production-line worker receives. So by and large they are cheaper and more adept at making small creative technical changes within strict guidelines—hitting the "target," in Sony jargon—than are the highly paid men in white coats in Silicon Valley.

However, in the mid-1980s Sony switched course. It set up four plants in Singapore, Malaysia, and Thailand. Given the rise of the yen in the late 1980s, Japanese laborers became among the highest paid in the world, but Sony could pay its 200 workers at its plant near Bangkok $2.90 a day. In 1989 Sony built a plant in the Philippines. Sony Electronics Malaysia now makes audio equipment in Penang and color televisions in Kuala Lumpur. Sony was also a latecomer in the race to the Mexican border. But in recent years it has taken advantage of the U.S. *maquiladora* program, which allows the more than 2,000 factories along the U.S.-Mexican border to export their products to the U.S. market with much-reduced duties. It built a factory in Tijuana to manufacture television components in the late 1980s at a time when Mexican industrial workers were getting eighty-nine cents an hour compared with $2.05 an hour in Hong Kong and $3.65 an hour in South Korea.[47]

By 1991, almost 200 Japanese companies had located factories in the border zone in response to strenuous wooing by Mexican politicians.[48] At the same time a number of U.S. companies pulled up stakes in Asia when wages rose and came home—to Mexico. But given the mounting U.S.-Japanese tension over the trade imbalance, the *maquiladoras* have an added attraction for Sony and other Japanese companies because of the magic of U.S. trade laws. Goods made in Japanese factories in Mexico and imported into the United States count as Mexican, not Japanese exports. Some members of Congress call the border zone a Japanese Trojan horse.

In the Ohga years Sony has counted on Asia to play the starring role in the company's global growth strategy. Singapore has been elevated from a place to make components to a regional headquarters on the same level on the organizational chart as Sony Corp. of America or Sony Europe. Sony understands that the trend in Asia is toward higher wages and that this is not bad news. Morita has become the ambassador of "consumerism." Having heard hundreds of lectures from Americans in recent years about how Japanese have to buy more foreign products if they expect to sell their own in foreign markets, he now envisions "the Asia-Pacific region" as "a big consumer society" where Sony and every other enterprising company can sell its products. He sees Asia not as an eastern clone of the European Community but more like a giant Hong Kong, a great free market to absorb the Japanese consumer products that the United States and Europe will more and more wish to keep out. "I see Singapore, Korea, Taiwan, Thailand, Malaysia, Hong Kong . . . buying lots of products from outside. So we get our economies growing.

We are getting to be stronger consumer societies. If we buy significantly from America and Europe, we can at the same time sell our products to those countries."[49]

Morita has a theory of how economic development is proceeding in Asia, and he understands that company strategy must fit the emerging pattern of development. The theory may well prove wrong. Obviously, there is more than creative tension between the cheap-labor strategy and the "consumer society" vision. "We realized we couldn't survive unless we started taking advantage of the lower labor costs in Southeast Asia," Mitsuo Kutsukake, managing director of Sony Corp. of Hong Kong explains.[50] But he also sees sales in Southeast Asia growing at 10–20 percent a year, far more than in the sluggish economies of Europe and North America. However, the host countries in Asia have the same view of "consumerism" that the Japanese government has had. Not yet. First, we work hard and create an export machine. Then we can afford to take home what we make, and only thereafter what foreigners make. So Thailand, for example, which granted Sony a three-year tax holiday to locate its plant near Bangkok, stipulated that domestic sales were to be limited to 20 percent of what the company produced in Thailand. For the foreseeable future the Asian tigers are willing to subsidize foreign firms to provide export muscle. Each of them sees Morita's dream of the "consumer society" as a distant goal—but at least for now, a dream best exported to other countries.

The third aspect of Sony's growth strategy for the 1990s has been to develop a philosophical and organizational definition of what it means to be a global company. Morita considers it the key to Sony's future success. He calls his concept "global localization," and it has fallen to Ohga to implement it. The basic idea has been to decentralize authority and to adapt working arrangements, product lines, and promotion ideas to local conditions, but all within the context of a coherent global strategy. It was not an original notion. Some years ago Coca-Cola adopted the slogan of the 1970s environmentalists, "Think Globally, Act Locally," as its own. IBM, which is a model for Sony in many ways, has tried for more than twenty years to develop protective local coloration for each of its foreign subsidiaries. It has decentralized its research operations, locating more than twenty in ten strategically placed countries around the world.

But Sony was determined to pursue its global localization strategy on a number of fronts. Its stock is traded around the world. It was the first major Japanese company to invite a non-Japanese on its board and now has two: Michael Schulhof, the vice-chairman of Sony USA, and Jacob Schmuckli, a Swiss who is chairman of Sony Europe, which is based in Cologne. (Translators whisper in their ears at board meetings in Tokyo.) Sony Europe, Morita explains, was trying "to become a proper European company" long before the further integration of the continent took effect in 1993.

Most of Sony's "leading edge" research is still carried on in the home islands, but gradually the all-important refinements and market-driven wrinkles that give new life to familiar products will take place in laboratories outside Japan. The company now has technology centers in Stuttgart and in Basingstoke, Hampshire, with more than 200 scientists. This will free the engineers in Japan to concentrate on the unsolved riddles of the twenty-first-century technologies now under development—an audiovisual entertainment center compact enough to be installed in front of a single tourist-class airplane seat, a tiny digital audiocassette tape recorder that can play for two hours using a cassette no bigger than a postage stamp, and high-definition television, on which Sony has pinned great hopes.

In 1991 Sony Europe performed better than Sony's divisions in either the United States or Japan. Sony sells about 30 percent of its consumer-electronics products on the Continent. The company says that its European factories use an average of 60 percent local materials and labor and in some cases, such as televisions, more than 90 percent.[51] Although it would be cheaper to ship components from Southeast Asia, "that is not corporate policy," says Schmuckli, who believes that being strongly tied into Europe is a more important consideration than labor costs. As Europe expands to include its eastern half, Sony is on the lookout for new factories and suppliers. Hungary has been picked as a promising place to make loudspeakers.

All operations in Europe are expected to report to Cologne, not Tokyo. Rainer Kurr, the general manager of Sony's European television operations, was removed from his position after stating publicly that Sony's factories in Europe were still controlled from Tokyo. "That's wrong," Schmuckli told a British business publication, "and that's why he is no longer in the job. Not because he said that, but because he did not understand the structure of the organization. He always felt it was quicker to go direct to Tokyo."[52] But the more decentralized Sony's global operations become, the harder it is to maintain a coherent strategy.

The fourth leg of Sony's global strategy to reinvent itself was the most critical and the most risky. In the late 1980s, the company acquired CBS Records and Columbia Pictures. Sony had suddenly become a major player in global entertainment software. The United States had surpassed Japan as Sony's largest market. More and more, as we describe in a subsequent chapter, the fate of the company hung on its American holdings and the American market.

CHAPTER THREE

A SMALL TOWN
GLOBAL GIANT

I.

BERTELSMANN IS THE SECOND-LARGEST MEDIA AND ENTER-
tainment conglomerate in the world, but its name is unknown to the
millions who devour its books and magazines or buy its hit tapes,
videos, and discs. The company owns book clubs, publishing houses,
record labels, mammoth printing operations, television and radio
properties, popular magazines, and newspapers across the world.
Unlike Time Warner, the world leader in entertainment revenues, this
German-based giant is not burdened with great debts.

For almost fifty years the fate of the company has rested in the
hands of one man. Reinhard Mohn is the great-grandson of the
original Bertelsmann, a printer in a small town in Westphalia who
started the business in 1835 to publish hymnbooks and religious
tracts. Quiet, driven, conscientious, and steely, Mohn was once identified by *Forbes* as Germany's wealthiest individual. He no longer
runs the company and has left the board, but he still owns 100
percent of the voting shares. "I am the annual shareholders' meeting," he once explained. More interested in making good investments
than good copy, he has avoided the celebrity lifestyle cultivated by
other global media lords like the late Robert Maxwell. His idea of a
good time is a long bird walk. On the eve of his seventieth birthday,
he made a solemn resolution to "relax while I work."

One hundred fifty-nine years after it began, Bertelsmann is a collection of more than 375 companies operating in thirty countries with about 44,000 employees. Almost a third of the company's worldwide sales revenue of $7.9 billion is earned in the United States. Despite Bertelsmann's considerable reach, the world headquarters is in a provincial city of 80,000 inhabitants on the Westphalian plain that is hard to reach by train and has no public airport within a hundred miles. In the early Cold War years Bertelsmann arranged with the Royal Air Force for the company jet to use a nearby British air base to fly its executives from Gütersloh to Bertelsmann operations around the globe.

From this remote command post the company management oversees its book and record clubs across the planet from New Zealand to Denmark. Bertelsmann also owns publishing houses in Germany, Austria, Switzerland, Spain, Colombia, Australia, and the United States (Bantam Doubleday Dell), and it operates a chain of bookstores in Germany. The Bertelsmann Music Group now operates in more than twenty-seven countries under many labels, including RCA and Arista, and features such stars as Whitney Houston, Grateful Dead, Carly Simon, Lisa Stansfield, Cowboy Junkies, James Galway, and Arturo Toscanini. In addition, Bertelsmann publishes more than a hundred magazines and newspapers throughout Europe and the Western Hemisphere, operates major radio stations in Hamburg and Munich, a radio news agency based in Bonn, three film companies in Berlin producing films mostly for TV, a pay-TV channel in Germany in partnership with Canal Plus France, and a 40-percent interest in RTLplus, the most powerful private broadcasting TV and radio network in Europe. European-wide syndication of its made-for-TV movies can command audiences of more than 200 million viewers. It also owns facilities in many countries for producing tapes, CDs, and music videos and is expanding its electronic-media division.

Above all else, the company is a huge reproducer and distributor of the printed word. It owns printing and paper plants in Germany, Spain, Colombia, Austria, Italy, Portugal, and the United States. One out of five of all paperback books produced in the United States is printed by Offset Paperback Mfrs., a Bertelsmann subsidiary in Dallas, Pennsylvania. Another Bertelsmann subsidiary in Minnesota prints 140 magazines, including all national and international editions of *Fortune* and regional editions of *Time, Sports Illustrated,* and *Business Week International*. Still another Bertelsmann acquisition in Virginia is a state-of-the-art book-printing facility that spits out copies of hardcover books every eighty seconds. Having acquired three leading publishing houses in the United States, Bertelsmann is a major force in the American book industry. Within its collection of subsidiaries around the world, the company owns everything it takes to make books, magazines, newspapers, maps, diaries, calendars, and brochures—except trees.

Although the company had been in existence for well over a hundred years, Bertelsmann had to reinvent itself from scratch at the end of World War II. Its reincarnation was based on a curious mix of serendipity and misunderstanding. Reinhard Mohn, who had been captured while serving with Rommel's Afrika Korps, spent almost three years in a POW camp in Concordia, Kansas. One day book carts began to appear at the camp bringing hand-me-down books for the prisoners. Although he was an engineer by training and had shown no interest in the book business, Mohn's curiosity was aroused. At about the same time he began hearing about the successful American publishing venture Book-of-the-Month Club, and somehow got the erroneous idea that the Club had sent the carts. (In fact it seems to have been the ladies' auxiliary of a local church.) He pictured the Club rolling its book carts filled with used books all across America, and it occurred to him that door-to-door bookselling would be a terrific business for postwar Germany.

The Germany to which Mohn returned in 1946 was devastated beyond belief. The round-the-clock bombing by the U.S. and British air forces had destroyed almost 40 percent of all German factories, including Bertelsmann's. The Nazis had distrusted the Bertelsmann family from the first because a year after Hitler came to power Mohn's father had published the "Tecklenburg Confession," a Protestant document that denounced the Nazi doctrine of state supremacy. Although young Reinhard Mohn served briefly in the Nazi *Arbeitsdienst* and then joined the air force, and the religious publishing house printed manuals for the troops all during the war, the Mohns did not demonstrate the zeal for *der Führer* the Nazis demanded. In 1944 the regime closed the company down on the flimsy ground that it had illegally imported paper from Finland.[1] A few months later the RAF reduced the Bertelsmann printing plant to rubble.

"If the war is lost," Hitler had told Albert Speer just before the end, "the nation will also perish." Hitler ordered everything destroyed—"all industrial plants, all important electrical facilities, water works, gas works, all stocks of food and clothing"—but although the orders were not obeyed, Hitler prolonged the resistance until his own bunker was in range of Russian mortars. The destruction of the final days finished what Allied bombers had been doing for more than three years. The daily ration in industrial regions of Germany fell to less than 700 calories a day. Konrad Adenauer, the future chancellor of the Federal Republic, shivered in his unheated room, sleeping in his suit and overcoat, and his driver slept in a hospital bathtub. In the small town of Gütersloh where the Bertelsmann enterprise lay in ruins life was somewhat easier, but not much.

Arriving back in Germany in early 1946 with a potato sack holding all his worldly possessions, Mohn, now barely 25, felt the weight of four generations of Bertelsmanns. His great-grandfather, Carl Bertelsmann, the founder of the firm, was the pioneer lithographer of Westphalia. When he opened a print shop in Gütersloh in 1824, he prospered almost immediately, and soon he was able to build an imposing residence to house both his business and his family. The Nazis razed the original Bertelsmann town house on *Kristallnacht* in 1938 because a Jew had been living in it. The company rescued a single beam, which is now set in a concrete wall in Bertelsmann's sprawling headquarters building on Carl Bertelsmannstrasse in Gütersloh.

The firm was born as a family project. In 1835 when Carl Bertelsmann applied for a license from the Prussian government to set up a religious publishing house, his main motive was to provide a publishing outlet for his son-in-law, who had compiled a collection of hymns. A few months after the press started, Bertelsmann published its first blockbuster, a hymnal for children entitled *The Little Mission Harp* that over the next few decades sold over 2 million copies. This could not help but be taken as a sign of divine favor, for the population in the German states was not prosperous, and only 40 percent of the people could read. The king of Prussia, though sympathetic to anything that encouraged piety, prohibited books on controversial current topics, and indeed, until the Revolution of 1848, even newspapers were barred from covering contemporary events.[2]

Carl Bertelsmann then decided he would publish a newspaper to reflect his own archconservative views, but when the editor he hired accepted an ad for a local carnival, he closed the paper down on the grounds that the promotion of ribaldry was a sin. In the revolutionary year of 1848 he brought out a violently antirevolutionary paper but quickly bowed to the spirit of the times and ceased publication after two issues. His son Heinrich then tried to organize a conservative party to oppose the rising social democrats of Westphalia, and this also failed. Heinrich's daughter married Johannes Mohn, Reinhard's grandfather, and since there were no male heirs with the Bertelsmann name, the Mohns took over the business.

Even as a 16-year-old boy, Reinhard Mohn was making solemn resolutions about his "responsibility" for other people. Now, next to the youngest of six children, he felt duty-bound to pick up the pieces of the family business. His father was in failing health. His oldest brother had been killed in battle, and another was missing in Russia. There was no one else to carry on. Mohn still remembers his father as "a very orderly man . . . eager to do everything right and to do his duty," who, to the boy's acute embarrassment, would say grace before dinner at restaurants in a commanding voice that provoked giggles and stares from some of the other patrons. Unlike most German high-bourgeois families, the Mohns were not permitted to have tobacco or wine in the house. But the elder Mohn was extravagant in other ways. An elephant was maintained at the family estate in the Harz Mountains to amuse the children. His father's piety never took hold in Reinhard's life, but the Protestant ethic did.

As Mohn set about to rebuild the company, he recalled that at the height of the inflation in the early 1920s the family business had been down to just six employees. But now there was nothing left but the family name. With the Kansas book carts in mind, Mohn decided to start with a scheme to distribute used books door-to-door. Because tens of thousands of private book collections had gone up in smoke, there was a lively market for anything to read. He began scavenging through rubble heaps and bombed-out libraries, collecting thousands of volumes that had escaped the bombs. A little later he managed to get a few presses working that he used to print labels for a local distiller, for which he was paid in whiskey. This was prime currency, better even than cigarettes. The bottles were traded for bricks to rebuild the publishing plant. By working other avenues of the barter system on which the German economy ran in 1946, Mohn got his hands on wastepaper. He then reopened C. Bertelsmann, keeping the old name but converting the operation into a publisher of general-interest books. Bertlesmann salesmen began knocking on doors and the book business took off.

On June 20, 1948, with no advance warning, the United States, Britain, and France imposed a currency reform. With the stroke of a pen the conquerors abolished 93 percent of the paper wealth of the German people living in the zones occupied by the Western powers. There were not many who had any interest in spending what was left on books. Unsold Bertelsmann books were returned to the publisher by the ton. But Mohn had an intuitive understanding of how to make money in bad times. He decided to expand his door-to-door operation and offer heavily discounted books promoted by salesmen with richly illustrated catalogs. The bookstores howled, and critics denounced Bertelsmann for corrupting the public taste, but by 1954 Germany's first book club had a million members.

In the early 1950s Bertelsmann branched out into the music business and started a record club. When the record companies began to question how smart it was to supply their records to a cut-rate competitor, Mohn established his own label, Ariola, along with a record factory to press his own discs, and soon he was a major figure in the music business in the new Germany. By the end of the 1950s Mohn had already achieved such a commanding position in the German entertainment industry that he began to collide with the antitrust laws. This roadblock, put in place by the American conquerors, forced the company onto what proved to be a golden path.

The company began to expand its book and record clubs abroad—first in Spain and Austria, and later in Latin America. In many countries Bertelsmann salesmen went door-to-door with books and records, even hut to hut. "Recently I was in Colombia," Mohn told an interviewer from *Forbes* in the late 1970s, "in villages of two thousand to three thousand five hundred people, all Indians. These are poor people, really. Still in those small villages we have one hundred to two hundred book club members."[3] By the mid-1970s Bertelsmann clubs—including the record clubs Mohn launched beginning in the 1950s—had 7.5 million members in eighteen countries. Today there are more than 25 million members of Bertelsmann book and music clubs across the world. The French book-club operation *France Loisirs*, in which Bertelsmann is a 50-percent partner with a French publisher, has 5 million members in France, Switzerland, Belgium, and Canada, and it is the largest book club in the world. On the eve of reunification, West Germany alone, a country the size of Oregon with a population of 60 million, had about 4.5 million Bertelsmann club members and nearly 300 retail outlets. Within a year of reunification in 1991 Bertelsmann had acquired a million new members in the former East Germany, a chunk of territory with a population of 17 million and an unemployment rate approaching 50 percent in some regions. For several years Bertelsmann has derived about two-thirds of its sales and profits from outside Germany.

II.

In 1968 Reinhard Mohn told the press that he had no intention of getting into the magazine business, but a year later Bertelsmann purchased a 25-percent interest in Grüner & Jahr, then the largest publisher of magazines in Europe. At about the same time Mohn entered into a secret deal to acquire a one-third ownership of the Axel Springer newspaper empire, a first step to a possible complete takeover. Springer was the biggest media operation in Germany at the time, and the owner was a prime target of student activists because of his reactionary views and his zeal in spreading them through his wide array of mass publications.

Stern, a sophisticated girlie magazine featuring excellent investigative reporting with a leftish slant, was Grüner & Jahr's biggest seller. Despite the fact that Mohn was now a major stockholder, the magazine published an exposé of the impending alliance of Springer and Bertelsmann. Springer backed out of the deal, saying that a publishing house should not be "a sort of department store where you can buy everything . . . from the leftist propaganda journal to the conservative newspaper." Mohn's revenge was to acquire controlling interest in Grüner & Jahr, and Bertelsmann soon surpassed the Springer operation in size and revenue.

Bertelsmann turned the magazine colossus, which had not been doing well, into one of its largest and most profitable subsidiaries. By 1990 the international magazine division was selling 550 million copies a year of its various periodicals along with 30,000 pages of advertising; in Germany alone the Bertelsmann empire offers twenty four different magazines that together sell more than 200 million copies a year. These include the most successful women's magazines as well as monthlies on travel, food, art, sports, gardening, interior decorating, and how to be good parents. The company also has a 25-percent interest in *Der Spiegel*, Germany's influential weekly news magazine.

Stern, the flagship of Bertelsmann's magazine empire, was the creation of a publishing genius by the name of Henri Nannen who developed the right mix of sexy pictures and antiestablishment politics to reach an affluent mass audience during postwar Germany's boom years. "He was the von Karajan," says Gerd Schulte-Hillen, head of Bertelsmann's magazine division and number-two executive in the company. "He could move his eye, and he could make people fly." (Literally, it seems. For one investigative project, the magazine hired five jets.) "When he left," says Schulte-Hillen, "the genius was gone, but the arrogance remained." Nannen would tell his editors, "First get the crowd into the church. Then you can preach." Although its circulation has fallen and is now surpassed by *Femme Actuelle* in France and *Parents* magazine in the United States, the German weekly still accounts for 15 percent of Bertelsmann's worldwide profits from magazines.

More than ten years have passed since the company fell for one of the century's most expensive and humiliating hoaxes. In 1983 *Stern*'s editor in chief, Peter Koch, with the approval of top Bertelsmann executives almost certainly including Reinhard Mohn, paid more than 9 million marks for "Hitler's diaries," and exploded into print. (The "find of the century" carried the endorsement of a famous Oxford professor.) The exposure of these bogus notebooks as a forgery, a clumsy one at that, was humiliating for a company that prided itself on prudence and meticulous preparation. The magazine had built its reputation on being right in its sensational exposés, and it has never fully recovered from the fiasco.

Gerd Schulte-Hillen is a sophisticated, worldly man who speaks several European languages. He started in the company as a young man, ran the company's printing operation in Spain, and quickly became one of Mohn's protégés (along with Mark Woessner, the chief executive officer, and Dieter Vogel, now the head of the great Thyssen industrial complex). He took over the magazine division just as the supersecret Hitler deal was being concluded, and he was the one who approved the checks. Even ten years after the event, questions about the hoax push this highly articulate, cool executive to the brink of incoherence as he tries to explain how he was taken in by a cast of improbable characters and overwhelmed by a chain of implausible events. (The reporter who procured the notebooks was a secret Hitler freak and the proud possessor of Göring's bathrobe.) How could one doubt the authority of three handwriting experts from three different countries who painstakingly ruled out all possible authors of the documents but *der Führer*, or question the judgment of three experienced editors who spent months studying the expensive texts, or not feel protected by the blessing of famous historians who congratulated the magazine on its stupendous discovery?

The media conglomerates, as the *Stern* saga shows, face a dilemma. On the one hand, as Schulte-Hillen puts it, "We are in the entertainment business." Mass magazines may instruct, but their primary purpose is to provide "a relaxing experience" for large numbers of people with disposable income during which they are exposed to the four-color fantasies of the advertisers. To intrigue enough people to sell 30,000 pages of advertising a year is a creative challenge. Creative juices do not flow on command, nor can people who are employed for their intuitive gifts be heavily managed. For this reason "freedom," "diversity," "decentralization," and "pluralism" are company buzzwords, and the concept of creative independence is enshrined in the Bertelsmann constitution. *Stern* developed its readership and reputation by twitting the German establishment even as it was signing up some of the country's leading advertisers. The strategy was surprisingly successful, despite boycotting by some leading banks and a few manufacturers.[4]

But for a large company, especially one as closely identified with one man as Bertelsmann has been, the pressures to restrict creative freedom are considerable. Reinhard Mohn's friends are bankers and industrialists who consider *Stern* a scandal, and over the years they have let him know what they think. He has felt social pressure from fellow tycoons to unload or discipline the magazine they consider a pest. *Stern* has helped popularize previously far-out positions. In the 1970s the magazine promoted Willi Brandt's *Ostpolitik* and abortion rights. In 1989 it took a distinctly cool approach to reunification, a position that directly collided with that of both business and financial elites and mass opinion. A year later it revealed that Thyssen, now run by a Bertelsmann board member, was selling Saddam Hussein machinery to make poison gas.

Some years ago Mohn acknowledged in an interview with *Die Zeit* that the relationship between top management and *Der Stern* as well as with other Grüner & Jahr publications has been "fraught with conflicts" and he predicted that it would take "years, even decades" to resolve them.[5] Bertelsmann executives point out that *Stern* is balanced off with two leading German business publications, *Capital* and *Impulse*, but *Stern* is always held up as the symbol of Bertelsmann's commitment to free expression. Mohn himself always made a point of distancing himself equally from Rupert Murdoch, who still uses his newspapers to press his conservative views, and from Robert Maxwell, who called himself a socialist and took a pro–Labor Party line in his British tabloids (even as he was speculating with the pension funds of his workers). A large publishing house, Mohn insists, should not represent the views of the owner. "Diversity of opinion must be assured and promoted by a liberal, permissive approach to publishing."

But it was hard for Mohn to keep his hands off. In the early years long before the *Stern* era, Mohn intervened periodically to make certain that sex remained an unmentionable in any Bertelsmann publication. He personally stopped the publication of Rolf Hochhuth's *The Deputy*—a devastating attack on Pope Pius XII for collaborating with Hitler—after it had been set in type. In 1976 the acting editor of *Stern*, Manfred Bissinger, already considered too far left by Bertelsmann management, published an article about Germany's leading tax evaders and capital exporters, a list that included Mohn himself. But he lacked the evidence to pin down his charges, and to the astonishment of no one but himself was fired. According to a former *Stern* editor, Mark Woessner, Bertelsmann's CEO, now insists on being told in advance what will be in the magazine each week. Nine editors have been dismissed since the Hitler fiasco. Michael Jurgs, the ninth to fall, believes that his skepticism about reunification was the reason why Schulte-Hillen handed him a 3-million-mark golden parachute exactly four weeks after being signed to a new four-year contract.

Mohn and his top managers in Gütersloh decided to discipline the magazine for the Hitler scandal by forcing a man of pronounced conservative views on the demoralized staff. The publisher of *Capital*, Johannes Gross, and the well-known writer Peter Scholl-Latour were appointed editors, but the staff occupied the magazine's offices and Mohn hired someone else. In the early 1990s, a former editor in chief at West German Television who had served as a public-relations man for Bertelsmann took over. The magazine is under control. No longer the free spirit it was, *Stern* causes Bertelsmann less trouble and still makes money.

III.

Mark Woessner has been running day-to-day operations at Bertelsmann since 1983. An engineer by training, he has spent most of his professional life at the company in the printing division, which he headed just before Mohn made him CEO. He is a smooth, silver-haired man who gives the impression of someone watching himself in the mirror. (A few years back *Bunte*, Germany's version of the *Na-*

tional Enquirer, listed him as the seventh best-looking man in West Germany.) As chief of a large, cash-rich company with neither serious labor problems nor risks of a hostile takeover, Woessner is enviably free of many of the problems facing his competitors in the industry. He is one of Germany's highest-paid executives, and his salary in 1990 approached $3 million a year.

But he serves at the pleasure of one man. Manfred Fischer, the first chief executive Mohn appointed when he reached 60, the mandatory retirement age the owner himself wrote into the corporate by-laws, lasted barely eighteen months. His basic mistake was his failure to grasp the fact that Bertelsmann, though a global giant, was still a family company. But Woessner, a long-time protégé of Mohn, has been careful not to make the same mistake. When he retired as top manager, Reinhard Mohn drew up elaborate plans for the continuation of Bertelsmann as a private company. He created a self-perpetuating board that included Woessner and Schulte-Hillen to manage the operation. The board members have twenty-year contracts beyond retirement, in effect positions for life. But everyone knows that the entire scheme could be revoked at any time of the day or night by the "annual shareholders' meeting." It would cost millions to buy up the contracts, but that has never been an obstacle to sudden dismissals at Bertelsmann.

Mohn has been scrupulous in withdrawing from day-to-day decisions since his retirement, but his interest in the quarterly reports are, if anything, greater than ever. Thus the urge to show the owner "beautiful figures" is also greater. Several top Bertelsmann executives told us that the big advantage of being a private company was its liberation from the tyranny of the quarterly statement and from the prying eyes of Wall Street analysts, but they acknowledged that one pair of eyes can be more intimidating than all the rest. Yet Mohn encourages the successful technocrats who manage the company to "feel like nineteenth-century entrepreneurs." Manfred Harnischfeger, the executive vice-president for public relations, explains: "This is a company run from the middle." Each manager of the 200 profit centers around the world is not only urged to innovate and thus to take risks, but he is liberally supplied with cash. Until he is perceived to have failed. "Anyone who doesn't perform gets the boot," as one of Mohn's industrialist colleagues puts it.

A favorite theme in Mohn's memos on company philosophy is the call for "dialogue and creative unrest." (The test of management, he maintains, is to "channel" this energy.) Top executives have some major differences of opinion about basic choices facing the company, and we found them surprisingly willing to voice them. Manfred Niewiarra, the general counsel, challenges a basic precept of company strategy—that Bertelsmann will never invest in any business outside the communications industry. In the 1970s the company acquired a large chicken farm with unhappy consequences. From then on Mohn's dictum has been: Buy only what you know how to run. If you don't know how to run it, buy a small piece and learn or make a coproduction arrangement. The company constitution makes it clear that nonmedia investments are off-limits. Niewiarra thinks this is logical but wrong given the fact that the world is on the threshold of a series of revolutions in media technology. In a decade or so books, book clubs, discs, and magazines may be obsolete, and the hardware companies like Sony may have an unbeatable advantage. Two students of the German media industry who have written extensively about Bertelsmann are skeptical about "diversity" and "pluralism" at Bertelsmann. They describe the atmosphere inside the company as "submissive." Reinhard Mohn may lecture his managers about how "the tranquillity of the graveyard leads us nowhere," but as one of their sources puts it, "I have never seen so many highly paid people cringe all at the same time."[6]

Mark Woessner has a large globe by his desk, but he stoutly denies that Bertelsmann is a global corporation. His office is ample, comfortable, and wood-paneled in contrast to the unrelievedly white look of the rest of the headquarters building, but not as sumptuous as senior partners in the largest American law and accounting firms normally insist upon. But like everything at Bertelsmann, the office is expected to communicate company values: The owner has no need to make a show, and his principal employees would be well advised not to try.

Woessner is skeptical about the hype in the business press about globalization. During an interview he pointed to our Sony tape recorder. "That's globalization. It goes anywhere. Cigarettes. Yes. Ford cars. Yes. But books, magazines, radio programs. They are local, regional maybe. We are an international company. But not global." It soon became evident that Woessner had a precise economic definition of what constitutes a "global" commodity. To qualify, a product must be able to travel easily around the world with only the most modest cosmetic retouching to appeal to local customers. (Coke is a little sweeter in some countries than others. On the Mexican border McDonald burgers come with peppers.) But a product achieves "global" status only if it is essential to sell it all over the world in order to recover the costs of production. In the media business, Woessner insists, this applies only to Hollywood productions with huge budgets and rock stars who command multimillion-dollar contracts. Unless you reach a world audience, you don't get your investment back, much less make money.

Despite the fact that CNN reaches hotel rooms around the world, television, according to the Bertelsmann CEO, is not global. It is not even pan-European. Woessner predicts that there will be no central booking for Europe-wide TV advertising for at least ten years. The agreements on European integration that went into effect in 1993 will have no effect on Bertelsmann's operations. "Zero." If there were a harmonization of rules limiting TV advertising, that would be significant, but it is not likely.

Bertelsmann operates as a network of national companies, each subject to the laws where it does business. Should we acquire TV stations in the United States? U.S. law limits foreigners to a 20-percent interest. "What do you do with 20 percent? We want control." A Hollywood studio? Woessner thought that maybe in twenty years the company would feel confident enough to try. "We don't know how to run a big studio." Several Bertelsmann officials were openly scornful of Sony's plunge into Hollywood. One predicted that the buttoned-up "Prussian" high-tech engineers in Japan would never be able to control the "longhairs," "beards," and temperamental creative geniuses of Hollywood. Bertelsmann for now will keep its distance. It will enter into coproduction arrangements but will avoid any attempt to digest the indigestible. Nonetheless, in the summer of 1993, Bertelsmann announced that it was actively seeking to acquire a film studio.

Despite Bertelsmann's vast international multimedia acquisitions, it is still basically a big printing operation. This in part explains the conservative approach to globalization Bertelsmann takes as compared with Time Warner, where pop music and Hollywood films account for a larger share of the business. Printed products do not travel easily. True, the *Herald Tribune* is printed at various places around the world. The *Wall Street Journal* has several regional editions, and the *Financial Times* is to be found in the farthest reaches of Britain's former empire. *Time* and *Newsweek* also have widely distributed international editions. But these publications reach an international English-speaking elite readership; to call them "global" products, as advertising copywriters sometimes do, is puffing. The

Reader's Digest is probably the closest approximation of a global magazine. By the mid-1980s it had forty-one editions in seventeen languages and was selling in the millions in Europe, Latin America, and Asia. Other U.S. magazines, including *Scientific American*, *Playboy*, *Penthouse*, and *Cosmopolitan*, have foreign-language editions but the number of readers worldwide is much more limited.[7]

Woessner confesses to having ambitious dreams. But reality intrudes. He turns over in his mind a book club in the USSR, which was still in existence when we talked. "Maybe in the next ten years." A Chinese encyclopedia on the model of Bertelsmann's most successful product in Germany? Impossible. The Philippines? Too small. Maybe a magazine in Indonesia some day. (Schulte-Hillen agrees. "They are beautiful people. Dutch-educated.") The recent experience in the former East Germany and in Eastern Europe has dramatized both the possibilities and limits of the internationalization of media. The book club in East Germany is a huge success. People are so hungry for ideas, for practical how-to-do-it advice on living under capitalism, on fixing up your house, taking care of children that they will buy expensive books despite the sorry state of the economy. After forty-five years of communism, they are still German, and "Germans think of books as being as essential to a house as furniture." The difference between Prague and Dresden, says Woessner, is "zero." Both are German cities, culturally speaking, but Czechoslovakia has two languages, and that presents problems. Poland, Hungary, and the rest are much more problematical.

Bertelsmann has bought tabloids in Berlin and Dresden and is developing more. Short, cheap, with a wholly local emphasis, they have been successful investments. But the effort to export West German magazines like *Stern* or *Spiegel* to the former East Germany have failed. They are too fat for a generation brought up on twelve-page propaganda magazines, and certainly too expensive. Unlike books, which are kept and loved, periodicals are throwaways and are seen as luxuries. East Germans still find the irreverence of western journalism toward German politicians unsettling. West German magazines, says Schulte-Hillen, are aimed at "nosy consumers" who like seeing their leaders cut down to size. The advertising of the west completely misses the mark in the east. In the affluent west the appeal is "You don't need this, but it will make you happy. It will excite you." But in the new eastern provinces of Germany there is real need. "The same advertising that is effective here is not doing the job there."

McKinsey & Co. argues that large media companies can survive only if they are strong in the three great world markets, the United States, Europe, and the Pacific basin. "I do not believe in such a theory. Why do I have to be in the Pacific basin?" Schulte-Hillen asks in response to a question about Bertelsmann's magazine operations. The "laws" of globalization promoted by industry consultants and business writers are seductive, fashionable, but an altogether flimsy basis for building a company. Experience is a better teacher, and Bertelsmann experience is to proceed step by step looking for market niches in any country with favorable political and economic conditions. German law is especially considerate of magazine publishers. As has been the case with book clubs almost everywhere, but contrary to American law governing magazines that requires periodic renewals, subscribers must actually cancel their subscriptions; otherwise they are presumed to be subscribers for life.

Grüner & Jahr, Bertelsmann's magazine division, is constantly developing new ideas, and it scans every continent—with the exception of black Africa, where, as one executive put it, "living standards are too low"—trying to find hospitable new markets for tried-and-true magazine concepts. A Bertelsmann employee spent more than three years in Japan researching the possibility of launching something in that "strange country," as more than one Bertelsmann executive describes it, but Schulte-Hillen is skittish. "Do I want to be responsible for a magazine I can't read?" The rise of commercial TV in Europe, a phenomenon of the 1980s, is accelerating the search for new magazines in other countries. Now that advertisers have much greater access to the electronic media, magazine advertising revenues in Germany are down.

Bertelsmann has developed a highly successful formula for women's magazines. In Britain it publishes the two best-sellers in this market; in France Bertelsmann's *Femme Actuelle* sells more than 1.8 million copies a year (the number-one seller worldwide of all Bertelsmann magazines in 1990). Fifty years ago, Schulte-Hillen notes, it would have been inconceivable to transplant any version of a German magazine to Spain. Now the differences are much less, and with careful adaptation the same concept can work in different countries. Although the competition is intense to extend magazines across national boundaries, there is no such thing, he insists, as global content; each magazine must be tailored to its own market. There are techniques for producing and placing photos, for creating attractive layouts that work anywhere, but the content must be rooted in the cultural differences. Schulte-Hillen, whose outlook is greatly influenced by his time in Spain, says, "You must love the differences. Otherwise you can't respect them."

IV.

Bertelsmann's major competitor in the print media in Europe, and more recently in the United States, is Hachette, a French publisher of schoolbooks founded a few years before Bertelsmann. For more than 150 years the company was run by the descendants of Professor Hachette and was known chiefly because Émile Zola had once been an editor at the house and the firm had managed the feat of producing a speller in French that sold 160 million copies. In 1980 the publishing house was taken over by one of France's top defense contractors, Matra, the maker of the Mistral surface-to-air missile. Jean-Luc Lagardère, the chairman of Matra, which also builds subways and telephone systems in various corners of the world, decided to turn Hachette into a media giant. Ten years later he had succeeded. Hachette had become the world's fourth-largest media company. Largardère's style is the antithesis of Mohn's. He is a highly visible figure on the French political scene, a supporter of French conservatives like former prime minister Jacques Chirac, and his efforts to recruit superstars for his Matra-Racing soccer team are well publicized.

Obviously energized by the prospect of a good fight—he says his hero is John Wayne—Lagardère appears almost obsessed by Bertelsmann. In an interview with the *Wall Street Journal* he described the competition with the German company as hand-to-hand combat. "I ask myself constantly how a company whose native language is spoken by so few people can become the biggest media company in the world. The answer is amassing financial resources and conquering the English-speaking world."[8]

At a time when the dollar was cheap, Bertelsmann was picking up properties in the United States, "a war chest for the real fight back home," as one knowledgeable observer described the strategy.[9] In 1988, the year after Bertelsmann acquired Doubleday and RCA Records, Hachette spent more than a billion dollars to acquire Grolier Inc. and Diamandis Communications, two U.S.-based publishers of encyclopedias and magazines. By these purchases the rapidly expanding company became the world's largest publisher of encyclopedias and magazines. By the end of the decade, in addition to the

Encyclopedia Americana, Hachette owned seventy-four magazines in ten languages selling some 650 million copies.

Hachette had begun its drive to head off Bertelsmann in the American market three years before. Despite the large number of home-grown competitors on American newsstands and checkout counters, the French company successfully launched a new women's magazine in partnership with Rupert Murdoch. *Elle*, a French fashion magazine that now sells in thirteen different versions including a Chinese edition, was "Americanized" but the "European flavor" was carefully retained. *Elle* became a hit with American women.

In the 1980s European magazine editors began running leading U.S. publications. Tina Brown, the editor of Condé Nast's British magazine *Tatler*, took over the company's foundering effort to revive the famous 1920s American magazine *Vanity Fair*. She succeeded by grasping the essential differences that divide the two countries with a more-or-less-common language. England is "small, bound together with the same assumptions about class and education," she notes. You can "assume everyone knows what you are talking about. In America you have to think big. You can't assume people are going to know what your in-jokes mean." In England you can be quirky, esoteric, and outrageously satirical, but in the United States people are drawn to the "time-honored, universal themes: love, passion, intrigue, money," and, she adds, they are much more easily offended.[10] In 1992 Tina Brown became editor in chief of the *New Yorker*.

Bertelsmann's experience in the American magazine business has been mixed. It acquired *Parents* magazine in the United States and made it one of its biggest sellers, but its ambitious effort to transplant to the United States a version of *Geo*, a German popular-geography magazine it successfully launched elsewhere in Europe, proved to be an expensive flop. This was an example, Bertelsmann executives admit, of overconfidence and failure to understand the market. "We didn't realize that *National Geographic* is not just a magazine but a cultural institution which commands great loyalty." The lesson cost $50 million.

V.

For almost fifty years Bertelsmann has been the project of one man, and although Reinhard Mohn has not been running the company on a day-to-day basis for more than ten years, the company is still strongly influenced by the philosophical precepts he developed over four decades. In 1960 the company adopted a set of corporate principles based on his ideas, and in 1973 they were enshrined in a company constitution that is amended from time to time. When we asked one Bertelsmann executive what aspect of the media business Mohn really cares about, he was momentarily stumped. Then came this answer: He is not much interested in publishing or printing or recorded music. He could just as happily sell anything that wasn't disreputable. His passion is to create a successful corporate structure.

On a visit to the United States in the 1960s Mohn was strongly influenced by the ideas of Alfred P. Sloan, the General Motors genius who popularized the concept that great corporations must decentralize their management, and Mohn is committed to the idea of "leadership from within." As Woessner puts it, "We try to provide management with working conditions that are as close as possible to those of an independent entrepreneur."[11] There are inevitable limits to decentralization in a company in which all the ultimate decision-making power is still concentrated in one pair of hands. Nonetheless, the decentralization idea is company gospel. Mohn tells the story of his conversation years ago with a manager of one of Bertelsmann's operations in Italy. He was growing increasingly annoyed that the Italian wasn't paying more attention to his recommendations, and the owner, then also the CEO, reminded this middle-level employee that he would do well to listen to the boss. The manager smiled and said, "Tonight you go back to Germany, and I'm the boss."

Mohn writes that family money is no longer an acceptable basis for exercising leadership in a corporation, and he has arranged affairs such that he will be the last of the Bertelsmann clan to run the company. But the culture of the family business still pervades the organization. Mark Woessner's brother Frank runs one of Bertelsmann's seven divisions.

In a media company it is especially important that managers at the operating level have free rein. Middle-level employees are given considerable latitude and paid extremely well. But a top official in Gütersloh complained that decentralization leads to the creation of baronies. It is not possible for him to call someone in New York "without that person running to Michael Dornemann" (the senior Bertelsmann executive in the United States). There is intense rivalry in the company at the top among Mohn's protégés. Schulte-Hillen, a cosmopolitan sort who lives in Hamburg, a great European city, has his loyalists, and they tend to regard Woessner, who has spent most of his professional life in Gütersloh, as a provincial. "The distance between Hamburg and Gütersloh is more than a five-hour train ride." Because Grüner & Jahr is not owned 100 percent by Bertelsmann, Schulte-Hillen has a certain independence in running the magazine division that other division heads lack.

An important influence on Reinhard Mohn was the Christian Democratic idea of a "social market economy" that was particularly strong in Germany just after the war. He is a fervent believer in the free market, but he is also strongly committed to the idea that "owners of large assets consisting of the means of production" need to "acknowledge their responsibility as trustees with regard to the general public."[12] Business must develop a new understanding of social responsibility, he writes, because the welfare state has reached its limit. "Taxes and benefit deductions have reached a level which is generally considered excessive. The temptation to evade this pressure imposed by the community is becoming greater." The opportunities are also greater, he might have added, because the increased mobility of capital allows global companies to locate their production and direct their profits to countries where the state demands little in the way of taxes and benefits.

From the start Bertelsmann was a benevolent, paternalistic employer. Long before Bismarck's social legislation was introduced in the late nineteenth century, Bertelsmann had its own safety net. The proprietor and his family looked out for the employees, visiting the sick, supplying chickens, old clothes, and help with doctor bills in emergencies. Mohn acknowledges that the rise of both the welfare state and labor unions has brought more security to workers. But having achieved great gains for workers over the years by "confrontation" and "class struggle," old-style unions are now obsolete, Mohn says, because the workers themselves don't find such tactics "convincing." Bertelsmann has unions, but only about a quarter of its work force in Germany are members. The only economic advantage is access to the strike fund, but since the company doesn't have strikes, for most employees this feature is not worth the dues.

German labor practice is based on ideas of codetermination, labor-capital partnership, and workers' councils, and Bertelsmann pushes these ideas to the limit. The head of the workers' council, a former accountant at the company, is an enthusiastic company booster, a quiet-spoken man about as far from a German Joe Hill as could be imagined. Bertelsmann workers by and large are financially more secure than in most other companies. The company spends considerable effort on internal communication and on the solicitation of employee reactions and ideas.

The most novel feature of labor relations at Bertelsmann is the company's profit-sharing arrangement. Mohn believes that to make the free-market system "just" there must be greater distribution of wealth. But as instruments of redistribution, both the state and unions have built-in limits, and in pushing beyond those limits, they jeopardize the whole system. It is management's duty to share the wealth, and that can be done effectively only at management's discretion. In the 1950s Bertelsmann issued profit-sharing certificates to its workers "which comprised almost the entire profit of the company," but the condition was that the employees had to lend it all back to the company to finance its expansion. "Only upon retirement did each employee have a right to payment of the funds." Thus at a time when banks looked askance at book clubs and novel notions of media development, the workers provided the money at 2-percent interest.

Since the 1950s Bertelsmann has not had to depend on workers' savings to finance its expansion, and immediate access to the profit-sharing dividends is much easier. Indeed, the only securities of the company traded on the open market are the profit-sharing certificates, and about 50 percent of these are still in the hands of Bertelsmann's workers, who own more than 600 million marks worth. Upon retirement, workers receive a combined income from the state pension (more than 60 percent of the last yearly net income), a Bertelsmann pension (25 percent of net income just before retirement), and profit-sharing income (which ranges from 25 percent to 100 percent of last net income). Thus retired workers can look forward to receiving monthly checks in excess of their last monthly paychecks, and in some cases almost double.[13] These provisions apply only in Germany, and while it is a company objective to harmonize employee benefits worldwide insofar as possible, it is very far from achieving this goal. (Indeed, the more likely prospect is a reduction of benefits in Germany.)

The owners of capital—the Bertelsmann Foundation, the Mohn family, and Gerd Bucerius, the publisher of *Die Zeit* (who traded his stock in Grüner & Jahr for a 10-percent share of Bertelsmann)—receive a return calculated on prevailing market interest rates plus an undisclosed "risk premium." If the company has made a profit beyond these obligations and the contractual obligations to employees for wages, salaries, and benefits, these earnings are divided equally between employees and the owners of capital.

Skepticism about government runs deep at Bertelsmann. Companies, Mohn argues, need to act more like governments within the corporate domain so that government can recede. He recommends that every company spend the hundreds of hours that Bertelsmann has invested in hammering out a constitution to regulate and clarify the interests of workers, owners, and managers. Although government regulation is a blunt and cumbersome instrument, there are times, he believes, when the state must step in. Mohn says that governments in the 1970s should have intervened to prevent the inflationary wage deals of that era. Peace in the workplace, he believes, was purchased by sacrificing the public interest.

Mohn is no more sympathetic to Europe-wide regulation than to national regulation. In 1990 in a speech on European integration at Frankfurt University he expressed skepticism that a European social charter, the set of guidelines on workers' rights, the environment, safety, consumer protection, and other social goals that has been pieced together since 1974, could be depended upon to make the market system work in a just and equitable way. Bureaucratic or political efforts to achieve Europe-wide standards may well threaten "the diversity of ideas and opinions in Europe," which "historically, has been the basis of its evolution."[14] These objectives can better be achieved by developing "a contemporary corporate structure in the best interests of human and economic progress."

Reinhard Mohn's elaborate vision of a postsocialist corporate order, a strategy for making profits in a human way and putting them to the service of a more equitable society, is reminiscent of utopian capitalist thinking of the last century. His vision depends heavily on the development of a new "corporate man." He does not use this term, but his emphasis on changing the consciousness of entrepreneurs and managers sounds in some ways like the optimistic notions promoted in the Soviet Union two generations ago. In that case the state was supposed to serve as the teacher and enforcer of the new morality. The hopes for the new corporate man rest on the development of a more subtle, long-term, and complex notion of self-interest that can be nurtured in a progressive corporate culture.

Mohn understands the contradictions. He notes that the entrepreneur's personal goals are those that only financial success provides in a market-oriented society—"wealth, power, and esteem." But in the right cultural milieu a manager can be socialized to pursue goals on behalf of the corporation that go well beyond "profit maximization," which he characterizes as a downright "dangerous" goal for both the corporation and society. There is no better test of individual entrepreneurial performance than profit, but corporations, Mohn says, must develop social goals more subtle, more flexible, and more responsible than can be achieved by slavishly following the dictates of the bottom line. The man who remade Bertelsmann and turned it into a global media empire amassed extraordinary personal economic power and political influence in the years when global economic growth was at its peak. Mohn's successors, lacking his flair and unique authority, are struggling to continue the founder's global strategy at a time when competitive pressures in an increasingly integrated world economy make corporate pursuit of social goals more difficult.

CHAPTER FOUR

OF THE MAKING OF BOOKS

I.

ON THE DAY THE TWO HALVES OF GERMANY WERE RE-
united in October 1990, 8,492 publishers from ninety countries gathered at the Frankfurt Book Fair to push 114,000 new titles and a global backlist of 268,000 books in print. The fair is an annual literary bazaar and carnival featuring rounds of cocktail parties, dinners, power breakfasts, and buffets where established authors like John Irving and Jean M. Auel and celebrities eager to sell their moment of fame—that year it was Ivana Trump—are brought in to kindle worldwide interest in their book projects. A star author whose output can mean the difference between profit and loss for the publisher understands that he or she is a "product," as the best-selling crime novelist Scott Turow once described himself in the *New York Times*.[1]

They came from all over the world—317 publishing logos from Eastern Europe alone, 100 from Japan—to set up their wares in booths that ranged from closet-size stands for small publishers to "Maxwell Row," a whole corridor given over to flashy exhibits of the new literary products of the Robert Maxwell empire, then already on the brink of collapse. Reading scouts for publishing houses scurried from booth to booth advising their clients on what to buy, and the agents and publishers of the English-speaking world made the rounds, selling what they promised to be next year's best-sellers to book clubs and reprint houses around the world. Bantam had bought *The Quark and the Jaguar* by the Nobel Prize winner Murray Gell-Mann, a book destined for even more commercial success, so its promoters claimed, than Stephen Hawking's *A Brief History of Time*. ("I will take the reader further, reaching for answers that people really want," the distinguished physicist promised.)[2] This was a "big book" of the fair, along with Katharine Hepburn's memoirs, and publishers from around the world eagerly bid for the foreign rights. (Gell-Mann's manuscript was eventually rejected and has yet to appear in print.)

The publishing industry has been transformed in the last thirty years as a result of a four-stage process of consolidation. First, beginning in the 1960s large corporations not previously in the print business began to acquire publishers of textbooks. These were mostly electronics-based conglomerates such as IBM, ITT, Litton, Westinghouse, Xerox, and GTE. The education market was growing rapidly as the baby-boom generation poured into the schools and government was spending more money on schools and universities. The makers of computers and related electronic hardware were convinced that the computer would be universally accepted as a primary teaching tool, and they figured that if they also controlled the textbook software, they could dominate another huge government-subsidized market.

Then in the 1970s mass-communications companies began buying up publishers of "trade" books, as books of general interest are known in the industry. RCA, which owned NBC at the time, took over Random House, CBS picked up Holt, Rinehart & Winston, and Gulf & Western, which has since become a media conglomerate, started off in this direction by buying Simon & Schuster. By the beginning of the 1980s only a handful of independent trade-book publishers remained. Most of these mergers, however, were ahead of their time. The hardware companies and TV networks had little understanding of publishing. They looked for quick profits, and mostly failed.[3]

The third stage in the takeover by large corporations of what had traditionally been a small and quirky business began when the owners of the television networks, with mounting troubles of their own, decided to unload their publishing acquisitions. A few U.S.-based print-media companies picked them up. In 1980 Newhouse, the fourth-largest newspaper and magazine chain in the United States, a privately held family corporation, took over Random House from RCA.

Shortly thereafter the fourth stage began. Non-U.S. media and publishing corporations with large international holdings moved in and took over leading U.S. publishing houses. Rupert Murdoch—originally an Australian citizen until he swore allegiance to the United States, thereby becoming eligible to buy a major TV property in Boston—added Harper & Row to his empire. Hachette bought Grolier, the publisher of *Encyclopedia Americana*; Pearson, a British publishing giant, bought Viking, Penguin, and New American Library; Robert Maxwell bought Macmillan and Scribner's; Bertelsmann acquired Bantam Doubleday Dell; and Matsushita bought the Putnam Berkeley Group as part of its acquisition of MCA. The dollar was cheap, and global conglomerates found the prospect of picking up famous old American houses at bargain prices irresistible.

It was a time of unprecedented book sales and extravagant talk. As the 1980s began, the business press and financial analysts burbled about the synergies that would result from combining books, book clubs, magazines, music, video, and films all under a single corporate roof. "The good companies must be integrated," Lee Isgur, Paine Webber's media analyst, declared. The pronouncement typified the fashionable wisdom of the Reagan era. The "information revolution" had arrived, and communication, so Wall Street promoters promised, was becoming the principal human activity. Any enterprise without a powerful communications capability would not make it in "postindustrial society." Billions of dollars were raised for the merger of Warner Communications and Time, Inc., which also owns Book-of-the-Month Club and Little, Brown, much of it by luring investors with the magic of synergy.

But putting books, movies, magazines, and clubs under one corporate roof has produced few miracles. By and large, books have to make it on their own. An order from conglomerate headquarters to its film company to make a movie of one of its literary properties that would not otherwise be selected is obviously not good business. It is not a good way to keep talented people who are employed for their intuition about what will and will not sell. In the book business, synergies have been most successful in the children's market. Disney's trademarked characters can serve equally well in books, films, T-shirts, and theme parks. Of the ten best-selling children's paperbacks of 1990, eight had "Teenage Mutant Ninja Turtles" in the title.[4]

By the end of the 1980s the production of general books of fiction and nonfiction in the United States had been substantially taken over by the global entertainment and mass-media conglomerates. The dreams of the global media conglomerates changed the culture of bookmaking, broadening, and frequently cheapening, the understanding of what a book is.

By tradition, publishing was a labor of love. Entrepreneurs became publishers primarily because they loved books at least as much as money, and they enjoyed being with writers. Others started bookstores because they delighted in introducing readers to books and counted it a bonus that they might even turn a profit. The great majority of writers, then as now, wrote because of a compulsion to put thoughts and feelings on paper, a conceit that these scratchings merited at least the few months of shelf life likely to be accorded them in the bookstore, and the hope that their work would inform or touch a few thousand readers. Money was distinctly secondary, as the odds against making any were considerable. When Joseph Heller delivered the manuscript for *Catch-22* in 1960 he received the final installment on his $1,500 advance. He had no particular reason to hope for more.

Writers and critics celebrate this golden age long gone when editors devoted themselves to writers, and Alfred Knopf reputedly would publish no author whom he would not invite to dinner. The industry attracted men and women with literary ambitions, at least literary tastes, who were willing to work long hours in dingy offices for small pay for the privilege of making books happen. Publishers were patrons of literature and learning, and occasionally a Bennett Cerf would come along with a commercial flair. But as the pace of contemporary publishing has quickened and the industry has become more commercial and less caring about individual books, the memories of the good old days become more idyllic and more mythic. Many trees were felled in the preconglomerate era to offer readers pulp, schlock, and indifferent literary products. (It takes seventeen trees to produce a ton of paper, from which about 2,000 300-page books can be printed).[5] Then as now a few authors made considerable amounts of money. And today most authors still write books for largely noncommercial reasons, which is fortunate since the overwhelming majority of books published sell fewer than 3,000 copies and most writers earn no more than $5,000 a year from books. But the globalization and commercialization of publishing are changing the way books are conceived, the way they are written and edited, and the cultural impact they are having around the world.

II.

Publishing has become a global industry. Owning publishing properties in several countries is no different from owning other commercial operations in a variety of places, except that it encourages dreams of turning books into global products. Despite the difficulties, the need for translation being only one of them, a few books such as Alex Haley's *Roots*, Umberto Eco's *The Name of the Rose*, and books by John Le Carré and Gabriel García Márquez have sold in large quantities all over the world. The same could have been said for *Anna Karenina* over a century ago, but the difference now is that global distribution is greatly speeded by copublishing arrangements and near-simultaneous launchings in a number of countries. Danielle Steel is a prolific and successful Bertelsmann author, along with two or three other authors the closest thing to a global best-selling book machine there is. But Dell, the Bertelsmann subsidiary in the United States that is her primary publisher, does not have the power to require this producer of yearly blockbusters to publish with Bertelsmann-owned presses in other countries nor to turn over the foreign rights. She herself is a global industry, and there are many agents and publishers waiting in line for a share.

Nevertheless, the number of manuscripts that turn into global books is exceedingly small. Film and music can be easily marketed as global products because their chief attractions are action, sound, and beat. A Pakistani audience can watch an action-packed Arnold Schwarzenegger film with Urdu subtitles and come away with just about everything the film has to offer. The essence of a book, on the other hand, is language. A translation is a reflection of a literary work as perceived by a translator who is usually not the author. Inevitably, a book displaying literary artistry or complex thought will be read by foreign readers as if reflected in a glass darkly. Even a brilliant translation is a different book. This reality sets limits to global marketing. Books do not travel well in their original language, unless it happens to be English, and then only a tiny fraction of the world's Coke-guzzlers or Madonna fans is likely to pick it up.[6]

But a very few books are now conceived from the start as global products. Mostly they are slices of American life written for a huge mass audience around the world modeled on earlier blockbusters and marketed like any Hollywood fairy tale. Indeed, such books are either inspired by a film or designed to whet appetites for the major motion picture that is soon to be. *Scarlett: The Sequel to Margaret Mitchell's Gone with the Wind*, published by Time Warner's Warner Books, was released simultaneously in forty countries in the fall of 1991, but this unprecedented global launching, which resulted in phenomenal sales, was possible only because 100 million readers had already read the original and hundreds of millions more had seen the movie. Shortly after the end of the Gulf War in 1991, General H. Norman Schwarz-kopf, who had become a world celebrity thanks to his nightly appearances on global television during the conflict, sold the rights to his memoirs to Bantam for somewhere between $5 million and $7 million and publishers virtually everywhere competed for the foreign-language rights. Madonna's *Sex* was launched simultaneously in five languages, but what sold the book needed no translation.

Even books from Britain encounter problems in the American market, despite the common language. Occasionally, the story lines of British novels are altered to accommodate American readers. In Jeffrey Archer's novel *First Among Equals*, a tale of British politics, the book was "recast" for the American audience. As Joni Evans, the editor of the American edition, explained, "The person who ended up being elected prime minister was not the same man who won in the British version. It was all with Jeffrey's approval. . . ."[7]

Readers buy books for all sorts of reasons—to give a gift, to satisfy curiosity, to gain wisdom, to experience the joy of learning or the sound of poetry, to escape into other people's lives through stories, plays, and novels, to devour gossip, to find the meaning of life, to spice an evening with the thrills of the chase or the bedroom, or to acquire useful information about how to bake a truly delicious carrot cake or to make a million dollars in hog-belly futures. A general-interest book is many things—an object to grace a coffee table, an illustrated manual on how to unclog the sink, a novel to last an airplane ride or to reread over a lifetime. According to tradition, when sheets of paper were bound in buckram the publisher was offering an implied warranty that the contents were worth keeping. Books were permanent acquisitions that became parts of one's life, unlike periodicals, which were for tossing after a quick read. But the distinction has become blurry.

As publishing has merged into the entertainment industry, books for the general reader now increasingly make the front page. Kitty Kelley's account of Nancy Reagan's alleged lunchtime trysts with Frank Sinatra and Bob Woodward's account of General Colin Powell's private agonizing over the Gulf War offered inside peeks into the corridors of power that became top news stories all over the world. Famous novelists such as Norman Mailer now find themselves reviewed on page one of the *New York Times*. Authors have become celebrities largely because of the money they are reported to earn. In the 1980s the public's interest in other people's money reached new heights as magazines and newspapers devoted ever more space to the salaries, bonuses, fabulous deals, and purported net worth of industry tycoons and media celebrities. A few star authors now joined their ranks, packaged and marketed like rock stars and sports figures, although neither the fame nor the money was quite on the same scale.

But trade-book divisions are at the mercy of customers' whims, changing fashions, and the competition from a variety of entertainment enterprises skilled in luring prospective readers to easy listening or mindless viewing. Publishers know that Samuel Butler, the great English novelist who was not hugely popular in his day, had it right: "God will not have any human being know what will sell."[8]

On the other hand, educational and scientific book publishing, though it rarely makes headlines or the *Today* show, makes money; profit rates range between 15 and 25 percent as compared with 5 or 6 percent for trade publishers if they are lucky. A business built on books that are required reading is obviously more stable than one built on catching the consumer's eye at a mall bookstore or hoping for the sort of publicity or reviews that make millions of people feel guilty or deprived if that book is not on their night table. Thus Simon & Schuster is a wholly owned subsidiary of an entertainment conglomerate, but it has also become the nation's largest educational publisher by paying over a billion dollars to acquire Prentice Hall, Ginn & Company, and other suppliers of marketable information to largely captive audiences. Trade publishing now accounts for just 23 percent of Simon & Schuster's total revenues.[9] Reference books have a much more predictable global market than trade books. At Robinson's Galleria in Manila, a huge shopping mall in a city with a sizable middle class and millions of wretchedly poor people, the *Encyclopedia Britannica* is available on easy monthly terms—literally a lifetime purchase.

There is a genuinely global market for scientific publishing. Most of it is in English, which is the accepted language of science and learning around the world. In the 1980s a major share of scientific publishing in the United States was taken over by foreign conglomerates. Von Holzbrinck, a German publisher, bought *Scientific American*. Elsevier owns Congressional Information Service and has recently acquired a number of other specialized publishers in the United States. This giant Dutch company, having acquired Pergamon Press, which is the British company Robert Maxwell used to build his fortune, specializes in scientific and scholarly publications. It publishes technical books and more than a thousand newsletters and journals for communicating professional, academic, scientific, medical, and technical research developments around the world. Wolters Kluwer, another Dutch company, owns the venerable U.S. publisher Lippincott and has also picked up many other publishing ventures in the United States. In 1990 these two global publishing companies sold more than $2.4 billion worth of books and journals across the planet, just about equaling the sales figures for that year of the two largest American publishers, Simon & Schuster and Time Warner. Foreign publishers had taken over a significant share of the nation's scientific-information industry, but this caused almost no stir. Hardly anyone outside the industry knew that it was happening.

As the publishing business became more international, more and more foreign media companies considered it essential to acquire major publishing properties in the United States. It is the largest national book market in the world, college-educated, middle class, affluent, and its literary products travel better than those of any other country. But the U.S. market has a built-in limitation. Most Americans are not avid book readers. In 1988, according to Jason Epstein, editorial director of Random House, Americans spent about $3 billion on "consumer" books—about as much as they spent that year "on turkeys and apples."[10] According to the *Economist*, it was more like $6 billion, a discrepancy attributable to wildly different understandings of what a "general fiction and nonfiction book" is and to the notorious state of record-keeping in the industry.[11] The Association of American Publishers reports that only 13 percent of Americans buy books.[12] Just 14 percent of the population say that reading is their favorite way to spend an evening—down from 21 percent when the same question was asked in 1938.[13]

However, what Americans read still sets fashions all over the world. A book that is popular in the United States is likely to sell well in Europe and Japan. It rarely works the other way around. The

American market is not only huge but it is, as Alberto Vitale, the head of Random House, puts it, "homogeneous." Popular attitudes are more "monolithic," he argues, because lifestyles are shared across class lines. The millionaire with forty-five acres and the clerk with a patch of green behind his tract house both care about their gardens in the same way. This makes it easier, he says, to sell books to a wide public.

III.

In the mid-1970s a revolution took place in what had been the weakest link of the book business, retail distribution. Shopping malls were sprouting all over the United States, and national chains of retail bookstores were put together to take advantage of a new mass clientele. The largest of them was Waldenbooks, a division of the phenomenally successful Kmart stores; by the end of the 1980s it had more than 1,250 bookshops around the country. The relocation of bookstores to the sites of America's great spending spree of the 1980s did wonders for the visibility and sales of general-interest books and the character of bookstores was transformed.

The idea behind the chains was to market "consumer" books like any other product using sophisticated merchandising techniques. The chains discovered that not only could they make best-sellers by concentrating on stocking "brand-name" authors in large quantities, but they could change the meaning of best-seller. Before the rise of the chains, even blockbuster novels could not aspire to sales of more than 350,000 hardcover copies, and commercial success on that scale was a rarity. In the 1980s a few of the biggest best-sellers, thanks to their promotion by the chains, were selling a million or more copies in hardcover.

The rise of the chains, as Robert Gottlieb, who was president of Knopf for many years, explains, had the effect of shifting responsibility for marketing from the publisher to the retailer. Old-fashioned publishers considered it their primary task to convey their personal enthusiasm for their books, first to the bookstores and then to the public. When the chains became bigger than the trade publishers, the chains took over this task. The chains decided which books they would feature, and because the orders were so huge, the chains had the bargaining power to decide which titles would be displayed in the window and which would receive the largest advertising promotion. As the volume of sales grew, they were able to offer such large discounts on hardcover best-sellers—usually 35 percent—that hardcovers could now be marketed much like mass paperbacks, but with much greater profit on each book sold.

Like any supermarket, the chain bookstore reserved its precious shelf space for products that moved. That meant brisk sellers; books that didn't move were packed up and sent back, usually within a few weeks. Anywhere from 20 to 40 percent of books "sold" to bookstores wind up unsold, and the publisher bears the loss. In the trade-book divisions, manuscripts were read with the requirements of the giant retail distributors in mind. Brand-name authors, formula fiction, and celebrity biographies were the staples of the industry. To some extent they always had been, but now the "big book" became much more of an investment. The Newhouse empire, Rupert Murdoch, and Robert Maxwell could provide a Random House or Harper or Macmillan with the cash to play in this high-stakes game. With a few notable exceptions, independent publishers without a corporation awash in cash behind them could not.

The chains wielded enough power over the publishers to force them to commit themselves to huge first printings so that the stores would not risk being out of stock of a hit book even for a few days. The titles that didn't turn out to be hits were returned—sometimes in the hundreds of thousands—to end their short lives as pulp. The exact dimensions of the mountain of pulp produced by Ronald Reagan's autobiography and speeches, for which he was paid a reported $8 million, is unknown.

The new dimensions of the book market have done much to change the culture of bookmaking at every stage of the process. Authors are now coached in television techniques in preparation for their coast-to-coast tours. In more and more cases, the author's good looks or mastery of the art of the sound bite is more important for selling the book than its contents. TV promos are carefully designed to excite bookstore buyers and TV-show publicists. But the first audience, and from a commercial standpoint the most important, is the sales force, which must be revved up to sell books few of them will ever read. Some editors resort to stunts to push their books. At Random House the editor of the life story of the founder of Domino's Pizza ordered pizzas for 135 sales representatives, and they arrived in exactly thirty minutes as promised.[14] At another house an editor passed out breakfast rolls at a sales conference made according to a recipe in a new cookbook the publisher was about to release, but they were leaden and the book died on the conference table.

In the increasingly commercialized environment of the 1980s publishing more and more mimicked the film and TV industries. Editors relentlessly looked for ways to repeat the successes of the past: combine a best-selling name with a book idea close to something already proved in the marketplace and enlist the enthusiasm of the chains. Books would be certain to fly off the shelf. Or so it was thought. However, best-sellers are still largely hit-and-miss affairs. Books still have to be published one by one, and while critics might complain that too many books are cut from the same cloth, as a technical matter this is only partially true. Each book, however indistinguishable from the next, is to some degree a custom product requiring individual judgments for which neither robots nor computers are yet suitable.

But the economics of the business has encouraged assembly-line publishing. Publishers can hedge against their own bad guesses on any single book only by publishing more titles, looking desperately for the winners to "flog" with big advertising budgets and continental tours. Publishers must keep putting out revenue-producing products—the so-called "midlist"—to take care of the light bill and to defray the costs of the many individuals whose judgment and energy are needed at every stage of acquisition, production, distribution, and marketing. Rather than let their book-publishing capacity lie fallow, publishing houses began to look like factories. Random House in its various divisions lists about 2,500 new titles a year. When the recession of the 1990s hit, publishers trimmed their lists, wrote off millions in advances that did not result in profitable books, and fired editors who did not pay enough attention to the bottom line. But the problem remained. Trade publishing was still a gamble. Even though they were now buttressed by elaborate computer projections, decisions involving millions of dollars were still seat-of-the-pants judgments.

IV.

When Bertelsmann decided to make a major investment in the U.S. publishing industry, it discovered how resistant the book world is to globalization. The top management of the company has a conservative view of what a global product is, an awareness that in the media business there are not many, and a skeptical view of how easily synergies can be achieved. At the same time it has an expansive view of global ownership. Since American books travel more easily than those of any other country, the company was determined to anchor its global expansion strategy to a major publishing acquisition in the United States.

In 1977 Bertelsmann bought Bantam, a leading mass-paperback publisher based in New York. Alberto Vitale, an Italian Jew who had spent his early years in Egypt, was brought in as head of the company. A graduate of the Wharton School and years of service at Olivetti and IFI, the Italian company that owns Fiat, he was a cosmopolitan businessman with no experience in trade publishing. However, he conceived what he proudly claims to be the book deal of the century, the ghost-written autobiography of Lee Iacocca, which he insists will outsell *Gone with the Wind* by the end of the century. As the chain discounts cut into mass-paperback sales, Bantam became a profitable hardcover publisher while maintaining its share of the mass-paperback market.

In 1986 Bertelsmann decided to buy Doubleday, an old and famous American publishing house for which it paid more than $475 million. The purchase included not only Doubleday and Dell publishing operations, but the Literary Guild, which is the second-largest book club in the United States, seven smaller clubs, 50 percent of a British book club, four printing plants, and a chain of bookstores. Not only did Bertelsmann share the general interest among European media companies in the newly concentrated book-publishing business in the United States, but it had particular reasons of its own to acquire Doubleday. Book clubs were the foundation of Bertelsmann's global business, and although Doubleday had a well-deserved reputation in the 1980s for being mismanaged and showed signs of floundering, Mark Woessner was confident that Bertelsmann could turn the operation around. Owning the book clubs was important for defensive reasons as well. There was always the risk that the American book clubs might embark on a campaign to seize part of the highly profitable European market.

The once-distinguished company had been run by the Doubledays for three generations. It was famous for publishing commercial blockbusters by such authors as Edna Ferber, Daphne Du Maurier, Herman Wouk, Leon Uris, and Victoria Holt. Unlike virtually every other publisher, it had its own printing plants. It had a roster of gifted editors. In 1978 Nelson Doubleday, Jr. had ascended to the president's chair. Almost immediately the company's problems multiplied. Book-club profits declined as the chains began offering discounts. While the last of the Doubledays in publishing devoted his attention to his prized possession and real love, the New York Mets, "armadas of vice-presidents," as a former senior editor at Doubleday put it, "tall[ied] up losses and constantly sound[ed] the alarm."[15] The company was slow to perceive that bargaining power had shifted to best-selling authors and their agents, and they lost Stephen King, Irwin Shaw, and other profitable literary properties by being inflexible and slow to react. The printing facilities aged, and the physical appearance of the books, in one competing publisher's words, became so "debased . . . that one wonders why they would produce books instead of baseball."[16]

Bertelsmann management was confident that it had the experience and sophistication to take Doubleday assets, combine them with other Bertelsmann operations, and show the American publishing industry what good management could accomplish. The man who had presided over Bantam's success, Alberto Vitale, was put in charge of Bertelsmann's publishing operations in the United States. When Vitale suddenly left three years later to take the presidency of Random House, Doubleday had undergone considerable reorganization. The list had been cut. All but one of the printing plants had been sold off along with the retail bookstores. Six hundred employees had been fired, given early retirement, or transformed into part-time consultants. More Doubleday books were appearing on the best-seller lists. But Bertelsmann's American publishing operation was still a disappointment. "The Germans have responded by assuming that what works in Europe works here, and it does not," a Doubleday editor explained.[17] Considerable money was spent on European-style expensive catalogs to shore up the declining book-club membership, but the extra attention inspired no new loyalty in the fading membership. Woessner conceded, "It was perhaps too much of an attempt to transfer European know-how to America."[18]

"God knows what they promised the Supervisory Board in Germany to sell this deal," says Vitale. The top managers who arranged the acquisition, including Michael Dornemann, had little understanding of the trade-publishing business. They were in a "political bind" since they had held out the prospects of profits they could not deliver, especially since the business climate in the United States had worsened. The primary interests of the Americans at Doubleday and the owners in Germany clashed. The Doubleday executives were interested in reviving a distinguished publishing house, not in Bertelsmann's bottom line. Bertelsmann executives were bent on convincing their board that they had not made a mistake. That meant trying to increase profits fast, a goal hard to achieve in any year in the industry but especially hard at the onset of a recession. Vitale says that there was no editorial interference from Germany while he was president, but there was pressure to cut costs, and as the years went by the pressure from Bertelsmann increased.

Bertelsmann kept replacing top executives of its publishing acquisitions. A 29-year-old American who had been at Book-of-the-Month Club was brought in to run the floundering book clubs, but he complained that he had to share authority with a German executive and quit after nine months. One executive said the arrangement was like teaming a rock-and-roll star with a Tibetan monk. Top executives and editors at Doubleday and Bantam were replaced, in some cases twice in a four-year period. German executives were brought in to rescue the floundering book clubs, and Bernard von Minckwitz, the head of Bertelsmann's worldwide book-publishing activities, began spending a month a year in New York. As the German executives played a more active role in overseeing their American media properties, language problems surfaced. (Stephen Rubin, the head of Doubleday, recalls telling von Minckwitz that "my hands were really tied, and he looked down at my hands.")[19]

But six years after the purchase, Bertelsmann's American book-publishing ventures were doing better. German book-club experts began to understand the American market, and developed new clubs for the women's market and for children. The Literary Guild had begun to be profitable. In July 1992 Doubleday, Dell, and Bantam had eleven books on the *New York Times* best-seller lists, three of them by John Grisham, a new star writer of crime novels. In the recession year 1992 Bertelsmann did $2.5 billion worth of business in the United States and Canada. Worldwide, Bertelsmann sales were up more than 10 percent, and virtually alone among the global media giants, Bertelsmann reduced its debt to almost zero.[20] The world's largest publishing company announced that it had bought a brand-new large office building on Broadway near Times Square in a bankruptcy sale after being offered a $10-million "tax incentive package" by New York city and state authorities. The building has been renamed the Bertelsmann Building, a clear statement that Bertelsmann is in the United States to stay.

V.

The internationalization of publishing is being driven by a number of political and economic developments. Because of the economic integration of the European Community, German, French, and Spanish publishing houses are all under greater competitive pressures to treat Europe as one great market. The largest publishers have little choice but to think globally. U.S. publishers are acquiring sister companies in Canada, Australia, and New Zealand and entering into copublishing arrangements in such places as Japan and Hungary. For a number of U.S. publishing houses, about a fifth of their sales and profits come from overseas, approximately four times what they were ten years ago.[21]

One indication of the growing importance of the global market for U.S. publishers is the number of foreign-born executives who run Boston and New York publishing houses. In 1990 an Iranian-born executive was head of Houghton Mifflin, a native of Italy ran the Random House publishing operation, a Cambridge-educated Indian was president of its Knopf division, and the former editor of the London *Times* ran Random House's principal trade imprint. The same phenomenon is occurring in many industries besides publishing. Top executives in all fields are increasingly mobile and have fewer ties to their countries of origin. But, as Peter Mayer, an American who is the chief executive of the Penguin Group with offices in London, observes, "There is an international component to large-scale trade publishing today," and "people who have international backgrounds" are in greater demand than ever before. "Heads of houses now have to have a much greater understanding of different markets and different economies," agrees Alun Davies, who is the president of Bantam Doubleday Dell's international division and a Welshman.[22]

Nonetheless, the global publishing industry faces obstacles to growth and further concentration. Despite global talk and dreams of synergy, nationalist and ethnic feelings are now stronger than ever in much of the world. True, in the United States there is so far relatively little backlash prompted by the increasing foreign ownership of major producers of entertainment and culture. One reason is that the products are still overwhelmingly identifiable as American and American culture is such a dominant force in popular culture around the world. Some people in the entertainment industry become wistful or angry at the thought of movie and recorded-music profits ending up in Japan. But hardly anyone who shops in bookstores or newsstands worries about a cultural "takeover" of the U.S. book and magazine industry by France, Germany, or the Netherlands, which, to no small extent, has already happened.

Because publishing involves the spread of ideas and information, which in the twentieth century are keys to the production of wealth and the exercise of power, governments take a keen interest in foreign books and magazines. In the United States the market is much more open, but some U.S. local governments become suspicious when American-history textbooks are published by British, German, or Japanese companies. There has been enough talk about foreign-owned textbook houses constituting a threat to "the American way of life" to discourage some prospective purchasers from abroad.[23]

During the Cold War, the Soviet Union, China, and many other countries barred all literature published outside the country from public sale. There were limited exemptions for technical and scholarly books, and government and party officials and a few scholars were allowed to pore over the New York Times and Newsweek to assemble evidence of corruption and collapse in the capitalist world. At the same time the state publishing houses flooded the country with the books it wanted citizens to read. Along with a number of other governments the Soviets and Chinese subsidized the export of huge quantities of books to the Third World.

In the 1950s and 1960s the United States joined the book war. U.S. Information Agency libraries in Western Europe offered an ideological weapon against the Left. Under the Marshall Plan, government funds were used to subsidize the export of American books and magazines provided they "reflect[ed] the best elements of American life and shall not be such as to bring discredit on the United States."[24] The taxpayer was paying thirty-eight cents of every dollar the publishers received.

Politicians and intellectuals in developing countries are the ones who still worry most about foreign cultural domination. As they struggle to define their own national identities, these leaders see the penetration of foreign print and TV news organizations, books, magazines, film, and television programming as a threat because global media products can overwhelm local cultures. But many of these same leaders want their people to have access to the scientific and scholarly books of developed nations, although some find the dependence on foreign brain power humiliating. As an official of the International Association of Scholarly Publishers put it in 1985, "The book flow has been and continues to be a one-way traffic—from North to South. . . ."[25] Even the flow of books between the United States and Japan has largely been a one-way street, despite the high quality of Japanese scholarship in many fields.

In the 1980s Third World politicians supported efforts by the United Nations Educational, Scientific, and Cultural Organization (UNESCO) to promote a "new international information order" aimed at equalizing access to information. Under its auspices the Nobel laureate Seán MacBride issued a report that was widely regarded in Europe and the United States as an attack on privately owned news organizations and publishers and an attempt to delegitimize international copyright protection at exactly the moment when piracy was threatening the economic basis of the global culture industry. The United States walked out of UNESCO. But with the collapse of socialism at the end of the decade and the resurgence of free-market ideology almost everywhere, the idea that information painstakingly developed by writers, artists, scholars, and computer engineers is either a free good or an instrument of imperialism was no longer fashionable. Piracy continued to flourish, but the "new international information order" disappeared and the United States returned to UNESCO.

However, the issues of cultural diversity and cultural dependence remain. Most underdeveloped countries have neither the political clout nor economic strategy to protect their local cultures from being overwhelmed by global information media. In the major markets of Europe and the growing markets of Canada and Mexico, however, these concerns about culture are still very much alive. The term "cultural identity" became a verbal weapon in negotiations with the European Community and within the Community. In Mexico and Canada feelings ran even stronger. When the U.S.-Canadian free-trade talks were announced in the mid-1980s, the outcry among Canadian artists, filmmakers, publishers, and others in the culture industry was so loud that the Canadian government was forced to announce that Canadian culture would not be on the table. Only on the emotionally charged issue of national control over strategic oil, gas, and uranium resources was a similar pledge given.

As Donald G. Campbell, the chairman of the board of the company that publishes *Maclean's*, Canada's principal weekly news magazine, puts it, "We use the word culture in Canada in its broadest sense: it refers to those characteristics which give Canada a sense of identity, thus distinguishing itself from other nationalities."[26] With the growing threat of the breakup of Canada, the issue of Canadian identity has taken on greater urgency. Noting that 77 percent of all newsstand periodicals and three out of four books sold in Canada originate in foreign countries, Campbell calls for protection of Canadian-owned media. According to a survey by *PW International*, "No foreigner has been able to buy a Canadian house for some years." France and Japan discourage foreign control of publishing houses and most developing countries "permit only minority partnerships by foreigners." A number of other governments flatly refuse to allow foreigners to invest in publishing properties. The United States is intent on including cultural products in future trade agreements with Canada and Mexico, but resistance to relaxing restrictions on American books, magazines, films, and TV programs remains strong in both countries.

VI.

The arrival of the electronic book has made it easier for books to cross borders. Though the hardware is still expensive, it is now possible to read a best-seller on a computer and to adjust the print size or command illustrations to appear by punching a key. But despite the elaborate electronic networks for the diffusion of information that increasingly define our age, books (in the old-fashioned sense of the word) and journals (usually bound for permanent library use) remain the principal communications media for the transmission of ideas. The great majority of people today pick up information from television and radio; they are entertained by video and film. But these increasingly globalized channels of communication do not lend themselves well to the exploration of ideas. What comes across the air waves, even in most public-affairs documentaries, is the simplification of thought. Often it is the vulgarization or distortion of ideas that first came to light in a book or an article. The electronic media are not substitutes for the printed word. They feed on it, usually transmitting snippets of thought as an obbligato to pictures or as teasers for ads. Books and literary or scholarly articles remain the only vehicles that permit the sort of prolonged intellectual encounter of one mind with another by which knowledge is transformed into understanding.

To be sure, books require active collaboration of the reader, a degree of concentration most people, bombarded and distracted by messages of all sorts, are unwilling or unable to dedicate to them. Henry David Thoreau was not thinking only of Goethe and Montesquieu when he wrote, "Books must be read as deliberately and reservedly as they were written," but presumably also of the dime novels of his day.[27] The two generations that have grown up with television have exhibited less patience for books demanding concentration than their parents had, and the MTV generation even less. Casual readers in the United States no longer peruse newspapers in the numbers or with the care that was typical even twenty years ago.[28] It is not surprising, therefore, that the publishing divisions of global entertainment conglomerates devote ever smaller proportions of their lists to poetry, essays, analytical history, or social critiques (as opposed to flashy manifestos). "One of a kind" books, as some publishers call nonformula books, are hard to sell. A few "difficult" books such as Paul Kennedy's *The Rise and Fall of the Great Powers* become fashionable, usually for extrinsic and entirely unpredictable reasons.

The "bottom line"—the accounting mantra old-line editors hate—echoes through the corridors in foreign-owned publishing houses in the United States just as in publishing houses that are still U.S.-owned. According to the publisher Andre Schiffrin, "For decades, the industry averaged a 4 percent after-tax profit. Now the conglomerates expect anywhere from 10 percent to 16 percent."[29] How driven a media conglomerate may be to reap quick profits has a great deal to do with the parent corporation's debt load or the promises made to sell the board on the acquisition and little to do with the color of the flag flying at world headquarters. Non-U.S. global media conglomerates mortgaged themselves heavily—in Maxwell's case to the point of extinction—in order to acquire global-scale publishing properties.

Media conglomerates, wherever they are based, pay attention to profits and market shares, and they are quite prepared to publish books critical of their countries of origin, provided there are good business reasons for doing so. Death warrants even for books already at the press are occasionally signed in the executive offices of corporate publishers because publication threatens to bring bad publicity, lawsuits, or the wrath of a powerful corporation or personage.[30] When executive censorship happens, it is an assault on editorial independence and free expression. But a foreign conglomerate in America is, if anything, more likely to be nervous about the negative effects of executive high-handedness than a U.S.-based company because it is more vulnerable to charges of cultural imperialism.

The ability of large publishing conglomerates to operate on a global scale creates both pressures and opportunities for the increasing commercialization of cultural products. New technologies are accelerating this process. "One day you'll go to your book store and you'll find a display rack with an electronic medium that lets you page through any book electronically," says Peter Yunich, Simon & Schuster's chief information officer. The prospective buyer can consult an electronic display to scan reviews or watch the author promote the book. "You tell the clerk which book you'd like to buy. He'll ask you whether you want it with a dust jacket and hardcover binding or as a paperback. . . . Three minutes later, you have your book with the specified typeface and bindings. The store carries no inventory, and its only investment is in a local reproduction device that produces bound books, probably laser-driven."[31] This technology, company officials say, will be available by the mid-1990s.

According to its chairman, Richard Snyder, Simon & Schuster is not "just a publisher anymore but a creator and exploiter of copyrights." Because the information is stored digitally, "We now can sell the same information in various forms." Production time will be cut in half. It will no longer be necessary to maintain large inventories or to contemplate huge returns. Computer-based information will be increasingly used in making decisions about which books to publish. All will be expected to show a profit.

The speedup in the flow of books and in the use of computers to keep track of inventory has greatly reduced the life span of the average book. From the 1930s even into the 1970s a book could stay on a bookshop shelf for months until the proprietor got around to doing a storewide inventory. This afforded time for the book to receive attention from reviewers and perhaps to catch on. Today, because inventory can be instantly monitored by computer, the shelf life of a novel by an unknown author can be little more than a month. The "bottom line" dictates the merciless pruning of backlists. Books go out of print when they fall below an arbitrarily set sales minimum, "cultural genocide by computer," as Lewis Coser calls it.[32]

The traditional vehicle for exploring ideas in depth and at length, the general-interest book designed for citizens rather than academics, is the only commercially distributed printed product not dependent on advertising. By almost any measure it is becoming more and more of a commercial product rather than a vehicle for spreading intellectual or artistic work. The French sociologist Pierre Bourdieu has a reasonably precise measure of what becoming "commercial" means. He points out that the Paris publisher of Samuel Beckett's *Waiting for Godot* sold an average of 2,000 copies a year in the first five years after publication. It eventually became a worldwide classic and still sells respectably. But today's computers are rarely programmed to show this sort of patience.

Some publishing executives argue that critics who decry the commercialization of literature are being elitist and antidemocratic. People are buying the books they want. It is the failure of the education system and the collapse of family discipline that is turning the United States into a land of illiterates. They point out that once-obscure Latin American literary figures and such writers as the Egyptian Nobel laureate Nagib Mahfuz would never have been known outside their own countries but for the global publishing conglomerates. If readers don't want to take Henry James, Faulkner, or Wittgenstein to the beach, that is not the fault of S. I. Newhouse or Reinhard Mohn.

Publishing executives like to point out that small presses have sprung up to fill the gap left by the decisions of the large commercial publishing houses to cut back on poetry, essays, literary novels, and analytical history by little-known authors. University presses have carved out specialized niches and flourished. Small, independent bookstores have expanded, using computerized merchandising and business-school management techniques, and a number of independent bookstores became "superstores," so successful, in fact, that the chains copied them or took them over. (Borders, the most successful of the independents, was acquired by Kmart.)

But there is something a little disingenuous about this. As the March Hare explained to Alice, "I like what I get" is not the same thing as "I get what I like." People are influenced by what is available, visible, and publicized. Small publishers do not have the financial resources to support full-time writers. Publishers' decisions about what gets published and *how* it is published are important in the development of public tastes.

Good books in ever greater quantities are being published by the conglomerates, but they are overwhelmed by much greater quantities of ever trashier books. The danger is that because trade publishers "are in the fashion business," as Richard Snyder puts it, they are using their market power, whether or not they intend to do so, to reinforce orthodoxy of ideas, styles, and forms at a moment in human history when new ideas and unconventional approaches are desperately needed. There is a certain irony in all this. Just as state control over the printed word appears finally to be weakening around the world, market forces are establishing their own orthodoxies, not by suppressing thought but by drowning it out.

CHAPTER FIVE

IF MUSIC BE THE FOOD OF LOVE

I.

Recorded music is one of the world's most widely distributed industrial products. A world-class pop singer is a global brand name like Coke or Marlboro. In the flesh, superstars come and go, but their shadows and voices live on for decades. Music travels well because the language is universal. The essence of the song is in the beat, and fully as important as the words are the nonverbal messages the performer communicates with voice, dress, electronically synthesized sounds, guitar, drum, and—on music video—body language.

The products of the global pop-music industry are American in beat and in feel, and the market is dominated by American artists, promoters, and songwriters. British artists like the Beatles and the Rolling Stones have also figured prominently in the music revolution of the past thirty years, but their art is traceable to the same African-American roots from which blues, jazz, swing, rock, and rap have sprung. The black experience in America—the yearning, pathos, intensity, and energy inspired by a mix of African rhythms, slave songs sung in a strange land, and the speed and din of life in America—produced a cultural mix that has excited people everywhere in the twentieth century. This authentically American art form touches people across divisions of race, nation, and class in ways no other musical experience can equal.

Marketable songs that can command a worldwide audience cannot be reproduced in a Japanese laboratory. Talent has to be discovered or purchased, and because the discovery process is uncertain,
Americans still make the industry go even though they no longer own
it. Warner Music is the sole remaining global record company still
flying the American flag. The industry depends so much on talent
that megastars like Michael Jackson, Madonna, Prince, and Barbra
Streisand can exact tens of millions of dollars from their Japanese
employers. In a 1991 press release Sony claimed that "Jackson's new
relationship with Sony could easily be worth more than $1 billion."

The songs on the great majority of pop records in the global
market are in English, although the queen might not always recognize it as such. But this poses little problem for the great army of
pop-music aficionados around the world, most of whom do not understand the words. In Portuguese-speaking Brazil, about 70 percent
of the songs played on the radio are in English.[1] Robert J. Morgado,
the executive vice-president in charge of recorded music at Warner,
estimates that about 80 percent of the music sold in Germany is in
English. "It's about 50-50 in Japan."[2] Some genres of pop music are
infinitely transplantable; others, like American country music, have
only a limited market outside the United States.

The six record majors distribute virtually all recorded music carried by record stores in the United States including the independent
labels, which for the most part no longer have their own distribution.
The consolidation process is speeding up. The six now have more
than 95 percent of the American and over half of the European
markets.[3] Increasingly, the majors demand an equity share in the
independent labels whose discs and tapes they distribute.

One company, Philips, sells about half of all the classical music
sold around the world. The concert- and chamber-music literature of
the seventeenth, eighteenth, and nineteenth centuries, which makes
up the bulk of "museum music" as some in the industry call it, never
had a mass audience even in its own day, and the entire symphonic,
operatic, and chamber-music repertoire now accounts for less than 8
percent of the global music market and less than 5 percent in the
United States.[4] But Pavarotti in the flesh, Horowitz from beyond the
grave, and a handful of others have become global stars. Pavarotti's
rendering of a Puccini aria climbed to the top of the pop charts in
England and has been used to publicize world soccer cup matches on
TV and radio. At least one teenage magazine has started a column on
classical music.[5]

In 1990 the world recording industry had sales of about $20 billion, $8 billion in Europe, $6.5 billion in the United States, $3 billion in Japan, and more than $2 billion in the less-developed world.[6] Local pop artists sell well in their own countries all over the world. As popular as American music is in Japan, three-quarters of all recorded music sold there is by Japanese artists. About a fifth of the global pop and rock repertoire is British. Recently, songs in Portuguese, Spanish, and French have been finding an expanding global market. "We're importing music from places like Bulgaria, France, and Brazil that either celebrates a great ethnic tradition or a life style, like the Gypsy Kings," Bob Krasnow, chairman of Elektra Records, explains.[7] But by a wide margin American artists, American musical tradition, and shifting American tastes continue to define the industry across the entire planet.

Americans have been spending on compact discs, records, and tapes roughly what they spend on breakfast cereal. But corn flakes are fungible, predictable, and reliable; rock stars are none of the above. Packaged pop culture may be the fastest-growing global product in the world, but can't-miss products are few and far between. Since Michael Jackson, Whitney Houston, Bruce Springsteen, and a few other superstars can mean the difference between profit and loss for a major record company, finding them, promoting them, and keeping them is the obvious road to riches. But for every star there are enough expensive flops to make up a sizable chorus. Less than 10 percent of single records make it to the hit lists. In the music business everything depends on signing artists who resonate with the public taste or, better yet, are compelling enough to transform the buying habits of pop-music fans and set new fashions. The competition for talent is fierce, and the competition to secure radio and television promotion time is equally fierce. Promotion costs have skyrocketed, and because of the increasing importance of music video, the artists have to have the right look as well as the right sound. What is right is not only mysterious but subject to sudden shifts in fashion.

As in the rest of the entertainment industry, the record business has always been an uneasy alliance of the "creative types" and the "suits." To be a "great record man"—there are very few women in these jobs—demands that an executive have "ears." He must be able to listen to music and sense whether or not it will sell, or at least be able to convince his superiors that he has such a gift. The "suits" have no such pretensions. They hire the "ears." Walter Yetnikoff, head of CBS Records when Sony bought it in 1988, once boasted in an interview that he was tone-deaf. "I mean I can't *sing*," he hedged somewhat. "My ear is okay, but somewhere between the ear and the throat there is something missing."[8] Artists' managers on the lookout for hot new talent, record company A&R (artist and repertoire) men who buy the talent, pick the songs, and remake the personas of the singers they contract for—though less of this happens now that top singers and their managers and lawyers wield such power in the industry—are temperamental and highly mobile. A singer's trademark is on his or her birth certificate or business card, and it can be moved to another company whenever the contract expires. Since the average life of most successful pop stars is no more than five years— three hit albums, at the most—loyalty is not a prime value for either the companies or the stars, and temperament is frequently put to the service of tough bargaining.

Singers are of course notorious for temperament; it was not uncommon for a great diva to walk out of the opera house just before a performance because of a slight, real or imagined, or for no reason at all. The business types can be just as temperamental as the artists. The great record entrepreneurs styled themselves as characters. Yetnikoff, who began his career as a buttoned-down corporate lawyer, reinvented himself as a show-biz personality, cultivating in the process a well-deserved reputation for rage and abusiveness. His screams shattered glassware, it was said, and he resorted to tantrums in which he pummeled walls and spit out curses. Usually there was method in his madness. He inspired loyalty by being attentive to the stars, jetting off to California "because Michael needs me," and he cultivated the myth at CBS, which was the basis of his power and his license to be outrageous, that the artists were really his, not the company's.[9]

Yetnikoff defended his management style by pointing out that this is a business "where the product can talk back to you, where it can *scream* back at you."[10] Clive Davis, Yetnikoff's predecessor as head of CBS Records, discovered that artists can express temperament in a variety of ways. When Davis signed Janis Joplin, she proposed that they sleep together to celebrate the deal. He apologetically turned down the offer, but promised that CBS wasn't as formal as it might seem. A member of the band then suddenly got up from behind the conference table stark naked. "This is how informal *we* are," Joplin is supposed to have said.[11]

Had anyone in 1975 predicted that the two oldest and most famous corporate producers and marketers of American recorded music would end up in the hands of German printers and publishers and Japanese physicists and electronic engineers, the reaction in the industry would have been astonishment. By the early 1980s the notion provoked nervous laughter. How would Bertelsmann and Sony ever be able to manage the weird cast of creative characters who make up the record business? Why would they want to try? By the late 1980s it had happened.

"We knew we had to be in the United States in a big way. It is the world's largest media market. To be just in Europe—it's too narrow," Michael Dornemann, the man who masterminded Bertelsmann's major acquisitions in the United States, explained to skeptical business reporters a few months after negotiating the purchase of RCA Records for what industry pundits considered a highly inflated price.[12] (In 1986, the year of purchase, the company lost $35 million.) Until the mid-1980s Bertelsmann was still primarily a publishing company; its European record company, Ariola, was no more than a promising sideline. But Mohn and Woessner decided that the company's growth strategy depended upon developing its nonprint business. Having determined in the early 1980s to get out of all unrelated businesses, Bertelsmann resolved to go after every phase of the media and entertainment business. As Dornemann explains it, "We are not a boutique. We have to compete in every aspect of media."[13]

Michael Dornemann is a tall, energetic man in his late-40s who skis in Zermatt and radiates enthusiasm about living in America. After acquiring a doctorate in economics, he began his career as a systems engineer, marketing representative, and business consultant. Before he was brought into Bertelsmann in 1982 by his friend Mark Woessner, who had just become president of the company, he sold office machinery for IBM in Europe and advised BMW, the German carmaker, on corporate acquisitions. In 1985, on the strength of his reputation for strategic planning, he became Bertelsmann's executive vice-president for corporate development and a member of the board.

Bertelsmann had decided to buy up major media properties in the United States, and Dornemann was handed the assignment of his life. He flew to the United States to find the right takeover candidate. Bertelsmann had plenty of cash. The dollar was down. The media industry was poised for a comeback after the lean years of the late 1970s and early 1980s.

But Bertelsmann had a mixed record in its earlier forays into the American market. Not only had its plans to transplant its lavishly illustrated magazine *Geo* from Germany to the United States proved to be a fiasco, but another $5 million was dropped testing the idea of a book club. The idea was to recruit members by knocking on doors as in Bertelsmann's hugely successful operation in Europe.[14] Morton Janklow, the literary lawyer and book agent who was consulted on the project, had advised against it. "I told them nobody would open the door. In Chicago?"[15] Nonetheless, a full-time sales force of eighty managed to get 45,000 doors to open, not only in Chicago but in Kansas City, Cincinnati, and Dallas as well. Yet American readers proved too fickle, jumping from one club to another to take advantage of introductory offers.[16] "They had no loyalty," Bertelsmann officials complained as they packed up the project. The same year that American Circle Book Club was scrapped, Bertelsmann bid $130 million for *U.S. News & World Report* only to be nosed out by the real-estate developer Mortimer Zuckerman.[17]

Undaunted, Dornemann spent more than two years commuting between Gütersloh and New York in quest of American media properties. He had instructions to buy magazines. The music business was in a global slump. Bertelsmann had already acquired a music property in the United States in 1979 when it had bought the small Arista label. But Arista was losing money in the early 1980s for reasons typical in the industry; its superstar, Barry Manilow, had faded. In 1983 Bertelsmann had sold off 50 percent of Arista to RCA in return for a 25-percent share in the larger company. Although the arrangement with RCA was carefully designed to facilitate a possible future takeover of what was once the most famous record company in the world, this was not in Mark Woessner's mind when he launched his takeover quest in the United States. He was hungry for another successful American magazine. Dornemann looked over more than twenty-five takeover targets, but Woessner and the board thought the prices were excessive.

Suddenly RCA's music business came on the market. In December 1986, RCA itself, including its line of household appliances and the NBC networks, was swallowed by General Electric after a secret weekend deal was arranged between the chief executive officers of both companies. It was immediately apparent that GE was uncomfortable with the music business, which bore too little resemblance to the electronics giant's primary products, household appliances and weapons. "Write me a memo on the moral and ethical problems of the music industry," John Welch, the chairman of GE, asked Elliott Goldman, who had just signed a four-year contract as the new president of the RCA music operation a few days before RCA was sold. Welch's request was a tipoff. "What did he want with sex, drugs, and rock 'n' roll?" Goldman concluded as he set out to raise $400 million to try to buy the company himself. But Bertelsmann had the cash in hand.

Not only was Bertelsmann already a part owner of RCA Records, but Bertelsmann's European label, Ariola Records, had been operating a joint venture with RCA for some time. While Dornemann was pondering the RCA deal, Arista struck gold. Clive Davis, Arista's president, was famous for having discovered Janis Joplin, and he had brilliantly guided CBS Records all through the 1960s rock revolution—until federal prosecutors discovered the phony invoices he had been using to charge the company for home improvements and a lavish bar mitzvah reception. But now, having managed to avoid jail and land another top job in the industry, Davis scored again. He signed a 19-year-old model by the name of Whitney Houston, and her first album of the same name—with an assist from a $2-million promotion budget—sold 20 million, thus rivalling Madonna as the most successful female recording star in history.[18] The worldwide pop-music business was reviving. If Bertelsmann was to be in the game, it had to have a major American music property. With RCA in hand, why could not Bertelsmann come up with even bigger successes than Whitney Houston?

II.

When it was announced that Bertelsmann had paid $333 million to pick up the rest of RCA Records, about seventy times earnings, the music industry was stunned. RCA was a troubled company with a glorious past. Years before, RCA Victor, with its trademark picturing the world's most famous dog listening raptly to a Victrola, had been the most illustrious classical-record label. In 1904 Enrico Caruso became RCA's first superstar on the strength of the scratchy echoes of his glorious tenor voice.[19] In the years when classical music had a much more significant share of the market, RCA had exclusive recording contracts with the great names of the opera house and concert stage: Flagstad, Melba, Pons, Pinza, Rachmaninoff, Heifetz,

Stokowski, and Toscanini. But RCA had lost the race to develop the long-playing record to CBS. The LP, which revolutionized the industry when it was introduced in 1948, revolved at thirty-three and a third revolutions a minute and could accommodate a half hour of music. RCA responded with the smaller forty-five RPM disc, which was ideal for single pop songs. As late as 1967 RCA, CBS, and Capitol each had roughly the same share of the market.

As the 1960s got under way and the Beatles and Rolling Stones were changing pop musical taste around the world on competing labels, RCA kept reissuing Bing Crosby. In classical music it banked heavily on a fading opera star named Anna Moffo, who had married its president, Robert Sarnoff, the son of the founder. As the market for classical music shrank and carloads of records by the Boston Symphony and the Philadelphia Orchestra came back from the stores, a sizable chunk of the promotion budget was lavished on the new Mrs. Sarnoff. The sixties rolled over RCA like a tidal wave. But fortunately, a few years earlier the company had paid $40,000 to Sun, a small independent label, to buy up the contract of a young singer by the name of Elvis Presley. In the end, Elvis's immortality saved RCA.

Now Bertelsmann resolved to make it great once again. Within a year of acquiring RCA Records, the new German owners had combined its worldwide music business with their European music operations into the Bertelsmann Music Group. The headquarters was in New York and the head was Michael Dornemann. RCA had never understood the global nature of the record business, Michael Dornemann explained. "A country manager in France had to report to a regional manager. The regional manager was a businessman. The businessman reported to an international manager. . . . He reported to the chief executive officer for records, and he reported to someone who was responsible for records in RCA and he reported to the RCA boss. This was wrong. Today, there is only one businessman, me, and then you go directly down to the creative people who are in charge in their own countries."[20] Bertelsmann cut costs at RCA by $17 million, which involved closing a record plant in Indianapolis and firing about a quarter of the administrative employees.[21] Dornemann, Woessner, and other Bertelsmann executives gave enthusiastic interviews to the business press. "We're number two in the U.S. now," Dornemann announced. "I think we'll be catching CBS very soon."[22] Industry analysts were puzzled by the claim, which neither sales figures nor the pop charts appeared to support. But within a year RCA records was showing a modest profit thanks largely to the phenomenal success of two sound-track albums from the hit film *Dirty Dancing*.

"You can't run an international music business anywhere but from the United States," Dornemann insists. Pop music is an American product. You are selling American dynamism, speed, openness, and possibility with every record. Americans have to be in charge of the creative process. "You have to understand what creative people are like, what egos they have, how they think they can conquer the world with their artists. You should not have many business people above them."[23]

Philips had tried to run PolyGram with a resident Dutchman in charge, and EMI had a British national running Capitol. Neither had worked well. Dornemann, however, was confident that he could run the American music operation because the Bertelsmann credo was to give the local managers plenty of space. But from the first there was a clash of style and culture. Top executives kept flying in from Gütersloh to look over their New York property and to oversee the hiring and firing. The top brass from Germany made a point of staying away unless there were major decisions to be made. But since they kept replacing top American executives with some regularity, the German owners could be true to their principles and still be much in evidence. When executives from Germany flew into New York and held meetings with RCA executives, they tended to break into German in side conversations with one another, and this struck the old hands at RCA as offensive and gauche. Dornemann, who is completely fluent in English, concedes that employees felt excluded when the bosses lapsed into German, but now there is no problem. The executives from Germany are more careful, and they don't come so much anymore. "If I speak German, I talk only to myself," Dornemann says.

But the language barrier remained even when Bertelsmann executives used their excellent English. In his first conversations with Elliott Goldman, Dornemann began to instruct the president of RCA Records on Bertelsmann company culture, which he said was premised on "transparent pockets" and "flat pyramids." We work as a team. There are no secrets. We treat our managers as entrepreneurs. We make a point of not interfering. True to his word, Dornemann left Goldman alone and was uninvolved in day-to-day affairs. But the more he repeated the company aphorisms, the more skeptical the top American managers became. Dornemann was not a "record man." He had made his name in Germany by solving a technical problem involving the music business, but he knew nothing about artists or their culture. To the Americans, he seemed arrogant and ignorant. To Dornemann, Goldman seemed erratic and cantankerous.

The German owners would suddenly make their presence felt in ways that infuriated the Americans, in one case forcing Goldman to fire the head of international operations, who had moved his family to New York from California, because he is "not our style." (With his golden parachute, Goldman gleefully points out, the man started a successful new label.) According to Goldman, Dornemann interfered with a major licensing deal, forcing Goldman to alter it in ways, he believes, that eventually cost the company millions of dollars. Goldman also says that Mark Woessner flew into New York and killed Goldman's design for a new logo for BMG with a wave of the hand and a "Was ist dass?" The American creators considered it an act of desecration. What did these printers from Germany know about the music business?

Bertelsmann faced not only the daunting task of consolidating its global music operation but also the special problems of doing business in the United States. A *Rashomon* drama developed over the subject of office sex. It was as if the buttoned-up German executives and the bohemian American creative types exchanged stereotypes. The German executives surprised, even shocked the Americans as swingers on the loose. The Americans struck the managers from Germany as prudish and hypocritical. Conduct considered well within permissible limits in Munich or Madrid, the Germans complained, turned out to constitute sexual harassment in New York. Incidents that would not have made a ripple in Germany demanded the attention of top management.

After five years under Bertelsmann management RCA profits grew and Arista was doing well, but neither company had yet to "break" a new superstar. Its biggest new artist, Rick Astley, was developed in the United Kingdom and licensed to Arista in the United States. His debut album sold 7 million copies. But given the huge costs of acquiring, cultivating, and promoting talent, even this was not enough to come close to the 15 percent return Bertelsmann's president was now demanding from its divisions. RCA had dumped faded stars like Barry Manilow and John Denver, but

Dornemann was unwilling to increase its 10 percent share of the U.S. market by buying one of the few remaining "hot" independent labels, such as Chrysalis or A&M Records. (The latter was bought by Philips for $500 million.)

Goldman was fired after a year. Bob Buziak, a former artists' manager, was brought in as president and he lasted about two years. Events will show, he told an Italian magazine shortly before he was replaced, that the music giants willing to spend "all that money" to acquire independent labels were "right." Dornemann complained about the two American executives. "I learned that if you leave Americans too much alone," says Dornemann, "they take a little too much power." Goldman says that he wanted to make major investments to improve distribution and to increase volume through global licensing arrangements. Dornemann says that the departed RCA president made some important decisions without consulting him and that he was bent on raiding other companies for rock stars.[24] Bertelsmann, he said, had built its empire by cautious step-by-step expansion. Top management had no intention of throwing money at rock stars.

In the early 1970s Clive Davis had built CBS records through what he called "the heaviest talent-raiding campaign ever conducted," paying about a million dollars for Pink Floyd.[25] The last major raid was in 1978 when Warner snatched Paul Simon from CBS. But the amounts of money involved are now so large, the time frame so long, that raiding is almost never a viable strategy. Companies usually sign renewals with their top artists when there are still three or four more albums due. Typically, the royalties on the remaining albums of the old contract are increased to entice the artist.

"You *develop* artists," Dornemann explained to us. "You can't make money buying them. This is a misconception." Goldman launched into the same lecture in virtually the same words. Each accused the other of wanting to throw money at rock stars. Another *Rashomon*. Executive-suite conflicts of this sort are played out every day, usually in corporations in which the protagonists all speak the same language. But the unlikely collaboration of German print executives and management consultants, on the one hand, and American ears on the other, to market a peculiarly American product around the world did nothing for the troubled company in its losing battle with the other global music giants.

To make matters worse, in 1990 BMG was hit by a scandal involving the German rock group Milli Vanilli. Robert Pilatus, the son of a German striptease dancer and an American soldier, and Fabrice Morvan, an aspiring French dancer of Caribbean descent, teamed up for an album called *Girl You Know It's True* for Arista which sold 10 million copies and won several awards, including a Grammy. "Musically, we are more talented than any Bob Dylan," Pilatus boasted at a press conference. "Mick Jagger doesn't know how he should produce a sound." Despite an aggressive stage presence that had captivated fans in Europe, the duo had heavy German accents and unimpressive voices. Neither sang a word on their best-selling album.

Confessing at a press conference that they had made "a pact with the devil," the duo appeared in their signature costume—braided dreadlocks and spandex pants—and said they were Milli Vanilli no more. They accused Clive Davis of having been in on the ruse, an accusation denied by BMG. The denial is not believed by experienced hands in the industry since it was an open secret that Pilatus and Morvan didn't sound like their famous record. *Variety* reported that "that synching feeling" was spreading throughout the music business as companies marketed more and more of their artists primarily for their looks. Bertelsmann, which had been trumpeting the artists a few months earlier as an example of the new international rock star— non-American, non-British, but popular in both markets—treated the incident as a regrettable case of mislabeling. "It was a team act; some dance and others sing." But aggressive lawyers managed to mobilize large numbers of fans for class-action suits against BMG that alleged that the deception had caused irreparable damage to their young psyches. For the company, it was like being attacked by a swarm of bees.

Bertelsmann had earned back its entire purchase price in three years. But after six years RCA was still a big problem; indeed, among the big players in the industry it was at the bottom of the heap. As the 1990s began, Dornemann conceded that its expensive acquisition was "in bad shape except for country music." Then, after a six-year drought, Whitney Houston had another enormous hit; Arista was selling more than 20 million copies of the sound track of her widely panned movie *The Bodyguard*. Clive Davis, who insists on total independence from his German bosses, orchestrated this triumph. But, Michael Dornemann was beginning to feel vindicated.

III.

Alexander Graham Bell, the inventor of the telephone, was one of the founders of Columbia Records in 1887. The company's first hit was a faint but rousing rendering of John Philip Sousa's "Washington Post March" recorded by the composer and the U.S. Marine Band on a wax cylinder. In 1938 CBS bought Columbia for $700,000. From the outset "my baby," as William Paley called his company, managed to hire people to run the record business who had an uncanny sense of what the public wanted to hear or would come to want to hear. John Hammond was a jazz lover who grew up in a Fifth Avenue mansion, a Vanderbilt on his mother's side. He liked to frequent Harlem speakeasies and roam about the Old South looking for talent in out-of-the-way roadhouses. In his nocturnal wanderings he discovered and signed up Billie Holiday, and then for fifty years at Columbia he kept finding the stars: from Count Basie to Bob Dylan to Bruce Springsteen. Mitch Miller, who became a famous TV personality himself late in life with the 1950s *Sing Along with Mitch* television program, was a classical oboist who discovered Rosemary Clooney, Tony Bennett, and Mahalia Jackson. Goddard Lieberson, the president of CBS Masterworks, was an Eastman School of Music graduate, a classical pianist, and cultivator of the famous. He captured Vladimir Horowitz and Leonard Bernstein for CBS and persuaded the company to finance the musical *My Fair Lady*, from which CBS made $32 million. In 1948 the company had patented the long-playing record, and an LP of this one Broadway hit sold an unheard-of 5 million copies; this triumph gave Lieberson room to indulge his own taste, which ran to rather more sluggish sellers like the complete works of Arnold Schönberg.[26]

In November 1988 CBS agreed to sell CBS Records to Sony for $2 billion. By this time only two other music majors were still American companies. But this deal was the first Japanese takeover of a major media company. The announcement of the merger churned the wave of rising resentment in the United States against Japan for its conquest of the American market in so many areas, for its purchase of national treasures like Rockefeller Center, for the trade deficit, and, above all, for the loss of American jobs. Japan-bashing and America-bashing were feeding on one another, launching political careers and best-selling books in both countries. "We're obviously very disappointed that a great American record company . . . has been sold to a foreign company," an executive of Warner lamented in the *Wall Street Journal*.

Some music columnists expressed outright grief. Pop music was not just a product but a part of America's soul. CBS Records owned "the greatest library of recorded music in the world," *Rolling Stone* pointed out.[27] The rights to one of the richest lodes of Americana—music and lyrics of Bruce Springsteen, Count Basie, Bob Dylan, and hundreds more—were now in the hands of the very company that was most famous for besting American industry in consumer-oriented high technology. The nation's cultural heritage was being sold off piece by piece. A few months later Sony bought Columbia Pictures. "Where Will Japan Strike Next?" screamed the headline on *Fortune*'s cover, catching the anxious public mood. As communism collapsed in Eastern Europe and the Soviet Union began to unravel in 1989, it was now commonplace to note that the Cold War was over, and Japan had won.

It seemed like an altogether strange match, a marriage of a high-tech hardware company and a music company utterly dependent on artists accomplished at making a scene, volatile characters like Yet-nikoff who knew how to scream back, and "ears" who could hear new, marketable sounds blowing in the wind. For Sony the purchase was a key step in its new global strategy of controlling entertainment software to feed its hardware products. The Betamax fiasco in the early 1980s had been a painful lesson. Morita and Ohga resolved to control the very best in software to assure a steady supply for its millions of Walkmans, CD players, tape decks, and Trinitron TVs around the world and, if possible, to sign up the talent that would sell the next generation of electronic hardware products still on the drawing board.

"Software and hardware," says Norio Ohga, "are two wheels of the same cart." Sony was under increasing pressure to acquire entertainment software, for there were few films available to fit Sony's new products like the tiny Video Walkman. "Unlike TV or radio, the equipment that's on the rise now is the kind that is worthless on its own without software," Akihiko Tsuda, senior manager of corporate planning at Toshiba, points out.[28] Not only did CBS records have the biggest stars in the music business, but its fabulous library of old favorites could be permanently recycled on into the next century. "Twenty years from now," Akio Morita declared after the deal was signed, "history will prove us right."

CBS, on the other hand, was thinking about the here and now. The troubled company was in the hands of its major investor, Laurence A. Tisch, a billionaire financier who had managed to use the family business, a small chain of run-down hotels in New Jersey, to build a multibillion-dollar empire that embraced Loew's hotels, the CNA insurance company, Bulova watches, Lorillard (the nation's fourth-largest cigarette manufacturer), and much else. He had bought up 25 percent of CBS stock, blocked a projected sale of the network to Coca-Cola, ousted the president, and taken over the company himself.

Tisch pronounced himself a "square" as far as the music business was concerned. From the days of "payola" in the 1950s to the mid-1980s when stories of the role of the Mafia in record distribution surfaced again on the nightly news, the shadow of drugs, bribery, and crime has hung over the industry. Charges that Yetnikoff himself was involved in payola were broadcast on NBC News. "Our licenses come from the Federal Communications Commission," said the new president of CBS, "and there are always questions raised about relationships within the record business." As the *New York Times* television reporter Peter Boyer notes, the $2-billion deal became possible because of "profoundly different business and cultural philosophies."[29] The American company had its eyes on the present value of its stock and thought that exchanging a volatile business for a massive infusion of cash was a good idea. The Japanese company was focused on future growth, and with the yen strong was willing to pay a price Wall Street considered excessive. In fact, by acquiring CBS Records for about nine times earnings Sony had landed a bargain.

In the early 1980s profits in the music industry had fallen precipitously as fans tired of the aging rock stars and disco styles of the 1970s and the new computer-game craze siphoned off teenage dollars. Video also cut into record sales. The new affluence and changing consumer culture of the 1980s had a depressing effect on the Japanese music market as consumers became more venturesome, spending more leisure time on travel, sports, and high living and less at home listening to tapes and discs. Almost exactly twenty years earlier the market for 1950s pop music had collapsed. By the mid-1960s the rock-and-roll revolution had come along to rescue the industry. Now history repeated itself. This time the music business was rescued by three revolutionary technological innovations: the compact disc, the satellites that made MTV possible, and cable television. The second half of the decade witnessed an historic growth spurt in the global music business. But Laurence Tisch had spent his life buying cheap and selling dear, and he wanted to unload CBS's music business before the next dive.

Sony, it will be recalled, had been operating a label in Japan jointly with CBS for twenty years, but although Morita was familiar with the American company and Ohga had been in charge of the joint venture, both were unprepared for a negotiation that took more than a year to complete.[30] William Paley, the man who built CBS, was reluctant to let the record company go. Walter Yetnikoff, the head of CBS Records, was making his own side arrangements with Sony (which included a $20-million multiyear contract, backing as a movie producer, and a promise of a corporate jet—a perk of the Warner Communications president that Yetnikoff had coveted for years). At the same time he systematically set about to infuriate Tisch so that Tisch would sell the company to get rid of him. He referred to him, among other epithets, as "the evil dwarf," and his views found their way into industry gossip columns. Yetnikoff was also expert at little touches of calculated madness, like the $50 glass of brandy he ordered at the end of a tête-à-tête at a restaurant to which his notoriously cost-conscious boss had invited him. "I think I was very instrumental by making Tisch crazy, so he had to sell the company . . . ," Yetnikoff boasted to the *New York Times*.

One incentive for Sony to make the deal was the prospect of owning Michael Jackson, the biggest star of the biggest record company in the world. His 1983 video "Thriller" had propelled him to the top of the charts, and it is still the all-time best-seller. Jackson's sell-out concert tour in Japan in 1987 was underwritten by Pepsi-Cola and Nippon Telegraph and Telephone. Even his pet chimpanzee Bubbles, which accompanied him to Tokyo, was put to profitable use promoting Hudson's Ice Cream. Plush replicas of Bubbles were sold at Hudson's twenty-two stores with a scoop of free ice cream, and the Santa Barbara–based company, only two years after entering Japan, consolidated its hold as that nation's number-one ice-cream retailer.

Michael Jackson had been an extraordinarily affecting artist since he made his debut as a child. His voice alone made him a global product, but he enhanced his audience appeal by styling himself as a freakish commodity; his well-publicized yearly model changes on his face via nose jobs and chin tucks, his predilection for going about in disguises, and his insistence on dating his autographs "1998" were all carefully created promotional lore to establish him as the king of global pop figures. A genius at self-promotion, he earned $9 million by putting his name on a line of athletic shoes almost nobody wanted to buy.[31] When he opened his estate in Encino to the major record retailers, he netted advance orders of 2.5 million copies of his latest album.

Morita had been taken with Michael Jackson when he had met him on his Japanese tour, and Sony was impressed that Pepsi-Cola had invested more than $50 million in Jackson commercials.[32] As pop-culture figures become products themselves, they are employed to sell other global products, and the exposure makes the pop star even more of a global icon. Pepsi spokesman Ken Ross explains, "When you are selling soft drinks what you need is excitement, and we believe that nobody can generate excitement like Michael Jackson." The Los Angeles television producer and entertainment writer Bridget Byrne thinks his carefully contrived looks hold the secret, "neither young nor old, neither black nor white, neither male nor female . . . the perfect marketing logo."[33]

"It's nice to be wanted," Walter Yetnikoff beamed as the Sony acquisition was announced. Soon he had the $20-million Falcon jet he had always said he needed to accommodate and to impress his stable of continent-hopping rock stars. The Sony executive who negotiated the deal for the Tokyo-based company, Michael P. Schulhof, was a physicist who had briefly worked as an assistant to the vice-president in charge of recording studios and record-manufacturing plants at CBS Records. He had collaborated with Yetnikoff on the Sony-CBS joint venture and had supervised the building of a speaker factory for Sony in Pennsylvania. When asked by reporters how "the orderly Japanese business mentality" would square with the "free-wheeling record business," Schulhof replied that Walter Yetnikoff would be in charge, and would have "a much freer hand in hiring people and compensating them based on industry standards, not Sony standards or CBS standards."[34] CBS Records would have a name change but it would stay an American company.

Walter Yetnikoff, caught up in the excitement of finding a Hollywood studio for his new employers, began paying less attention to his superstar clients, Bruce Springsteen and Michael Jackson. As he drank more wildly, he fought more and screamed more—at the wrong people, including on occasion his new bosses. Yetnikoff alienated Michael Jackson and his powerful lawyer by refusing to let Jackson sing on a sound-track album for Geffen Records because of his long-standing feud with David Geffen, the label's founder. Bruce Springsteen also publicly broke with him.

In 1989 Sony paid more than $5 billion to purchase Columbia Pictures from its principal stockholder, Coca-Cola. It was Yetnikoff who arranged for two flashy Hollywood characters, Jon Peters and Peter Guber, to take over the artistic direction at Columbia Pictures as part of Sony's acquisition of the studio. However, the two movie producers, who were in great demand because of *Batman* and other blockbusters, had just signed a contract with Warner. Yetnikoff considered this a minor detail. Sony lawyers had insisted on noting in the original announcement that the Peters-Guber involvement was conditional upon Warner's releasing them. But Yetnikoff threatened to resign if Sony did not announce the whole deal as done, and this the new Japanese owners did without securing Warner's agreement, giving Warner legal grounds for a suit for interference with its contract. Allowing themselves to be intimidated by Yetnikoff eventually cost Sony more than $500 million in settlement costs and legal fees. (Warner executives quietly passed the word to stock analysts that the figure was closer to $800 million.)

Yetnikoff was made chairman of a committee to oversee the studio, but Peters and Guber made certain that the committee never met. He stopped drinking after a month at a rehabilitation clinic. But in its first year as a Sony company CBS Records lost an "astounding" share of the U.S. market, according to Russell Solomon, the chairman of Tower Records, a leading retail chain. Like RCA under Bertelsmann, CBS Records under Sony was having trouble finding and breaking in young artists, although Sony was much freer with money.

Unfavorable publicity about Yetnikoff kept mounting, culminating in a devastating portrait in the best-selling book *The Hit Men*. The industry executives, lawyers, and agents whom he had routinely called "Nazis," "liars," and "pricks" over the years began striking back. At the same time the Columbia Pictures deal, in which Yetnikoff had been much involved, was also generating expensive lawsuits, expensive settlements, and bad publicity for Sony, a company that had built its whole business on image and a reputation for innovation and shrewdness. On September 4, 1990, Sony announced that Yetnikoff had decided "to step down as head of the company." Barred from setting foot in the company premises, his mouth sealed by his severance agreement, Yetnikoff walked away with $45 million, leaving Sony dazed but presumably wiser.[35]

IV.

In 1991, a year in which politicians heralded the world economic recovery even as the effects of the recession deepened, Sony and its competitors in the electronics-hardware business saw their profits drop. Although Sony's lightweight camcorder was a great success, consumers around the world were anxious about their own economic prospects, and too few of them were ready to pull out their credit cards and take home Sony's latest electronic novelties. Even the Japanese, who could always be counted on for their insatiable appetite for Sony products, grew cautious and sales were flat. In the first quarter of 1992 profits plummeted.

Even a year earlier Ken Iwaka, Sony's deputy president in charge of corporate strategy, had given an uncharacteristically downbeat interview in which he admitted that company "miscalculations" had much to do with Sony's problems. For years Japanese electronic companies had counted on high-definition TV (HDTV) as the frontier technology that would symbolize Japan's global leadership in electronics in the twenty-first century. "We thought high-definition TV would become a real business," Iwaka explained. But the company had run into all sorts of problems. "Now it has more confusion. We're not quite sure if we wait, will it come?" The company had also pinned its hopes on multimedia hardware, that is, equipment to mix sound, text, video, and graphics, but this market too was disappointing. "We spent a lot of money on this area, but still we don't have the answer yet." Sony's foray into the personal-computer business was not a great success either. The result, Iwaka conceded, was that the archcompetitor, Matsushita, "has really hit Sony across the board."[36]

As the recession worsened, Michael P. Schulhof, who was put in charge of Sony Music and Sony Pictures, became the only top company official to exude the old Sony confidence. Having personally participated in and negotiated seven out of the eight corporate acquisitions Sony had made, he remained relentlessly bullish about the gains Sony had scored by marrying hardware and software. In Sony's fiscal year ending March 31, 1992, operating income (revenue minus expenses) for the company's entertainment divisions was up 14 percent while that of the electronics divisions fell 55 percent. Schulhof predicted that the entertainment business would eventually contribute as much to Sony's operating income as the electronics business. Software, Schulhof argued, would not only help to sell hardware, and vice versa, but music and motion pictures were now the most promising profit centers for the company. As profit margins in the electronics business became slimmer because of fierce competition, the key to Sony's future growth was entertainment software.

In the 1980s the entertainment industry discovered the word "synergy." Originally a seventeenth-century medical term to describe the interaction of two or more drugs, in the late twentieth century the word acquired magical properties. Synergy was the key to riches. Companies able to use visuals to sell sound, movies to sell books, or software to sell hardware would become the winners in the new global commercial order. On such dreams the great media conglomerates were built. Synergy was a one-word reason to gather all sorts of entertainment and communications properties under one corporate roof. The signs were favorable. Michael Jackson began selling millions of records only after his video "Thriller" had captured the hearts of teenagers around the world. Madonna's leather-and-lace look aroused interest well before her voice did. The billion-dollar record "Purple Rain" by Prince was turned into a movie that made several hundred million more. The sound track of *Dirty Dancing* sold more than 22 million copies and put RCA Records in the black after Bertelsmann took it over.

Sony's experience with music and film has been an unending drama in which the abstract notion of synergy keeps colliding with the concrete realities of the global entertainment business. The Sony story dramatizes both the possibilities and difficulties of combining hardware and software under one roof. From the viewpoint of corporate accountants, hit records and movies are miracle products. Their markets are not bound by time or space, and as they are purchased, played, or shown around the world, they keep earning money for the producers without incurring any additional costs. By contrast, every tape recorder or television set shipped across town or across the globe involves added expense for Sony that must be subtracted from the sales revenue. But like major technological innovations, global hits usually require substantial development costs up front, and substantial interest must be paid while the producers wait for the miracle to unfold. Often it never does. This is the basic problem for producers of commercial sounds and images: Every film and record is a new invention.

Sony has been remarkably prolific in producing innovative products, but its commercial success has depended upon taking a relatively few basic inventions and dressing them up or down for a variety of markets. Once the popularity of Walkman was established, it was reasonably easy to predict how the various new models with small eye-catching changes would sell. But records and movies are much less predictable. Hollywood investors favor formulas and sequels, such as *Batman II* or *Teenage Mutant Ninja Turtles III*, but they are often disappointed.

Five years after its takeover of CBS Records, Sony management was still trying to fathom the mysteries of the music business. On the one hand, the company had scored some impressive successes. Michael Jackson's album *Dangerous* sold 11 million in the first six months, 7 million outside the United States. Other stars such as Michael Bolton and Mariah Carey also hit the top of the charts.

As global sales in records settled on a disappointing plateau in the early 1990s, Tommy Mottola, the head of Sony Music, concluded several multimillion-dollar record deals, including the highly publicized one with Michael Jackson that Sony said could be worth a billion dollars. ("Michael is a god in Japan. . . . They were afraid of losing him and upsetting the Japanese," an executive of a rival label gossiped to the *New York Times*.) The rock group Aerosmith was signed for a reported $25 million even though their contract with another label would not be up for several years, by which time, some industry analysts concluded, they would be too old for their pubescent fans. Mottola also helped build Mariah Carey's career with generous financial arrangements; when they married, eyebrows were raised in the industry and there was a brief flurry of bad publicity.

Sony, ignoring the endless gossip and *schadenfreude* on which the music industry runs, continued to assert that it was the world's number-one record company. But by 1992 the fight for world leadership was no longer a Sony-Warner duel. EMI paid almost $1 billion to acquire Virgin Music Group, and PolyGram also grew much larger because of major acquisitions. One top industry analyst told us that by his calculations Sony had now dropped to fourth place, a conclusion Sony vigorously disputes. As global competition intensifies, the record majors are increasingly closemouthed about supplying the figures to determine their respective shares of the market.

"The synergy is working better than I hoped," Schulhof declared soon after he was put in charge of Sony's new entertainment division.[37] Sony Music made a music video of the title song of the Sony film *My Girl* and released it weeks before the film came out, and this helped the film considerably with its carefully targeted teenage audience. "Usually," Schulhof explains, "film people don't want to allow scenes from the film to be shown in a filmclip prior to the film's release . . . it's very uncommon to get use of film scenes before a theatrical release."[38] Sony shot extra footage for its film *Dracula* for use in one of its CD-Rom-based video games.[39] Schulhof promoted the film *Hook* in Europe with a fifteen-minute video called "The Making of *Hook*" that played on Sony television sets in 5,000 windows of retail outlets across the continent well before the motion picture was released. The film made even more money in Europe than in the United States. At the same time the glamour of Sony films, Schulhof promised, would give new luster to Sony VCRs and television sets. Putting hardware and software under one roof had made it all possible, Schulhof claimed, but other industry executives point out that these techniques had been used before.

Yet no miracles occurred. Sony's disastrous experience with digital audio tape players (DAT) was not averted because the company could put some of the world's hottest music properties on its digital tape. Fans could hear them on CDs, music videos, and old-fashioned tapes that were much cheaper. It was becoming equally clear that owning software was not the only way to assure access to it. Licensing arrangements are an alternative, and usually cheaper. The market itself makes it dangerous for companies to engage in economic warfare by trying to deny entertainment software to their hardware competitors. Sony and Philips squared off against each other in 1992 for a global fight over whether the home-recording format of the decade would be the Japanese-designed Mini Disc or the Dutch-designed digital compact cassette (DCC), or neither as many expect. As each entertainment-hardware conglomerate aggressively lined up its own stars, Sony announced that it would make tapes to fit Philips's new machine. "Every record company will put music out to support any legitimate hardware format—which includes DCC," Schulhof declared. "If the Mini-Disc hardware takes off, it will create business not only for Sony Music, but for all record companies."[40]

The point seems clear, but it does raise the question why the cohabitation of hardware production and artistic creativity under one corporate roof is such a good idea, especially when it requires the outlay of billions. No doubt, the search for synergy through corporate acquisitions has handsomely benefited some of the owners of the acquired companies. When Matsushita acquired MCA, Lew Wasserman, the chairman, sold his stock to the Japanese electronics giant for $327 million; David Geffen had done even better when he sold his record company for $710 million worth of MCA stock.[41] But for Sony the experience has confirmed some of the predictions expressed by Bertelsmann executives and others in the industry about what was lying in wait for it once it tried to harness Hollywood and Broadway types to engineers and promoters of hardware.

The simmering conflicts between Sony's hardware and software divisions became public knowledge when Ron Sommer, the head of the company's consumer-electronics business in the United States, diplomatically but unmistakably rebuked Schulhof in an interview about public statements the latter had made about impending decisions on new hardware. The attempt to realize synergies around *Hook* also stirred up controversy within the company. The hardware division had pushed for tie-ins that would use the movie's fame to sell Walkmans and camcorders, but Steven Spielberg, the director, resisted for fear that some of Sony's marketing ideas would "cheapen the movie and jeopardize his chance of winning critical awards," perhaps reminding old-timers of Depression days when movie theaters gave away dishes.[42] One of the cultural divides between creative types and hardware executives is that the former, though they obviously like big money, often act out of noneconomic motives, such as the desire for personal fame and prestige or the satisfaction of grabbing a famous star away from a rival, never mind what it costs.

A year after the purchase of Columbia Pictures, Sony's president, Norio Ohga, promised that it would be kept "totally as an American company." Sony would be "bashed" if it started to act "like the American occupation army in post-war Japan. . . ."[43] Schulhof is the bridge between the "creative types" in New York and Hollywood and the "suits" in Tokyo. "I give him three things," Peter Guber said of Schulhof after they had been working together about two years. "Balance—he doesn't get ruffled easily. Intelligence—he has a high quotient of intelligence. And No. 3, he speaks Japanese. I don't mean he literally speaks Japanese, but after 18 years in the company, he understands the significance of what's not said."[44]

Schulhof knows that in the Columbia Pictures deal he negotiated for Sony he paid a premium to buy synergy, and he is determined to prove to his employers in Tokyo that they made a good investment. But he is too shrewd and too experienced to believe that the synergies for which Sony has paid well over $9 billion since 1988 will materialize on command. Everything depends on the people. This is a business, Schulhof told us, where the "assets" go down the elevator at the end of the day. Sony let it be known when it bought its American music and film properties that it would not be afraid to spend money in the fight for market shares, and the creative managers at Sony Music and Sony Film, all of whom are Americans, have been extremely generous in handing out Sony millions to pop stars, movie actors, and directors.

Thanks to *Bugsy, Terminator 2, Hook, Prince of Tides*, and a few other big hits, Sony had a 20-percent share of the U.S. film market in 1992, more than any other entertainment company, and it showed a 33-percent increase in operating income in the first two years after acquiring Columbia. But unlike CBS Records, the picture studio had been no bargain. Despite the string of box-office successes, it was not at all clear when, if ever, Sony would realize its investment.

The first three years had been more than normally chaotic. Guber and Peters paid $1.2 million for the script of *Radio Flyer* and another $1 million to the director they fired, and after they had spent $41 million altogether, Sony earned back a little over $4 million.[45] *Hudson Hawk* became world famous in the industry as a turkey, and there were a number of others. Producing turkeys is of course a normal business risk in Hollywood, but Sony was more than normally generous in sharing the profits of its successes with the actors and directors. Forty percent of the box-office take for the hit movie *Hook* went to Steven Spielberg and the stars. The television division of Sony Pictures Entertainment accounted for a major chunk of the profits, most of it for reruns of television programs, but when it had sold the rights to its big hits, *Jeopardy, Married with Children*, and *Wheel of Fortune*, it began raiding other companies for producers and writers, "paying people two or three times what their previous contracts had been."[46]

Jon Peters, who had gotten his start as Barbra Streisand's hairdresser and for whom the kindest epithet in the Hollywood gossip circuit was "erratic," left suddenly. Columbia's head of production and the entire top marketing staff also moved on. Sony executives dismissed the negative buzz in the financial world about Sony's fortunes in Hollywood as just one more bit of evidence of the American obsession with short-term profits. Sony's published record of how well it was doing was much more upbeat but hard to read. Accountants who work in the entertainment business are no less creative than those who mix marketable sounds or splice shadows for the screen. Sony does not break down its profits in such a way that anyone outside the company can understand the financial picture. Creative accounting can turn short-term losses into long-term investment.

In late 1992 Peter Guber declared that if he had known what he was in for, "I'm not sure I'd have come."[47] This must have grated some on the sensitive ears of Akio Morita, who by some accounts had paid more than $1 billion to get him and his departed partner. Repeatedly asked whether he was still comfortable with Sony's investment in movies, Morita replied, "Comfortable is a very delicate word. Once we get the return on the investment, we will be comfortable."[48]

CHAPTER SIX

GLOBAL
ENTERTAINMENT
AND LOCAL TASTE

I.

WHEN THE BERLIN WALL CAME DOWN IN LATE 1989, EAST German families flocked to West Berlin to taste the pleasures of capitalism; what they wanted most were oranges and pop-music records. In Rio, school kids adorn their workbooks with pictures of Michael Jackson. In Kashmir, teenagers hum Beatles songs. Vegetable stalls in Madras still feature "disco" cauliflower. All over the world people are listening to pop music and watching videos that offer excitement, escape, and the feeling of connectedness to a larger world. Most of these consumers of global cultural products are young.

As governments, families, and tribal structures are thrown into crisis by the sweeping changes of late-twentieth-century society, pop artists have emerged as global authority figures. Thanks to the microphone and camera, a few megastars can communicate power and the appearance of strong commitment at great distance. Unlike parents, mullahs, chiefs, bureaucrats, and politicians, they ask little of their fans except to enjoy themselves and to keep buying.[1] On the few publicized occasions when rock stars call upon their worldwide audiences for personal contributions—for rain forests, famine relief, political prisoners—the global outpouring is astounding.

Global entertainment companies are pinning their hopes on the two-fifths of the people on earth who are under 20. The competition to hook millions of new fans at increasingly early ages is intense. Sony has expanded into the children's market with its "My First Sony" line of toylike radios, its new Sony Kids' Music label, and an expanding Children's Library of videos.[2]

The most spectacular technological development of the 1980s for expanding the reach of global entertainment was MTV. By the beginning of 1993 MTV programming was beamed daily to 210 million TV households in seventy-one countries. The cable network, which began in August 1981, claims to have 39 million viewers in Europe and well over 50 million in the United States. It has already spun off a second network called VH-1. Viacom, the parent company, also has a channel aimed at children called Nickelodeon. (In the early 1990s its hit attraction was the *Ren & Stimpy Show*, a cartoon saga of a hyperactive Chihuahua and a cat that spits up hair balls.) The owner of this global network of networks is Sumner Redstone, a Boston multibillionaire who made a fortune in movie theaters. Although his name is unknown to the general public, he has become one of the most influential educators of young people in the world. As MTV was announcing plans to extend its worldwide home-entertainment networks to China, Korea, and Taiwan and to launch *Ren & Stimpy* in Europe, Redstone was celebrating the arrival of the global child. "Just as teenagers are the same all over the world, children are the same all over the world," he declared.[3]

Although hundreds of millions of children and teenagers around the world are listening to the same music and watching the same films and videos, globally distributed entertainment products are not creating a discernible global consciousness—other than a widely shared passion for more global goods and vicarious experience. Because of the great range of personal experience consumers bring to global cultural products, the emotional impact on fans can differ widely in unpredictable ways. Depending on who you are and where you are, you can listen to the same song and hear different voices. Hearing the same music, playing the same globally distributed games, or watching the same global broadcast do not appear to change people's sense of who they are or where they belong. Serbs and Croats, Sinhalese and Tamils, listen to the same Michael Jackson songs as they take up arms against each other. The exotic imagery of music video offers the illusion of being connected to cultural currents sweeping across the world, but this has little to do with the consciousness philosophers from Kant to Marshall McLuhan have dreamed of, an identification with the whole human species and the welfare of the planet itself.

II.

The spread of commercially produced popular music, most of it conceived in the United States, is speeding up as once-formidable ideological barriers come down. The collapse of communism makes it easier to export music, film, and video to Eastern Europe, the former Soviet Union, and China. But integrating vast reaches of the world into a global story-and-song market is not a simple task. In 1990 Rudi Gassner was president of BMG International and was in direct charge of Bertelsmann's music business. "Our priority," he says, is "signing acts on a worldwide basis exclusive to BMG for worldwide exploitation." Months before the reunification of Germany was completed, Bertelsmann had hired someone to head its sales force for the German Democratic Republic, where, Gassner says, he is counting on picking up an additional 15 million customers. (As noted, there are only 17 million people in the former East Germany.) "Our next target group," he wrote in an internal newsletter for BMG management in 1990, includes "Hungary, Czechoslovakia, and to a certain extent, Poland." But he anticipated "enormous problems for us because of the currency constraints. . . . We will not make money immediately; we will not be able to take the money out. But I feel that long term we should be there and be one of the first, if not the first, . . . for political and strategic reasons."

The dream of supplying a billion Chinese with a Coke a week, a tape a week, or anything a week has been part of American business culture since the nineteenth century, the inspiration for political careers, quick fortunes, and wars.[4] But the head of BMG International is wary of falling prey to fashion, and he is more skeptical of the potential of the Russian and Chinese markets than are some industry enthusiasts in the United States. "I think it's very chic, very sexy in international circles to say, 'I'm going to be there; my artists are going to be there,' " says Gassner. But Russia and China "have to put their houses in order first, in my opinion, before we can make any reasonable assessment." Because of their "one-way education of the past forty-five years" their managers don't understand free trade, balance sheets, or profit-and-loss statements. "These territories will take a very long time to penetrate. . . ."

The strongest remaining ideological barrier to American music, television, and film is Islamic fundamentalism. In the Khomeini era in Iran American cultural products were the supreme symbols of satanic decadence. The more fanatical Iranian and Saudi authorities became in their attempts to purify their traditional cultures, the more people were drawn to forbidden music and films. Underground video clubs sprang up all over Iran, and crowds came to watch tapes of the latest American network programs, and of course X-rated films. Pirated Michael Jackson videotapes were available for $50, and underground discos abounded. The Islamic Guards regularly raided all these activities, but in recent years there have been a few signs of liberalization. The technologies of penetration are so powerful that the industry is planning for the day when Iran will rejoin the global market in music and film. In Saudi Arabia, where Western rock was equally abhorrent to the ruling family, except when they were out of the country or throwing a party in the privacy of their own homes, the arrival of a half-million American soldiers and Desert Shield Network FM-107 with its dozen or more transmitters all over the country produced a cultural shock. Once the war ended, however, the religious police stepped up their campaign to rid the desert kingdom of all cultural traces of their protectors. But ultimately, it is a losing battle.[5]

The biggest growth potential for pop music is in Latin America and Asia. (Africa is almost never mentioned.) BMG Ariola Discos Ltda. operates in Brazil and has 55 percent of the market. About 80 percent of the records sold are by local artists. A country with a yearly inflation rate of 1,800 percent is not an easy place in which to do business, and when it suddenly drops to zero it is no easier; you have to assume that next year it will again be closer to 1,800. But despite Brazil's political and economic difficulties, BMG remains bullish. Today only 50 million of Brazil's 150 million people buy records. But in a few years, Gassner predicts, "another half will be active economically, doubling our market potential."[6] Bertelsmann has plans to launch Brazilian artists into the international market, along with artists from some of the other twenty-eight countries where it owns record labels. "Local talent must be cultivated for a territory to have a constant stream of product to secure and build outward from the domestic market," says Gassner. "These are the two streams

[English and local-language repertoire], and the kids don't really care; the question is the quality of the music."

Gassner says that Third World governments "see us as 'The Great Multinationals' controlled by companies in Germany, England, the United States, etc. They're sure all we want to do is exploit international repertoire in their country, take the money out, and run. . . . BMG International can say to them, 'Now wait a minute. I can do something for you. I can take care of your local artists.' . . . And all of this accrues over time into a viable, profitable working arrangement. . . ." If the global music vendors can help increase local revenue and jobs and hold out the possibility of breaking the first world-class Filipino or Indonesian rock star, the theory goes, local governments will join forces to protect intellectual property rights and show greater zeal in fighting the record pirates.

Hardware products are routinely copied, as everyone with a Korean clone of an IBM personal computer knows. But there is also a thriving business in evading government restrictions on imported brand-name entertainment products. For years ads have appeared in Indian newspapers for Sony tape recorders, televisions, and VCRs despite the fact that until recently the sale of these Sony products has been barred by Indian law. (In the 1990s India has become more accommodating to the global companies.) The prohibition of imported luxuries was an austerity measure to save foreign exchange. At the ports of Calcutta and Madras there were rows of shacks— even some modern warehouses—where illegally imported recorders and other electronic equipment were stashed. Occasionally the police would raid these establishments; but usually they would just show up for their *hafta*, the monthly bribe. For years customers could not find a Sony product displayed in the shops, but a request would produce one within the time it takes to run down the street to the store's not-so-secret cache.

The same technology that has made commercially recorded music one of the few truly global products also makes it one of the world's most stealable. Stars can now count on being seen and heard somewhere around the world many times a day. But the bigger the hit, the more likely it is that its creators and owners will have to share the profits with pirates. While intellectuals and politicians in poor countries denounced the "cultural imperialism" of the global media giants, underground entrepreneurs did something about it.

In Asia, which Mark Woessner hopes to make "the fourth pillar" of Bertelsmann's worldwide business, the unlicensed copying of tapes, records, videos, and films is rampant. Not so long ago hit songs were routinely pirated all over the Third World. Even in China, says Gassner, they "pirated and copied like hell and traded tapes through underground channels." According to a Bertelsmann in-house publication, in the People's Republic "hundreds of millions of dollars each year are siphoned away from the major labels and their artists."

But other Asian governments, anticipating important revenues from the record business, have begun to crack down. Singapore, a small island republic of malls and assembly plants, is totally depen-dent on exports. Its authoritarian government has gone out of its way to cooperate with the music giants by enacting a draconian copyright law that provides for five-year jail sentences and $50,000 fines for possession of pirated tapes with intent to sell. Teenagers can earn up to $150 by acting as informants for the police.[7] But such laws work only as well as the local culture permits. In many parts of the world the tradition is that music belongs to the community, and an edict to treat a song as a piece of property is greeted by ordinary people with puzzlement and anger.

Industry executives now pronounce Singapore and Hong Kong, once the headquarters of Asian pirating operations, to be "clean." So are Malaysia and Indonesia. Bertelsmann has operations in the Phil-ippines and Thailand, which no one yet claims are "clean," and is planning to set up companies in Taiwan, Korea, and Indonesia. As one executive at Warner put it, the new concern about property rights among Asian governments "means that we can sell into a market that a few years ago we couldn't sell to at all."[8] But illegal copying of audio- and videotapes continues all over the world, in-cluding the countries pronounced to be "clean." Performances of Madonna on films and videos are taken off television sets and movie-house screens in India; the copies, still fuzzy but less so as the tech-nology of piracy improves, are sold by the hundreds of thousands. The local tape industry, which offers Indian music and pirated global pop music, has taken off.

In South Korea about 85 percent of the 30,000 video shops in the country openly stocked pirated tapes as recently as 1990. A com-mercial tape sells for $27, a pirated version for half. Richard O'Neill, a former Green Beret who received a Silver Star and six Bronze Stars in the Vietnam War, now hunts video pirates in Korea on behalf of the Motion Picture Export Association of America. By leading the police to more than 700 bootleg video stores where they seized over 140,000 tapes, O'Neill managed to double U.S. video sales to Korea. "It's Genghis Khan," he explains. "You burn one village and leave a few survivors to tell the rest." The Korean government, eager to increase its exports to the United States, not only permits this private American police operation (posing as a market survey) on its territory, but encourages the use of similar methods against purveyors of fake Louis Vuitton bags and ripped-off Lotus software. O'Neill has extended his operation to Thailand.[9]

Many governments, however, are reluctant to act against their own bootleggers. Pirating recorded music and video is a major source of income and jobs, and since the "informal economy" is all that stands in the way of total economic and social collapse in many places, governments are ambivalent about cracking down. Besides, bootleggers are infinitely resourceful. As the sale of pirated videos through legitimate stores becomes more of a problem in Korea, entrepreneurs are hooking homes up to illegal cable systems that will play pirated videos. Profit-threatening ideas travel no less swiftly than global goods.

The music industry is worried about other ingenious ways to turn expensive software into free goods. Bertelsmann executives fear that as radio stations proliferate and broadcast music becomes more diverse, the market for canned music is becoming saturated. It was "crazy" to give away free records to radio stations back in the 1930s, one told us; the "free advertising" ultimately cuts into the market. Now the industry is hooked. By the end of the 1990s canned music products in all forms could be obsolete. The technology is on the drawing boards to connect a giant data bank of sounds and sights with home computers, VCRs, and recorders. For a small fee the listener will be able to retrieve a blues song, a Madonna video, or a symphony. This is possible, Bertelsmann's Michael Dornemann concedes, but he does not appear to be worried. Old habits die slowly. The pre-computer-age generation will have a hard time adjusting to the notion of "accessing" sound instead of owning it. Perhaps. But teenagers, the mainstay of the market, are quite at home with computers; property rights are increasingly based on "access" rather than "ownership."

The computer-based global music library for home listening is still years away. But meanwhile the conflict over new technologies for playing prerecorded music is intensifying. Sony developed a high-fidelity digital audiotape (DAT) for mass marketing in 1990 and sold

150,000 digital tape players, mostly in Japan where new gadgets are snapped up more avidly than anywhere else. The music industry became extremely worried about piracy because DAT, unlike the CD, can be copied. CDs are coated with a chemical that precludes their being used again. When unsold compact discs are returned to the manufacturer, they are ground up and used as trays for new CDs. The music industry worried that since Sony's hardware business is so much bigger than its software divisions, its interests in rapid technological innovation and mass production of high-profit consumer-electronics devices would continue to outweigh its interests in protecting songs and films from the ever more resourceful pirates— who also turn out to be highly successful promoters of Sony hardware in developing countries that try to keep Sony products out.

Sales of Sony's digital audiotape, however, were disappointing. A year later Sony announced that it had developed the Mini Disc, which is a diminutive version of the compact disc and, like DAT, is "rewritable," that is, it can be used to copy either a tape, radio broadcast, or another Mini Disc. Philips has brought out the digital compact cassette, also "rewritable," and is counting on grabbing off a large share of the market from Sony because its hardware will work not only for the new high-fidelity tapes but for the billions of conventional tapes already stored in homes around the world. Philips, a giant in both music hardware and software, teamed up with Sony's archrival, Matsushita, which, having acquired MCA, now also had a major record division. Together they mounted a campaign to use the new tape technology to overwhelm Sony's drive to flood the world market with relatively low-cost Mini Disc players.

The hardware companies believe that the battle of the new technologies will ultimately be decided by which company controls the most marketable music. When DAT was launched, the hardware and software companies in the music industry squared off. For the hardware companies, the ability to record two hours of music with near total fidelity on a cassette half the size of an analog cassette was a feat to trumpet far and wide. For the record companies, it meant that an infinite number of copies could then be made with no loss of sound quality.[10] While Bertelsmann executives lose few opportunities to express scorn for Sony's venture into Hollywood and the music business, behind the derision is cold fear. Bertelsmann and other music companies spent years lobbying for a law requiring the makers of DAT playback machines to insert a chip rendering the machine incapable of making recordings. The Japanese electronics giants were predictably unenthusiastic about hobbling their new invention in this way; before its purchase of CBS Records, Sony retained lobbyists to oppose legislation imposing copying restrictions.

In 1991 a shaky truce was reached in the battle over DAT just as that technology was about to be overtaken by newer technologies. Under new legislation passed by Congress manufacturers of blank digital tapes and discs are required to pay a set sum into a fund to compensate composers and artists.[11] But the battle of chips, cards, and other technological fixes leaves the basic issues far from settled. All sorts of new wrinkles in hardware development could eventually render the compromise between the producers of sound equipment and the producers of music obsolete. Electronics-hardware companies have picked up three of the six record majors and several of the most successful independent record labels. This means that future fights over entertainment technology will increasingly take place inside megacorporations rather than between them.

Public concern with protecting the rights of creative artists is less developed in the United States than in Europe. Although the United States is the pioneer producer of computer software, there is little stigma in this country attached to the unauthorized copying of computer programs. A 1985 study of software use in corporate offices found that 52 percent of all data-base programs, 52 percent of all spreadsheet and accounting programs, and 45 percent of all word-processing programs were pirated, and the result was a loss of about $600 million in revenues. In 1992 the estimated global loss of revenue due to piracy of software of all sorts reached $60–70 billion. The record industry and the music publishers have sponsored focus groups to determine how open their customers might be to compensating the creators of pop music when their work is copied. For Bertelsmann and other music companies not owned by hardware manufacturers, the results were discouraging. It usually takes about two hours before randomly selected groups of American consumers see any great reason to compensate the rich pop stars who make the music possible, much less the global record companies.

IV.

The six giants of the recorded-music industry are now better able to take advantage of the global dimensions of the market than they were a decade ago. They can offset losses in one region with profits from another. They can now create global superstars—although with no greater predictability than before—and they can sell their fame in new ways. MCA has a division that sells posters, T-shirts, hats, and buttons, and Sony is getting into this business. New Kids on the Block, the favorite of the preteen set at the beginning of the 1990s, made $400 million in merchandise sales in three years. The manager of one British rock group boasted that on its American tour "we made more from music merchandise—junk we would have sneered at 10 years ago—than we did from ticket sales."[12] At the same time, the music majors are consolidating their control over the world's distribution channels, at least the legal ones.

What does this extraordinary market power mean? For music fans? For artists? For creativity? Industry spokesmen argue that oligopoly is good for both the consumer and the artists. The fierce competition among five or six companies for the global market, they contend, drives record prices down and forces companies to make fabulous financial commitments to artists in great demand, a state of affairs from which artists all down the line also benefit. The evidence does not support the industry's contention about prices with respect to music software. The costs of making CDs have come down dramatically, given the huge volume and the vast opportunities to re-release the backlist of old recordings. Retail prices did come down sharply in the early years of the CD era, but in 1992, even in the midst of a deep recession, they went up. The markup on CDs is much greater than it was on LPs or tapes, and fans now pay 30 to 50 percent more for the same music.[13] CD albums of popular artists now command as much as $10.70 wholesale, which means that the retail list price can be as high as $17.98. Royalties are going up as artists like Prince receive $10-million advances per album. But even so, the cost to produce an expensive CD, royalties included, is no more than $4.20. The profit, according to the knowledgeable industry observer John Pareles, is somewhere around $2. Other analysts say it can often be more.[14]

Each record company has a monopoly with respect to its own artists. Sony can charge what the market will bear for a Michael Jackson release, knowing that no other company can compete with this unique product. On the other hand, in the music hardware business, as Sony has discovered, keeping prices high is not a reliable strategy in a fast-changing industry heavily dependent on technological innovation and volatile consumer tastes. The electronics giants of Korea and Taiwan have entered the global market and are able to offer quality products at cut-rate prices. So the six majors have a common interest in keeping software prices high, and while the competition involving Sony, Philips, and Matsushita in consumer-electronics hardware is intense, they all have an interest in not pushing the fight over market shares too far lest the new Asian challengers end up the winners.

The greatest impact that the recording giants have on music around the world is their power to decide what music they will promote and distribute. Small independent labels used to serve as hothouses to develop whole new genres that the big companies would then exploit—often years later. Now, as the pop-music-industry analyst Simon Frith notes, the small independents—the most successful ones have been acquired by the majors—serve more as talent scouts for the global music companies and they are regularly "fished" for ideas, styles, new and distinctive sounds, and, of course, artists. The system is now quirkier and more irrational than in the past. In the old days there was a long ladder to the top, and artists competed with one another rung by rung. The lowest rungs were live performances at local clubs, and the next was the competition for local press attention, and then local radio. If the artist stimulated enough "buzz," he or she would make it past the "gatekeepers"—agents, disc jockeys, record critics, columnists, and industry gossips—to the next rungs, first regional, then national and international. This was the route the Beatles took—from Liverpool to the global stage. Now the making of a pop artist is more a matter of luck. It depends on whether he or she has been heard by one of the industry's "ears." The big companies choose artists who can be sold globally, and they prepackage these candidates for global stardom years before they are launched, long before most fans have heard of them. They are then relentlessly promoted in every available medium. As Frith puts it:

> Who gets selected for success seems a matter of chance . . . and success itself is fragmented, unearned, impermanent. The "creative" role in this pop scheme is assigned to the *packagers*, to record producers, clothes designers, magazine editors, etc.; they are the "authors" of success, the intelligence of the system.[15]

At the same time the market for sound has expanded well beyond the retail market. Pop songs are now regularly sold or rented to the media and to advertisers. According to Frith:

> Thus a business that has long been organized around the vagaries of public taste and the problems of overproduction, now enjoys the ben-

efits of *preselling*: the programs are designed and sold to advertisers, cable companies, and/or station programmers before they're even made.[16]

Most video-pop channels now have to pay to use "promotional" clips. Old songs can now be resold to promote all sorts of products. In Europe, Cream's "I Feel Free" has been used to sell Renault cars; the Doors' "Riders in the Storm" has pushed Pirelli tires; and Nike marketed a new generation of sneakers with the aid of the Beatles' "Revolution." But now new songs can be promoted and at the same time generate substantial revenues via global TV ads. In 1989 Pepsi-Cola marketed two minutes of prime time in each of forty countries ranging from Finland to the Philippines to launch a commercial featuring Madonna introducing her new song, "Like a Prayer."[17] (It was withdrawn from the U.S. market, however, after the American Family Association threatened a Pepsi boycott.)

Record-company executives like to call recorded music "the world's most customer-driven product." The "kids," as industry marketers tend to refer to their primary market, are both vulnerable to fashion and capable of overwhelming sales resistance. Clearly, that which hits the airwaves and the record stores establishes the menu. Until that point the fans have no more role in the process than they do in deciding what films reach the screen or what magazines reach the newsstand. Investors, producers, and editors bank on their fans' previous enthusiasms for similar sorts of music, films, and features, but the notion that the record companies can create taste and force artists on the public through sheer promotion is mostly myth. To be sure, consumer tastes have less to do with the making of stars than in the days when performers had to pay their dues to local audiences and work their way up to global fame. But no amount of promotion can sell an artist the fans do not like.

What gets distributed and how it is promoted can reinforce fashions, but what next year's marketable sounds will turn out to be is unknowable. Promotion can drive smaller companies from the marketplace or force them to sell out, but it cannot guarantee the production of hit records. The story of the so-called independent promoters, known as "indies," is instructive. In 1985 the industry was spending somewhere between $60 million and $80 million a year on "indies," whose job was to talk local radio stations into repeated airings of their clients' prospective hit songs and to keep competitors' records off the air. An informal alliance of "indies" was established in 1978 that was known as the Network. The members divided up the U.S. market; each member claimed a "territory," a group of radio stations he could influence.

But more than sales patter and personality was involved. This heavy expenditure of the U.S. record industry for "indie" promotion—some 30 percent of pretax profits, according to one estimate—involved the liberal use of kickbacks. Fredric Dannen describes how it worked:

> The former program director of a medium-sized California radio station, for example, admitted in 1987 that he had taken about $100,000 in cash from an independent promoter over a three year period. Every week he got a "birthday card" in the mail, delivered to a post office box he had set up under an assumed name, as instructed by the indie. Each week he added three or four songs for the promoter and found between $500 and $1000 in his birthday card.[18]

The station would play the songs in return for birthday cards, cassettes, and record jackets stuffed with cash or for a supply of cocaine. The promoter would get a "spiff" of $7,500 from the record company each time a station reported to *Radio & Records* that it played the right song, but station managers often lied or played the song at 2:00 A.M. The result was that many aggressively promoted songs didn't sell. "The Network was not a good investment," Dannen concludes. Nevertheless, the "indies" have made a comeback in the 1990s.

V.

While the global spread of pop music originating in the English-speaking world has been greeted enthusiastically by hundreds of millions of fans, it has elicited cries of "cultural imperialism" from politicians and citizens groups around the world. France, Canada, and other industrial countries try in various ways to restrict foreign music. The French government is encouraging the development of a French superstar to compete with American rock stars on the global stage. U.S. record-company executives say they are not worried. "You know the French. It's a pride thing like the *force de frappe*. Europop doesn't travel like American rock." Canada has a "domestic content" law for AM radio; 30 percent of the music played must be Canadian.

In Tanzania the government records local music and plays it over the state-controlled radio. A few years ago the Ministry of Housing employed a Tanzanian-style jazz band to record a song to popularize a new way to build huts.[19]

Musicians, social critics, and politicians in poor countries of Asia, Africa, and Latin America worry that the massive penetration of transnational sound marketed by the Big Six will not only foreclose employment opportunities for local artists but will doom the traditional music of their local culture. "My fear is that in another 10 or 15 years' time what with all the cassettes that find their way into the remotest village, and with none of their own music available, people will get conditioned to this cheap kind of music." This remark by a Sri Lankan musician typifies the anxieties throughout the nonindustrialized world that industrial musical products will sweep away hundreds, perhaps thousands of years of traditional music. "However small a nation we are, we still have our own way of singing, accompanying, intonating, making movements and so on. We can make a small but distinctive contribution to world culture. But we could lose it. . . ."[20]

In the 1980s the environmental movement began to popularize the important idea that biological diversity is a precious global resource, that the disappearance of snail darters, gorgeous tropical birds, and African beetles impoverishes the earth and possibly threatens the survival of the human species. The cultural-environment movement has no powerful organizations promoting its message, but it has a large, unorganized global constituency. The feeling that world culture will be degraded if diversity is lost is widely shared among artists, cultural conservatives, and nationalists. Yet these concerns are overwhelmed by the sheer power of global popular culture, which threatens local cultural traditions and the traditional communities from which they spring. Bertelsmann and its competitors are acutely conscious of these feelings, and that is one reason why they go out of their way to promote and market local artists. The other reason is that local music can be a profitable market.

In the early 1980s Roger Wallis of the Swedish Broadcasting Corporation and Krister Malm, the director of the Music Museum in Stockholm, conducted a four-year study of what was happening to local music in twelve countries around the world as a result of the rise of the global music industry. The arrival of the Beatles and Rolling Stones in Sweden in the 1960s stimulated more than a thousand Swedish pop groups who sang in English, but most of them disappeared by the end of the decade. In the 1970s Swedish groups began singing more in Swedish, and the songs had more political content—anti-Vietnam War, antiestablishment, celebration of the "back to nature" movement. Meanwhile, the Big Five (MCA was not yet a big player in those days) were "increas[ing] their share of the lucrative Swedish market by buying up local producers, distributors, and retailers."[21] One Swedish group, ABBA, became a huge international success.

Many of the same consequences were documented in the other countries studied. On the one hand, local music groups in Wales, Sri Lanka, Trinidad, and other cultures were excited by the arrival of the cassette, and they began recording and distributing local songs, gathering an audience on a scale hitherto unknown. As early as 1984, when the Sri Lankan Broadcasting Corporation made a survey of a small village of 1,360 families, the researchers found that more than a third had cassettes, and in remote fishing villages new audiences for the traditional Baila-style songs supported a burgeoning local industry. But increasingly, cheap pirated versions of Anglo-American pop music became the status symbol. The local songs were rarely played by the Sri Lankan Broadcasting Corporation because of the "subject matter"—the lyrics of local songs sung in Sinhalese often have political overtones the government finds "unhelpful"—or because the tapes were not of broadcast quality.

The impact of the global music industry on the character of local music has been significant. The Indian pop star Babydoll Alisha sings Madonna songs in a Hindi rendering. Tunisian artists now routinely use synthesizers to accompany the traditional bagpipes at live concerts. The need for financing for expensive electronic instruments and the dependence on access to electricity is changing the local music culture. In Trinidad the introduction of multichannel recording has transformed the employment prospects of the famous steel bands. It used to be that a hundred musicians would be crowded into someone's backyard, each with his own tuned oil drum, and two microphones would pick it all up to make local tapes. Now, as Wallis and Malm report, a few of the best musicians are brought into a studio and they now "record all the various parts on different channels on the tape recorder at different times. The final mix . . . might be technically perfect, but it no longer represents the collective communication of 100 musicians and their audiences."[22]

The globalization of the music market and the technology of multiple-channel recording has made it possible to create fresh sound for the world market with musical exotica from all over the world. Everything from *zouk*, *rhi,* and *jit* from Africa and *salsa* from the Caribbean islands to the chants of India known as *bhangra* are mixed with a variety of American pop genres to produce a blend that is promoted around the world as "world beat."[23] "Lambada," promoted by French entrepreneurs as the dance craze of Brazil, is Bolivian in origin. A recorded version of this music performed by mostly Senegalese musicians became a global hit.[24] Paul Simon used South African singers and songs for his hit album *Graceland*, but he wrote his own words and the political message was diluted.

Local musicians are of course excited by the audiences, fame, and money that the international record companies can provide, but some are uncomfortable that their rich cultural traditions are being fished and skimmed to make an international product. The companies, though much agitated about the protection of their own intellectual property from pirates, feel no compunction about uprooting the music of indigenous artists from its native soil and treating it as a free good until they have blended its rhythms and melody into a global commodity. To be sure, painters and composers have often borrowed from folk art and folk music; world cultural creations are indebted to many different artistic traditions. Picasso's use of African images and Dvorak's renderings of folk dances in sophisticated works of chamber music are examples. But there is a fine line between tapping into an exotic musical tradition and stealing uncopyrighted songs, and sometimes the line is crossed.

Technology is increasingly rendering ancient art forms seemingly obsolete. Amplification—electric guitar and the microphone for the human voice—has a deskilling effect on local musicians, who no longer need to preserve the techniques of making themselves heard on traditional instruments. Gainful employment, recognition, even fame flow from the integration of local artists into an international industry. Paul Simon may not be a purist when it comes to South African music, but without his fame and initiative there would be nothing like the audience for it outside of South Africa he has developed. There is growing alarm around the world in communities not yet overwhelmed by the global commercial culture that ancient art forms are headed for extinction as surely as the endangered flora and fauna of the hacked-up rain forests. This may well turn out to be too pessimistic. Some genres and traditions will no doubt disappear, as has happened all through history. But there is a process of local resistance and renewal under way as well. The invasion of global culture is reawakening the appreciation of local cultural traditions and the preciousness of cultural diversity. Still, the power of global commercial music grows with each new breakthrough in the technology of reproduction.

VI.

"From the outset," Tom Freston, chairman of MTV explains, "our vision has been that this would be a worldwide rock-and-roll network." MTV alone claims to have a regular audience in the hundreds of millions. An increasing number of imitators are reaching tens of millions more. Even though the figures given out by the music video networks tend to be hyped—a former MTV executive says that in the early 1990s not more than 200,000 households in the United States were tuning in during any fifteen-minute period—the music video now commands a vast world audience.

An enterprising Hong Kong–based company is beaming MTV into 400,000 households in India, to the delight of the middle-class kids whose families have the satellite dishes to receive it and to the consternation of the government. Mahesh Prasad, India's secretary of information, worries about the social impact: "Our own social ethos, our cultural values—we would not like them to be subverted." Even though India is reversing nationalist policies of the past, he is concerned that satellite television is giving poor people "dreams which cannot be fulfilled. It can create social tensions." Intrusive technology is overtaking long-standing government policy. Ads for such items as jewelry and baby food that are well beyond the reach of most Indians were banned on state television for fear of stimulating envy and greed. But thanks to powerful boosters used by unregulated cable companies, politically incorrect commercials, rap singers, and rock nymphets from faraway places are entering Indian homes.

Music video is not only forcing changes in culture but also in politics. In 1984 Ronald Reagan rested his case for reelection on an eighteen-minute mix of music and story on television. Four years later George Bush's campaign chief released a notorious TV commercial featuring Willie Horton and the garbage in Boston Harbor that bore the telltale traces of music-video artistry. The use of this powerful new commercial art form is now standard in elections in the United States and in many other countries. Its influence on Hollywood films and TV series such as *Miami Vice*, where all car chases were accompanied by blaring rock, is unmistakable. As the critic John Pareles notes, even self-described news programs, like CBS's now departed *West 57th Street*, thanks to its frenetic cutting and rock obbligato, were children of MTV.[25]

A pop video is many things but it is always an ad—for itself, for other songs, rock groups, concerts, the latest fashion in teenage apparel, or Hollywood films from which bits of sound track may be included. Nonmusic products are relentlessly plugged. RC Cola financed a Louise Mandrell video that featured so much RC sipping that it made its debut at the National Soft Drink Association convention in 1985 before being shown on TV and marketed in stores.[26] The performances and the ads merge to create a mood of longing for someone to love, for something exciting to happen, for an end to loneliness, for things to buy—a record, a ticket to a rock concert, a T-shirt, a Thunderbird. The advertising is all the more effective because it is not acknowledged as such.

The juxtaposition of music and story has a long history—from the epic tales of Homeric bards to Walt Disney's *Fantasia* to the Beatles' *A Hard Day's Night*. But the blurring of advertising, fashion, heavy beat, ecstatic melody, dance, and story, the quirky camera angle, the quick cutaway, the split-second succession of dream snippets, the floating, disconnected pictures, and the daring lyrics and images command an unprecedented global audience. The sheer power of combining sight, sound, fashion, and dance and the fast-paced film-camera technique originally developed for advertising spots have whetted appetites around the world for recorded music, Coke, and all sorts of clothes that are meant to look like Madonna costumes.

MTV is the premier example of synergy at work twenty-four hours a day. Its success helped rescue the music industry from its slump at the beginning of the 1980s, and as it became a global network for promoting pop music, it acquired enormous power to decide what kind of music to play and what artists to push. Because of the considerable market power of MTV and its imitators across the globe, the promotion and advertising budgets of the global packagers of sound, and their increasing control over the local music industry everywhere, MTV has drawn fire from an array of critics across the political spectrum. "From the beginning, we made a lot of hay out of the fact that MTV was meant to alienate a lot of people," Tom Freston recalls. "It was meant to drive a 55-year-old person crazy."[27]

Bertelsmann, Sony, and their four global competitors in the music business have been caught in the cross fire.

In an era when massive shifts in cultural values were continuing to transform families around the world, creating a political backlash in the United States in defense of "family values," the culture industry found itself almost everywhere welcomed as a liberator but also attacked as an alien and subversive force. During the 1980s and into the 1990s value questions rather than economic issues dominated American political rhetoric. Until the idea took hold in 1992 that the United States might be facing a structural economic crisis, voters appeared to be more easily mobilized by political rhetoric about flag salutes, school prayers, abortion, sexual harassment, and condoms in the public schools than about jobs or health care. The media, so it was charged by political figures and social activists appealing to fundamentalist religious values and parental fears, bore heavy responsibility for the moral crisis in America.

Popular music has always interested social critics. Some, as David Riesman noted in 1950, are highbrows who "fear poaching on their preserves." Rap music communicates messages of social criticism to audiences considerably larger than the readership of the *New Republic* or the *Kenyon Review*, or even Dan Rather's viewers. Riesman observed that academic critics in the early postwar years automatically equated commercialization and the vulgarization of taste. Marxist critics have traditionally attacked pop music as an antirevolutionary narcotic that celebrates hyperindividualism, narcissism, sexism, and violence. Feminist and African-American, Hispanic, and other minority groups point out that music videos often reinforce race and gender stereotypes.

When it comes to violence, critics on the left are joined by critics on the right, but the conservatives' main target has been "explicit sexual content" rather than violence, as if there is much of a distinction in many cases. Within the Right only the small libertarian enclave opposes the rising clamor for censorship. The Parents Music Resource Center was founded in 1985 by Tipper Gore to organize parents as a lobby against erotic and satanic lyrics and explicit sexual imagery. When her husband ran for vice-president in 1992, she went out of her way to assure the fans that she was a rock-music fan even as she took on the role of symbolizing the Democratic Party's commitment to "family values."

But the backlash against global commercial culture is fed by even deeper springs. Few places in the world can escape these cultural currents. Especially in so-called traditional societies, there is mounting anxiety about the impact of mass entertainment on the most basic, the most emotionally explosive issues of daily life—men-women relations, sexual morality, and the obligations of parents and children. In the United States people are still sorting out the revolutionary cultural, social, and political changes of the 1960s, which have been sources of great hope for many but which have also elicited great anger and much confusion on all sides. Old certainties about how human beings should behave have been shattered by new social and sexual mores that the global media have helped to spread. At the same time established authority structures are increasingly powerless to reassert traditional values. Not even in Iran, after thousands of executions in the name of purity and holiness, could it be done.

Increasingly, neither parents, teachers, priests, nor mullahs can hold back the tides of change, and the levels of frustration are rising. Families cannot control what their children see and hear or how they spend their time, and teachers cannot compete with highly professional global media that preempt more of their students' waking hours than they do. According to a Nielsen survey conducted over two months in 1989, the average American household has the TV set on 50.1 hours a week. (In black households the set is on 77.3 hours a week.)[28] In a society where most women work and most children are in day-care arrangements that depend heavily upon the sedative effects of television, the love-hate relationship between Americans and the tube is boiling over.

Ten-year-olds who are glued for two or three hours a day to TV or who dream away the afternoon with the aid of CDs are neither exercising their brains, developing their own aesthetic sense, nor coping with reality. In an increasingly atomized society, packaged fantasies serve to cut off real human relationships, for which they substitute stereotypes; the beat and pictures touch basic feelings of impressionable preteens about race, gender, love, and social interaction, and, in ways we understand only dimly, help mold the personality of the adolescent by offering role models.

By the time the average American child has completed elementary school, a 1992 report of the American Psychological Association estimates, he or she will have witnessed 8,000 make-believe murders and 100,000 acts of violence. The APA report notes that more than

3,000 studies show a consistent correlation between "viewing violence and aggressive behavior." On an average diet of films and TV, according to several of these studies, the child is not only likely to become fearful of being a victim of violence, but also callous about violence directed at others.[29]

Movies are more violent than network- or cable-television fare. But critics have been gentler with movies than with television, presumably because movies do not intrude into the home in the same way. A small child can turn on the tube, become transfixed, and watch for hours.

MTV has a code of conduct that limits nudity and violence. But in schools of communication and media, earnest graduate students are cataloging instances of "crotch-grabbing hands, gyrating pelvises, and perfect curves bursting out of molded spandex" in music videos and counting acts of violence.[30] One research team, after watching 100 hours of music-video programming, found that there were eighteen violent or hostile acts either actually depicted on the screen or communicated in lyrics every hour. "Heavy metal rock lyrics and music videos routinely romanticize bondage, sexual aggression, and death; and popular teen movies are showcasing role models engaged in the most criminally indulgent, morally ambiguous and self-destructive forms of behavior," another researcher concludes.[31] Much of the violence is subtle. Most of it is against women. It all takes place in a dreamy setting in which there are no consequences.

MTV has invited special scrutiny not only because of its success but because of its hyperbolic claims. "MTV provides reason to live," the twenty-four-hour-a-day cable channel promises, an escape from the "botched world" portrayed by network news programs.[32] MTV founder Robert Pittman claims that "TV babies" think fundamentally differently from their parents, who grew up in the pre-TV world. "The pre-TV adults," he says, "are the 'one thing at a time' generation. . . . The TV babies, by contrast, seem to be processing information from different sources almost simultaneously. They can do homework, watch TV, talk on the phone and listen to the radio all at the same time. It's as if information from each source finds its way to a different cluster of thoughts. And at the end of the evening, it all makes sense." Pittman proposes that the new communications techniques be imported into the classroom.[33]

But many teachers believe that TV has quite enough influence in the classroom already. Zapped by hours of video, the TV babies, far from the virtuoso information processors who can simultaneously listen, talk, dream, and study, have trouble sitting still long enough to grasp any information more subtle than a flash of color, an insistent beat, or an orgasmic look. Learning math, history, or language, despite all sorts of innovations in teaching methods, is still a slow, linear process offering neither instantaneous change of pace nor much in the way of sex thrills, and only the tame violence of battles fought long ago. Video is so formidable a competitor for the attention of 9- and 10-year-olds that frequently teachers, especially in the demoralized classrooms of American inner cities, and stretched-out mothers trying to earn a living and keep house (and fathers when they are there) serve neither as effective communicators nor role models. True, the TV set, unlike the teacher, cannot command the child to sit down or even to watch, but for that very reason its influence may be greater.

As traditional family authority continues to weaken, and public education fails to prepare American children to cope either with the responsibilities of citizenship or with the challenges of a changing job market in a changing world or to develop the critical faculties citizens need so as not to be gulled by their leaders, children are being instructed by shadows on the screen on how to become precocious consumers and debtors. At a formative stage in their development, boys and girls are under the influence of highly creative communicators with no interest at all in their education.

Michael Dornemann insists that Bertelsmann is not in the business of creating taste but of satisfying the widest range of tastes and keeping up with changes in taste as fast as they occur. People who own or run music companies, says Dornemann, should not be missionaries for one set of sounds or another. A music company is like a big department store. A babel of sound is released, and the ring of the cash register decides what stays in the store and what comes back to end up as CD trays. This is a prudish country, he complains. "A 3-year-old can't walk up and down the beach without wearing a bathing suit." When we asked how he deals with the problem of potentially offensive lyrics, he replied, "I ask my lawyer, 'Is it legal?' If it is, okay. Do I like this stuff? No, I like jazz," says Dornemann.

When we pointed out the many research studies that attempt to correlate the escalating juvenile suicide and crime rates with TV violence or that purport to demonstrate the negative impact of pop-music addiction on social attitudes and school performance, his response was a quizzical look and a shrug. What kind of science is that? To prove the connection between what is watched on television or heard on tapes and CDs and what is going on inside a child's head is impossible. True, you can find child psychologists who say that healthy children in stable homes are no more likely to be harmed by TV and movie violence than their grandparents were by being read scary bed-time stories from *Grimms' Fairy Tales*. But it is precisely the growing number of children without stable homes on whom the impact of popular culture is most powerful and most negative. At best, the hours a child spends in front of the television or the boom box are hours devoid of learning and loving relationships.

BMG says that it is in the business of selling music. It is the job of parents to educate their children and to instill the strength and discipline they need to grow up. Media companies are not nursemaids, and they should not try to play any such role. Bertelsmann obviously opposes censorship in all its forms. The industry has reluctantly agreed to attach warning stickers to music products destined for the U.S. market that alert parents to lyrics the companies judge to be sexually explicit, but company executives do not like it, although they think it undoubtedly increases sales.

The result is that no one—least of all the "family values" preacher/politicians—is taking responsibility for major influences on children and young people in their formative years. Movies, TV, pop music, and advertising, given the doses now being administered to young children around the world, do affect their ability to learn, to think, to imagine, and to love, and the predictable consequences for their relationships to their families, for their future job prospects, and for the society as a whole are not at all encouraging.

In the United States global cultural products may outrage local sensibilities, but at least they are mostly made in the USA. In Latin America and parts of Asia, American films and TV programs dominate the airways. It costs next to nothing to air an old Hollywood "B" film or a rerun of *Lucy* or *Mr. Ed*. Even less antique programs like *Dallas* or *L.A. Law* are much less expensive to run than a local program with local talent, and the American product is likely to draw a bigger audience. Of the 4,000 films shown on Brazilian TV, according to the Brazilian film producer Luis Carlos Barreto, 99 percent are from the rich countries, mostly from Hollywood. Television is the most powerful force for mass education in most poor countries. Cultural nationalists in Latin America and in pockets of Asia are enraged that the most influential teachers of the next generation are Hollywood film studios and the global advertising agencies. But recent trends all over the world—advances in intrusive technologies, privatization, deregulation, and commercialization of electronic media—are making it increasingly difficult for families and teachers to compete with the global media for the attention of the next generation.

PART TWO

THE GLOBAL SHOPPING MALL

CHAPTER ONE

THE GLOBAL CUSTOMER

I.

IT HAS BEEN LITTLE MORE THAN FIFTY YEARS SINCE JOHN MAYnard Keynes proclaimed, "Ideas are made to travel, but let goods be homespun." The notion had a certain quaintness to it even in Keynes's day. Since ancient times, gems, ivory, household goods, wines, fine cloth, and other products mostly for affluent customers have made their way to distant markets. But as recently as World War II most people in the world had no choice but to content themselves with what was grown or made close by, much of it in the plot or the shed behind the house.

In industrial countries today few people grow their own food or make their own clothes. Imports are within reach of almost everybody, and more and more products are hybrids combining capital, labor, and materials from all around the world. Many of the materials and much of the labor originate in the former colonial appendages of Africa, Asia, and Latin America. Here flowers for export are grown, television sets for the world market are assembled, and data are cheaply processed for transmittal across the world. Hair from Pakistan and India is sold in the beauty parlors of Brooklyn—at a little over $100 a pound. Sand from the coral beaches of the Philippines is marketed in Japan. At the same time, global goods are making their way into once-remote regions of developing countries.

Chopsticks from Minnesota are sold across Asia. Marlboro country is everywhere.

Since Hugh Prather developed the first planned shopping center in Dallas, Texas, in 1931, more and more of the world's goods have been sold in suburban clusters of stores or enclosed malls in urban centers. In the United States in a typical month about 175 million adults shop in at least one of the country's 36,650 shopping centers. Almost a tenth of the work force is employed there.[1] Malls have become premier tourist attractions. In Virginia, a state rich in historical sites—Colonial Williamsburg, Monticello, Mount Vernon, Civil War battlefields—none of these attractions drew numbers even approaching the 12 million people who came to shop at Potomac Mills Mall in 1990.[2] In the age of the mall, shopping has become a favorite recreational activity. These sprawling consumption palaces are designed to combine the pleasures of shopping and shopping for pleasure. The tired shopper can take in a movie, have a drink, work out in a glitzy gym, or have a massage. "Shopping is the No. 1 attraction in the tourist business," says Nader Ghermezian, developer of the world's most colossal mall, which is located in West Edmonton, Canada.[3]

The line between malls and theme parks is being erased. Mall of America, conceived at the height of the consumer-spending craze of the mid-1980s, is the second-largest mall in the world. This 4.2-million-square-foot colossus on the outskirts of Minneapolis counts among its major backers Mitsubishi Bank and Mitsui Trust and Banking Co.[4] The mall includes a seven-acre theme park with a water flume ride in the company of Snoopy, a 1.2 million-gallon walk-through aquarium, a two-story eighteen-hole miniature golf course, the largest Lego structure ever built, four huge department stores, and about 400 specialty shops.

Japan has traditionally been a nation of mom-and-pop stores. But because of increasing pressure from the United States and Europe to import more, the government is encouraging more consumer spending and is a bit more welcoming of foreign goods. This means that, despite the fact that the home islands are among the most cramped industrial regions of the world, downsized versions of the suburban bazaars of America are springing up along the highways. About ninety Japanese shopping centers opened in 1991 just as the consumer-spending frenzy of the 1980s was cut short by a recession. Japanese malls lure customers with such features as aquariums, ferris wheels, even an indoor ski slope. Twenty miles south of Tokyo there is an "American" mall complete with boutiques carrying the "Fifth Avenue" line, a gadget store called So-Ho, and a seventy-ton fish tank called Fisherman's Wharf. "It may not be what America is really like," a spokesman for Nichii Co. explained. "But it's an America that Japanese consumers dream of." The mall itself is called MyCal Honmoku. (MyCal is an acronym for the developer's slogan in English—Mind Young Casual Amenity Life—but it is meant to sound like "My California.")[5]

If you drive into Manila from the airport past the main intersection where hundreds of thousands of Filipinos stood up to the dictator Ferdinand Marcos's tanks in 1986, you will see a statue suggesting the Virgin Mary put up by Cory Aquino's government to commemorate the event that propelled her into the presidency. Some Filipinos call the memorial "Our Lady of the Malls," for in its shadow have risen two of the largest shopping paradises in all of Asia. Giant flashing electric billboards welcome the throngs in the names of Coca-Cola, 7Up, Pepsi, McDonald's, Sony, Samsung, Sharp, Nestlé, Nike, Shell, and the Japan Tobacco Corporation's Mild Seven.

Filipino factories, except for the spotless buildings where semiconductors are manufactured, have a shabby look, but the malls are immaculate. Here is where much of the new investment into the islands has streamed in recent years. Most of the financing for mall construction is Chinese capital from Taiwan and Hong Kong, where investors with ample cash continually scan the globe for safe and profitable investments. John Gokonwei is a Chinese Filipino who has built Robinson's Galleria, a state-of-the-art mall and one of the country's largest. On four floors are jammed fifty-one fast-food shops—among them Wendy's, McDonald's, Shakey's Pizza—sixty-two boutiques, and dozens of video-game arcades, flower shops, photo studios, bakeshops, tailors, movie theaters, pet shops, and a Catholic chapel.

The Levi Shop beckons shoppers with three oversized Sony televisions playing Madonna videos nonstop. Few Filipino workers are willing to come up with two weeks' pay for a pair of jeans, but for the thousands of bureaucrats on international salaries at the Asian Development Bank next door, $40 is not an obstacle. A couple of shops away is the Blue Magic Shop, where Marlboro piggy banks and Winston tin boxes are on display under photos of Tom Cruise and Demi Moore. Toby's Sports Shop greets customers with a life-size cardboard cutout of Magic Johnson. In Rino's Arcade, under flashing lights kids pump pesos into video-game machines with names like

Robocop and Moonwalker. The walls of the upscale clothing store, Pop Studio, are covered with U.S. advertisements from the 1950s; next door, Comic Book Story features personalized nameplates for kids, who have a choice of having them adorned with either Batman, Superman, or Spiderman. Shoppers strolling along the corridors connecting the shops are bathed in piped-in American pop music.

Less than 10 percent of the population can afford to buy anything at Robinson's Galleria other than a soft drink or a small bag of potato chips. Oscar de la Renta designer clothes are available, but most of the crowd is there to window-shop in air-conditioned splendor and to escape the pollution outside. The scene is duplicated in big cities across Asia, Latin America, and in a few places in Africa.

By 1990 34 percent of people in developing countries were living in cities where daily exposure to global products through television, radio, and billboards was inescapable. Even in the rural areas of the Philippines any city of over 20,000 will have at least one "supermarket," usually a one-room affair about the size of an old New Hampshire general store. In the fishing and rice-farming town of Balanga, Bataan, the San José Supermarket offers Philip Morris's Tang and Cheez Whiz, Procter & Gamble's Pringle's potato chips, Hormel's Spam, Hershey's Kisses, RJR Nabisco's Chips Ahoy, Del Monte's tomato juice, Planter's Cheez Curls, and Colgate-Palmolive's toothpaste. Above the cash register is a large poster celebrating "Sweet Land of Liberty" with a picture of the American flag.

Alongside several boxes of locally made Jack & Jill cornflakes is the sole remaining box of Ralston Purina's Batman cereal. Ralston pays royalties of 3 percent or more for logos that children the world over recognize, including Cabbage Patch Kids, Hot Wheels, and Ghostbusters. Renting Batman's fame is a way to cut advertising costs. "If your name is Kellogg's and you've got Corn Flakes, you don't have to deal with Ninja Turtles," as one analyst of the global cereal market explains it. But if you are less well known, it is a bargain to be able to ride the latest Hollywood hit for eighteen months until the next one comes along.[6] All over the world, more and more of what children eat, drink, wear, ride, play with, and sleep on are influenced by such product promotions, the fruits of corporate deals between the licensing departments of Time Warner or Sony or Nintendo and the manufacturers of food, beverages, and toys.

The 1980s began and ended with periods of economic recession in much of the world, but it was a decade of unprecedented consumer spending. In the years just before the crash of communism it was no longer a badge of degeneracy for Soviet citizens to yearn for capitalist goods, and by 1992 leaders of post–Soviet Russia were offering to sell off mines and other national assets to get a free-market consumer economy going. Pepsi was running ads on Russian television, and McDonald's was raking in rubles near Red Square. The hunger for things to eat, drink, and wear was overwhelming, but Pepsi and Big Macs aside, global goods were beyond the reach of all but a small class of new entrepreneurs; the economy lay in ruins and foreign exchange reserves were exhausted. With infusions of capital from their compatriots in the west, former East Germans looked as if they might soon become a promising new market for international products, but elsewhere in the former Soviet empire the short-term prospects were not encouraging.

China announced its determination to raise the gross national product and the standard of living, and suddenly the old American dream of the China trade came alive again. American businessmen flocked to the Great Wall Hotel in Beijing to make deals, dreams of China's 1.1 billion potential consumers dancing in their heads. Consumer spending exploded in the mid-1980s. By 1987 35 percent of urban Chinese households had color TV, up from less than 1 percent at the beginning of the decade. Two-thirds of urban households had washing machines.[7] But these appliances were mostly produced in China. Japanese companies managed to sell a few cars and VCRs in the fast-growing Chinese economy, but the China trade in imported consumer goods did not become promising until the 1990s. Even as the Chinese government cracked down on political dissent after the massive show of force at Tiananmen Square in 1989, it encouraged consumer spending and liberalized its policies on imports. Retail sales rose more than 13 percent in 1991 and reached $173 billion, five times what they were in 1978.[8]

Of course, most consumer spending was in the developed capitalist world. According to the 1991 *Economic Report of the President,* annual spending on personal consumption in the United States jumped by $682 billion during the decade.[9] The Reagan administration encouraged easy consumer credit, and American banks, having exhausted the profitable possibilities in lending vast amounts to near-bankrupt Third World countries in the previous decade, now turned to consumers at home. Incomes of the very rich and near rich rose spectacularly in the United States and in other islands of affluence spread around the world. Middle- and working-class incomes in the United States dipped over the decade, but easy consumer credit lured unprecedented numbers of customers into the malls, where they parted with astonishing numbers of dollars. Japanese assembly-line workers and hardworking salarymen began consuming more as the government in Tokyo, battered by its angry trading partners, let it be known that saving could be overdone and that it was no longer always unpatriotic to buy things made by foreigners. Year after year affluent Germans managed to save more and to spend more at the same time.

II.

As global competition intensified, marketing became the preoccupation of the great corporations. At the end of the decade, forty-seven chairmen of global companies, including the heads of IBM and AT&T, were polled about the future of their companies, and most of them said that they expected to recruit their successors and other top executives from their marketing divisions.[10] Heineken, the Dutch brewer, proudly called itself a "marketing company with a production facility."[11]

In the early 1970s Lee S. Bickmore, then chairman of Nabisco, mused about his plans for a global TV ad that would project a box of Ritz crackers on screens around the globe and reach 2 billion potential munchers. It was a time of lyrical celebration of the multinational corporation, but the age of globalization had not yet come. Nabisco's global commercial never appeared. The cookie company, having been swallowed up by a tobacco company, became the target of the largest and most famous leveraged buyout of the 1980s.

But in the 1980s the age of the global ad finally arrived. The best-known advocate of global marketing was Theodore Levitt, a professor at Harvard Business School. Arguing that "the products and methods of the industrialized world play a single tune for all the world and all the world eagerly dances to it,"[12] he insisted that companies should start thinking of themselves as global rather than multinational. "The multinational operates in a number of countries, and adjusts its practices in each—at high relative costs." The global corporation "sells the same things in the same way everywhere." It is no longer necessary, he argued, to be so "respectful" of local differences, tastes, quirks, and religions. Push your products in the right way, and the local customs will fall away. Surely Hindus and Muslims both need to brush their teeth.

It was an immensely appealing idea that a company could sell its products in exactly the same way and with essentially the same words in Katmandu as in Peoria. The global expansion of the largest advertising agencies grew with astonishing speed in the 1980s as they convinced clients that cultural diversity was no longer an obstacle to reaching the global customer. "A lie has been perpetuated for years and years," Norman Vale, the international area director for Grey Advertising Agency, told the editor of *Management Review*. "The lie is that people are different. Yes, there are differences among cultures, but a headache is a headache."[13] And aspirin is aspirin. The right message on television or on the back of the bus, so the ad-makers' self-promotion went, was all-important in insuring that people reached for the right bottle.

Coca-Cola vies with Marlboro cigarettes as the most famous brand name of all; the company sells nearly half of all the soft drinks consumed on the planet.[14] What was once advertised across America as "The Pause That Refreshes" now takes place 560 million times a day every day in 160 countries. Roberto C. Goizueta, chairman of the Coca-Cola Company, notes that "people around the world are today connected to each other by brand name consumer products as much as by anything else." Logos on bottles, boxes, and labels are global banners, instantly recognizable by millions who could not tell you the color of the UN flag. Tokyo, New York, London, and Los Angeles now resemble one another much more than they did twenty-five years ago because, Goizueta suggests, "their residents' tastes in consumer products have converged."[15] The availability of global products means that masses of people separated by great distances now want the same things to eat, drink, play with, and wear, and larger numbers of a global minority can satisfy these wants.

Coke's top executives pride themselves on "thinking globally" and "acting locally." In 1992 Coke aired its first truly global commercial; Coke drinkers all across the world could watch the same message at the same time. At the Winter Olympics Coke's "sing-a-long commercials" were broadcast in twelve languages to what advertising agencies claimed were 3.8 billion viewers in 131 countries.[16] "The world has now come so close together, we can cut costs and achieve more by doing one promotion globally," declared the director of global marketing. Coke's universal theme is "joy, laughter, sport, and music," says the chairman, and that is why the Hollywood entrepreneur Michael S. Ovitz was brought in as consultant on the global commercials. "The cultural agenda of the globe is set by the U.S. film, music, and entertainment industry and Mike sits at the apotheosis of that," another Coke official explained.[17]

The company sells its product through more than 1,000 bottling companies and a much larger number of distributors around the world. The latter are the foot soldiers in Coke's global army, the ones who act locally and end up in the chairman's speeches: the Mazzas who drive through the Australian outback delivering Coke to "isolated pockets of consumers"; Pops Valentine, a 73-year-old Filipino who works at least twelve hours every day selling ice-cold Coca-Cola, "refusing to leave the marketplace until he has sold 50 cases"; Larbe Lahgui, "loading donkeys with Coca-Cola for transport through the steep, narrow streets of Fez in Morocco."

Goizueta, who was born in Cuba, notes that already 80 percent of Coke's operating income "comes from outside the United States, and that proportion is absolutely destined to go higher."[18] The company proudly sells an "American" experience with the aid of American pop culture, but the chairman is quick to point out that 95 percent of the world lives outside the United States, "and that's where the money is."

In the 1980s advertising agencies, following their clients, became global operations. A wave of mergers swept over the advertising industry as over every other global business, and by the end of the decade the top ten advertising conglomerates accounted for well over a quarter of global advertising billings, more than double their share when the decade began.[19] Charles and Maurice Saatchi started in a modest office in London's Soho district in 1970, but by 1986 they were the world's largest advertising agency with offices in major cities around the planet. In 1992 they were earning half their revenue from campaigns that spanned five countries or more.[20] All but one of the forty largest agencies in the United States and Britain had departments specializing in single global ads; five years earlier barely a third were in this business.[21]

Global advertising campaigns face a number of daunting problems. One is language. When Coca-Cola returned to China in 1979, it discovered that Mao's simplification of Chinese characters had turned the literal meaning of Coca-Cola into "Bite the Wax Tadpole." The solution was to come up with four Mandarin characters meaning "Can Happy, Mouth Happy," which seems to work. The literal Spanish rendering of Frank Perdue's widely broadcast TV spot aimed at the Hispanic population in the United States came out something like "It takes a sexually excited man to make a chick affectionate." Subtle differences in taste across the world are another hurdle. The opulent bouquet in the perfume ad for the New York market must be replaced with a single exquisite rose if the ad is to work its magic in Rome.

Global advertisers have also learned from experience that local sensibilities must be respected. You can use aging celebrities to sell Polident anywhere, but do not try selling shampoo aimed at "the over-40 woman" in Spain. She will not identify herself by stepping up to the cash register.[22] Japanese mothers found Procter & Gamble's ads for Pampers overbearing. On the advice of local specialists the company introduced pink diapers for girls and blue ones for boys, pushing both with a television spot in which a talking diaper promises that it will not leak. Pampers now sell well in Japan.

Advertisers are learning which products can travel the world via a single ad and which cannot. Levi Strauss, which used to film its ads for the world market in various locations, now shoots a global jeans ad twice a year in Los Angeles. Using 1960s American rock music and silent actors, the ad stresses "the ruggedly American virtues of its jeans" and is used without alteration in Latin America, Australia, and Europe. (However, the ad has to be reshot by local crews in Australia because of the ban on imported advertising.) Global ads for shampoo, disposable diapers, diamond watches, scotch, and many other household and luxury products are now being aired across the world.

It was the extraordinary reach of television in the 1980s that made global advertising possible. According to a *Wall Street Journal* survey, CNN reaches 78 million homes in more than 100 countries. The MTV networks claim more than 200 million viewers. There are more than eighty pan-European TV channels. The Middle East Broadcast Center reaches audiences in North Africa and the Middle East with programs in Arabic. Deregulation of media and the merging of markets mean that a single ad can now reach a Europe-wide audience. Although Switzerland no longer requires that television commercials feature dwarfs in children's roles, other national obstacles remain. In Poland, lyrics must be sung in Polish. Brazil has a "local content" law that requires global ads to be redone in Brazil. Norway prohibits beer commercials aired elsewhere in Europe.

The simultaneous rise of global markets for consumer goods and global media for promotion has boosted worldwide expenditures on advertising. In 1989 corporations were spending over $240 billion on advertising and another $380 billion on packaging, design, and other eye-catching promotion.[23] The combined total amounts to

$120 per person around the world, almost double what the average citizen of Mozambique earns in a year.[24] Close to half the advertising dollars spent across the world flow into the United States, the world's most developed consumer market.

Each year well over 15,000 new products are introduced into American supermarkets. The fight for attention, name recognition, and shelf space is fierce, and the dizzying menu of possible media outlets changes constantly. Of the top ten global spenders on advertising eight are U.S.-based firms: Procter & Gamble, Philip Morris, RJR Nabisco, Kellogg, General Motors, Sears, Pepsico, and McDonald's. The only non-U.S. companies to make it to the big-spenders list are the British-Dutch and Swiss global food- and home-product giants Unilever and Nestlé.[25]

At the beginning of the 1980s the average consumer in the United States was exposed to something like 1,600 advertising messages from the instant the clock radio went on in the morning until the television set was turned off at bedtime. At the end of the decade it was more like 3,000.[26] Direct-mail appeals, advertising inserts in the ad-filled morning paper, telemarketing—"Hello, I'm George," announces the computer selling radon detectors in the midst of dinner—and fifteen-second television spots by the thousands across a hundred or more cable channels twenty-four hours a day bombard the consumer daily.

There is no escape. Former sanctuaries such as public radio and TV and national parks are disappearing as ad-free zones. Snappy sales pitches or product reminders now routinely appear on buses, taxis, ski lifts, cereal boxes, blimps, pinball games, and less frequently on boxer shorts (Diet Pepsi), on parking meters, and above urinals. Even the sky is put to good use. Doritos and BMW have projected their messages onto the clouds over San Francisco via laser beams. For air travelers there is the twenty-acre ad for Absolut vodka that can be seen on takeoff from the Kansas City International Airport.[27]

The mad proliferation of ads reflects the fragmentation and proliferation of media. Not long ago the three major television networks in the United States could deliver 93 percent of American homes to advertisers; by the end of the 1980s it was barely 60 percent. There is much more advertising on the airways, but because consumers now have hundreds of cable channels to choose from if they have the latest equipment, the chances are greatly diminished that the right viewers will be tuned in when any particular ad is aired. It is a long time since all of America gathered around the Dumont to watch *I*

Love Lucy, and longer still since Sunday night at seven o'clock meant Jack Benny and Jell-O. Jell-O is still around, but prospective Jell-O eaters are now undependable grazers of TV fare. The same development has occurred in print media. The mass weeklies with a huge national readership such as *Life* (now a monthly) and *Look* are long gone. A profusion of magazines on every conceivable subject lure advertisers into a maze of "market niches." Most advertising is aimed at specialized audiences and uses carefully gathered data about their tastes, dreams, and quirks.

National, ethnic, generational, and local differences, it turns out, matter considerably. Niche marketing takes many forms. A marketing unit of Dun & Bradstreet enlists home-economics and gym teachers to pass around samples and coupons to 2.4 million junior-high- and high-school students.[28] The Agricultural Products Division at Anheuser-Busch targets Chinese, Korean, and Japanese communities across the country for its sticky California rice, and varies its ads by using the characteristic rice bowl of each ethnic community it is trying to reach.[29] Nestlé prides itself on being able to make its ground coffee taste German in Germany and Brazilian in Brazil. Its worldwide ad campaign celebrates diversity. "Whatever good coffee means to you and however you like to serve it, Nescafé has a coffee for you."[30]

Marketing increasingly involves the use of alternatives to advertising. Mail-order catalogs, many of which bypass ad agencies altogether, are becoming global marketing tools. L.L. Bean has opened an operation in Japan. Its hometown, Freeport, Maine, is itself a virtual mall attracting consumers from all over the world looking for bargains. Other towns around the globe are converting themselves into showcases of "factory seconds" and "discontinued styles" for the global bargain-hunter. Direct marketing by telephone has become a predictable harassment of the dinner hour in a number of countries. The home telephone is no longer a private channel of communication, the journal *Direct Marketing* cheerfully notes, but one that is now profitably open to "the commercial verbiage of everyday life." Direct marketing is becoming a major source of minimum-wage jobs and a $3-billion growth industry. Information such as the weather outlook in Penang is sold by telephone. All sorts of other services as well as goods can now be ordered by phone from almost anywhere to be delivered anywhere. A $6.95 call to 1-900-VIP-BUGS is all it takes to hire Bugs Bunny to call up a friend and wish her happy birthday.[31]

Ironically, the sheer volume of advertising, along with the rise of competing marketing strategies, actually undercut the power of mass advertising even as the global ad was becoming fashionable. Consumers were becoming more cost-conscious, and famous advertised brands were losing some of their allure. A 1990 survey by DDB Needham Worldwide Advertising found that only 62 percent of consumers said that they were buying advertised brands—down from 77 percent in 1975. As the recession deepened and as ads kept offering more mood music and less information, consumers reached for cheaper unadvertised brands. Many companies cut their advertising budgets, causing what *Business Week* called "the deepest and most prolonged ad drought in 20 years."[32]

III.

Virtually the entire globe now welcomes advertising, but no particular ad, however many millions see it, can be relied upon to deliver enough customers to justify the cost. The polyglot, multicultural world market poses all sorts of problems for global marketers, but it is a bonanza for the mushrooming market-research industry. Outdoor Advertising International, Ltd. handles global airport billboard campaigns for companies such as Mazda, advising them on such important realities of international life as the common practice in the Ivory Coast in West Africa of tearing billboards down because they make excellent roofs for huts.[33] Careful study has also been made of "the consumer-parking meter interface." Adapting some of the same techniques that are employed to study workers on the assembly line, researchers have established that the average man spends twelve seconds putting money into a meter. This is only a little less than the duration of many TV spots, and since most parkers are on their way to shop, parking-meter ads are a last shot, like campaign literature outside the polling booth.

With the exception of the laboratory mouse, the global customer is the most studied mammal on earth. Market research has established that the French consume four times as much yogurt as the British, that Americans reach for canned food only one-third as often as Britons, and that Germans eat three times as much beef as Swedes. Teenage Research Unlimited of Northbrook, Illinois, has discovered that 13.4 million American youths 12 to 15 have $10.5 billion a year to spend as they wish, and much more because working parents send the kids to the store. The Griffin Bacall Agency specializes in marketing to children. The agency calculates the annual combined income of children 6 to 15 to be about $15 billion. (At age 9 kids become more interesting since about a fifth of them get part-time jobs yielding $6 billion a year.) Perception Resources Services tests *Playboy* ads in "a small darkened booth . . . in a Florida shopping mall." As the subject turns the pages, an invisible beam of infrared light focused on his eyes maps exactly what he is gazing at so that advertisers can be informed whether their messages are stopping the eye or are being skipped on the way to the centerfold.[34] Another company uses encephalography to track brain waves of subjects watching commercials.

Since most ads are designed to create a mood, research into the psyches of global customers is a growth industry. How can you tell what makes people in Luxembourg or Indonesia feel good—or feel anxious, because for some products eliciting anxiety sells better than promising bliss—unless you study them? Asking them is one way to do it, and there has been an explosion of questionnaires and telephone interviews. In one year the toy maker Mattel queried 70,000 children and their parents.[35] Giant data banks are being created from the telltale traces of supermarket and mail-order purchases. The scanner at the supermarket checkout counter identifies each customer's purchases, and this information is processed into a customer profile to be sold to "micromarketers" around the world.

Demographics—age, sex, size of car, number of rooms, graduate degrees—are fed into the computer and supplemented with "psychographics"—scraps of data about values, lifestyle, behavior—to provide customer profiles that are then sold to companies. SRI International prepared a report for a food-industry association dividing the U.S. population into the "harried" (prime targets for fast food, steak houses, and frozen boneless chicken), the "traditional" (aging newspaper readers and afternoon TV watchers who are not adventurous eaters), the "financially restricted" (big consumers of canned goods), and the "working singles" (who account for 22 percent of health-food sales).[36] Then they sent an eighty-five-page questionnaire to 1,635 persons and took another cut, this time dividing the American population into "belongers," "outer directeds," "inner directeds," "need drivens" (poor people), "emulators," and "achievers."

IV.

Viewed from the moon, the Global Shopping Mall looks a good deal shakier than is suggested at advertising conventions and in marketing journals. Trillions of dollars are bet each year on the faith that a steadily expanding global civilization built on mass consumption is at hand. But there are major obstacles in the path. Despite all the free-market talk of recent years, trade barriers remain formidable and have been growing. Between 1975 and 1992, the share of U.S. imports subject to quotas or other forms of protection rose from 8 percent to 18 percent.[37] As tariffs have come down, quotas and other nontariff barriers have gone up. Some countries have proved to be ingenious at locating their health inspectors in places so hard to reach that it becomes prohibitive to ship goods there. Global retailers must often make deals with local entrepreneurs, legal or otherwise, to insure a warm welcome for their products. Often they must conform to foreign investment codes they consider onerous. In the fierce competition for shelf space, retailers exact substantial bribes, known in the trade as "slotting fees."

But as the ideological climate shifts in favor of a more "open and integrated" world, restrictions on trade and investment do not appear to be the most important limitations to the growth of the global consumer economy. The specter haunting the Global Shopping Mall is demographics. About four-fifths of the world's buying power is concentrated in countries in which less than a quarter of the world's population lives. The real shoppers who can afford everything from electronic sound systems and video entertainment centers to commercially produced toys amount to no more than 1.7 billion people. The universe of purchasers of new cars is a fraction of this number. The competition among corporations based in a handful of developed industrial nations to reach the affluent and the credit-worthy is so intense that issues of trade are becoming the national-security preoccupation of the 1990s. A world in which national purpose is defined by global economic competition just as it was once measured by territorial expansion is vulnerable to global economic warfare. The limits of the global market are pushing nations into economic and political conflict even as the scarcity of living space and natural resources not so long ago pushed them into wars of conquest.

The success of Benetton, Philip Morris, Coca-Cola, and a few other large corporations in developing global brands has helped to create the impression that a homogeneous global consumer society is emerging. Enthusiastic marketers celebrate the homogenization of tastes as a singular advance in the human condition. Surely people who open the same Kellogg cereal package, though separated by thousands of miles or by religion or color or economic status, have no reason to fight one another. No one as yet has suggested that there is a worldwide communion of Coke and Tang sippers, but some of the advertising agencies' self-promotion comes perilously close. Commercialization has invaded every area of contemporary life in more and more once-remote regions of the world. Human relations that were once defined by family ties, tradition, and philosophical or religious beliefs now increasingly rest on the production, marketing, accumulation, and exchange of commercially produced and globally distributed goods. People everywhere, especially children, are attracted to global goods. Ninety-five percent of American girls aged 3 to 11 own Barbie dolls—indeed, on the average, they own seven of them.[38] Mattel now produces black, Hispanic, and Asian Barbies for the world market.

The itch to accumulate, however, is not genetically programmed. Indeed, poor people the world over are often berated for their lack of acquisitive drive. Yet as the traditions of precapitalist societies fall away and socialist societies in the Soviet orbit are revealed to have had the aspirations of a mass-consumption capitalist order without a notion of how to achieve it, visions of organizing social systems on values other than frantic consumption have dimmed. The message of the Global Shopping Mall is ascendant almost everywhere. Industrial countries now pin their hopes for prosperity and political stability on an expanding global market for mass consumer products.

Yet even for those who feel most alive when they are shopping, the message is neither inspiring nor ultimately satisfying. At times we all feel the inexplicable sadness of the child after all the presents are opened. More and more of us are working for our cars, furnishings, and appliances rather than the other way around.[39] The disorders and dangers of the contemporary world somehow conspire to push those who have much to accumulate more. Brand-name luxuries are the badges of achievement and the trappings of power. Those who have little feel the spurs of envy as they come to the Mall in search of the good life they have seen on television.

The environmentalists Paul and Anne Ehrlich point out that, because of Americans' extravagant consumption habits, "a baby born in the United States represents twice the disaster for Earth as one born in Sweden or the USSR, three times one born in Italy, 13 times one born in Brazil, 35 times one in India, 140 times one in Bangladesh or Kenya, and 280 times one in Chad, Rwanda, Haiti, or Nepal."[40] They worry that a Midas curse might actually strike impoverished countries, and that someday they will figure out how to ape the profligate consumption habits of the United States to the ultimate ruin of the earth. The display of obscenely unequal consumption may well be a political time bomb, but except in China, where a middle class numbering in the hundreds of millions is growing rapidly, the Midas curse is not likely to hit soon.

The planet is not turning into a single global village but into a collection of highly segmented clusters of consumers sharing a common lifestyle despite being separated by great distances. "Eighteen-year-olds in Paris have more in common with 18-year-olds in New York than with their own parents," William Roedy, director of MTV Europe, says. "They buy the same products, go to the same movies, listen to the same music, sip the same colas. Global advertising merely works on that premise."[41] People at the top of the income scale provide the inspiration and the energy for the Global Shopping Mall. They make heavy use of global products. The family car, the home entertainment center, the liquor cabinet, and the kitchen look remarkably similar once a certain income level is achieved, whether one lives in Detroit, Geneva, Delhi, or Caracas. Jerome Pickholz, an executive in a global advertising firm, monitors what the top strata of the global elite wear to international meetings. Ferragamo suits, Christian Dior shirts, Gucci shoes, Paco Raban cologne, Hermes scarfs, Gold Cross pens, and Rolex watches comprise the uniform whether one has jetted in from Tokyo, Paris, or Buenos Aires. The jet-age nomad represents a market niche especially favored by American Express; in the 1980s all it took to order Ferragamo's clothing directly from Italy or from Harrods in London was the right credit card and the international 800-number for free global teleshopping.

Marketing departments of global corporations focus on the two dozen wealthiest countries of North America, Europe, and East Asia. North America and Europe each account for 31 percent of the world's economic activity; Japan takes up 17 percent.[42] In these countries in the 1980s, more than 90 percent of people who wanted to work had a job but unemployment is rising in the 1990s. The affluent middle classes of the industrial countries are still the world's preferred customers. In these countries when people who look as if they belong to the bottom tenth show up at shopping centers, they risk being invited to leave. One attraction of malls is that they are well patrolled. As one retail consultant puts it, "The fact is, the public areas in malls are better than Main Street. They have created the ambiance without any of the problems."[43]

The price of an affluent society is high productivity and a low birthrate, and one consequence is an aging population. In the United States, Europe, and Japan, near-zero and even negative population-growth rates are giving these advanced societies more and more of a geriatric look. In the United States over half of all disposable income is in the hands of people over 50. A large number are over 65, and there are armies of 80-year-olds with money left over from doctors' bills. But even the energetic among them can take only so many trips a year. The annual trade-in of golf clubs has yet to take off as a national custom. In the twilight years, the enthusiasm for a new refrigerator flags.

Three-quarters of the world's population lives in 130 poorer countries. In these countries of Latin America, Africa, and Asia, the majority of the population do not have either steady jobs or secure incomes. The explosion of urban populations, particularly in what used to be called the Third World, will bring more and more people into contact with shopping centers and malls, and they will be subjected to more and more advertising messages. But the very processes of urban growth—mainly the huge migrations into the cities—leads to further impoverishment for large numbers of people. The world's urban population is projected to grow by 29 percent during the 1990s, about three times the projected growth in rural areas, but most of those pouring into Mexico City, São Paulo, and Calcutta have little more than the clothes on their backs.[44] The ones most likely to succeed will do so by bartering in the informal economy. Most will not have spare change even for Pringle's or Cheez Whiz.

Over the past decade, as the Third World debt crisis deepened, most of these people watched their real incomes shrink. In the Philippines, as in most countries of Asia, Latin America, and Africa, well over half the national income is earned by the top 20 percent of households. (In the United States, less than 40 percent of income goes to the richest 20 percent of households).[45] Brazil is the world's fourth most populous developing country, and because of debt burdens and economic stagnation income distribution is becoming more unequal. Between 1981 and 1989, the share of national income that went to the top 10 percent of the population grew from 46.6 percent to 53.2 percent. The top 5 percent increased its share from 33.4 to 39.4 percent, and the share of the top 1 percent jumped from 13.0 to 17.3 percent.[46] In the Philippines in the mid-1980s the average Filipino family was spending over half its income on food and beverages. The rest went for housing, utilities, transportation, and education, almost all of which were locally provided.[47] Unless the Philippines becomes another "newly industrialized country" like South Korea, and the prospects for this in the next decade are minuscule, this densely populated archipelago, like most other countries where most of the world lives, offers little prospect of becoming a major market for global companies.

V.

Even before the onset of the 1990 recession there were signs that market saturation was setting in across the developed world. Francesca Turchiano, the president of a New York consulting firm, concluded that shopping centers in the United States were "on the brink of a mega-decline." She predicted that 20 percent of the regional shopping centers operating in the United States would close by the year 2000. Even when it was still morning in Reagan's America, the *Wall Street Journal* had detected signs of "shopping fatigue." Three-quarters of respondents in a national survey said that "they had fulfilled most, if not all, of their material needs."[48] As famous high spenders landed in Chapter Eleven or in jail, poverty and homelessness in America were splashed across the front pages. Corporations cut back on expense accounts, more and more people woke from dreams of extravagance and malls became less happy places.

"Consumer confidence," a barometer of how comfortable people feel about parting with their money, plummeted in the recession of the early 1990s. Many Americans found that they were not as rich as they once thought; their major asset, their house, had lost value, and in many places it was hard to sell at any price. The restructuring of the economy not only eliminated millions of jobs, but it destroyed myths of middle-class stability that had undergirded American society since World War II. The promise of new job-creating initiatives helped Bill Clinton get elected in 1992 and gave a lift to consumer spending in the postelection Christmas. But when he took office, the limits on what could be done to stimulate stronger consumer demand in the United States became clearer.

The U.S. market remains the flagship for the marketers of global goods, but because of the demographic and structural changes just discussed they are looking more and more to a few promising countries in Asia. In addition to China, South Korea and Taiwan have had the most impressive expansion in their middle-class populations, but they have highly protected markets. Global companies are determined to crack these barriers. Coke's president looks hungrily at Indonesia: "When I think of Indonesia—a country on the Equator with 180 million people, a median age of 18, and a Moslem ban on alcohol—I feel I know what heaven looks like." Nevertheless, with the aid of labels sporting the colors of the national flag, the local bottled drink Tehbotol has so far beat back a major push by Coca-Cola. (Indonesians drink four Cokes a year; Mexicans drink 263.)[49]

Still, as Donald Halper and H. Chang Moon, who are professors of international business, point out in *Management Review*, some countries such as India, Indonesia, and Brazil are so populous that even a small percentage growth can deliver a highly profitable market to the suppliers of global goods. "India has a low per capita income of $350, but it also has an expanding middle class, currently estimated at 100 million citizens" (the upper 12 percent of the population). Sales of consumer goods are rising 10 to 20 percent every year.[50] Not surprisingly, these numbers intrigue the global corporations. The Japanese believe that they have a significant edge in these markets.

They have already moved into the world's most populous country and fastest-growing economy. In Shanghai the Yaohan Department Store Company of Japan is building a department store with about 20 percent more selling space than Macy's flagship store at Herald Square. Coke, Tang, and Head & Shoulders shampoo are advertised on Chinese television, and Sony and Sanyo laser-disc and tape players are now on display in stores open to Chinese. Kazuo Wada, Yaohan's president, plans to build 1,000 supermarkets in China before the end of the century.[51]

At the end of the 1980s the Chinese government decided to stand Soviet *perestroika* on its head. The Communist Party cracked down on political dissent and opened up the consumer-goods market. "Consumer" was no longer a dirty word in the People's Republic. "People want to have some fun when they go shopping these days," the deputy general manager at the state-run Shanghai No. 1 Department Store explains. They are willing to pay more for foreign goods with "style." Foreign retailers are now permitted to import 30 percent of their merchandise. China is still a poor country where, as recently as 1992, the average annual income was less than $500. But more than 300 million live in cities, and many of them earn considerably more. U.S. companies such as Johnson & Johnson and Procter & Gamble now have wholly owned factories in China producing for the domestic market.

In poor countries where extremes of poverty and wealth coexist, global corporations carefully match the various items in their product lines with the particular slice of the market that can afford them. For Philip Morris, RJR Nabisco, BAT, and other tobacco transnationals, almost everybody is a potential customer. Cigarettes are sold on the street by the "stick" (in the jargon of the trade) to millions too poor to buy a pack. Coca-Cola and Pepsico can expect to sell their soft drinks to large numbers of people except in the bottom 30 percent of the population; below that level they are more likely to buy a cheaper local cola or stick to water. Nestlé and other purveyors of infant formula can count on reaching significant numbers above the bottom 30 to 40 percent of the female population. Philip Morris's Kraft-General Foods division, Procter & Gamble, Unilever, and other producers of food and personal-care products (soap, shampoo, toothpaste, detergent, beauty products) target about the top half of the income ladder. Johnson & Johnson, Merck, Hoffmann-La Roche, Bayer, and other pharmaceutical firms, depending on the product, can expect to reach less than half the population. Brewers Guinness and Heineken can reach only around the top fifth because far cheaper local alcoholic beverages are available all over the non-Muslim world. Producers of cheap household appliances and consumer electronics can reach up to the top tenth in developing countries; in the Philippines where income distribution is especially skewed, Sony and Matsushita can expect to reach no more than the 3.5 percent of the population that earn $5,000 a year or more.[52]

At the top of the mass-consumption product ladder is the automobile, the foundation of the modern American consumer culture and the machine that made the shopping center possible. Of the more than 400 million motor vehicles on the planet in 1980, 150 million were in the United States, 36 million in Japan, 24 million in Germany, 1.7 million each in India and China, and 180,000 in Nigeria. Close to 50 million automobiles are produced annually around the world, but for years there has been a glut of new cars. In the mid-1980s there were nearly thirteen people for every car in Brazil. Only one out of every seventy-seven South Koreans has one. There are 677 Chinese for every car in China. For the vast majority of human beings even to buy a used car can take the entire family income for five or ten years.[53]

Over the past two decades *images* of consumption have been transmitted across the planet, but for most of the world the dreams are unrealizable for both economic and psychological reasons. About two-thirds of the people on earth cannot connect most of the glamorous products they see on billboards and on television with their own lives of poverty and struggle. The expanding cornucopia of globally distributed goods is largely irrelevant to the basic needs of most people in the world.

New islands of affluence—in China and in a few other countries—are appearing on the horizon, but whether these enclaves are big enough to absorb the already huge but expanding global capacity for producing and distributing goods and services is dubious. Global companies dream of building a smoothly functioning global machine for the distribution of goods and the accumulation of wealth. But they do not consider it their responsibility to ponder the long-term social, political, and ecological consequences, much less deal with them. Global marketers are missionaries. As Stuart Ewen puts it, "Rather than being perceived as having another way of life, people in other societies, especially the less industrialized societies, are seen as people waiting to be ushered into the church."[54]

CHAPTER TWO

MARLBORO COUNTRY

I.

THE CIGARETTE IS THE MOST WIDELY DISTRIBUTED GLOBAL consumer product on earth, the most profitable, and the most deadly. In 1992 tobacco products, according to top public-health officials, were the cause of 434,000 deaths in the United States, more than all the deaths caused by homicides, fires, alcohol abuse, suicides, motor-vehicle accidents, AIDS, and illegal-drug use combined.[1] William Foege, former director of the Centers for Disease Control, estimates that smoking causes 3 million deaths on the planet each year, and he predicts that tobacco will become the leading cause of death in developing countries during the next decade.[2] The Oxford University epidemiologist Richard Peto, in a study of lung-cancer rates published in *Lancet*, predicts that without large reductions in smoking there will be 21 million smoking-related deaths in the industrialized world before the end of the decade.[3] Earlier studies estimated that across the entire planet "over 200 million of today's children and teen-agers will be killed by tobacco" by the second quarter of the next century.[4]

In 1991 Philip Morris, the world's largest distributor of cigarettes for the global market, produced about 11 percent of the 5.5 trillion cigarettes sold that year. The company's rapid-fire automated rollers spit out more than 640 billion cigarettes, roughly 17,000 a second twenty-four hours a day every day. (The state tobacco monopoly in

China makes about three times as many—more than 1.5 trillion a year—but they are all smoked in China.)[5] Philip Morris has cornered more than two-fifths of the U.S. cigarette market, and Marlboros, the most popular brand in the world, are to be found in every country on earth.

When the Soviet Union was beginning to dissolve in 1990, Philip Morris airlifted 20 billion of the world's favorite consumer product to Russia. Waving a pack of Marlboros was about the only way to get a taxi in Moscow, but a pack could cost as much as $25. Cigarettes were disappearing from the stores. Heavy smokers were flinging themselves across trolley tracks in protest. Soviet Foreign Ministry spokesperson Gennady Gerasimov clowned on U.S. television, "There is a discussion in my country about a new name for the U.S.S.R. . . . Philip Morris is sending us billions of cigarettes. . . . So some people suggest our new name should be Marlboro Country."[6] In 1992 after the collapse of the Soviet Union Philip Morris took over three cigarette factories in eastern Germany and announced plans to build a new plant near St. Petersburg to produce 10 billion cigarettes a year.[7]

There is no simple explanation for the phenomenal success of the global tobacco industry in marketing a lethal product that leaves a trail of disease, misery, and rising health-care costs across the world. Crucial to the growth of the global tobacco companies is the fact that the cigarette is the world's most profitable globally distributed consumer product. According to Roy Burry, a tobacco-industry analyst at Kidder Peabody, the average profit margin on a cigarette has been about 35 percent—thanks largely to the availability of cheap foreign tobacco and the successful automation of the cigarette-making process. This means that Philip Morris and its five global competitors who dominate the world market have large sums to advertise and push their wares, to curry political support, to court potential adversaries, to do conspicuous good works, and to sponsor entertainment, culture, and sporting events across the planet.

The extraordinary profits in making cigarettes are directly traceable to the pharmacology of tobacco. Nicotine is more addictive than either alcohol or cocaine. According to research findings publicized by the surgeon general of the United States in 1988, it appears to be as habit-forming a substance as heroin. The difference is that the feelings and behavior associated with smoking are more socially acceptable. For over 400 years human beings have derived pleasure and relief from the mood-altering properties of this acrid weed. Tobacco can help people relax, or it can provide a mild stimulus to get through the day, or it can offer relief from anxiety. Cigarettes are especially welcome as an antidote to boredom in the workplace, and there is some evidence that it improves job performance for truck drivers and factory workers and helps writers to concentrate. The feel of "doing nothing while still doing something," as David Krogh puts it, is pleasurable, and it has the added advantage—no small matter to the large number of people who regard excess fat as the ultimate symbol of failure—of keeping pounds off.

Entire generations have grown up associating smoking with power, glamour, and drama—Franklin Delano Roosevelt looking benignly imperious, puffing through a long cigarette holder, Humphrey Bogart enveloping Ingrid Bergman in swirls of smoke, condemned murderers taking a final puff as they walk the last mile to the electric chair, ecstatic jazz drummers with cigarettes drooping from their lips, and wartime buddies blowing smoke in each other's faces. Much of this smoke is still swirling on TV reruns. In real life cigarettes are also used as props to strike a pose or to signal anger, boredom, or an interest in a sexual encounter.

Until research findings were published in 1983 indicating that nonsmokers who keep company with smokers can end up with tobacco-related diseases and none of the pleasure, tobacco addiction was widely regarded as an entirely personal matter. If someone wanted to court lung cancer or set oneself up for a heart attack, that was his business. Unlike alcohol, which alters drinkers' moods in ways that sometimes impact unpleasantly on others—from the noise levels of cocktail parties in the next apartment to wife-beating and child-molesting to drunk driving—smoking has been thought to make people more relaxed, fun to be around, even sexy. The alcohol culture with its incapacitating three-martini lunches, assembly-line absences, industrial accidents, and five-car crashes takes its toll on productivity. The cigarette culture extracts money from society more quietly. The best estimates are that the social and medical consequences of alcohol consumption are about twice that of cigarette consumption even though cigarettes kill many times more people.

The cigarette companies' internal documents make it clear that the companies took seriously the scientific evidence of the health risks of smoking right from the start. As early as 1956 Philip Morris's own scientists were writing memos to top executives confirming that carbon monoxide and nicotine cause "harm to the circulatory system as a result of smoking," but the company joined in an industrywide campaign to confuse the public. In November 1961 Helmut Wakeham, research director for Philip Morris, wrote a memo for executives that listed fifteen compounds in cigarette smoke "identified as carcinogens," and he listed two other smoke ingredients as cancer promoters. Wakeham said it was possible to develop a low-carcinogen cigarette for about $10 million.[8] The decision was made not to market the product because it would raise questions about the high-nicotine products that were the mainstay of the company, notably Marlboros.

The public position of the industry was that the smoking-cancer link was "inconclusive" because the data were merely "anecdotal." Companies promised to conduct more research themselves and to support research. However, as Robert Seligman, vice-president for research at Philip Morris, wrote his counterpart at Lorillard, the industry had strict internal guidelines about what sort of research they would consider backing. Specifically excluded were "developing new tests for carcinogenity" and "conduct[ing] experiments . . . to show addictive effects of smoking."[9]

Nevertheless, Philip Morris and its competitors saw the handwriting on the wall. The American cigarette market was no longer a secure money machine. By 1964 the surgeon general of the United States had released the first report on the hazards of smoking based on the 7,000 articles in the world biomedical literature already available. By 1972 a vice-president of the Tobacco Institute, the industry public-relations and lobbying arm, was writing memos about the industry's "brilliantly conceived and executed strategy" that made "an orderly retreat" possible.[10]

As the antismoking campaign scored successes in the United States, Philip Morris put more and more of its efforts into developing overseas markets. In the 1980s the company became a global producer and distributor of grocery and household products by acquiring General Foods, Kraft, Jacobs Suchard, and several smaller food companies. Philip Morris now rivals Nestlé as the world's largest food corporation and is the seventh-largest industrial corporation in the United States. About 10 percent of everything on the shelf in American supermarkets is a Philip Morris product. But in a recent year, domestic cigarette sales alone acccounted for over 60 percent of "Uncle Phil's" worldwide profits, as its well-paid employees affectionately call the firm. Philip Morris is making ever greater efforts to present itself to investors and to the public as a purveyor of coffee and ice cream, but it makes a point of reminding its employees of its primary product. On the stubs of payroll checks appears the legend: "THIS IS TOBACCO MONEY."

II.

Although Philip Morris manufactures more than 160 other cigarette brands in some 170 countries, Marlboros have been the key to its global success. A succession of marketing entrepreneurs steered the company's phenomenal expansion. But the most valuable figure in the company by far is the mythic billboard idol, the Marlboro man. *Forbes* magazine once estimated that the Marlboro man by himself had a "goodwill" value of $10 billion.[11]

Each pack of Marlboros is emblazoned with the corporation's coat of arms and the slogan "*Veni Vidi Vici*," "I came, I saw, I conquered." But for years the company was far from the Julius Caesar of the cigarette industry. In fact, as former chairman Hamish Maxwell recalls, "when Marlboro was reintroduced [with the cowboy] in 1954, Philip Morris was the smallest of the six major tobacco companies."[12] But it had been around for more than a hundred years. In 1847 a young man by the name of Philip Morris set up a tobacconist shop on Bond Street in London and a few years later began making his own cigarettes, but the company remained small even by nineteenth-century standards.

In 1902 the company set up a subsidiary in New York. At that time the American Tobacco Company, under the command of James Buchanan Duke and his brother Benjamin, was in the mopping-up phase of a fierce "cigarette war." American Tobacco took over rival companies, established a near stranglehold on the American market, invaded the British market, and divided up the rest of the world with Imperial Tobacco Company, the British trust that was organized to fight them. In 1911 the U.S. Supreme Court broke up American Tobacco. Four American and two British firms emerged from the litigation, and these dominated the industry until the 1950s.

Amid these giants Philip Morris was a pygmy. It had entered the American market trumpeting the royal warrant appointing the firm "Tobacconist to His Majesty King Edward VII," hoping that more American smokers would be impressed than proved to be the case. In 1919 a group of American investors decided to buy out the struggling company with the intention of concentrating on exports to the Orient and of developing a promising new "specialty" market in the

United States—women smokers. By 1929, the year of the great stock-market crash, Philip Morris was a small American company turning out cigarettes in Richmond, Virginia.

The Depression proved to be Philip Morris's opportunity. In the tradition of the industry, American Tobacco, R. J. Reynolds, and the other major companies had all jacked up their prices. Philip Morris decided to undercut them, and it put the company name on an economy brand. A midget bellhop by the name of Johnny Roventini was discovered working in the lobby of the Hotel New Yorker. Outfitted with a tiny pillbox hat worn at a rakish angle, Johnny's squeaky cry "Call for Philip Morris" on coast-to-coast radio became one of the most famous sounds in America, and his picture was plastered on billboards all across the country. By the end of World War II, thanks to Johnny and discount prices, Philip Morris was the nation's fourth best-selling brand.

In 1954 the company hit upon the promotional campaign that would make it a global giant. In response to mounting concerns about cancer, R. J. Reynolds had introduced a filter-tip brand called Winston and was achieving great success. Philip Morris decided to push its own filter-tip cigarette as the way to reduce the risks of smoking without reducing its pleasurable effects. Most important, the new "safe" cigarette had to avoid making male smokers feel like a "sissy." (Extensive marketing surveys by Elmo Roper had identified the "sissy" problem.) The Marlboro name had been a company asset for years. In 1924, just as women were beginning to smoke in great numbers, Philip Morris had launched Marlboros as a cigarette for the female market. Under the slogan "Mild as May" the original Marlboro had strived for the carriage trade.[13] "Women quickly develop discerning taste," the original Marlboro ad read. "That is why Marlboros now ride in so many limousines, attend so many bridge parties, and repose in so many handbags."[14] An ivory tip was added for class, but so many women complained that the long white cigarette smeared too easily with lipstick that Philip Morris killed the Marlboro brand in the midst of World War II. Not even the substitution of a red tip could save it.

When Marlboro was reintroduced in 1954, it became the world's most successful global brand in an astonishingly short time. Coca-Cola had been around since 1886, but in less than a quarter-century even more men, women, and children all over the world were puffing on Marlboros than sipping Cokes. The Marlboro miracle began when Joseph Cullman III was put in charge of marketing. A fourth-generation member of a prominent American tobacco-growing family with blood ties to the Rothschilds, Loebs, and Lehmans, Cullman had a feel for what moved smokers. Within three years he was the top man at Philip Morris. Leo Burnett, the creator of the global advertising firm that still bears his name, conceived the Marlboro man. "What's the most masculine type of man?" he asked his writers as they gathered at his Wisconsin farmhouse one weekend. Everyone nodded when someone said, "Cowboy." Cullman recalls Burnett striding into his office and slapping a page down on the table. "Here's your ad. Says it all right there. New from Philip Morris. The cowboy, a symbol of masculine virility. Filter, flavor, flip-top box." Cullman later wrote, "We ran Burnett's ad in *The New York Times* and the other newspapers. Thirty days later, Marlboro was the best-selling cigarette in the city."[15] Don Tennant, a former writer for Leo Burnett, recalls that his boss got the idea from a black-and-white photograph of a cowboy on a *Life* magazine cover. A tattoo on the cowboy's arm was the crowning touch.

One can imagine archaeologists in some dim future trying to trace the frontiers of a lost twentieth-century empire called Marlboro Country, a land of freedom, independence, autonomy, fresh air, and radiant health. In the advertising world, explanations abound for the phenomenal global impact and longevity of the cowboy. Former Philip Morris president George Weissman says, "We chose the cowboy because he's close to earth. He's an authentic American hero. Probably the only one. And it worked."[16] Others attribute the triumph of the Marlboro man to the Hollywood Western. Philip Morris was profiting from synergy long before the word had become fashionable in the business world. Philip Morris's ad was a still shot from a Western, and the whole world loves Westerns. "Foreigners associate America with the cowboy image, primarily because of Hollywood westerns," one industry analyst concludes. "There is something in all this foreign ambivalence toward America: simultaneous admiration, envy and resentment. Marlboro seems to elicit the admiration rather than the envy." So many people around the world want to emigrate to America, and Marlboros represent an inexpensive "psychic downpayment on achieving that American dream."[17]

Some Philip Morris executives think the key element in the ad is the Great Outdoors. The Marlboro man is leading the simple life, the stuff of dreams for harried urban smokers. Richard W. Pollay, a professor of marketing at the University of British Columbia who specializes in research on cigarette advertising, believes that the ad succeeds so brilliantly because it is a celebration of self-reliance and independence. "These are precisely the well researched and known needs of adolescents at the age of breaking away and standing on their own two feet. Marlboro channels that need into cigarette demand."[18]

Of course, the ad itself is a crafted dream. The cowboy radiates good health as he inhales carcinogenic particles. A symbol of virility, the Marlboro man makes men feel comfortable about smoking filter-tip cigarettes instead of pipes or cigars, which are considered more masculine in many parts of the world. (At the dawn of the twentieth century cigarettes, but not cigars, were banned in the U.S. Navy because the former was regarded as "a debasement of manhood.")[19] Philip Morris marketers are so proud of this supremely successful global advertising campaign that they have taped hours of reminiscences and presented them to the Smithsonian Institution. (A condition of the gift was that the names and affiliations of all researchers using the archive be reported to Philip Morris, a detail that the Institution apparently feels no need to pass on to the researchers.[20]) "Very few brands have a global character," Elizabeth Butson, a marketing vice-president, explains on the tape. "Marlboro certainly does." Philip Morris's lead cigarette is not only the number-one brand in Mexico City, but is growing by leaps and bounds in Brazil, and is big in Greece. For this reason, she observes, the company has not "allowed people to fool around" with the Marlboro man, except for slight alterations dictated by local culture.

The director of marketing services for Leo Burnett in São Paulo points out that what unites people everywhere is "pleasure-seeking, hedonism, fun." The Marlboro man riding out into the wide open spaces symbolizes freedom, independence, and infinite possibility. But Brazilians found "Marlboro Country" too confining, and so the ad in that market featured a more expansive "World of Marlboro." Argentina has its own cowboys, but the gauchos are regarded as menial servants, not lonely heroes; Burnett's Buenos Aires office secured permission to use sports figures in local ads instead. Hong Kong was a big problem. In 1977 Marlboro had only 0.3 percent of the market. Burnett went to work with a campaign to promote name recognition featuring a lottery in which the prize was the winner's weight in gold. Later, the company ran ads on the front page of every Hong Kong daily made to look like news reports announcing that Marlboro was now the number-one cigarette in the United States.

Unfortunately, the cowboy came across as a coolie. The solution was to focus on the horse, which Chinese love and admire, and to make the horse white because heroes ride white horses. A major ad campaign was timed to appear in the Year of the Horse in the Chinese calendar. It all worked, and Marlboros, despite government restrictions on cigarette advertising, became the leading brand even though Marlboros cost more than all the others. In Mexico, despite initial skepticism about the image of cowboys, the campaign had good results. However, responsibility for a sudden outbreak of hepatitis in the army caused by dirty tattoo needles was laid at the door of the Marlboro man. Mexican military officials maintained that the ads had started a barracks fad. Philip Morris removed the tattoo from its Mexican ads, and soldiers stopped visiting the tattoo shops.

To insure that the Marlboro man comes across as the soul of honesty, Philip Morris stopped using actors and found real cowboys. Marlboro men are "sworn to secrecy" about every aspect of their work, according to the company. But one former cowboy model, Wayne McClaren, just before he died of lung cancer in July 1992, claimed he had briefly been a Marlboro man. "I'm dying proof," McClaren told reporters, "that smoking will kill you." Philip Morris admitted that he had been a cowboy model for its Marlboro Texan Poker Cards, but disputed the claim that he was ever a Marlboro man. To counteract the bad publicity, a company spokeswoman pointed out that the current Marlboro man, Darrell Winfield, who was discovered on a Wyoming ranch, has been appearing for nearly twenty-five years on billboards around the world and feels just fine.[21]

III.

The ability of the tobacco industry to survive and prosper in the face of overwhelming evidence of the damage its products do is a tribute to the extraordinary ability of human beings to deny what they do not want to hear. Both producers and consumers are virtuoso deniers. "Maybe I'm addicted, but so what?" a 19-year-old college sophomore in Washington, D.C., tells a reporter. "I don't want to be caught 90 years old playing bingo in a church." Most people who smoke don't get cancer, emphysema, or anything else that you can pin on cigarettes. Cigarette-company executives see themselves as last-ditch defenders of the First Amendment, rugged individualists who will not let health nuts and killjoys impose their own squeaky-clean notions on the hundreds of millions who enjoy smoking. "Only gurus on Himalayan mountaintops are pure," says a former Philip Morris chairman. Some in the industry have persuaded themselves that advances in genetic science are just around the corner that will make it possible to pinpoint the particular genes that render smoking relatively safe for some and a death sentence for others. In the meantime, convinced of their own rectitude, they have no problem sowing doubt, skepticism, and confusion about smoking anywhere they can.

"This business of constantly being under attack is a marvelous thing in a certain way," former Philip Morris chairman George Weissman claims. "It makes our people feel cohesive and put-upon."[22] Like jujitsu artists, the marketing departments of the tobacco companies were for many years able to turn virtually every effort to curb smoking to their own advantage. Before taking his seat on the U.S. Supreme Court, the Washington lawyer Abe Fortas succeeded in watering down the label proposed by health experts and the government on behalf of his client, Philip Morris. For almost seven years the package carried an innocuous Sphinxlike message, "Smoking may be harmful to your health." (Like too much mashed potatoes, addicts reasoned as they took another puff.) Thanks to the skill of the artists, the small print at the bottom of billboards is anything but arresting.

The banishing of all cigarette advertising from television proved to be the making of the Marlboro man. By 1970, the year the tobacco companies in the face of a threatened ban agreed to stop using this medium, Americans were already so much at home in Marlboro country that the loss of TV as an advertising medium worked to the advantage of Philip Morris. The cowboy was even more commanding on billboards and back covers of glossy magazines than he was on television, while the competing brands, notably Winston, had trouble moving from the electronic age back to ink. Even as the warnings grew more dire, Philip Morris's clever advertising kept targeting its core market, smokers who cannot quit, with challenges to the official scoldings they were forced to carry on every pack. The message was subtle but unmistakable: Whom do you trust? Some faceless bureaucrat with a fancy title you can hardly read? Or the man everyone knows? The Marlboro man.[23]

According to Joseph Cullman, the rise in excise taxes that was designed to discourage smoking also helped the company because it demonstrated how unresponsive to price hikes its customers really were. "Tobacco was a low margin business. When the state and Federal governments began to raise the excise taxes, we naturally thought that consumption would go down. Instead the customers kept buying the product. We found that we could charge a realistic price."[24] In the 1960s, according to Tobacco Institute figures, despite the surgeon general's warnings, cigarette sales rose 11 percent even as prices rose 42 percent. Highly addictive products distributed by a handful of companies were for many years exempt from the discipline of the marketplace since price was no object for hard-core smokers. But higher taxes in a number of countries, including Canada, have cut cigarette consumption substantially. The cigarette companies, however, have successfully resisted tax hikes in the United States. In 1992 the average tax on a pack in the United States was fifty-one cents. In many countries it is over $3.00.[25]

In the recession year 1992 Philip Morris finally discovered that even in Marlboro country the limitations of the real world intrude. After their price was raised seven times in a little over two years, many smokers abandoned Marlboros for cheaper brands, enough in fact to cause the steepest drop in sales since the Marlboro man first appeared. Many Marlboro puffers switched to Philip Morris's popular discount brands, so the company was prompted to take drastic action. In early 1993, Philip Morris announced plans to slash Marlboro prices by as much as 20 percent, and its stock plunged 23 percent in one day. This unexpected pressure on the world's most successful brand reverberated throughout the consumer products economy, and many other companies with famous trademarks felt the effects.

Despite the millions spent by the tobacco industry to prevent it, there has been a major cultural shift in the United States in one generation. In 1964 over half of the adult population of the United States smoked. By 1991 only 26 percent did, and many of these inveterate smokers found themselves unwelcome at social gatherings, even forced to take furtive puffs in the backyard. The pressure on smokers stepped up as the dangers of breathing other people's smoke became front-page news. In 1992 a study released by the Environmental Protection Agency attributed 3,000 deaths a year and widespread lung disease in children to "passive smoking."

The antismoking movement is now a global network. International meetings to share experiences of lobbyists, activists, physicians, and scientific investigators take place all over the world. Fresh data documenting the health hazards are available almost instantly any place that can receive a fax. The World Health Organization, national medical societies, organizations concerned with the prevention of cancer and heart disease, consumer unions, and antismoking citizens' groups such as the Advocacy Institute and Americans for Nonsmokers' Rights collect information and swap experiences in collaboration with antismoking groups around the world. By 1986 fifty-five countries had passed laws limiting the advertising of tobacco products; twenty (including the heavily addicted Soviet Union) had total bans. Forty-seven countries had some legislation designed to control smoking in public places, and eleven had laws limiting smoking in the workplace.[26] Canadian federal and provincial governments more than quadrupled cigarette taxes in the 1980s, and per-capita consumption has fallen by over a third since 1982. In 1992 the European Community enacted a ban on cigarette television advertising and was debating a European Commission directive that would banish the Marlboro man from billboards, newspapers, and magazines across the entire European market.

IV.

Philip Morris has mapped a global strategy of "orderly retreat" in face of the worldwide antismoking campaign in collaboration with its competitors and the Tobacco Institute. The company gives no ground in attacking its attackers. By 1987, forty states had passed laws restricting smoking, and about 800 cities and counties had enacted antismoking ordinances.[27] Philip Morris and RJR Nabisco organized a "smokers' rights" movement, using "action alert" newsletters to mobilize opposition to antismoking legislation. In 1988 alone the Tobacco Institute was involved in efforts to defeat some 200 proposed laws; it dispatched experienced lobbyists to instruct local restaurant and tavern owners in the techniques of fending off antismoking ordinances. When the City Council of Rancho Mirage, California was considering one such measure, RJR Nabisco threatened to move its Nabisco–Dinah Shore Ladies Professional Golf Association Tournament to another locality. At a stormy meeting that had been inundated with Tobacco Institute fliers, the ban was watered down. "It was close to a mob mentality," Mayor Jeffrey Bleaman told the *New York Times*. "There was screaming and booing. . . . It was as if we were passing an ordinance to ban sex."

At the same time Philip Morris aggressively targeted potential new smokers to take the place of those who had stopped. According to the National Center for Health Statistics, 43 percent of blue-collar men smoke as against 28 percent of white-collar men; 38 percent of blue-collar women smoke as against 30 percent of white-collar women.[28] Stored in the cigarette-company computers are telltale bits of information such as the fact that only 2 percent of Harvard's incoming freshmen smoke and that the most promising growth market for new smokers is women who earn less than $5,000 a year.[29] Since the 1920s tobacco companies have regarded women as their most promising growth market, and they have not been disappointed. Marlboro's market share among women aged 18 to 24 is over 48 percent.[30] Philip Morris introduced Virginia Slims as a cigarette designed for females with the slogan "You've Come a Long Way Baby." Both Virginia Slims ads and the Marlboro man sell freedom, and they make the same appeal: Take charge of your life by puffing tobacco. Young women now represent the fastest growing U.S. smoking population. In the 1960s about a third of the smokers in the United States were women; by the early 1980s it was about half.[31]

In February 1990, an antismoking group leaked confidential documents from Philip Morris's chief competitor, RJR, describing a new brand under development to be called Dakota. Within the company work on the new cigarette was known as "Project Virile Female." The targeted customers were low-income women aged 18–20 with the right "psychographics," that is, women whose primary aspiration in life is to have a stable relationship with a man and whose favorite pastimes run heavily to "drag races, tractor pulls and wrestling."[32] As RJR took heat from the press, Philip Morris quietly repositioned its Benson & Hedges brand for the blue-collar market, carefully removing its former heavy-handed snob appeal with a $60-million-a-year ad campaign.[33]

As better-educated and health-conscious Americans stop smoking, the cigarette companies have aimed more and more of their promotional energies at poor people. Much of Harlem looks like a war zone, but the ubiquitous billboards featuring scantily clad women advertising Kools, Camels, and Virginia Slims and the fully clothed cowboys welcoming all to Marlboro country are bright and shiny. In early 1990, the *New England Journal of Medicine* published the shocking findings that black men in Harlem were less likely to reach the age of 40 than men in Bangladesh.[34] Six of the top seven killers in Harlem are, according to the great weight of medical opinion, tobacco-related or alcohol-related. According to the Centers for Disease Control, cigarettes and alcohol are the two most heavily advertised products in African-American and Latino communities. Indeed, about 90 percent of all cigarette and alcohol billboard advertising in the country is located in these communities.[35]

At the same time the tobacco industry has been a pioneer in supporting African-American causes, especially Philip Morris. In the 1950s the white-supremicist monthly *White Sentinel* tried to organize a boycott against the company, noting that "Philip Morris, Inc. has the worst race-mixing record of any large company in the nation . . . the first in the tobacco industry to hire negroes instead of Whites for executive and sales positions . . . the first cigarette company to advertise in the negro press."[36] In a recent year Philip Morris gave over $2.4 million to 180 black, Hispanic, and women's groups and it is the number-one advertiser in the Hispanic press. It is money well spent. When the New York City Council was considering an indoor-smoking ordinance, the NAACP, the National Black Police Association, and other black organizations that had been recipients of tobacco-company largesse showed up to oppose it. The *National Black Monitor*, a monthly insert in eighty African-American newspapers, called on its readers to oppose antismoking legislation, terming it a "vehicle for intensified discrimination against this industry which has befriended us . . . in our hour of greatest need."

Early addiction is a powerful foundation on which to build brand loyalty. The younger and less well educated the target population, the less likely it is that smokers will kick the habit in later life, or even that they will try. According to the 1989 Surgeon General's Report, 90 percent of smokers start before their nineteenth birthday; about half begin before the age of fifteen.[37] Cigarette companies claim that they do not target the youth market, but the evidence suggests otherwise.[38] No company has been nearly as successful in marketing cigarettes to juveniles around the world as Philip Morris; in the United States about two-thirds of all young smokers use Philip Morris brands.[39] In the late 1980s, however, RJR Nabisco, which at times had less than 1 percent of the youth market, launched an aggressive campaign aimed at preadolescents. By making use of a cartoon camel with an ostentatiously phallic face to promote Camels, its high-nicotine cigarette that makes no pretence of being good for you, RJR almost managed to double its share of the 18-to-24-year-olds market and to snare almost a third of the nation's child smokers.[40]

Philip Morris spends more than any other corporation in the world on advertising. The company regularly introduces model changes to keep customers interested, a softpack in 1958, a menthol in 1966, Marlboro 100s in 1967, Marlboro Lights in 1972, and so on. Different colors are introduced on packages and ads to attract different customers. Thus red supposedly promises flavor, and it appeals to men. Gold connotes fashion and attracts women. Green appeals to blacks. Flip-top boxes are popular in cities on the East and West Coasts, but rural and blue-collar smokers in the Midwest and South go for softpacks.

Each new Philip Morris brand takes $100 million to $200 million in advertising and promotion costs to launch.[41] These advertising budgets have allowed Philip Morris to answer each attack by antismoking forces with a new promotional campaign or an innovative assault on another market niche. Because these advertising campaigns are so expensive, it has become virtually impossible for newcomers to assemble the necessary cash to break into the U.S. cigarette market. Philip Morris and its two closest competitors, RJR Nabisco and British American Tobacco, controlled about 80 percent of the market all through the 1980s. In 1993, Philip Morris's share of the U.S. cigarette market was a formidable 43 percent.

V.

As the war over smoking in North America intensifies, Philip Morris looks to the overseas market for profits and growth in the next century, particularly to the developing world. The nation's leading tobacco company has conducted its "orderly retreat" from its home market by taking advantage of the global marketplace. The long-term rear-guard defense of its most profitable market combined with overseas expansion has been a success. Despite the victories won by the antismoking movement around the world, more cigarettes are being sold on the planet than ever before.

In recent years the leadership at Philip Morris has been international. The chairman and CEO in the 1980s was Hamish Maxwell, who grew up in Liverpool. The chief financial officer, Hans Storr, is German. The president of the international division is Australian, and the president of Philip Morris USA is an Israeli. In 1991 Michael Miles, an American who is a food-marketing expert and the first nonsmoker to rise to the top at Philip Morris, narrowly edged out the head of the company's worldwide cigarette operations to become CEO.

Maxwell had built his career at Philip Morris by developing its overseas subsidiaries. He calls Philip Morris's international business the company's "first—and, to some extent, most successful—diversification."[42] By the late 1980s, the wisdom of looking to the global market was apparent. In just one year cigarette sales had dropped 6 percent in the United States. Philip Morris was the only company whose overall sales grew slightly, but this was only because its overseas sales grew by 8 percent. In Asian markets the growth was spectacular, well into the double digits.[43] Per-capita cigarette consumption in most underdeveloped countries remains at just about a tenth of what it is in the United States, and so the potential for growth is enormous.[44] As the stresses of modern industrial life find their way into underdeveloped countries, compounding the familiar problems of hunger, lack of water, and joblessness, nicotine addiction is spreading. Marlboro's growth market for the twenty-first century is the teeming world of Asia, Africa, and Latin America.

American analysts often attribute Japan's phenomenal success as a trading nation to the close working relationship between the Japanese government and the country's leading corporations. Business leaders routinely suggest that the American system be revamped to enlist government more actively in the service of U.S. exports. In the world of tobacco, however, the government-industry partnership has been in place for years. As the Tobacco Institute notes, "Tobacco was our first cash crop, the salvation of the struggling Jamestown Colony 350 years ago. It was our first step into international trade. . . ."[45] In the seventeenth century the weed smoked by native tribes in North America quickly became the leading export from Britain's North American colonies to the mother country.[46] In the Revolutionary War, Jefferson and Franklin used tobacco as collateral for French loans.[47] In the Civil War, Lincoln imposed a stiff excise tax on tobacco to support the Union war effort.[48] In World War I, the cigarette companies supplied packs of cigarettes to Pershing's army for free distribution to the troops. This patriotic act not only created a ready mass market for what was then an elite product, but it associated smoking in the public mind with youth and heroism. Cheap cigarettes are one of the perks of military service. In the Gulf War, Philip Morris airlifted 10,000 cartons to the troops with the full cooperation of the Pentagon.

Since the 1930s hundreds of millions of dollars of Commodity Credit Corporation loans and price-support programs have flowed to American tobacco growers, inducing them to produce more tobacco than they otherwise would. Thanks to subsidies, farmers can earn from an acre of tobacco sixteen times what they can earn from an acre of soybeans.[49] Under the "Food for Peace" program, the federal government purchased U.S. agricultural surpluses and shipped them at subsidized rates to the Third World.[50] North Carolina senator Jesse Helms, the leading protector of the tobacco growers in the U.S. Congress, insisted that cigarettes be included in the food program on the grounds that "historically these sales have developed new markets for American tobacco."[51]

Ironically, Helms was also a major supporter of the appointment of C. Everett Koop as surgeon general. The Philadelphia surgeon, known mostly for his strong antiabortion views, became a fierce warrior against smoking, to the great surprise of the tobacco industry. Helms set about to correct his miscalculation. "Once, at a Washington reception," Koop writes, "not long after a devastating report on the consequences of smoking, he patted me on the back and said, 'Keep up the good work, son; you are doing the Lord's work.' " Not long afterward, he made an official request that Koop be investigated for improper conduct in releasing a report on nicotine addiction.[52]

By the mid-1980s the trade deficit was a major political issue in the United States. U.S.-based tobacco companies began working more closely with the U.S. trade representative to pry open foreign markets for U.S. cigarettes. Philip Morris's 1989 *Annual Report* proudly announced that "Our gross contribution to the U.S. balance of payments was $2.4 billion."[53] By 1990 the overall surplus of U.S. tobacco and cigarette exports over imports was $4.54 billion, more than double what it had been four years earlier.[54] The U.S. Commerce Department estimates that $1 billion worth of trade creates 25,000 jobs; hence over 110,000 jobs were created as a result of the 1990 tobacco trade surplus. The number of people around the world who are significantly dependent on tobacco for their livelihood is estimated by the Tobacco Institute to be at least 47 million.

Tobacco exports are one of the few bright spots in the nation's generally depressing international trade experience in recent years, but they are entirely accounted for by a cigarette exports blitz directed at the Far East markets of Japan, South Korea, and Taiwan. Over half of the world lives in Asia, about 3.1 billion out of 5.4 billion, and cigarette consumption there is rising at more than 5 percent each year. Cigarette exports from the United States jumped from 64 billion cigarettes in 1986 to 142 billion by 1989; Marlboro and other Philip Morris brands beat out all rivals with 78 billion of the 1989 total.[55]

The key figure in promoting the cigarette export boom was the U.S. trade representative in the Reagan administration, Clayton Yeutter. On the day George Bush announced that he had picked Yeutter to be his secretary of agriculture, the former trade negotiator was the guest of honor at a Philip Morris reception. George Knox, a Philip Morris spokesman, explained, "Our company is the largest processor of agricultural products in the United States with Kraft, General Foods, Miller Brewing and the tobacco division. So we thought it would be nice and appropriate to celebrate the selection of an eminently qualified man" for the top agriculture position.[56] That evening, in a show of evenhandedness, Yeutter and his wife were guests of RJR Nabisco at a $1,500-a-plate inaugural dinner.

In the 1980s Clayton Yeutter did more to advance Philip Morris's cigarette business than anyone except the Marlboro man. Section 301 of the 1974 Trade Act permits the U.S. government to take severe punitive action against nations that are found practicing "unfair" or "discriminatory" trade restrictions against U.S. exporters. In the early 1980s the major nations of Asia with large cigarette-smoking populations—Japan, Taiwan, South Korea, China, and Thailand—were tightly controlling their highly profitable domestic markets. Brandishing Section 301, Yeutter first went after Japan, Taiwan, and South Korea, since these three nations together accounted for at least a third and in some years a half of the U.S. trade deficit all during the 1980s. Much as the British East India Company had forced Indian opium on the Chinese market during the nineteenth century to turn around a trade deficit, Philip Morris and Clayton Yeutter descended on Asia waving the same free-trade banner.

Dr. James O. Mason, assistant secretary of health and human services, told the 1990 Seventh World Conference on Tobacco and Health that the tobacco transnationals "play our free trade laws like a Stradivarius violin, pressuring our trade promotion agencies to keep open—even force open in some cases—other nations' markets for their products." Mason was rebuked by the Bush administration for expressing these views and was forbidden to testify before a House subcommittee that had invited him. Dr. Mason, who soon left the government, said that the tobacco companies' "bottom line is to at least replace the 2.5 million customers they lose every year to death and disease because of their products—and to replace the millions more who quit."[57]

For years there have been deep divisions within the U.S. government about smoking. Vice-President Dan Quayle reflected the traditional view that the tobacco industry is a national treasure. In 1990 he told a group of North Carolina Republicans that tobacco exports should be expanded aggressively because "Americans are smoking less."[58] An Interagency Committee on Smoking and Health had scheduled a meeting to address the collision course between Koop's aggressive antismoking campaign and Yeutter's crowbar tactics to open foreign markets, but the White House canceled the meeting. "Son, you've got your hands in my pants," a senior trade official told Dr. Ron Davis, the director of the Office of Smoking and Health who was arranging the meeting, "and I want them out."[59]

The cigarette market in Japan yields about $23 billion a year, but as recently as 1985 foreign cigarettes had captured no more than 2.3 percent of it.[60] Japan kept the market safe for its giant monopoly, Japan Tobacco Inc., by putting up high tariffs, prohibiting foreigners from producing cigarettes in Japan, and imposing all sorts of restrictions on the advertisement and distribution of foreign cigarettes.[61] Well over 60 percent of Japanese men are smokers, but consumption had been falling slightly before Marlboro and other world brands invaded the market. Lung cancer among Japanese men is now thirty-four times what it was in 1956.

In late 1985 the Reagan administration threatened an investigation preparatory to imposing Section 301, and within a few months the tariff walls came tumbling down, along with many of the other restrictions. By 1990, the global tobacco companies had grabbed 15.5 percent of the market, of which 10 percent fell to Philip Morris.[62] The Marlboro man was once again flashed across television screens as tobacco advertising in Japan tripled. Japan Tobacco Inc., whose Mild Seven brand had been second in the world only to Marlboro, reacted as sluggishly as Detroit did to the Japanese car onslaught; its worldwide sales fell from $23 billion, the year the tariffs were dropped, to $20 billion in 1990.[63] In Taiwan, tariffs had kept the price of foreign cigarettes three times that of local brands, and the result was that foreign brands all together had only 1 percent of the market. Threats to invoke 301 had the same magical effect as in Japan. Tariffs were eliminated in early 1988, and within one year foreign imports took over 21 percent of the market.[64]

The hardest market to crack was South Korea.[65] Three-quarters of Korean men are smokers and, together with a rapidly rising number of women, they consumed 91 billion cigarettes in 1989. About 4.5 percent of these were supplied by Philip Morris and the other tobacco transnationals. Four years earlier these same foreign companies had split 0.2 percent of the market.[66] South Korea operated a government tobacco monopoly on which it depended heavily to finance its economic miracle, and it viewed the foreign tobacco companies as enemies and anyone who collaborated with them by puffing their products as no better than a traitor. In the 1980s almost 10 percent of the government's general budget was financed from cigarette taxes, and as many as 130,000 farming households were engaged in tobacco farming.[67] Before the United States began its campaign to crack the Korean market, anyone caught smoking a foreign cigarette faced a fine of up to $1,250 and imprisonment. In 1984 the Korean government carried out a crackdown, and over a twenty-day period netted 407 offenders, including two members of the National Assembly and dozens of businessmen.[68]

The global tobacco companies hired former Reagan administration officials to lobby in Seoul and Washington. R. J. Reynolds retained Reagan's former national security adviser, Richard Allen. Philip Morris took on Michael Deaver, who was not only a member of the Reagan inner circle but had personal access to Korea's President Chun Doo Hwan. In July 1985 he met for seventy-five minutes with the president on behalf of Philip Morris.[69] Yeutter and Philip Morris had a strong card to play. South Korea was the world's sixth-largest exporter of tobacco leaf, and about 30 percent of their crop shipped abroad went to the United States.[70] In 1988 South Korea capitulated to the pressures of the U.S. government and the American tobacco industry. Of the foreign tobacco companies Philip Morris was in the best position to expand into the Korean market because it was already there in another guise; for twenty years its General Foods subsidiary had been producing Maxwell House coffee in a joint venture with a Korean food company and had cornered 90 percent of the Korean coffee market.[71] We have identified at least one former CIA covert operator that Philip Morris has hired to advise and to assist its sales force in getting its products into stores where storekeepers are opposed or local opposition is intense. As a result of all such efforts to push American cigarette exports, cigarette consumption in Japan, Korea, and Taiwan increased from 410 billion in 1986 to 455 billion in 1989.

Since 1974 the Thai government had been a pioneer among developing countries in trying to curb smoking, and the smoking population declined significantly from the mid-'70s (when the government's antismoking campaign began) until the late 1980s. The Thai government banned all foreign cigarettes, but Marlboros and other U.S. and British cigarettes were smuggled into the country in such numbers that they accounted for between 5 and 8 percent of the market.[72] Such is the power of the Marlboro man that many Thais buy domestic cigarettes and stuff them into old Marlboro boxes. The U.S. Cigarette Export Association, which Philip Morris had created in 1981 in collaboration with R. J. Reynolds and Brown & Williamson, petitioned the Bush administration to open up Thailand for American tobacco products, and once again threats to impose prohibitive tariffs succeeded.

The last two great markets that remain to be cracked by Philip Morris are China and India. The latter country is firmly in the hands of the British firm BAT, which has about half the market.[73] The Chinese still in China smoke 28 percent of all the cigarettes sold in the world.[74] The China National Tobacco Corporation limits foreign-cigarette sales to duty-free shops, international hotels, and Friendship Stores, but the black market in Marlboros is a big business. As exports from China to the United States grow, the global tobacco companies are counting once again on the help of the government.

The tobacco industry shows its appreciation for all the official efforts in its behalf in many ways. Cigarette companies are among the nation's largest suppliers of campaign cash. In the 1986 elections one tobacco company alone gave out more than $500,000 to members of Congress.[75] In the 1992 presidential election campaign RJR and Philip Morris each gave both candidates more than $100,000 each. The industry established the "Tobacco Heritage Committee" made up of CEOs of the big tobacco companies to raise more than $1 million to refurbish the Treaty Room of the State Department. The remodeling featured wall paneling with tastefully carved figures in the shape of tobacco leaves and elegant rugs with a similar motif.[76] Until the arrival of the Clinton administration, tobacco companies also provided free cigarette packages stamped with the presidential seal for the White House mess.[77]

VI.

In 1950 the average U.S. cigarette contained no more than 6 percent of imported tobacco, but ever since 1984, when American growers aided by U.S. government subsidies began to price themselves out of the market, the foreign content of the average American cigarette has been going up. In 1954 tobacco was grown on 512,000 farms in the United States, but by 1987 there were only 137,000 left.[78] Over roughly the same period U.S. tobacco production fell from 2 billion pounds to 1.2 billion.[79] The United States is still the world's largest exporter of tobacco, but it is now also the largest importer.[80]

The survivors are well looked after. "When you come down to it," says one North Carolina tobacco grower, a devout Methodist who is troubled about what his crop does to people, "we farmers try to grow a lot of crops but it's tobacco that pays the bills." In the early 1980s an acre of tobacco yielded a profit of $1,200 and an acre of soybeans $72.[81] For over half a century U.S. government subsidies have helped keep domestic tobacco prices artificially high. The tobacco growers have powerful support in Congress because tobacco is grown in twenty-one states. One consequence of the price supports is that the price differential between U.S. and foreign-grown tobacco widened dramatically over the last quarter-century. When U.S. tobacco prices reached their peak in 1983 and 1984, they were about double the prices in the other major tobacco-growing countries such as Brazil, Thailand, Malawi, and South Korea.[82] Ever since World War II the major tobacco companies have been encouraging the cultivation of tobacco across the Third World so that they could manufacture cigarettes inside the local markets. When U.S. tobacco prices rose, the companies had a ready alternative source.

In 1970 when home-grown tobacco was selling at seventy-three cents a pound, the foreign tobacco in the average cigarette in the U.S. market amounted to about 14 percent. In 1981 the price of American tobacco had climbed to $1.70, and more than 30 percent of the average American cigarette was cheaper tobacco, mostly from the Third World. By the mid-1980s, it had become clear to the U.S. Department of Agriculture that "tobacco price supports were too high for domestic tobacco to compete in world markets."[83] The supports were cut, U.S. tobacco prices fell, but tobacco imports by the American-based tobacco companies, though reduced, remained significant.

Growers and manufacturers no longer always have the same interests. Philip Morris has forged alliances with the domestic tobacco growers when it is useful to do so, but has systematically undercut them by making increasing use of cheaper foreign tobacco. The company has no interest in subsidizing American farmers at the expense of its own bottom line. Nor does it feel the need to pass along the savings from cheaper raw materials to its customers. In the 1980s, a period in which the Reagan antiinflation medicine worked well, cigarette prices increased more than 100 percent in the United States, double the average rise in consumer products.[84]

Producers of tobacco for the world market such as Thailand or the Philippines regularly import cigarettes of far greater dollar value than the tobacco they export. Indeed, just as sugar-producing countries import their own sugar in the form of Nestlé's chocolate (at a wildly inflated price per unit of sugar used), so tobacco producers often find themselves in the position of importing their own tobacco in the form of Marlboros. That is the normal order of things in the age of globalization. But for poor countries it poses a problem. In 1989 the five Asian countries that imported over half of all U.S. cigarette exports incurred a drain on their foreign exchange reserves far in excess of what they earned from tobacco exports.[85]

More than three-quarters of all tobacco imported into the United States comes from thirty developing countries.[86] Most of the world's tobacco crop is grown by small farmers in poor countries who have exclusive contracts with a subsidiary of Philip Morris or another of the tobacco giants. A few developing countries have become heavily dependent on tobacco exports. Half of Malawi's export earnings come from tobacco and a quarter of Zimbabwe's.[87] In Brazil, the world's third-largest tobacco producer and one of its fastest-growing consumers, the cigarette market is dominated by Philip Morris, RJR Nabisco, and BAT. The British giant got to Brazil first, and it still has four-fifths of the domestic market thanks to its Brazilian subsidiary Souza Cruz. Much of the tobacco for BAT's Brazilian cigarettes is grown in Brazil's southern province of Rio Grande do Sul. Peter Taylor interviewed many small farmers in that province who had been set up in business by BAT:

> The companies arrange loans to set the farmer up in business, enabling him to buy equipment and build a curing barn; they provide him with free tobacco seed; they sell him fertilizer and insecticide at cost price, as well as lending him the money to buy it; and they see he is visited

regularly by an agricultural instructor (Souza Cruz employs around 700 in the south of Brazil). . . . The farmers have to grow tobacco to pay off their debts, as no other crop will bring in enough money to meet the repayments. In turn, they too become dependent on tobacco.[88]

For farmers to switch to another crop would require alternative financing. But banks in developing countries rarely lend to small independent agricultural producers. However, if the farmer has a guaranteed market thanks to a tobacco company, banks become interested. From Costa Rica to India to Kenya, scarce government and private finance is being siphoned off to tobacco farmers.[89] Tobacco raising is an attractive proposition for small farmers because the returns per hectare are much higher than for food crops, and unlike fruits and vegetables, which are highly perishable, tobacco is easy to store and to transport with minimal loss.

Moreover, governments eager to promote tobacco as an export crop have been generous with subsidies. In the 1950s the Philippine government offered financial inducements to encourage tobacco cultivation that permitted farmers to earn from a hectare of tobacco about four times what they could earn from rice.[90] Much of this assistance to small tobacco farmers has been facilitated by rural development loans of the World Bank, which has seen fit to promote its ideas of export-led development by financing tobacco dependence in such poor countries as Pakistan, Tunisia, Brazil, Paraguay, Malawi, and Tanzania.[91]

The effects of tobacco on the land where it is grown are only marginally more gentle than its effects on smokers' hearts and lungs. In India, Sri Lanka, Kenya, and Malawi there has been massive soil erosion in the vicinity of tobacco farms.[92] Tobacco production typically makes heavy use of pesticides and depletes soil nutrients at more than twice the rate of many other crops such as coffee.[93] In Brazil alone 60 million trees a year are felled to provide fuel for tobacco curing. Across the globe, year after year, specialists in environmental management have calculated, "the equivalent of some 1.2 million hectares of open forest is stripped of wood for tobacco curing." This is an expanse roughly the size of Connecticut.[94] Another environmentalist has calculated that for every 300 of the trillions of cigarettes the smokers of the world buy in a single year, someone somewhere has killed a tree.[95]

CHAPTER THREE

THE GLOBAL GROCER

I.

THERE HAS BEEN A REVOLUTION IN EATING OVER THE LAST thirty years. Where food is grown, who grows it, how it is grown, where people can find it, what it tastes like, where and how it is eaten, how nourishing it is, and what it costs are not what they were even a generation ago. Political, social, technological, and economic developments at each stage of food production—from grasses, seeds, and fertilizers at one end to the supermarket scanners, microwavable cookies that erupt like volcanoes, rush-delivered pizzas, and irradiated strawberries at the other—are transforming the world food system. Many important changes have taken place in the last ten years.

Growing food is a quintessentially local activity. What can be grown depends upon the qualities of the soil and the climate conditions of a particular place. Yet over the past two generations farmers everywhere have been drawn into an increasingly globalized food system. The most striking result is that all over the world fewer and fewer people are growing food, and more and more former farmers are flocking to the cities. In the United States farmers now constitute just over 1 percent of the population.

While somewhere between a quarter and a half of the people in the world still grow at least a substantial share of their own food, the number of people who no longer do so has risen sharply since the 1970s for a number of reasons. The rise of global agribusiness is putting the family farm out of business in large areas of the world. In the United States, more than a million family farmers hang on to a life of hard work and financial insecurity for many different reasons: love of the land, escape from the city, passion for a way of life that means more than money, or just plain Vermont cussedness. Small farms can be more efficient than large ones, and farmers who care about the land can still earn a living. But the great industrial farms have the capital, technology, markets, and global political connections that are needed now to make large sums.

Food has been exported since the beginning of trade. Indeed, the philosophers who conceived modern economics used natural products to illustrate one of their chief discoveries, the "law of comparative advantage." England should raise sheep for wool on its misty meadows and weave it into cloth for export; sunny Portugal should grow grapes to make port for English gentlemen. By trading with one another, each would grow richer than if all the wool and wine stayed at home. But the overwhelming majority of agricultural products never traveled far from where they were grown because there was no efficient way to transport, package, or distribute them, and no reliable way to keep them from spoiling. It was only in the early years of this century that refrigeration equipment suitable for long voyages was widely installed in oceangoing vessels. This enabled the symbiosis that developed between international agribusiness and banana republics. By World War II, the colonial pattern of trade was well established throughout the world. Southern countries exported food, fibers, and minerals in exchange for the industrial products of the north.

Until the Middle Ages most food exports—salt and a few other life-sustaining products aside—were exotic treats for the rich rather than staples for the masses. Ethiopians discovered the coffee bean around the fifth century, but they regarded it as something to chew; by the thirteenth century Arab traders had discovered that coffee tastes better brewed than chewed, and coffee entered international trade. With the Age of Discovery, world food trade exploded. In 1492 Christopher Columbus brought to the New World sugar, bananas, and citrus fruits, which had been found centuries before in China and India, and he took corn, pineapples, and cocoa from the Caribbean back to Europe. Sixteenth-century Spanish traders brought chilies from Mexico to Sichuan Province in China.[1] Centuries later there was another spurt in world food trade that promoted the industrialization of Europe. In 1846 Britain repealed the barriers to grain imports known as the Corn Laws, and foreign grain flooded the British Isles. Local farmers, no longer protected from foreign competition, left the land in huge numbers to enter the factories of Birmingham, Manchester, and Leeds.

Food products now account for about 10 percent of world trade. But because food is so basic a commodity, the global trade in agricultural products has profound political and economic consequences. For the United States, food is the largest single category showing a positive trade balance, and this has been the case for most of the last twenty years. In 1969 U.S. exports of agricultural products stood at $6 billion; by 1981 they had jumped to $44 billion.[2]

In the warm, poor regions where the majority of the world's population lives, most of the arable land has been used for thousands of years for subsistence farming. But as the forces of globalization close in, acreage once used by people to raise food for themselves and their families has become too valuable to remain outside the money economy. With the encouragement of national governments looking for export earnings and tax revenues, large food producers buy up land or contract with landowners, usually the larger ones, to convert the land to the production of flowers, coffee, bananas, strawberries, and a host of other products that wind up in supermarkets around the world. Millions of subsistence farmers over the last generation have suddenly found themselves without land of their own. Some locate jobs in factories making goods for export, or in food-processing plants, or in the tourist industry. Many more who are now dependent on the money economy but have no money become poorly paid hands on the plantations where once they farmed for themselves. Millions more make their way to Mexico City, Manila, Jakarta, Rio, Bangkok, Calcutta, and other centers of urban sprawl around the world. As food becomes more and more of an industrial commodity, money becomes the ration card.

Across the world infant mortality has declined sharply in the last fifty years, thanks mainly to improvements in sanitation and public health. But 35,000 children still die every day, mostly because they do not get enough to eat.[3] Many of these 13 million or so infants and toddlers who have their lives cut short every year, according to the UN Food and Agriculture Organization, live in countries where the total food supply is ample. But a growing population of landless families no longer able to feed themselves lack the connections, information, and most of all money to put their hands on the food their families need. More than ever before, decisions taken thousands of miles away influence what people eat. The globalization of food production has increased total food stocks thanks to mechanization, chemical fertilizers, and the development of new varieties of rice, corn, and wheat, but the commercialization of food production has put much of this food beyond reach for hundreds of millions of poor people around the world. More food is now grown in the world than ever before, but the world food situation is increasingly precarious because of distribution problems compounded by the alarming population growth rates in many poor countries.

Mass starvation in a world of plenty is due partly to physical changes—soil erosion, environmental abuse, and drought—but also to equally significant changes in the way the world food system is now organized. The contract pickers, field hands, and factory workers who plant, pickle, can, and freeze the food products that reach supermarket shelves all across the world number in the millions. But most of these former farmers are not paid enough to buy industrial food products other than Cokes and small snacks. The poorest 1.7 billion inhabitants of our still-bountiful planet eat mainly what they grow in back of the house or just down the road. And it is not enough.

II.

Just five years after the world's premier tobacco company decided to become a global grocer, Philip Morris was running neck and neck with Nestlé as the number-one processor and distributor of packaged food products on earth. Before 1986, except for its acquisition in 1969 of Miller beer, a product classified in the industry as "food," and brief, unhappy experiences with chewing gum and a soft drink, the world's premier tobacco company had never been in the grocery business. But in just five years it became the world's second largest grocer. Its world-famous brands now include: Maxwell House, Jell-O, Kool-Aid, Cheez Whiz, Philadelphia cream cheese, Breakstone's, Oscar Mayer, Kraft's Miracle Whip, Breyers and Frusen Glädjé ice creams, Tang, Parkay margarine, Sanka, Post Raisin Bran, and Toblerone chocolates.

The food market is seemingly limitless since there is no more basic human need than nourishment. Across the planet many people are eating more than their parents did. In the judgment of physicians and diet specialists, increasing numbers are eating better, but much of the world is still malnourished in one way or another. About a billion people are "severely malnourished." Hundreds of millions more have protein deficits, some significant percentage of which are serious enough to cause retarded growth, loss of energy, learning problems, and even irremediable brain damage.[4] Many of the billion or so people who live in the United States, Japan, and Europe often eat too much of what the body does not need and would be better off without.

Americans alone spend well over a half-trillion dollars a year on things to eat at home, at restaurants, at workplace cafeterias, at their desks, or on the run.[5] Across the entire globe over $2 trillion is spent on food, which is about 10 percent of all the measured economic activity in the world. Since food has first claim on consumer pocketbooks even in bad times, it is no mystery that Philip Morris, faced with ever sharper attacks on its profitable cigarette business, opted to become a purveyor of milk, cheese, coffee, and Jell-O. By the late 1980s the U.S. food-processing industry was already generating $18 billion in exports and accounted for almost 1.5 million jobs.[6] Packaged food has its critics, and the Food and Drug Administration has in recent years become tougher on hyped nutritional claims on food packages, but Philip Morris can be confident that it will not be pilloried as a drug pusher and poisoner for marketing Cheez Whiz and Tang.

Philip Morris has been the preferred tobacco stock of pension-fund and portfolio managers, who typically choose only one cigarette company. But tobacco stocks had been undervalued for years as investors, prematurely it turned out, feared for their future. Philip Morris executives understood that major appreciation of Philip Morris stock in the coming decade would depend upon the company being perceived by investors as something other than a cigarette maker. By 1990 the giant global grocer was no longer listed as a tobacco company in the *Fortune* 500 rankings but as a processor and distributor of food. Hamish Maxwell, the Philip Morris chairman who accomplished the transformation, believed that it would not only rescue Philip Morris's company image but would be a winning strategy for managing the decades-long transition from cigarette dependence that lay ahead.

Philip Morris has been masterful in using its worldwide market clout to rise to the very top of the food business. The key to the company's strategy was its ability to leverage the economic power generated by cigarette profits. "Most companies have a core business," Alan Kaplan of Merrill Lynch Research explains, "a cash cow. But Philip Morris's is something special. It gives pure cream."[7] In 1985 cigarettes still accounted for 90 percent of the company's profits. (The only other products were Miller beer and 7Up, a soft drink with flat sales that the company unloaded the following year.) Thanks largely to rising overseas cigarette sales and regular price increases, Philip Morris had enormous cash reserves. Vice-chairman William Murray bluntly instructed a *Forbes* reporter on why the company was able to raise cigarette prices in good times and bad: "We've done it because we thought we could get away with it, and we have. That's what you're in business to do."[8]

In late 1985 Philip Morris made a sudden bid to take over General Foods, eventually paying $5.7 billion. Three years later it took over Kraft Foods for $13.1 billion, and in 1990, confounding expectations that it was about to pick up another U.S. food giant—even Pepsico was a widely rumored target—Philip Morris spent another $4.1 billion to acquire Jacobs Suchard, a Swiss chocolate and coffee operation. "We have lost a piece of Switzerland," the Bern paper *Bund* mourned.

Hamish Maxwell, the strategist of these lightning takeovers, is a tough, chain-smoking, soft-spoken, rumpled man who looks a bit like Charles Laughton. He grew up in Liverpool and studied history at Cambridge. His father, Sir Alexander Maxwell, was a tobacco-leaf dealer like his father and grandfather before him, and during World War II he had served as Britain's comptroller of tobacco. Hamish served in the RAF, then in the early postwar years went to work for Thomas Cook and Sons selling tours. Assigned to New York, Maxwell met his future wife, Gee-Gee, who was a receptionist for Cook. "My wife said she wouldn't marry me unless I got a well-paying job," he explained, and so armed with a letter of introduction from Sir Alexander to Philip Morris's CEO, Maxwell landed a job as a cigarette salesman in Richmond. Like all who have become top executives at Philip Morris, he had the marketer's instinct. Hamish Maxwell grew up with tobacco, but this affable young man who was comfortable talking to anyone about anything could have sold refrigerators or diamonds as easily.[9]

Maxwell worked his way up through the marketing division and early specialized in the company's international distribution and marketing. He was head of all Philip Morris operations in Asia during Marlboro's big growth spurt in the Orient. When he became chairman in 1984, he was still doing the family shopping himself, as he liked to tell reporters, but once his company entered the food business he was more careful to fill his cart with Maxwell House coffee, Miller beer, Oscar Mayer bologna, and other Philip Morris staples.[10] Like virtually all Philip Morris executives of his generation—with the conspicuous exception of his successor as chairman Michael Miles—he was a defiant smoker until the day he retired, despite having had coronory-bypass surgery. "I have no feelings of guilt, no trouble sleeping at night," he would respond coolly to hostile questions. Cigarettes, like alcohol, can be abused, "but each gives pleasure and has social value."[11] He would tell visitors that he stops from time to time "just to show I can; it's not addictive."[12]

III.

In the feverish culture of hostile takeovers and leveraged buyouts that characterized his years as chairman, Maxwell moved like a panther, striking terror in boardrooms of potential acquisition targets. Even before taking over the top position, he had acquired a reputation as one who could make and break deals merely by getting on an airplane. In 1981 he had flown into Johannesburg just as R. J. Reynolds was about to take over the South African cigarette-maker Rothman's distribution in Britain, and by courting the major stockholder "snatched the deal out of Reynolds's briefcase," as one incredulous observer put it. He was unfailingly diplomatic. When Ross Johnson, the head of RJR Nabisco, tried to interest him in merging Nabisco and General Foods in the summer of 1988, he pronounced the proposal, which for many reasons was absurd on its face, to be "a brilliant idea," then courteously lighted up a Winston, RJR's premier brand. After a decent interval, he called to say no.[13]

Philip Morris had two problems that were the direct consequence of its Midas touch. One was an image built on cigarettes, at once the world's most profitable consumer product and, increasingly, the most loathed. The other was the cash surplus built on smoking profits. In the predatory climate of the 1980s, as Maxwell knew well, a company awash in cash could suddenly find itself financing its own takeover by outside looters. The cash had to be invested. Maxwell was determined to make Philip Morris a global presence in food just as in cigarettes.

Like most top managers of the 1980s, he believed in the magical powers of synergy. Experience gained in one line could be applied to another, and the cross-fertilization would eventually help both. The company could draw on its expertise and experience in advertising, marketing, and distributing the world's most popular brand of cigarettes to sell anything you put in your mouth. Philip Morris was no stranger to supermarkets. The more products Philip Morris acquired, Maxwell reasoned, the more weight it would have in negotiations with supermarkets over price and shelf space. Like the cigarette market the core of which are heavy smokers who cannot quit, the food industry offers staples that consumers cannot do without (along with thousands of items that could disappear tomorrow without any consequence whatever). Like tobacco, the products have an agricultural origin. As in the cigarette business, competitive success is achieved by packaging, advertising, and promotion; in each case what makes the difference is the distributor's willingness to shelve the product at eye level, a good-looking box, and the seductive appeal of ad copy promising health, happiness, and convenience.

It took Maxwell only sixteen months to launch his takeover strategy. Philip Morris offered more than $5 billion for General Foods, pronouncing their initiative to be a "friendly" takeover. Indeed, Wall Street analysts thought that Philip Morris's offer was more than generous. Some said it was a marriage proposal only a fool could turn down and only a fool would make. But General Foods executives did not consider the takeover friendly; a number of them had moral qualms about working for a tobacco company and were reluctant to take orders from their new cigarette-smoking bosses, who clearly intended to shake things up. "Lackluster" was the conventional Wall Street euphemism for the venerable food conglomerate that for years had been doing about half as well as its principal competitors, a bureaucratic, stodgy, badly managed operation that was better at acquiring product lines than making sales.

Nonetheless, General Foods still had many of the most famous grocery-store products that had been invented in its laboratories over ninety years. As the 1980s began, the company employed more than 1,600 food technologists to concoct new products, mostly for the microwave, to rejuvenate its old-fashioned desserts, and to recover its once-dominant share of the coffee market. The company had picked up one brand after another as successful family food businesses decided to sell out rather than to keep fighting General Foods for shelf space. The oldest General Foods product dates from 1765, when Dr. James Baker, a physician in Dorchester, Massachusetts, launched the first chocolate factory in America, but General Foods itself dates from the early 1890s.

The company, which eventually became the world's largest seller of coffee, was founded by a health-food enthusiast who hated all stimulants, especially coffee. Charles W. Post was determined to get Americans to change their drinking habits. He developed a cereal beverage he called Monk's Brew, and when he changed the name to Postum, it took off. He then marketed a granola he called Grape-Nuts. In 1904 he came out with a corn-flakes product under the name Elijah's Manna that languished on the shelves until it was renamed Post Toasties. On the strength of these virtuous products the company grew year by year as it picked up Jell-O, Kool-Aid, Gaines dog food, Birdseye frozen foods, Calumet baking powder, Swans Down flour, SOS scouring pads, Entenmann's baked goods, and on and on.

Maxwell had spent a year studying the sluggish food giant before making his sudden offer. He considered the executives "tentative and overanalytical," and the performance record in recent years altogether unpromising. Despite all these problems, Maxwell counted on the newly acquired company to serve as a building block in his global strategy to remake Philip Morris. "We want to be known as a consumer-products company."[14] After taking over General Foods, Maxwell poured an additional $1.4 billion into it over the next four years and fired most of its top executives. When Kraft was acquired and merged with General Foods in 1988, the combined operation retained only two General Foods holdovers at the top management level. As the new owners cut away layers of bureacracy, they launched seventy-five new products.[15] After just three years, during which Philip Morris was piling up cash at a rate of almost $190,000 an hour, the costs of the General Foods acquisition were paid off.[16]

The takeover of Kraft was unmistakably unfriendly. Almost as old a company as General Foods, Kraft was founded by the son of a Canadian Mennonite farmer who arrived in Chicago in 1903, acquired a horse and wagon, and began selling cheese to grocers. By the outbreak of World War I, James L. Kraft and his brothers were selling thirty-one varieties of cheese throughout the Midwest and beyond. Kraft became a national dairy company by introducing foil-wrapped cheeses in wooden boxes in the early 1920s. It then merged with competitors and picked up such long-established lines as Breyers ice cream, which dates from William Breyer's ice-cream business started a year after the Civil War, and Breakstone's, the outgrowth of Isaac and Joseph Breakstone's dairy store on the Lower East Side of Manhattan that opened in 1883. In the early 1980s Kraft had been briefly merged with Dart Industries and had acquired nondairy businesses, including the maker of KitchenAid home appliances, but the mix of hardware and cheese was not a happy one, and Kraft executives had rid themselves of their nondairy businesses just before Hamish Maxwell moved in on them.

On October 17, 1988, Maxwell called John M. Richman, Kraft's chairman, with an offer to buy all the company's stock at $90 a share. It was a call Richman had been expecting. He was as well aware as Maxwell that predators were lurking about looking for corporations with treasuries ample enough to finance their own demise. He knew that his company was a likely target because of what once were considered prudent business practices. Its pension plan was fully funded. Its earnings were high. Its debt was low. Twice a year he had been assembling his stable of lawyers and investment bankers in a "fire drill" just in case "I got a call some afternoon." The hypothetical enemy in the war-gaming of a hostile takeover bid was always Philip Morris.

The telephone finally rang. "It's nothing personal," said Maxwell, "but business is business."[17] "Dear Hamish," Richman replied in a letter three days later, "You did not see fit to discuss your takeover attempt when we were together at the Grocery Manufacturers of America meeting last Wednesday and Thursday, nor did you see fit to tell me that you were planning on filing a bizarre and baseless law suit against me and our Board of Directors on Monday. . . ." The next day Maxwell wrote back: "I would have preferred to discuss our offer with you prior to taking the actions we commenced. However, in the current legal environment in which we live, I accepted the advice to proceed as we did as a business decision. . . . Yours sincerely, Hamish Maxwell." Another four days passed. Then on October 25 Richman wrote a categorical refusal of the Philip Morris offer. "Dear Hamish: . . . Kraft was not 'for sale' and is not 'for sale.' "[18]

The resistance struggle lasted only one more day, culminating in a three-hour negotiation between the two corporate heads alone in a hotel room at O'Hare Airport. Under the terms of the agreement struck at 1:00 A.M., Kraft became a division of Philip Morris, to be merged with General Foods and thenceforth known as KGF. Richman's consolation was a few months tenure as vice-chairman of Philip Morris and a $22.4-million golden parachute. Kraft had a reputation as a well-managed company. As part of the deal fifty-three Kraft executives agreed to stay on after the merger and were rewarded with "golden handcuffs" amounting to more than $14.5 million.[19] The investment bankers who advised both marriage partners ended up with commissions of more than $45 million.[20]

An important reason why Maxwell was so eager to digest Kraft was that the dairy-foods giant fitted perfectly into Philip Morris's strategy to establish a worldwide presence. The company's success with cigarettes depended heavily on its international operations; 47 percent of cigarette revenues came from overseas. But only 20 percent of its food sales took place outside the American market.[21] Maxwell considered Kraft "the strongest of the American-owned food companies internationally." The company had successfully found niches for its dairy line in Italy, Germany, and Australia.[22] Since General Foods was strong in France, Britain, Japan, and Korea, Philip Morris now had a good foundation for its global food business. Kraft dominated the refrigerated-foods section of the supermarket, a major source of supermarket profits as more and more consumers in the 1980s displayed their willingness to pay a premium for frozen "freshness." Traditional General Foods products, mostly dry, canned, or boxed, are unavoidable in the rest of the store. The market power of the faster-selling products would allow Philip Morris to make sure that the supermarket chains accorded its slower-selling products proper shelf space. Combining the two food companies also made it possible "to swap secrets on marketing and food technology."[23]

IV.

As part of the Kraft deal, Philip Morris secured the services of the company president, Michael Miles, to whom Maxwell turned over the combined food operations. In short order Miles slashed the work force by 2,500, and with this and other cost-cutting measures he was able to increase the combined food divisions' earnings by 26 percent in the first year. He refurbished aging products like Cheez Whiz and brought them into the microwave age; the "mature" cheese-spread, as the company called it, was put into a new microwavable package and repositioned as an exciting melted-cheese dip. Sales shot up 35 percent.[24]

Forbes magazine called the world's largest food merger "one of the fastest consolidations of two huge companies ever seen."[25]

A few months after the Kraft merger Maxwell was dropping hints that he was about to move again on another food company. "You never get to where you can just sit back and say, 'Okay, I've now created the world, I'll rest.' "[26] Nestlé was still the world's largest food company, and in Europe Unilever was also bigger. "To strengthen our food business internationally—and we are concerned that we should do it sooner rather than later—," Maxwell mused aloud, "we need acquisitions. We cannot do it in one big acquisition. . . . So it's more a matter of picking up bits and pieces."[27] In 1989, Philip Morris paid less than $100 million for Fini, an Italian pasta and cold-cuts company.

The next year, long before most industry analysts thought Philip Morris would be finished digesting its last multibillion-dollar acquisition, Maxwell was ready for another. To be a truly global food giant, Maxwell and Miles realized, Philip Morris had to have a major European food company. The European Community appeared to be moving rapidly toward economic integration. Most European nations west of Poland had agreed to form a single market embracing 340 million customers by the beginning of 1993. It was important to hedge against the possibility that the EC would erect tariff barriers against the outside world even as they lowered them within Europe. Jacobs Suchard would give Philip Morris a place inside "Fortress Europe," if that is what it were to become.

The year Philip Morris bid to take it over, Jacobs Suchard was selling about 13 percent of all the candy sold in Europe and about 20 percent of the coffee. It was especially strong in Europe's premier national market, West Germany. With the acquisition of the Swiss chocolate-maker, Philip Morris became the world's number-one consumer-products company. By the same stroke it became the third-largest food company in Europe, a $700-billion-a-year market that was once the exclusive domain of Nestlé, Unilever, and a host of other smaller Old World companies.[28]

One motive behind Philip Morris's transformation into a food company was the hope of becoming recession-proof. As Maxwell puts it, no matter how bad things get "you can bet your life they'll keep on eating."[29] As food companies merged and expanded in the 1980s and the prices of their stock surged, they looked impervious to fluctuations in the economy. In the recession that began in 1989 a relatively small number of people in the United States went to bed hungry, but more than 25 million received food stamps.[30] Many shoppers stopped buying expensive brands and turned to cheaper foods. Philip Morris, as in its tobacco business, had been hiking the prices of its cheese products and frozen dinners about 5 percent every year. Even Kraft loyalists balked at paying eighty-nine cents for a boxed macaroni-and-cheese dinner when there was a box with a less famous label right next to it that cost under half.[31] As food sales in the United States flattened, Philip Morris looked more and more to foreign markets. But so did competing food companies like Kellogg, which built factories in Latvia, India, and China.

Economic integration generated great hopes in the food industry, but the psychological barriers in the global food trade are even more formidable than tariffs. The grocery business is much more country-bound than the cigarette trade, a hostage to local tastes and social customs. Brand loyalties are often quirky. Nestlé had an astonishing 70 percent of the coffee market in Japan as late as the 1980s because of the Japanese custom of giving one another 10 million gift boxes of Nescafé every year. This peculiar custom dates from the days of the American occupation when a few ounces of Nescafé were as good as gold on the black market. Nescafé is still a prestige symbol that is helping turn this once tea-imbibing society into coffee drinkers.[32] Japanese yuppies now prefer ground coffee, a product in which Philip Morris is better able to compete.

Philip Morris is betting that the psychological barriers to unfamiliar foods will continue to crumble. Michael Miles counts on being able to develop and market what he calls "pan-European brands" to fill shopping carts from Portugal to Russia. James M. Kilts, president of Kraft USA, an operating unit of Kraft General Foods, believes that "the application of similar ideas across the global marketplace *is working* today as consumer needs for taste, convenience, nutrition, and value become more internationally entrenched. . . ."[33] Just before he retired, Hamish Maxwell cast a last look to the East. "A lot of opportunity is going to come our way in Asia as Asians develop tastes for Occidental food."[34] By coordinating its international cigarette- and food-marketing operations in Asia, the company has been able to turn many of its new Marlboro smokers into nibblers of Kraft cheese and Suchard chocolate as well.

About 35 percent of everything that the United States exports to Japan is food. No trade issues arouse more rancor on both sides than Japanese barriers to American-grown, American-processed, or

American-owned food. The United States has been trying without success to open the richest rice-eating nation in the world to American rice. Japanese farmers, who grow hundreds of strains of rice, are a powerful political constituency. The rice issue transcends economic interest. It is a cultural symbol and a focal point of anger. Though stalled on the rice front, the U.S. government, with the powerful backing of the food industry, has forced the Japanese to open their market to other previously restricted products, notably oranges and beef. Just as Philip Morris had convinced the U.S. government to press the Japanese to open the door to Marlboro cigarettes a few years earlier, now the company persuaded the Bush administration to open the way for Kraft General Foods to become a major Japanese importer of processed cheese slices, Philadelphia cream cheese, and Oscar Mayer processed meats.

When George Bush took a planeload of top executives from auto and electronics firms to Japan in January 1992—the Philip Morris CEO was invited but declined—the president announced that his visit was essentially a trade mission and that his goal was "Jobs. Jobs. Jobs." But it has become a fact of life that in the new world economy firms flying the American flag export commodities produced thousands of miles from the United States. Thus Philip Morris's Japanese subsidiaries import Philadelphia cream cheese from Australia, soft white cheese from Denmark and Italy, and chocolate from Germany and Switzerland.[35] The U.S.-based food giants have resorted to rhetorical flag-waving and calculated self-congratulation as the companies best able to redress America's trade deficit with Japan. Their campaign to persuade the U.S. government to help them elbow their way into the Japanese market has been largely successful. But the result, while it is always helpful to Philip Morris and its U.S.-based competitors, often has no discernible impact on either stimulating U.S. exports or easing unemployment in the United States. Just as "American" televisions are made in Korea, so "American" cheese can be produced any place with cows.

In 1991 Michael Miles succeeded Maxwell as chief executive officer and chairman of Philip Morris. By background and training an advertising man, he worked first for Leo Burnett, the discoverer of Marlboro country. For Procter & Gamble, then the world's largest advertiser, he developed winning ad campaigns for the deodorant Secret and other products, then moved to the beverage and fast-food giant Heublein as corporate vice-president of marketing. He became famous in the marketing world for resurrecting Kentucky Fried Chicken, a Heublein acquisition that had fallen into a sea of troubles. Miles devised a strategy he dubbed "QSCVFOOFAMP" (pronounced *qui-SIV-o-famp*)—the acronym for "quality, service, cleanliness, values, facilities, other operating factors, advertising, merchandising, and promotion"—which amounted to a battle plan to transform the company from head to toe. He started a Chicken School modeled on McDonald's Hamburger University to train the help, and he introduced fresh-buttermilk biscuits. The results were stunning, and his ability to breathe new life into Colonel Sanders's chicken chain made him the obvious candidate for the presidency of Kraft in 1982.[36]

Michael Miles is a cool, controlled man who arrives at the office by 6:00 A.M.; when asked by *Fortune* what he did besides work, he answered, "Sleep."[37] (The magazine pronounced him to be "pragmatic, ruthless, focused, and lucky . . . the very model of the new breed of manager that has climbed out of the rubble of mergers and restructurings across corporate America.") In his last year as CEO, Maxwell was paid $1,877,000; Miles took $500,000 less. The Philip Morris chairman is a confirmed nonsmoker who is quite prepared to coexist with the smokers of Philip Morris. He says that he sees "nothing morally wrong" with the tobacco business. He compares the health risks of tobacco to those of cholesterol, a potential problem in almost any traditional Kraft product. It's up to the consumer to decide whether he wants to smoke or go heavy on the mayonnaise. Philip Morris extends the invitation as persuasively as it knows how. But no one is forcing you.[38]

V.

Philip Morris's chief competitor in the food business is Nestlé S.A., a $36-billion Swiss corporation that makes 98 percent of its sales outside its home country. Its world headquarters is located in the little town of Vevey on Lake Geneva, wedged below a panorama of Alpine peaks, surely the most picturesque company town on earth. The world's largest food company operates on five continents and is a truly multinational corporation in culture as well as reach. As the 1990s began, its chief executive officer was German and five out of ten of its general managers were also not Swiss. An American was in charge of selling pet food in Japan. An Indian was running the coffee operation in Australia. A Scotsman was handling yogurt sales in France. In Nestlé's Asia-Pacific territory the top marketing managers represented ten different nationalities.[39] So determined to adapt to local conditions is Nestlé that it even has a factory in the Ivory Coast to produce dehydrated yam flakes.[40]

With the acquisition in the 1980s of such familiar U.S. brands as Chase & Sanborn and Hills Bros. coffees, Oh! Henry, Chunky, and Raisinets candies, Carnation milk products, and Stouffer's foods (along with Stouffer's hotels and restaurants), and of established European products such as the Buitoni pasta line and Perugina chocolates, both sold widely in the United States, Nestlé entered the 1990s with the world's largest food operation. Nestlé's nonfood business is still relatively minor—a few California wineries, an ophthalmological laboratory in Texas, and Cosmair, one of the top five U.S. cosmetics companies—but in recent years it has launched an ambitious expansion program with its hostile takeover of Source Perrier, the famous water-bottler.

Nestlé traces its roots to two milk-products companies established right after the American Civil War, one in a small town on Lake Zug in the central German-speaking part of Switzerland, and the other in French-speaking Vevey 120 miles away. In 1866 it occurred to Charles A. Page, who was the American consul at Zurich, that Switzerland was an ideal place to manufacture canned condensed milk, a product that the American inventor Gail Borden had developed ten years earlier. At exactly the same time Henri Nestlé, a German-born inventor with a French name, hit upon a milk-product substitute for mother's milk and built his factory in Vevey. For almost forty years Nestlé and Page's operation, Anglo-Swiss Condensed Milk Company, fought one another for shares of the expanding world market for condensed milk and infant formula. In 1905, the year after Nestlé started making chocolate, they merged.

Henri Nestlé's original motivation in developing infant formula was to do something about the tragic infant-mortality rate in Switzerland, where one out of five babies died in the first year of life. (Borden had started with the same motivation. The idea of sterilizing milk by dehydration occurred to him on a voyage during which infants died from contaminated milk.) Ironically, in the 1970s Nestlé became the target of a worldwide boycott organized under the banner "Nestlé Kills Babies" because of the company's crude campaign to push its expensive infant formula in poor countries. The company used saleswomen dressed up as "milk nurses" in Third World countries who would give away free samples to nursing mothers. This had the intended effect of discouraging breast-feeding as well as the unintended but predictable effect of increasing infant diarrhea, since in many countries the packaged product was almost certain to be mixed with contaminated water.

A Nestlé lawsuit cooled the rhetoric of the global campaign to force the giant company to change these practices but not the activists' determination. After several years of a worldwide boycott of Nestlé products, the company agreed to most of the activists' demands. Although the company's compliance with the agreement has been far from perfect, the Nestlé boycott was probably the most successful transnational consumer effort to hold global corporations accountable to ethical and health standards. The humanitarian impulses on which Henri Nestlé started the company had been long forgotten, and the "Boycott Nestlé!" campaign failed to note the irony. In 1987 the company that had been started to save babies was caught selling adulterated apple juice for infants through its baby-food subsidiary, Beech-Nut. Nestlé was embarrassed and unloaded Beech-Nut two years later.

In the business world Nestlé has had a reputation over the years as an easygoing company, even cowlike. Over a century ago it bought a milk factory in the United States and tried to edge its way into the American market then dominated by Borden. But the original condensed milk company, despite the sweet, maternal image projected a generation ago by Elsie the Borden Cow (an advertising character as successful in its day as the Marlboro man), ran Nestlé out of the country by putting out price-slashed "fighting brands." In 1985, just as Philip Morris was gearing up for its European invasion, Nestlé paid $3 billion for Carnation, which included its Friskies pet-food line. But in the 1990s American dogs were eating more Purina and less Friskies; indeed, Nestlé's performance in the United States was unimpressive, revealing a lack of the organization and drive that characterized the U.S. food giants. The top executives at Vevey were accustomed to operating in the underdeveloped world, where they had little competition, and in the more genteel climate of Europe, where competing giants specialized and divided the market, using their market power against weaker and smaller family food businesses more than against each other. But the entry of one of the most aggressive American companies accelerated changes in the competitive climate of Europe.

Nestlé's global business is built on Nescafé much as Philip Morris's is built on Marlboro. Philip Morris is, of course, a coffee roaster too. Indeed, in 1990 Kraft General Foods had the largest single share of the American coffee market, about 35 percent. But coffee accounts for about 40 percent of the Swiss-based giant's global earnings. Thus the world's two largest food companies are sustained by two products each of which is purchased primarily for its pharmacological impact on the human body. It would not be inappropriate to list both Philip Morris and Nestlé as drug companies.

However, there is a huge difference between coffee and cigarettes when it comes to profits. Because of the well-publicized fall of world coffee prices and the huge increase in advertising costs in the fierce battle among the coffee roasters over market shares, profits come to no more than a penny a cup. Maxwell House tried to market a "gourmet coffee" of the sort that fancy delis offer at $6 a pound, but supermarket customers would have none of it. The roasters then came up with a well-worn but effective solution to falling profits; they reduced the size of the can from sixteen ounces to thirteen ounces and, where they could, they raised the price.[41] Meanwhile, Philip Morris, Nestlé, and Procter & Gamble were working hard to perfect new refrigerated "gourmet" coffees in the hope of extracting another forty or fifty cents for a thirteen-ounce pound.

Nestlé has worked more zealously, and certainly longer, than the other food giants to cultivate a truly global market. Nescafé, which was introduced in 1938, dominates the coffee market in low-income countries, but it is a prestige product many people cannot afford. Nestlé makes a point of understanding and catering to local tastes. Its managers, like missionaries in days gone by, stay in foreign countries for years, learning the language and food quirks. "That's where Nestlé wins hands down," Joel M. Glasser, a vice-president of Philip Morris's food operation in Japan, concedes. Nestlé, which is the most successful foreign food company in Japan, offers Japanese families packaged cereals that taste like seaweed, coconuts, and papaya and has made many converts in a country where people traditionally begin the day with fish and rice. In contrast, Kellogg, which has dominated the global cereal market for almost a century, has kept pushing Sugar Pops on Japanese kids with little success so far.[42]

Nestlé's strategy is to work patiently to build up markets, counting on the huge populations in underdeveloped countries and improvement in living standards to yield new customers in the coming century. In Indonesia, which currently accounts for no more than one-third of 1 percent of Nestlé's global sales, the company has a powdered-milk processing operation in eastern Java. It is hard to think of a less promising place to put one. Java is an island of scrawny cows subsisting on tropical grasses. But Nestlé teaches village farmers how to care for their cows and to transport their milk in cans one at a time to collection stations from which they are trucked a harrowing hour's journey to the processing plant on the coast. The powdered milk is sold mostly in stalls in open markets. Nestlé is willing to nurture such low-yield operations because it is counting on the world's fifth-most-populous nation to develop enough in the early years of the next century to provide 50 million new customers for Nestlé products. A few years ago, Nestlé's CEO, Helmut Maucher, was flying over Pakistan. Surprised to see so many electric lights in Karachi, Maucher quickly calculated that there must be 100 million people down there. "What are we doing in Pakistan?" he asked. Shortly thereafter a Nestlé factory went up in Lahore, one of more than 420 Nestlé plants in sixty countries across the globe. There were sixty-seven in the United States at last count.[43]

As the 1990s began, Philip Morris posed a growing global threat for the venerable Swiss-based food giant. The American-based company had doubled its presence in Europe with the purchase of Jacobs Suchard. As he girded for "the global battle to feed the world," the hyperbolic rendering in the business press of what is known in economics jargon as "global oligopolistic competition," Maucher called a press conference and predicted a "harsher, more competitive environment." In private asides he made it clear what he meant. "Philip Morris has teeth."[44]

VI.

The 1980s was a decade of large-scale consolidation, dismemberment, and disappearance of food companies. The era of hostile takeovers and leveraged buyouts coincided with an explosion in foreign investment in food manufacturing. The agricultural economist John M. Connor has calculated that "between 1977 and 1987 foreign investment in food manufacturing industries in the United States soared 790%."[45] About 90 percent of this buy-up of American food-processing facilities occurred through mergers.[46] In the food-and-drink industry in Europe between 1989 and 1991 there were 450 mergers. In the U.S. retail food industry there were 387 mergers between 1982 and 1988. European automobile makers tried to solve their mounting problems by acquiring food companies. The Agnelli family, the owners of Fiat, attempted to buy a controlling interest in Perrier, the world's largest distributor of bottled water and owner of the famous Chateau Margaux vineyards, but Nestlé, a major water bottler itself, snatched the company away. Volvo, the Swedish car company, merged with a large Swedish food company. Just as the U.S.-based food giants were making more and more of their sales outside the United States—Coca-Cola and CPC International sell more than 50 percent of their processed food from their foreign subsidiaries—so foreign food firms have moved into the American market and bought up famous U.S. brands.

In the merger mania of the 1980s Beatrice Foods, the purveyor of Orville Redenbacher's popcorn and Hunt's ketchup among many other products, vanished from view in a leveraged buyout by Kohlberg Kravis Roberts. (This was the same Wall Street firm that bought Philip Morris's chief cigarette competitor, RJR Nabisco.) Once the most ambitious conglomerate in the industry after having acquired more than 400 companies, Beatrice was systematically pulled apart by its new owners. Its last remains were sold off in the early 1990s. ConAgra, a major devourer of former Beatrice operations and originally a Nebraska flour-milling company, had a spectacular rise from $1 billion in sales in 1980 to almost $21 billion by the beginning of the 1990s as a result of picking up more than fifty businesses, including the two most famous meat-packing brands, Swift and Armour. It is hard to stop at the frozen-foods section for frozen shrimp, chicken, or enchiladas without putting some ConAgra product in your cart. But few outside of food-industry mavens and investors have ever heard of it.

Sara Lee became famous in the United States in the 1950s for its frozen cheesecake, but in the last ten years it has been operating in twenty-three foreign countries, specializing in panties, bras, shoe polish, and Fuller brushes as well as sweets and rolls. Sara Lee sells $3 billion worth of cakes, underwear, wine, and coffee in Europe, about a fourth of its worldwide sales. The company is one of the leading coffee roasters on the Continent, and its Kiwi shoe polish, which has 90 percent of the market in the United States, is sold in 130 countries. H. J. Heinz is run by an Irish entrepreneur, a former rugby star who owns six newspapers and two castles in his native land. By the end of the 1980s the world's number-one ketchup company was making 40 percent of its sales outside the United States and was developing joint

ventures in China, Zimbabwe, and Thailand. But even with its famous brand name and worldwide operations, its global sales are
about a fourth of Philip Morris's food sales. All together, the ten
largest food companies are responsible for one-third of all U.S. food
exports, but most of their foreign sales are made from their foreign
subsidiaries, which operate plants inside their many markets around
the world.

By tradition, the food industry in the United States has been less
concentrated than, say, the auto or steel industries. In the 1950s there
were more than 2,000 companies selling canned dog food in the
American market, and by one count 1,200 of them, despite the
merger wave, are still in business.[47] In Europe the food industry had
been made up of small firms, about 100,000 of them in the 1980s.
When the 1990s began, the top two dozen food companies in Europe
had only 15 percent of the Continental market. But the threat of
takeovers from outside Europe whetted European appetites for mergers within the Continent. Not only would larger companies yield
better economies of scale in reaching the new integrated European
market, but bigness was becoming a strategy for survival in the new
corporate culture. The choice was now "eat or be eaten," and for
more and more food companies the goal was to achieve such size as
to be indigestible.

In this atmosphere of intense, often brutal competition, Philip
Morris has one great advantage: cigarette profits. RJR Nabisco, the
number-two U.S. cigarette company, which owns such supermarket
staples as Oreo cookies and Ritz crackers, generates cigarette revenues as well, but the company spent $25 billion to become a private
company and, after selling off much of its snack-food business and its
Del Monte fresh- and canned-fruits business to reduce its debt, it was
still strapped for cash. "There's no such thing as 'petty' cash,"
Nabisco informed its employees in an internal company communication. "In today's environment, cash is king."[48]

Philip Morris is doubly fortunate in not only having an obliging
cash cow but a chief financial officer who knows how and when to
milk her. Hans Storr is a German-born accountant with a flair for
thinking and acting globally that is legendary in the world of international finance. All during the 1980s when the dollar was fluctuating wildly, Storr hedged by moving in and out of exotic currencies
and financial holdings such as 17.5-percent New Zealand bonds.[49]
As a child in Germany before World War II he came across bundles
of worthless Reichsmarks in the attic, all that remained of his father's

business that had been wiped out by inflation and then the Depression. "It left a tremendous impression on me as to what is value." In 1984 he anticipated that the U.S. trade deficit would undermine the dollar, and he moved $2 billion into foreign currencies. Betting against the dollar netted Philip Morris an extra $400 million in three years.[50] He went to Europe and Japan to raise almost three-quarters of the $5.6 billion needed to finance the purchase of General Foods. Philip Morris has had even better credit ratings in Switzerland and Germany than in the United States.

To execute the hostile takeover of Kraft, Philip Morris needed to borrow $9.6 billion. Secrecy and speed were critical to the success of the operation. If word leaked that Philip Morris was about to bid, Kraft stock would shoot up. Within twenty-four hours, thanks to his carefully cultivated relationships with sixty-five banks across the world, Storr had offers of more than $19 billion. Philip Morris's "money magician," as *Business Week* calls him, not only has a reputation for being showered with more money than he can use, but he is also known for getting money cheap. Philip Morris acquired General Foods within months of R. J. Reynolds's acquisition of Nabisco. To finance Philip Morris's acquisition, Storr secured an interest rate almost a full percentage point less.[51] He also oversees Philip Morris's own profitable multibillion-dollar bank that offers financing to cigarette and beer distributors. But this fanatical company loyalist, who insists upon being photographed with a lighted cigarette and has been known to urge nonsmokers who drop by his office to take up the habit, is under no illusions. "There's nothing scientific about it." He calls himself a shaman rather than a prophet. At a meeting in Nigeria for senior managers, he put on an African mask and waved a wooden snake to make the point. He knows that when he telephones for money, he is certain to get it because his request is backed by the full faith and credit of the Marlboro man.

VII.

Globalization has transformed the world food industry at every point. The global grain market has become more concentrated. Cargill, the nation's largest privately held corporation, and five other grain companies have in recent years controlled 96 percent of all American wheat exports and 95 percent of American corn exports. The same companies handled 90 percent of wheat and corn trade in the Common Market, 90 percent of Canada's barley exports, and 80 percent of Argentina's wheat exports. In 1921 there were thirty-six firms that handled almost all U.S. wheat exports.[52] A larger and larger share of the fruits and vegetables consumed across the planet have come under the control of a few global food conglomerates and retail chains.

In the early 1980s an average of thirty-eight large food-manufacturing companies a year disappeared because they were gobbled up by larger companies. As in previous merger waves in the U.S. food industry, foreign investors played key roles. The British firm Grand Metropolitan, to give one example, acquired Pillsbury, Green Giant, and Alpo.[53] In the same years, packagers and distributors stepped up their competition by shifting more and more of their production and processing of supermarket staples to poor countries with long growing seasons and an abundance of low-wage farm workers. They also began importing massive amounts of beef from ranches under their control in Latin America. The dependence of the United States on food imports virtually quadrupled from $6 billion in 1971 to $23 billion in 1992.[54] As in other industries, globalization and concentration fed on one another. Supermarkets became larger, and many smaller ones went out of business. This created a niche for "convenience stores" like the 7-Elevens, and these franchised mom-and-pop stores, which carry a few of the most popular brands offered by the food conglomerates, increased by more than 50 percent during the 1980s and extended their operations in many countries.

Lawyers, economists, and social critics have argued for years about the consequences of concentration. There is a good deal of evidence that large firms are less creative than small ones. The electronics and software industries, to give two examples, suggest that this is so. Although there are exceptions—Bell Labs, IBM in the 1960s, and pharmaceutical companies are a few examples—big companies tend to buy the fruits of creativity; the creators work in smaller, usually humbler surroundings. Larger firms tend to be more capital-intensive; small businesses create more jobs per investment dollar.[55] In recent decades the random collection of new assets by U.S. corporations has smacked more of empire-building than clever strategy, and some of the most avaricious corporate octopuses of the late 1960s and 1970s were themselves dismembered in the 1980s and 1990s.

The agricultural economist John Connor estimates that concentration in the United States has raised prices somewhere between 6 and 10 percent above what they would have been given less concentration.[56] Such analyses are controversial, however, since they depend on widely differing and disputed assumptions. But there is a good deal of anecdotal evidence to support the view that concentrated market power has a big impact on consumer pocketbooks.

A *Washington Post* survey, for example, tracked the cost breakdown of Kellogg's corn flakes as follows: The farmer receives ten cents and the grain elevators and millers four cents. Kellogg's processing, including labor, freight, and packaging, costs fifty-two cents. Kellogg then spends fifty-two cents on advertising and marketing to the retailers, and another fifty-five cents on warehousing, depreciation, taxes, overhead, and the like. The box is sold to Safeway for $1.73. It is then marked up to $2.25. The rival retail chain Giant was selling its own brand, identical in taste and crunch as far as most consumers are able to tell, for $1.69. But Kellogg sells 40 percent of all the cereals sold in the United States and has dominated the industry for almost ninety years thanks to the power of advertising and consumer habit.[57]

By tradition, the U.S. political system has been much more hostile to cartels and mergers than either the nations of continental Europe or Japan. At the end of World War II, the American occupiers of the defeated Axis powers broke up the great business combines of Germany and the *zaibatsu* of Japan on the ground that they were incompatible with democracy. American business history is the story of four great waves of mergers, each followed by efforts to control or reverse this phenomenon through legislation such as the Sherman Act of 1890, the Clayton Act of 1914, and the Cellar-Kefauver Act of 1950. However, the merger wave of the Reagan era took place in an atmosphere of deregulation that shows no sign of being reversed. Emboldened by permissive tax laws, an administration in Washington that embraced laissez-faire with the zeal of a Savonarola, and a culture of greed encouraged by the White House, corporations ingested almost twice the share of total industrial assets in the country in takeovers in 1985 as in 1968, a previous peak year for mergers.

By digesting General Foods and Kraft, Philip Morris now controls about 10 percent of the entire array of food products on U.S. supermarket shelves. Because of global competition from giant corporations in Europe and Japan, a de facto consensus has developed in the United States in recent years that the antitrust laws are a relic of a bygone age. Global markets invite global corporate giants, and global competition demands it. American advertising and marketing strategies are transforming the business culture of Europe, and to a lesser extent that of Japan too, but the fight over the global food market is also changing long-established ideas in the United States about government-business relationships, concentration, and corporate size.

A MATTER OF TASTE

I.

As anyone who has sat through a business lunch, prayer breakfast, or family get-together knows, food has a larger, more complex role in the human drama than to supply calories. To be sure, every baby instinctively apprehends from its very first moments on earth that regular intake of food is necessary to life. The passion to consume that propels the global industrial economy is rooted, some believe, in primal food anxieties; like Scarlett O'Hara, we are determined never to be hungry again.

Indeed, the need for nourishment is so basic in so many ways that food serves a variety of social and cultural functions in human society everywhere. From the first bite of the apple in the Garden of Eden to the breaking of bread at the Last Supper, eating is a mystical or sacramental act in both the Old and New Testaments. Muslims are commanded to share food with the stranger at the door. The Bantu make contracts with one another by exchanging food, establishing thereby what they call a "clanship of porridge."[1]

Weddings, funerals, bar mitzvahs, confirmations, graduations, homecomings, anniversaries, and birthday celebrations all over the world come with good things to eat, even when the hosts are poor. In the United States, food is often used as glue to hold fractionating families together; invitations to a meal are occasions for delivering messages of family love and obligation: "Home for Thanksgiving."

"Sunday dinner at Grandma's." "If you miss Seder again this year, it will break your mother's heart."

For thousands of years the tastes, aromas, sizzling sounds, and sensuous look of beautiful meals in a dimly lit room have awakened sexual hunger and served as appetizers to a night of love. The private dining room or elegant restaurant is also the preferred ambience for striking commercial deals. A profitable niche in the restaurant industry has been carved by opulent establishments to serve the expense-account trade. A surcharge can be levied because customers can drop the names of celebrities at the next table long after they have forgotten what they ate.

Food also has served over the ages as a weapon to insult and anger fellow human beings whose food taboos are at odds with one's own. Thus cultural differences among Hindus, Muslims, and Jews about pigs and cows have provoked considerable bloodletting over the centuries. Bread, corn, potatoes, rice, horseradish, and many other commonplace items on supermarket shelves are religious symbols for one or another people, and some—the bit of bread known as the communion wafer is an example—are believed to partake of the divine when properly consecrated. "The ancient Egyptians," Diane Ackerman writes, "thought onions symbolized the many-layered universe, and swore oaths on an onion as we might on a Bible."[2]

In theory, the fact that we must all eat is a common bond uniting humanity. But since human beings eat almost anything that can be digested, other people's tastes in food can strike those who do not share them as nauseating, even as proof of belonging to some lower order. Well-to-do Aztecs ate roasted hairless dogs. Rats, known as "household deer," were relished by the Chinese of the Chou dynasty. The Masai find drinking cow's blood refreshing. Italians eat deep-fried songbirds.[3] Grasshoppers, snakes, and bats are delicacies in various corners of the globe. The insect and rodent eaters remind us of the diversity of human taste and culinary tradition. Food evokes strong feelings among people belonging to widely differing cultures with idiosyncratic tastes. Nevertheless, global food companies are betting substantial sums on the coming McDonaldization of the world.

II.

A great many things have happened over the last two generations to revolutionize and standardize diet. The fast-food industry is globalizing tastes. In Korea, young girls are spending the whole afternoon nibbling french fries, sipping Coke, and listening to American rock music at McDonald's or Wendy's or Burger King or Kentucky Fried Chicken just as kids their age are doing in Peoria or Johannesburg. (McDonald's alone had 760 restaurants in Japan and fifty-one in tiny Hong Kong at last count.)[4] In his classic treatise on eating, the eighteenth-century French gastronome Anthelme Brillat-Savarin wrote that food was the key to understanding human beings. "Tell me what you eat, and I will tell you what you are."[5] If, indeed, we are what we eat, a lot of us, despite vast cultural differences, language barriers, and great distances, are becoming more alike.

Changes in global food technology are accelerating this process. Thanks to advances in refrigeration, packaging, and transportation, New Yorkers can fill their market baskets with Mexican strawberries or New Zealand kiwis in the dead of winter. Grapes are now routinely eaten in February in Chicago that just ten days before were growing on a vine in Chile. London supermarkets feature snow peas from Kenya, garlic from Egypt, baby corn from Zambia, starfruit from Malaysia, and papayas from Brazil. Between 1970 and 1989, Americans increased their per-capita consumption of vegetables by 42 percent and of fruit by 22 percent.[6] Partly, this had to do with growing concern about the effects of diet on health. But this major dietary change could not have happened had the global food companies not been able to take advantage of Southern Hemisphere growing seasons (which coincide with North American winters) and of sunny climates in other once-inaccessible places. Today New York, London, Paris, Geneva, and Tokyo grocers, except in poor neighborhoods, are seldom without fresh grapes, asparagus, strawberries, and peaches.

Not surprisingly, grapes hauled 6,000 miles or more are expensive; at each stage of their journey from the vineyard to the delivery platform at the supermarket, they depend upon a complex chain of refrigerated storage areas inside freighters, trains, and trucks. Tropical fruits such as atemoya, breadfruit, starfruit, and lychee can command especially high prices because these products of poor countries are exotic novelties in affluent neighborhoods across the Temperate Zone. Some of the poorest countries in the world, therefore, are increasingly basing their economies on the export of fresh fruits and vegetables to upscale markets in the industrialized countries. Fresh fruit is Chile's major export after copper, and it is available all over the world. But of the four largest Chilean fruit shippers, only one is still owned by Chileans.[7]

The principal social consequence of "counterseasonal" food production has been to develop a mass middle-class clientele all year round for a rich variety of fresh fruits and vegetables, many of which were unknown in the Temperate Zone a generation ago, except occasionally in gift baskets. The influx of refugees from war and the importation of migrant workers into the United States and Europe over the past generation have further helped to enrich and expand diets. Thanks largely to the prolonged wars of Central America and the mounting economic distress in Mexico in the 1980s, sales of salsa and other piquant Latin sauces overtook ketchup in American supermarkets in the early 1990s.[8] The influx of Caribbean peoples into the United States created a market niche for plantain, but like many other foods introduced by immigrants, this once-exotic fruit has entered the American diet.

In the 1960s lettuce in the United States meant essentially one thing, the tightly rolled iceberg lettuce wrapped in plastic, a product unknown in Europe. Today baby lettuce, Boston lettuce, radicchio, arugula, and many more compete for space in produce bins with the hardy iceberg, a product that for years sophisticated French, German, and Italian visitors to America have scorned but that is now catching on in Europe. The mass clientele for fresh garden products has grown as more people in the Temperate Zone encounter strange fruits and exotic vegetables in their travels.[9] A major result is that millions of acres once used to feed poor families in poor countries are now used to grow kiwis, asparagus, strawberries, and baby carrots for upper-middle-class consumers who can now eat what was once the fare of kings—365 days a year.

III.

The global food industry spends billions trying to persuade its customers what they should eat. But it also keeps careful track of their shifting tastes by monitoring what they buy. In 1991 food companies placed more than 6,000 new things to eat onto supermarket shelves, pushing unknown numbers of older products off. By 1992 many of these new wrinkles in familiar products, exotic taste thrills, and innovative packages had themselves disappeared. Seldom does a food packager start a fashion in the way a Paris dress designer can influence next season's mass-market styles. Food fads are mostly unpredictable expressions of mysterious cultural shifts that food companies cannot orchestrate but can accommodate or co-opt with great skill. The food companies are resourceful in giving (or appearing to give) modern-day eaters what they say they are looking for.

Take "freshness," "naturalness," and "health." One of the lasting effects of the global countercultural movements of the 1960s that originated in the United States and Europe was a deep distrust of everything artificial, unnatural, or adulterated. Sixties people, some of whom formed the core of the environmental movement that took off a decade later, were unhappy about many aspects of bourgeois life, but they reserved a special loathing for things plastic and processed. In the 1970s the polling industry devoted much attention to the "sea change" in values that had gripped consumer culture in affluent countries, and their research showed that for the upscale market the promise of freshness had great appeal. Since successful packaged food products must not only taste good but if at all possible make the consumer feel virtuous, the major food distributors began to stress the "healthy, natural" look. By the 1980s medical research had established links between cholesterol and certain saturated fats, on the one hand, and heart disease, diabetes, cardiovascular disease, cancer, and early death on the other. By then, more and more affluent Americans, having spent $80 or more for running shoes, were now committed to panting along the road twenty miles a week or more in pursuit of a long, healthy life, and they resisted undoing their good work with eggs, butter, and filet mignon. Fresh vegetables and low-fat meats and pastas became the staples in yuppie households.

The food companies' response was immediate. First, they advertised "no cholesterol" on fatty products that have none, such as peanut butter and potato chips. This provided time to develop a line of "lite" products low in fat. Kraft, a company built on butterfat, had by 1990 introduced seven "no-fat" product lines with dozens more on the way, including salad dressings, ice cream, cheese, and yogurt. Philip Morris's Entenmann's baked goods line now featured the fatless cake marketed under the ad slogan "You Can Eat Cake!"[10]

However, selling health rather than taste involved some risks for the food companies since many of their products are still loaded with fat, oils, sugar, and other nutritionally weak and artery-clogging ingredients that have made them taste good to generations of Americans. Philip Morris and its competitors worry about making too much of the health issue in their marketing because of their fear of what the president of Kraft USA calls "cannibalization." It is not a felicitous word in the mouth of a food-company executive, but Kraft General Foods worries about devouring its own customers when it touts a new line of "healthy foods," fearing that by implication it is branding its established product lines as unhealthy. There is a further risk of turning shoppers off altogether by calling their attention to hazards of which they were happily unaware. As one independent food marketer told the *Wall Street Journal,* "We can't sell food safety because that says everything else isn't safe."[11] Healthy food has become just another market niche. Foods with genuine old-fashioned buttery taste can still be sold in great quantities to the millions who are still largely untouched by the changes in food consciousness, the millions more who are confused by it all, and even to the health-conscious as a well-earned respite from what steak and butter die-hards scorn as live-forever diets.

In the 1980s a rash of food scares swept over the United States as consumers became concerned about chemicals, additives, and pesticide residues in foods offered at the supermarket. Two grapes from Chile mysteriously injected with cyanide prompted the U.S. government to ban all Chilean grapes for a time and destroy $100 million worth of Chilean fruit. The *60 Minutes* television show, the movie star Meryl Streep, and the Natural Resources Defense Council marshaled their efforts in the fight against Alar. This antiripening agent that keeps apples hard long enough to survive long-distance travel was denounced for its alleged carcinogenic effects. The industry was forced to stop using the agent, and wholesale apple prices plunged more than 50 percent.[12] Unsettling stories in the media about contaminated food products on supermarket shelves—botulism in honey, aflatoxin in corn, chemically tainted milk, salmonella in poultry, and toxic shellfish—helped turn organic food, once a cottage industry serving health faddists, into a $1-billion-a-year business.

Food distributors made important changes in response to popular concerns about health. It was not a small matter for McDonald's, which feeds 22 million people on the planet every day, to stop using beef tallow to fry the mountains of potatoes served in its more than 10,000 restaurants around the world. (The two largest are now in Moscow and Beijing.) It took a certain courage to develop the McLean Deluxe, a burger of reduced fat content thanks to a bit of a seaweed-derived chemical and a flavor enhancer to trick the palate.[13] But the McLean Deluxe was a modest seller; only a small proportion of the great global mass of McDonald patrons could be coaxed into eating a virtuous burger that didn't taste very good. Still, the company kept trying to establish a reputation for nutritional concern by introducing carrot sticks. McDonald's employed forty-five Ph.D.s in food science to get the carrots just right. Kentucky Fried Chicken, the pioneer of the global fast-food chains with more than 3,000 locations outside the United States, is also lightening up with a lower-fat line.

But critics believe that Philip Morris and its competitors have hyped their health claims and misled consumers with labels containing a mass of confusing numbers and terms. In the early 1990s the Food and Drug Administration became concerned about "no cholesterol" and other misleading claims that lull consumers into eating heavy fat and high-calorie diets, and Congress was persuaded to pass the National Labeling Education Act requiring much more nutritional information on food packages. In 1991 only about half the food products on the supermarket shelf offered the buyer even a clue as to what was in them.[14] Kraft voluntarily dropped some of its "low fat" claims in anticipation of the regulations. But for the company, demystification of its product lines will be an expensive process. Designing and printing new labels on some 15,000 Kraft products costs tens of millions of dollars. The other big food companies are in the same situation, and many complained that the new labels would be as confusing as the old ones. But as Tom Pirko, a Los Angeles food and beverage consultant, points out, the food giants' concern is different: "It's very hard to describe a product fairly and accurately and still make it saleable."[15]

Moreover, the companies are well aware, as Mary Ann Schmidt, group director for Burke Marketing Research, puts it, that while many consumers may say they are worried about health, salt, and cholesterol, "when it comes down to it, factors such as easy preparation, taste, package size, and appeal to children dominate their buying behavior."[16] The primary purpose of food advertising is to evoke mouth-watering fantasies and fond memories. Sizzles, crunches, and creamy smoothness turn customers on in ways that promises of potassium, thiamine, or riboflavin seldom do. The only truly "natural" foods are nuts and berries one plucks oneself and pops into the mouth on a summer afternoon's walk in the woods or the organically grown spinach from the patch in the backyard. Once food is shipped great distances, what is "fresh" and "natural" is all a matter of definition. Apples are untimely ripped from the tree so that they will be firm, hard, and rosy when they arrive at the supermarket. They are bred for hardiness, appearance, and longevity, and there is a tradeoff in loss of flavor. For those consumers fortunate enough to have experienced old-fashioned apples just picked from the tree, the perfectly shaped, shiny red, unbruised fruit that beckons the supermarket customer is something of a misleading label in itself. It does not taste the way apples should. A tomato prematurely plucked from the vine and gas-ripened for long-distance travel is not a gourmet experience either. Despite the rise of a large industry devoted to the development of chemical additives to enhance flavor and fragrance in all sorts of products, global, even continental, journeys take their toll on taste.

IV.

Between 1970 and 1990, according to Judy Putnam, a U.S. Department of Agriculture researcher who has been tracking her compatriots' eating habits for over twenty-five years, Americans consumed more food per capita than ever before. If this trend continues, she laughs, "we're going to be blimps by the year 2000."[17] But what Americans are eating has changed radically: not just more fruits and vegetables but more cereal, pasta, rice, and fajitas and less steak and bacon. Since 1984 crop-based foods now dominate the American diet; a decade earlier American cuisine was still heavily dependent on animal products—beef, pork, chicken, and eggs. But despite the much-publicized "health craze" encouraged by a burgeoning fitness industry all during the 1970s and 1980s—health clubs, Exercycles, running shoes, and the like—and the barrage of solemn warnings in the same period from physicians and diet specialists, overall consumption of fat went up.

Shoppers simply reached for vegetable oils, some in bottles marked as such, more of it lurking in the cornucopia of junk food encountered at supermarkets and vending machines. Americans now get 43 percent of their total calories from fat. (In 1900 it was 32 percent. The American Heart Association recommends that calories from fat be kept under 30 percent.) Sugar consumption is also way up. Americans consumed fifteen pounds more sugar per person in 1990 than they did in 1970, thanks largely to the explosion in bakery products, soft drinks, and sweet cereals at the supermarket.[18] The $12-billion-a-year popcorn, chips, nuts, cookies, cakes, crackers, and processed-cheese snack industry, as one would predict, prefers to describe junk food as "savories" and "snacks." According to the Snack Food Association, the average American consumes more than eighteen pounds of snacks a year, the equivalent of 294 small bags of potato chips. The U.S. snack-food market grew 88 percent between 1979 and 1988, and the rest of the developed world followed suit. Snacking in Europe grew at almost the same rate. In Japan about $3.5 billion worth of chips, cookies, candy bars, and popcorn were sold in 1988, and the market is growing. Of course, the global food companies must accommodate local tastes. According to Peter Tettweiler, a flavor specialist for a German company, the British like their potato chips to taste of salt and vinegar or cheese and onion. The Dutch and French favor a seafood taste. Scandinavians have a passion for dill. Japanese are tiring of "piquant snacks" and showing a preference for milder seasoning on their chips, pretzels, and minipizzas.[19]

The food industry spends millions trying to reach the next generation as early as possible in the hope of inculcating food habits that will last a lifetime. In recent years the food companies have aimed ads at very young children, using cartoon characters. Pepsico's Frito-Lay launched a Saturday-morning cartoon featuring Chester Cheetah, a cool cat who becomes ecstatic when munching Chee·tos. Kraft developed a TV kiddie cartoon featuring the star of its macaroni-and-cheese ads, a cheese-colored dinosaur known as Cheesasaurus Rex. Targeting children with cartoons featuring characters transplanted from ad copy produced a certain backlash from consumer groups, and Pepsico promised that Chester Cheetah would swear off Cheetos for the few minutes he was entertaining the children Saturday mornings.

The food industry has no interest in making a sharp distinction between eating for nourishment and eating for fun. Since eating has always been an aesthetic and social experience, not merely a bodily function, people everywhere are drawn to foods that not only taste good but also have the right feel, look, sound, and, above all, smell. Although some harassed office workers grab chips and a candy bar to get through the day because they cannot spare time for lunch, snacking is mostly pure entertainment. It can be a social experience but need not be. Solitary snackers constitute a major market. However, *Snackertainer*, a publication of the Snack Food Association and the National Potato Board, offers tips for home-video parties where the snack is part of the show: Shove *Knute Rockne* into the VCR and serve "First-Down Franks" smothered in crushed potato chips or, if you prefer the 1960s counterculture movie *Easy Rider*, complete the experience with a "Psychedelic Dip" of raw vegetable hunks, crushed potato chips, sour cream, and grated cheese. If your taste runs to a Japanese film like *Tampopo*, why not serve your favorite tempura coated with crushed potato chips and deep-fried to golden brown?

Food engineers constantly try to enhance the entertainment value of food by assaulting as many senses as possible.[20] David Bodanis describes how eating potato chips is a source of aural as well as oral pleasure. Chips, being 80-percent air by volume, are what he calls "total destruction foods." The high-frequency shattering is an essential part of the experience. Potato chips must not be "slurpy" or "crunchy." They are designed to be too large to fit into the mouth so that snackers will keep their mouths open, which is essential for creating the right acoustic ambience for the enjoyment of crispness.[21]

As food companies vie with one another for shelf space, the role of chemical synthetics has become increasingly critical. A can of chicken soup fortified with a powerful flavor enhancer needs only traces of chicken; the more effective the flavor additive, the cheaper the product becomes to produce and the higher the profit margin. Flavor companies most consumers have never heard of have developed everything from artificial baked potato, anchovy, and lemon flavors to synthetic Tex-Mex, Cajun, and other ethnic tastes. Extract of wood smoke helps sell hams.

Food technologists are also innovative in designing new shapes for fun foods as a result of what one food technologist terms "the triumphant progress of extruded snacks." A cereal mass is subjected to high pressure and temperature and expelled through a nozzle when the pressure is suddenly released. As the concoction is extruded, the unappealing mess is molded into stars, curls, lattices, and squiggles. The intrinsic flavors of extruded snacks, a food scientist writing in *Food Technology* concedes, "are usually not only undesirable but could actually be classified as unpalatable. Thus it is no wonder that all the stops on the flavor-imparting keyboard have been pulled by flavor chemists and food technologists . . . ." When extruded snacks reach the international market, they might well taste of steak au poivre, Chinese cabbage, or piña colada.[22]

Philip Morris and its competitors have also tried to meet the growing environmental concerns of their customers. But the claims of the food companies are bewildering, and the hard information they offer is scarce. A number of claims that packaging has beneficial environmental impacts have turned out to be either untrue or unknowable.

Dennis Hayes, the founder of Earth Day, says that "you could easily make buying a roll of toilet paper subject to a master's thesis."[23] "Green" products come in "ungreen" packages and "ungreen" products come in recyclable packages. Coffee shoppers do not have the information to decide whether Melitta's "natural brown" filter for "coffee lovers who are also concerned about the environment" is a more responsible purchase than the company's white filter, which is "oxygen cleansed" and "environmentally friendly." Bleached-paper products contain dioxin, a potent carcinogen in animals, but this important fact is not mentioned on either the brown- or white-filter packages. Some ecologically correct claims have been patently misleading. Mobil was forced to remove its "biodegradable" claim for its Hefty trash bags, most of which are destined for landfills where nothing degrades. Thirty-year-old hot dogs retrieved from landfills have been found to be virtually in mint condition.

Combining convenience, taste, tempting looks and smells with assurances of good nutrition and concern for the planet is a daunting task. But supermarkets in affluent neighborhoods in the United States and elsewhere in the developed world are making major efforts to do this. These temples of abundance with aisle after aisle of dazzling choices, all well lighted, well heated, and well cooled, are open twenty-four hours a day, offering a pleasant, safe environment in which all sorts of food fantasies can be indulged. Supermarkets are increasingly in the business of selling time in the guise of selling food. Not only do they promise to save hours in the kitchen with microwavable cuisine and to shrink the dinner hour to twenty minutes with all sorts of "ready to serve" and "quick eating" products, but they have developed technology to compress the amount of time spent shopping. Scanning devices will soon be widely installed in shopping carts and the total price will be instantly available by the time the shopper is ready to leave the store; lines at checkout counters will become as obsolete as the long pole with which the corner grocer used to pull cereal boxes down from the top shelf.

Yet in Harlem, the South Side of Chicago, and other depressed areas throughout the United States, choices are limited. Supermarket chains have abandoned many of these neighborhoods to local grocery stores and bodegas. The produce is old and wilted, and the prices are significantly higher than in better-off neighborhoods. Choices run heavily to aging brands of canned meat and Fritos, Cheetos, Snickers, white Wonder Bread, and Little Debbies cupcakes, all of which are products that have become somewhat harder to sell to better-educated, health-conscious suburbanites or affluent city dwellers.

African Americans are especially susceptible to cardiovascular problems for which low-sodium diets are routinely prescribed. Campbell's has a line of low-sodium soups, but to find a can of Special Request anywhere in Harlem is a project, and if a diligent shopper chances upon one, according to a *Wall Street Journal* survey, it is likely to cost fourteen cents more than the same soup with salt. "We like to fish where the fish are," Brent Walker, a Campbell's marketing manager, explains. Sodium and cholesterol are not high on the list of things people who are eking out an existence count as pressing problems. As one poor young black woman explained to a reporter after looking at a television ad for Special K showing a svelte suburbanite by the family swimming pool, "The nutrition obsession is for rich people with real nice houses and lawns. . . ."[24]

Food companies reject the notion that they have any responsibility for bad dietary habits in poor neighborhoods. "We aren't a miniature Health and Human Services Department," says Michael Mudd, a Kraft General Foods spokesman. "A company doesn't have a social obligation to instruct consumers on the best way to handle their health."[25] Kraft General Foods gives money for nutrition education, but its major contribution to public education about what to eat is in its ads.

V.

According to the U.S. Department of Agriculture, of every dollar Americans spend on food seventy-five cents goes to the processors, marketers, packagers, and distributors; twenty-five cents is left for farmers.[26] The system is highly efficient in prolonging the useful life of food products, proliferating product varieties, and relieving consumers of the burden of cooking. But it is wildly inefficient in energy use. Chickens can be raised anywhere, but our increasingly centralized food system subjects the average chicken product to truck or train rides of a thousand miles or more. Refrigeration is not only energy-depleting, but it is a major source of ozone-depleting gases. The United States devotes 4 percent of its total energy use to the packaging of food, about as much as comes through the Alaska pipeline. The metal, glass, paper, cardboard, and plastic containers that Americans pile into their shopping carts end up as 36 million tons of solid waste every year, "about 20 percent of the nation's tonnage of municipal solid waste, according to data from the U.S. Environmental Protection Agency." This amounts to 290 pounds per person.[27]

According to Fergus M. Clydesdale, professor of food science at the University of Massachusetts, this is the food future for affluent consumers in the developed world:

> Biosensors built into packaging materials to give consumers a digital readout of the degree of freshness, the presence of pesticides, and the relative risk of the food compared to others. Stable colors and flavors developed within the plant or animal by genetic engineering, and putrid, fishy, or rancid flavors eliminated through an understanding of the molecular basis of such events. Computer models in the home to provide consumers with a diet customized to fit their genetic individuality, which will have been predetermined by simple diagnostic tests.[28]

In the 130 poor countries in which 75 percent of the world's population lives most shoppers encounter a very different reality. Open markets are colorful, noisy, and alive with conversation. The market is a place to gossip and bargain. Indeed, this is one of its great attractions. But instead of the array of enticing packages now standard in American, Japanese, and European supermarkets, the shopper is likely to encounter burlap bags of grains and legumes. Fruits and vegetables are available in season only, and increasingly the best is shipped abroad in one form or another. Flies buzz about the food, and much of what is unsold at the end of the day begins to spoil and is eaten by the vendors' families or thrown away.

According to Ricardo Bressani of the Institute of Nutrition of Central America and Panama, despite the great advances in food technology over the past fifty years the nutritional status of the 75 to 80 percent of the world population living in poor countries "is only slightly better than 50 years ago."[29] Protein deficiencies are common. High-quality products using local resources such as Protina have been developed for Central America, but such protein-rich products, though they are far more nutritious and a much better value, have trouble competing with well-advertised nonnutritious global brands that are high in what nutritionists call "empty calories." The development and marketing of protein-rich food for poor, malnourished people excites neither local entrepreneurs nor the global companies.

A United Nations–sponsored study in the Philippines found that Coke and Pepsi "have virtually wiped out from the market all traces of indigenous beverages like kalamansi (local lime) juice, buko (coconut water), and gulaman (seaweed gelatin with sugared water or coconut milk.)"[30] (These traditional drinks are now found mostly in tourist restaurants or are consumed at home on special occasions.) Thanks to McDonald's triumph in Japan and the success of the U.S. beef industry in penetrating the Japanese market, that nation for the first time in its more than 2,000-year history now consumes more beef than rice. One consequence of the Westernization of the Japanese diet (accompanied by the rise in smoking) is a significant increase in cancer and heart disease.[31]

In Mexico City, small children beg for pesos to buy Frito-Lay's Sabritas, Doritos, Ruffles, and Rancheritos because they have become entranced by the TV ads. Frito-Lay runs as many as four consecutive ads on local Mexican television. A 1981 survey of the National Consumer Institute in Mexico found that "gradeschool children spend more time watching television than in school and have more knowledge of TV ads than of Mexican history."[32] In the state of Michoacán, according to a study conducted in one Indian village, as the villagers spent more time watching television, "their strong social structure began to erode. . . . The children began to eat more junk food and constantly complained of hunger." Elsewhere in Mexico workers are turning away from the traditional lunch of tortillas and beans, which are no longer cheap, and filling up on cupcakes and soda pop, which cost more. Not only do these dietary shifts adversely affect nutrition but they cause very poor people to pay more money for less food. As Jorge Calderón, a Mexican agricultural researcher, sums up the impact of global food products: "Sabritas [Pepsico] buys potatoes in Mexico, cuts them up, and puts them in a bag. Then they sell the potato chips for a hundred times what they paid the farmer for the potatoes."[33]

Diets almost everywhere are becoming more Americanized as global television ads, packaged-food products, and fast-food chains make their way into traditional societies around the world. Even in remote mountain regions, international foods are incorporated into the local cuisine. The anthropologist Mary Weismantel reports that in the Andean parish of Zumbagua Quaker oatmeal (pronounced *kwacker*) is strained and fermented to make *aswa*, the mild alcoholic drink these Ecuadorean people consume at weddings.[34] In some cultures, India, for example, traditional diets remain largely undisturbed; by and large they are supplemented rather than supplanted by global food products.

Across the world traditional diets vary widely in their nutritional value, but they serve a common social function: local food prepared according to time-honored custom serves as a cultural bond, a link with a shared past, and a source of pride. Clearly, not every loss of traditional dietary customs need evoke nostalgia. There are a number of societies in which girls are not allowed to eat until the boys have had their fill, and across the world females are more likely than males to suffer the effects of malnutrition. But, as Dr. Abdulrahman O. Musaiger, a nutrition expert in the Ministry of Health in Bahrain, notes, the penetration of global food products into the underdeveloped world has produced radical changes in diets in many countries, and some of the major health consequences are not favorable: "The consumption of fat and sugar has risen steadily, while the intake of fiber and complex carbohydrates has declined. . . . These changes, together with the adoption of sedentary lifestyles by many people, account for much of the increase in chronic disease. Hypertension, heart disease, obesity, dental caries and some cancers are already major problems in many countries of Africa, Asia, and Latin America."[35]

VI.

The microwave, the liberator of the overworked, has revolutionized eating in industrialized countries. Partaking of food has become less of a stylized ritual, less hierarchic, less formal, possibly more hygienic. In three of every four households in the United States, food is regularly "zapped." The microwave revolution is somewhat less advanced in Europe and Japan, but small, hygienic-looking, snazzily wrapped plastic containers of frozen bits of meat, vegetables, and pasta are making their way in ever greater quantities all across the world, including poor countries.

Increasingly, Americans feel rushed. Numerous polls indicate that, despite the profusion of time-saving devices, people in developed countries feel that they never have enough time. In most American families both partners now work, and at almost every social level— from busboys to blue-collar mechanics to $1-million-a-year Wall Street lawyers—Americans who work are working harder than ever.

After long grueling hours at the office sandwiched between two te-
dious, often harrowing commutes on jammed highways, fewer and
fewer of us are in the mood to make dinner. The situation is becoming much the same in a number of European countries and in Japan.

For more than seventy years, food companies have looked upon
kitchen drudgery as a market opportunity. Before then, it was expected that "the woman of the house" would spend much of the day
in the kitchen. But as far back as the early 1920s, the home economist Christine Frederick could write, "The American housewife is no
longer a cook—she is a can-opener."[36] As more and more women
went to work and American life became more harried, the idea of
hiring Campbell or Borden or General Foods or Birdseye to cut up
your vegetables and to precook dinner became increasingly attractive. In the 1930s, however, guilt about shirking kitchen responsibilities was still sufficiently strong that General Mills decided to leave
the egg out of its Betty Crocker prepared cake flour in order to give
housewives something fulfilling to do.

These are not the problems of the 1990s. As marriages and sexual
mores changed, many males without steady partners willing to cook
for them soon discovered that their very survival depended on pre-
cooked food. For the companies, the mass processing of food was
profitable. "Convenience," a code word for "saving time," became
the industry's fastest-growing product. However, as Margaret Visser,
who is a classics professor and a food historian, notes, the microwave
has achieved more of a cultural throwback than a revolution. She
writes that before the eighteenth century "people drew up benches to
the hearth and sat down in relays to eat."[37]

Then for 300 years the dining-room table became a pivotal social
institution, the centerpiece of the daily dramas of family life. (In
some households the kitchen table served the same function.) Family
dinner in America, immortalized in Norman Rockwell's *Saturday
Evening Post* covers of the 1940s, was the apotheosis of togetherness.
Attendance at dinner was mandatory, and the communal meal served
as a socializing ritual where children learned patience and manners.
The requirement that all family members living at home gather together at the same time daily in a special room, sit up straight, abide
by a complex set of table manners, and touch the food only with
approved instruments, as Visser notes, "imposed a degree of physical
constraint that is quite rare in the history of human mealtimes."[38]

But the microwave has changed all that by reintroducing serial
eating. The kitchen, Visser says, has become "a sort of filling sta-

tion," and the microwave is the perfect self-service pump. Family members arrive when they want; a food container is taken from the shelf or the refrigerator. In seven minutes or less its contents are ready to be eaten without even a transfer to a plastic plate. Other family members return from work, school, or play on their own schedules, and they cruise by the kitchen when they like. Communal meals, the traditional bonding rituals of American family life, are becoming rarer and rarer. Even in Malaysia, the traditional dinner hour in many homes is falling victim to television and, increasingly, the microwave. Whether the passing of the Norman Rockwell family dinner (in all its various ethnic guises) is counted as liberation or as a giant step toward social disintegration depends upon one's memories of family dinners. For many of today's toddlers, the question will never arise. Even when the family is gathered at the table, the chances are that the television will be on.

VII.

From the end of World War II to the early 1970s, the world food system operated in accordance with the rules of the world trading order established at Bretton Woods. These rules were made for a world of sovereign nation-states. In 1945 the United States reigned supreme, the producer of two-fifths of all the marketable products on earth. But within ten years the war-damaged industrial states of Europe and Japan recovered, and dozens of new nations carved from collapsing colonial empires were recognized. For most nations, food self-sufficiency was an important goal, although for many it could not be achieved. Nations regulated, protected, and subsidized their agricultural sectors. In turn, farmers everywhere subsidized industrial development based on mass consumption by working long hours to produce food that governments kept relatively cheap. In developed nations, most notably the United States, the share of the family income spent on food kept going down.

These were the golden years of Pax Americana, and the United States was the dominant force in the international system. Despite growing competitive strains in the 1960s, world food markets remained relatively stable until the Bretton Woods system itself began to collapse in the early 1970s. The reasons are complex. But the driving force behind this historic shift was the rise of transnational commercial and financial relations and the consequent undermining of national sovereignty. The world food system organized under what the economist Susan Strange calls a "state-centered paradigm" began to come apart as nations resorted to dumping, protectionism, and export wars.[39]

For the last decade or so, classic free-trade notions of the nineteenth century have been revived with all the passion of a proselytizing religion, but they have been used as the intellectual underpinnings of a radically new twenty-first-century global food order. Under the powerful influence of the United States, which increasingly exerts that influence through key international institutions such as the World Bank, the International Monetary Fund, and the General Agreement on Tariffs and Trade, one powerful idea has come to dominate the thinking of governments virtually everywhere. The road to economic prosperity and political stability is foreign trade. Let capital, goods, and people willing to perform marketable services move freely. When IBM executives listened to Paris students chanting "Down with borders!" in 1968, they heard welcome echoes of their own revolutionary slogan "World Peace Through World Trade." In the intervening years, countries that sought to base their social systems on the strict control of trade have been torn apart, notably the former communist countries of Europe.

In Japan, a country with few natural resources and scarce land for growing food, no one needs to be convinced that the country must earn foreign exchange by exporting massive amounts of cars, televisions, and other industrial products. The United States is more than twice as dependent on foreign trade than it was twenty years ago, but compared with countries like Japan, Switzerland, or Germany, the export sector appears small. In 1990 exports of goods accounted for only 7.1 percent of GNP. (In Japan exports account for 10 percent of their gross domestic product, in West Germany 35 percent, and in Singapore 100 percent.) Though small in comparison to the economy as a whole, the export sector has a disproportionate share of the well-paid jobs in the United States.

Poor countries have always been in desperate need of foreign exchange in order to buy the machines that they hope will bring industrial development and prosperity. Increasingly, however, they need foreign exchange to feed their populations. The message of the World Bank to poor countries is "Export or die!" The export market, however, is notoriously volatile, and poor countries that depend on exporting one or another agricultural or mineral product can suddenly face ruin when world market prices drop. There was a coffee boom in the mid-1970s, then prices plummeted more than 60 percent.

Advances in food technology also threaten to undermine development strategies for poor countries based on agricultural exports. Consumer-health advocates in the United States have run full-page ads denouncing "tropical oils" as health hazards, and various products now carry labels assuring the customer that they are free of all such potentially cancer-causing substances. The market for artificial sweeteners and fats developed in American, European, and Japanese laboratories flourished while the market sagged for palm oils and tropical sugars on which many poor, hot countries depend. World Bank officials, most of whom are fervent believers in free trade as the answer to poverty in underdeveloped countries, concede these problems. Global consumers soon will have a choice, according to a Bank report, between Kenya AA coffee, which is justly famous, and biocoffee beans made in laboratories in the United States. Laboratory-produced vanilla has threatened the livelihood of 70,000 vanilla-bean farmers in Madagascar. Bioengineered celery, which promises to be crunchy, stringless, and long-lasting, has been test-marketed under the brand name Vegisnax. Waiting in the wings are freeze-resistant chrysanthemums, carnations, tomatoes, and strawberries into which DNA has been cloned. The DNA is configured to reproduce an "antifreeze" protein much like the one that protects fish in Arctic waters.[40] Thanks to new biotechnologies and advances in gene-mapping, agroindustry has conceived and is about to give birth to a "supercow" that will give 25 percent more milk than an average cow, and all of it will be high in protein and low in fat.

Farmers in poor countries without access to patented seeds and cows will have problems competing in the global market. But the prevailing development orthodoxy holds that if poor countries are to feed their people they have no alternative but to plant high-margin export crops, such as flowers and upscale vegetables and fruits, in order to earn the cash to buy imported food. But this can be risky. Shifts in dietary habits can play havoc with export crops, and these are even harder to predict than breakthroughs in food chemistry or fluctuations on the London or Chicago commodity markets. Thus in the 1980s advisers from aid agencies urged the Philippines, Taiwan, Thailand, and Indonesia to become major exporters of prawns. It seemed to be an ideal export crop because world prices were high and the profit margin substantial. Moreover, prawns harvested in the region enjoy a rich and ready market. The Japanese have a passion for prawns and consume 80 percent of the prawn output of Asia. But a freakish disaster occurred. Emperor Hirohito lay dying. Who could know that he would take almost half a year to die, and that millions of Japanese would honor him by giving up prawns and other luxuries all during the imperial deathwatch? By the time it became clear what was happening, entire communities that had been drawn into the prawn economy had been reduced to penury.

In the 1970s world grain trade expanded by 60 percent, and the United States had four-fifths of this market. Secretary of State Henry Kissinger believed that America's "food weapon" could be the answer to the "oil weapon" in the hands of the Arab oil cartel. The United States became the breadbasket for much of the world, pushing subsidized grain into Asian, African, and Latin American countries. Because of liberal government subsidies, U.S. marketers could undersell local producers. They could offer rice at $4 a hundredweight when other countries like Thailand, which depends upon rice to earn 15 percent of its foreign exchange, could not afford to charge less than the world-market price, which was $8.

As a result of the food-export blitz, which all the grain-exporting countries joined, some of the poorest countries in the world, including Somalia, Mozambique, Bangladesh, Sierra Leone, Togo, and Angola, became dependent for the first time on imported wheat, corn, and rice. In a number of these countries, foreign-grown food now represented over a quarter of all imports.[41] Both local economies and local diets were transformed.

Some of these same nations and many others began exporting ever larger quantities of coffee, flowers, and other high-value luxury products for the international market. The predictable result was that commodity prices fell. Some regions in a few countries prospered by moving into cash crops, but the overall global effect was a loss of self-sufficiency in the ability to feed large elements of the local population. Per-capita food production reached new and impressive levels, but food distribution in many poor countries worsened. Millions who went to bed hungry lived within sight of rich agricultural lands producing bumper crops for export. Some of the results were glimpsed when the world's television cameras were briefly aimed at Somalia. The confrontation between U.S. marines and marauding Somali warlords who stole bags of food destined for starving children was the focus of the nightly news. The political and economic decisions that had left Somalis and poor people in other ravaged countries without enough land or credit to grow their own food were not.

The tranformation of the global food system has also had consequences for the Western Hemisphere. From 1940 to 1960 Mexico was self-sufficient in food. The country was able to increase its food production at a rate double that of its very high population growth rate. Mexican governments pursued a nationalistic economic policy, and foreign investment was strictly controlled. Maintaining self-sufficiency in food was a foundation of government policy. By the early 1980s, however, Mexico's situation had changed dramatically. Industrialization was stalled. The oil boom was over. Inflation was rampant. Market forces played a cruel trick on the Mexicans. Mexican farmers could get higher prices for animal feed for the livestock industry than for corn or beans, and so acres once devoted to these staples of most Mexicans went into sorghum and other higher-priced grains to feed the livestock that would eventually end up on the grills of affluent beef-eaters, mostly abroad.

Since the mid-1980s Mexico has liberalized its trade and investment laws as the country shifted its economic strategy in favor of increased integration into the global economy. Government investment in support of domestic agriculture declined by 70 percent. By 1990, 40 percent of the beans consumed by Mexicans were imported as was 25 percent of the corn and 30 percent of the sugar. Imported beans are obviously more expensive than beans grown by the side of the house, and per-capita consumption fell 28 percent. Fresh-milk consumption fell by 21 percent, and meat by over 30 percent. Not surprisingly, large numbers of Mexicans, whose buying power in the 1980s declined almost 60 percent, could not afford what was once the daily bread of Mexican life. According to a report of the National Chamber of Hospitals, almost a half of all children in rural Mexico suffer from malnutrition.[42] Our nearest neighbor to the south is becoming one of the seriously malnourished nations in Latin America.

The North American Free Trade Agreement envisions a vast area comprising the United States, Canada, and Mexico with a combined gross national product of $6 trillion and a market of 362 million consumers. The last two Mexican governments have become enthusiasts in large part because trade liberalization solves two immediate problems. It creates a favorable climate for foreign investment, something Mexico now seeks under almost any terms. Second, it creates jobs. The agro-export sector in the state of Sinaloa alone employs 180,000 people.[43]

But the export model appears to doom increasing numbers of people in the country to poverty and hunger. According to a study carried out by the Center of Economic Studies of the Colegio de Mexico, 30 percent of Mexico's agricultural workers will be pushed off the land once the North American Free Trade Agreement goes into effect; small corn and grain farmers cannot compete with heavily subsidized, machine-produced U.S. grain exports.[44] Official policies that drive them off the land make a certain amount of economic sense: Many (but by no means all) small farmers are "inefficient" producers. That may be so, but there is no evidence that alternative sources of livelihood for these former farmers can be created in a country with a real unemployment and underemployment rate approaching 50 percent.

According to the free-trade ideology, the freer the exchange of goods and services can be, the faster the world economy grows and the better the prospects for everyone. But recent history is not reassuring on this score. In the 1980s investors and business owners in Mexico increased their share of the national income from 55 percent to 71 percent while the impact of government austerity measures insisted upon by the International Monetary Fund and foreign creditors was felt by the poor majority, as access to health facilities, schools, drinking water, jobs, and food declined precipitously.

About a quarter of all the fruits and vegetables imported into the United States, including canned and frozen vegetables, come from Mexico. In recent years the state of California has been the place where the great food companies have grown and packaged about half of all the fruits and vegetables Americans eat. But a major shift in production to Mexico has begun. Pepsico's food division bought Grupo Gamesa, Mexico's largest snack-food company. Pillsbury, now owned by the British food giant Grand Metropolitan, has moved its Green Giant frozen broccoli and cauliflower operations from Watsonville, California, where it was paying employees as much as $9 an hour, to the town of Irapuato, about a 150 miles north of Mexico City, where it pays local workers as little as $4.28 a day.[45] A number of large U.S. food companies have set up processing plants in the Mexican-border area to take advantage of the same favorable treatment U.S. law has long accorded the automobile and electronics *maquiladoras*. Many agricultural products processed in the border zone enter the United States duty-free. Thus J. R. Simplot shut down two frozen-vegetable packing plants in Salinas, California, laying off 530 workers, and moved much of the operation to Morelia. "We just couldn't compete in California," a company spokesman explained. Almost half the board members of the Western Growers Association lease land in Mexico and farm there. "The peso is so low that there's almost a built-in profit," one California grower put it.[46]

Cheap labor and favorable exchange rates are not the only attractions. Land is cheap, and environmental laws are easily circumvented. (Sewage from Nogales, Mexico, flows down hillsides into Nogales, Arizona, which now has hepatitis rates twenty times the national average.) The Mexican government has little bargaining power to enforce environmental regulation on the foreign companies on which it has come to depend, but the effects are felt not just by Mexicans but also in the United States.[47] Companies able to buy up or lease the scarce arable land are siphoning off scarce water for irrigation. Mexico is a big country, but much of it has excellent soil for growing cactuses and not much else. Two-thirds of the arable land already shows the effects of serious erosion, and only 25 percent of the arable land can be irrigated.[48]

Smaller U.S. producers fear that they will be driven out of the market by companies operating in Mexico free of the financial obligations to protect the environment demanded of companies operating in the United States. Florida and California have been hurt badly because the giant food-processing companies have moved so many of their operations across the border.

Globalization of the food system is taxing the capabilities of national governments to maintain their own standards for the food their people eat. As more and more foreign fruit and vegetables enter the United States, American consumers face potential new health hazards. A number of pesticides banned in the United States are widely used in Mexico by U.S.-owned companies and contract farmers producing for export to the United States. All food from abroad is subjected to inspection by the Food and Drug Administration. But only about 1 percent of U.S. food imports are actually inspected. At the inspection station in the Arizona border town of Nogales 800 trucks arrive daily from Mexico. There are two inspectors on hand who take five to ten samples a day on the 2 billion pounds of Mexican produce that comes through each year.[49]

Unfortunately, some of the greatest health hazards resulting from global food movements elude border inspection altogether. Mexican sewage seeps into thousands of wells on the U.S. border where packing houses draw water for ice to cool Mexican fruits and vegetables on their way north. Health specialists are suspicious that dirty ice used to pack Mexican lettuce in Nogales may have caused an outbreak of hepatitis in Louisville, Kentucky.[50]

As large American growers abandon major operations in the nation's two largest agricultural states, the implications for the American people are much the same as in the shift of automobile and electronics production to foreign shores. But there has been no more citizen debate on this issue than there was when the U.S. government began rewarding U.S.-based companies for locating their manufacturing plants anywhere but in the United States.

PART THREE

THE GLOBAL WORKPLACE

CHAPTER ONE

MASS PRODUCTION IN POSTMODERN TIMES

IN THE SECOND HALF OF THE TWENTIETH CENTURY THE GLObal productive system was transformed. The appearance of the factory floor, the sex, race, and nationality of the work force, changes in labor-management relations, and the ever increasing numbers of foreign flags flying in front of corporate headquarters around the world heralded a new era in the history of work. Mammoth assembly plants of the sort that thrilled Henry Ford and Joseph Stalin are still in evidence, many of them now in out-of-the-way places, a few bigger than ever, but less and less of the world's work is done there. One reason is that the production of goods is dispersed to smaller facilities around the world, to subcontractors, suppliers, and casual workers, many of whom cut, sew, and punch data at home. But the main reason is that more and more of the world's work is not in manufacturing.

Vast numbers of workers around the world are engaged in producing, marketing, and distributing paper and electronic data of symbolic value. All sorts of marketable information such as insurance policies, bond offerings, investment tips, legal opinions, and shopping guides are pouring forth into the world marketplace. Word-processed promises, advice, and opinions now figure among the world's most profitable products. Even more workers are engaged in feeding people all over the world, curing, comforting, and entertaining them, or picking up after them in their houses, hotels, and other public places. Armies of service-providers of all sorts are employed by large global networks—ad agencies, law firms, investment houses, airlines, restaurants, hotels, hospitals, clinics, media complexes, and waste-removal companies. According to the *Random House Dictionary*, "any place producing a uniform product, without concern for individuality" is a factory. By this definition more and more of us are factory workers.

The Ford Motor Company ushered in the era of mass production. Indeed, modern capitalism is sometimes described as "Fordism," a word that connotes the marriage of mass production based on well-paid jobs on the assembly line and mass consumption of affordable, standardized products. In 1903, when Henry Ford started making cars, each assembler was responsible for putting the whole car together himself, and it took 514 minutes, almost nine hours, to turn one out. For five years the young mechanic experimented with ways to speed up the assembly process. In 1908 he hit upon a new way to make an automobile.

The Model T was a black, square vehicle so simple to drive and so easy to repair that Ford called it the "universal car." Ford had already discovered that if workers used the same gauging system throughout the whole manufacturing cycle, the parts would not have to be custom-crafted car by car but would fit any car of a given model. With the Model T, Ford achieved what he had been looking for. Parts were now uniform and interchangeable.[1] Each assembler now performed just one task, and as a result the task cycle for the average Ford assembler fell from 514 to 2.3 minutes.[2] With the introduction of the moving assembly line at Ford's new Highland Park plant in 1913, the cycle time was cut another forty-four seconds.

More fascinated by factories than cars, Henry Ford built his company on these innovations in mass production. By drastically reducing the time needed to make an automobile, Ford found that he could cut the cost to the consumer by more than one-half, from $780 in 1910 to $360 in 1913.[3] In the second decade of the century well over half the cars sold in the world were Model Ts. By 1923 Ford was producing 2.1 million perfectly identical cars and still had 50 percent of the world market. "Every time I reduce the price of the car by one dollar, I get one thousand new buyers," Henry Ford exulted.[4]

In January 1914 Ford announced that he would thenceforth pay his workers a minimum of $5 a day, more than twice the existing minimum. "I can find methods of manufacturing that will make high wages," the inventor announced to incredulous reporters. "If you cut wages, you just cut the number of your customers." (The *Wall Street Journal* denounced Ford's high-wage scheme as an "economic crime.")[5] For almost seventy years a social system flourished in the United States, thanks in large part to the labor movement, that was based on high-volume assembly-line production employing well-paid workers who could afford to drive Fords to work. Ford's vision eventually led to big factories, big cars, and big unions. Henry Ford didn't like unions or bankers or a good many other aspects of contemporary life in the United States, but he was glad to take the credit for the transformation of small-town America. When John Dahlinger, reputed to be his illegitimate son, once reminded the aging entrepreneur that this was the modern age, Henry Ford stopped him short: "Young man, I invented the modern age."

By 1914, the year World War I broke out, Henry Ford had become the premier automaker in Britain. His highly publicized efforts to keep American boys out of the trenches aroused such anger that he had to take in British minority shareholders to cool nationalist feelings. By the mid-1920s Fords or Ford parts were coming off the line in nineteen foreign countries.[6] The company had assembly operations in Argentina, Brazil, India, South Africa, Mexico, Malaya, Australia, and Japan. Its Yokohama plant established in 1925 soon took the largest share of the Japanese market. "Fordo" became a generic term for car in Japanese. Militarists and nationalists kept squeezing the company and calling for Ford's expulsion, but Henry Ford's operation in Japan was still managing to produce 12,400 cars a year when it was shut down two years before Pearl Harbor.[7]

Unlike GM, a public corporation run by mostly anonymous bureaucrats, the Ford Motor Company has always been a family business. Though the company's stock is publicly traded, the Ford family retains 40 percent of the voting shares. According to former CEO Harold A. Poling, two great-grandsons of the founder, Edsel B. Ford II and William C. Ford, Jr., "aspire to run the company at some time."[8] Irritation with the "Ford boys" for demanding titles to match their voting power rather than their experience or responsibilities helped push Poling's predecessor as chairman into early retirement.

Tension between owners and managers is an old story at Ford. For almost eighty years two quirky owners, each in his own way an unforgettable character, ran the company. As David Halberstam puts it in his examination of the auto industry, *The Reckoning*, the creator of the Ford Motor Company became its destroyer.[9] The inventor of mass production could not see its flaws. After years of driving black, look-alike vehicles, customers were becoming wistful about the bygone age of elegant craftsmanship when each carriage and motorcar had a custom look. As America prospered, the car became a primary locus of recreation, a badge of affluence, a power fantasy on wheels, a gleaming sex symbol, and customers resisted buying thrifty boxlike vehicles year after year. Alfred P. Sloan, whose management ideas made General Motors work for nearly ninety years, had the vision to introduce variety into mass production and to tailor lines and models to different markets. He developed the organizational and marketing techniques that made General Motors possible, and by adapting the Fordist strategy to the changing requirements of the market, he prolonged its life—even as he very nearly ran Henry Ford out of business.

By the late 1920s Henry Ford had encountered another problem. His assembly-line workers were becoming restive. The men who had been drawn to Ford's Highland Park plant in the early years of the century—no women allowed—came from virtually every country in the world and, according to a 1915 survey, spoke fifty languages. Most of them planned to save up enough money to return to the Old Country. But as their take-home pay rose and the job became too good to give up, dreams of returning home faded. Work on the fast-moving assembly line, immortalized by Charlie Chaplin in *Modern Times*, was not a restful or uplifting experience. Spending one's day putting two nuts on two bolts every 1.19 minutes became intolerable for many workers once they realized that they might be doing this for the rest of their working lives. From the sit-down strikes of the 1930s to the rising incidence of absenteeism and sloppy work of the 1970s, the human cog in the Fordist machine became an ever increasing problem for the company.

Year by year Henry Ford grew more cantankerous and tyrannical. He flatly refused to change his models or colors to keep up with the times or to finance the purchase of his cars, all of which the upstart General Motors was doing with great success. The man who was briefly hailed as a messiah by labor in 1914 a few years later hired an ex-sailor and barroom brawler by the name of Harry Bennett to bust the union. "Can you shoot?" Ford demanded when they met at lunch, explaining that his workers were tough. Bennett took the cue and became expert in roughing up troublemakers, a term that was liberally applied to the whole work force. He steadily increased his power in the company as Henry grew old and ever more isolated.

Meanwhile, General Motors raced ahead to become the world's number-one auto manufacturer.

In World War II Ford, already thoroughly demoralized, became the nation's third-largest military contractor in the war against Hitler and Japan. Without this flow of cash from the U.S. Treasury the Ford family empire might well have collapsed.[10] In 1945 the family finally wrested control of the company from the old man. His grandson, Henry Ford II, was 28 years old and serving in the Navy. President Roosevelt ordered his early release to save what was once the greatest car company in the world.

In his way Henry II was as autocratic as his grandfather. He inherited the most international of the U.S. auto companies, but his outlook was not exactly cosmopolitan. When one of his executives put Michelin tires on a Mustang, he was angry. "I don't like frog tires," he warned. The same went for "goddam foreign steel in my cars."[11] He seldom failed to remind people who disagreed with him of the name on the company door. Unlike his grandfather in that he was neither a populist, a pacifist, nor a famous anti-Semite, the young Ford was a rather staid young man when he took over the company. But by the 1960s he was a gossip-column celebrity thanks to his lavish jet-setting lifestyle and indiscreet liaisons. His divorce and arrest for drunk driving became front-page news. The second Henry's views on the auto industry were widely quoted, but they were not always helpful to the company, which now increasingly bored him. His response to the suggestion that the age of gas-guzzlers was over was to observe that "minicars earn miniprofits," a truth that the public-relations department wished had been left unspoken.[12]

When he took over in 1945, Ford was losing $10 million a month. He fired Harry Bennett and hundreds of others, invested $1 billion in new plant and automated machinery, liberalized old Henry's Neanderthal labor practices, and decentralized management along GM lines. He brought in a team of ex–systems analysts from the Air Force known as the "Whiz Kids" that included Charles B. "Tex" Thornton, later the founder of Litton Industries, and two future Ford presidents, Robert S. McNamara and Arjay Miller. By 1954 Ford had surpassed Chrysler. When the reign of Henry II ended, Ford had become a major automaker in Europe, had more than tripled its global work force, and had increased its annual vehicle production from 900,000 to 6.5 million. The original Henry Ford hated banks, but under his grandson the Ford Motor Company operated one of the biggest. By the beginning of the 1990s Ford's various banking subsidiaries had a loan portfolio of $115 billion, exceeded in the United States only by Citicorp.[13]

Yet in 1980, the year he resigned as chairman, Ford had the worst year in its history up to that time, losing $1.5 billion. Ten years earlier foreign imports had already grabbed off 10 percent of the U.S. car market, and the figure was growing each year. It turned out that more Americans were looking for cheap, fuel-efficient, parkable automobiles than Henry II had thought.[14] Only in 1976, three years after the oil panic following the Mideast war, did the Ford Motor Company begin to develop a small car. The Panther was designed with the Ford balance sheet in mind by executives in the finance department who knew what the boss wanted. To avoid expensive retooling, these accounting experts prescribed stripping down Ford's medium-size model and keeping its rear-wheel drive although the front-wheel drive was a major selling point for the increasingly successful foreign imports. The products that came off the line reflected the reigning confusion in the executive suite. Ford is not a car; it's an acronym, the current joke went: "Fix or Repair Daily."

The renewed energy crisis caused by the 1979 Iranian revolution and the resulting world "stagflation" badly hurt the entire industry. Ford, however, had its own special problems. While the Edsel had been a famous and expensive flop of the 1950s, the Pinto fiasco of the late 1970s was more serious. The car was a menace since the fuel tank sometimes went up in flames in the event of a rear-end collision, and Ford was paying millions in lawsuit settlements and legal fees. Moreover, Ford automatic transmissions had an unfortunate habit of slipping into reverse when drivers thought they were in park. This defect, according to the National Traffic Highway Safety Administration, caused 3,700 accidents resulting in sixty deaths and 1,100 injuries. The findings were publicized in a national magazine and did nothing for Ford's morale, car sales, or its stock.[15]

The company's problems were compounded by the influx of foreign imports, which more than doubled in the 1970s. Between 1980 and 1983 Ford lost almost $3.5 billion. Philip Caldwell, a plodding man—"plain vanilla," a rival for the top spot described him—had taken over as chairman. In the first profitable year after several years of devastating losses, he paid himself $7.3 million in annual salary and stock options.[16] The Ford Motor Company, once the worldwide symbol of American ingenuity and enterprise, was now regularly roasted in the press as the symbol of all that was wrong with American industry.

II.

It fell to the Japanese to modify the mass-production process, and their reward was to take over a third of the U.S. car market. In this they had considerable American help of all sorts. By reducing much of Japanese prewar industry to rubble, American bombs forced the Japanese to conceive a new production system. There was no money to buy factory technology from abroad. It had to be invented, and it was. Americans, notably the quality-control expert W. Edwards Deming, were influential contributors to this process.

Japanese carmakers, trying to rebuild their plants, made a virtue out of necessity. In the prewar years the Toyota Motor Company, founded in 1937 by a wealthy family that had been in the textile business, specialized in military trucks. Since its prewar factories lay in ruins and hardly anyone was in a position to buy a car in 1945, Toyota and its competitors were forced to develop a new production system. The Japanese combined innovations in engineering with innovations in social organization that fit the new technology and Japanese culture.

The International Motor Vehicle Program at MIT conducted a five-year study of the system Toyota developed, which it calls "lean production."[17] The first element in the process was to develop ways to stamp auto parts in very small batches. Toyota needed a production system that did not create large inventories. In 1950 it was making only 2,685 automobiles a year; Ford was producing 7,000 a day in just one plant. Taiichi Ochno, the engineering chief at Toyota, had by the late 1950s succeeded in reducing the time needed to change dies used for stamping and forming metal parts from a day to three minutes. Dies are metal mold halves held in huge stamping presses. Sheet metal is inserted between the mold halves, which are then brought together to form the distinctive shapes of fenders, hoods, and the nearly 300 other metal stampings that go into an automobile. Changing dies often and quickly meant that defects showed up quickly and much waste was eliminated. Instead of employing specialists to change the dies as in Detroit, he trained the production workers to do it themselves, thus both saving labor costs and making the workers' jobs more interesting.[18]

Douglas MacArthur, the conservative American general in charge of the Japanese occupation, had introduced into Japan a series of labor laws prepared by his liberal advisers that were far more stringent—and for Japanese companies far more expensive—than anything that had been enacted in the United States during the New Deal. Strengthening unions was part of the American program of democratization and reeducation to destroy militarism in Japan. The right to lay off workers was limited, and powerful unions exacted many concessions, including profit sharing. (In the United States, by contrast, the Taft-Hartley law, enacted in 1946, severely cut back labor's bargaining power.)

MacArthur also instituted draconian austerity policies designed to squeeze inflation out of the postwar Japanese economy. There was tremendous pressure on corporations to cut costs. Kiichiro Toyoda, the president of Toyota, attempted this by firing a quarter of his labor force. The workers occupied the factory. But from the settlement of this strike the postwar Japanese labor compact was born. A quarter of the workers were indeed dismissed, but the rest received the promise of lifetime employment. As the summary of the MIT study, *The Machine That Changed the World*, puts it:

> In short, they became members of the Toyota community with a full set of rights, including the guarantee of lifetime employment and access to Toyota facilities (housing, recreation, and so forth), that went far beyond what most unions had been able to negotiate for mass-production employees in the West. . . . Thus in every plant workers became as much a fixed cost as the machinery, but, unlike machines, workers gained in skill over their working life.

When Taiichi Ochno, the chief engineer at Toyota, visited Ford's Rouge plant in Detroit in 1950 he was astonished by both the expanse of the plant, which could never be duplicated in the squeezed cities of Japan, and by the waste. Even in the 1980s auto plants using traditional mass-production methods had to dedicate 20 percent of plant area and 25 percent of man-hours to fixing mistakes.[19] Ochno discovered that assembly workers had a much lower status than the specialists who were employed to discover and correct their mistakes. On his return to Japan he organized workers into teams, gradually gave assembly workers additional responsibilities such as tool repair and quality checking. The emphasis was on collaborative team effort. In U.S. plants only the line manager could pull the cord that brought everything to a halt so that the "rework" specialists could undo the damage done days earlier. In Toyota plants, Ochno decided, any worker should be able to stop the line. This emphasis on preventing errors and solving problems early in the production process resulted in a dramatic increase in productivity and quality.

The most famous aspect of post-mass-production manufacturing is the "just in time" supply chain, known as *kanban* in Japan and JIT in the United States. The idea was to calibrate the flow of supplies so that large inventories became unnecessary. The parts would arrive at the time they were needed in the production process. This would eliminate the need for storage space and the costs of idle time on the production line as a result of supplier delays. The production of parts would be dictated by the immediate requirements of the next stage in the production process. Each container of parts was returned to the supplier as soon as the parts were used up, and this was the signal to send more.

Lean production also seeks to reduce production costs by introducing a flexibility that enables producers to adjust to changes in consumer tastes. Toyota is half as big as GM but offers as many models. The average Japanese model is kept in production for only four years while U.S. and European companies keep them almost ten years; production runs are half the size. This greater facility in adapting models to changing customer tastes is backed up by a sophisticated marketing system.

In the American system, dealers have served historically as "shock absorbers" for the carmakers. In slow periods the manufacturers would reduce their factory inventory by forcing dealers to take more cars on their lots than they could sell. In contrast, Toyota and other Japanese companies made much greater efforts to adjust the production process to the market and to develop the market by aggressive monitoring of the shifting attitudes of customers and assiduous cultivation of the best prospects. In Japan, Toyota sales representatives made house calls to drum up business. In the United States, Toyota, Honda, and the other Japanese manufacturers devoted substantial resources to building up a large data base on customer tastes and preferences. Old customers were treated as members of the "Toyota family."[20]

The Ford Motor Company became the pioneer U.S. automaker to revamp its production line using Japanese models and experience. Lean production was no more dependent on Japanese culture, Ford executives came to believe, than old-fashioned mass production depended on growing up in Detroit. To be sure, Japanese practices had to be modified. The manager of Ford's Wixom plant, which is the largest manufacturing facility in North America, told us he had observed Japanese workers running from one work station to another, something American workers will not do. But Ford has adapted many Japanese techniques to its North American plants, and these are almost as productive as the average Japanese plant. One Ford factory in Mexico, according to the MIT study, had the best assembly-plant quality of the entire global sample, better than the best of the Japanese auto plants.[21]

In 1985 Donald E. Petersen became chairman of the Ford Motor Company, the first engineer to head it since the founder. It was a difficult period for the U.S. auto industry, but Ford surged ahead of its American competitors and for several years it was the most profitable American automaker. Understanding the extent and chronic nature of the global overcapacity of the industry more quickly than its competitors, Ford cut payrolls, closed factories, and figured out how to make attractive and reliable cars more cheaply.

Ford had already carried out a major retooling of its production facilities all over the world, investing $28 billion to automate production and to eliminate excess capacity. The company's global work force was cut from 506,500 to 390,000. Most of the cuts were in the United States. Over a nine-year period, the number of robots in the North American plants rose from 236 to 1,300, and more than 80,000 hourly workers and 16,000 salaried white-collar workers were discharged.[22] The number of hourly workers fell by 47 percent and productivity increased by 57 percent; labor costs per car were now $800 less than at GM.[23]

Computer-driven machines to weld, stamp out parts, and schedule, control, and monitor production were introduced into Ford plants in Europe as well as in North America. Ford also adopted "just in time" production, enabling the company to reduce its inventories from three weeks to one week; in just one engine plant this innovation resulted in a $30-million saving. In Spain, a complete production line for Escorts was installed in a space previously used to store parts.

III.

The question was whether Ford had the time to catch up with its Japanese teachers. Much depended upon whether the company could once again become a globally integrated business enterprise. Ford's president Philip Benton points out that the company began as a global company, exporting the same cars everywhere. Soon thereafter, however, "we became a multinational company with separate operations overseas." In 1904, the year after the company was organized, Ford set up assembly plants in Canada and Ireland and supplied them with identical parts to make identical cars. Interchangeable, look-alike Fords were sold all over the world. But in the 1920s Ford Europe and Ford North America began to evolve in ways that were different from one another. Each subsidiary "had its own product development capability," Benton explained. "We were producing different cars for different parts of the world." In the Depression the differences became more pronounced. Governments began to insist that foreign companies produce cars with more local parts if they wanted access to the local market. That meant adapting the cars to the local labor force and to local suppliers. "Now we are moving into phase three," Benton continued, "where we are moving from multinationalism to globalism once again. . . . With product-development costs increasing geometrically, we must coordinate product development."

Ford had been slow to integrate its non-U.S. operations. Not until the early 1960s did Ford bring its Canadian and U.S. manufacturing operations together by exchanging parts and rearranging assembly. The push behind it was to qualify for favorable tariff treatment. Then in 1967 the company integrated its plant at Cologne, Germany, with its factory in Halewood, England, to produce the Capri. For Ford it was a fortuitous decision. Britain was on the brink of a wave of strikes and labor conflict. (In 1970 alone Ford experienced 155 strikes in Britain.) Integration made it possible to shift production from the British to the German plant since a single model—except for the location of the steering wheel—was now produced for both the British and Continental markets.

In the 1970s Ford began to integrate its U.S. and European operations, which for years had been treated as completely different markets. America was a land of big cars and cheap gas. Europe, on the other hand, was a continent of narrow streets and fiercely taxed gas, and small cars were a necessity. However, minicars not only meant miniprofits but, conventional wisdom had it, Americans would not buy them. Profit margins are higher not only on big cars but on trucks and vans because "the companies which produce and participate in that field have chosen to keep the price up where everybody makes a very good margin," according to Benton. They didn't conspire, he hastily assured us. All the makers had the same interest in preventing another round of price wars as had happened when the Japanese entered the U.S. car market. There is also another reason why automakers like big vehicles that he did not mention. Pickups and minivans qualify as "trucks," with much less stringent gas-mileage regulations than apply to cars. Since they involve less expensive development costs, profit margins are much higher. About a third of all passenger vehicles in the United States are "trucks," as far as the environmental laws are concerned.

All during the 1970s Ford had tried to bring its two regionally integrated operations of North America and Europe together with its far-flung manufacturing operations in Brazil, Argentina, Australia, South Africa, and Mexico to produce a "world car." The goal was to manufacture a vehicle that would sell well in the U.S. market, break into the Southern European market, and eventually penetrate the Latin American and Asia-Pacific markets. The Fiesta was conceived by a new Product Planning and Research team made up of 700 engineers, designers, and support staff. Ford's operation in Dunton, England, took responsibility for the engine. A group at Merkenich, Germany, was assigned the job of developing the drive train, brakes, and some of the styling. A group in Detroit concentrated on the interior. The axles would be made in Bordeaux. Overall assembly was assigned to the Ford plant in Almusafes, Spain, which offered cheap labor, one of the world's fastest-growing automobile markets, and an ideal location for shipping Fiestas to southern France and Italy. Plans called for assembling the car in Germany for the North European market and producing the same vehicle at a later stage in Brazil.

The first world car did not live up to its name. In Brazil inflation, rising oil prices, and the government's protectionist response made it impossible to build Fiestas there. The Escort, an enlarged Fiesta, was the second attempt at a world car. It was the first Ford car to be designed totally by computers; design and development groups in the United States, England, and Germany were linked to the Ford Engineering Computer Center in Dearborn. The Escort had wheel nuts and glass from the United States, a French alternator, a cylinder head and defroster from Italy, an air filter and mirrors from Spain, speedometer gears from Switzerland, radiator and heater hoses from Austria, seat pads from Belgium, rear-wheel spindle and clutch from West Germany, hose clamps from Sweden, and exhaust flanges from Norway.[24] "We had two separate product-development activities," Jack Eby, head of Ford's strategic planning, explained. "They were supposed to get together and agree to a set of parameters for the vehicles. [It was] impossible." The much-ballyhooed global vehicle still fell short of Ford's goal, a car assembled on one continent that could be sold with only trivial modifications on all the others.

Petersen now made a third attempt at global integration. Top operating executives with engineering and marketing experience in Europe, where Ford had been relatively more successful in recent years, were brought to world headquarters in Dearborn. At the same time overseas plants were given global responsibilities. Ford's Bordeaux plant became the source for all automatic transmissions wherever the cars were assembled. The German operation became Ford's global center for all advanced research and development.[25] But because of corporate confusion and rivalries, the Escort still ended up as two different cars, one for the United States and the other for Europe. The only part they shared was "a water-pump seal the size of a thumbnail."[26]

In 1993 Ford pinned its hopes and $6 billion on still another effort to produce a world car when it unveiled the Mondeo in the European market. Ford Europe, once the pride of the company, had lost more than $1 billion a year for the previous two years. An additional 10,000 employees received pink slips. It was not an auspicious moment for the car industry in Europe, but Ford was banking on the Mondeo to come close to being global; at least 75 percent of the parts in the U.S. and European versions are the same.[27]

IV.

Ford received a much-needed boost in the 1980s by developing a set of strategic alliances with non-American automakers. Joint ventures between U.S. and Japanese auto companies became fashionable when U.S. automakers discovered that they could market under their own names popular Japanese compacts that they had neither the capital, the lead time, nor the know-how to reproduce themselves. A U.S. carmaker would open the way for a Japanese company to build a plant in the United States, run the facility, import 80 percent of the components from Japan, and attach a GM, Ford, or Chrysler nameplate. The U.S. company would get a high-quality fuel-efficient car for its fleet, and the Japanese company would have a secure footing inside the American market. Most of these marriages proved to be happier experiences in Tokyo than in Detroit.

The Ford-Mazda marriage began as a version of this model. Henry

Ford had been rebuffed in 1971 when he had tried to buy a piece of Mazda, then known as Toyo Kogyo Co. But after the oil crisis of 1973 had left Mazda reeling because its rotary engines were exposed as gas-guzzlers, Mazda and its chief financial backer, Sumitomo Bank, began courting Ford. Sales were down and an infusion of $130 million or so was desperately needed. In 1979 the deal was struck, and Ford became the owner of a quarter share of what is now the fourth-largest Japanese maker of small cars and trucks.[28] (As part payment, Ford swapped the land on which its Yokohama assembly plant once stood.)

"We would much rather have Ford of Asia," Benton explained. "If we had been in Japan the same way that we are in Europe, they'd never have caught us off guard." Ford considered taking over a Japanese firm, but "it is hard. There is that very strong element of pride." Ford's goal is to work with Mazda "without significantly diminishing Mazda's independence." Benton explains how Ford, despite its minority share in Mazda, is "the senior partner" in the alliance. Joint projects have come "mostly from us. They are very wary of us."

From the beginning the alliance with Mazda was a learning experience for Ford. In the disastrous years 1980–83 the Mazda connection helped Ford survive; the beleaguered Detroit auto giant sold Mazda compacts under the Ford name all over Asia before the Escort was ready.[29] In 1984 Mazda announced that it would manufacture Mazdas at Ford's idle facility at Flat Rock, Michigan, enabling Ford executives and workers to monitor Japanese production without leaving the state. A third of the vehicles were to be outfitted with Ford engines. Mazda promised that 50 percent of everything that went into its Michigan-produced cars would be of local origin.[30]

On their many trips to Japan the Detroit-based executives were astonished to find that the Japanese could design and market a car in three and a half years instead of five. They could utilize 90 percent or more of their capacity instead of 60 or 70 percent, as in Detroit. "We were being dramatically outperformed by the Japanese in units produced per employee, capital per unit produced, process-yield versus planned capacity, inventory management and plant space utilization," Petersen publicly admitted in 1983.[31]

That same year Ford commissioned Mazda to design and build an updated Escort. The vaunted world car was by now the most popular car on earth but not a profitable one. Thanks to its heavy development and engineering costs, every Escort was sold at a substantial loss.[32] Ford had counted on turning over the production of a redesigned Escort to Mazda, which would have meant that the parts would have been 80-percent Japanese. But a problem surfaced. Changes in U.S. law required that Ford's entire fleet average 27.5 miles a gallon. In order to keep selling high-margin, gas-guzzling Continentals and Town Cars on which the company's profits depended, Ford had to average-in the fuel-efficient Escort. But the small car could not be counted for this purpose unless three-quarters of everything that went into it was made in the United States. So Ford agreed that it would design the outside of the car and Mazda would engineer the inside. The assembly would be divided between the Ford plant at Wayne, Michigan, after it was extensively retooled, and the company's state-of-the-art facility at Hermosillo, Mexico. The suppliers would be primarily American.

It was an exciting relationship but not an altogether smooth one. Bilingual marriages pose an added risk of miscommunication. Mazda president Yoshihiro Wada estimates that when he and his top executives would meet their counterparts at Ford, about a third of everything said was lost or garbled in translation.[33] Even more serious, as Dee Kapur, Ford's manager of the project, soon discovered, "the design and specification systems" used by the two companies "were completely different. Like night and day." The computerized engineering system in Detroit could not talk to Mazda's computers in Hiroshima.[34]

Mazda insisted on specifications for materials and parts that Ford executives and suppliers found astonishingly (and maddeningly) exacting. How were Detroit engineers supposed to know that Malaysian license plates are oversize and wouldn't fit Ford's design for the license-plate recess? Mazda engineers insisted that deadlines be met; missing even a day or two could produce anger and scorn. Ford managers found themselves working eighty-hour weeks.[35]

Despite the $200 million Ford had been obliged to invest in its Michigan plant (not to mention the $120-million inducement package offered by the State of Michigan, including worker-training subsidies, road and rail-spur improvements, and $80 million in tax abatements), Ford believes that it got its money's worth.[36] Thanks to Mazda's strict scheduling, the new Escort had about 60 percent fewer last-minute expensive design changes. The target of 34.2 miles per gallon had been exceeded. To be sure, had the American company done the project by itself, it would have cost $600 million less, Kapur estimates. But the education of the Ford Motor Company was an investment in the company's future. Company executives say that they didn't expect the new world car to make money—"just lose less than its predecessor."[37]

The Ford-Mazda alliance has surmounted growing tensions between the United States and Japan for almost a decade and a half because both companies have been determined to make it serve their interests. Because of the connection, Ford became the best-selling foreign nameplate in Japan. Ford workers were put under increasing pressure to get jobs done on time and to work more efficiently. "Nine times out of 10," the manager of the Ford-Mazda Escort project recalls, "we came up with a technical solution faster than they would. Implementation-wise, process methodology, discipline, that's where we are killing ourselves."[38] American executives learned to pay more attention to what the workers thought about improving production. Top management learned that up-front investment to retrain workers (especially if the government paid for it), the organization of a "downsized" work force into "quality of work" teams, and the modernization of plant and machinery would pay off in future profits. Among the three Detroit automakers, the Ford Motor Company, the world's first teacher of mass production, emerged as the most eager student in the American auto industry of what it would now require to make profits in a world in which auto companies have the capacity to produce 57 million cars and trucks a year—11 million more than anyone wants or can afford to buy.

V.

Because of the size and importance of the industry, the loss of American jobs in auto production has been front-page news for many years. But the same pressures and incentives operate in virtually all other industries and in many other industrial countries. The financial rewards in closing factories in the home country and opening them in low-wage enclaves of Latin America and Asia have been especially irresistible for U.S. companies, however, because of a variety of government policies—credits, tax breaks, tariff exemptions, and insurance against overseas losses—that have accelerated the deindustrialization of the United States.

Poor countries with unorganized work forces are attractive production sites for global companies, whatever flag they fly. Higher profits, labor peace, access to natural resources of the region and to local markets are powerful incentives to relocate factories. The countries spread across the planet along what professors like to call the "periphery" of the world economy and most people still call the Third World have little in common beyond rapidly growing non-white populations, histories of colonialism, hot weather, and tenacious poverty. In the years 1962–71 imports of manufactured goods from underdeveloped countries into the United States increased by almost 18 percent a year.

However, a large share of the imports were from U.S.-owned factories in the former colonial world.[39] Bulova, for example, began to manufacture its watch movements in Switzerland and ship them to Pago Pago in American Samoa, where they were assembled for the U.S. market. The cost of transportation was more than offset by the happy circumstance that goods from American Samoa enter the United States free of tariff. "We are able to beat the foreign competition," Bulova president Harry B. Henshel explained, "because we *are* the foreign competition."[40] By 1991 more than half of all U.S. exports and imports were transfers of components and services within the same global corporation, most of them flying the American flag.[41]

European companies such as Philips, Nestlé, and Siemens, all based in small countries like Holland, Switzerland, and the former West Germany, outgrew their home markets years ago and began deriving ever greater shares of their profits from foreign sales. It made economic as well as political sense to locate factories close to new expanding markets to save transportation costs. France encouraged its corporations to establish operations in its former colonial possessions in West Africa. British corporations gravitated to the more promising newly independent countries of once-British East Africa, notably Kenya.

Then the Japanese joined the exodus, although at a slower pace. In the 1960s, as wages at home rose and pollution problems became an issue, textile manufacturers and apparel makers shifted operations from the home islands to East Asia, particularly Hong Kong. In the next decade a sizable chunk of the electronics industry moved offshore. According to the Japanese Electrical Machinery Industry Association, 193,000 workers were employed in the 1980s by Japanese electrical-equipment affiliates throughout the world, and of these 134,000 were in East Asia.[42]

These transformations in the geography of production changed the face of all industrial countries, but the changes have been especially dramatic in the United States. In 1950 about a third of all American jobs were in manufacturing; by the mid-1980s factory employment accounted for only 20 percent of the work force, and by the early 1990s only 16 percent.[43] During the 1970s, to give two examples of a widely imitated cost-cutting strategy, General Electric added 30,000 foreign jobs and eliminated 25,000 American workers from its payroll; RCA laid off 14,000 workers in the United States and hired 19,000 abroad. In the 1990s workers in Australia, Ireland, and the United Kingdom can be hired for 60 percent of a U.S. hourly wage, and Mexicans, Brazilians, and South Koreans still work for 10 to 15 percent of U.S. labor costs. Fiber-optic systems, regional telecommunications, satellite teleports, telefax, microwave communications, and specially wired "smart" buildings make it possible for world headquarters of global corporations to adapt some of the technologies of command and control developed for the military to their commercial and financial operations spread across the globe.[44]

Although the loss of industrial jobs is most pronounced in the United States, the same trends are evident in other great manufacturing centers in the industrial world. In the United Kingdom there was a net decline of more than a million manufacturing jobs between 1966 and 1976. Employment in the motor-vehicle, shipbuilding, metal-manufacturing, mechanical-engineering, and electrical-engineering industries fell from 10 to 20 percent in that decade alone. In the West Midlands, a leading industrial region, 151,117 more manufacturing jobs were lost than were created in just three bad years, 1978–81. In Lancashire the textile industry lost a half-million jobs. In the industrial areas of northeast France and western Belgium unemployment rates shot up from 1 to 2 percent in 1973 to a range of 8 to 12 percent by the mid-1980s. Traditional industrial regions in northern England, Northern Ireland, Wales, Hamburg, Nordrhein-Westfalen, Saarland, Auvergne, and the Paris basin became pockets of severe and chronic unemployment.[45]

The closing of factories that had been located in or near the heart of America's industrial cities caused an exodus from what came to be known as the "inner city." The term dates from the early 1960s. A generation before, many of these same blocks and census tracts were the heart of the city; now people spoke of them as if they were abscesses. Not all the downtown factory closings were prompted by decisions to move out of the country altogether; corporate flight to the suburbs also played a role. In the postwar boom years, huge suburban housing tracts sprouted all across the country, and women (who typically earned 60 percent of what a male earned for equivalent work) entered the labor market in droves. This new labor market, along with cheap land and lower taxes, attracted corporations out of the older urban industrial regions into the surrounding rural areas where clean, safe "bedroom communities" were sprouting.

The result was that virtually all the older cities developed "inner-city problems"—50-percent unemployment rates for undereducated youth, crime, declining educational facilities, inadequate health facilities—and, as cities became increasingly expensive, unpleasant, and dangerous places to work and live, the exodus of large corporations accelerated. As stories of inanities and violence in the schoolroom, traffic jams, soaring real-estate assessments, and random killings were becoming staple dinner-party talk among their executives, a number of top manufacturing companies resolved to relocate their world headquarters to less stressful surroundings.

As firms scanned the globe for the best places to relocate their production facilities, countries and regions all over the world, including the Sunbelt in the United States, hungrily competed for jobs with offers of tax holidays and other benefits that cost-conscious companies could not pass up. What was still being produced in the advanced industrial countries, what neighborhoods, cities, and regions were attracting the production, and what the work force was coming to look like were all caught up in a vortex of change.

As the great corporations merged, automated, exported jobs, and relied increasingly on subcontractors and temporary employees, the Global Workplace took on a new look. Old jobs were lost by the millions, but new manufacturing and related jobs in substantially lower numbers were created in high-technology industries—aerospace, robotics, synthetics, chemicals, and ceramics—in the technology of sophisticated assembly, and in the fashion industry—clothes, furniture, specialized fittings of all sorts for the upscale market. All this changed the way cities looked. Right next to row on row of dilapidated buildings where former factory workers waited for government checks and young men without hope of jobs supported themselves running drugs or by violent crime, there rose gleaming miracle miles of shopping malls, hotels, and globally connected offices.

For some workers, regions, and city blocks around the world, this shift in production brought unparalleled prosperity and for others crushing poverty. Everywhere the gap between neighborhoods with a future and those with memories of a once-prosperous past widened. As the 1980s began, local politicians in the United States with presidential ambitions claimed that the economic surges in Massachusetts and other parts of the country based on the influx of advanced high-tech hardware factories and information software companies were models for the renewal of the American economy as a whole. But by the end of the decade many of these "miracles" had lost their luster. California and the East Coast industrial corridor were hit hard in the recession of the early 1990s, while enclaves within the old Midwest "Rustbelt" that had diversified their manufacturing bases and were now producing specialized industrial products for export were doing better than the rest of the country.[46] As the impact of the new global production system began to be felt, the fissures dividing the winners and losers grew deeper. The "gales of creative destruction," as the economist Joseph Schumpeter termed the processes of capitalist change, could sweep through a neighborhood as a gentle breeze or an ill wind, depending on whether people who lived or worked there found themselves in or out of the prospering sectors of the global economy.

Arcane matters of trade suddenly became highly charged political issues. As hundreds of thousands of American autoworkers lost their jobs, a few vented their anger by kicking in Honda fenders. Matt Darcy, a Chevrolet salesman from Garden City, Michigan, was interviewed on *60 Minutes* and said he had qualms about urging customers to buy American products when they were inferior to what foreign competitors were offering. He was summarily fired for disloyalty to his car and country.[47] Some U.S. politicians attempted to capitalize on public anger about the loss of American jobs by resorting to voodoo; one congressman took a sledgehammer to a Toshiba television set, and the picture flashed across the world via CNN.

From Japan came return fire, some from prominent political personalities who raised the decibel level: The world's sole remaining superpower was suffering from a lazy, illiterate, mongrelized work force run by avaricious executives who paid themselves fat salaries for producing shoddy products. Such America-bashing remarks circulating in Japan had a good chance of being instantly picked up in the United States, and on one occasion when this happened Senator Ernest F. Hollings of South Carolina told a group of cheering American factory workers to send the Japanese a picture of a mushroom cloud with the message underneath it: "Made in America by lazy and illiterate Americans and tested in Japan."[48] Just as the mayor of Chicago in the 1920s used to run against King George V, now White House aspirants ran against Toyotas. "Buy American" became the cry of the 1990s as the president, the Republican Party, and some prominent American companies took the pledge.

The trouble was that, however heartfelt the patriotic desire to patronize American products, the pledge could not be kept. In the age of globalization, insistence on purity of lineage in cars, radios, indeed most products in international commerce, makes about as much sense as notions of racial purity. There is little of either in the world today, and the illusion of purity of origin, whatever form it takes, can drive human beings to irrational, indeed murderous behavior. What is an "American" car? A Geo Prizm, which is really a Toyota Corolla made in California? A Geo Metro, marketed by GM but made by Suzuki and Isuzu? What is a "foreign" car? A Jaguar made in England by a wholly owned Ford subsidiary? A Mazda Navaho, which is really a Ford Explorer made in Kentucky?[49]

Some companies, including Monsanto, promised to pay as much as $1,000 to any of their employees who bought an "American" car. But all had different definitions of what an American car was. (Franklin Bank of Southfield, Michigan, devised a Buy American plan for its employees under which it rejected Hondas made in Ohio but allowed Chrysler minivans made in Canada.) As the 1992 presidential election campaign got under way, the Bush-Quayle campaign announced its Buy American plan and boasted that its fax machines came from Texas and its computers from San Jose. But one company was Japanese and the other Korean. A spokesperson explained, "We did try very hard to get American-made PC's, but the ones available were way out of our price range."[50]

A key to the American strategy to save jobs in the United States once U.S.-based manufacturers had fled American shores was to insist that foreign companies manufacturing in the United States include substantial "local content." But the concept leads inexorably into a thicket of legal complexity and logical confusion. For example, Hondas made in Canada, according to the Customs Service, do not qualify for tariff-free treatment because they fall short of the required 50-percent "North American content." It is not that Canada is not North American, but that too many parts can be traced back to a network of Japanese suppliers. The Japanese government maintains that more than 60 percent of 931 Japanese-owned companies in the United States obtain "two-thirds of their materials in America," but many of these "American" suppliers are Japanese-owned. Moreover, legal legerdemain and accounting alchemy can turn American parts into Japanese parts and vice versa. Robert Reich, who became secretary of labor in the Clinton administration, gives a graphic illustration of some of the problems of basing a nation's employment policy on the pedigrees of globally produced machines:

When an American buys a Pontiac Le Mans from General Motors, for example, he engages unwittingly in an international transaction. Of the $10,000 paid to GM, about $3,000 goes to South Korea for routine labor and assembly operations, $1,850 to Japan for advanced components (engines, transaxles, and electronics), $700 to the former West Germany for styling and design engineering, $400 to Taiwan, Singapore, and Japan for small components, $250 to Britain for advertising and marketing services, and about $50 to Ireland and Barbados for data processing. The rest—less than $4,000—goes to strategists in Detroit, lawyers, bankers in New York, lobbyists in Washington, insurance and health care workers all over the country, and to General Motors shareholders all over the world.[51]

It is now a fact of global life that multinationals, whatever flag they fly, can use overseas subsidiaries, joint ventures, licensing agreements, and strategic alliances to assume foreign identities when it suits their purposes—either to help them slip under tariff walls or to take advantage of some law of another country. Thus the American subsidiaries of Japanese and European global companies are going into American courts as zealous protectors of American jobs, bringing antidumping suits against low-wage Korean and Taiwanese competitors. "When we go to Brussels, we're a member state [of the European Community]," an executive of the U.S. pharmaceutical firm SmithKline (now merged with the British-based drug company Beecham) explains. "And when we go to Washington, we're an American company, too."[52]

To look like a "stateless corporation" is becoming more and more of a corporate goal, and to a limited extent the goal is achieved. "IBM, to some degree, has successfully lost its American identity," according to C. Michael Armstrong, senior vice-president in charge of IBM World Trade Corp. The *Economist* puts it more strongly. "One of the secrets of IBM's success is that IBM Europe is a European company just as IBM Japan is a Japanese one." IBM-Japan is Japan's biggest exporter of computers.[53] There are no more American-sounding brand names than General Electric and RCA, but a French firm with an English name, Thomson, owns these famous trademarks for its consumer-electronics line.[54] The Japanese government observes the Arab embargo of Israel. Japanese cars are banned by the Taiwanese and South Korean governments to protect local industry. But by the miracle of globalization "Japanese" cars are transformed into "American" cars as Honda ships its Accords to Taiwan, Korea, and Israel from its Ohio plant. The rise of regional trading blocs in Europe, North America, and East Asia is encouraging a number of world corporations to develop what *Business Week* calls "chameleon-like abilities to resemble insiders no matter where they operate."[55]

VI.

As the global market becomes more important for American firms, the less invested they become in the territory of the United States. Reich has argued that these firms "are rapidly becoming global entities with no special relationship to the United States economy."[56] He says that foreign-owned companies willing to employ, train, and offer job security and good working conditions to American workers by locating production plants and advanced research facilities in Ohio or Tennessee are more "us" than nominally American companies that have fled American shores.

There is truth to his proposition, but it is not the whole truth. The problem of defining corporate identity in a world of nation-states and transnational markets is not a new one. In 1972 Carl A. Gerstacker, chairman of the Dow Chemical Company, confided to the White House Conference on the Industrial World Ahead that he dreamed of buying "an island owned by no nation" and on "such truly neutral ground" he would locate the world headquarters of the Dow company so that "we could then really operate in the United States as U.S. citizens, in Japan as Japanese citizens, and in Brazil as Brazilians rather than being governed in prime by the laws of the United States." (He promised to pay any natives handsomely to move elsewhere and was promptly offered a Pacific atoll.) Corporations dream of escaping the laws of any nations that restrict the free movement of goods, information, and profits.

But at the same time global companies everywhere look to their home governments to protect their existing markets and to provide muscle for penetrating new markets, to keep labor and environmental costs down, and to subsidize their operations in various ways. The relationship between large corporations and the governments of their home countries varies. In Japanese culture an arms-length, not to say adversarial, relationship between the government and big business is considered bizarre. In the United States the relationship is not as intimate as in Japan, but thanks to the deep involvement of corporations in the political process, it is hardly as adversarial as corporate executives often claim. Theoretically, the leverage federal and local governments have over global companies flying the American flag is greater than over foreign-owned companies since U.S.-based corporations are creations of U.S. laws and they are usually more dependent on the American market than are foreign corporations.

Government treatment of their home-based corporations can result in competitive advantages or disadvantages. The Japanese government does not offer its corporations the same tax incentives to abandon the home country as are available in U.S. law. Thanks to a clearer consensus on the national interest with respect to economic matters than exists in the United States, the Japanese government employs a heavier hand over its corporations to ensure that the long-range needs of Japanese are met. How much home governments are willing to spend on health, education, ports, roads, and other public-infrastructure needs and how they spend it can translate into competitive advantages or disadvantages for their home-based corporations. Clearly, Japanese corporations have benefitted from the decisions of Japanese governments to invest in primary and secondary education. In this sense the playing field is never quite level. The national origin of a global business corporation matters less than it once did, but in a world of nation-states it still matters.

CHAPTER TWO

THE NEW DIVISION OF LABOR AND THE GLOBAL JOB CRISIS

I.

IN THE AGE OF GLOBALIZATION, HUNDREDS OF MILLIONS OF people are waking up to the fact that they are competing for their jobs with people who may live on the other side of the world. This is not a wholly new state of affairs, but rather a continuation of the same dynamic process that spelled the decline of the mill towns of New England. As textile factories, shirtmakers, tanners, and shoe manufacturers moved south and west in droves beginning in the 1920s in quest of cheaper nonunion labor, many eventually leaving the country altogether, the economies of once-stable industrial communities were shaken. What is new is that industrial restructuring is happening on a global scale—and with accelerating speed.

In the 1990s the global division of labor is markedly different from what it was forty years ago. Where manufacturing, agricultural, and service activities are taking place and how the work is done have changed radically. In the early 1950s the world's production of manufactured goods was still largely confined to twenty-four industrialized countries within which advanced research facilities were concentrated in a few capital cities and university centers. Most of the rest of the world was lumped together, designated the Third World, and generally regarded as a supplier of natural resources. (In the Cold War years, the Soviet empire and China, the so-called Second World, were largely outside the world economy; so few links remained between the capitalist and communist spheres that the impact of the huge Eurasian landmass on the international division of labor was minimal.) Today the world's work is divided up according to a more complex pattern among seven groups of nations. What people do—indeed, the very nature of work itself—differs in each of them.

Almost four-fifths of the measured economic activity on earth is still generated by two dozen richer countries: the United States, Canada, Japan, Australia, New Zealand, South Africa, and the nations of Western Europe. All but a handful of the world's top 200 corporations are based here. Most of world trade and investment takes place within this collection of nations. The United Nations estimates that of the $196 billion in new overseas private investment made in 1989, over four-fifths flowed back and forth among twenty-four affluent countries. Only a sixth of the total flowed into the poorer nations; less than 2 percent flowed into Africa.[1]

Eight countries, though still poor by many measures, have entered the industrial age to become large-scale manufacturers of a broad range of products. This second group is made up of nations aspiring to become the middle class in the global economic hierarchy: Brazil, Mexico, Argentina, India, but especially the so-called Asian tigers—South Korea, Taiwan, Singapore, and Hong Kong. In the lingo of development economics, all but India are often referred to as "newly industrializing countries," NICs for short. (India has been in the process of industrialization for a long time. Heavy industry was well established on the subcontinent before the outbreak of World War II.) Several of the other countries in this group had developed a scattering of manufacturing facilities in textiles, apparel, steel, shipbuilding, chemicals, and other advanced industries as early as the 1930s because of the breakdown in world trade in the Great Depression years. But the drive to industrialize began in earnest only in the late 1950s and early 1960s. Despite impressive efforts to train engineers and scientists and to invest in their own research and development capabilities, all these countries remain technologically dependent on American, Japanese, and European corporations in a number of ways.

A third group of nations has achieved some limited industrialization but they are still predominantly dependent on agriculture. Typically, elites in such countries dream of escaping poverty by digging up rice paddies or bean fields to build factories. But only a very few have any real prospects of becoming members of the industrialized world soon or ever. Among some two dozen aspiring nations, China, Thailand, Indonesia, and Malaysia appear to have the best chances, especially China, but global economic conditions are less favorable than in the boom years when the Asian tigers achieved their remarkable transformations.[2]

Over the past two decades the aspiring NICs have organized a variety of enclaves to assemble consumer products for the world market. However, unlike the NICs, which built up networks of integrated industries in accordance with national development strategies, the would-be NICs for the most part have not had either the resources or the political culture to follow such a course. Their strategy has been to integrate their labor forces into global production chains that are outside their control. This they do by inviting foreign-owned, labor-intensive assembly operations into their territories. Taiwan, Korea, Singapore, and Hong Kong had a different approach; these governments promoted foreign investment in local factories but took a heavy managerial role in economic development, and the result was dramatic economic growth. In recent years production enclaves have spread to such places as Mauritius, Jamaica, Guatemala, Panama, St. Lucia, Sri Lanka, the Philippines, Barbados, Belize, Costa Rica, and Haiti, where the governments have neither the resources nor the inclination to follow the interventionist policies so successfully pursued by South Korea and Taiwan.[3]

The former communist countries of Eastern Europe make up a fourth group of producers for the global market. Despite the relatively high state of industrialization some of them had achieved before World War II, with the exception of the former East Germany most are finding it difficult to compete for foreign investment with the industrializing enclaves of Asia and Latin America. The formerly communist countries are caught up in the throes of revolutionary change, and the path to capitalism is proving to be painful and difficult. But there are considerable differences among the former Soviet satellites. Even under communism Hungary had gone farther than the other East European countries in pushing market-oriented economic policies. Because of its relatively strong economy and its aggressive efforts to persuade global corporations to set up factories on its territory, Hungary attracted about half of all the foreign investment in Eastern Europe in the first two years after the crash of communism.[4] General Electric is making light bulbs there, Schwinn has a bike factory, and Levi's has opened a jeans factory. Strikes are unknown and labor costs are astonishingly low.

Foreign companies are attracted to the region by the prospect of picking up former state enterprises at bargain prices. Between September 1991 and April 1992, U.S. firms took over all or part of twenty-four Czech firms. Philip Morris arranged to purchase the state company that controlled 56 percent of the Czech cigarette market. (Czechs buy 30 billion cigarettes a year.)[5] But wages were so low in Czechoslovakia in the early 1990s that sales of goods produced for the domestic market were sluggish; large inventories piled up in warehouses. The newly privatized, foreign-owned factories of Eastern Europe are selling most of what they produce in Western Europe. Foreign investors were also attracted to the former Soviet Union by the lure of Russia's mineral-rich expanse, cheap wages, and an educated work force hungry for consumer goods. But conditions have remained so unsettled that foreign companies have concluded very few deals to produce goods in the former Soviet republics for either the domestic or global market.

Most of the dozen oil-exporting countries belonging to the Organization of Petroleum Exporting Countries (OPEC) constitute a fifth set of countries with a special niche in the world economy. OPEC is dominated by feudal desert kingdoms in the Middle East. These countries have been able to import whole factories along with a wide range of industrial products for their suddenly affluent populations, but by and large they lack the scientific and engineering expertise to develop their own industrial bases. In the oil-boom years of the 1970s and 1980s, these sparsely populated oil monarchies attracted millions of guest workers and also provided considerable business for large American, European, and Japanese construction and engineering firms. But this activity left no more than a veneer of industrialization.

A sixth set of countries is made up of forty or so poor countries that are situated just above the bottom of the global economic pyramid. Some are in Asia, but the vast majority are in Africa and Latin America. These countries still play much the same role in the world economy they played in the colonial era. They have little industry beyond a few packing and processing facilities. They are suppliers of one or two raw materials for export, and most people who earn money in the legal economy do so by participating in this process. Thus copper accounts for 98 percent of Zambia's export earnings; coffee for 95 percent of Uganda's; cocoa for 59 percent of Ghana's; natural gas for 49 percent of Bolivia's (if you don't count the booming but not easily calculable coca trade); tea for 35 percent of Sri Lanka's.[6]

The fate of these countries has always depended on the weather and the commodity markets, which are equally capricious. But recently, corporate plans to increase reliance on laboratory substitutes for tropical oils, cocoa, sugar, and other products on which hot, poor countries depend are threatening a number of them with economic catastrophe. Foreign corporations select as their principal suppliers of raw materials countries that are good prospects for foreign investment, and they do not hesitate to abandon those that fall behind. Ghana, once the world's leader in cocoa, has lost much of its market to Malaysia because the country has failed to thrive.

The poorest of the poor are forty-seven so-called "least developed countries," almost all of them in Africa, and these make up the seventh group. They are so poor that their economic connection with the rest of the world is pretty much limited to cashing relief checks and opening bags of food from government and private relief agencies. They export small quantities of primary commodities, but they remain locked into a cycle of poverty and dependency. When executives of global corporations scan the world for materials, labor, or markets, their eyes never light on these nations at the very bottom. In executive suites they are not regarded as part of the world economy.

II.

Economists and development experts by and large do not permit the vastly different stages of production and consumption in these seven sets of countries to interfere with well-established theory. Economic development has become a leading twentieth-century secular religion, although its roots are in the eighteenth century. If belief in the inevitability of progress toward good, just, and happy societies has been shaken by the collapse of socialism and the perils and inequities of late-twentieth-century capitalism, the faith that there is basically one road to riches remains. Nations, like flowers, unfold by using their resources in prescribed ways, in short, by proceeding along a well-trodden path to something called "development." Indeed, the very word connotes a process of enhancing a potential already in place, as in developing muscles or developing pictures. Adam Smith described the stages by which the wealth of nations is achieved—

from societies of hunters and gatherers to pastoral societies and thence to agricultural communities, ascending finally to the full stage of development as commercial and manufacturing nations. Karl Marx had a surprisingly similar notion about the stages of development from feudalism to capitalism, although he had other ideas about what constitutes the ideal society and how change takes place.

After World War II, faith in development dogma was at its height. As an answer to the communist credo of development, Walt Rostow, an economic historian at Massachusetts Institute of Technology, articulated an influential capitalist theory that set out five "stages of growth." He argued that poor nations could direct investment into "leading sectors" of their economies and ascend to each of these higher stages, finally achieving a self-sustaining prosperity based on mass consumption.[7] But, as it has turned out, Japan's ascendance as a global economic superpower and the success of the newly industrializing economies of Asia, now viewed as models by dozens of other countries, stand out as puzzling exceptions to what is a rather pessimistic global picture of stubborn poverty.

A global brotherhood of development advisers, consultants, and experts has grown up in the last forty years; most of them are employed by universities, ministries, banks, and international agencies. By and large, they are optimists since they are in the business of selling hope to investors, foundations, and governments. World Bank economist Bela Balassa, for example, has laid out a neat theory of salvation for poor countries. He speculates that countries will develop in stages by playing a sort of economic musical chairs. Thus "countries at lower stages of industrial development" will take over light manufacturing—textiles, clothing, shoes, toys, and the like—as the more successful countries, South Korea, for example, move up to become global players in high technology.[8] But it has not worked out quite this way. South Korea and Taiwan, for example, had no interest in giving up their hold on the textile and apparel industries merely because they had become successful producers of computers, cars, and microchips, although their entrepreneurs relocated factories to lower-wage countries just as the first-rung industrial nations did. As the growth of the world economy has slowed significantly in the last quarter century, it appears that most developing countries, as they are indiscriminately called, appear locked into place. If they are indeed on any path at all, for most countries in Africa and many in Latin America it is downhill.

III.

All across the planet the standard answer to poverty is to produce more goods and services for the world market. But in recent years conventional economic wisdom has clashed with a growing awareness that industrial processes are ruining the environment. No one denies that factories create waste and pollution. The environmental debate is about how much pollution can be tolerated as the price of industrial growth and who will bear the economic, social, and political costs of living with the effluents of mass production and mass consumption.

Production itself is threatening the environment at four distinct stages in the process. Factories are principal emitters of greenhouse gases, ozone-depleting chemicals, and toxic pollutants. So polluting are petrochemical plants, oil refineries, and steel smelters, still the foundations of the production system even in the age of software, that they are being spread around the world to countries willing to exchange breathable air for jobs. (The Japanese have been pioneers in relocating their dirtiest factories outside the home islands.) The distribution, packaging, and transportation of factory-produced goods, much of it by truck, has further polluting effects. Packaging makes huge demands on trees and other natural resources. Once they are purchased, many of the products themselves contribute to the environmental crisis either because they run on internal-combustion engines—trucks, cars, lawn mowers, power boats—or on electric power, much of which depends upon burning dirty coal or creating nuclear wastes. Finally, the production process creates waste, much of it toxic.

The fourteen-month globe-circling voyage of the *Khian Sea* is but one of over 1,000 documented efforts to export toxics to faraway places. In this case the vessel set sail in October 1987 with more than 13,000 tons of toxic incinerator ash from Philadelphia bound for Haiti, which had agreed to accept the ash under the impression that it was fertilizer. The ash was dumped on a beach. When the Haitian government discovered what it really was and complained, the crew shoveled most of the ash back onto the ship, leaving 2,000 tons or so on the sands. The *Khian Sea* then put in at ports on five continents seeking to unload its poisonous cargo, but fourteen countries, including Senegal, Cape Verde, Sri Lanka, and Yugoslavia, turned the ship back and the toxic ash was eventually dumped into the Indian Ocean.[9]

Since the pollution of oceans is hurting the fishing industry and killing marine life of all sorts in many parts of the world and the earth is supplied with but one ozone layer, the prudent policy would be to take the disturbing evidence on which environmental scientists across the world base their grim predictions, as inconclusive as some of it may be, a good deal more seriously than the reassurances of politicians and shamans of development. Perhaps it will turn out that the environmentalists were overwrought after all, and the earth is more patient than they believed. But nothing would be lost if industrial civilization were a bit cleaner, a tad more cautious, a little more saving than it absolutely needed to be for survival. Should the positive thinkers turn out to be wrong, and there is considerable data to suggest that they are, the flooding and scorching of the earth that might have caused them to change their minds will destroy a good deal more than their reputations as prophets.

The overriding political argument for dismissing urgent warnings of environmental hazards as "extreme" or "not proved" is jobs. Without continuous economic growth fueled by the production of goods and services, it is asserted, billions of people across the planet will have no livelihood. Self-described environmental "moderates" who oppose any environmental safeguards that slow economic growth are proposing a Faustian bargain—the spending down of irreplaceable capital in the form of breathable air, drinkable water, and endangered plants and animals, all of which are necessary for producing future wealth, in order to generate employment and income now. Why worry about global hazards tomorrow when there is no food on the table today? It is a plausible argument everywhere, and the poorer and more desperate a country is, the more compelling it sounds to governments. But because of the restructuring of production and the new division of labor brought about by these structural changes in the global productive system, the trading of environmental security for jobs makes no sense. We end up with foul air, dirty water, and disastrous climatic changes that threaten long-term prosperity and genuine economic development and ultimately accelerate the loss of jobs across the world.

IV.

Mark Twain's famous division of the universe of disinformation into lies, damn lies, and statistics comes to mind when we turn to the unemployment problem. Who is working, who wants to work, who has given up looking for a job, and who is "underemployed" are all difficult to calculate. Except for a handful of countries with labor shortages, the actual state of unemployment around the world is something rulers have every reason to hide. Their own job security depends on it. The assumptions behind the elaborate number-crunching of labor economists, whether they work for the government, or a union, or a business group, are politically charged and they are usually not disclosed. Nonetheless, even the overly optimistic official figures from around the world make a stark picture of a global human crisis. As subsistence agriculture declines everywhere, hundreds of millions are drawn into the money economy and need jobs in order to live. But for vast numbers of them there are not enough opportunities to earn a living wage.

The nature and consequences of unemployment differ with the state of development. In Europe, which traditionally had a much lower unemployment rate than the United States in the post–World War II boom years 1955–75, the percentage of the work force without jobs has climbed steadily for almost twenty years and now exceeds that of the United States. By mid-1993 the rate in the twelve countries of the European Community was a chronic 10.3 percent. (In Spain, where wages are among the lowest in the region and many foreign companies have moved in, it was over 19 percent.[10])

In July 1992 the official U.S. unemployment rate stood at 7.8 percent. If discouraged job-seekers who had stopped looking and part-time workers wanting full-time work were included, the actual percentage of jobless in the United States that year stood closer to 14 percent or more than 20 million men and women. As factories closed in the late 1970s through the early 1990s, job-seekers and their families fled the major industrial centers of the United States: by 1988 Detroit had lost 19 percent of its people, St. Louis 27 percent, and Buffalo 23 percent.[11] For skilled industrial workers relocation more often than not meant a fall in living standards. Using data from the Social Security Administration for the years 1957–75, economists Barry Bluestone and Bennett Harrison found that ex-autoworkers two years after being laid off were making 43 percent less than workers who were still making cars. Large numbers had found jobs in places like Kmart and McDonald's, but the hopes engendered by the theorists of "postindustrial" America that the workers from dying smokestack industries would end up in well-paid, clean jobs in newer high-technology industries were not realized. Of 674,000 workers in New England displaced by the closing of textile mills, shoe factories, and the like, only 3 percent were able to make it into the high-tech sector. In 1992 a Pennsylvania steelworker who had just been laid off after twenty-five years explained why he was attending restaurant school: "Who's going to send overseas for a hamburger or a coq au vin?" But hamburger slingers and kitchen assistants even in fancy restaurants do not make anything remotely like steelworker wages.[12]

In the previous chapter we talked about some of the physical consequences of factory relocation in the United States—the hollowing out of older cities and the transformation of once-remote farmland into enclaves of new production. The direct and indirect economic costs of deindustrialization—in unemployment and welfare benefits, added strain on the health, police, and penal systems in stressed-out communities across America—add up to a catastrophic loss.

But the human costs of chronic unemployment—family breakup, alcohol abuse, crime, and violence—represent an even greater loss. Dr. Harvey Brenner of Johns Hopkins University statistically correlated a 1-percent increase in the aggregate unemployment rate with 37,000 deaths, 920 suicides, 650 homicides, 4,000 admissions to mental hospitals, and 3,300 admissions to state prisons over a six-year period.[13] All such correlations are easily attacked on methodological grounds, but elaborate social science is hardly necessary to establish that the loss of a job or the loss of hope of finding one takes its toll on individuals, families, and communities. This is especially true in the United States and other meritocracies in which work and achievement are so important in defining an individual's worth. When the unemployment rate reaches 50 percent, as it has among young African-American men in major cities along the east coast of the United States and in many other places, the unwanted and unneeded pose a threat to the social order, whether they end up as criminals, victims, or just wasted human beings. In 1991, 42 percent of young black males in Washington, D.C., were embroiled in the judicial or penal systems.[14]

Bluestone and Harrison calculate that between 1969 and 1976 22.3 million jobs disappeared as a result of plant closings and the removal of production to other states or overseas. "When we extrapolated these numbers to the entire decade of the 1970's, we concluded that somewhere between 32 and 38 million jobs had disappeared in this 10-year period."[15] At the same time, millions of new jobs were created, a larger number than the jobs that were lost, as the Reagan and Bush administrations kept repeating. But by far the greatest number were low-skill service jobs much farther down on the pay scale (with fewer benefits and less security) than the jobs that were lost. The Bureau of Labor Statistics predicts a continuation of this trend for the rest of the century. There will be millions of new jobs created in the United States during the 1990s—most of them for people able and willing to work as retail salespeople, nurses and health aides, janitors, maids, waiters, and waitresses.

Increasingly, the global labor market, including its North American component, is relying on "contingent workers" (in simpler times the term was "day laborers") and "flexible scheduling" (spurts of overtime in busy seasons interspersed with long periods during which the worker waits by the phone or on the street corner that serves as a hiring hall for small construction and cleanup jobs). Between 1980 and 1987 about half of all the new jobs in the United States went to "temporary workers, part-time contractors, and independent workers,"[16] the majority of whom are women who earn on the average 69 percent of what males earn.[17] Health insurance and other benefits associated with the era of mass production are not typically provided. These shifts have a major impact on young workers, especially blacks who once had career opportunities in heavy manufacturing industry but are now competing for (or rejecting) jobs at or near the poverty level.

One effect of the massive restructuring of the labor market in the United States during the last two decades is that average real wages (adjusted for inflation) are roughly 9 percent below what they were in 1973.[18] Throughout the 1970s and 1980s family income kept ahead of inflation thanks to the contributions of second and third wage earners and to moonlighting, but in the recession year 1991 gains in family income for the first time in the post–World War II era failed to keep pace with the inflation rate. According to 1990 census data, over 14 percent of Americans are now living below the official poverty line.

V.

In the developed world, the labor pool is growing relatively slowly. The documented work force in the United States is expected to grow at about 1 percent a year through the 1990s. (The number of undocumented workers who slip into the country from abroad has been growing faster.) In most of the developed countries in Europe the native working population is growing about half as fast as in the United States.[19] Except for two industrializing nations in Asia (South Korea and Taiwan) that have been highly successful in creating jobs and building a middle class, two commercial city-states in the same part of the world (Hong Kong and Singapore) that are free from typical Third World population pressures, and China, which is growing fast, the rest of Asia, Africa, and Latin America face chronic unemployment problems on a scale far beyond anything encountered in Europe, Japan, or the United States even in the Great Depression. This includes a number of nations that are aggressively pursuing strategies of industrialization.

If we look twenty years ahead, over 700 million men and women will reach the legal working age throughout the underdeveloped world. Thus, around 38 million will be looking for work in underdeveloped countries each year, adding to the 700 million already unemployed or "underemployed." (These United Nations figures are extremely rough estimates. But it can be safely assumed that the national and international officials involved in compiling this data have no interest in inflating the numbers.)[20] In countries with the highest population growth rates, such as Mexico, Kenya, and Pakistan, the labor pool is growing at nearly 3 percent a year. In India and China the growth rate is down some, but the new job-seekers are additions to what in 1985 was already a combined labor pool of nearly a billion men and women. Progress in public health resulting in lower infant mortality and prolonged working life has further diminished the prospects of finding enough work at a living wage for the hundreds of millions seeking jobs.

The "feminization" of work is also changing job prospects around the world. As traditional cultural barriers give way, large numbers of women have entered the labor force in Asia, Africa, and Latin America. Because of their numbers, skills, and the worldwide practice of paying women much less than men, the "feminization" of work exerts two pressures on the global job market. First, the entry of women into jobs once reserved for men lowers labor costs dramatically. In South Korea in the late 1980s female earnings in manufacturing were 50 percent of male earnings in the same industries.[21] In the 1980s deregulation of the workplace was the trend all around the world. A number of governments seeking to build up their export sectors repealed regulations on workplace conditions, refused to renew their adherence to International Labor Organization conventions for the protection of workers to which they had previously subscribed, and stopped enforcing regulations still on the books.[22] In large part, this reflected the reality that governments around the world feel less pressure to protect female workers than males, who by and large are more likely to vote or make trouble.

However, in much of the world it is becoming less difficult for women to find paying jobs than it is for men, especially in developing countries. It is not only that they can be paid less and worked harder or that the state is less interested in protecting such rights as they may have, but women can be fit more easily into the flexible production systems that are becoming ever more important to global corporations. More and more females are working in what Ann Misch of the Worldwatch Institute calls the "shadow economy," cutting rubber, punching data, and performing a variety of other tasks at home. She draws on anthropological studies from all over the world. In Turkey women sit all day and well into the night weaving carpets. In northern Greece women with children at home work at least twelve hours a day stitching or sewing clothes in addition to looking after the children and doing the housework. In the Netherlands they attach fasteners on brassieres. In Italy they stitch shoes. In Mexico they assemble toys and pens. Because of the influx of migrant labor that accelerated in the 1970s and 1980s, the United States now has Third World enclaves in virtually every major city. As Susan Cowell of the International Ladies' Garment Workers' Union puts it, "Homework is an integral part of the production system in the U.S. garment industry." In busy seasons sewing is contracted out to women working at home so that sufficient quantities of the new fashions will arrive at the store in time for the Christmas or Easter rush.

One consequence of all this is that more and more men find that they have no place in the job market. This second impact of the "feminization" of work has social implications as important as the first. All over the world men are discovering that the traditional role of breadwinner is not open to them, and this is not only a blow to male pride but it calls their very reason for existence into question. What are they supposed to do all day? The opportunities to hunt and fish are shrinking, thanks largely to industrialization, overfishing, and bad management of the forests. The opportunities to make a living in traditional crafts are shrinking. Because of the end of the Cold War, the prospects for a stable job in the army or navy are not what they were. Though the opportunities to participate in the violent struggles of breakaway nations are already ample and are growing, the pay is low and there is little job security. As young men wait on street corners or in the village square for jobs that do not exist for them, the message becomes clear: you have no place here. As anger and despair well up within them, increasing numbers are driven to crime and violence.

Across the world the male worker is an endangered species. More and more men are opting out of civil society, refusing to act as fathers for children they cannot or will not earn enough money to support. Others are missing their children's formative years as they seek work thousands of miles away to send enough money home to keep the family fed. Forced separation of families because of economic necessity is now a fact of life all over the world, but it is a social disaster and a human tragedy.

VI.

The failure of national economies, especially in Asia, Africa, and Latin America, to provide enough jobs at living wages for the swelling numbers of job-seekers has coincided with labor shortages in a few countries and in certain job categories and locales in a number of other countries, including the United States. These great disparities in employment possibilities have helped stimulate mass migrations on a global scale. By the early 1990s some 75 million people from poor countries were leaving their native lands each year. Some were refugees from war and oppression, but the vast majority were leaving home in search of jobs.[23] In the early 1970s hundreds of thousands of young men from India, Jordan, Pakistan, and Bangladesh flocked to the oil-rich, thinly populated kingdoms of the Middle East to work in the oil fields or to sweep floors. Turks in large numbers arrived in Germany as "guest workers" to wash dishes and clean streets. Algerians looking for work arrived in Paris in droves. By the late 1970s more than 20 percent of the Swiss work force was made up of foreign workers.

More recently, as Japan, Taiwan, Korea, Singapore, and Hong Kong have prospered, they have served as magnets for large-scale flows of migrant workers from Indonesia and the Philippines. Indeed, in today's world the importation of labor is often an important indicator of a rising standard of living and changing cultural attitudes about work. For example, as Clark Ellis of the American Institute in Taiwan explains it, in that country many laborers have worked their way up from the assembly line to "more technical, skilled positions at their company" and others have moved into "Taiwan's expanding financial services sector." So difficult has it now become to find Taiwanese who want to work cleaning other people's houses or digging ditches that an estimated half-million illegal immigrants are filling these jobs.[24]

The global traffic in human labor has become critical to the economies of both sending and receiving countries. In the oil-boom years, Kuwait desperately needed foreign workers to do the menial work the feudal elite and their suddenly rich subjects had no interest in doing. On the eve of the Gulf War of 1990–91 over a million of the 1.8 million people in Kuwait were foreign workers. When the war broke out, 2 million guest workers lost their jobs in Kuwait and Iraq, and countries such as Egypt, Jordan, and Bangladesh lost millions of dollars in remittances from their workers abroad. The official total of what guest workers around the world send home to their families is estimated at more than $28 billion a year, but the real figure is probably many times this amount since so much money is transferred through informal channels that cannot be monitored.

For such countries as Jordan and Bangladesh, workers are the number-one export; indeed, before the Gulf War Jordan earned more foreign exchange from its construction workers abroad than from all its export products, and when they lost their jobs the Jordanian GNP fell by 25 percent.[25] Bangladesh earns over $700 million a year in hard currency from money its workers send home, more than it receives for the sale of jute, its principal crop. In the 1990s the governments of Egypt, Portugal, Pakistan, Indonesia, the Philippines, Bangladesh, and most recently China have encouraged foreign companies to come in and recruit their citizens for contract employment in such places as Kuwait, Hong Kong, and Australia. The U.S. government has generally discouraged such practice. Indeed, immigrants arriving at Ellis Island during the great migration waves of the last century, bursting with pride that they had jobs already lined up, were turned back as soon as they told immigration officials that they had been recruited in their home countries. But recently American hospitals, driven largely by the shortage of nurses and an ever growing need to staff AIDS wards, have been recruiting in the Philippines, the world's number-one exporter of nurses.

The United States has been shaped by five major streams of migration. The first migration waves are thought to have begun around 30,000 B.C. when the Asian ancestors of American Indians crossed the Bering Straits. The second stream began at the end of the fifteenth century A.D. when Spanish, French, and British explorers claimed pieces of the North American continent. A few years later colonists began to arrive in St. Augustine, Jamestown, and Plymouth, and their descendants settled the thirteen colonies that became the United States of America. From the first, the new nation was torn by the consequences of a third stream of migration that had begun in 1619. From that year until the early nineteenth century African and Caribbean peoples in large numbers were brought to North America in chains; nearly four centuries after the slave trade began in Virginia, American society is still struggling with the legacy of this commercial traffic in human beings.

The 35 million people who made up the great European migration that occurred between 1800 and 1914 constituted a fourth stream. These immigrants, who willingly braved long, harsh voyages for a chance to make a new life in the New World, eventually succeeded in turning the former English colonies into a multiethnic nation. Poles, Irish, Germans, Jews, and Slavs were joined by Asians, most of whom entered the work force at the very bottom in dangerous, exhausting, and pitifully paid jobs. Chinese who came to California in search of gold ended up in backbreaking work on the railroads. Japanese, Korean, Indian, and Philippine immigrants did much of the work to transform California's Central Valley from a near-desert into one of the world's most fertile agricultural regions.

Since 1965 a fifth migration wave has once again transformed the landscape of the United States, turning it more than ever into a multiracial society, swelling the work force, and creating a new set of social tensions. In 1990 the flow of legal immigrants reached more than 1.5 million, a number about equal to that of Ellis Island's peak year.[26] Millions more entered the United States illegally in the 1980s, most of them crossing the largely unpoliced 2,000-mile border with Mexico. How many millions no one really knows. The official number of undocumented entrants apprehended in a single year had reached 1,346,299 by the mid-1980s, but a relatively small percentage are caught.

Before 1965 the majority of immigrants were still overwhelmingly European, and in the early post–World War II years they were largely middle class. Many refugees from Hitler's Europe were highly educated. But by the 1980s immigrants from Asia, Latin America, and the Caribbean accounted for 83 percent of the new influx.[27] While large numbers came to escape the wars and repression in such places as El Salvador, Guatemala, Ethiopia, Cuba, and Vietnam, the primary motive for most, as in the great migrations of the nineteenth century, was to earn a living.

What prompts millions of people at a particular historical moment to pick up stakes and move thousands of miles to start a new life? Conventional explanations based on the "push" of poverty and the "pull" of economic opportunity in distant lands are too mechanistic. Neither poverty, overpopulation, nor economic stagnation in themselves serve to trigger mass migration, although they obviously play some role.[28] By and large it is not the poorest countries that mobilize the armies of foreign workers around the world, since most people in these countries still have little contact with the outside world. (The exodus from Somalia and Haiti, which rank among the poorest, can be explained not only by war and oppression but by their relatively easy access to the world beyond their shores.) The newly industrializing countries that have been major recipients of foreign investment are also among the greatest exporters of migrant labor. One of the arguments for development aid and private investment has been that improved living standards in underdeveloped countries would keep their people at home and out of other countries' job markets. But it seems to have had the opposite effect.

"The clearest proof of this," writes Saskia Sassen, a professor of urban planning at Columbia University who has done pioneering work on migration trends, "is the indelible fact that several of the newly industrializing countries with the highest growth rates in the world are simultaneously becoming the most important suppliers of immigrants to the United States."[29] These new immigrants come mostly from eleven countries that have experienced "higher than average rates of economic growth and industrial development in recent decades."[30]

The allure of modern urban life is attracting rural folk to factory jobs even as the processes of industrialization are throwing them off the land. Even if they want to remain subsistence farmers, millions no longer have the choice since "market forces," personified by local landlords and political chiefs, preempt their land for some profitable use. A 1983 World Bank "country paper" on Haiti, which is the third largest supplier of migrants to the United States, outlines the future that the Bank has in mind for that country. "Haiti's long-term future will be urban. This migration [from the countryside to the city] will sustain the development of assembly industries, cottage industries, and other urban labor-intensive activities consistent with export-led growth."[31] Since the new industries cannot absorb anything approaching the numbers leaving the land and still compete in the international market, this development model virtually guarantees that a steady stream of people will continue their attempts to emigrate to the United States.

The pull of the city for poor people from the country is a familiar story ever since the Industrial Revolution, especially in the twentieth century. But it is only in the last twenty-five years or so, thanks to the global spread of American movies, television programs, and other Western cultural products, that New York, Los Angeles, London, and Paris have become worldwide symbols of the good life. Well-advertised jet air routes and cheap fares turn cities thousands of miles away into magnets for millions of people who leave their homelands in search of the more glamorous and exciting life they have seen on the screen or heard in the beat of a rock song.

The increasing mobility of labor is a largely unanticipated response to the extraordinary global mobility of capital in recent years. (According to United Nations figures, the sales of foreign affiliates of global corporations more than doubled between 1982 and 1990.) The new wave of immigrants into the United States can be thought of as unanticipated imports from "export-processing zones." Much of the sewing, stitching, assembly, and packing of global consumer products now takes place in these duty-free, largely tax-free enclaves dedicated to light assembly and production. (The Shannon International Free Port at the Shannon, Ireland, airport, which opened in 1958, was the first.) Korea, Taiwan, Hong Kong, and Singapore were early centers of "export platform" production. Years later these countries used their experience to launch their own overseas factories.

When foreign firms began to invest in assembly operations in places such as Taiwan, they attracted large numbers of women from rural areas. Only a fraction who went to the city for jobs actually ended up with one. But they had made the momentous decision to leave their villages. Many of those who did secure employment later lost their jobs, some because their eyesight failed, others because the foreign company decided to shift production to a cheaper labor market, and still others because employers automated their assembly operations or made increasing use of temporary employees.

But having already taken the decisive step into the modern world, these young women did not wish to return to the village. In some cases going back to planting vegetables was no longer an option because neither the family plot nor the village still existed. In other cases women feared the stigma of returning to the village because in many cultures the villagers suspect that all single women who go off to the city end up as prostitutes. Most important, as Saskia Sassen argues, employees in the export-processing zones in their own countries encountered the American dream in all sorts of ways: magazines, toys, consumer goods, stories from friends and family members writing back from Los Angeles, encounters with recruiting agents looking for disciplined, accommodating workers to fill jobs somewhere across the seas, and of course American rock music, Hollywood films, and television programs, which stimulate longings to seek one's fortune in the land of the free and the rich. Almost half the new immigrants have ended up in the New York and Los Angeles areas, which are long-established centers of Asian and Caribbean immigration but also the favorite setting of Hollywood movies and TV dramas.

In the modern enclaves of their own traditional societies young workers develop a new outlook about their own possibilities, and the most adventurous among them a new willingness to seek new lives even across the world. The more political, economic, and military connections their country has with the United States, Sassen's research suggests, the more likely they are to end up in America. (The influx from El Salvador and Vietnam makes her point.) She believes that the nature of the foreign investment has more influence on immigration flows than the source of the investment. Thus Japanese foreign investment in the 1970s in labor-intensive export production in Asia "may well have ultimately promoted migration to the United States," because of the "greater number of other linkages" the United States had with developing countries and its reputation for welcoming immigrants.[32]

VII.

By far the greatest number of new immigrants to the United States are eking out livings waiting in parking lots for the trucks that might bring them to a day's work at a construction site, or cleaning houses or hotel suites as maids, or picking fruit in Oregon or Florida, or washing pots in restaurant kitchens or sewing apparel in city sweatshops. They are the most vulnerable workers in the society, underpaid and often cheated. But other new immigrants have been so successful that their prosperity exacerbates racial and ethnic tensions. According to a 1987 Census Bureau study, one out of every ten Korean-Americans owns his or her own business; for African-Americans the figure is one in sixty-seven.[33] In the 1992 Los Angeles riot, Korean stores were special targets of black rage.

In the New York City area, 40 percent of the gas stations are owned by recent immigrants from Punjab. In Los Angeles, Koreans have what the *New York Times* calls a "quasi-monopoly" on gas stations. Indians and Pakistanis have a "virtual monopoly" on New York City newsstands. There are only 4,000 Afghans in New York City, but they have managed to start a chain of fried-chicken restaurants. Indians and Pakistanis are challenging the once-exclusive control Hasidic Jews have had over the diamond trade in New York. Other ethnic and racial minorities have established highly visible niches in local economies in major American cities—as taxi drivers, owners of ethnic restaurants, greengrocers, fruit stores, and many more.

Like the Jews, Greeks, and others before them, many of the new ethnic immigrants have succeeded in carving out places for themselves and their compatriots by making use of the traditional transnational networks of poor people. Typically, pioneer immigrants who find jobs send for their families and friends. Once a family is established in an American city, word gets back to the village. Family, friends, and neighbors make plans, save up for plane tickets, and another stream of migration begins to flow. The economically successful immigrants in the United States form tight networks for economic survival. Koreans, Ethiopians, and other ethnic groups pool their money to start small businesses, usually in poor neighborhoods of the inner city. Their primary source of capital beyond the savings of their extended family and friends is free labor; family discipline and loyalty are the critical assets. The crisis besetting so many African-American families has economic as well as social consequences. The growing number of single-parent families and the loss of the tight family structure that once was more typical of many black families in the United States now make it much harder for African-Americans to start family businesses. Increasingly, the mom-and-pop stores in black neighborhoods are owned by Asian families.

Immigration from Mexico follows a different path. Philip Martin and Edward Taylor of the University of California have studied some of the networks that link Mexican villages with U.S. employers. This is one way the system works. Typically, a Mexican worker finds a low-status factory job outside of Chicago and proves to be a hard worker and more eager to please the foreman than are frustrated American employees, whose morale has dropped along with their real wages. When the American workers quit or are fired for coming in late or talking back, the foreman asks the Mexican worker to recruit replacements from his friends and relatives back in the village.

The connections between remote Mexican villages and job sites in the United States are surprisingly sophisticated. A telephone call can produce Mexicans ready to work three days later in Washington or Chicago. In small, rural communities, it is common to encounter long lines of Mexicans waiting patiently to receive wired money from relatives working illegally in the United States. A Michigan farmer maintains an 800 number in a village in Michoacán province so that "my" Mexican workers, as he terms them, "can call to find out when the seasonal work will begin." The Immigration Reform and Control Act of 1986 was designed to stop such recruiting networks for illegal immigrants. U.S. employers who knowingly hire undocumented workers are subject to fine. But the Act gave rise to a thriving industry in false documents throughout Mexico and was probably more a stimulus of illegal migration than a deterrent. Two years after the legislation was signed into law, Martin and Taylor report, whole villages were "virtually emptied of adult men . . . as Mexicans streamed north."[34]

According to neoclassical economic theory, labor migrations are an inspiring example of the invisible hand at work. Thus Julian Simon of the University of Maryland observes, "The overall effect of the migration on the average standard of living of the world's people is positive . . . the migrant goes from a place where he or she is less productive to a place where he or she is more productive."[35] But the impacts of mass migrations on the countries of origin, on the receiving countries, and on the migrants themselves do not conform to a neat win-win schema.

For the receiving countries, mass immigration is a mixed blessing. Corporations operating on their territory clearly benefit from an ever widening choice of cheap, nonunionized, and substantially nonorganizable labor. At the Seattle Sheraton, as in most urban hotels in the United States, the hotel's housekeeping and dishwashing staff is foreign-born. "We don't have American-born people apply for those positions," the manager explains.[36] A large influx of immigrants, many of them illiterate and without either legal status or technical skills, helps to change the local labor-relations culture. Workers without a green card that grants noncitizens the right to work in the United States are not easily persuaded to join picket lines. Indeed, immigrants have traditionally been employed as strikebreakers. The earlier immigration coincided with the rise of mass production, but the new immigration has arrived in the era of flexible production. Temporary workers are hard to organize even when they are native-born Americans. The presence of large numbers of unorganized, exploitable foreign-born workers has a depressing effect on the wages and working conditions of all nonskilled workers.

Compared to those who came in the immigration waves from Europe a hundred years ago, the new immigrants on the average are poorer, and more of them are female. For these reasons many have a harder time blending in the American melting pot than earlier generations of immigrants. The economic necessity of sticking together for economic survival often makes them appear more clannish than they would otherwise be. Many hang on to their languages and cultures as a way to develop the financial resources from within their own communities as well as the inner strength to face a society that is often less than welcoming. On the other hand, the United States in recent years has benefited from an influx of skilled, motivated, and highly educated workers. More than 1.5 million college and university graduates arrived in the 1980s, many with advanced degrees, and American high-tech industry has increasingly come to depend on Indian, Korean, Filipino, and Chinese scientists and engineers. In 1989, foreign-born students received almost half of all the math and computer science doctorates in the United States, and over 50 percent in engineering.[37] The preparatory-schooling costs for these new productive American workers paid for by the Indian or Korean government is a form of reverse foreign aid.

But the United States and the other receiving countries import problems along with the migrant labor force. The major problem is social tension, which becomes especially serious when the economy is weak and jobs are scarce. In a 1992 *Business Week*/Harris poll, "68% of respondents said today's immigration is bad for the country." (Seventy-three percent of African-American respondents were convinced that "businesses would rather hire immigrants than black Americans.")[38] Some U.S. unions call migrants "indentured servants" and complain that they take jobs away from union members. But the complaints are overdone. Most of the jobs are at the low end of the scale, and most union members would not take them in any event, at least as long as any social safety net remains. For American workers, the competition from foreign workers who stay home is a much greater threat. And that threat is growing. College attendance for blacks in the United States dropped by 7 percent in the 1980s, and the high-school dropout rate for Hispanics, the fastest-growing group of new entrants into the U.S. labor market, is even higher than it is for blacks, about 40 percent.[39] As the education crisis deepens in the United States, educational levels in the more successful developing countries are rising fast. By the year 2000 almost 80 percent of the high-school graduates across the world will be found in (and increasingly from) poor countries on their way up. According to the U.S. Department of Education, high-school students in Singapore, Hong Kong, Poland, and Hungary outperform U.S. high-school students on standardized tests in chemistry and physics.[40]

Immigrants in the United States receive an estimated $5 billion a year in welfare. The fact that they pay more than $90 billion in taxes does not lessen the resentment of many native-born citizens. By 2025, according to some projections, it will cost about 50 percent of the U.S. federal budget to maintain present benefit programs—retirement, Social Security, pensions, health insurance, disability entitlements, and the like. One reason why immigrants who are off the books and willing to do the work natives do not wish to do are so attractive to corporations and are tolerated by governments is that they do not have the right to make expensive long-term claims on national treasuries. But they do end up making demands for public funds one way or another. Their children go to school. They show up at hospital emergency rooms. Others live at taxpayer expense in prisons or other public institutions for the disabled.

The countries of Western Europe are experiencing some of the same tensions as a result of importing guest workers. Despite high unemployment rates, the pressures to bring in workers from abroad remain. The Continent faces the prospect of an aging population and a shrinking labor force. For years both halves of Germany have had negative birthrates. Thus there are unfilled jobs at both the top and the bottom of the employment ladder in certain population centers across Europe. The sudden availability of a vast labor pool in Russia and Eastern Europe may well encourage corporations in Europe to export production instead of importing more Asian and African workers. But economic conditions there are uncertain, and there are large numbers of immigrants already settled in industrial Europe.

Despite the more conservative governments of recent years, the countries of Western Europe retain a social-democratic culture. On much of the Continent, retirement and welfare benefits are liberal, far more so than in the United States, but the reserves to fund the benefits are not. Almost half of all men between the ages of 55 and 64 on the Continent and virtually two-thirds of the women are retired.[41] Many European workers fear that their pensions and other entitlements will be cut because foreign workers are skimming off benefits that should not be going to people who mangle the French language or look so out of place in the Rhineland. Neo-Nazis in Germany and reactionary nationalists in France have viciously attacked "the foreigners in our midst." As ethnic identity becomes more of a political force in Europe, foreign workers are faced with murderous harassment and threats of expulsion.

Japan, thanks to its rapid economic growth over the last forty years, its negative birthrate, and its relatively controllable borders, has for years been the one world economic power without an unemployment problem. (In the recession year 1992 for the first time in many years there were slightly more people looking for work than positions waiting to be filled.) But the Japan Federation of Workers has called the labor shortage "the most difficult problem facing Japanese companies."[42] According to a survey conducted by Japan's Ministry of Labor at the end of the 1980s, 268 companies reported that they were unable to hire even a quarter of the new young workers they were seeking. Sony officials say they have trouble recruiting enough engineers in Japan, and this is one reason why more research facilities are being shifted overseas. But Japan has been reluctant to encourage immigration as the answer to its labor shortage.

Most Japanese oppose liberalizing their stringent immigration laws, which have helped to preserve a single national culture and a racial "purity" that some claim is the key to Japan's phenomenal postwar success. (Even the presence of 1 million Koreans and 25,000 Ainus, the remnant of the original islanders, amid 122 million Japanese is a considerable source of tension.) Japan has preferred to rely on internal rather than transnational migrations. In the years of great economic growth, 1950 to 1970, the percentage of the Japanese population in agriculture declined from 50 percent to 19 percent. Entire villages voted to abandon their settlements and move *en masse* to factory jobs in the cities.

But the pressure to recruit from abroad has been mounting. In 1988, 80,000 legal migrants were admitted into the islands, but 88 percent were sports figures and "entertainers," the latter category made up mostly of Filipino or Korean women who end up as prostitutes or domestics. Low-skilled Asian males stay on illegally after entering as tourists and they find work in the major cities. There were, according to the Japanese Ministry of Labor, about 210,000 of them in 1991, mostly working on construction jobs and in restaurant kitchens.[43] According to International Labor Organization estimates, there may have been as many as 500,000.

The experience of being a worker in a foreign land can be anything from the hell of a sweatshop to the American dream come true. Many migrant laborers in the United States and Europe find themselves the most isolated members of what they see as a hostile and terrifying society. Others are embraced by ethnic communities that provide the sort of financial and emotional support Americans long for but fewer and fewer find.[44] Some are the most productive members of American society by any definition.

The same technologies that enable a global commercial culture of American origin to penetrate traditional societies and to overwhelm local cultures make it easier for ethnic minorities in America to preserve their cultural identities. Thanks to satellite communication, Taiwanese in Texas can gather around the TV and watch their favorite programs from back home. At neighborhood video stores and ethnic restaurants, new immigrants can rent the hit movies of Mexico, Brazil, India, the Philippines, and Vietnam. Vietnamese "boat people" who arrived penniless in the United States were so eager to have a television and VCR that they would often scrape together the money a few weeks after arrival. Street vendors, ethnic-based churches, clubs, and restaurants transplant distant cultures and transform the landscape in suburbia.

The new immigration, like those before it, enriches, fertilizes, and renews the older American community, but it also subjects it to strain just when the sinews of nationhood are fraying for all sorts of other reasons. The arrival of Latinos in large numbers has transformed the once-depressed inner-city Adams-Morgan neighborhood in Washington, D.C., into a lively center of ethnic music, sidewalk stands, and markets. The restaurants, boutiques, and parking lots do a brisk tourist business. But in a time of high unemployment, many African-Americans, who make up 65 percent of the population of the nation's capital, resent the success of the newcomers. Even those at the top of the society, though they increasingly depend on immigrants to look after their babies, to do their washing, and to fix their cars, feel inconvenienced by the babble of foreign tongues. Senator Robert Byrd complains that he cannot understand the Russian auto mechanic at the repair shop he has patronized for years. Elementary-school teachers complain that the children of the new immigrants are not learning English. Increasingly, the sound of conversation on the Washington, D.C., Metro has turned into a polyglot hum; the employees of Giant, the largest food chain in the area, speak twenty different languages. (The company has added signs in Vietnamese and Spanish in forty-five of its stores.) In Miami, three out of four residents speak a language other than English at home. In New York City, 41 percent of the residents speak a foreign language in their homes; 40 percent of the people in Los Angeles are foreign-born. For the nation as a whole, according to the 1990 census, the figure is 32 million.[45]

"Multiculturalism" has become a heated political issue in the United States, Britain, France, Germany, and other industrial countries that have received large immigrant populations. The new immigrants are largely nonwhite, and increasingly they are insisting that their cultures be studied and honored. The United States is approaching the time when it will no longer be a white country of primarily European origin. In important metropolitan centers such as Miami and Los Angeles this is already true. But power, money, and status still overwhelmingly belong to the descendants of European immigrants.

Britain is a small island with its own ethnic minorities—even after more than 900 years of British rule the Welsh have refused to become English—and, like the United States, the former world empire is facing a cultural crisis because of the nonwhite immigration of recent years. In a time of ethnic politics and multiracial immigration, national identity is becoming a more confusing idea. A school principal in an English state school, where daily Christian prayers are a long tradition, could not conceal her fury as she recalled for us the terrible moment when an Indian student dared ask for class time to talk about the *Bhagavad Gita* and chant Indian prayers. "We will lose our culture. The foreigners in our midst should do in Rome as the Romans do." British laborers were infuriated when a Sikh worker was excused from wearing a hard hat because his religion required him to wear his turban, and the matter became one more symbol of loss. In Germany neo-Nazis resorted to fire and murder against Turkish immigrants, and the government deported large numbers of Gypsies. A civilized society ought to be able to accommodate cultural differences and be enriched by the languages, music, and customs of many countries. But in bad economic times, when native-born citizens are unsure of their own place in society, the polyglot hum takes on a threatening tone.

Mass migration is an obvious strategy for poor countries with large unemployed populations and little else to export. But there are costs. The men and women who rise to the challenge of jobs abroad are likely to be the more intelligent and the most self-confident, entrepreneurial, and adventurous among the working population. These are precisely some of the qualities most needed by developing countries. The negative impact of losing skilled workers and professionals is obvious. The term "brain drain" usually refers to the loss of doctors, teachers, and engineers, but the loss of people lower down on the job-skills ladder who are healthy enough, energetic enough, and resourceful enough to make their way to a foreign society also takes its toll.

CHAPTER THREE

THE TRANSFORMED WORKPLACE

I.

THE GEOGRAPHICAL SPREAD OF PRODUCTIVE FACILITIES HAS been accompanied by far-reaching changes in the workplace all over the world. Union power has steadily eroded in the last twenty years for many reasons, but the most important has been the increasing difficulty of protecting the interests of relatively immobile workers in a global economy in which capital is in constant motion. Workers face hardships in pulling up stakes or in leaving the family for a distant job, though more and more people are being faced with the need to do it. But capital has no home, and money in the trillions moves routinely across the world at the punch of a key. Twenty years ago, corporations could shift jobs around the world only in certain light-manufacturing industries, such as textiles and consumer electronics. Today, business enterprises have options to pick and choose workers from all over the world to fill a whole range of agricultural and manufacturing jobs and increasingly service jobs as well. This loosening of geographic ties gives them greatly enhanced power in dealing with organized labor. Automation, the increasing use of part-time labor all across the world, and the opening up of a truly global labor pool have speeded the loss of factory jobs in the industrial world and cut into union membership.

All these changes have so curtailed labor's bargaining power that the strike is no longer an effective weapon except in the rare cases where a union is willing either to risk putting the target company out of business, thereby losing the jobs permanently, or it is desperate enough to put its own survival on the line. In the United States, strikes involving 1,000 workers or more have fallen from an average of 300 a year in the 1960s to forty in 1991.[1] With neither a labor party nor a strong social-democratic tradition in back of it, the U.S. labor movement has been more vulnerable than those of some other industrial countries. In the early Cold War years legislation cut back on union prerogatives won in the New Deal years. The problems of organized labor have been compounded by policies of the federal government that encourage companies to locate plants abroad. By the beginning of the 1990s just 16 percent of the U.S. work force belonged to a union, the lowest percentage anywhere in the industrialized world except for France and Spain.

For almost three decades the power of unions in the United States and Europe was formidable enough to keep hard-won wage gains intact. But beginning in the mid-1970s this changed. Labor governments were voted out of office in what a few years earlier were the most congenial political environments, such as Scandinavia and the Netherlands, and in 1992 the British Labor Party suffered a stunning defeat in the midst of a recession following more than a decade of Conservative rule. In Italy and France, where communist parties used to be the dominant forces in the labor movement, the collapse of these once-formidable political players has left organized labor in a confused and more vulnerable position. Even as early as 1985, an OECD report concluded, "Labor power as measured by union membership and strike activity has fallen to postwar lows in most countries. . . ."[2]

In Japan the unions, thanks to the economic chaos and the democratization policies of the occupation, wielded considerable power right after World War II, but since the mid-1950s they have become essentially company unions; wages are set in an amicable "spring offensive," a nationwide collective-bargaining ritual culminating in what is really a prenegotiated national wage adjustment. Labor relations are smoothed by efforts on both sides to establish an atmosphere of trust and to involve workers in workplace decisions. This makes factories more tolerable for workers with lifetime employment, despite the long hours and great stress under which they work. Permanent workers, however, are becoming a shrinking and increasingly less-secure segment of the total labor force as the Japanese economy loses steam. The prevailing culture of workplace cooperation diminishes the attraction of unions. Japanese unions and the employers' association have each made a videotape on labor relations that they show visitors. The two are virtually identical, and each could comfortably screen the other's as its own.

The wide range of options open to employers to relocate, restructure, reorganize, and redefine work in the midst of a worldwide economic slowdown has made it necessary for unions to change their traditional adversarial tactics. Mass production ushered in the era of strong unions and plentiful, steady jobs. Lean production and "just in time" inventory control are designed to reduce the number of steady jobs. Larger numbers of workers who are hired by suppliers and contract operations are on tap when needed, and most are not paid when they are not needed. In the executive suite, labor is regarded as a commodity and as a cost. This has always been the case. But in the flood tide of the mass-production era even corporations like Ford that had engaged in aggressive union-busting activities came to understand the advantages of making long-term arrangements with unions. Organized labor could be counted on to provide skilled workers at a price that could be kept stable for a term of years. The union, though it pushed wages higher, was in a position to smooth over problems caused by periodic layoffs and to maintain peace in the workplace. Auto companies would bargain hard over sharing the fruits of rising productivity with workers, but before the effects of global competition hit the industry, it was assumed by all parties that wages would keep going up. How otherwise could Ford workers keep buying Fords?

In the 1970s, however, the Detroit Big Three, reacting to global competition, became persuaded that high labor costs and an overvalued dollar were the prime reasons that foreign imports assembled with cheap labor were now grabbing ever larger shares of the market. The companies now had greatly increased bargaining power in labor negotiations, thanks to the increased flexibility offered by globalized production. As it became easier through advances in technology to transmit skills to inexperienced workers in low-wage countries and the number of essential core workers in the U.S. auto industry declined, the companies felt less and less commitment to protect the jobs of long-term workers.

In the United States what happens to workers when they lose their

jobs is largely the individual's responsibility, and to the extent prescribed by law, the government's. The United Auto Workers (UAW),
however, was able to negotiate substantial support from the automakers for retraining and retirement benefits for laid-off workers
that cost GM alone about $3 billion in the early 1990s. But usually
protection for American workers when companies eliminate jobs
falls far short of what exists in Germany and in a number of other
countries.

The global options now open to car companies under increasing
pressure of global competition hit skilled workers the hardest. They
were living out Henry Ford's dream, earning $25 an hour or more
with houses in the suburbs and children in school. Financially and
psychologically, they were tied to a place. The Ford Motor Company,
on the other hand, could shift production by simply buying, building,
or renting a plant somewhere else in the world or by concluding a
transnational deal. Ford and its competitors made it clear to the
UAW that if the union refused to make wage and other concessions
to keep the industry competitive, plants in the United States would be
closed.

Between 1979 and 1989 membership in the union fell by 500,000,
about a third of its total. Part of this loss occurred when the Canadian affiliates left the UAW, but the loss of membership was a blow.
Beginning in 1982 the UAW adopted a less adversarial labor-relations
strategy. In return for job security for the core workers who remained, the union recognized a shared responsibility for keeping the
Big Three competitive. In turn, the companies agreed not to close any
more plants than were agreed upon in the contract. It was clear to
both the unions and the carmakers that global competition required
a much greater degree of cooperation for their mutual survival.

The auto industry offers a particularly dramatic example of a more
general phenomenon. As recourse to the global labor pool became
easier for corporations, there was a downward pressure on wages in
all the long-established industrial economies. This trend hit the
United States especially hard. In the OECD countries real wages
actually dipped for a couple of years during the recession at the
beginning of the 1980s, but unlike the United States, this was a
short-term blip. Higher wages came at the price of higher unemployment, the European unions understood, but they counted on liberal
government benefits to protect the unemployed. In recent years take-
home pay in Europe has not increased significantly, thanks to aus-

terity programs, the imposition of strict limits on cost-of-living indexes, and wage ceilings in countries such as Denmark, Italy, and France. Nonetheless, measured by the purchasing power the average worker can generate in an hour, employees in Sweden and the Netherlands earn 15 percent more than what a U.S. worker earns. For workers in manufacturing the disparities are even greater. A production worker in a West German plant takes home 30 percent more than what his U.S. counterpart receives. Because of the strong yen, Japanese industrial workers now make among the highest wages, as calculated in international purchasing power. However, food, housing, and consumer products cost much more in Japan and in many other industrial countries, and so the bigger paychecks do not necessarily provide a higher standard of living even in societies with liberal government subsidies for health and retirement benefits.[3]

II.

On his visits to Japan in the 1980s, Ford CEO Donald Petersen discovered what he calls "the real secret" of Japan's industrial success. The Japanese companies "organized their people into teams, trained their workers with the skills they needed, and gave them the power to do their jobs properly."[4] The top executives of all three Detroit automakers began to see that the culture of cooperative labor relations that prevails in Japan, Germany, and other advanced industrial countries had something to do with their success in producing better cars with fewer costly errors along the way. Highly skilled workers who feel humiliated, ignored, or degraded have many opportunities to subvert the production process, and this they are known to do, sometimes consciously, sometimes not.

Since the 1970s, ideas for reorganizing work to make it more human while making it more efficient had been circulating in a number of industrial and service corporations. Auto factories were prime candidates since the price of a good job on the assembly line was a boring, stressful life in an ear-shattering, high-speed environment. As its power began to weaken, the UAW agreed to experiment in bringing some Japanese-style notions of team production to the factory floor. The strategy of building mutual trust between workers and managers changed the atmosphere in those plants where managers took workers' needs and feelings seriously. They became happier places to work, and the quality of the cars reflected it. The team concept was an essential component of lean production, and the new buzzword on the shop floor was "jointness."

There are a number of different ideas involved in lean production. One is job rotation. Each worker is given more than a single repetitive task to perform; workers become expert in accomplishing many different operations. Another is that worker teams take greater responsibility for the production process, for insuring quality, for managing their own schedules, and for assigning work to one another. The role of supervisors is reduced, and worker teams are encouraged to take pride in the product and to feel part of the corporate family. The worker recovers some of the autonomy of the craftsman lost long ago on the assembly line. Though workers have the opportunity to do more than one job, the high-speed pressures for each task are as stressful as ever, sometimes more so.

These innovations in the culture of mass production often contributed to the improved productivity in U.S. auto plants. But the team concept was oversold in the business press. Some autoworkers in the United States became "multiskilled" and felt that they enjoyed more freedom to control their work, but many did not. Others felt that the only real change was that they were working harder than ever. The "mind-numbing stress" of mass production had by no means disappeared, and the notion of "comfortable factories" was still an oxymoron. A 1990 survey of UAW workers at the Mazda assembly plant in Flat Rock, Michigan, for example, found that only one out of seven workers "said that they could consistently count on their supervisor . . . to implement the company philosophy of participatory management," and that lean production, with its emphasis on eliminating wasted motion and filling idle time, meant that workers had to work faster and harder. In a poll of workers in the Mazda plant, over 70 percent subscribed to the statement "If the present level of work intensity continues, I will likely be injured or worn out before I retire."[5]

At the state-of-the-art Ford plant at Wixom, Michigan, that produces Lincoln Continentals, Town Cars, and Mark VIIIs, many aspects of lean production have been introduced. Because of computerized just-in-time production methods, all sorts of parts arrive at the plant within an hour of when they are needed, and seldom do components sit around more than a week and a half. The plant manager boasts that the 4.2-million-square-foot factory has no more than $3 million tied up in inventory; twenty years ago it was more like $20 million. But the plant seldom tries job rotation because it is too expensive to train workers to manage the robots that install the engines, delicately drop the windshields into place, spray multiple coats of paint, and weld body parts under flying sparks. The best and most experienced workers get the favored jobs and generally keep them. But workers are encouraged to take the initiative to catch errors early in the production process, and some worker suggestions are adopted. The plant manager told us that a special robot was designed to install the sixty-pound carpets that line every Lincoln because workers complained that repetitive lifting was taking a toll on their backs.

The team concept has not turned postmodern factories into a workers' paradise, but it has been a factor in achieving stunning productivity increases in some cases. Toyota and GM introduced the team concept in their joint venture in Fremont, California. According to a 1985 internal video for GM managers, it took only fourteen hours of direct labor for worker teams to turn out a Nova; in the same plant before the merger with Toyota, a roughly equivalent car took twenty-two hours. But some unionists argue that the team concept is just a way to exact more work. How effective or fair these innovations are depends almost wholly on the commitment of managers and workers to create a better, more cooperative working environment.[6] The introduction of the team concept into U.S. auto plants permitted management to eliminate unneeded jobs once protected by union power, but the key to greater productivity and peace in the workplace is a sense of mutual trust between managers and workers. This can be achieved with or without teams.

Ford executives point out that one consequence of world economic integration is that recessions now overlap in many parts of the world. When the company has trouble selling cars in all its major markets, the drive to increase labor productivity and to cut costs becomes more intense. As the balance of power in the labor market has shifted against the unions, they have felt compelled to give greater due to management's overriding interest in cost-cutting and productivity and less to their traditional concerns with employee benefits and job security. Some unionists charge the UAW with selling out, but they offer no more convincing strategy for protecting American autoworkers in a world in which auto companies have the capacity to produce several million more cars each year than consumers have either the inclination or the funds to drive off the lot.

III.

The massive layoffs of the early 1990s soured the atmosphere in GM, Ford, and Chrysler plants in the United States and Canada. The prospect of more plant closings had a chilling effect on workers; yet even though auto-industry jobs were becoming increasingly less secure, there was no significant revival of labor militancy in the United States. In the boom years of the auto industry, federal and state governments in effect subsidized the carmakers' strategies for cost-cutting and streamlining production by providing unemployment benefits. But some of the same economic pressures rooted in global competition that have prompted U.S. automakers to cut payrolls have also forced government to cut back on support for unemployed workers. The unions have looked to Congress for legislative help in curbing strikebreaking tactics, but none has been forthcoming. Here again global competition is used as a powerful argument against more government intervention to protect what remains of the bargaining power of organized labor.

In March 1992, after suffering an $8.7-billion loss from its North American car business, at the time the largest one-year loss in U.S. corporate history, GM announced that it was closing its Willow Run plant at Ypsilanti, Michigan, along with twenty other plants in the United States and Canada, all with the announced purpose of eliminating 74,000 jobs.[7] GM executives declared that they would close either the Ypsilanti plant or a plant in Arlington, Texas. A 1988 internal "plant competitiveness" study at GM had given Willow Run a 4.1 rating on a five-point scale and the Texas plant only a 1.5, mostly because of high shipping costs. But GM opted for the Texas plant because they could absorb the Michigan workers more easily in other plants and thereby avoid high retraining and moving costs required by their contract with the UAW. But there was another important consideration. The Texas workers had agreed to a three-shift, round-the-clock production schedule without overtime pay. In announcing the decision, GM chairman Robert C. Stempel warned GM workers in other plants that similar "innovative labor agreements and work arrangements" would influence the company's decisions about which plants to close in the future. Employees were now on notice that a plant offering a compliant work force was much more likely to stay open.

Worker solidarity was the principle on which the industrial unions were built. But increasingly, flexible production made it possible for the companies to shave their labor costs by pitting workers in one plant against workers in another, even when they belonged to the same union. As part of its 1992 plan for massive plant closings, GM decided to shut down its Flint, Michigan, V-8 engine plant that had been hailed as a model of labor-management teamwork in the new era of lean production. Workers set their own production schedules, their own hours, and decided themselves on the number of hands needed to do a job. The company had promoted this plant (as well as others previously closed) as an example of the productivity increases that flow from giving workers responsibility and challenge, and these claims were fully justified. The peremptory announcement that the plant would close provoked howls of protest from workers and from some UAW officials. But there was little the union could do about it. Despite the cooperation of the unions, the export of jobs from the industrial heartland of the United States to low-wage countries continued.

The Mexican workforce is young and eager, and U.S. companies find the low wages irresistible. A welder at Chrysler's Sterling Heights, Michigan, plant with seventeen years service earns $16 an hour and substantial benefits. A welder at the Chrysler plant at Toluca, Mexico, with five years service is delighted to receive $1.75 an hour, vacation pay, a Christmas bonus, and a subsidized lunch that costs about a penny. (Starting pay is $1 an hour, attractive-sounding pay in a country that has witnessed a several-hundred-percent devaluation of its currency in recent years.) At GM's plant at Ramos Arizpe, judged by *Business Week* to be the giant automaker's number-one plant in the world, workers switch jobs with agility, act as tough taskmasters for one another, and work long hours to the accompaniment of recorded songs of fellow workers celebrating quality welding and tight-fitting parts.[8]

The country has a history of largely nonconfrontational unions. The Confederation of Mexican Workers (CTM), which represents about 90 percent of Mexico's organized work force, is a pillar of the ruling party, the PRI, that has governed Mexico without interruption since the 1930s. It has neither the interest nor the power to make life difficult for corporations wooed by government promises of a cooperative, hardworking labor force. The U.S. auto companies were careful not simply to close a plant in the United States and open an identical one in Mexico. The transfer of jobs was a more subtle process. The automakers carried out largely nontraceable shifts in production to widely dispersed company facilities and contractors within the United States and abroad, and runs in plants already established in Mexico were increased.

Harley Shaiken, a University of California professor who is a specialist on the impact of automation on employment, conducted a five-year intensive study of Ford plants in Mexico, to which he was granted unusual access. (A condition of his study was that he not name the company, but we have ascertained independently that Ford facilities were the subject of his research.) For an investment of $250 million, Ford built a state-of-the-art engine factory at Chihuahua that can turn out 400,000 engines with what Professor Shaiken calls a "slender" 1,100-member work force. The plant is divided into "a labor-intensive assembly line" and four capital-intensive "transfer lines, each as big as a football field. . . ."[9] The labor force brought in to work the plant was young and literate, but untrained. Ford elected to install the most advanced technology and to use sophisticated training methods to instruct the workers how to use it rather than to put in less complex, more labor-intensive machines, which had been the normal practice. The company could be picky about whom to hire. "Some 3000 people applied for the 250 production jobs" Ford needed for start-up, Shaiken writes, "and 1500 applied for 125 skilled jobs."[10]

The plant boasts laser-guided precision drilling tools, automated tools to hone parts to tolerances up to ten times thinner than a human hair, 100-foot machine complexes, some over a story tall, and a computer-controlled line turning out 150 cylinder blocks an hour with only sixteen human beings in attendance. Clearly, training is the critical component in making this marriage of a low-wage labor force and highly automated capital-intensive machinery work. The initial training is performed at a local technical college. Workers are called *becarios* or scholarship students, and when they graduate, they receive diplomas and Ford's blue-and-white uniform and are addressed as "operators" or "technicians."[11]

Managers, engineers, and outside specialists are brought in to supervise, train, and solve problems resulting from the workers' inexperience and lack of skill. But Ford assiduously avoids the practice common in the United States of treating new workers as apprentices to senior workers, fearing that old hands will "bring traditional attitudes and work practices into the plant." The union has virtually no say about what happens on the shop floor. Ford is able to pay wages one-half of what it paid in its older Mexican plants, and to slash benefits by two-thirds. "As far as I'm concerned," one U.S. manager put it, "there is no union here."[12]

Ford's high-tech assembly facility at Hermosillo in northern Mexico is the showcase plant celebrated in the MIT study discussed earlier. Originally, about 65 percent of the parts came from Japan, but by the early 1990s a majority of the components were produced in North America. It is Ford's best plant in North America, with a quality level and productivity rate surpassing all Japanese competitors except for the Honda Civic. A virtual clone of the most advanced Mazda plant in Japan, the Hermosillo plant, Shaiken reports, was paying its workers $2 an hour in wages and benefits compared with $30 in Detroit, a saving of $672 in hourly labor costs per vehicle.[13]

In 1987 Ford responded to a strike in its twenty-three-year-old plant in Cuautitlán on the outskirts of Mexico City by closing the factory for a few weeks and then reopening it with a new pay scale about half what it was. Henry Ford once said that history is bunk; more than forty years after his death, the Ford Motor Company abolished history at the Cuautitlán plant; when the plant reopened, rehired workers had lost all seniority rights and pension credits. The workers were infuriated, and support for a radical alternative to the official union grew. As protests mounted, the workers were assured by the leadership of the Confederation of Mexican Workers that a new union election would be held in 1990.

Instead, more than a hundred armed men hired by the CTM were given access to the plant, and issued uniforms and ID badges. The idea was to intimidate the workers, not injure them, but once inside some of the goons opened fire on unsuspecting workers who were waiting at their work stations until the company agreed to the election. One worker was killed and eight were wounded. Despite Ford's denial of involvement in the incident, an investigating committee that included the archbishop of Hermosillo concluded that Ford was complicit in the attack on the workers. It attached to its report records showing that the company had put the thugs on the payroll (using falsified social-security identification numbers) two days before the incident—and that it discharged them all soon after.

IV.

For all the mounting job insecurity and downward pressures on their pay, Ford, Toyota, and Volkswagen workers are still among the privileged elite of the Global Workplace. The majority of human beings who stand over assembly lines or sit at workbenches around the world are engaged in light manufacturing—mostly such consumer goods as television sets, calculators, radios, shirts, suits, belts, ties, underwear, shoes, sneakers, toys, and luggage—and by and large they labor under worse conditions than exist in auto plants and other heavy industries, and they earn considerably less money. Much of this work is done in export processing zones. These enclaves in developing countries, which are designed to generate foreign exchange, are usually not otherwise integrated into the local economy.

Almost 4 million workers are employed in these factories across the world. More than 2.6 million are women. Almost half of this global work force is in the special economic zones of China. Even here they operate under their own rules and customs, which often are at odds with the prevailing economic culture in the rest of the country. In subtropical islands of Southeast Asia and the Caribbean, assemblers, weavers, and processors, young females mostly, are still selling their labor for as little as fifteen cents an hour, a state of affairs long past in Taiwan and Korea. There are well over 175 such manufacturing centers around the world that attract not only corporations of U.S., European, or Japanese origin, but also firms from Korea, Taiwan, and Hong Kong. Governments of poor countries with massive unemployment on their hands attract global companies to their shores with tax holidays, subsidies, duty-free entry of raw materials, and a strike-free environment.

Foreign manufacturers, mostly from Japan and Europe, set up factories in the United States in the 1980s as the superpower became a marketplace for relatively cheap labor. Mostly, foreign corporations wished to establish themselves inside the world's largest market, but the increasingly advantageous labor costs were an additional attraction. Wages in the United States were falling in real terms, and the decline of the dollar made it cheaper still for foreign companies to meet payrolls in America. Much of this new foreign investment is in small industrial centers in border states like Tennessee and Kentucky and in the Deep South. The highest concentration of foreign investment is in South Carolina, which is now home to 185 non-U.S. companies. BMW is likely to pay around $12 an hour in South Carolina rather than the $28 it has to pay in Germany.[14]

Dothan, Alabama, is a hundred-year-old community set in the southeastern corner of Alabama. This small city with a population of about 50,000 advertises itself as the "Peanut Capital of the World." A quarter of all peanuts grown in the United States come from within a seventy-five-mile radius. The National Peanut Festival draws

200,000 visitors every year who come to witness the coronation of the Peanut Queen. Agriculture is still the largest economic activity in the Dothan area, but since the 1970s the town has made itself into a small industrial park.

After Sony opened its first factory in the United States in 1972, a large television plant in San Diego, the company began to look for a site to locate a second factory to make audio- and videotapes, two of Sony's big sellers around the world. A site-selection team from Tokyo traveled about the country collecting attractive offers from such cities as Dallas, Nashville, and Tallahassee. Just as Sony was about to decide on Tallahassee, the Dothan city fathers heard about it and quickly devised a plan to lure the plant to the Peanut Capital. A team of local Chamber of Commerce and state officials requested an audience at which they presented irresistible incentives for coming to Dothan. The executive vice-president at the plant, Barry Singletary, recalls that the most persuasive aspects of the offer were these: excellent weather; cheap land; an abundance of workers with a good "work ethic"; a state industrial development bond with substantial tax benefits; and free training for workers offered by the Alabama industrial development training organization worth in itself about $1 million. In 1976 Sony broke ground for what is now a million-square-foot factory employing 1,400 workers. The company has invested well over $100 million in its Dothan plant.

Other non-U.S. firms have come to Dothan, including Michelin, which has a large tire plant a mile or so from the Sony plant, but Sony is by far the largest industrial employer in the area. The plant operates around the clock to produce over 60 million videocassettes, 55 million audiocassettes, and tens of millions more floppy disks a year. Production is closely coordinated with a twin-plant Maquila operation in Laredo, Texas, and Nuevo Laredo, Mexico, employing 2,000 workers. Although a small team of Japanese engineers has come to Dothan, research and development on products produced at the plant is still concentrated in Japan.

Dothan is not easy to get to, but the plant management is in constant communication with headquarters in Japan. They also exchange information with Sony plants making the same products in France, Italy, and Japan. Sony officials told us that labor costs are cheaper in Dothan than in Japan or Europe. Alabama is a "right to work" state, and Dothan civic leaders proudly offer foreign firms a union-free atmosphere. There have been several attempts to form unions at Sony's plant in Dothan, but none came even close to succeeding. In one case, Sony officials told us, a covert union organizer managed to slip by company interviewers and was hired, but when he started soliciting workers, they complained to management and he left town.

The work force is about equally divided between men and women. About 80 percent of the workers are white, which roughly reflects the racial balance in the immediate Dothan area, and the overwhelming majority are from hardworking, religious farm families. (Dothan's 130 churches are matched in number only by the banks that dot the city, often next door to a church.) Wages and benefits are good for the area. The average hourly wage is $10.40, and this is supplemented by liberal benefits including profit-sharing, pensions, and a program under which the company matches workers' savings up to a point. Sony employees have a choice of working eight- or twelve-hour shifts. Workers on the twelve-hour shifts receive two fifteen-minute breaks and a twenty-minute lunch period. When we asked one woman in her mid-30s whether she had children, she laughed and said that she was much too busy; after three days of twelve-hour shifts her interests were sleep, her dog, and her boyfriend—in that order.

Sony is the third-largest taxpayer in the community. The company tries to purchase as much of its raw materials in the United States as it can, preferably in Alabama, but over half of its inputs, mostly chemicals, come from Japan. Sony officials say that U.S. suppliers often cannot satisfy Sony's exacting technical requirements but that their technicians are working hard to find ways to use more local materials. Sony seeks to be a highly visible community booster, and Akio Morita himself has come on several occasions to play that role. Local company officials are regularly photographed at presentation ceremonies in town, giving away videotapes and color televisions or making small contributions to the Boy Scouts or the March of Dimes, altogether about $200,000 a year.

Twice a week Sony delivers large quantities of defective tapes and floppy disks to a local center for the mentally handicapped. With the aid of electric screwdrivers supplied by Sony, workers disassemble and sort the various components, which are then shipped to recycling centers. As a result, what used to be waste material destined for the landfill can now be used again, and the workers take pride in being useful and able to earn small amounts of money.

Sony executives in Dothan, including those from Japan, insist that this conservative community has no negative feelings about a Japanese company in their midst. In what not so long ago was among the most racially segregated corners of America, Japanese engineers are welcomed at the Dothan Country Club. One employee remembers that her father, a World War II veteran, was angry when she told him she was going to work for a Japanese company, but this has not been a problem for years. Sony is a mainstay of Dothan, and many local citizens do not even know that the company is Japanese. The president of the Chamber of Commerce makes regular trips to Japan to seek out new investors.

Tapes and floppy disks are by no means the most sophisticated products Sony makes, but the Dothan plant is heavily automated. In the department where the plastic for cassettes and floppy disks is molded, a large overhead sign proclaims "People, Pride, Performance." But there are few people in sight. The handful of human beings on the floor are mostly technicians who check the machines and program the robots that do most of the work here. The assembly line for audiocassettes is made up of row upon row of machines, each feeding the next. Just a few years ago almost twenty workers were needed to operate the machines that wind the tape coming off giant spools onto each cassette and to make the appropriate cuts. Today one person presides over this fully automated operation. Nearby, an automated forklift silently lumbers down the aisle. Suddenly it veers off to the side toward the storage area. A steel pincer, obedient to the unseen computer controlling its every movement, reaches out to pluck a small box of parts from a high shelf and heads for Work Station 18. The only old-fashioned manual labor on the entire line we could discern was at the end of the process; a worker collects the neatly boxed tapes and places them in a larger box for shipment.

We asked Sony officials whether the company could continue to be a mainstay of the Dothan economy given its need for fewer and fewer workers to produce cassettes in ever greater quantities. In the past Sony has managed to avoid laying off workers by finding new markets for expanded production, and executives assume that this will continue. But the work force in Dothan is expected to be trimmed somewhat. New workers will be hired only as others retire, leave, or are dismissed for cause. The jobs in Dothan will be secure only if Sony succeeds in increasing its share of the global tape and floppy-disk markets. In its pursuit of this goal, quality control is a passion. Not even a microscopic speck of lint must light on the spools of tape during the production process for fear that it might compromise even a millisecond of sound. For this reason all persons on the floor must take air showers and wear special protective clothing. These hygienic precautions are stricter than those customarily in place to protect sick babies in newborn nurseries or the critically ill in intensive care units.

V.

Despite automation, there is still much work left for human hands. Especially female hands. "The manual dexterity of the oriental female is famous the world over." So begins the siren song of a Malaysian investment brochure of the late 1970s. "Her hands are small and she works fast with extreme care. Who therefore could be better qualified by nature and inheritance to contribute to the efficiency of a bench-assembly production line than an oriental girl? . . . Female factory workers can be hired for approximately US$1.50 a day."[15] In 1990 a private business group in El Salvador placed an ad in *Bobbin*, the magazine of the U.S. spinning industry, singing the same tune. It was a celebration of young, attractive Rosa Martinez, pictured at her sewing machine: "You can hire her for 57 cents an hour. Rosa is more than just colorful. She and her co-workers are known for their industriousness, reliability, and quick learning." The business group that sponsored the ad received 94 percent of its budget from the U.S. Agency for International Development, just one more example of government financial incentives for U.S. companies to locate factories outside the United States.[16]

Nike is the number-one maker of sport shoes in the world. Founded in 1964 by Philip Knight, a former University of Oregon accounting student and running enthusiast, the company sells $2 billion worth of basketball, track, and running shoes a year. In 1990 Nike had 40 percent of the basketball-shoe market in the United States. In the 1980s Nike stock, of which Knight himself owns more than 90 percent, jumped almost 600 percent in value. Its headquarters in Beaverton, Oregon, is made up of a series of low buildings each named for a sports superstar like Michael Jordan, Joan Benoit, John McEnroe, Alberto Salazar, and others whose promotional efforts were critical in propelling Nike to the top.[17] From this complex, surrounded by $1 million worth of Japanese cherry trees, Nike executives preside over a global network of production facilities around the world, only a few of which Nike owns.[18] As Neal Lauridsen, vice-president for Asia, puts it, "We don't know the first thing about manufacturing. We are marketers and designers."

Virtually 100 percent of Nike's shoe assembly is in Asia. In the last five years the company has closed down twenty production sites in South Korea and Taiwan as wages have risen and opened up thirty-five new ones in China, Indonesia, and Thailand, where wages are rock bottom. The company has a global payroll of over 8,000, virtually all in management, sales, promotion, and advertising. The actual production is in the hands of about 75,000 Asian contractors.[19]

Along with Reebok and some other large global distributors of high-price running and tennis shoes, Nike purchases a significant share of the sporting shoes it distributes around the world from contractors in Indonesia. Four of the plants are owned by South Korean companies that formerly made the shoes in Korea, and two are local Indonesian enterprises. Nikes made in Indonesia cost $5.60 to produce, and sell on the average in North America and Europe for $73 and as much as $135.[20] The Indonesian girls who sew them can earn as little as fifteen cents an hour. (A 1991 survey of Nike-licensed plants reported in *Indonesia Today* put the average wage for an experienced female worker at $.82 a day.[21]) Overtime is often mandatory, and after an eleven-hour day that begins at 7:30 A.M. the girls return to the company barracks at 9:15 P.M. to collapse into bed, having earned as much as $2.00 if they are lucky.

A research institute in Bandung and the Asian-American Free Labor Institute complained that Nike was profiting from the exploitation of Indonesian workers. "Exploitation?" John Woodman, Nike's general manager in Indonesia, responded to an American journalist. "Yes, they are low wages. But we've come in here and given jobs to thousands of people who wouldn't be working otherwise."[22] The statement is undoubtedly true. But it neatly skirts the fundamental human-rights issue raised by these production arrangements that are now spreading all across the world. In the free-trade zone near the Colombo International Airport in Sri Lanka, to give an example that could be duplicated in almost any poor country, the textile factories have served as magnets drawing young women from distant villages. The Australian reporter Peter Mares reports what they experience when they come:

> . . . they barely earned enough to survive; there was no spare earning to send back home as they expected. Sleeping six or more to a tiny

room with one tap and one toilet for 30 or 40 women, they told me stories of sexual harassment, of repetitive strain injury, of eye problems and respiratory diseases caused by poor working conditions and hours of enforced overtime. If they return to their home villages, their chances of marriage are damaged by the reputation of sexual promiscuity that is attached to women who go on their own to the city. . . . "We have nowhere to go," one woman told me. "I feel like a refugee in my own land."[23]

In Indonesia the reserve army of the unemployed is vast. Two and a half million people enter the labor market each year; most end up without jobs. Foreign investors eager to employ what government brochures call "nimble fingers" can set their own terms, for they know that the government is so eager to have their factories that it will usually wink at violations of the minimal labor standards on the books. The consequence is that desperately poor people can be induced to make a high-margin product at less than a living wage. (The minimum wage for a seven-hour day in Indonesia is $1.06, but the Labor Ministry calculates that $1.22 is required to meet a worker's "minimum physical needs.")[24] According to the Institut Teknologi Bandung, the shoe factories often pay below the minimum wage.

Some workers know that they are being exploited. Enny, a worker at Nagasakti Para shoes, told Adam Schwarz of the *Far Eastern Economic Review* that the workers "are terrified" of the South Korean managers. "They yell at us when we don't make the production quotas and if we talk back they cut our wages." (Enny earns $7.70 for a fifty-hour workweek.)[25] But for others, possibly the majority, exploitation is not a category they easily comprehend because the alternatives are so bleak. Riyanti, a worker at an Indonesian-owned plant who works unbelievably long hours for unbelievably low pay, tells a foreign reporter, "I am happy working here. I can make money and I can make friends." The company provides meals.[26]

Some Indonesian officials and a few union activists are appalled by the working conditions; angry workers in all six factories producing Nikes, Reeboks, and the more downscale L.A. Gear point to violations of labor regulations. The South Korean managers are particularly brutal, in part because they are frustrated by the gentle, easygoing ways of the Indonesians, who are much less money-driven than Korean workers. Lee In Jae, the managing director of a plant that sells more than 2 million pairs of sport shoes to Nike a year, complains about the lack of discipline and low productivity.

Consumers around the world who are unaware or unconcerned

about the conditions under which they were made are persuaded to part with $60 or $100 for bits of rubber and nylon mesh. In 1990 the wholesale market for athletic shoes of all sorts in the United States was $7.6 billion, although an estimated 80 percent are worn on the street and never make it to the track or the basketball court. This extraordinary popularity of fancy sports footwear is largely due to the aura surrounding these products from endorsements by Michael Jordan and other global sports figures. For promoting Nikes across the globe Jordan reportedly received $20 million in 1992, an amount greater than the entire annual payroll of the Indonesian factories that make them. Asked about labor problems in Nike's contract factories, Woodman answered: "It's not within our scope to investigate." He was aware, he said "of labor disturbances in the six factories that make Nike shoes," but he did not know what they were about and had not asked. "I don't know that I need to know."[27]

One important indication of the increasingly global character of production is the inability (and increasing disinclination) of governments to maintain their own labor standards within their frontiers. The International Labor Organization estimates that informal-sector production—the term economists commonly use for economic activity that is under the table or off the books—accounts for anywhere from 5 to 35 percent of the gross domestic product of the various developing countries for which it has gathered data. Most of this production takes place under exploitative conditions. It would be a mistake to assume that casual workers for global companies are subjected to worse treatment than workers for local enterprises.

Take the Indian cigarette manufacturing industry, for example. According to a study by the Worldwatch Institute, there are an estimated 5 million women making cigarettes at home in India. In Vellore, a city in southern India, Gulzar Begum earns fifty-seven cents a day rolling more than a thousand cigarettes from just before dawn into the evening. The tobacco is rolled and sewed up inside a leaf to make *beedi*, the local cigarettes smoked by India's poor workers. The product is marketed only in India. Since in many parts of India it is not considered seemly for women to work outside the home, the manufacturer's agents deliver the tobacco, collect the cigarettes, and make the payments, but they regularly cheat the poor women either by claiming that cigarettes are missing or by exacting a "penalty" for supposedly shoddy work. There is no recourse. Gulzar Begum and her children have tuberculosis and do not make enough money to get the food they need. That which makes part-time female workers so eminently employable—whether they work for global or local companies—is their availability to work for pennies, and this of course is what keeps them poor.[28]

Bishwapriaya Sanyal, a professor at the Massachusetts Institute of Technology, estimates that 50 percent or more of the urban working population in poor countries is in the informal sector. Some of this activity is criminal. Much of it is innovative, productive, and a source of pride and independence, but poor entrepreneurs and craftsmen feel the pressures to exploit suppliers, family members, and temporary employees. In the face of absurd and contradictory government regulations, corruption, and harassment, poor people in many parts of the world survive by their wits, energy, and entrepreneurial skill. By the side of the road or in the midst of a slum they set up shop—as tailors, barbers, fixers of cars, makers of furniture. In the midst of what is reputed to be the worst slum in Africa, local entrepreneurs in Kenya put up a roof-tile factory that employs 300 women. The primary means of transportation in that country are *matatus*, minibuses owned by small entrepreneurs who pay the drivers by the trip and number of passengers. The predictable result is they are impossibly overcrowded and always speed. The wreckage of overturned *matatus* can be seen on any highway. But for most Kenyans they are the only affordable means of transportation.

Anthropologists, travelers, and journalists give us glimpses of what vast numbers of people working in the informal economy across the world actually do, how many hours a day they do it, and what they can expect to earn. Bloodless bureaucratic terms such as "underemployed," "part-time workers," and "contract employee" conceal a vast population that is uncounted, unregulated, and unprotected. The shadow economy helps to explain why unemployment rates approaching 50 percent, which are commonplace in vast regions spread across the belt of hot, poor countries around the world, result in malnutrition, disease, and misery, but not mass starvation in the hundreds of millions.

VI.

As borders become more porous and more workers migrate, as global corporations farm out more and more of their production and supplier operations to independent contractors all over the world, and as these local entrepreneurs keep slashing labor costs to meet

foreign competition, a certain convergence of pay and working conditions is occurring around the world. We have mentioned the influence of Japanese production innovations on the U.S. and European
car industries. There is a global trend toward greater equalization of
pay, although the gaps remain staggering. Wages in some less-
developed countries are going up, thanks to union organizing, productivity increases, and the manufacturers' marketing skills, and real
wages of American workers are going down, thanks to the weakening of unions and the pressures of global competition.[29]

In boom times globalization has the effect of bringing some poor
countries up; in lean times the trend toward greater equalization
comes about because the economies of the richest countries are depressed. Even in prosperous times workers in rich countries feel the
negative impact of global competition. In the boom years of the
1980s, which coincided with Central American wars and massive
migration from Asia, what *Newsweek* calls "vanquished old-style
sweat shops" opened for business in virtually every major city in the
United States:

> Once again, pieceworkers attach beads to belts in decrepit manufac-
> turing lofts in Manhattan where piles of fabric block fire exits; seam-
> stresses stitching together denim togs in El Paso are denied wages
> when owners make ends meet by stiffing their workers. . . . Most
> sweatshops today, as a century ago, are in the garment trade, where
> cutthroat competition from abroad has made it imperative for makers
> to slash costs.[30]

According to a 1989 Government Accounting Office report, over
half of the 7,000 apparel factories in New York, which employ an
estimated 50,000 workers, are sweatshops. There are 400 garment
shops in Chinatown paying "barely half the union wage."[31] The
International Ladies' Garment Workers' Union reports that a quarter
of the garment workers in California do their cutting and sewing in
airless firetraps for less than the minimum wage, with mandatory
overtime compensated at the same pay scale, and sometimes the boss
just decides not to pay. The workers, mostly foreign, many without
legal immigration status, are not in a good position to complain. An
El Paso jeans factory suddenly closed down one night in May 1990
owing the workers weeks of back wages. Official investigations of
thirty-nine sewing factories in the area ascertained that twenty of
them were in arrears to their workers by as much as $85,000. One

indication of the downward pressure on wages in the United States is the clientele now being served by soup kitchens. In Washington, D.C., a city with a large minority and refugee population, Martha's Table serves thousands of free meals each week; 62 percent of those who stand in line for a cup of soup are part of the growing army of the working poor. In 1993, 18 percent of the U.S. work force was working forty hours a week or more for wages that put them below the poverty line, as defined by the federal government.

The number-one garment company in the world is Levi Strauss. It built up a reputation not only for treating its workers decently but for its generous support of civic and charitable activities, mostly in the San Francisco area. The company devotes 2.5 percent of pretax profits to charitable contributions, much higher than the average among U.S. corporations. In 1990 the 140-year-old company became a family-owned enterprise once again, thanks to junk bonds and the miracle of the leveraged buyout. Levi's products are sold in 70 countries; the brand name is almost as well known as Coke or Marlboro. About a third of Levi Strauss's sales revenue comes from outside the United States. But thanks to global competition, the company has come to feel increasing pressures to cut costs.

In the 1980s the company closed thirty-two of its sixty-six production facilities in the United States, and corporate plans call for accelerating the shift from what its annual report calls "owned-and-operated production" to "fast, flexible, and responsive" production facilities. The company owns only fifteen plants outside the United States, more than half of which are in Europe. In 1992 it opened a $20-million jeans factory in Plock, Poland, a depressed industrial city eager for the 1,000 jobs the factory will generate.[32]

But the investment in Poland with its vast labor pool and promising domestic market for jeans is an exception. For the most part the company is not acquiring factories but is moving rapidly to implement a double-edged global strategy. In its remaining factories it is introducing lean production, in effect adapting the approach of high-skills industry to low-skill jobs. Workers in the reorganized plants no longer wait for a bundle of shirts to arrive at the work station so they can sew on the pockets. Now a team of thirty to fifty workers makes the whole garment, and they, rather than supervisors, decide how to eliminate bottlenecks in the line. The result is that plants that used to take six days to make a bundle of thirty jeans now can do it in seven hours.[33]

At the same time, the company is expanding its network of

contracted-out, "just in time" production. It now has over 600 contractors in more than thirty countries.[34] In 1990, to give just one example of the new company strategy, Levi Strauss closed a sewing plant in San Antonio with a work force of 1,100 earning an average of $5.57 an hour and moved the production to the Dominican Republic. In 1990, the company proudly reported that 90 percent of its jeans sold in the United States were still being made in the United States. But Peter Thigpen, senior vice-president, telegraphed the company's plans for the new decade: "American consumers value high quality, style, and price—and don't care too much where the garments come from."[35]

In 1991 it came to light that some of the contractors selected by such leading retailers as Sears and Levi Strauss had subcontracted with Chinese prisons to produce consumer goods for the U.S. market. Stung by union charges of exploiting "slave labor," they have established corporate codes of conduct promising not to sell prison-made goods, which is a federal crime. (The penalty for knowingly importing prison-made goods is $1,000.) Sears has promised to conduct surprise inspections of facilities in China and to secure pledges that its suppliers do not use "gulag labor." Levi Strauss has launched a global audit of all its contract suppliers around the world and has drawn up plans to visit each one. It has dropped a Saipan supplier that was imposing slavelike working conditions on imported Chinese workers, and is gradually pulling operations out of China on human-rights grounds.[36]

The voluntary codes and audits establish an important principle of corporate responsibility. But until such codes are expanded and toughened, U.S. consumers will continue to wear blouses, jeans, trousers, shirts, and underwear sewn by women and children who must submit to indignities and abuse that violate the most elementary standards of decency. In the late 1980s clothing became Guatemala's number-two export. There are some 250 apparel assembly operations in Guatemala that supply leading U.S. retailers such as Sears, Gap, and Kmart. The Reverend Thomas E. Trimmer of the Episcopal diocese of Michigan visited a Maquila in Guatemala City and reported on the working conditions:

> In order to go to the bathroom, a woman needs a pass from her supervisor, which may involve sexual favors. Many women have been beaten and sexually abused. One factory [foreman] regularly beats women on the stomach every 15 days to weed out those who may be

pregnant. . . . Some plants actually padlock their doors to keep people from leaving until 2 to 3 A.M.[37]

In the Philippines, according to a study of subcontracting in the garment industry in the town of Angono just south of Manila, 1,447 children are employed in sewing, stitching, or packing baby dresses. The typical work week is seventy-seven hours, 7:00 A.M. to 7:00 P.M. seven days a week (with an hour off for lunch.) Four-to-six-year-olds receive five pesos a day; an 11-year-old can earn as much as ten. The legal minimum wage in the area is sixty-nine pesos.[38]

Increasingly, as workers everywhere fall into the same global labor pool, the effects of exploitation in Guatemala or Haiti or China are felt by workers in New York, California, and Texas. Child labor is on the rise in the United States as the competitive impact of the employment of children and other grossly underpaid workers around the world are felt in U.S. labor markets. According to the U.S. Department of Labor, the number of minors illegally employed in sweatshops increased 128 percent in the second half of the 1980s. The United Farm Workers of America estimates that 800,000 children and teenagers are working as migrant laborers. According to estimates of the American Academy of Pediatrics, 100,000 children are injured on the job in the United States each year.[39] The choice is clear. Either global standards will be raised to some decent minimum, or workers everywhere will be dragged down together by the forces of international competition.[40]

Establishing minimum standards in a world of huge economic inequalities and cultural differences is obviously not easy. The gaps cannot be closed overnight but without the will to make human rights in the workplace a global priority, it can never happen. Yet the problems are great. As more and more of the world's work is contracted to small mom-and-pop operations around the world, the local cultural context assumes greater importance. This is especially true with respect to child labor. Consider the Lopez family in Bagong Silang, a city neighborhood on the outskirts of Manila. When a reporter for the Philippine *Globe* visited the Lopezes, she found the whole family squatting on the floor cutting and trimming rubber thongs for slippers to be sold under the Rubberworld name. Jobert, the youngest of twelve, is 3½, and he works a long day.[41] If the family were still farming, the child would have been expected to do his share of chores, although the work would have been less repetitive and possibly more fun. Who should tell the Lopez family what chores may be asked of Jobert, and who could enforce the restrictions?

VII.

The production, processing, and selling of information is the number-one growth industry in the world. Increasingly, the path to profits is the manipulation and packaging of ideas and data. In one way or another all five of the great global companies on which we have focused our account of the age of globalization are major beneficiaries of the "information revolution." The production of information is shaping the politics and, by default, establishing new rules for postindustrial society. The information-based economy is changing the way cities look and how they function. Robert Reich has written convincingly of how the manipulators of information, individuals whom he calls "problem-solvers" and "strategic brokers," have become in recent years key sources of high value in the space-age business enterprise.

For more than thirty years the coming of the postindustrial age has been celebrated as a milestone in the liberation of humankind from the tyranny of work. The prophets of the new age of plenty have promoted dreams of a world where homes are turned into "electronic cottages" and people interrupt lives of leisure and self-development with occasional work as needed to pay the bills. Thanks to the modem, fax, and fiber optics, postindustrial knowledge workers can plug themselves into the global economy whenever they like and cut out when the spirit moves them. The result will be to revive warm and loving family life that will no longer be held hostage to bumper-to-bumper commutes and other frazzling demands of the economic rat race. Thanks to the huge global market in intangibles, workers will no longer be locked into a place. A few hours of highly paid symbol manipulation can support days of leisure.

Such predictions of life after the "information revolution" romanticize and obfuscate what has happened. Given their hourly pay, jet-age nomads—rock stars, sports superstars, producers, agents, and brokers in the entertainment industry—can make more than enough money to live sumptuously by working less than a day a week. But by and large this is not what happens. Their jobs require long hours that conform to other people's schedules. Clients, investors, fans. Global advertising agencies, accounting firms, and law offices also employ well-paid, footloose individuals with specialized knowledge that can be put to profitable use all over the world. The world's largest transnational law firm, Baker & McKenzie, has more than thirty offices around the world and serves global operations like Levi Strauss.[42] CEOs and subordinate managers of global enterprises are not likely to be found at home; they are working somewhere in the world all day long, and often much of the night. Judged by the bottom lines of their corporations, it can be said that they are often paid more than they are worth, but no one can argue that they fail to give full measure of time. Nor can they avoid commutes, whether from the suburb to the office or to the branch plant in Kuala Lumpur. They spend a good chunk of the year in the air. Corporate presidents and managers whom we have interviewed all stressed the importance of face-to-face contact in building a successful global business.

The great majority of jobs created by the information revolution have none of the glamour of global deal-making. As the world economy becomes more and more dependent on the transmittal of information and the storing of data, someone must punch the data into the machines that make it all possible. The self-loading computer has yet to be invented. To be sure, scanning devices can eliminate hours of painstaking reading and eyestrain. But the copying of data into data banks is drudgery; the worker is riveted to a chair in front of a cathode tube for long hours. As in production lines in the auto industry before the era of lean production, professional data-punchers perform a single task all day long and they are under steady pressure to increase their output.

Although there is nothing revolutionary about how most of the work is done in the information industry, there has been a revolution of a different sort. More and more information that used to be freely available is free no more as the technology of assembling and packaging facts is perfected. Not so many years ago, anyone in Washington, D.C., could dial 411 and learn any local listed telephone number gratis. Today each such call costs seventy-five cents. In the 1980s a considerable amount of information supplied free or at nominal cost by government agencies was eliminated on grounds of cost-cutting and reducing "paper flow," and much of the information was turned over to private data banks. In 1982 the Census Bureau for a modest fee gave exclusive rights to a private consortium of fifteen companies, including Sears, Time Inc., and Montgomery Ward, to prepare their own tabulations and then sell the information for many times the price that the Census used to charge. Under the banner of streamlining government, eliminating red tape, and "getting the government out of business," a considerable amount of information once in the public domain has been transformed into commercial products.[43]

As information becomes increasingly important to corporate profits, more and more global companies have turned to outside companies to set up private data networks. Unilever has a computer network involving 500 separate companies in seventy-five countries. More and more global giants are contracting out the running of their data networks to IBM, Digital Equipment, and other companies with global telecommunications services. The oldest global institution still functioning, the Roman Catholic Church, employs GE to run the global data network linking the Holy See with dioceses and church installations around the world.[44]

Because of the explosion of sophisticated communications hardware, people can be employed anywhere to punch and store data. Thus it is now cheaper for Manhattan law offices to fax draft letters to an anonymous woman employed by a data firm in Barbados than to hand it to the secretary in the next office. The Washington, D.C., operator who now is willing to reveal addresses along with telephone numbers for seventy-five cents sounds as authoritative as ever. But it is quite possible that she has never even been to the nation's capital. The information-dispensers for the Chesapeake & Potomac Telephone Company are located in West Virginia, where jobs are scarce and wages are low.

But most menial data-processing jobs have been exported to places where wages are far lower. Advances in telecommunications make it simple to farm out even sophisticated data-processing. Equidata Philippines, Inc., founded by an American in 1985, employs well over 100 college-educated data-punchers who must punch a minimum of 10,000 characters an hour, for which they are paid $150 a month plus free medical care—and a few grams of rice if they do not miss a day of work. The compensation package altogether comes to about a sixth of what an entry-level data processor in Europe could earn.[45] Employees at Saztec, one of the oldest "custom software" firms to set up shop in the Philippines, the researcher John Maxwell Hamilton reports, punch "American patient records for hospitals in Pomona, Calif., or Greensboro, N.C.; consumer credit reports on British citizens; names and addresses of Stride Rite shoe clients in the United States; switching networks for the Mountain Bell and Pacific Bell telephone systems; articles in *Playboy* and the *Christian Science Monitor*; U.S. presidential speeches; French novels; European patent records; and the Helsinki, Finland National Library Book catalogue." Saztec has its headquarters in Kansas City, where, in addition to its full-time staff, it employs about eighty more local residents "who work part-time on personal computers in their homes."[46]

However, much more sophisticated software production is also being contracted out to "cottage industry" operations in low-wage countries. In 1990 Texas Instruments, the Dallas-based semiconductor firm, set up 41,500 computer terminals in its operations across the world, more than one for every two employees, to link up the "cottages." To cut costs more and more, microchip design is done in places like Baguio, a mountain city in the Philippines, and in Bangalore, India, where engineering talent costs a fraction of what it costs in Texas. The design specifications are transmitted by computer. With the collapse of the Soviet Union, global companies are farming out advanced engineering work to highly skilled Russian and Ukrainian scientists and engineers who are now global bargains.

Since the age of telecommunications began, it has been generally true that the capitals of poor countries are more closely and more efficiently linked to distant world commercial centers—the so-called "global cities" like New York, London, Paris, and Tokyo—than to the rest of their own countries. Twenty-four hours a day, information now travels distances of 5,000 miles or more after being bounced off satellites in space to arrive almost instantaneously at a globally wired port of entry, either a computer terminal, a telephone exchange, or a television facility. But the next leg of the journey into the interior can take hours or weeks. The transmission of data received in a globally wired office in the commercial district of the capital even to a *barrio* within the same city may well not happen because the local phones don't work. In many parts of the world, information that has been faxed or bounced off satellites into a "smart" building in a poor country may well go no further since the rest of the journey depends upon ancient buses, mules, camels, or goat carts. More than half the population of the planet lives in countries with fewer than one telephone for every 100 persons.[47] Information is becoming an ever greater source of value, and information technology plays an ever greater role in the global production system. But the gap between those who have access to information and those who do not is growing.

Increasingly, hundreds of millions of men and women who will enter the labor market in the less-developed countries over the next few years will be directly competing with workers in advanced industrial countries to produce the same basket of goods or to render identical services. Hundreds of millions of other human beings in this global labor pool will never find jobs in the Global Workplace or steady work of any kind. Without a role as producers or servicers of industrial commodities, they will not be consumers of global goods either. The cycle of unemployment, poverty, underconsumption, and stagnation of national economies is already shaking the new world of the great corporations.

POLITICS, MARKETS, AND JOBS

I.

GOVERNMENT HAS PLAYED A CRUCIAL ROLE IN CHANGING what factories look like, what jobs they offer, and where they are. Changes in tax laws and industrial regulations, the elimination of many barriers to border crossings of all sorts, and the orchestration of economic incentives to influence corporate behavior have encouraged the radical reorganization of global production. Ironically, one result of all this is that national governments have less power to maintain high levels of employment than they once had. A number of strategies formerly used to put people to work are no longer politically or financially feasible.

Public employment in state bureaucracies and state enterprises was used throughout the Third World to keep unemployment down, but with few exceptions, public enterprises were inefficient and corrupt. Indeed, many were public in name only since the profits often flowed into the very private pockets of the politicians and generals who were running the state. Under pressure from the International Monetary Fund and private investors, governments began to "privatize" state enterprises and to cut payrolls that had been bloated to buy social peace. The process was repeated in Eastern Europe and is being attempted in the former Soviet Union.

In the industrial world, public payrolls grew—even under regimes such as Margaret Thatcher's and Ronald Reagan's that had been elected on government-bashing rhetoric. But government funding for public-service jobs grew at a slower rate, and some of the most labor-intensive programs were cut. All this reduced the capacity of governments everywhere to conceal the extent of their unemployment problems, much less to solve them. As we have seen, more and more jobs were lost in the private sector under the pressures of global competition. As labor costs rose in the home islands in the 1980s, to give one example, Japanese firms were capturing foreign markets by making increasing use of part-time workers who get low pay and no benefits. (In 1980 there was one temporary employment agency in Tokyo; five years later there were nearly 150.) The practice quickly spread around the world. Swedish firms directed more and more work to nonunion part-time workers. By the late 1980s a quarter of the jobs in Sweden were part-time, about the same as in the United States.[1]

Over the last twenty years, governments have largely failed to deliver economic growth without inflation. As wages and living standards stagnate or fall, secessionary pressures are felt all over the world. As long as central governments in the Soviet Union, the Balkans, and Eastern Europe could repress dissent and deliver well enough on economic promises to maintain the legitimacy of multiethnic states, these secessionary impulses could be kept under control. But since the Cold War ended, the splitting of nations on ethnic or religious grounds, or along the fault lines of battles fought long ago, looms as a problem from hell, as Secretary of State Warren Christopher described the bloody mess in Bosnia.

Most of the reborn or newly created nation-states are too small or too poor to operate successfully in the world economy. Since even well-established sovereign states lack the power to control their own economies, breaking off from a large nation to become a small one is not usually a promising strategy for economic development. Yet however dubious a strategy secession may be, in many countries the national capital has become the symbol for all that is wrong in people's lives. The reflex reaction is to opt out of failing political communities. Ethnic or religious bonding becomes the surrogate for a functioning political order.

National governments lack both the strategic vision and the managerial tools to play an integrative role in the societies they are elected to govern because to a considerable extent they have lost control of the levers of economic change. The breakup of nations is in large part attributable to the failure of politicians who run democratic governments (or governments trying to become democracies) to offer the prospect of economic security. As special interests become more insistent in demanding the entitlements of money and power, it has become more difficult for the central governments of nation-states to play the socially integrative role they played in certain periods earlier in this century. Thus it was a policy of the New Deal to develop national markets and a national consciousness and to reduce regional inequalities. Liberal postwar administrations pushed racial integration across the nation. In Europe, postwar social-democratic governments pursued "full employment" and generous welfare policies. But the intrusions of the world economy now make it harder to play this role.

Some nations, of course, do better than others. While class divisions were widening in the United States in the 1980s, West Germany was still able to give its people generous social benefits, high wages, a shorter workweek, and longer vacations, and German industry could still compete effectively in the global economy. But this combination of a high standard of living, improvement in the quality of life, and a healthy foreign-trade surplus depended on a high level of taxation, discipline in public spending, regulation of the financial system, and a relatively modest defense burden. Because of the staggering costs of reunification, however, the German welfare state and the liberal social policies it fostered are now under great strain.

In contrast, the United States during the 1980s pursued a policy of debt-propelled growth that guaranteed greater inequality in income distribution and social disruption. Politicians won the presidency on promises of tax cuts and greater market freedom even though the skyrocketing deficits that followed, thanks to sharply increased defense spending, were entirely predictable. The limits to deficit spending in support of the domestic economy have become clearer in the 1990s as economies become more and more dependent on foreign trade for growth and jobs and foreign competition becomes more intense. Many countries have debt burdens that approach or exceed their gross national products and they can borrow no more.

The United States, the world's number-one debtor nation, is still welcome at tellers' windows. But the cost of servicing an ever increasing national debt to raise cash to run the government is so staggering as to undercut the long-term prospects of the American economy. As the deficits continue, new borrowings are constantly needed to pay the vast number of federal employees, to fund entitlement programs, to support a still large defense establishment, and to pay annual interest obligations that now rival the Pentagon budget. Interest on the $4-trillion national debt is a source of income for the small number of Americans with money to lend, but deficit-driven austerity measures are a cause of pain for the much larger numbers who depend upon public transportation, education, and other government-funded services.

Ronald Reagan characterized government as "the problem," and he won the presidency on the cry that bureaucrats and politicians should "get out of the way" and let the creative energies of business rescue the economy. The retreat of government in many places around the world has left a power vacuum that corporations have rushed in to fill. But business corporations are not chartered to solve social problems or to support communities. Indeed, their primary interests are not centered on particular places anywhere. They are in business to make products and sell services anywhere they can to make money. For these reasons, corporate behavior is having the unintended effect of breaking up communities and widening the gap between the beneficiaries of successful market strategies and the losers. The consequences can be felt in virtually every city in the United States and they are magnified in the Third World.

The men and the handful of women who run U.S.-based global corporations are subject to none of the illusions about their own organizations that are often voiced by high-ranking officials in the Pentagon and the Treasury. Whereas top bureaucrats talk as if global giants with their headquarters in Detroit or their charter from Delaware are national assets of the United States and instruments of national policy, corporate officials are much more candid in saying who they really are. The heads of global companies do not claim that the great generators and spreaders of capital they run are "American." They commonly describe their corporations as "stateless." The key to corporate survival is flexibility. Neither factories, products, nor a loyal work force can be regarded as permanent. As Martin S. Davis, chairman of Paramount, puts it, "You can't be emotionally bound to any particular asset."[2]

II.

Even as U.S.-based corporations are renouncing any special relationship to America other than to be favored merchants in the world's richest national market, they have greatly increased their political influence in the United States. Indeed, thanks to the decline of the labor movement around the world as a countervailing political force and the increasing costs of campaigning for office almost everywhere, the commanding role of corporations over the electoral process around the world is greater than at any time since the 1920s. Nowhere is this important shift in political culture clearer than in the United States.

"Corporations, by their nature, do not function as democratic organizations," William Greider notes in *Who Will Tell the People?*, his searing account of the state of democracy in America, "yet it is they who have seized the political ground left vacant by citizens, the political parties and other mediating institutions." He argues that the democratic process itself has been captured by money. The role of private money in electoral campaigns, much of it given by large corporations, their top executives, and major stockholders, is now critical to the electoral process. In 1992 Ross Perot ran for president on the claim that a multibillionaire with his heart in the right place would look after the people's interest better than hungry politicians beholden to various moneyed interests. His promise to buy the election for the people appealed to 19 percent of the voters, and it underscored the corruption of the electoral process more dramatically than all the calculations of reformers about how many millions it now takes to get elected to virtually any office.

But as Greider shows, large corporate interests inject massive amounts of money into the system to influence legislation and policy at many other points in the process. Legislators are always looking for contributions to their campaign chests, even if the election is six years away. A number perform services for private interests in return for speaking fees and junkets. The role of flattery in obtaining political favors should not be underestimated, but effective flattery— "roasts," awards, honorary degrees, ambassadorial appointments —costs money. Senator Jake Garn, who was ranking Republican on the Senate Banking Committee, set up the Garn Institute, a mini– think tank "financed by tax-deductible donations from banks and other financial institutions." Representative Les Aspin, chairman of the House Armed Services Commitee and later secretary of defense, set up a similar operation financed by defense contractors.[3] Hardworking staff members for key congressional committees that write tax laws and banking regulations are regularly tapped by large corporations and banks and given the opportunity to undo whatever damage they may have done to private interests while serving the public, at salaries that make their government pay look like pocket money.

Philip Morris pours money into all sorts of good causes to improve its public image and to buy influence in Washington and in other world capitals. In 1991 the company tried to hire presidential spokesman Marlin Fitzwater to oversee its government relations, which extend, as one former executive puts it, to "just about every regulatory agency" in Washington. When Fitzwater turned the job down, Philip Morris hired Craig Fuller, who had been George Bush's chief of staff when Bush was vice-president, at an annual salary of $500,000.[4] Former British prime minister Margaret Thatcher received $825,000 from Philip Morris for unspecified duties in the service of the cigarette giant.

Criminal conduct in the relationship between business interests and politicians is reported on the front pages from time to time. But most of the strategic infusions of cash into the political system from large corporations violate no laws and receive no public notice. One reason why corporations have plenty of spare cash to spread around is that their tax burdens, compared to their revenues and profits, are light, and they have been getting lighter. (In the 1950s corporations operating in the United States paid an average of 39 percent of all federal income taxes, but in the 1980s it was just 17 percent.)[5] Over the past forty years the tax burden has been shifted to individuals. The Tax Reform Act of 1986 sharply curtailed interest deductions for individuals but not for corporations. Mergers and leveraged buyouts that eliminated tens of thousands of American jobs were financed by borrowing hundreds of millions of dollars and deducting the interest payments. As corporations reduced their tax liability in this way, more and more of the burden fell on individual citizens who in effect were subsidizing the very processes of industrial restructuring that were putting many of them out of work.[6]

In the age of globalization a basic problem for government is how to collect enough revenue when the most powerful institutions that shape the economy have the mobility, expertise, and political clout to minimize their tax obligations. Both political parties in the United States are so dependent on corporate money that neither is willing to take the issue of corporate power head on. The appointment of industry executives to run the regulatory agencies that police corporate conduct is an old story dating back to the Progressive Era at the beginning of the century.[7] Large corporations exert massive influence on political parties and on the legislative process, thanks not only to campaign contributions but also to the battalions of lawyers, lobbyists, and public relations advisers in their employ. (In 1981 Robert Reich calculated that there were "12,000 lawyers in law firms representing business before courts and regulatory agencies, 42,000 trade association lobbyists and employees, 9,300 public affairs and public relations specialists.")[8]

Foreign-owned firms operating in the United States present special problems for government. In the boom year 1987, 59 percent of these non-U.S. companies reported no profit in the United States and paid no tax. In the previous three years the revenues of these companies had jumped 50 percent, but their U.S. taxes went up 2 percent.[9]

State governments have searched for ways to collect a fair share of taxes from their corporate guests from foreign lands. The basic problem is "transfer pricing." Corporations with operations around the world can arrange their transactions so that profits show up in jurisdictions with kinder, gentler tax collectors, or none at all. Since a large percentage of international transactions take place within centrally managed corporations either as sales between subsidiaries or as sales between parent and subsidiary, the prices are not set by arms-length market forces. These are administered prices much like prices set by government planners in the old Soviet Union, except that the motivation is financial, not political. Transfer prices are set with tax returns in mind; profits (or losses) show up where they will do the most good for the corporation's global bottom line. A few years ago the Internal Revenue Service gathered such overwhelming evidence that Toyota had been consistently overcharging its U.S. subsidiary on most of its cars, trucks, and parts sold in the United States that the Japanese automaker, although it denied improprieties, settled for a reported $1 billion.[10]

To deal with the problem of transfer pricing, California came up with the notion of unitary taxation. Since a foreign firm's actual California profits were unknowable and the profits declared in California were likely to be a fictional figure, state tax experts devised a complicated formula. Put simply, worldwide profits were estimated on the basis of sales, employees, and assets. The proportion of sales, employees, and assets in California to the global total would establish the percentage of worldwide income deemed to have been earned in California and thus subject to California tax. Under the formula a company could have an actual loss in California and be taxed on a substantial imputed profit.

When he heard about what California was up to, Akio Morita did not like it. By Sony's calculations its San Diego plant was in fact losing money. He complained to Governor Jerry Brown at a reception in Tokyo where the governor was trying to persuade more Japanese companies to set up plants in California. That is no way to do it, Morita told him. Sony went to work to organize a coalition of global companies, mostly non-U.S.-based, that included such giant firms as Unilever, Nestlé, and ICI, to fight state laws on unitary taxation.

Sony handed out $29,000 to California legislators to fight the unitary tax legislation, mostly in tickets to fund-raisers, and organized other companies to add another $108,000 to the kitty. Morita also took the lead in mobilizing a major Japanese business coalition (Electronic Industries of Japan) in what he called long-term lobbying to reach "ordinary Americans." The campaign sketched out a grassroots political organizing campaign including plans for "managing debates and seminars in states and localities; instituting exchanges with state universities and think tanks; contacting state economic development bureaus, local chambers of commerce, and state offices of U.S. senators and representatives; and organizing exchanges with local consumer groups."[11]

Company executives directly communicated threats to state officials that they would pull their plants out if the objectionable tax remained. Twenty-seven states had followed California's lead in adopting the unitary tax, but one by one they repealed it. California alone kept the tax law on the books, but it added a provision allowing corporations to buy an exemption by paying a modest fee. Sony won the battle.

In recent years corporations, whatever flag they fly, have made greater use of the mass media to sell not just their products but themselves. Brief reminders of the public-spiritedness of large corporations now appear on National Public Radio and public television and even on exercise equipment in national parks. Global industrial companies have bought major media outlets, and successful media operations, like CNN, have become global giants. "The United States, along with other major democracies," Ben H. Bagdkian, former dean of journalism at the University of California at Berkeley writes, "is moving swiftly toward media control by a handful of gigantic multi-national corporations." In 1988, just twenty-nine corporations controlled "most of the public information available to Americans."[12]

GE, which in addition to its traditional electronics business also owns what amounts to the fourth largest commercial bank in the United States, the Kidder Peabody brokerage firm, and the nation's second largest plastics-manufacturing operation, is a major player in the media business. It owns the NBC network, seven local television stations, and TV holdings in three foreign countries. Most viewers of NBC's *Nightly News* have no way of knowing that program segments, such as the fourteen minutes over three nights devoted to a new breast-cancer-detection technology in 1990 or the trumpeting of the nuclear-power industry in France, though newsworthy, were also promotions of GE products.[13] The ways in which large corporations operating in the United States exert their influence can be subtle, but often they are not.

It is not exactly news that business enterprises and wealthy investors buy or rent politicians all over the world. Compared with the systems in some other countries, the U.S. political culture is a model of civic virtue. The longtime corruption of Italian politicians, including Mafia connections, was revealed in the early 1990s to be so extensive as to be almost surreal. In Japan members of the Diet and cabinet ministers frequently expect cash payoffs in return for legislative favors or inside information, and these are discreetly delivered in envelopes, attaché cases—or as in one case where $4 million was delivered to Shin Kanemaru, perhaps Japan's most powerful politician—in a grocery cart. Japanese officeholders are under pressure to obtain large amounts of cash to hand around to their constituents. The typical Diet member raises and spends about $2 million every two years, one prominent Japanese political consultant estimates; much of it is spread around to the voters as part of an informal welfare and income distribution system of the sort found in many countries in Asia, Africa, and Latin America.[14] Voters expect their representatives to show up from time to time with presents.

U.S.-based global corporations complain that U.S. law prohibits them from bribing foreign officials, even where nothing can be done without it, and that this puts U.S. firms at a competitive disadvantage. But global companies, including U.S.-based firms, are resourceful, and they are often able to use their considerable economic power in innovative ways and thus take advantage of the culture of corruption in which stressed-out governments are mired without risk of prosecution.

III.

In an integrated world economy the line between public authority and private power has grown murkier. The decline of the political power and technical means of national governments to regulate the behavior of global corporations operating on their territories has helped to bring about an ideological shift that makes a virtue out of this reality. The legitimate role for government spending to promote the common good is much reduced although government spending continues to grow. This, we believe, is a consequence of the failures of national governments to deliver on promises of economic stability and growth. Because traditional Keynesian strategies for tinkering with interest rates and taxes no longer enable politicians to deliver on campaign promises of full employment, governments have lost public confidence and a large measure of legitimacy. All this has made political authorities everywhere more dependent on powerful private economic institutions, not only for electoral support but for the economic health of the nation. If a government seeks to impose regulations a company considers intolerable, the company can move out from under that government's authority in all sorts of ways.

The decline in effective public authority is introducing instability into the international economy. In a world in which corporations have wide latitude to go anywhere, make any product, or perform virtually any service, or remake themselves by going into whatever new business looks profitable at the moment, this cornucopia of private choices without clear rules of the road established by effective public authority makes navigation profitable but hazardous. Corporations bump up against each other in international waters, devouring and being devoured. The result is an increasingly volatile global economic environment. Spectacular losses follow spectacular gains with dizzying speed. In key sectors of the economy fewer and fewer corporations survive as the losers are either swallowed up or go bankrupt. The dangers of a system out of control are becoming clearer.

IV.

The redefinition of the role of government is at the core of the heated debate about "free trade." The term is misleading for two reasons. First, a sizable chunk of what passes for free trade is a good deal less free than it sounds. As the Council of Economic Advisers reported in the mid-1980s, "the world is moving away from, rather than toward comprehensive free trade" because even as tariffs go down, an increasing share of total manufacturing is "subject to nontariff restrictions. . . ." (import quotas, foreign-exchange controls, and other barriers to trade).[15] Second, some of the most significant issues in the free-trade debate have to do with investment, only indirectly with trade.

For the last twenty years the organization of the world economy has been commonly described as being "in transition," but to what is not yet clear. The period has been notable for the lowering of tariff barriers within trading blocs—inside the European Community and across North America—but at the same time for an increase in nontariff barriers and protectionist sentiment. In these years there has also been a rise in government-managed trade, a weakening of consumer demand as real wages have stalled or fallen, a global glut in automobiles, steel, and other industrial products, and a decline in the price of raw materials on which developing countries of Asia, Africa, and Latin America heavily depend.

The barriers to the flow of investment capital have come down, and large amounts have flowed, as we have described, to where goods can be made most cheaply. Corporations feel increasingly pressed to compete with one another by slashing the costs of production. Unlike the optimistic, expansive Bretton Woods era, the last two decades have witnessed a global race to cut labor costs and reduce job security, a deflationary strategy not calculated to encourage steady growth either in the numbers of consumers of global goods or in what economists call "consumer confidence," that happy state of affairs for merchants when people jam the shopping malls and car lots because they feel relaxed about their economic future.

From the time of Adam Smith the argument for free trade has been, as Robert Gilpin puts it, that "the key to national power" is "economic growth," which is "primarily a function of the division of labor. . . ."[16] If nations specialize in what they do best and exchange their products, markets will expand and the wealth of nations will increase. According to neoclassical theory, every trading partner will be in a better position than it would have been without trade, but some will gain more than others. From Alexander Hamilton to the economic nationalists of our own day, the opponents of free trade have emphasized its costs. Hamilton was concerned that reliance on foreign trade compromised a nation's independence. His theory of

economic development stressed the importance of building up domestic manufacturing and a domestic market. "Not only the wealth,
but the independence and security of a country," the first secretary of
the Treasury wrote in 1791, "appear to be materially connected with
the prosperity of manufactures. Every nation . . . ought to endeavor
to possess within itself . . . the means of subsistence, habitation, clothing, and defense."[17]

Today almost no one argues for autarchy or total self-sufficiency.
The memories of the vicious bouts of protectionist retaliation of the
1920s and 1930s that contributed to depression, totalitarian nationalism, and war are still too fresh and the penetration of the world
economy everywhere is already too deep. From 1950 to the mid-
1980s there was a tenfold expansion in the volume of world trade,
and the General Agreement on Tariffs and Trade (GATT) deserves a
share of the credit. But opposition to strengthening GATT and to the
North American Free Trade Agreement negotiated by the Bush administration increased in the 1990s. It stemmed from a fear that
while trade can increase the variety, quality, and low cost of goods,
totally deregulated trade can override national laws and policies to
protect small business, farmers, workers, and the environment.

Unelected bureaucrats in Brussels, Geneva, Rome, and Washington have become supranational deregulators. Under current provisions of the treaty setting up the European Commission, these largely
anonymous employees of international organizations have considerable latitude to decide when local laws enacted by democratically
elected legislatures for the protection of consumers, workers, the
physical environment, and local culture and tradition constitute an
unfair restraint on the free movement of people, goods, and money.
The Bush administration supported far-reaching changes in GATT
that would give international civil servants even greater authority to
override U.S. laws for the protection of consumers on the grounds
that they are trade barriers.

Not many Americans have heard of the commission charged with
enforcing the Codex Alimentarius, a small group in the United Nations Food and Agriculture Organization's World Food Program in
Rome that sets global food-safety standards. Even fewer are aware
that U.S. negotiators in the GATT talks in the early 1990s were
proposing to "harmonize" global standards by treating higher safety
standards as illegal "nontariff barriers." If GATT obtains the powers
global corporations want it to have, bananas with fifty times more
DDT than the traces now allowed by the U.S. Food and Drug Ad-

ministration, broccoli and lettuce with thirty-three times presently accepted DDT levels, and carrots and potatoes with twenty times more pesticide than present FDA standards permit could be on supermarket shelves across the country. GATT reforms would impose on national governments the obligation to sacrifice local and state laws that protect consumers, the environment, and a variety of other local interests.[18] Free trade of this sort sets global standards in health, safety, working conditions, and environmental protection based on the lowest common denominator.[19]

Hard-won victories at the national level for the protection of the environment have already been challenged at the supranational level. In 1991, for example, a GATT panel reviewed a complaint from Mexico that the U.S. Marine Mammal Protection Act unfairly discriminated against Mexico's exports of tuna to the United States. The Act, which the U.S. environmental movement considered a major achievement, prohibited the sale of tuna caught in a manner that killed too many of the dolphins that often travel with tuna. (Large multinational companies can afford to fish in the remote western Pacific waters where fewer dolphins swim with tuna; Mexican and Venezuelan fishermen often cannot.) The GATT panel recommended that the United States suspend the Act or face possible retaliatory trade measures from Mexico. As the North American Free Trade negotiations heated up, both countries decided to defer the fight. The dolphins are still endangered.

British Columbia was pressured by the United States to stop its publicly funded tree-planting program on the grounds that it was an "unfair subsidy" to the Canadian timber industry. In 1981 Denmark tried to ease its garbage crisis by requiring that beer and soft drinks be sold only in returnable bottles that could be recycled. The European Commission sued Denmark in the European Court of Justice on the grounds that this was too much environmental protection. Denmark won, but the government was forced to scrap plans to insist upon refillable bottles. Memories of supranational interference with progressive national policies played a role in the 1992 decision of Danish voters to reject the Treaty of Maastricht, which strengthens the Commission's hand in the domestic affairs of the members. Denmark secured some concessions and the Danish public approved the agreement the following year.

In the mid-1980s the Reagan administration developed plans to broaden GATT's mandate by extending its police powers to the areas of foreign investment and trade in services. If such reforms are enacted, GATT will have the authority to remove barriers to foreign investment and to override or knock out local laws for protecting a nation's insurance, brokerage, and banking businesses. The purpose was to allow global corporations greater freedom to shift investment to any country where profits could be made. But for newly industrializing countries eager to build locally based financial sectors, the new GATT agreement is likely to lead to the takeover of profitable financial enterprises by global corporations and banks, and financial sectors will be even less responsive to local needs such as affordable housing and small-business expansion than they are now. Money will flow to where it can count on less risk or a higher return.

The GATT reform movement is overwhelmingly a corporate movement even though the long-term effect on consumers, workers, and communities is, if anything, even greater than on corporations. The corporations that sit on the various trade-advisory panels are in constant touch with government negotiators. As negotiations on difficult technical issues arise, computer technology allows government bureaucrats in Geneva to be in split-second contact with corporate advisers. Corporate lawyers are on tap to fax answers to tough questions in the midst of Geneva negotiating sessions. A study by Public Citizen, a group organized by Ralph Nader, found that of the 111 members of three key trade-advisory committees, 108 represented corporations or industry trade associations, and noted that among the corporate members were twenty-four of the fifty largest spewers of toxic pollutants in the United States.[20] The move toward transnational regulation of economic activity is proceeding in fits and starts, but corporations around the world are adapting to regional and global levels the same strategies for protecting their interests they have pursued so successfully in national politics.

V.

Corporate influence over the agendas of supranational institutions that are in the business of promoting global economic expansion grew in the 1980s. The World Bank and the International Monetary Fund were the critical pillars set up under the Bretton Woods system. The Bank was established to finance the reconstruction and development of war-torn Europe. The Fund had the task of providing short-term loans to ease liquidity problems. European recovery was so successful that these institutions were soon able to turn their attention to the developing world. The World Bank began by setting a goal of "rapid industrialization." This meant financing huge projects—dams, roads, tourist meccas—that would generate growth and foreign capital. The benefits, so the theory went, would eventually find their way to the poor. When Robert McNamara became president of the Bank in the late 1960s, he insisted upon paying special attention to the "basic needs" of the "poorest of the poor." But faced with the world recession of the early 1980s in the wake of the "oil shocks" and the resulting trillion dollars of Third World debt, the Bank switched course again. It shed its social-worker guise and became a stern economic taskmaster.

The Bank began tying its loans to the willingness of poor countries to make "structural adjustments" in their feeble economies. To qualify for a structural-adjustment loan, governments had to agree to devalue their currencies, reduce government payrolls, encourage export sectors, let markets set food prices, and cut back health, education, and welfare programs to what they could actually afford. These austerity measures, applauded by bankers and businessmen as long-overdue doses of realism, were denounced by some Third World governments as "neocolonialist" schemes to take over their countries. But given the shortage of public development funds and the highly selective strategies of the global companies for investing private money in developing countries, these governments had little choice but to take the medicine the Bank offered along with its money.

At the same time, the International Monetary Fund became a global financial policeman, enforcing the draconian reductions in spending on domestic programs that international bankers now demanded. The Fund acquired greatly increased influence in the early 1980s because of the debt crisis in much of the Third World. A number of poor countries had debt loads approaching their gross national products, and they could not repay the loans. The IMF took on the task of enforcing austerity measures that would enable the banks to recoup at least some of their money. The Fund's seal of approval became the key that opened the door to new loans to cash-strapped poorer nations. By using their power to promote export dependence, the Bank and the Fund played key roles in opening up national economies for global corporations. One consequence of IMF pressure has been a significant decline in social spending in a number of developing countries, which has led to increasing malnutrition among the bottom 40 percent of the populations in those countries.

In the boom years, roughly 1950 to 1973, when world trade expanded rapidly year by year, the industrial countries offered the developing countries not only substantial aid but trade concessions, making it easier for poor countries to gain access to the markets in the rich countries. But with the slowdown in the expansion of trade in recent years and the shortage of investment capital, trade concessions for developing countries have been cut. The theory behind free-trade agreements is that there should be no special treatment. Under proposed GATT reforms, weak, poor economies would lose the power to protect domestic manufacturing industries and local providers of marketable services. Foreign banks would have to be accorded the same treatment as domestic banks.

While Third World countries under the proposed GATT reforms would lose the right to protect local business, the industrial countries are demanding much greater protection of patents, trademarks, and other potentially profitable (and counterfeitable) intellectual property. Over 80 percent of the patents in Third World countries are owned by foreigners, mostly by global corporations. Only 5 percent are actually used in production in these countries.[21] Developing countries are fighting the proposed reforms on intellectual property because in a knowledge-based global economy they see increased legal protection of ideas as a way for the industrial countries to keep a lock on innovation. The effect, they say, will be to prevent would-be industrial countries from ever catching up since the very strategies of development pursued by the United States, Japan, and other developed countries would be denied to them. Some face the prospect that their own homegrown seeds and other biological materials will be converted into global products and priced beyond the reach of their people. Third World consumers would have to pay much more for patented drugs. (In the 1970s Italy did not allow patenting of drugs but Britain did. According to the British Monopolies Commission, while the British subsidiary of Hoffmann-La Roche was paying its parent $925 per kilo for a patented tranquilizer, the same substance could be obtained in Italy for $22.50 per kilo.)[22]

Some Third World politicians charge that the proposed GATT reforms amount to a deliberate strategy to keep the new nations carved from the former colonial world from becoming formidable industrial competitors like Korea and Taiwan. Motivation aside, the effect will be to limit the power of poorer and weaker governments to pursue their own development strategies. So far only those developing countries with governments strong enough to set their own priorities have succeeded in becoming industrial nations.

VI.

Even as the Bush administration was pressing hard to reform GATT, it launched a parallel initiative on the regional level. The decision to push for a free-trade zone in North America, like the push for the European Community that began in the early postwar years, stemmed from a political concern that transcends specific economic interests. The fear of Japan's surging economic power and the prospect of a united European Community of 360 million customers stimulated the Bush administration to design a U.S.-dominated economic bloc that would eventually encompass the 700 million people of the Western Hemisphere. With the end of the Cold War the NATO alliance was a ghost of itself; the major U.S. allies in the fight against the Soviet Union were now the home countries of the most formidable corporations and banks challenging American industry and finance. The Bush administration feared that the United States would be isolated in the new world economy. Substantial Japanese and European capital was already flowing into the Western Hemisphere. Taiwanese, Korean, and Japanese firms entered Mexico and set up factories to make such things as baseball caps, toys, furniture, and bicycles. Nissan became one of the largest carmakers in Mexico, and about 100 Japanese, Korean, and Taiwanese plants moved in to produce consumer electronics along the Mexican side of the border with the United States.

The creation of free-trade blocs was sold to voters as an answer to the "competitiveness problem" on which unemployment and the lack of job opportunities are usually blamed. In the late 1980s Mexico was the fastest-growing market for U.S. exports as Mexico recovered from the previous decade during which real income had fallen by 40 percent. Caterpillar reported to the Business Roundtable in 1991 that it expected its sales of heavy equipment in Mexico to double every year for the foreseeable future. GE reported that it expected its exports of locomotives, power generators, and diagnostic imaging equipment to Mexico to quadruple every three years in the 1990s. Sandra Masur, an adviser to the chairman and CEO of Kodak on trade matters, predicted that if Mexico kept growing at 5 percent a year in the 1990s, at the end of the decade it "would be like having Korea next door as a market for U.S. goods and services, but without the import restraints."[23]

U.S. Treasury officials counted on the Mexican economy to continue its growth of recent years as it removes the remaining barriers to foreign investment. Since 1965 more than 1,800 plants employing more than 500,000 workers have been built in Mexico. Most of this industrialization of Mexico represents a shift in production from the United States carried out by U.S. corporations.[24] More good jobs will come to Mexico, and workers will have more money to spend for American products, so the theory goes. Mexican prosperity in turn will mean more American jobs.

But cheaper Mexican labor will obviously cost jobs in the United States. The process by which those jobs are lost is a familiar story since it has been going on for more than a quarter-century. The process by which the "greater number of new U.S. jobs" held out by advocates of the free-trade agreement will actually materialize is much more speculative, and the historical evidence to support such claims is confusing at best. Calculations of the number of new U.S. jobs resulting from trade liberalization are disputed, and the evidence strongly suggests that most come with considerably lower pay than the disappearing factory jobs. According to the International Trade Commission, a U.S. government agency, unskilled workers are likely to suffer a "slight decline" in income once the North American Free Trade Agreement goes into effect.[25] The Commission failed to note, however, that the workers who would lose ground constitute 70 percent of the U.S. work force.[26]

There is strong political opposition in Canada because of fear that the weaker partners will suffer at the hands of the stronger, and that the unique social and cultural character of these great expanses on the northern and southern ends of the continent will be lost. In the four years after Canada concluded a bilateral free-trade agreement with the United States in 1988, manufacturing employment in Canada fell over 15 percent as hundreds of thousands of industrial jobs, particularly in the auto and food-processing industries, moved south to low-wage areas of the United States and Mexico.[27] Officials of the Bush administration had no patience with such concerns. "The countries that do not make themselves attractive will not get investors' attention," declared David Mulford, undersecretary of the Treasury in the Bush administration. "This is like a girl trying to get a boyfriend. She has to go out, have her hair done up, wear makeup. . . ."[28] To many Canadians and Mexicans, however, the far-reaching changes in domestic life urged by the United States in the name of free trade—the selling off of profitable state-owned enterprises and the cutting of government spending on health care, welfare, and social security—are more like an afternoon at the dentist than at the beauty parlor.

The history of the last quarter-century suggests that the Mexican market is not likely to end up as a U.S. preserve. Non-U.S. firms are already well entrenched in Mexico, Panama, Brazil, and elsewhere in North and South America. Moreover, a political strategy of dividing up the world market into regional blocs does not square with either the self-image or strategy of many global companies. Corporations compete with corporations. They do not see themselves as foot sol- diers in global economic battles between countries or regions. Thus Sony, its vice-president in charge of government relations in the United States told us, approached the NAFTA negotiations exactly as if it were an American company with subsidiaries in Mexico. The company formed alliances with IBM and General Motors on some issues, worked with other U.S. firms on others, and, where it served its interests, opposed the lobbying efforts of other Japanese firms.

Whatever advantages they may offer, trade agreements and other policies that pin economic hopes on exports widen the gap between well-educated and highly skilled workers and unskilled, poorly edu- cated workers. By and large, the former do well when international trade grows, and the latter do not. In the United States, according to the Economic Policy Institute, real wages of high-school dropouts "have fallen by up to 20 percent since 1979, while real incomes of employees with more than four years of college have grown by 8 percent. . . ."[29] In post-baby-boom America, good jobs in engineer- ing and design are going begging, while millions who could be trained for productive work in the reorganized global labor market—but are not—face bleak prospects. Accelerating economic inequality and po- litical instability go hand in hand. Governments that are unable to address basic human needs and appear callous in the face of wide- spread economic injustice cannot govern democratic societies.

No one is in charge of the extraordinary economic changes that have transformed politics around the world. To relocate and redis- tribute power and responsibility among national governments, local communities, international organizations, supranational authorities, corporations, workers, and ordinary citizens is the fundamental intellectual and moral challenge of the new century. Government is in itself neither the problem nor the solution. But the lack of governance on behalf of people who are neither rich, educated, nor "skilled" as the word is understood in the Global Workplace—that is, most people—is exactly the problem.

PART FOUR

GLOBAL MONEY

CHAPTER ONE

BANKERS IN A WORLD OF DEBT

I.

As archaeologists who come upon old coins in strange places keep discovering, money has always crossed borders and banks can be found almost anywhere. In Egypt, Babylonia, and throughout the ancient world, financial services were offered in holy places. When Jesus drove the money changers out of the temple, he was overturning a long tradition. By the tenth century, monasteries had begun to lend money, and in medieval cities Jews, and later goldsmiths from Lombardy, dominated the business. Historians usually locate the roots of modern international finance in thirteenth-century Italy when Italian banks set up temporary foreign branches to facilitate trade. But permanent transnational branch banking of the sort that is now commonplace in much of the world dates only from the nineteenth century.

As early as the 1830s British financial institutions began to expand their networks of overseas locations. As the British Empire stretched across every continent, so did British banks; international banking was both a by-product and facilitator of nineteenth-century imperialism. Other imperialist powers followed suit. German banks opened branch offices in London and established subsidiaries in Latin America and elsewhere. Belgium's largest bank, Société Generale, acquired a French bank in 1890. French banks acquired substantial shares of the leading banks in czarist Russia. The Japanese government set up

Japan's first multinational banking operation, the Yokohama Specie Bank. But it was the British who continued to dominate international finance until 1945.

The one major industrial nation with only minor multinational banking interests in the nineteenth century was the United States. Until the Federal Reserve Act of 1913, U.S. law prohibited national banks from establishing foreign branches.[1] Americans have been suspicious of big banks ever since the founding of the nation. By tradition, banks were supposed to serve the neighborhood and local business. For much of American history, law and custom encouraged the proliferation of small banks under regulations that restricted the scope, character, and geographical reach of their activities within the United States. Yet as U.S. corporations moved more and more activities abroad, so did the largest banks. Under the pressures of global competition, the U.S. banking system was transformed in the 1970s and 1980s. But as late as 1960 only eight of the 13,126 banks in the United States had their own permanent foreign operations.

One of the eight was National City Bank. (In 1974 the bank, now wholly owned by the one-bank holding company Citicorp, changed its name to Citibank.) For most of the twentieth century Citi has stood above the crowd in international banking, the nation's premier multinational banking corporation. Chartered in 1812 by a group of New York merchants, City Bank grew by financing the companies that turned the United States into an industrial nation, in the beginning mostly railroads. After the Panic of 1837, the bank was rescued by John Jacob Astor, the richest man in the country at the time, who sold it to Moses Taylor in 1856. Taylor had made a fortune in the Cuban sugar trade, and he parlayed it into major interests in four railroads, New York Gas Light Co., Lackawanna Iron, Western Union, and much else. He became president of City Bank, and for the next generation the bank's main activity was to serve his sprawling empire. Until 1891, as the authorized history by former vice-president Harold van B. Cleveland and Thomas F. Huertas puts it, City had became "one merchant's bank."

In 1891 James Stillman became the major shareholder and president of National City Bank. He had even larger personal holdings than Taylor, including New York Life Insurance, New York Central Railroad, and Riggs National Bank of Washington. As the United States entered the final years of the nineteenth century, President McKinley ordered American forces into Cuba and the Philippines. Secretary of State John Hay promised to use the nation's new power to open up China and much of the rest of the world to American business. American commerce was following the flag into distant lands, and Stillman was determined that his bank would service the nation's greatest enterprises as they set forth to conquer overseas markets. Stillman began to turn City Bank into a major underwriter and specialist in foreign-exchange transactions. To gather support for its overseas expansion he put Cyrus McCormick, E. H. Harriman, William Rockefeller, and other titans of industry on his board. Two of his daughters married into the Rockefeller family.

City Bank established an office in Shanghai in 1902 and its first foreign branch in Buenos Aires in 1914. The following year the bank acquired the International Banking Corporation of New York, which had overseas branches in Shanghai, Yokohama, Hong Kong, Manila, Singapore, Calcutta, and ten other locations, mostly in Asia.[2] During World War I and the immediate postwar period, companies like U.S. Steel, Armour, Du Pont, International Harvester, and many others kept urging City Bank to set up more foreign branches. To encourage the bank to expand its overseas services, U.S. Steel promised to make available credit files on its foreign customers and to make a substantial deposit.[3]

Far more than any other U.S. lending institution, Citibank has grown because of its overseas business. The bank lost a considerable amount of money in the United States during the Depression, but as John S. Reed, Citicorp chairman and CEO, points out, "it was the dividend from the Shanghai branch that kept us going." Citi's international success has depended upon its ability to distance the company from U.S. foreign policy when it suits its interests. "We didn't get thrown out of China until 1950," Reed notes, "and it was the Korean War, not the coming of the Communists that made the difference. We've never closed our branch in Managua."[4] By 1988 the company had 2,135 offices in eighty-nine countries outside the United States.[5] Two years later, in the midst of a worldwide recession that caused other U.S. banks to cut back their foreign operations, the Citicorp network had expanded and now included ninety-two countries. "No other bank in the world approaches Citibank's global reach," the 1991 annual report proclaimed. In the 1980s Citicorp was twice as big as any other U.S. banking company, and despite major bank mergers in the 1990s, Citi still has more assets than any other American bank.

As recently as 1984 it was also the world's largest, but by 1992 it ranked number twenty. Of the ten largest banks in the world, eight are Japanese and two are French. In 1991, Citicorp announced that it had lost almost a half-billion dollars and it suspended the dividend on its common stock for the first time in its 179-year history. In his somber preface to the bank's 1991 annual report, Chairman John Reed promised that Citicorp would recover by providing every service a bank can offer "anywhere in the world."

II.

For almost a quarter-century just two men have been in charge of Citicorp. Both Walter Wriston and John Reed were drawn by the seemingly limitless possibilities of global markets for financial services; each, as Reed put it, was determined to make Citicorp "the world's first truly global financial institution."[6] Walter B. Wriston, a rangy, restless, and combative man with a sharp tongue and a reputation as a visionary in a stodgy industry, took over as chairman in 1970. Over fourteen years he turned the company from a bank into a global financial supermarket. While Citibank kept providing ever-expanding services to the largest U.S.-based industries, it also went into the insurance business, became a major mortgage banker, and sold electronic banking services.

Walter Wriston was the son of the president of Brown University, Henry Wriston, an infinitely quotable Establishment figure whose opinions on virtually anything found their way into the newspapers of his day. Walter became the most famous banker in the United States thanks mainly to the extraordinary changes he made in banking; but the pungent quips and flashes of learning he liked to display helped. He cultivated an image as the worldly philosopher of the banking world who could quote Plato to excite investment analysts about Citi's stock. As for his own philosophy, he once put it this way: "Be nice, feel guilty, and play safe. If there was ever a prescription for producing a dismal future, that has to be it."[7]

Wriston had no intention of being nice. As he drove his subordinates to meet his demand for a 15-percent annual growth in profits even as Citicorp reported record earnings, he loved to rail against the government red tape that was strangling the U.S. banking industry. His predecessor, George Moore, had talked his way into a Capitol conference room in 1933 and helped rewrite the landmark bank-regulation bill that was passed as the Glass-Steagall Act, pleased that he had been able to "minimize the damage," as he wrote in his autobiography.[8] Forty years later Wriston was still jousting with the regulators, but he did more to change American banking by simply outmaneuvering them. Using creative legal arrangements to circumvent U.S. banking laws that were designed to keep banks local, he ran end runs around the regulations and effectively turned Citicorp into an interstate bank. Other walls Congress had erected to keep banks out of businesses that went beyond what commercial bankers traditionally did were scaled with equal dexterity.

Wriston had made his name in the bank's international operations, and under his reign Citibank pushed more and more into overseas markets. By 1965 187 firms accounted for 75 percent of all U.S. foreign direct investment in manufacturing, and all but twenty-two of these had accounts at Citi. Wriston's offshore operations provided the bank's large corporate customers with the most sophisticated services for foreign-exchange transactions and also offered expertise in the booming Eurodollar market that was transforming international finance.

The concept of Eurodollars—U.S. currency held by banks abroad—was an invention to accommodate the government of communist China. Since the dollar was and remains the world's reserve currency and the primary exchange medium in foreign trade, the Chinese could not do without dollars. Fearing that the Truman administration would seize their assets in the United States, the new Chinese government consolidated its dollar accounts in one U.S. bank and then ordered the funds transferred to a Soviet-owned bank in Paris. Until the 1960s, as Paul Einzig, author of an early study of the Euromarket, has written, "The Eurodollar market was for years hidden by a remarkable conspiracy of silence." Concerned that they would be criticized for being bankers to communists or, worse, that loose talk would draw competitors into a profitable business they wanted to keep for themselves, bankers refused to talk about the booming secret money market. Other governments, corporations, and individuals had a variety of other reasons, some of them criminal, for keeping dollar accounts beyond the reach of the U.S. government. Under Walter Wriston, the bank became the world's leader in all sorts of cross-border financial transactions. By 1977 Citicorp derived 82 percent of its earnings from outside the United States.[9] In 1984, the year he retired, the bank had built up its domestic business, but it still earned well over 60 percent of its profits outside the United

States. Its financial-services holding company in Brazil, to give one example of the seemingly limitless possibilities abroad, was earning a 43-percent return.

Walter Wriston found John Reed at MIT's Sloan School of Management in 1965. The young man had grown up in Buenos Aires, where his father managed Armour Meat Co. subsidiaries. "Get me a new generation of banker," Wriston had demanded of his recruiters, "the sort of people who cause problems."[10] Reed was clearly bright. He had MIT degrees in both metallurgy and business management, and was a top student despite unhappy early school experiences due to dyslexia. (He still scrambles letters.) "I learned to push on despite bad report cards," Reed says. "I developed some scar tissue."[11]

Citibank was especially impressed with his overseas upbringing. His Spanish is still fluent, and he can get by in Portuguese. At age 26 Reed was excused from the usual stint as trainee and put directly on Wriston's planning staff to chart the expansion of Citibank's global business. Wriston was taken with him from the start. Reed liked to think big, and he enjoyed taking risks for big rewards, like the chairman himself. "They have that far-sighted, iconoclastic approach. That's the bond between them," a former associate said when Reed's appointment as Wriston's successor was announced. Colleagues and subordinates were more likely to use words like arrogant, brash, and abrasive.

Reed climbed to the top by taking on two quite different projects that helped change Citi in the Wriston era. After he had been at the bank only three years, he was asked to overhaul the check-processing operations. The "back room," as bankers call it, was a shambles. Each year expenses were going up as much as 15 percent. The backlog of uncorrected errors stood at 25,000, and the employee turnover rate was 50 percent. Reed summarily fired workers for minor mistakes. He maneuvered tired check-handling executives into jobs where they could do less damage or deftly out the front door, sometimes with great charm. In his effort to develop a "back-office assembly line" he brought in the latest technology and technocrats from Ford and Grumman to figure out how to make it work. The browbeaten work force was in rebellion, and Reed hired a Harvard human-relations expert to help him quell it.[12] In two years his office speed-up campaign had succeeded in cutting the delay in the flow of paper from two weeks to two days. What many an envious colleague had hoped would be a dead-end job propelled John Reed into the higher reaches of the Citicorp hierarchy.

In 1974, having become an executive vice-president, he was ready for his next major project. Reed asked to be put in charge of a study of Citicorp's consumer-banking activities. Traditionally, by far the greatest share of the bank's funds still came from the same sort of large corporate depositors that had been doing business with Citi since before the Civil War. But Wriston was eager to develop a retail business to lessen the bank's dependence on a relatively few giants and to exploit the consumer-credit market that he was sure was about to take off. His protégé discovered that the consumer-banking operations were actually losing money, and he pushed for more investment—in the credit-card business, in automated tellers, in offices and branches to serve small customers around the country and in the great cities across the world. Just as he had hoped, he was put in charge of the expansion program. Under Reed's leadership, Citi poured millions of credit-card applications into the mail and pioneered the installation of thousands of automatic teller machines, first around New York City, then around the world.

In 1977 Citi sent out 26 million letters inviting people across the country to apply for one of its array of cards—Visa, MasterCard, Diners Club, Choice, and Carte Blanche. By the time Reed took over as chairman, the bank had, according to Spencer Nilson's credit-card newsletter, 16.7 million cardholders and about 10 percent of total U.S. card revenues.[13] Wriston had managed another end run, this time around New York's usury law by locating the headquarters of the credit-card operation in South Dakota, where the sky is the limit. But even charging 19.8-percent interest on credit-card balances produced big losses since the cost of money to banks had soared at the end of the Carter administration, reaching a climax in Reagan's first year. Under Reed's management consumer banking was growing fast, but the losses from credit-card delinquents and the financial burden of the massive new investment in technology over which Reed presided amounted to hundreds of millions of dollars. Rumors flew on Wall Street that Reed was through. Walter Wriston laid down the law. "This talk will end here and it will end now."[14]

III.

Walter Wriston left John Reed with a rapidly expanding business. In addition to Citi's traditional large corporate customers and the millions of new small depositors and cardholders he had attracted into his financial supermarket, Wriston had vigorously pressed loans on a variety of Third World governments and entrepreneurs around the world all during the 1970s and early 1980s. Citi was the leader in plunging into this market, but it was by no means alone. Even mid-sized regional banks would send traveling salesmen on month-long trips to the Middle East and North Africa knocking on doors in government offices, renting money not just to the state but to the relatives and cronies of political leaders. When finance ministers met in Washington for the annual meetings of the World Bank and the International Monetary Fund, one of them told us, they were literally accosted on the street by loan hawkers. On the short walk between the Shoreham and Sheraton hotels the finance minister from one poor Latin American republic was stopped by five of them.

Thanks to the huge rise in oil prices beginning in 1973, the oil-producing nations, most of them in the Middle East, were sitting on hundreds of billions of dollars, much of which they deposited in U.S. banks. The largest of these deposits were at Citi. Wriston believed that recycling the "petrodollars" as loans to other governments was a surefire way to make big profits. Other governments around the world were forced to borrow large sums to import the expensive oil, or even to stay afloat as prices of everything rose everywhere. As the Citicorp CEO kept repeating until the day he left office, the chances of the bank's losing the money were small. "Countries don't go broke."

All during the 1970s Citi was earning record profits on its loans to foreign governments, quasi-governmental enterprises in Latin America and Asia, and private entrepreneurs. The bank lent several hundred million dollars to the Chilean dictatorship of Augusto Pinochet, and by 1987 Citibank's exposure in Chile was about $500 million. As with many other loans, a portion of this sum was guaranteed by the U.S. government's Export-Import Bank, in effect by U.S. taxpayers, but most of the debt was not guaranteed other than by the financially shaky sovereign states themselves. Wriston also pressed more than a billion dollars on the Philippines in the time of Ferdinand Marcos, much of it directly to Marcos's cronies, guaranteed by the dictator's government. This included $100 million for a nuclear reactor, a Westinghouse project that brought crowds out into the streets because the selected site had a history of earthquakes and was dangerously close to two active volcanoes.

Citicorp's net income from Latin America jumped from $8 million to $29 million between 1972 and 1974. Earnings from South Asia, the Middle East, and Africa rose from $11 million to $26 million in the same period. Another former Latin American minister of finance recalls how "the bankers tried to corner me at conferences, to offer me loans. They wouldn't leave me alone. . . . It's terribly tempting to borrow money instead of raising taxes, to put off the agony." The loan-selling campaign may have given the minister gray hairs, as he put it, but Wriston was elated. The "developing world"—a euphemism for a mixed bag of insolvent countries, some with potential for long-term growth, some with virtually none—was becoming Citi's cash cow. As Wriston liked to say, "Around here, it's Jakarta that pays the check."[15]

Wriston, as he was no doubt aware, was repeating history. National City Bank, the analyst Raul Madrid points out, was the premier bond salesman in Latin America during the 1920s, aggressively pushing bond issues to Latin American governments totaling more than $721 million in the years just before the Great Depression. In 1925 a National City vice-president had dismissed the notion that Latin American governments would default on their bonds; it was axiomatic that "a borrowing country must at all costs keep good its foreign credit, on which its commercial life depends."[16] In the competition to sell bonds National City, together with another investment bank, paid $450,000 to a group of agents, including the son of the president of Peru. Bribes constituted an ordinary and necessary expense of doing this sort of business. Chase National Bank made many personal loans to the Cuban dictator Gerardo Machado and employed his son-in-law, which may have had something to do with Chase being awarded two major Cuban bond issues.

In 1930 National City had sixty-seven branches in the developing world. But many of these it would soon close. When the Depression in the industrialized world hit Latin America in 1931, debt service absorbed 20 to 30 percent of the export earnings of several countries. Brazil, Bolivia, Chile, Peru, and Uruguay defaulted. Mexico negotiated an 80-percent reduction in what it owed the foreign banks. National City shut down thirty of its branches, twelve in Cuba alone.

Now in the mid-1980s history seemed to be repeating itself. During the Wriston era Citicorp had been earning almost half of its profits from its Third World operations. Even more than in the 1920s Citi was the undisputed leader of the herd of banks that had descended on poor countries around the world. But trouble began in the late 1970s. High interest rates, falling prices of minerals and other natural products on which underdeveloped countries depended for export earnings, and a worldwide economic slowdown brought a number of countries to the point where their indebtedness approached or even exceeded their entire gross domestic products, and they were out of foreign exchange. They were, Walter Wriston to the contrary notwithstanding, "broke," at least that is what they said and that is how they looked. To the delight of the large cast of characters in the financial world who had felt the sting of a Wriston barb over the years, the philosopher-banker had been exposed, his bank considerably more so.

To make matters worse for the debtor countries, between 1979 and 1982 well over $100 billion in capital fled the Third World, and this flight continued throughout the decade. But in the short run this was hardly bad news for Citi. Because it had become a financial supermarket, the bank was able to help people with money protect themselves from the improvidence of their governments. Even as Citi's loan pushers continued to visit government offices of insolvent countries, Citi's private bankers were arranging for the transfer of billions in personal and corporate funds from these same financial disaster areas to the safety of a Citi account in the United States or elsewhere. While Brazilian, Mexican, and Argentine business and professional people stockpiled dollars in suitcases under the bed to hedge against their own falling currency, Citi, according to the former bank economist James S. Henry, was intent on helping the superrich preserve their assets by getting them out of the country.

The bank assembled a list of "global elite" made up of "the 5000 or so people around the world who are supposed to have individual net worths greater than $100 million." American Express was courting the same select group of Paraguayans, Bolivians, and Argentineans by offering its Black Card, "the ultra VIP credit card that has a credit line of $500,000 and offers services such as private planes, bodyguards, and access to Fifth Avenue stores in the wee hours of the morning for 'solo shopping.' "[17] But Citi was the most aggressive facilitator of the exodus of capital from shaky Latin American economies thanks to its worldwide private banking network. "The problem is not that Latin Americans don't have assets," a member of the Federal Reserve Board remarked in the mid-1980s. "They do. The problem is, they're all in Miami."[18] Henry calculates that in 1984 Mexican funds in U.S. banks exceeded the amount Mexico owed U.S. banks by somewhere between $40 to $60 billion.[19]

As the tumultuous 1970s ended, over forty developing countries, including all the major Latin American borrowers, were in arrears on debt-service payments to private banks. Finally, in the summer of 1982, Mexican officials traveled to Washington to announce that they were insolvent, and dozens of other governments declared themselves broke. The lending bonanza was renamed the Third World debt crisis. By 1985 Citibank had $15 billion in Third World loans on its books, more than $10 billion of which was owed by five financially strapped Latin American countries with neither the wherewithal to pay it back nor the intention of doing so. These billions in bad loans raised doubts about Citi's own solvency. Citicorp stock fell. Yet all during the early 1980s the bank's operations in Latin America were extremely profitable. As late as 1986 Brazil, which at the time was the world's largest debtor, generated 16 percent of Citi's worldwide profit.[20]

In 1987 Reed suddenly announced that Citi was adding $3 billion to its reserves against losses on loans to developing countries, in effect devaluing the loans by an amount that exceeded any write-off in U.S. banking history. It was a realistic and courageous move that forced other banks to follow suit. Reed's initiative was part of a larger strategy to reduce Citi's risk, but it showed up as a substantial loss on the bank's books. Reed made it clear that he was not giving up on the loans, nor was Citi prepared to forgive any part of them. But by devaluing its debt portfolio the bank was showing the world that it could withstand a major default. In this way Reed hoped to convince Wall Street that Citicorp stock was a good investment, and for a time the stock did well.

The new chairman also set about to reduce Citi's debt portfolio by swapping the debt, selling it at a discount, or converting it into equity investments in the debtor countries. Reed had thought that by taking the initiative Citi could recover the influence it was losing in the continuing negotiations between the private banks, multilateral lending institutions (World Bank and IMF), and the U.S. government, on one side, and the debtor governments on the other. But the U.S. banks had no common approach. Competitors like Bankers Trust were more prepared to wait for their golden eggs in the interest of keeping the hen alive. Citi was usually the hard-liner in the group, demanding to be paid and calling for more austerity in the debtor nations. The U.S. government also had political concerns about the negative effect of squeezing strategically located nations too hard and on occasion sided with debtor governments against the major American banks. Citi's decision to prepare for defaults emboldened the Latin American countries to ask for debt forgiveness and other concessions, and Reed reportedly came to regret his decision.[21]

Nevertheless, by the end of the 1980s the Third World debt crisis appeared to be over, at least as far as the banks were concerned. Banks quietly began to swap the debt of various countries at discount rates, and a new profitable global market was created. On a given day in the late 1980s a bank could buy $100 million in Mexican loans for $50 million in cash and then trade the Mexican paper for $60 million in Argentine paper, and so on.[22] Citi and its competitors found that they could swap debt instruments of doubtful value for promising equity investments in Brazil, Chile, Argentina, and other places. Citi became the largest debt-equity investor, swapping loans for stock in Chilean paper companies, Mexican industrial conglomerates, and Brazilian electronics companies.[23]

In defusing the debt crisis in this way the foreign banks were able to build up global networks of productive assets. As the ideology of free trade spread across Latin America, spurred by the end of the Cold War, industries that had been off-limits to foreign corporations, such as communications and financial services, could now be bought at bargain prices in exchange for wiping away debts. By 1989 Federal Deposit Insurance Corporation chairman William Seidman was able to report to Congress that the nine banks with the greatest exposure in Third World debt could "write off 100 percent of their outstanding loans" to the largest debtor countries and "remain solvent."[24] However, all the major debtor nations still faced dire economic problems. By the end of the 1980s underdeveloped countries were paying about $50 billion a year more in debt service to global banks and governments than they were receiving in new loans, a reverse Marshall Plan of sorts.

The Third World debt crisis was often described in the press as a morality play, a story of greed, corruption, naïveté, and unbankerlike behavior. But the drama had a surprise ending. The rashness of the banks and their success in yoking the Third World to a load of crushing debt did not produce the collapse of the global financial system some pundits had predicted. Walter Wriston, it turned out, was right. The countries all had resources of one sort or another to keep going, the most important of which was the determination of governments in the developed world and of global banks to keep insolvent countries in business. All this helped the debt crisis to disappear from the front pages while the crushing consequences continued to be felt by millions of people squeezed by the austerity programs imposed upon the debtor nations. The main reason people stopped talking about the crisis in the rich countries was that the banks had sold enough of their dubious loans or converted enough of them into long-term bonds or equity investments to appear solvent once again. In October 1992 Reed announced that Citi would sell $600 million in Latin American equities to offset its losses in real-estate and consumer loans. Once more the bank's international operations, even its bad loans to foreign governments, were shoring up its failing operations at home.

IV.

John Reed came to the chairman's office with the strong conviction that the key to the bank's future growth was in the global consumer lending market. Financing the 1980s consumer spending spree was a much more stable and reliable business than deal-making and deal-backing. The Donald Trumps come and go, but the expense-account crowd at fancy restaurants, harried families at the local pizza parlor, shoppers for dresses, ties, jewelry, and underwear, consumers of entertainment, and travelers across the globe cannot get through the week without flashing a credit card at some waiter, clerk, or ticket seller somewhere. Citi was determined to be banker to the crowd. Any crowd, anywhere.

Citicorp's "individual bank," as the company called it, grew spectacularly throughout the decade. By 1987 Citi's Visa, MasterCard, and Diners Club cardholders were charging almost 1.5 percent of all retail sales in the United States. Two years before, Richard Braddock had taken over the consumer-banking operation from John Reed with the determination to run it like any consumer operation. Credit could be sold to millions of people who never had had anything to do with banks, except possibly for small checking and savings accounts. As with any consumer product, the keys were smart packaging and aggressive promotion. Braddock had had considerable experience with both. He went to work in General Food's marketing department after receiving a Harvard Business School degree and rose to become product manager for Tang. His triumph at General Foods, he once said, was orchestrating the debut of Stove Top stuffing.

Arriving at Citi in 1973, he made a loan to a Westchester County construction project, and when the borrower defaulted on several million dollars, he resolved never to make another. Instead he presided over the $100-million-a-year laboratory that tests consumer-banking technology. At a secret location, bank scientists measure audience reaction to the quips and pleasantries on Citi's touch-screen ATM and perfect the "enhanced telephone" that enables depositors to examine their bank balances on a screen in the privacy of their homes. For years even the existence of the lab was closely held within the bank.[25] Reed was convinced that if Citi could continue to pioneer dazzling consumer-services technology, the bank's bright future would be assured.

After spending a decade lending billions to insolvent nations and defaulting developers, Citicorp officials found the idea of spreading the risk around in short-term credits at high interest to tens of millions of people around the world very attractive. Since the credit-card business depends on high volume, defaults are treated simply as a cost of doing business. Citi's credit-card centers in Hagerstown, Maryland, Las Vegas, and Sioux Falls, South Dakota, routinely mailed 21 million statements, handled 4 million calls, and processed 855,000 applications every month. The computerized command center in Hunt Valley, Maryland, that controls all these geographically scattered operations reminds one of NASA's Launch Control.[26] The business tripled in five years and, according to industry analysts, generated about $600 million in 1989, which was not a good year for Citi. The bank sent out tens of millions of application forms, took back tens of thousands of completed applications, and, after scanning the current lists of bankrupts, sent off cards without any further credit check.

In 1987 Pei-yuan Chia, a former General Foods product manager for Brim then in charge of credit cards, explained that cardholders in arrears are permitted, as *Fortune* put it, to "charge away for a year or two simply to get a better statistical fix on how deadbeats behave."[27] As long as the deadbeat ratio does not exceed one in twenty, his successor, James Bailey, explained in a 1990 interview, there is no problem. In his view, of the 150 million adults in the United States, all but 20 million to 30 million would qualify for one or another Citibank card.[28] (One marketing program aimed at college students seeks to sign up 500,000 new cardholders every year.) By 1990 Citicorp had 36 million cards in circulation around the world. Although borrowers continue to be dunned, credit-card balances overdue by six months or more are written off, a cosmetic practice to tidy up the bank's books. (Unlike the commercial real-estate market, there is no large backlog of nonperforming debt, to use the bankers' euphemism for default on interest payments.)

The Reagan administration saw the national shopping spree of the 1980s as the preferred pump-priming strategy for the economy and did all it could to encourage it. High living on consumer credit and tax cuts would (along with military spending) finance recovery from the 1980 recession and restore robust economic growth. Citi took the lead in making easy money available for shoppers everywhere. Most of those who produced a credit card for a meal or a trip or a pair of shoes were neither yuppies nor deadbeats. As real income in manufacturing jobs declined over the decade, more and more Americans were using their cards just to make it through to payday. Citi officials were aware that behind the "We're number one" rhetoric of a flag-waving administration, there was a different reality. Incomes in America for the middle class were falling, and so was the standard of living. Credit cards constituted a privately financed safety net that kept tens of millions of Americans from falling too far or too fast for a while. But using credit cards to supplement falling incomes works only so long even when the economy is not in recession.

Citi was forced to write off $1 billion in U.S. consumer debt in 1991. At the same time, according to *ABA Banking Journal* estimates, Citicorp was investing roughly the same amount in its expanding consumer services, but as in previous recessions most of the new investment was concentrated overseas. At a Frankfurt press conference John Reed declared that "Europe was now more important to Citicorp than was North America," and bank officials announced plans to lure 5 to 6 percent of European consumers by the end of the decade with twenty-four-hour-a-day banking services everywhere on the Continent.[29] Citicorp's consumer services now reached 13.8 million households in thirty-seven different countries. Plans called for thousands of branches, regional processing centers, and automatic teller machines all across the world. Citi was already a member of the Cirrus ATM network of 55,000 teller machines in twenty countries, but it counted on the much larger profits that would flow once its own ATMs were on-line. "It's not just the size of our capital base," said Executive Vice-President Thomas Jones as he explained Citi's ambitious expansion plans in Asia, Latin America, and Europe, "it is also the size of our appetite. It's the psychology here. We're really global in our thinking."[30]

As the recession dragged on, Citi continued to suffer big losses from its consumer business in the United States. But once again foreign markets helped the bank to stay afloat. Reed was convinced that Citicorp's "foreign legionnaires" held the key to the bank's future success. "Our global human capital may be as important a resource, if not more important, than our financial capital." Almost 75 percent of the top policy-making officials of the bank have worked outside the United States. Half speak a foreign language and more than a quarter speak two or more languages besides English. "Compare that with single-culture competitors. . . . They may be fine in commodity banking like foreign exchange, but when it comes to the customer interface, . . . they don't feel comfortable in global-customer or originating interactions."[31]

Citi had discovered the global customer early on. Starting in 1974 Reed began flying around the world, first to Belgium "and all around Europe," then to Hong Kong and "all around Asia. We made an important discovery that drove everything we did later. . . . People's attitudes about their finances are a function of how they're raised, their education, and their values, not of their nationalities. What works in New York also works in Brussels, Hong Kong, and Tokyo," says Reed, who believes that by virtue of its long experience Citi's "global vision" is a unique advantage. He was determined "to eliminate the psychological notion that we are a geographically organized bank."[32]

Global consumer banking is Citi's "growth engine," Reed told a conference of investors in 1992. Thanks largely to its expanding business in Asia and Latin America, the bank earned $260 million in the first quarter of 1992 from offering a variety of financial services directly to the public. In the late 1980s Citi aggressively expanded in Asia and the Pacific. The bank bought 400,000 new credit-card customers by purchasing Australian Card Services. As Bank of America, once a power in Asia, and other U.S.-based banks retreated from the region because of financial difficulties, Citi expanded its beachheads in South Korea, Japan, Hong Kong, and Taiwan. Between 1986, when Citi's push in Asia began, and 1992, the bank increased its checking and savings accounts in the region from 1 million to 5 million; profits jumped almost tenfold.

Citi aggressively marketed its services by featuring its technological virtuosity; brochures depicted depositors banking in eight different currencies, moving their money twenty-four hours a day by making use of "banking by phone." In prosperous Singapore, Citi courted the status-conscious by specializing in the financing of golf-club memberships that cost more than $100,000 each. Citi's credit cards had become the core of its consumer business, and its major marketing efforts in Asia were designed to sign up new cardholders. By using what *Business Week* calls "Asia's slickest, steamiest ads," crafted by J. Walter Thompson Co. and Leo Burnett Co., Citi captured 6 percent of Singapore's credit-card business in less than a year.[33] Where other banks feared to tread, Citi began mailing out credit cards—in India, Indonesia, the Philippines, and Thailand. By 1992 the bank had already signed up 3 million accounts, but it was targeting the 10 million individuals in Asia outside Japan and China who make $30,000 a year or more. Pei-yuan Chia, head of Citi's global consumer operations, counts on this number tripling by the turn of the century as Asia's consumer economies continue to grow.

India, to be sure, has little experience with credit cards and as late as 1990 had no centralized credit bureau. But Pei-yuan Chia says it does not matter. "Forget about 90 percent of the people and focus on the top 10 percent. That's 80 million people," he pointed out in a 1990 interview, "larger than West Germany, and if you look at their standard of living, it's higher than the average German's."[34] How do you find them? Simple. Use the phone book. With very few exceptions, only the wealthy have phones. If you can afford one, Citi can afford to offer you credit. In Indonesia Citi targets the TV satellite dish owners. In Africa credit checkers obtain the membership lists of exclusive clubs. The Middle East Credit Company (MECICO) will provide credit information on anyone anywhere. A reading on an individual in Tunisia costs $66; checking up on someone inside Cuba costs $214. Financial information gathering by some other organizations can be a primitive process involving mostly neighborhood gossip and, in certain places, solicitation of finance department bureaucrats for tax data.[35]

In Thailand, a country without a credit bureau, Citi issued 70,000 cards in less than two years and in the Philippines 20,000 in the first five months of its campaign. Mohan Kulkarni is the head of Citibank's Card Products Group in the Philippines and also vice-president of the Credit Cards Association of the Philippines. Any Filipino earning $4,600 a year, he says, can qualify for a Citibank MasterCard, which allows the holder to pay off the balance in thirty-six monthly installments. Kulkarni is proud that the bank is bringing the "democratization of credit" to his country.[36]

V.

When he took over America's largest bank, John Reed had talked glowingly of limitless horizons and long-term plans. "It's as though you were a painter," he said, "and someone gave you the ceiling of the Sistine Chapel to paint on."[37] But unlike Wriston, Reed usually tried to keep out of the papers. Indeed, in the early years of his chairmanship he was barely visible inside the bank. "Few Citicorp employees beyond a small circle of executives and directors have ever met with him," *Institutional Investor* reported. "The multitudes view their leader on videotaped messages he prepares each quarter." He had an Oriental rock garden installed just off his office, and there he spent tranquil hours thinking about the future, insulated from the problems of the day.[38]

The bank's rating for financial strength was downgraded by Moody's in Reed's second year as CEO. By 1986, it was now clear, Citi faced two big immediate problems. The first was to remove the debris of the Third World debt crisis from Citi's books as fast as possible. The second was to raise revenue fast to cover the losses that the bank now acknowledged. When Reed took over, it was "morning in America," the golden years of junk bonds, leveraged buyouts, and quick money. Donald Trump and Michael Milken were culture heroes. Making money the old-fashioned way by lending large sums to the soundest and most powerful businesses around to finance productive investment was becoming harder because the global competition kept getting more fierce. Japanese banks, thanks to the high value of their currency and their access to cheaper capital, could undersell Citi, and the Tokyo-based giants rushed into the U.S. commercial loan market in the late 1980s.

The deregulation of the U.S. banking system that Walter Wriston and the other heads of large banks had worked so hard to bring about had been a source of great profits for Citi, but it had the side effect of opening up Citi's traditional domestic market to a horde of players that had never before been in the game. Financial institutions that traditionally were legally bound to deal only in one or another moneylending market were now free to compete with Citi across the board. Banks could now court customers in all sorts of new places, but as the regulations came tumbling down, borrowers could find a variety of new places to put their money and an expanded array of suppliers of credit—money-market funds, savings-and-loan institutions, credit-card companies, and brokerage houses.

Just as in its earlier campaign to lend money to Third World governments, Citi's loan officers competed with one another to make the most loans, with only casual concern about whether the borrowers would be able to make their interest payments. Fees were earned by committing money, lending money, and finding additional money by syndicating loans with other banks, not by turning down loans. In the boom years Citi officials had no incentive to be choosy about who took their millions. The bonus system reflected the go-go culture of the day as well as Reed's own penchant for risk-taking. Young, relatively inexperienced bank officers received fat bonus checks based on the quantity of dollars they lent out. The loans were made on the basis of overly optimistic economic assumptions and revenue projections. When the economy turned down in 1989, many of the borrowers could not make their payments. By December 1991 Citi had amassed a record $7.8 billion worth of bad commercial loans.

These loans could not have been made without the encouragement of top management. Reed became CEO just as leveraged buyouts became the craze on Wall Street. In the next four years Citi (along with Manufacturers Hanover Trust Co. and Bankers Trust) put themselves in a dominant position to finance the wave of mergers and leveraged buyouts. The junk bonds sold by Drexel Burnham and its imitators on Wall Street became famous as the primary means of financing corporate takeovers, but supplementary financing was almost always crucial, and the three big banks dominated this market. As the main banker for Drexel Burnham, Citi was the leader in what came to be known in the industry as HLTs (highly leveraged transactions). In the good years Citi earned substantial fees for its work on leveraged buyouts and hostile takeovers. By the late 1980s Citi, Manufacturers Hanover, and Bankers Trust thought nothing of lending money to a number of rival bidders intent on devouring the same corporation. Loyalty to old established clients was sacrificed in the scramble for quick profits. Thus Citi bankers agreed to finance a hostile bid to take over Gillette, a long-standing customer; Gillette's management promptly cut all ties to the bank.[39]

In the second half of the 1980s, as Reed himself later put it, Citi bankers became "deal junkies." By the end of the decade Citi was tied with Manufacturers Hanover for the dubious distinction of having put more money into highly leveraged transactions than any other bank, about $6 billion. By 1991 almost 20 percent of this portfolio was nonperforming. Citi was the agent for a $4.2-billion loan to the Canadian developer Robert Campeau nine months before he filed for bankruptcy and lent a sizable chunk of the $425 million Donald Trump borrowed to purchase the Plaza Hotel. (In 1990 Trump stopped paying interest.) Citi also laid out a major share of the $6.5 billion showered on Rupert Murdoch before the cracks in his over-extended media empire had begun to appear. When his troubles became apparent, Citi and the other creditors treated the Australian-born entrepreneur much like a less-developed country—too big to go broke—and, in the tradition of lending to poor countries, they advanced him more cash to help him make his interest payments.[40]

Reed split off a new investment-banking unit from the traditional corporate-banking operation and at the same time let it be known that consumer banking, which had been the major stepping-stone of his career, was the bank's great hope. Without meaning to, the chairman was spurring internal competition among the divisions to put out more loans and to throw caution to the winds. The fees and commissions on leveraged transactions were considerable, more than $207 million in 1989; quick profits generated by such deals were needed to balance off the losses from the Third World debt crisis and other reverses. Wriston's target of a 15-percent annual growth in profits was still in force. The loan officials who studied Campeau's multi-billion dollar request thought he was "a wild-man entrepreneur," but top management "seemed more concerned about competing with Bankers Trust in HLT's than about Campeau's ability to meet his obligations," and the word came down, "Don't be negative."[41]

In 1982 Congress had passed a major piece of legislation for the further deregulation of banks and thrifts known as the Garn–St. Germain Act. One of its provisions eliminated banking regulations that had restricted their investment in commercial real estate. Spurred by bullish 1980s talk about how the information revolution would fill towering office buildings all over the country with an ever-expanding supply of lawyers, accountants, brokers, and deal-makers and by generous tax-abatement packages offered by local governments, banks across the country invested more than $350 billion in real estate. Of all the office space in the United States, 32 percent was built in the 1980s, and much of it still lies empty.

It was official lore at Citi headquarters that, just as countries never go broke, real-estate values never go down. By 1991 Citi had the largest real-estate portfolio of any U.S. bank, $13.3 billion, and almost a third of this figure was made up of loans that would almost certainly never be paid back. The failures were there for all to see. In

1987 developers broke ground and erected a gleaming green-glass 42-story tower at 1540 Broadway financed by Citi. The real-estate market in New York City promptly collapsed after the stock-market crash in October of that year and the building remained vacant for years. (This is the building Bertelsmann bought at a great bargain for its U.S. headquarters.) Citi was also overextended in the residential real-estate market. In the boom years the bank had run ads promising to approve loans in fifteen minutes. By September 1990 its defaults on mortgage payments were five times as high as the nationwide delinquency rate, as reported by the Mortgage Bankers Association.[42]

Reed, who prided himself on his knowledge of sophisticated information technology, had made matters worse by making a serious strategic miscalculation. He purchased Quotron, an electronic stock-quotation-information system; like his predecessor, he believed that in the age of global banking selling rapid information about money is the key to making money. But Quotron's customers were brokers and managers of other financial institutions. Citi was a competitor they saw no reason to patronize, and Quotron lost 40 percent of its customers; the net loss for Citi was another $1 billion.

Another profitable idea that has since been successfully developed by others turned sour for Citi. The bank was a pioneer in gathering consumer data by wiring cash registers to a national data base. The Reward America program recorded every purchase made at grocery-store checkout counters for a group of selected products. Consumers were rewarded with rebates, but their names were sold to direct-marketing organizations. Citicorp made the tactical error of demanding that grocers pay for the data generated at their own cash registers, and they were infuriated by Citicorp's arrogance and foggy notions about how grocery stores actually work.[43] By the end of the 1980s the project was as good as dead; another 174 pink slips were put into mailboxes. Meanwhile other entrepreneurs, appreciative they said for the opportunity to learn from Citi's mistakes, were doing well in the consumer-data-gathering business.

At the end of the decade John Reed seemed more like Job than Michelangelo. Day after day there was a stream of bad news from many fronts. Nine of the ten largest banks in Texas had gone under because of the same sort of disastrous commercial-real-estate loans that had so attracted the chairman of Citicorp. John Dingell, a powerful Michigan congressman on the House Banking Committee, declared the bank to be "technically insolvent," and the next day there was a run on the bank's Hong Kong branch. Citicorp stock dived. J. P. Morgan ran pointed ads aimed at the $5-million-and-up market about "the security of your assets," and in addition to luring some of Citi's private investors, Morgan and other competitors also cut into Citi's share of the "swaps" market. Corporations wondered whether it was any longer prudent to count on a long-term relationship with the nation's largest bank.[44] Even the good news was embarrassing. A 36-year-old Saudi Arabian prince by the name of Alwaleed bin Talal bin Abdulaziz al Saud became Citi's largest stockholder with a welcome infusion of nearly $800 million and a warning that he would keep his eye on management, which he said, had "to be more in touch with reality. . . ."[45] Eyebrows were raised. It was one thing for Moses Taylor or James Stillman to own America's premier bank, but a Saudi prince? Critics broke into print with elaborate (and exaggerated) calculations on how Citi had been taken.

In November 1990 John Reed was summoned to a secret meeting by the president of the New York Federal Reserve Bank and the director of the Fed's division of bank supervision in Washington and informed that he would now have a partner in all important decisions affecting the future of the bank: the federal government. Then for two and a half years the Federal Reserve, the American version of a central bank, and the Office of the Comptroller of the Currency literally moved in. Reed was required to attend monthly meetings with the regulators at which mounting pressure was exerted on him to cut costs, slash dividends, fire staff, and unload investments to build up cash reserves. Ironically, Citi's international business, which had been its salvation at so many points in its history, was now regarded in one important respect as a vulnerability. A significant share of Citi's funds were in large overseas corporate deposits not protected by federal deposit insurance, and the Fed feared that nervous depositors might withdraw these funds and precipitate a crisis. At one point there were more than 300 bank examiners going over Citibank's books. In August 1992 the regulators turned up the pressure and issued a memorandum of understanding that amounted to a formal reprimand of Citi's management for not moving fast enough.[46]

Reed was now under fire from three directions. Investors had driven the stock down to $8.50. The board of directors, it was widely reported, was getting ready to fire him. The regulators were demanding more draconian measures. At a board meeting in Mexico City Reed persuaded the directors to hang in with him. He then cut the dividend almost by half, and over the next year and a half he replaced five of his six top executives and cut 11,000 jobs. By the end of 1992 Citi had recovered enough to convince investors to pay $30 for the stock. Reed's job (and his $2.2-million annual compensation package) seemed safe. Ironically, the U.S. bank that had done more than any other to escape federal regulators had been saved by Uncle Sam.

VI.

As Citibank officials bet the future of the bank more and more on the financing of consumption rather than on the financing of production, they are counting on governments everywhere to abandon their old-fashioned Benjamin Franklin outlook on the world and give a green light to heavy consumer debt. The success of the Global Shopping Mall depends upon the expansion of consumer credit across the world. The goods on display, the physical appearance of the shops where they are sold, and the ways they are advertised and promoted from Taiwan to Santiago are more and more clones of American originals. The missing ingredient for replicating the American boom in consumer spending in other places is easy consumer credit.

But is the global consumer-credit system a house of cards? There are built-in limits, cultural and legal, that could dash Citi's hopes. In Chile, for example, people use personal checks to pay bills instead of credit cards since they are almost universally accepted. (Writers of bad checks are hauled off to jail.) Germans refrain from running up large credit-card balances because the culture historically frowns on debt. (The German word for debt and guilt are the same. Citibank avoids this unfortunate association by using a coined expression *Ruckzahl-Wahl*, which roughly means "credit that empowers.")[47] In Asia the governments of Malaysia and Singapore, worried about poor people hurt by a spending-on-credit binge, have stepped in to raise the minimum-income requirements, and this limits Citi's market to well under 10 percent of the population.

The fundamental limitation on the global consumer-credit market is demographics. John Reed points out, "There are 5 billion people living on earth. Probably 800 million of them live within societies that are 'bankable' and probably 4.2 billion are living within societies that in some very fundamental way are not bankable. I think it's a great danger as we look out between now and the turn of the century that this distinction between the bankable and the unbankable parts of the world could become more aggravated."[48]

In the United States the democratization of credit closed the gap in lifestyles and buying habits between the very rich and the middle class. People who in other circumstances could never afford them could buy houses, cars, TVs, dresses, and summer vacations on credit. Consumer credit helped convince almost 90 percent of Americans that they are card-carrying members of the middle class. But in a world in which jobs cannot keep pace with population growth, the pressures of global competition are pushing real wages down. The percentage of the world's population able to pay off credit-card balances is small and it is not growing fast.

In most countries Citi and its competitors send applications to no more than 10 percent of the population. Yet every city dweller is exposed to credit-card promotions on billboards and TV commercials, and more and more people now pass by as their better-off compatriots extract bills from money machines. The credit revolution is thus creating new sorts of social divisions within countries that may well have important political consequences. As national boundaries lose much of their significance, different consumption patterns are splitting the world in new ways. There is a Global North that now embraces city blocks and affluent suburbs in and around Manila, Mexico City, Santiago, and Nairobi, and there is a Global South that now claims stretches of Los Angeles, Chicago, and Hartford.

CHAPTER TWO

MONEY WITHOUT A HOME

I.

MONEY HAS VALUE BECAUSE OF THE INFORMATION IT CONveys. Coins can be sold for the bits of gold or silver they contain, but paper money or promises to pay money have no intrinsic value. Confederate money and czarist bonds instantly inform all but the most unwary that they are museum artifacts. In the Gold Rush days, some bearer bonds redeemable in gold at a named bank deliberately omitted an essential piece of information: the bank was hidden away at the end of an unmarked, virtually impassable mountain road. Today, thanks to sophisticated information technology, money in its various guises is shuttled around the world, and the conditions under which promises to pay are redeemable can be excruciatingly complex.

Most business and personal financial transactions still involve cash, that is, the exchange of coins and bank notes issued by treasuries and central banks. According to the Federal Reserve, about 85 percent of dollar transactions are in cash at banks, supermarkets, gas stations, restaurants, and the like. But the trillions sloshing back and forth between countries, within and between corporations, and between large investors and entrepreneurs, are transferred from one account to another by entering data into an electronic network. Unlike withdrawals at ATMs, these transactions do not take place in public view. The number of electronic transfers amounts to only 2 percent of the total transfers; yet five out of every six dollars that move in the world economy are involved.[1]

Traders still shout at one another at exchanges around the world, buying and selling money in one form or another, but more and more dollars, yen, or lire move from one account to another hundreds or thousands of miles away because someone in a quiet room hooked into a global electronic network has punched a key. Well over $2 trillion a day travels across the street or across the world at unimaginable speed as bits of electronic information. A treasury bill, as James Grant, the editor of *Grant's Interest Rate Observer*, puts it, "no longer exists except as an entry on a computer tape."[2] Information technology has transformed global banking more than any other economic activity. The software that guides electronic networks now permits twenty-four-hour trading in a wide variety of money products all across the planet, and it has changed the human relations of banking. As Felix Rohatyn of Lazard Frères puts it: "People buy and sell blips on an electronic screen. They deal with people they never see, they talk to people on the phone in rooms that have no windows. They sit and look at screens. It's almost like modern warfare, where people sit in bunkers and look at screens and push buttons and things happen. . . ."[3]

The sheer size of global financial operations is reducing costs substantially. Any multimillion-dollar transfer across the globe can be accomplished for just eighteen cents. Financiers have always profited from advances in communication. Nathan Mayer Rothschild employed carrier pigeons to bring him advance news of the Battle of Waterloo, and the timeliness of the information was literally worth a fortune. By developing the most advanced foreign-exchange software, Bankers Trust was able to achieve a ten-second advantage over other traders, enough time, according to a 1987 Office of Technology Assessment study, to execute four or five trades.[4] The opportunity to react to new information a few seconds ahead of the market can be worth billions.[5]

The introduction of state-of-the-art information technology has changed what banks are and what banks do. Computers and electronic communications networks have expanded the markets for money products and reduced the costs of making transfers, in large measure by eliminating thousands of jobs for clerks, tellers, messengers, and the like. But the installation of the automated systems has required huge capital investments. In 1990 commercial banks in the United States spent $15 billion on information technology. The need to amass large investment funds for such purposes has encouraged the consolidation of investment and banking corporations; firms merge to save costs by sharing expensive data systems. These systems facilitate the speedy settlement of money transactions, and this usually reduces the risks of money trading; even a few seconds of exposure before a transfer is settled can spell disaster if millions of dollars are involved.

Information technology also makes it easier to check creditworthiness and the identity of the parties to money-transfer transactions even at great distances. The real value of a bank's loan portfolio depends upon the accuracy and timeliness of the information available to it about its borrowers and applicants for loans. But thanks to the spread of the technology for checking credit, banks no longer have the near monopoly on credit information they once had. Brokerage houses, insurance companies, and industrial giants like Ford and GE now have access to credit information as good as that available to banks, and they are now better able to compete with banks for the good credit risks. The result, according to one leading bank economist, has been a decline in the "average quality of banks' loan portfolios."[6]

All this means that global banking has become highly dependent on a few centralized information operations to accomplish and monitor the transfers. Behind "a maze of locked anterooms, rigged to trap, or at least slow, a determined intruder," Peter Passell of the *New York Times* writes, sits "the computer system that is the heart of global capitalism."[7] CHIPS is the New York Clearing House Interbank Payment System. Inside a reinforced-concrete-and-glass office building on a run-down block on Manhattan's West Side, two Unisys A-15 J mainframe computers about the size of refrigerators dispatch funds across the earth. Requests for payment stream in through 134 telephone lines, and after being screened for possible fraud by twenty-two electronic black boxes, the mainframes move the money, as Passell puts it, in the form of "weightless photons through the electromagnetic ether."

CHIPS is a privately owned project of eleven large New York banks. The service is available to 142 participating banks around the world, and through them to thousands of others. An overwhelming percentage of all dollar transactions in the world pass through the Unisys A-15 Js in Manhattan, more than 150,000 international transactions a day. CHIPS is by far the largest global electronic-transfer system, but it interacts with SWIFT (Society of Worldwide Interbank

Financial Telecommunications), a Belgian-based bank-to-bank system that links about 1,000 banks. Bankwire is another small link in the system that involves 200 U.S. banks. Fedwire serves the Federal Reserve System. The British contribution to the settlement of international accounts is called CHAPS. (The original acronym was FISH on the theory that it would connect nicely with CHIPS.)

As bankers contemplate this electronic money web, the nightmare—which most discount—is that a flash of lightning, a massive fraud, or a diabolical computer virus could trigger power failure, scrambled money messages, gridlock, and breakdown in the global banking system and lead to the world's first computer-driven worldwide financial panic. CHIPS takes this all seriously enough to adopt elaborate security arrangements, to put in auxiliary power and water systems, and to replicate the entire Manhattan operation just across the river in New Jersey down to the maze of white-walled rooms, network of telephone lines, Halon fire-protection system, and water-resistant ceilings. The backup operation has had to be used just once, CHIPS officials confirm, when both mainframes in the Manhattan office broke down on October 18, 1991, but the only consequence was a five-minute delay in processing transfers.

Theft is difficult. The perpetrator of electronic fraud would not only have to tap into secure phone lines and know the multiple authentication codes, but he or she would also have to figure out how to get ahold of the cash at the close of day before the fraud was discovered. Nevertheless, according to Passell, a $20-million theft did occur in 1989, a fraudulent transfer from a Zurich bank to the State Bank of New South Wales via its New York branch. A Malaysian con man secured the cooperation of two employees of the Swiss bank and conjured up a fictitious bank in Cameroon to work the scheme. The thieves were caught and convicted. The $20 million had been transferred in a fraction of a second, but recovering it took longer. Three years later $12 million of it was still missing. Despite all the technological precautions and hurdles, even more imaginative inside jobs on an even larger scale are possible.

John Lee, who is president of the New York Clearing House Association, estimates that 99 percent of CHIPS transactions are legitimate. That may well be true, given the huge volume of daily transactions. Nevertheless, the speed and anonymity of the global money-transfer system presents an opportunity for large-scale criminal operations and tax fraud. Any day, there are likely to be a number of transactions that are lawful in themselves but unlawful in their purpose. Large accumulations of cash often represent the fruits of unlawful activities to be kept hidden from regulators, police officials, and tax collectors. In 1989, according to a U.S. State Department report, annual worldwide drug profits were estimated to be $110 billion. A year later banking officials of the leading industrialized nations raised the estimate to $300 billion, a sum larger than the annual U.S. Pentagon budget.[8]

Global computer networks have revolutionized money laundering, but hiding money is an ancient art. Organized crime developed its own financial networks in the 1920s to handle gambling, drugs, and liquor revenues, and in 1932 the mobster Meyer Lansky began making use of secret Swiss bank accounts to squirrel away illegal and untaxed profits. In gratitude for Governor Huey Long's agreement to let the mob set up slot machines in New Orleans, the gangster set up a Swiss bank account for him. In the old days money left American shores in suitcases and wallets as cash, traveler's checks, cashier's checks, or stock in the name of nominees. After being cleansed of all criminal taint by discreet Swiss bankers who treated it like any other money, it was returned to the United States in the form of fictitious loans. Lansky and many others would simply pay interest into the secret Swiss bank accounts of their own dummy corporations and take a U.S. tax deduction.[9]

Today scrubbing dirty money is easier. Electronic transfers are secret. Anyone with funds in the bank who prefers to hide them from regulators, creditors, wives, or husbands can communicate with the bank by fax or modem, and order wire transfers across the globe without ever speaking to a bank officer.[10] Tax havens are nesting grounds for criminal gains or untaxed profits. Indeed, most of the deposits sitting in these out-of-the-way places are there to avoid scrutiny by regulatory and taxing authorities. Typically, tax havens are tiny—Cayman Islands, Bahamas, Bermuda, Cape Verde, Hong Kong, Bahrain—mostly islands featuring warm weather, good flight connections, and plenty of faxes. Grand Cayman's financial district is reputed to have the highest concentration of fax machines in the world to serve its 548 banking outposts, which hold assets of about $400 billion.[11] "I can hide money in the twinkling of an eye from all the bloodhounds that could be put on the case," William Mulholland, chief executive officer of the Bank of Montreal, explained to a parliamentary committee.[12] Anthony Ginsberg, a student of money traffic, estimates that "perhaps half of the industrialized world's stock of money resides in or passes through tax havens."[13]

The volume and reach afforded by instantaneous banking transactions across the world make global banking highly profitable, but some economists fear that these same characteristics could also be its undoing. On a typical day well over a hundred banks are sending and receiving pay orders via CHIPS at the rate of $2 billion a minute. Unlike payments in currency, which are final the instant bills and coins change hands, electronic orders to pay are not settled until the close of the business day, and then the accounts are cleared multilaterally. Peter Passell likens the process to a poker game: "Each institution that is in arrears makes payments into the kitty much the way the 'bank' settles accounts for a half-dozen players" when the game breaks up.[14] Should a bank lack the funds to settle accounts at the end of its business day, the electronic entries would be reversed— "unwound," in global-banking lingo—and every bank engaged in a transfer to or from the defaulting bank would feel its effects. The gridlock caused by the hundreds of corrections, especially if multiple bank defaults are involved or a stock-market crash is also occurring, could trigger a chain reaction of bank failures. The system could be shut down for weeks, during which time corporations would be starved for working capital. Bankers profess great confidence that such scenarios are highly improbable, but they acknowledge that the complexity, speed, and dynamism of global-banking arrangements expose the system to hazards we cannot even imagine. That, they say, is always a risk of any technological advance.

II.

David Edwards, an eager young man from Wichita Falls, Texas, landed a job as a supervisor of foreign-exchange operations in Citibank's Paris branch in the mid-1970s. He was just 30 years old. After a time he became suspicious that tax evasion and currency-trading violations were going on in his department, and when one of his traders confirmed this, he reported his concerns to his boss. He expected to be congratulated, perhaps even promoted for his initiative. Instead, he was told to forget about it, and when he kept on questioning his superiors up the line, he was fired for acting "in a manner that is detrimental to the best interests of Citibank." He cleaned out his desk and also took a carton of internal bank documents he had happened upon, which included the bank's manual on how to cover up illegal currency transactions. These he handed over to the Securities and Exchange Commission.

The documents not only showed how Citi evaded currency regulations and circumvented tax laws, but they also suggested that Walter Wriston and top management approved what one Citi vice-president in an internal memo termed Citibank's "rinky-dink deals . . . to get around the local regulations and locally imposed limits." The use of off-the-books transactions, bogus transfers, and double sets of accounts were routine. Arthur Natvig, a Citibank vice-president and auditor, noted that management "feels it can defend all the tricks it is presently engaged in . . . [and] receive no stronger than a sharp reprimand and a 'don't do it anymore.' "[15] This assessment of the bank's risk was prescient. The prolonged SEC investigation made the front pages and was embarrassing for the bank, but the SEC enforcement staff decided to take no further action since the shady practices accorded with "reasonable and standard business judgment."[16]

The technology of moneylending and the explosion in money-packaging have outraced banking regulations designed for a simpler and slower age. The pressures of globalization have been used as arguments to remove regulations of all sorts from the financial-services industry; U.S. banks are subject to more regulations than their German and Japanese competitors and therefore, it is argued, the global playing field is not level. Bigger German and Japanese banks with broader powers are outcompeting global banks that fly the American flag.

Some of the largest U.S. banks, but not Citibank, have pulled back from their overseas operations because they lack the sheer power to stand up against the competition. This they attribute in large measure to the growing gap between what they consider the still highly regulated environment at home and the rapid deregulation elsewhere. Banks operating in Europe now have a "single passport" to pursue a wide range of financial activities anywhere in the European Community. Changes in Japanese banking regulations are also putting Tokyo-based banks in a stronger competitive position. Two weeks before the 1992 presidential election, Secretary of the Treasury Nicholas Brady gave a speech to bankers in which he said that increasing the competitiveness of the U.S. financial-services industry was critical to stimulating growth in the U.S. economy. The key, he said, was to eliminate "the old arbitrary legal framework that governs the banking system," especially "outdated restrictions on products and geography."[17]

The argument that globalization requires deregulation is at least a quarter-century old. Deregulation of the American financial-services industry has actually been going on for years, part of a global shift in the relationship between governments and banks all over the world. To a great extent the U.S. financial-services industry deregulated itself. By resorting to creative corporate rearrangements such as holding companies and mergers, the banking, brokerage, and insurance industries had slipped out of the legislative restraints intended to limit their geographical reach and their permissible activities well before Congress acted to loosen them. Through its parent corporation, which is not a bank under the law, Citibank could operate as a credit-card banker in all fifty states, rendering irrelevant and unenforceable the New Deal legislation that was supposed to keep banks serving their own communities. To get around legal requirements that banks lend only a certain percentage of their cash reserves, Citibank could sell its loans to Citicorp, which is not subject to these requirements.

Congress had not anticipated that the nation's largest bank would make such effective use of the one-bank holding company to escape regulation, and friends of the banking industry in the Senate effectively blocked efforts to plug the loophole. By the 1980s banks were not only operating across state lines, but they had become sellers of insurance as well. Brokerage houses and automobile manufacturers were now deeply involved in the real-estate market. All had one way or another jumped over the fences Congress had put up to separate investment banks from commercial banks and to keep brokerage firms, insurance companies, and thrifts concentrated on the businesses for which they were chartered. Thanks to information technology and the ingenuity of lawyers, money now traveled faster, farther, and in ways never envisioned by banking legislation and regulatory authorities. As the *Economist* puts it, deregulation "is often no more than an acknowledgement that the rules are no longer working."[18]

But deregulation, whether by circumvention of official policy or by law, had unanticipated and extremely unpleasant consequences. Like war plans, bank regulations are written with the catastrophes of the last generation in mind. After the Great Depression, when the national banking system collapsed because of risky loans, the Federal Reserve was given authority to set interest-rate ceilings on deposits.

Regulation Q, as this grant of regulatory authority was known, was designed to stop banks from competing for deposits by offering higher interest rates. The theory was that if banks were paying high interest, they would have to earn more on their loans and would be under pressure to take big risks with the depositors' money. Since these deposits were now insured by the Federal Deposit Insurance Corporation, the risk would eventually fall on the taxpayers if the economy turned sour. In normal times the fees paid by all the member banks are sufficient to cover the deposits of banks in trouble, but if failures were to reach a certain point FDIC reserves would be exhausted and Congress would have to come up with the money to pay off depositors. This is, of course, exactly what happened in the late 1980s.

All through the Cold War years, Americans were putting more of their savings abroad to take advantage of the higher return. In 1966, under pressure from lobbies representing elderly and retired persons, the Federal Reserve Board agreed to let financial institutions such as brokerage houses and insurance companies charge market rates on consumer savings accounts. It was unfair, the Fed agreed, that retired persons could get no more than 3.5 percent on their savings when corporations could put millions into certificates of deposit in commercial banks and earn a 6-percent return. These new accounts offering higher returns for consumers were known as money-market funds. As nominal interest rates soared in the 1970s, money-market funds accumulated hundreds of billions of dollars. By 1979 savings banks, savings-and-loan associations, and credit unions, which had their deposits tied up in long-term low-interest home mortgages arranged before inflation became rampant, tottered on the edge of bankruptcy.

Congress came to the rescue with two pieces of legislation, one known as the Deregulation and Monetary Control Act of 1980 and the other the Garn–St. Germain Act of 1982, which we have already mentioned. Essentially, these laws phased out regulatory limits on interest rates for savings institutions, allowed them to offer interest-paying checking accounts, and granted authority to make all sorts of loans. Previously, thrifts had survived by lending most of the home-mortgage money in the nation, but now they were permitted to make consumer loans, farm loans, and commercial-real-estate loans. At the same time companies like Sears, GM, and Prudential could expand further into the commercial mortgage market, and so could the commercial banks. By tradition and by law, these banks were in business to supply working capital and investment funds to industry. But now they rushed into the real-estate market. Citi increased its mortgage portfolio from $100 million to $14.8 billion in just ten years. All this competitive zeal to finance unneeded office buildings spelled disaster for the S&Ls. Half of them disappeared. Our children and millions more taxpayers yet unborn will have to come up with something under $1 trillion to repair the damage.

III.

All through the last thirty years U.S. banks pursued another strategy to escape the regulators. They shifted more and more of their activities beyond American shores well out of reach of the Treasury or the Fed. Here too regulators inadvertently spurred the process. As American corporations, American armies, military installations, and government aid programs spread around the world in the 1950s, all spending billions in U.S. currency in other countries, the glut of dollars in the hands of foreigners became a serious world problem. By this time Germany, Japan, and the other industrial countries were recovering from the shocks of World War II and were producing a flood of goods. It was neither necessary nor advantageous to import so much from the United States. The result was that non-Americans had accumulated hundreds of billions of dollars more than they could possibly use to buy goods or services from the United States. Except for the fact that the dollar was the world's reserve currency backed by gold, these overvalued offshore dollars were becoming risky holdings. If the holders of offshore dollars were to cash them in, the United States would face financial catastrophe because the Treasury promised to redeem dollars with gold at $35 an ounce. The obvious alternatives for the federal government were either to scale back expensive military commitments or to devalue the dollar. But both were inconsistent with America's self-image in the 1960s as the world's number-one superpower.

For the first time the nation experienced severe balance-of-payments problems. As foreigners piled up unwanted, overvalued dollars in banks in London, Paris, Geneva, and Hong Kong, the doors of the gold depository at Fort Knox kept swinging open to accommodate the heavy traffic in gold bars bound for Europe. To stanch the flow of gold, the Kennedy and Johnson administrations tried to limit the amount of dollars U.S. banks could lend to foreigners and taxed foreign bonds issued in the United States. But these measures only succeeded in accelerating the outflow of dollars. American banks, led by Citi, were now firmly established in Europe and Asia, and offshore lending exploded in reaction to the U.S. government's efforts to keep Wall Street banks from lending to foreigners.[19]

By the 1970s for every dollar American banks were lending to non-Americans from their home offices, they were lending six or seven more from offshore facilities that came to be called the Euromarket. This pooling of funds, mostly in dollars, started in Europe, it will be recalled, to accommodate the needs of communist China, but it soon became a global money pool that could be used by borrowers anywhere. The distinguishing feature of the Euromarket is that the money is denominated in a currency different from the official currency where the deposits are located. All such money is largely beyond the reach of national regulators in the countries of origin.

When U.S. companies in need of capital abroad resorted to the Euromarket, they were complying with U.S policy to restrict capital outflow from the United States. But the buildup of this huge pool of offshore dollars created a formidable alternative to the U.S. capital market. IBM was the pioneer U.S.-based company to make creative use of the Euromarket, but soon many American companies operating outside the United States were financing their overseas operations without resorting to banks in their home country. The Euromarket expanded into bond issues and then began offering a menu of increasingly arcane money products. Soon it was serving as a "connecting rod" for financial markets around the world that once were entirely separate.[20]

Money itself was becoming a truly global product. In 1973 the gross sum in Eurocurrency accounts all over the world was $315 billion; by 1987 the total was nearly $4 trillion.[21] This fantastic expansion was hastened by the series of deregulations of international money transactions that began when the Nixon administration forced the end of fixed exchange rates in August 1971 and governments everywhere lost much of their power over money. The value of money was now set in the increasingly integrated global marketplace as foreign-exchange traders around the world haggled over how many lire or drachmas an ever-fluctuating dollar could buy at any instant in time. In the 1970s the eminent economist Milton Friedman had convinced the Chicago Mercantile Exchange, which had established a lively futures market in hog bellies and other agricultural products to protect farmers and food companies from the volatility of farm prices, that a futures market for money products would be a smart idea. The more exchange rates fluctuated, the more interested investors would become in hedging their bets with contracts to buy or sell at a set price on a set date. The betting possibilities were limitless. By 1989, 350 varieties of futures contracts, most of which were financial, were traded in Chicago and in the more than seventy new exchanges that had sprouted up across the world.[22]

American officials played the key role in the transformation of world financial markets, most notably on two occasions. The first was in 1971 when Nixon closed the "gold window." No longer was it possible to redeem dollars for gold. For non-Americans this meant that they had to keep their dollars on deposit somewhere in the world or convert them into some other currency. The second event came eight years later when Paul Volcker, chairman of the Federal Reserve Board, tried to fight inflation in the United States by cutting the money supply. He used the standard tool, charging substantially higher interest rates to commercial banks to obtain dollars from the Federal Reserve. Since the dollar was the reserve currency for the world, however, the Fed had unwittingly raised interest rates everywhere, and both interest rates and exchange rates began fluctuating wildly. As Michael Lewis puts it, "Overnight the bond market was transformed from a backwater into a casino."[23] The buying, selling, and lending of monetary products worldwide became businesses in themselves. Most of it had little or nothing to do with investment in either production or commerce. (However, as exchange rates became more volatile, hedging became almost a necessity for some transnational businesses.) Foreign direct investment in the Third World fell as the leading commercial banks of the world saw that they could reap quick profits in commissions, fees, and interest by "recycling" tens of billions of "petrodollars" from the coffers of Kuwait and Saudi Arabia to the governments and their business associates in poor countries.

IV.

"Deregulation and liberalization," Richard O'Brien, chief economist of American Express Bank, notes, "clearly encourage globalization and integration. Liberal markets and systems tend to be open, providing greater ease of access, greater transparency of pricing and information." The flow of accessible information offers a global environment that is hospitable to homeless money, promoting what O'Brien calls "the end of geography" in the finance and investment business.[24] Even Switzerland, under outside pressures, has had to give up a little of its great national asset, the assurance of absolute secrecy and anonymity for bank accounts within its borders. Thanks to the Euromarket, Switzerland no longer had a corner on this trade. Already in 1970 Julien-Pierre Koszul, a Citibank official, had noted that the Euromarket constitutes "a marvelous platform from which it is easy to rebound, in any direction, to any country, into any currency—and with anonymity."[25]

The rise of global financial markets makes it increasingly difficult for national governments to formulate economic policy, much less to enforce it. In the increasingly anarchic world of high-speed money, the dilemma facing national political leaders is clear. Impose regulations, and sit back and watch how quickly financial institutions slip out from under them by changing their looks, disappearing into other corporations, or otherwise rearranging their affairs to make life difficult for the regulators. At the same time, bankers argue that to the extent the regulations are observed, they pose a handicap in international competition. Yet the history of deregulation is littered with scandals and financial foolishness for which a handful of bankers, but mostly millions of taxpayers and depositors, have paid a heavy price.

Governments are periodically taught chilling lessons about how much control they have lost over the money they print. In September 1992 a frenzy of twenty-four-hour-a-day trading in European currencies forced the central banks of Finland, Italy, Spain, and Britain to devalue their currencies and to spend 24 billion marks to prop up the lira and 10 billion pounds to keep British currency afloat. The British prime minister, who had made a public vow never to do what currency speculators around the world forced him to do, could not defend the pound even after the Bank of England raised interest rates five percentage points.[26] The exchange of one currency for another, according to estimates of the Bank of International Settlements, is now about $640 billion a day. Not more than 10 percent of this huge volume of currency trading that causes governments to quake and some to fall has anything to do with normal commercial transactions in which people or companies actually need to convert one currency to another to purchase foreign goods or services.[27]

The currency market never closes. About 30 percent of trading activities occur during the hours the Asian markets are open, 45 percent during trading hours in Europe, and only 15 percent when U.S. trading facilities are open. Currency traders in the world's least regulated market work long hours under great strain. At Chemical Bank's London operation the working day begins at 7:00 A.M. and ends at 6:00 P.M. A skeleton crew stays all night. The typical trader, in his 20s, his eyes glued to a green computer screen, a telephone receiver squashed against his ear, shouts bids across a roomful of high-decibel babble. "They start young and they burn out young," the recruitment director for the London headhunting firm Jonathan Wren explains. Aggressive young men eager to play for high stakes are recruited at $65,000 a year. A momentary lapse of attention or slip of the tongue can lose a ten-second trading opportunity and cost somebody millions. But for those who can stand the pace, the rewards in buying and selling fluctuating currencies are considerable, and, as the British prime minister can testify, the collective power of currency traders is formidable. Citibank typically earns about $150 million every quarter from its currency-trading operation. The financier George Soros personally earned $117 million in 1991 primarily from betting right on the German mark. A year later, he accumulated nearly $1 billion betting on the pound.[28]

V.

For most of this century world's fairs and theme parks have celebrated the promise of science and technology to transform the lives of ordinary people—bullet trains that ride on air, bubble-encased temperature-controlled cities, instantaneous delivery systems, and other wonders to turn homes and workplaces into a science-fiction world of convenience and fun. An amazing amount of it materialized, and much did not. The most spectacular technological advances over the past generation, however, did not take place in consumer products, and certainly not in the delivery of public services, but in the delivery of private services. The computer and related products for the manipulation of information have provided much of the drive for economic growth in the past quarter-century, playing a role much like that of the internal-combustion engine a hundred years ago. No industries are as dependent on information as money-traders and moneylenders. Innovation in information technology has had a more pronounced impact on the financial-services industry than on any other sector of the world economy.

It is almost a cliché in the industry now to say that information about money is as important as money itself. "From the first telegraph links and telephone exchanges in the late nineteenth century to the development of fourth generation computer languages today," Bernard Hoekman and Pierre Sauve write, "every major advance in information-related technologies has tended to find its first commercial application in the financial sector." The information revolution opened up the banking business to all sorts of newcomers, and this explosion of competition changed what a bank looks like, indeed what it is.

On October 27, 1986, the "Big Bang," as the chairman of the London Stock Exchange first called it, went off in the City of London, ending 200 years of comfortable, stately, and expensive trading practices on the London Stock Exchange. Overnight the market was deregulated and opened to foreign banks and securities firms of all sorts. An electronic marketing system modeled on the new American computer-age stock exchange, NASDAQ, was installed to take the place of old-fashioned floor trading. The London Stock Exchange was a centerpiece of world capitalism years after the British Empire had faded, but it had been run much like a gentleman's club. The Exchange was in a position to exact high fees and charges for the privilege of trading on its floor, and to be extremely choosy about whom to let in.

By the 1980s, however, stuffiness and monopolistic practices could not withstand the onslaught of telecommunications technology. Traders could now bypass London and deal directly with markets in New York and Tokyo at much less cost. Deregulation was a strategy for trying to get lost business back. As the New York Stock Exchange had done more than ten years earlier, the London Stock Exchange abolished fixed commissions for traders, and it now permitted firms to act as both wholesale dealers and brokers. Suddenly, U.S. commercial banks that were barred from the securities business at home could plunge into this market in London, neatly jumping over the wall of separation between investment and commercial banking provided under the Glass-Steagall Act of 1933, the cornerstone of modern U.S. banking regulation. (With the Great Crash and its consequences still fresh in mind, the Act was intended to forbid banks to act as underwriters for corporate securities.)

The global expansion through large corporate mergers and acquisitions gathered steam in the 1970s, and this global restructuring of industry required the amassing of huge amounts of capital. At first, large banks dominated this market because they were the ones with the financial power and connections to syndicate large loans through networks of foreign banks. But in the 1980s, as capital needs mushroomed, corporations in need of funds found that it was much cheaper to raise the capital by issuing bonds and other sorts of commercial paper. Financial institutions of all sorts packaged a bunch of small loans and sold them as securities on world markets. Small borrowers are sometimes unaware that their notes have been sold and resold. Nor is the borrower told that an inexplicable denial of mortgage money has nothing to do with his or her personal credit rating or the house to be purchased; the mortgage simply does not fit the profile of a globally salable loan.

"Securitization" of the banking business, as bankers call it, posed commercial financial institutions with the choice of either getting into the securities business or losing business. According to Professor Donald N. Thompson, "From 1980 to 1985 the volume of international loans fell from about $100 billion a year to about $25 billion, while new notes and bonds quadrupled from $50 billion to $200 billion." Securities went from a quarter of the Eurodollar lending market in 1980 to 85 percent in 1986. Foreign companies snapped up nineteen of the top twenty stock-brokerage firms in the United Kingdom. Citi acquired two of them, and in anticipation of the impact of the Big Bang it increased its London payroll to 3,400 employees.[29] But within a year it was losing $5 million a month on its acquisitions. "Big commercial banks," the *Economist* reported, "—notably America's Chase Manhattan, Citicorp, and Security Pacific—have throttled their London securities operations to extinction."[30]

Borrowers all over the world, including the largest corporations, could now shop around the world for money, and they could borrow it in many different forms on a wide variety of terms. Investors could hedge against risks in one national economy or in one industry by buying foreign stocks. Global markets in securities offered opportunities for diversification. Laws and regulations that had previously put international investments out of bounds came tumbling down. Markets in securities were losing what few geographical ties were left. It was now possible to invest in the New York market by buying

New York Stock Exchange index shares on the Chicago Board Options Exchange.[31]

The Big Bang triggered an explosion of deregulation in other financial centers all over the world. Screen-based markets offering instantaneous flows of global information took over an ever larger share of business from traditional floor trading. In addition to the speed and convenience, there were fees and taxes to be saved. Stocks in foreign companies became internationally traded products. London, Amsterdam, Paris, Frankfurt, and Zurich competed in offering the most cosmopolitan menu of stocks, options, swaps, and futures in companies around the world. By 1990 the buying and selling of foreign equities on the London Exchange exceeded that of British equities. The New York Stock Exchange and the Tokyo Exchange still deal primarily in the stocks of companies based in their own countries, but to attract international business, according to New York Stock Exchange chairman William Donaldson, American traders will have to put an end to parochialism and encourage more deregulation: "If this nation is to be the international market for securities, we must recognize the obvious, that not all the quality companies in the world are U.S. companies, nor are all U.S. accounting standards and practices necessarily the only way of approaching disclosure."[32]

In France the socialist government relaxed exchange controls and restrictions on banks, reorganized the money and government-bond markets, offered tax breaks to investors, and let banks and brokerage firms buy one another. Spain introduced computer-driven continuous trading and allowed foreign firms to buy into brokerage houses. But in other countries in Europe cultural traditions that have protected the local financial-services industry for generations still show signs of life. In Italy, for example, two-thirds of the capitalization on the Milan Stock Exchange is controlled by a handful of family holding companies like Fiat, which is owned by the Agnellis, and Italy has been slow to deregulate its financial services.[33] Germany has also hesitated to deregulate because the Bundesbank, reflecting the nation's historic fear of inflation, is concerned that the proliferation of financial instruments would encourage speculation and lessen the central bank's control over the money supply.

In most poor countries around the world foreign banks are welcomed as servicers of foreign corporations, sellers of retail credit, and providers of capital under controlled conditions. But foreign banks have with few exceptions been prohibited from buying into the commercial-banking sector. Since finance is central to development, so goes the standard nationalist argument, the financial-services industry should remain in domestic hands. The United States aggressively challenged this notion in the Uruguay Round of the GATT negotiations, arguing that efficiency and fairness required that foreign banks be accorded "national treatment." The GATT negotiations stalled for more than seven years; in the meantime, the U.S. pushed deregulation of financial services with Mexico, and secured an agreement that the American negotiator says will give U.S. banks "dramatic new opportunities" in that country with a growing consumer market. In an effort to sell NAFTA, another Treasury official bragged at an off-the-record briefing, "They gave us their financial system."

Thanks to the proliferation of money products through "derivative markets"—swaps, stock-index options, futures, and the like—under current law regulators cannot keep up with the swoosh of homeless money. Unregulated speculation is a major threat to the world economy and global regulation is clearly a formidable task. That said, there are a number of concrete steps that can be taken at the local, national, and supranational level to assure more public accountability in the global money market and to insure that a much larger share of global capital is used to meet the needs of people, communities, and the small enterprises that generate most of the world's jobs. We will suggest some of them in the next chapter.

CHAPTER THREE

GLOBAL FINANCE AND AMERICA'S BANKING CRISIS

I.

THE CHRONIC TRADE AND BUDGET DEFICITS OF THE UNITED States reflect two realities: One is that Americans buy more goods and services from overseas than they can sell abroad. The other is that the U.S. government has been able to spend much more than its income because of borrowing, much of it from foreign sources. In the process, the United States, still the world's leading creditor nation as recently as the early 1980s, has become the world's largest debtor nation.

How this happened is better understood now than when it was taking place. Over forty years have passed since the head of General Motors declared that he knew what was "good for America" because he knew what was good for his company; they were the same, Charles E. Wilson told a congressional committee. In 1992 one of his successors was ousted because he did not seem to know what was good either for General Motors or the country, and the president of the United States was rejected by the voters a few weeks later for essentially the same reasons.

By the 1980s Japanese prosperity had come to symbolize America's troubles. After three decades of extraordinary growth and expansion, Japan emerged in the early 1980s as a dominant force in the world economy, eager to profit from the economic troubles of its principal ally, but not their primary cause. Since the 1960s seven administrations had consistently underestimated Japanese industrial prowess. At the same time they assumed that America's hegemonic power meant that Japan, not the United States, would have to change course to avert a collision. Neither the government nor the largest manufacturing corporations had adapted to the new global environment or changed old habits fast enough to compete effectively with Japanese firms that had been focused on the global market for decades. Instead, increasing pressure on Japan to change its ways of doing business became the centerpiece of American strategy for dealing with its growing deficit.

In a world of complicated, often mysterious global connections, however, getting your way can turn out to be a curse. In the early 1980s U.S. negotiators insisted that the Japanese build cars in the United States, and the result was that the Japanese took over a still bigger share of the U.S. market and extended control over the automobile parts and accessories business. In 1984 Secretary of the Treasury Donald Regan went to Tokyo to demand that the Japanese open up their financial markets to U.S. firms and raise the value of the yen. Regan was emphatic. "The message that I'm giving to your Ministry of Finance . . . is: action, action, action, that's what I want now. I'm through with patience. . . ."[1] The top Japanese businessmen who made up the audience got the point. A Yen/Dollar Agreement was reached in which, according to a top adviser to the negotiation, "the U.S. side got almost all it asked for."[2]

Only when it was much too late did the U.S. government discover that the major triumphs it scored over Japan at the negotiating table in the 1980s would drive the nation deeper into debt. There were two conventional, plausible, but wrongheaded assumptions behind the American demands. They proved to be expensive. One was a belief that once the Japanese financial industry was more open to foreign investment, Wall Street banks and securities houses would devour a sizable chunk of the Tokyo capital market. The thought that Japanese banks, insurance companies, and securities firms, having accepted the invitation to compete on a global scale, would proceed to take over Wall Street firms and California banks occurred only to people who understood something about Japan. They were not in charge. Thanks to its huge trade surplus, Japan had enormous capital reserves that its financial industry used to buy into or buy up major assets across America.

The second assumption was that a weaker dollar would improve the U.S. trade balance without shifting the balance of world economic power. Cheapening the dollar did cause U.S. exports to surge by the end of the 1980s, including a modest increase into Japan's still tightly controlled market. But the export gains lagged behind the unprecedented flood of Japanese goods into the United States, which were snapped up by Americans with credit cards. The value of the dollar against the yen fell one-third between 1983 and 1986; devaluation made U.S. real estate and corporations of all sorts irresistible bargains for Japanese investors.

Thanks to the strong yen and its trade surplus, Japan was awash in cash. The huge capital accumulation was also helped by the extraordinary savings rate encouraged by Japanese culture and government policy of four decades. By 1989 the thirteen largest Japanese banks were capitalized at $500 billion, more than five times the value of the fifty largest U.S.-based banks. These bulging coffers contributed to the low cost of capital for Japanese corporations. U.S. banks had to pay almost twice as much for the money they lent. In the mid-1980s the Ministry of Finance began urging Japanese financial institutions to put their mammoth accumulations of surplus cash to work outside the country to minimize the domestic inflationary impact of Japan's commercial success. Fortunately for Japan, the world's second-largest economy found itself flush with cash at an historical moment when almost anything anywhere in the world could be bought. Neither pride nor national-security worries nor fame nor long tradition could prevail against the new power of money.

The results of prodding the Japanese into world financial markets and simultaneously devaluing the dollar were substantial[3]:

—By 1992, eight of the world's top ten banks, ranked by assets, were all Japanese; Citibank was the world's twentieth.

—By 1989 Japanese banks held almost 11 percent of U.S. banking assets, up from 2.3 percent in 1974.

—Between 1981 and 1989 Japanese banks increased their share of the assets of the world's top 100 banks from 25 to 46 percent, while the share of U.S. banks fell from 15 percent to 6 percent.

—By 1989 Japanese banks were providing 20 percent of all credit in California.

—By 1988 Nomura Securities, with twenty times the capital of Merrill Lynch, the largest U.S. brokerage house, bought a 20-percent share of Wasserstein & Perella, the leading merger-and-acquisition broker. Nikko Securities purchased 20 percent of the Blackstone Group. Sumitomo Bank bought a significant interest in Goldman

Sachs, Nippon Life a substantial share of Shearson Lehman, and Yasuda Mutual Life a major minority position in PaineWebber.

Just before he stepped down as chairman of the Federal Reserve Board, Paul Volcker observed, "We are obviously in danger of losing control over our own economic destiny."[4] He was referring to the fact that the U.S. government was becoming increasingly dependent on foreigners to finance its operations. In the Reagan years the annual budget deficit hovered between $150 and $250 billion, a state of affairs guaranteed by the administration's decision to increase federal spending while cutting tax rates. Every three months the U.S. Treasury holds a global auction of long-term bonds and short-term Treasury bills. Between 1984 and the end of the Reagan administration, Japanese securities firms were the best customers in the world for the highly prized obligations of the United States, still regarded as the world's most stable society and the best credit risk on earth. At one auction in 1986 Japanese investors bought 80 percent of the issue. As Daniel Burstein observes, "If Japanese investors hadn't bought $90 billion worth of U.S. government debt in 1986, the U.S. budget deficit would have intruded painfully on American life in forms ranging from sharply higher mortgage rates to higher taxes and deeper, more socially divisive cuts in government programs."[5]

The Japanese role in financing America's debt became a matter of concern on Wall Street, especially in the spring of 1986 when Japanese securities houses seemed to be hoarding U.S. Treasury bonds. Panicked Wall Street traders who were deluged with orders from all over the world suspected some political motive behind this unaccountable behavior; the Japanese, some bond traders charged, were "doing to us on the long bond what they did to us at Pearl Harbor." The explanation offered by Americans working for Japanese securities firms was that the bond "squeeze" was dictated not by fiendish design but by the peculiarities of the Japanese tax laws that made it disadvantageous to sell at that point. Whatever the real explanation, the basic lesson was the same: The globalized capital market allows the United States to conduct its short-term financial affairs with minimum pain, but the cost is long-term dependence on the goodwill, agendas, quirks, and business cultures of foreign creditors, who are in a position to do great harm to the United States whether or not that is their intention.

The problem of U.S. dependence on foreign credit is more basic than the challenge of Japanese competitive power. To be sure, in a globally integrated economy nations are influenced and constrained by the ways their trading partners and creditors organize their affairs. What "fair trade" means or what would constitute a "level playing field" for commercial competition are important questions, and new rules and understandings are needed. But the globalization of finance would still seriously limit choices national governments can make in trying to solve what we still call domestic problems even if Japan Inc. were to transform itself into an American clone or to disappear.

Indeed, as the 1990s began, Japan suffered a series of severe economic reverses. Thanks to the trade surplus, strong yen, and cheap capital, the Japanese real-estate market had boomed in the 1980s. Stretches of land no bigger than California, this string of cramped islands of shoe-box houses now had a paper value exceeding that of all the real estate in the United States. The market capitalization of the Tokyo Stock Exchange exceeded that of the New York Stock Exchange. But in 1990 the Japanese stock market collapsed, losing more than half its value. The real-estate bubble burst as land values in Tokyo fell 30 to 50 percent. Suddenly Japanese banks found that they were carrying somewhere between 20 and 50 trillion yen in bad real-estate loans (about $186 billion–$465 billion in July 1993).[6] The Japanese government, partly in response to American pressure but mostly to control the wild speculation of the 1980s, removed the ceiling on interest rates. The end of cheap money further cut into the profits of Japanese banks.

Talk of retrenchment could be heard in the great Tokyo banks. The Bank of International Settlements in Basel, which has limited regulatory authority under international agreements, had announced minimum capital requirements for international lending, and Japan had agreed to observe them. But this made the drive for growth more difficult. Japanese bankers, like their compatriots in manufacturing, had consistently sacrificed quick profits for long-term growth. Now this was becoming more difficult. A number of banks had fallen below the BIS capital requirements described by the deputy president of Sanwa Bank (then the world's fourth largest) as a "silk stocking strangling us."[7] Japan, it turned out, was not exempt from the vicissitudes of the same global economy it had so successfully ridden to the heights of power.

By 1991 Japan's financial juggernaut appeared stalled. A year later the Japanese economy was in recession. Japanese banks cut back on their international lending, and the Japanese takeover of U.S. companies and prime pieces of real estate slowed. But America's problems of debt and dependence remained.

Every day an estimated $150 billion in U.S. government bonds changes hands across a global computerized trading network that virtually never stops. By late 1992, the U.S. government owed $2.7 trillion in Treasury obligations to private investors—17 percent of these bondholders were outside the United States—and another $1 trillion to itself, that is, the bonds were held by federal-government agencies. Since the nongovernment bondholders are free at any time to sell millions of dollars of long-term U.S. securities literally in seconds, they hold enormous power over the economic decisions of any president. Bill Clinton was elected in part on a promise to get the economy moving with the aid of a "stimulus package," the infusion of tens of billions of new investment funds. But already during the transition he was made acutely aware that, as Robert Hormats, vice-chairman of Goldman Sachs International, puts it, "the global bond market can be a very tough disciplinarian." If the president is perceived to be pursuing an inflationary policy by thousands of bondholders across the world, who generally exhibit what Hormats calls a "very conservative bias," they are almost certain to unload their fixed-income securities. This would drive interest rates up, slow the economy, and effectively cancel the effect of the new investment. As Clinton took office the budget deficit stood at a record $290 billion, up from $74 billion at the end of the Carter administration. "By having such a big deficit," Edward Yardeni, chief economist at C. J. Lawrence Inc., notes, "we have created a situation that puts a lot of power in the hands of money managers all around the world. We created the monster, and now it's coming back to tell us what we can and can't do."[8] Clinton's stimulus package was killed at birth.

For the United States, as for every other country, the price of economic integration has been a loss of political autonomy. For years managers of the U.S. economy assumed that because America was the flagship of the world economy, indeed the printer and prime manager of the world's reserve currency, the country was relatively free to tune its own economy by raising and lowering taxes and adjusting interest rates. But by 1990 crucial decisions that were traditionally the exclusive province of the president and the Federal Reserve Board were now held hostage to international pressures.

Indeed, the need to accommodate Japan and the failure to influence Germany to keep interest rates down may well have cost George

Bush his reelection. The president infuriated his right-wing support-
ers by going back on his "no new taxes" pledge. It was, as C. Michael
Aho and Bruce Stokes point out in *Foreign Affairs*, "no coincidence"
that Bush called for a second reading of his lips just days before the
Structural Impediments Initiative talks with Japan were concluded.
Bush's agreement to a tax hike—his biggest mistake, he later said—
was intended as a demonstration to the Japanese of the nation's
willingness to reduce its budget deficit. Given the enormity of the
deficit and the large numbers of foreign bondholders, the U.S. government was no longer able to count on the traditional instruments
of monetary and fiscal policy to lift the U.S. economy out of recession.

II.

Several months before the 1992 election Roger J. Vaughan and Edward W. Hill published a detailed study of the financial health of
commercial banks in the United States. They reported that there were
2,000 "troubled banks" in the nation, that 1,200 of them would fail
or be forced by regulators into mergers, and that at the heart of the
banking crisis were "14 banking holding companies each with more
than $10 billion in assets." Were their portfolios given "honest mar-
ket valuations," all would show a negative net worth. Although only
about 10 percent of commercial banks were in serious difficulty,
these included some of the biggest. In 1992 Congress passed a law
requiring federal regulators to take over failing banks once their
losses reached a certain point. As Bill Clinton took office, he faced
the prospect of having to preside over a rescue mission for the nation's failing commercial banks on a scale approaching that of the
savings-and-loan bailout.

How and why the United States was faced with a string of bank
failures beyond anything experienced since the early 1930s is a tan-
gled tale with many subplots. Bankers with tens of billions of other
people's money to lend, impelled by the large fees to be made by
lending large sums, piled up an unprecedented number of imprudent
loans, knowing that the federal government would ultimately pay off
their depositors if the loans turned sour. The wreckage caused by
human frailty on Wall Street, State Street, LaSalle Street, and other
citadels of American capitalism have been documented extensively in
recent years, and films, novels, and exposés of the business culture of

the Reagan-Bush years have entertained millions of its victims.[9] The role that the global transformation of finance played in compounding America's money troubles is a less familiar story.

To a casual visitor, all banks look more or less alike, wherever they happen to be located. But their social, political, and economic roles differ widely from country to country. As banks in the major industrial countries compete ever more fiercely in the global marketplace, the differences in the ways national banking systems are organized become more important. Historically, the banking system in the United States has been highly decentralized. At the end of the 1980s, despite the bank mergers that occurred in that decade, there were still 14,000 commercial banks in the United States. Japan had exactly 158.[10] This is one reason why only a handful of U.S.-based banks are important players in the global marketplace, and why many small U.S. banks, lured in the 1980s into foreign operations, found that they could not compete and had to pull back. Only banks the size of Citicorp, Bankers Trust, and J. P. Morgan had the resources to play in this game, and even they, as we have seen, were often overtaken by Japanese, German, Dutch, and French giants.

In Germany and Japan, banks have a more prominent role in the economy than they do in the United States. The typical Japanese firm borrows about 80 percent of its capital, most of it in the form of bank loans, not bonds. U.S. firms are much more likely to borrow no more than half their capital needs, and much of this debt is in the form of securities.[11] This much greater dependence on the stock market is one important reason why so many U.S. firms are so terrorized by their quarterly statements, and so concerned with short-term profits that they neglect the long-term investment needed to compete effectively over a long period of time.

In Japan, two-thirds of all corporate stock is held by institutions, mostly by a bank or trading partners with a long, intimate association with the company. Thus Mitsubishi Bank owns stock and shares directors with the other Mitsubishi companies. Sony, though not a *keiretsu* member, is nonetheless closely linked to its major lender, and through that bank to a loose association of other companies.

The cozy relationship between banks and industrial companies has offered certain advantages to Japanese industry. Capital is cheaper and more reliably available than it would be if there were a purely arms-length relationship between borrower and lender. German and Japanese banks do not demand high dividends on the corporate stock they own; industrial companies substantially owned by banks are thus able to accumulate savings for long-term investment. In the first half of the 1980s, for example, Toyota paid out a 1.3-percent dividend to its shareholders compared with 7.1 percent at General Motors.[12] Moreover, by owning major shares of their borrowers, Japanese banks have a pecuniary interest in rescuing troubled industrial corporations before they go bankrupt.

But with the growing speed of high-tech finance and the increasing irrelevance of national frontiers, national differences in the ways banking systems operate across the industrial world are giving way. Global competition has become a powerful argument almost everywhere for reshaping national banking systems. The boom in trading financial instruments on the global market in the last decade has coincided with record defaults in bank loans, particularly in the United States and Japan. The European and Japanese banks competed successfully in those years because a great share of their assets were in large blocks of stock in their nations' most powerful corporations to which they supplied cheap credit. The Japanese also made huge profits by buying up takeover firms and financing leveraged buyouts in the United States, a risky activity that was out of bounds in Japan. When some of their major debtors began to default, the Japanese firms pulled back, and this helped bring the go-go years on Wall Street to an end.

The largest U.S. banks began to respond to the pressures of the global marketplace and moved from lending money to trading securities. In the 1970s, U.S. banks of all sorts lent out 85 percent of their assets, but as the 1990s began, they were, on the average, lending out only 50 to 60 percent. (In 1992 Bankers Trust was lending out only 16 percent of its assets.)[13] The Fed reduced the prime rate to the lowest point in many years, but banks preferred to put their 3-percent money into Treasuries yielding 7.5 percent or into credit-card loans at 19 percent rather than lend it to home owners with shaky job prospects, or to entrepreneurs with small businesses, many of which fail.[14]

Global competition has forced changes in Japan, too. Under international pressure, interest rates have been deregulated, and banks can no longer offer their industrial clients the favorable terms they once did. In anticipation of the opening of the Europe-wide market, there was a wave of mergers in France, Holland, Belgium, and Spain in the 1980s. Banks consolidated rapidly in the belief that only larger banks would have the clout to compete in their own countries with the U.S. global banks—Citicorp, Bankers Trust, and J. P. Morgan—

and the Japanese, Swiss, and French giants. By 1989 the three largest banks in Holland held 70 percent of the deposits in the country. According to a McKinsey & Co. study, the five largest banks in France and Spain had between 60 and 70 percent of all deposits.[15]

As the 1990s began, U.S. bankers warned that American banks would be overwhelmed in the global marketplace unless the U.S. banking system changed even more than it had in the 1970s and 1980s. "Clearly, the geography thing killed us," John Reed declared, "and the degree to which industrial companies are in our business." Charles S. Sanford, Jr., chairman of Bankers Trust, agreed. "Not having securities powers makes U.S. banks less competitive with European banks, and this will be exacerbated when Japanese banks get more powers." German and Japanese banks can operate anywhere in their own national markets. They can sell stocks, bonds, and insurance. They can provide a fuller range of services to their customers in the United States than can U.S. banks, which, despite deregulation, still face what E. Gerald Corrigan, former president of the New York Fed, calls a "crazy-quilt pattern" of state and federal laws and regulations.[16] Faced with growing problems in their own home markets, including the entry of foreign banks, many U.S. banks began to unload or severely cut back their overseas operations.

The new international standards prescribing tougher minimum reserve requirements for banks, which became operative in 1993, mandated more conservative lending policies and reduced worldwide lending. Although money was now cheaper, U.S. banks had less of it for hire. Large banks increasingly preferred to trade securities rather than to make commercial loans, and in the global recession this made credit even tighter. Investment bankers and academics argued about whether there was a worldwide capital shortage, yet the hundreds of billions of dollars that banks have steered into leveraged buyouts and other speculative instruments in recent years suggest that the shortage is man-made. The small farmers, small businesses, and prospective home buyers who could not get financing did not need to be convinced that they faced a credit crunch.

At the same time, the Federal Deposit Insurance Corporation acquired increased powers to close banks in the United States or to force them into mergers. Within the banking industry sudden growth by merger became the preferred strategy for confronting foreign competition. Nineteen ninety-one was a year of megamergers: Bank America and Security Pacific became the giant of the West, Manufacturers Hanover and Chemical Bank the giant of the East and the number-two bank in the country, and North Carolina National Bank (NCNB) and C&S/Sovran joined forces to become the giant of the new South. Five of these six banks ranked among the U.S. lending institutions with the greatest exposure in commercial real estate. The mergers in the name of competitiveness and efficiency cost about 35,000 jobs, but this addition to the ranks of the unemployed solved none of the structural problems of the industry, neither the patchwork of regulations (and the small army of encircled regulators who try to administer them) nor the pressures that incite bankers to chase risky deals.[17] Nor, most important, did they resolve the underlying confusion about what a bank is and what social role, if any, it ought to serve.

III.

American history books are filled with the names of famous bankers—Gallatin, Biddle, Morgan, Mellon, Warburg, Giannini, Wriston—who changed the face of the nation. But bankers almost never become American culture heroes because in the popular consciousness they are in the business of denying credit to needy widows and families about to lose the farm. In the days of vaudeville and Depression-era movies, bankers and financiers were stock characters because audiences so enjoyed hissing them. Edward Arnold made a career out of looking like a financier even in the rare roles that did not call for him to be one. Audiences responded because these films mirrored their own experience. Unmarried women could not open bank accounts, and lots of families lost the farm.

The only heartwarming banker to emerge from Hollywood was George Bailey in *It's a Wonderful Life,* who was so responsive to his neighbors' needs that his bank had to be bailed out by an angel. In fact, as Michael Thomas notes, the angel was not needed to pay off the depositors, who were covered by FDIC insurance, but supernatural intervention was necessary to rescue George from the shame of bankruptcy and to preserve his "Godgiven entitlement to feel good about himself."[18] When this early postwar film reemerged as a Christmas favorite in the 1980s, however, bankruptcy was no longer a badge of shame but a widely used financial option.

As the 1990s began, lurid tales of criminal banks were splashed across front pages. The dimensions of the money mania and its costs were becoming clearer. The United States faced another round in its

200-year self-examination of the role of money in American life. (These periodic bouts of introspection normally follow on the heels of guilded decades, panics, and depressions.) Although democracy and plutocracy have coexisted in the United States since the beginning, the tension was becoming more obvious in the 1990s as record numbers of votes were snared through multimillion-dollar campaigns financed by private contributions. According to Craig McDonald and David Eppler of Public Citizen, in the 1990 election campaign the largest source of business PAC contributions "came from financial, insurance, and real estate interests, who gave a total of $25 million."[19]

Banks play two important but distinct economic roles in shaping society. One is to meet the credit needs of large business enterprises. The other is to lend money to the millions of small depositors from whom banks raise capital. After the financial crisis of the Great Depression, new forms of government-sponsored, government-organized, and government-funded credit institutions sprang up in the United States to serve farmers, home buyers, and small businesses. In the years of America's extraordinary growth, roughly 1945–73, the system worked well. GI mortgages financed two generations of home owners of modest incomes, and GI loans enabled millions to acquire a liberal education and marketable skills. Private local banks financed thousands of small businesses, which employ well over half of the work force in the private sector.

But in the last twenty years the allure of quick profits in distant markets and the press of global competition have undercut the two functions that the U.S. banking system was created to serve. Debt relief for Donald Trump's casinos is on the scale accorded debtor nations, but the banking system seldom facilitates the financing of long-term investment to expand employment. The money of local depositors is being sucked into speculative global securities and away from local communities badly in need of financing for housing, small business, and local services. Family farms face a severe credit crisis and great numbers of foreclosures and bankruptcies continue across the country. First-time home owners, low-income families unable to afford mortgages at market rates, and small businesses have also been hit hard. Who can get credit and who cannot is a critical determinant of social and political development. What banks do or refuse to do has considerable influence on how a society functions and what a nation looks like. If there is no adequate credit for affordable housing or for small business, the predictable consequences are homelessness, racial tensions, and unemployment.

IV.

Governments can no longer keep money from fleeing the country, nor can they keep foreign money out, even when they try. But they can set standards and create incentives to encourage capital to flow where it is needed by changing some of the rules of the game. Government still has instruments, especially the power to tax, that can influence banks in the direction either of long-term investment or short-term speculation. How it exercises these powers can influence the behavior of banks in a number of ways.

Bank reform is high on the political agenda in the 1990s, thanks to the financial crises created in the 1980s. But bank reformers have very different things in mind, depending upon where they sit. By and large bankers everywhere want more deregulation. In the United States the financial industry continues its relentless lobbying to get rid of what is left of the Glass-Steagall Act so that the remaining barriers between commercial and investment banking will be eliminated. In Europe banks are urging that they be allowed to own major shares of industrial corporations, as in Japan. In all three banking centers of the world, financial firms, arguing that global competitiveness requires it, are taking aim at the remaining barriers to the free flow of capital.

Reformers who worry about the credit crunch for affordable housing, the launching of small businesses, and other local community needs have a quite different agenda. Martin Mayer, who has written extensively about banking, says that the savings-and-loan crisis "provides convincing evidence that the government cannot afford to give total insurance to principal and interest on public deposits and permit banks to invest other people's money entirely at their own discretion. Either the insurance must be restricted, or the use of the money must be controlled by law."[20] Under present law banks have an incentive to maximize earnings by placing insured deposits in speculative securities and real-estate investments.

Some reformers call for a two-tier banking system. Banks covered by the Federal Deposit Insurance Corporation should be required to lend a given percentage of their assets in the local communities in which they operate to meet the short-term credit needs of local business and to facilitate home ownership. Large banks operating primarily in global credit and securities markets would remain free to speculate with their depositors' money, but the deposits would be uninsured and the depositors, not the taxpayers, would bear any loss. Lowell Bryan, head of the banking group at McKinsey & Co., argues for the two-tier system. "Core banks," as he calls them, would accept government-insured deposits, but their activities would be restricted to what he calls "low-risk businesses," government securities, and consumer loans. "Wholesale or commercial finance banks" could do as much risky trading and lending as they liked, but there would be no bailout.[21]

William Kistler, who runs a diversified investment fund, notes that the income tax on gains from a security held for ten seconds is the same as on a security held ten years. To steer capital to long-term investment he suggests staggering the tax rate, for example, 50 percent on securities held less than six months, 35 percent on securities held from six months to three years, and as low as 10 percent on securities held more than three years.[22] The economist Howard Wachtel points to another lever that could be used to encourage long-term investment. Federal regulators could set lower capital-asset requirements for banking activities on which local communities depend, such as lending to small businesses or home buyers, than for global banking activities. Former chair of the House Banking Committee Henry Reuss believes that the Community Reinvestment Act, which was designed to encourage banks to lend in the local community, should be strengthened and more zealously enforced. William Greider argues that the nation's housing crisis "could be resolved directly and efficiently if the financial system were required to pool sufficient capital to provide below-market mortgage rates for first-time home-buyers and low-income housing construction. The government could require financial institutions to accept a modest social burden in exchange for the protections that government provides them."[23]

As the Clinton administration took office, the stubborn character of the economic crisis in America was becoming apparent. Despite signs of recovery, the hemorrhaging of jobs continued. The four largest employers in the nation, GM, Sears, Ford, and IBM, laid off tens of thousands of workers in 1993, and it was now clearer that the largest several hundred corporations would continue to play a diminishing role as job providers. (Between 1979 and 1992, the largest

500 U.S.-based industrial corporations cut 4.4 million workers from their payrolls.)[24] Although the often-expressed concerns about the state of American education were justified on many grounds, the hopes that better technical and scientific training of the American work force would improve "competitiveness" and thereby solve the unemployment problem were to a considerable extent illusory. Too many jobs in large corporations requiring specialized skills were disappearing, and the pressures to employ cheap labor abroad were greater than ever.

The hopes for job creation were in smaller enterprises serving local community needs that global corporations are unable to provide for or uninterested in doing so, and these required different sorts of training and support. Opening up lines of credit to those who will never successfully compete for the ever scarcer jobs in global enterprises to enable them to participate in the rebuilding of local economies is a sensible and achievable goal. The redirection of credit is an essential component of a more credible long-range strategy. It certainly makes more sense than a global productivity race that pits American workers against Chinese.

There are many ways to change the incentive system that has directed credit away from where it is most needed to renew American communities. Tom Schlesinger of the Financial Democracy Campaign and banking specialist Jane D'Arista argue for much greater community involvement in the banking process at every stage.[25] They propose that all financial institutions operate under renewable licenses, as television stations do. Every few years banks would need to demonstrate their financial and managerial soundness and their record of performance with regard to community obligations already on the books, such as the Community Reinvestment Act, Home Mortgage Disclosure Act, Truth-in-Lending Act, and Equal Credit Opportunity Act.

Another proposal has been put forward to create an American Investment Bank, financed in part by a share of the pension funds of American workers. There are more than 100 community efforts around the nation to generate and direct capital to where it is most needed. The South Shore Bank in Chicago, mentioned frequently by President Clinton during his campaign, is one example. Another influential model has been the Grameen Bank in Bangladesh, which now grants thousands of loans to small rural enterprises in that country. (The average loan is around $60.) Because the bank lends money to a group of farmers or small entrepreneurs who are accountable to one another, the default rate is amazingly low. These ideas are being tried in American cities.

At the same time, international regulation is badly needed. Euro-currency markets are still largely unregulated. The Basel Group of central banks, reacting to the BCCI scandal and a number of others less celebrated, issued new guidelines for international bank supervision calling on governments to monitor the global activities of their home-based banks and to share information with one another. But, as Gary Kleiman, who is an international banking consultant, points out, these rules are inadequate since they "make no provision for when a country is unwilling to share data. . . ."[26] Kleiman calls for a new international coordinating body within the Basel Group to help resolve disputes between central banks and investigate complex multinational cases like BCCI. Howard Wachtel calls for a reserve requirement on Eurodollar accounts. The higher the reserve requirement, the more money would flow back into national banking systems.[27]

Our point in this brief survey of alternative directions for the banking industry is that, despite the globalization of finance, territorially based governments still have many resources to influence capital flows in ways that can meet the credit needs of communities, families, and citizens. Traditional monetary and fiscal policies, the tools invented by governments two generations ago to steer capital, do not work well anymore. New approaches are needed to carry out these functions in the new global environment. After all, banks are still instruments of the political communities from which they derive their legal powers and to which they look to guarantee the underlying credibility of the credit system.

CONCLUSION

GLOBAL THINKING IN A DISORDERLY WORLD

I.

"THINK GLOBALLY!" IS GOOD BUMPER-STICKER ADVICE, but it is a daunting task. In poetry, pictures from space, or in religious teachings a vision of the earth as a whole can touch and inspire us, but in the practical decisions of daily life it is hard to go about embracing a planet. Most of us have trouble even thinking of our own nuclear family as a unit. In the worlds of commerce and politics all global visions are partial. Corporate leaders talk about producing "global products" even though most people in the world cannot afford to buy them. National political leaders talk about meeting the "challenges of globalization" through economic strategy and foreign policy. But what they have in mind are subsidies, incentives, and sanctions to combat the threats to the "domestic" economy posed by "foreign" competition. No world authority exists to define global welfare, much less to promote it.

Commercial culture—music, video, and film—has a truly global audience, and the technology exists to reach billions of people even in the same instant of real time. Fantasies of affluence, freedom, and power flash across the earth as movie and TV images, offering the poor of the world a window into a fairy-tale world of money, thrills, and ease, but no door. Goods can now be made everywhere and sold anywhere, and more and more services, even highly skilled and specialized services, can be performed at great distance. There is an ever-expanding global labor pool as more than 47 million men and women enter the job market each year. But there are not enough good jobs, that is, secure jobs with decent working conditions that pay enough, nor are there encouraging prospects that such jobs will ever be available in sufficient numbers. Because of the downward pressures on wages in many places in the world in recent years, the class of global consumers is not growing rapidly enough to keep the global mass-production system humming.

Viewed as a whole as if from space, this system appears fragile. The built-in pressures to cut jobs and wages are intensifying because of chronic overproduction and global competition, and advances in automation and training make it easier to relocate factories and to slash payrolls. Production becomes more "efficient" in an economic sense, but the next generation faces declining prospects of stable, well-paid jobs and more of the world's population are fated to be window shoppers, not customers. Finance is now global, but most people in the world cannot get a loan to build a house, plant a field, or start a business.

As they look out on this world, CEOs, presidents, prime ministers, and chancellors feel that they do not have the luxury to adopt the astronaut's angle of vision, much less the prophet's. They are players in a highly competitive game, not lofty observers. Each has his (occasionally her) own responsibility only for a piece of the playing field. The collapse of communism has dealt a blow even to the sort of global thinking that characterized much of world politics over the last fifty years. The Cold War was a truly worldwide struggle, a long peace in Europe, North America, and Japan accompanied by wars and threats of wars almost everywhere else. Even regimes in remote places deemed to be under Soviet influence or in danger of becoming subject to such influence were objects of American attention, either as recipients of guns and dollars or targets of military and paramilitary operations. Sporadic military interventions continue. But with the end of the Soviet Union and its far-flung political interests around the world, the leading industrial nations that formed a global alliance to oppose it have turned inward.

The United States is engaged in an uncertain effort to renew an overstretched and abused economy through cost-cutting and modest social reform. Germany is focused on integrating itself and finding ways to pay the heavy costs of reunification without wrecking what has been the strongest economy of Europe. As the decade began, Japan, the world's chief supplier of foreign capital, seemed to be on the threshold of a grand entrance onto the world stage, but mounting political problems at home, the sharp decline in its wildly inflated real-estate and financial markets, and the continuing world recession have dictated a more cautious role. Russia is in the throes of painful change, lurching from one set of economic ideas to another in the effort to stave off chaos.

The result is that while there is a crying need for political vision at the global level, national leaders seem unable to take even small steps toward effective global action. Thus Serbia's war of aggression against Bosnia, despite the danger that it could escalate to a wider Balkan war, did not prompt an even remotely adequate European response, much less a global one. The United States and other major military powers exhibited a certain amount of guilt and much frustration at their inability to stop an expansionist war likely to embolden ambitious leaders elsewhere. But all the major powers refused to be distracted from problems closer to home until it was too late.

Given the present state of the world, global political norms, global economic rules of conduct, a global legal order, and effective global authorities to undertake preventive diplomacy, the settlement of disputes, the containment of war, and the enforcement of peace are urgently needed. But in the closing years of the twentieth century the "deglobalization" of world politics is occurring even as the globalization of economic activities proceeds. The great powers are all uncertain about what they should be doing and how to define their interests in the disorderly world about them. Dean Acheson's remark about Britain—that it had lost an empire but not yet found a role—is now applicable to all the prime political actors on the world stage.

As the world economy becomes more and more integrated, the processes of political disintegration are accelerating. The prospect of further rapid integration of Europe has dimmed. Political agreement at the global level, whether on the environment, immigration, labor standards, human rights, trade, or investment is proceeding slowly. There appears to be a direct connection between economic integration and political dissolution, and throughout the book we have included specific illustrations of how and why this perverse relationship exists. Bringing global economic institutions under the authority of political institutions is essential to protect the environment, human rights, and job possibilities around the world. Making both accountable to the people is essential if the new world order is to be democratic, and if it is not democratic it will enjoy neither legitimacy nor stability.

No world political figure is grappling with the sorts of political challenges that the radical technological and economic changes of the last quarter century have thrust upon us. By default, business enterprises are wielding political power in many important ways. Global financial markets increasingly dictate the limits of domestic political strategies to fund environmental clean-up or to create jobs. Corporate managers have neither the consciousness, the incentives, nor the inclination to take on public responsibilities that governments are unable to perform. To be sure, there are many companies only too happy to perform services once provided by government such as running prisons or delivering the mail. But the idea that the national unemployment rate ten years hence should figure in a CEO's decision today about where to locate a plant or whether or how to automate strikes most business people as the quickest path to early retirement or Chapter Eleven.

Most corporate leaders, while proudly exercising their constitutionally protected right to influence elections and legislation, deny that they are making public policy merely by doing business. They do not accept responsibility for the social consequences of what they make or how they make it. That is government's job, but one, they believe, that must defer to market freedom. If the people want a product or a service, government should not act as a nanny or a censor. Public accountability is an important criterion by which to judge presidents, bureaucrats, and senators but not CEOs of great corporations. Because business enterprises have outgrown political institutions at the local, national, and supranational levels, national leaders are exerting less and less control over economic issues. As a result the world faces an authority crisis without precedent in modern times.

II.

Economic ties across national borders have become so strong, so deep, and so complex that political leaders can no longer make successful use of traditional strategies to deal with such problems as unemployment, ecological deterioration, and the corrosive effects of chronic poverty. Lavish government expenditures to soften the impact of these problems are no longer available, except perhaps in Japan, which is still flush thanks to its trade surplus. Authoritarian governments that tried to solve political problems by suppressing the market have been forced to shift course. Even the heavily managed market economies such as those of Korea and Japan, after achieving the most spectacular growth in the last twenty years, are bumping up against the limits all national governments feel.

Because global corporations are the prime actors in the economic transformation of the last quarter century, they have inspired flights of hyperbole from many different quarters. In the early 1970s CEOs and business philosophers rhapsodized about IBM, GM, Pfizer, and other U.S.-based giants being "the only force for peace," or "the most powerful agent for the internationalization of human society," or even as one business-school dean put it, "the prologue to a new world symphony." Critics predicted that a few multinationals, most of them chartered in the United States, would soon be running the world. The French publisher Jean-Jacques Servan-Schreiber became famous in the late 1960s by calling on Europe to resist the "American challenge" from U.S.-based multinationals by launching its own transnational enterprises. Gaullists and communists alike took to the barricades against the "Coca-colonization" of the Old World.

The world looks different today. In 1970, according to the UN Center on Transnationals, there were 7,000 multinational companies in the world, and more than half were based in the United States and Britain. But by the early 1990s there were 35,000 multinationals, and the United States, Japan, Germany, and Switzerland combined had less than half. In the early 1970s a professor at the Wharton School predicted that by 1985 about 80 percent of all productive assets in the noncommunist world would be owned by 200 to 300 corporations. According to back-of-the-envelope calculations by the editors of the *Economist*, the world's top 300 industrial corporations now control more like 25 percent of the world's $20 trillion stock of productive assets.[1] But these footloose business enterprises in a world of weakened governments hold the power to veto a range of crucial political decisions across the planet. In the world economy, as in a large public corporation, powerful minority stockholders can end up in control.

The editors of the *Economist* call multinationals "everybody's favourite monster," a double entendre that suggests how ephemeral opinions in economic matters turn out to be. Their point is that the same multinationals that inspired such concern in the 1970s are seen today "as the embodiment of modernity and the prospect of wealth: full of technology, rich in capital, replete with skilled jobs." The editors admit that this may overstate the positive assessment of global corporations, and they worry that excessive expectations will produce a backlash. But it is indeed true that governments in developing countries (and state governors in the United States) "are queuing up to attract multinationals." The job crisis and cash problems in poor countries are so severe that any number of new jobs, any boost in foreign exchange, is welcomed. Still, the courting of global corporations has more to do with the absence of alternatives than with enthusiasm for foreign firms.

Political leaders in populous developing countries are eager to attract foreign capital since global companies offer a small number of skilled jobs with higher pay in many cases than the prevailing local rate, a larger number of semiskilled assembly jobs, and a still larger number of low-wage jobs for suppliers or contract labor. Debt-ridden countries need foreign exchange, and global corporations with local export operations are sometimes the only available source. Developing countries that sharply restricted foreign investment in the 1970s have now opened their doors to such firms because they see no other way to solve balance-of-payments problems. Other paths to development that they had hoped to take have turned out to be dead ends. When China, despite its huge resources, abandoned Maoist autarchy, political leaders in poor countries rethought the practicality of "self-sufficiency." The collapse of socialism in Russia, the exposure of the corruption and bankruptcy of so-called "African socialist" countries, and the trend toward "privatization" and "marketization" almost everywhere have altered the way foreign capital is perceived. The radical dreams of the 1970s—massive government-to-government transfers, Marshall Plans for the Third World, a global North–South bargain, the New International Economic Order, massive South–South trade—have become casualties of the global shift in ideological fashion. A more sober and realistic understanding of the global power relations now reigns. For all these reasons, the bargaining power of governments vis-à-vis foreign capital has declined.

The critics are now confronted by the astonishing size, pace, and diversity of transnational economic activity. The face of the foreign company has become blurry. Corporations chartered in Delaware present themselves as American corporations when it suits their interests and emphasize their "statelessness" when it does not. Alliances struck between competing firms mostly based in the three affluent regions of the industrialized world—North America, Europe, and East Asia—complicate the meanings of domestic and foreign, friend and foe, us and them. Twenty years ago the words "foreign capital" evoked images of dark, dirty, and dangerous mines, polluting refineries, airless electronics assembly operations, and plantations. All of these still exist, but they are less visible because they are enmeshed in complex transnational networks of many other sorts. Finance, accounting, legal, and engineering services, media, entertainment, and information processing now also have a global reach. At the same time companies with transnational operations are now so ubiquitous that they have become part of the landscape. Virtually all business enterprises beyond a certain size do business across national frontiers.

Yet the signs of fragility in this increasingly unregulated and ungoverned system are growing. GM and IBM are prime examples of how size does not guarantee success or even survival. Giant companies that have controlled substantial shares of the world market have sustained gargantuan losses in recent years. The competition from smaller firms sharpens as the technology and know-how to develop transnational enterprises become cheaper and more widely available. Because incremental technological changes come so fast and have such an unpredictable impact on the market in electronics, drugs, and computers, for example, even within the largest firms with long track records and deep roots in many countries, there is a growing sense of impermanence.

The fierceness of global competition in many industries in a time of prolonged global recession is producing a certain convergence in business cultures around the world. Social democracies are cutting back on high wages, secure employment, and liberal benefits. In the United States, corporations are making greater efforts to conserve energy and other resources. But the pressures of competition driven by trade deficits and falling market shares are forcing even corporations accustomed to taking the long view into greater concern for cost-cutting strategies that reduce employment security and threaten the environment.

III.

The surplus of gifted, skilled, undervalued, and unwanted human beings is the Achilles heel of this emerging global system. The problem is starkly simple: An astonishingly large and increasing number of people are not needed or wanted to make the goods or to provide the services that the paying customers of the world can afford. The gathering pressures of global competition to cut costs threaten the vast majority of the 8 billion human beings expected to be living on earth in the first quarter of the next century with the prospect that they will be neither producers nor consumers.

Hopes for full employment have traditionally rested on the assumption of technological rescue. Aging markets, obsolete factories, and unneeded jobs are swept away and replaced by bigger markets and higher-paid jobs. The makers of buggy whips enter the middle class by landing jobs at a Ford plant. The pace of technological rescue slowed in the 1930s, but was revived by World War II. The postwar prosperity was generated mostly by consumer spending in entertainment, travel, and electronics made possible by adaptations of military technology—jet aircraft, computers, transistors, and telecommunications. The promising commercial technologies of the near future—improvements in TV reception, interactive TV, and high-tech information technologies—appear to offer consumers new wrinkles, styles, and games, but not fundamentally new products that can create and satisfy new human needs, thereby triggering what Robert Heilbroner calls a "transformational boom."[2]

Like digital technologies, biotechnology, on which perhaps the greatest hopes for transforming society are pinned, is anything but labor-intensive. (In 1992, Amgen, the largest biotechnology company, employed a mere 2,335 people.)[3] Indeed, biotech products threaten to become large-scale job destroyers. Were the bovine growth hormone to become widely used, according to some estimates, 7.5 million "supercows" could furnish the same quantity of milk now provided by 10.8 million ordinary cows, and the number of commercial dairy firms would be cut in half. Genetically engineered food products that bypass farming altogether could have a revolutionary effect on the hundreds of millions of people in the world who are still dependent on farming.[4] It is simply not prudent to count on technological rescue to solve America's job problem, much less the global job problem of which it is an inextricable part.

The jobs crisis raises the most fundamental question of human existence: What are we doing here? The global economic system prizes the efficient production of goods more than the dignity of human beings. (Even in economic terms, if we take into account the costs that damaged, displaced, and despairing people exact from the taxpayer—bills for running prisons, hospitals, welfare programs, unemployment insurance, and the like—this sort of efficiency is no bargain.) Contemporary society is built on a social system in which the individual's livelihood, place, worth, and sense of self are increasingly defined by his or her job. At the same time the jobs are disappearing. The global economic system is fragile because it depends on growth fueled by the expansion of consumption, but the fierce drive to eliminate work and cut wages is clearly not the way to bring the crowds to the shopping malls and car lots.

Yet there is a colossal amount of things waiting to be done—building decent places to live, exploring the universe, making cities less dangerous places, teaching one another, helping to raise our children, visiting, comforting, healing, feeding one another, dancing, making music, telling stories, inventing things, and governing ourselves. But much of the essential activity people have always undertaken to raise and to educate their families, to enjoy themselves, to give pleasure to others, and to promote the general welfare is not considered work and is not packaged as a job.

There is a rich range of ideas around in the United States about how to create jobs: worker training, reorganized management, more direct government assistance. But most thinking at the pinnacle of government and in corporate boardrooms concerns national and corporate strategies for competing more effectively *within* the existing global system rather than strategies to push the system itself in other directions. Only a fundamental rethinking of values and priorities can stop the human assault on human beings we call the jobs problem.

Globalization is not really global. Transnational business activities are concentrated in the industrial world and in scattered enclaves throughout the underdeveloped world. Most people are outside the system and the ranks of the window-shoppers and the jobless are growing faster than the global army of the employed. Yet the processes of globalization are altering the character of nations everywhere and the quality of life within their borders.

At the same time nationalism is on the rise. The power of national governments over the two most critical functions of the nation-state—security and economic development—have eroded, but the myth of national sovereignty is as strong as ever. The result is the new sort of power vacuum we have described. Yet the gridlock that traps public authority combined with the disclaimer of public responsibility by the private sector guarantees a world economy out of control. Public accountability is the essence of democracy. But the institutions for assuring corporate accountability at the local, national, and international levels are extremely weak. In the absence of public policies developed and enforced at the international level, the sum of individual corporate decisions is, as we have said, determining the character and dimensions of the job market, the quality of the physical environment, and the experience of childhood.

Ever since the Industrial Revolution, business enterprises have been buffeted by swings in the popular mood as dreams of steady progress and prosperity have been swept away by crashes, depressions, and the scandals of greed. Because the operations of global corporations and banks are intrusive, and to a great extent unregulated, they often threaten such basic human values as stability, community, family, and cultural identity. If prosperity is widely distributed, people accommodate themselves to forced relocation, revolutions in living arrangements, and culture shock. But membership privileges in what we have called the Global North are not what they were, and most of the Global South is in despair.

IV.

The intersecting webs of economic activity we have examined in this book make up a global system—a global system in trouble. Political rhetoric these days is virtuous, even inspired, but neither politicians nor corporate managers have been willing or able to make resource conservation or ecological balance central political values. The result has been a bizarre sacrifice of what is needed to sustain life, beauty, and the natural order. Every day real wealth—breathable air, drinkable water, human imagination and energy, and the health and development of children are sacrificed for mere symbols of wealth, mostly pieces of paper and bits of electronic data that tell us how rich we are.

The human species has proved to be remarkably adaptable. One can imagine different global dreams that inspire the development of sustainable economies and less brutal social systems. The present inability of government to regulate and to manage the economic system is dictated by political decisions based on a particular set of assumptions, priorities, and values that we rarely examine. Living in a time of momentous transition—to what we do not yet know— brings with it more suspense than most of us like. In a chaotic and puzzling time, when ideas for navigating the new world disorder are not yet in place, it is easy to become immobilized by the false cheer of self-serving political promises of better times ahead. Or by despair. But to succumb to either robs those waiting to be born of their chances. They may well be better able to think globally than we are.

The global consciousness that could begin to build a genuine global community has yet to take root within either governments or business enterprises. Most leaders are embodiments of the dominant culture, not transformers of the systems in which they have risen to power and wealth. On the eve of the new millennium, politicians and executives of business enterprises all across the planet are much more likely to be punished than rewarded for taking a broad global approach. The global consciousness on which human survival depends requires changes in education, in the way we reward, encourage, and nurture leadership in both government and the business world, and in the ways we define success.

From where then will the political energy come to redefine the roles of government so that the political and economic systems can be brought into greater harmony and the global gridlock can be broken? Local backlash against the new world order in many different guises is evident all around the world. Most expressions of local resistance to global culture and celebrations of ethnicity, nationalism, religion, and hallowed territory that we see as TV snippets—militant fundamentalism, wars of ethnic purification, and the like—appear reactionary and dangerous. But there is another side.

Globalization from below, to use Richard Falk's term, is proceeding much faster than most of us realize.[5] Local citizens' movements and alternative institutions are springing up all over the world to meet basic economic needs, to preserve local traditions, religious life, cultural life, biological species, and other treasures of the natural world, and to struggle for human dignity. Because the global economic and political systems are out of synch, and therefore unresponsive and unaccountable, people are staking out their own living space. Exiles from the new world order, they spend their lives building the small communities that give their lives meaning, establishing links with other communities with common interests. These communities can be based on anything from geography and ethnicity to a shared concern for the fate of endangered forests and fish.

More and more people who are bypassed by the new world order are crafting their own strategies for survival and development, and in the process are spinning their own transnational webs to embrace and connect people across the world. On dreams of a global civilization that respects human diversity and values people one by one, a global civil society is beginning to take shape—mostly off camera. It is the only force we see that can break the global gridlock. The great question of our age is whether people, acting with the spirit, energy, and urgency our collective crisis requires, can develop a democratic global consciousness rooted in authentic local communities.

NOTES

Introduction. The Age of Globalization
1. "A Survey of Multinationals," *Economist*, Mar. 27, 1993, pp. 5–6.
2. James Robinson, CEO, American Express, to Executives Club, Chicago, September 1989.
3. *Wall Street Journal*, Sept. 18, 1992.
4. In 1965, the figure was 10.8 percent; in 1990 it was 25.9 percent. Calculated from Council of Economic Advisers, *Economic Report of the President* (Washington, D.C.: U.S. Government Printing Office, 1991).

Part One

Chapter One. Global Dreams
1. John Huey, "America's Hottest Export: Pop Culture," *Fortune*, Dec. 31, 1990, p. 50.
2. Fredric Dannen, *Hit Men* (New York: Times Books, 1990), p. 112.
3. Huey, "America's Hottest Export," p. 51; John Micklethwait, "The Entertainment Industry," *Economist*, Dec. 23, 1989, p. 3.
4. Micklethwait, "Entertainment Industry," p. 4.
5. Carl Bernstein, "The Leisure Empire," *Time*, Dec. 24, 1990, p. 56; Micklethwait, "Entertainment Industry," p. 3.
6. Karl Heinrich Russmann, "High Noon," *Manager Magazin* (Bertelsmann translation), June 6, 1989, p. 4.
7. U.S. Bureau of the Census, Mar. 11, 1993.
8. Recording Industry Association of America, 1991 Consumer Profile.
9. *New York Times*, May 26, 1991.
10. *Ibid.*
11. *Ibid.*

12. Robert W. Rydell, *All the World's a Fair* (Chicago: University of Chicago, 1984), p. 2.

13. *Ibid.*, p. 3.

14. *Atlanta Constitution*, Oct. 30, 1990.

15. *New York Times*, May 26, 1991.

16. *Washington Post*, Mar. 31, 1991.

17. *Ibid.*

18. *Ibid.*

19. Rydell, *All the World's a Fair*, p. 4.

20. *New York Times*, Feb. 12, 1992.

21. Micklethwait, "Entertainment Industry," p. 3.

22. David King Dunaway, "Music as Political Communication in the United States," in James Lull, ed., *Popular Music and Communication* (Newbury Park, Calif.: Sage, 1987), p. 36.

23. Mary Harron, "McRock: Pop as a Commodity," in Simon Frith, ed., *Facing the Music* (New York: Pantheon, 1988), pp. 185–186.

24. Jane D. Brown and Kenneth Campbell, "Race and Gender in Music Videos: The Same Beat but a Different Drummer," *Journal of Communication*, Winter 1986, p. 100.

25. Harron, "McRock," p. 184.

26. Neil Postman, *Amusing Ourselves to Death: Public Discourse in the Age of Show Business* (New York: Viking, 1985), pp. 155–156.

Chapter Two. The Technology of Pleasure

1. Akio Morita, *Made in Japan: Akio Morita and Sony* (New York: NAL, 1988), p. 17.

2. *Ibid.*, p. 52.

3. Connie Bruck, "Leap of Faith," *New Yorker*, Sept. 9, 1991, p. 39.

4. "The Global 500," *Fortune*, July 27, 1992, p. 179.

5. Nick Lyons, *The Sony Vision* (New York: Crown, 1976), p. 19.

6. Clyde Prestowitz, *Trading Places* (New York: Basic Books, 1988), p. 29.

7. Lyons, *Sony Vision*, p. 11.

8. Prestowitz, *Trading Places*, p. 125.

9. Morita, *Made in Japan*, p. 72.

10. Kumi Hirai, "Sony Makes What Its Staff Wants to Make," *Tokyo Business Today*, April 1991, p. 42.

11. Peter Ross Range, "Playboy Interview: Akio Morita," *Playboy*, August 1982, p. 70.

12. "Sony: Sorting Out the Sales Suspects," *Business Marketing*, August 1988, p. 44.

13. Hirai, "Sony Makes," p. 42

14. Range, "Playboy Interview," p. 72.

15. Morita, *Made in Japan*, p. 90.

16. Nigel Cope, "Walkman's Global Stride," *Business* (U.K.), March 1990, p. 58.

17. *Euromoney*, September 1984, p. 157.

18. Prestowitz, *Trading Places*, p. 93.

19. Morita, *Made in Japan*, p. 93.

20. *Ibid.*, p. 140.

21. *Ibid.*, p. 143.

22. *Ibid.*, p. 138.

23. Werner Funk and Viziano Terzani, "Japan as Global Superpower," *World Press Review* (translation reprinted from *Der Spiegel*), February 1990, p. 62.

24. *New York Times*, Oct. 1, 1989.

25. Norman Jonas, "The Hollow Corporation," *Business Week*, Mar. 3, 1986, p. 58.

26. Stephen S. Cohen and John Zysman, *Manufacturing Matters* (New York: Basic Books, 1987), p. 4.

27. Milton Moskowitz et al., *Everybody's Business* (New York: Doubleday, 1990), pp. 114–115.

28. Robert Reich, *The Work of Nations* (New York: Alfred A. Knopf, 1991), p. 134.

29. Robert Reich, "Who Do We Think They Are?" *American Prospect*, Winter 1991, p. 50.

30. Lee Smith, "Sony Battles Back," *Fortune*, Apr. 15, 1985, p. 28.

31. Michael Cieply, "Sony's Profitless Prosperity," *Forbes*, Oct. 24, 1983, p. 129.

32. Mark Clifford, "Taking on the Titans," *Far Eastern Economic Review*, Oct. 31, 1991, p. 66.

33. Smith, "Sony Battles Back," p. 38.

34. Larry Armstrong, "Sony's Challenge," *Business Week*, June 1, 1987, p. 65.

35. "Sony Fights So That You Don't Have to Switch," *Industry Week*, Apr. 4, 1983, p. 78.

36. Smith, "Sony Battles Back," p. 36.

37. Morita, *Made in Japan*, p. 131.

38. David E. Sangler, "Sony's Norio Ohga: Building Smaller, Buying Bigger," *New York Times Magazine*, Feb. 18, 1990, p. 61.

39. James Lardner, *Fast Forward: Hollywood, the Japanese, and the Onslaught of the VCR* (New York: Norton, 1987), p. 53.

40. Morita, *Made in Japan*, p. 114.

41. Lyons, *Sony Vision*, p. 11.

42. *Washington Post*, Aug. 6, 1989.

43. "Bringing Sony into Line," *Management Today*, July 1985, p. 74.

44. *Washington Post*, Oct. 7, 1991.

45. Morita, *Made in Japan*, p. 85.

46. Cieply, "Sony's Profitless Prosperity," p. 133.

47. *Los Angeles Times*, Dec. 22, 1989; Carl Goldstein, "Sound Electronics Strategy," *Far Eastern Economic Review*, June 16, 1988, p. 120; *Business Trends*, June 15, 1988, p. 22.

48. David Clark Scott, "Mexico Attracts Japanese Investors," *Christian Science Monitor*, Mar. 20, 1991, p. 40.

49. Gerald Delilkhan, "Asia's Role Is a Great Free Port," *Asian Finance*, February 1990, p. 17.

50. Goldstein, "Sound Electronics Strategy," p. 120.

51. Cope, "Walkman's Global Stride," p. 53.

52. *Ibid.*, p. 54

Chapter Three. A Small Town Global Giant

1. *German Media Dynasties* (internal Bertelsmann company history), p. 6.
2. *Bertelsmann USA*, Bertelsmann brochure, p. 6.
3. Milton Moskowitz, *The Global Marketplace* (New York: Macmillan, 1987), p. 70.
4. Interview with Michael Jurgs.
5. "Reinhard Mohn: Der Bertelsmann," p. 310.
6. *Ibid.*, pp. 308–309.
7. Lionel Kaufman, "Are Our Print Media Going Global?" *Marketing and Media Decisions*, December 1984, p. 72.
8. *Wall Street Journal*, Apr. 25, 1988, p. 11; Ben Bagdikian, "The Lords of the Global Village," *Nation*, June 12, 1989, pp. 805, 818.
9. *Wall Street Journal*, Apr. 25, 1988, p. 11.
10. Stuart J. Elliot, "Foreign Execs Put U.S. Books in Focus," *Advertising Age*, June 22, 1987, p. S-14.
11. Dr. Mark Woessner, "Bertelsmann's Strategies for Growth Markets," (Bertelsmann brochure), 1990, p. 8.
12. Reinhard Mohn, *Success Through Partnership* (New York: Doubleday, 1988), p. 121.
13. *Ibid.*, p. 27.
14. *Bertelsmann Management News*, August 1990, p. 2.

Chapter Four. Of the Making of Books

1. *New York Times*, Mar. 25, 1990.
2. Herbert R. Lottman, "Reunification Frankfurt," *Publishers Weekly*, Nov. 2, 1990, p. 18.
3. Ben H. Bagdikian, "Assembly-Line Publishing," *Tikkun*, May/June 1990, p. 44.
4. "Goodnight, Goodnight Moon?" *Harper's*, June 1991, p. 59.
5. *Wall Street Journal*, Mar. 28, 1990.
6. Interview with Tom Englehardt.
7. *Wall Street Journal*, Oct. 8, 1992.
8. James D. Hart, *The Popular Book* (Oxford: Oxford University Press, 1950), p. 288.
9. *New York Times*, June 30, 1991.
10. Jason Epstein, "The Decline and Rise of Publishing," *New York Review*, Mar. 1, 1990, p. 8.
11. "The Diseconomies of Scale," *Economist*, Apr. 7, 1990, p. 25; *New York Times*, Mar. 18, 1991.
12. *New York Times*, Mar. 5, 1990.
13. Rebecca Piirto, "I Love a Good Story," *American Demographics*, July 1989, p. 38.
14. *New York Times*, Dec. 10, 1990.
15. *New York Times*, Oct. 2, 1986.
16. *Ibid.*
17. *New York Times*, Feb. 21, 1990.
18. *Wall Street Journal*, Feb. 21, 1990.

19. *New York Times*, Oct. 18, 1992.

20. Herbert R. Lottman, "Bertelsmann Sales Worldwide Up 10% in Past Year," *Publishers Weekly*, Sept. 21, 1992, p. 9.

21. *New York Times*, Nov. 5, 1990.

22. *Ibid.*

23. Gordon Graham, "Nationalism and the Book Business," *PW International*, Mar. 16, 1990, p. S2.

24. Curtis G. Benjamin, *U.S. Books Abroad: Neglected Ambassadors* (Washington, D.C.: Library of Congress, 1984), pp. 17–18.

25. Quoted in Irving Louis Horowitz, *Communicating Ideas* (Oxford: Oxford University Press, 1986), p. 119.

26. Donald G. Campbell, "Free Trade: Implications for the Canadian Culture/Communications Industries," *Business Quarterly* (Canada), Spring 1986, p. 33.

27. John Y. Cole, ed., *Books in Our Future* (Washington, D.C.: Library of Congress, 1987), p. 90.

28. American Society of Newspaper Publishers, Monitor Radio, July 22, 1991.

29. "Books and the Bottom Line," *Voice Literary Supplement*, June 1992, p. 12.

30. Books that have been killed or delayed by publishers include: Marc Elliot's *Walt Disney: Hollywood's Dark Prince* (by Bantam), Thomas Hauser's *Missing* (by Harcourt and Dell), Bret Ellis's *American Psycho* (by Simon & Schuster), Peter Matthiessen's *In the Spirit of Crazy Horse* (by Viking), and Roy Rowan and Sandy Smith's *Connections: American Business and the Mob* (by Little, Brown). See Jon Wiener, "Murdered Ink," *The Nation*, May 31, 1993.

31. Thomas Weyr, "The Wiring of Simon and Schuster," *Publishers Weekly*, June 1, 1992, p. 32.

32. John Y. Cole, *Responsibilities of the American Book Community* (Washington, D.C.: Library of Congress, 1981), p. 19.

Chapter Five. If Music Be the Food of Love

1. Carl Bernstein, "The Leisure Empire," *Time*, Dec. 24, 1990, p. 56.

2. David Lieberman, "Now Playing: The Sound of Money," *Business Week*, Aug. 15, 1988, p. 87.

3. "Sony Sees More than Michael Jackson in CBS," *Economist*, Nov. 28, 1987, p. 65; *Billboard*, Aug. 29, 1992, p. 48.

4. Interview with Michael Dornemann.

5. "Even Classic Music Makes Its Impact in the Hit Parade," *Fortune Italia* (English translation), August 1990, p. 2.

6. Giancarlo Radice, "A Business at Full Blast," *Fortune Italia* (English translation), August 1990, p. 1.

7. *New York Times*, Jan. 3, 1990.

8. Fredric Dannen, *Hit Men* (New York: Times Books, 1990), p. 19.

9. Peter J. Boyer, "Sony and CBS Records: What a Romance!" *New York Times Magazine*, Sept. 18, 1988, p. 42.

10. *Ibid.*, p. 40.

11. Dannen, *Hit Men*, p. 76.

12. David Manasian, "Bertelsmann's Stairway to Stardom," *International Management*, November 1987, p. 38.

13. Interview with Michael Dornemann.

14. Manasian, "Bertelsmann's Stairway," p. 38.

15. Interview with Morton Janklow.

16. "Bertelsmann Scraps U.S. Book Club Operation," *Publishers Weekly*, Sept. 7, 1984.

17. Manasian, "Bertelsmann's Stairway," p. 38.

18. Dannen, *Hit Men*, pp. 246, 86; "The Selling of Whitney Houston," *Newsweek*, July 13, 1987, p. 58.

19. Interview with Michael Dornemann.

20. *Wall Street Journal*, Dec. 20, 1988.

21. *Ibid*.

22. Richard C. Morais, "The Latest U.S. Media Giant Isn't Even American," *Forbes*, Apr. 25, 1988, p. 70.

23. *Wall Street Journal*, Dec. 20, 1988.

24. *Wall Street Journal*, Feb. 21, 1990.

25. Dannen, *Hit Men*, p. 79.

26. *Ibid*., pp. 58–63.

27. Fred Goodman, "CBS Records Sold to Sony," *Rolling Stone*, Jan. 14, 1988, p. 17.

28. *Wall Street Journal*, Dec. 30, 1988.

29. Boyer, "Sony and CBS Records," p. 36.

30. The history of Sony is introduced in Chapter Two.

31. *Los Angeles Times*, Sept. 12, 1990.

32. *Los Angeles Times*, Oct. 11, 1987.

33. Bridget Byrne, "Michael Jackson," *Los Angeles Times Magazine*, Oct. 11, 1987, p. 31.

34. *Wall Street Journal*, Dec. 30, 1988.

35. *New York Times*, Oct. 19, 1989; Fred Goodman, "Yetnikoff Steps Down," *Rolling Stone*, Oct. 18, 1990, pp. 21, 24; *Los Angeles Times Calendar*, Apr. 22, 1990; Eric Pooley, "Spinning Out: How Record Heavyweight Walter Yetnikoff Took the Big Fall," *New York*, Nov. 5, 1990, pp. 43–50.

36. *Wall Street Journal*, Jan. 7, 1992.

37. Ken Terry and Chris Morris, "Sony Music Group Generates Major Profits for Corp.," *Billboard*, June 6, 1992, p. 1.

38. *Ibid*.

39. Robert Neff, "Sony's Recipe: One Part Hardware, One Part Software," *Business Week*, Sept. 7, 1992, p. 64.

40. Maggie Mahar, "Adventures in Wonderland," *Barron's*, Oct. 7, 1991, p. 28.

41. *New York Times*, Mar. 1, 1992.

42. *New York Times*, Aug. 11, 1991.

43. *Washington Post*, Oct. 1, 1989.

44. Mahar, "Adventures in Wonderland," p. 9.

45. Ronald Grover, "Is Sony Finally Getting the Hang of Hollywood?" *Business Week*, Sept. 7, 1992, p. 77.

46. *New York Times*, Feb. 23, 1992.

47. Grover, "Is Sony Finally Getting the Hang of Hollywood?" p. 77.

48. Mahar, "Adventures in Wonderland," p. 28.

Chapter Six. Global Entertainment and Local Taste

1. Will Baker, "The Global Teenager," *Whole Earth Review*, Winter 1989, p. 12.

2. Janet Schnol, "Sony Music Video Creates Children's Programming Division," *Publishers Weekly*, June 14, 1991, p. 34.

3. Mark Landler, "The MTV Tycoon," *Business Week*, Sept. 21, 1991, p. 57.

4. See John K. Fairbank, *The United States and China* (Cambridge: Harvard University Press, 1973).

5. See Andrew Philips, "Infidels on Holy Land," *Maclean's*, Jan. 28, 1991, pp. 26–27; *Atlanta Constitution*, Sept. 22, 1990.

6. *The World of Bertelsmann Music Group*, Summer 1990, p. 20.

7. Christie Leo, "Singapore IFPI Offers Cash for Fingering Music Pirates," *Billboard*, May 13, 1989, pp. 70, 72.

8. David Lieberman, "Now Playing: The Sound of Money," *Business Week*, Aug. 15, 1988, p. 89.

9. *Wall Street Journal*, Jan. 28, 1992.

10. David H. Horowitz, "The Record Rental Amendment of 1984: A Case Study in the Effort to Adapt Copyright Law to New Technology," *Columbia-VLA Journal of Law and the Arts*, March 1988, p. 69.

11. P.L. 563, signed Oct. 28, 1992.

12. *New York Times*, Jan. 8, 1991.

13. *New York Times*, Sept. 20, 1992.

14. *Ibid.*

15. Simon Frith, "Video Pop: Picking Up the Pieces," in Simon Frith, ed., *Facing the Music* (New York: Pantheon, 1988), p. 113.

16. *Ibid.*, p. 94.

17. *New York Times*, Mar. 2, 1989.

18. Fredric Dannen, *Hit Men* (New York: Times Books, 1990), p. 14.

19. Roger Wallis and Krister Malm, "The International Music Industry and Transcultural Communication," in James Lull, ed., *Popular Music and Communication* (Newbury Park, Calif.: Sage, 1987), p. 125.

20. Roger Wallis and Krister Malm, "Patterns of Change," in Simon Frith and Andrew Goodwin, eds., *On Record* (New York: Pantheon, 1990), p. 160.

21. Wallis and Malm, "International Music Industry," p. 114.

22. *Ibid.*, p. 128.

23. Steven Mills and Melanie Menagh, "Rock Stars Score the Future," *Omni*, June 1990, p. 47.

24. Craig Bromberg, "Lambadimizing Culture," *Omni*, June 1990, p. 12.

25. *New York Times*, Dec. 10, 1989.

26. Pat Aufderheide, "Music Videos: The Look of Sound," *Journal of Communication*, Winter 1986, p. 62.

27. *Washington Post*, Dec. 13, 1989.

28. Paul Carton, "Mass Media Culture and the Breakdown of Values Among Inner City Youth," *Future Choices*, 1991, p. 7.

29. *Washington Post*, July 1, 1993.

30. *New York Times*, Apr. 22, 1990.

31. Carton, "Mass Media Culture," p. 1.

32. Aufderheide, "Music Videos," p. 64.

33. *New York Times*, Sept. 30, 1990.

Part Two

Chapter One. The Global Customer

1. International Council of Shopping Centers, *The Scope of the Shopping Center Industry in the United States 1991* (New York: International Council of Shopping Centers, 1991), p. 1.

2. *Washington Post*, Sept. 8, 1991.

3. *Washington Post*, June 30, 1991.

4. *Wall Street Journal*, Oct. 30, 1990.

5. *Wall Street Journal*, Feb. 11, 1991.

6. *Washington Post*, July 16, 1991.

7. Worldwatch Institute, *State of the World 1991*, cited in *Co-op America Quarterly*, Winter 1991, p. 10.

8. *New York Times*, Oct. 11, 1992.

9. Council of Economic Advisers, *Economic Report of the President* (Washington, D.C.: U.S. Government Printing Office, 1991), p. 303.

10. "The Advertising Industry," *Economist*, June 9, 1990, p. 6.

11. *Ibid.*

12. Theodore Levitt, "The Globalization of Markets," *Harvard Business Review*, May 1983, p. 92.

13. Anthony J. Rutigliano, "The Debate Goes On: Global vs. Local Advertising," *Management Review*, June 1986, p. 28.

14. *New York Times*, Nov. 21, 1991.

15. Roberto C. Goizueta, "Globalization: A Soft Drink Perspective," *Executive Speeches*, September 1989, p. 2.

16. *Wall Street Journal*, Aug. 27, 1992.

17. *New York Times*, Nov. 21, 1991.

18. *Ibid.*

19. In 1989, the top ten had billings of $65.9 billion out of global billings of $240 billion. See the *Economist*, June 9, 1990.

20. *Wall Street Journal*, Aug. 27, 1992.

21. *Ibid.*

22. Ed Fitch, "Marketing to Hispanics," *Advertising Age*, Feb. 9, 1987, p. S-23; Rutigliano, "Debate Goes On," p. 28; Philip Geier, "Global Products, Localized Messages," *Marketing Communications*, December 1986, p. 26.

23. *Economist*, June 9, 1990, p. 3.

24. Mozambique per-capita income for 1991 was $70. World Bank, cited in *Washington Post*, Jan. 5, 1993.

25. Ranking in 1988. Source: *Advertising Age*, quoted in *Economist*, June 9, 1990, p. 8.

26. *Ibid.*, p. 6.

27. Peter Carlson, "It's an Ad Ad Ad Ad World," *Washington Post Magazine*, Nov. 3, 1991, p. 18.

28. *Wall Street Journal*, July 17, 1990.

29. Maria Shad et al., "Suddenly, Asian-Americans Are a Marketer's Dream," *Business Week*, June 17, 1991, p. 55.

30. Gordon Link, "Global Advertising: An Update," *Journal of Consumer Marketing*, Spring 1988, p. 72.

31. Robert Ingenito, "It's Your Call: 900 Numbers," *Direct Marketing*, September 1990, p. 49.

32. Mark Landler et al., "What Happened to Advertising," *Business Week*, Sept. 23, 1991, p. 66.

33. David Kalish, "Out of Home, Around the World," *Marketing and Media Decisions*, February 1990, p. 14.

34. Eric Clark, *The Want Makers* (New York: Viking Books, 1988), p. 59.

35. *Ibid.*, p. 79.

36. Joe Schwartz, "Bitestyles of the Rich and Famished," *American Demographics*, October 1988, p. 10.

37. Institute for International Economics, quoted in *New York Times*, Jan 26, 1992.

38. "November Almanac," *Atlantic Monthly*, November 1991, p. 28.

39. *Washington Post*, Jan. 18, 1992.

40. Paul Ehrlich and Anne H. Ehrlich, "Too Many Rich Folks," *Populi*, March 1989, p. 25.

41. *Wall Street Journal*, Aug. 27, 1992.

42. Calculated from figures in World Bank, *World Development Report, 1990* (Washington, D.C.: World Bank, 1990); and *The 1990 Information Please Almanac* (Boston: Houghton Mifflin, 1990), pp. 138–141.

43. John Barber, "Courting Commerce," *Equinox*, November/December 1990, p. 83.

44. United Nations, *World Economic Survey, 1990* (New York: United Nations, 1990), p. 205.

45. Calculated from data in various issues of *American Demographics* and *Consumer Markets Abroad*.

46. Data supplied by the research group PACS, based in Rio de Janeiro, November 1990.

47. "Metro Manila: The Urban Challenge," *Consumer Markets Abroad*, June 1987, pp. 7–8. The per-capita GNP figures are for 1988; see World Bank, *World Development Report, 1990* (Washington, D.C.: World Bank, 1990), p. 178.

48. Quoted in Francesca Turchiano, "The (Un)Malling of America," *American Demographics*, April 1990, p. 39.

49. *New York Times*, Nov. 21, 1991.

50. Donald G. Halper and H. Chang Moon, "Striving for First-Rate Markets in Third World Nations," *Management Review*, May 1990, p. 21.

51. *New York Times*, Oct. 11, 1992.

52. The figures in this paragraph are the authors' estimates based on articles in *Advertising Age, American Demographics*, and *Consumer Markets Abroad*, as well as interviews with marketing experts.

53. "Pedaling East: First Time Car Buyers Don't Live in the West Anymore," *Consumer Markets Abroad*, Sept. 12, 1988, pp. 12–13.

54. *Washington Post*, June 14, 1992.

Chapter Two. Marlboro Country

1. American Public Health Association, Apr. 16, 1993.

2. Testimony before the Senate Labor and Human Resources Committee on May 4, 1990, cited in *Washington Post*, May 5, 1990.

3. "Ashes in Their Mouths," *Economist*, May 30, 1992, p. 86.

4. Morton Mintz, "Tobacco Roads," *Progressive*, May 1991, p. 24.

5. *Philip Morris Annual Report 1991*, p. 6; "The Search for El Dorado," *Economist*, May 16, 1991, p. 22.

6. Quoted in *Newsweek*, Oct. 22, 1990, p. 17. The $25 figure is from *Christian Science Monitor*, Oct. 30, 1990.

7. *Washington Post*, Sept. 5, 1992.

8. *Washington Post*, Feb. 5, 1988.

9. Quoted in Morton Mintz, "The Pro-Corporate Tilt," *Nieman Reports*, Fall 1991, p. 28.

10. Document reproduced in *Harper's*, June 1988, p. 25.

11. Jerry A. Trachtenberg, "Here's One Tough Cowboy," *Forbes*, Feb. 9, 1987, p. 110.

12. Quoted in *ibid.*, p. 108.

13. See Fred Danzig, "The Big Idea," *Advertising Age*, Nov. 9, 1988, p. 16, and L. J. Davis, "Philip Morris's Big Bite," *New York Times Magazine*, Apr. 9, 1989, p. 32.

14. Peter Taylor, *The Smoke Ring: Tobacco, Money, and Multinational Politics* (New York: NAL, 1985), p. 40.

15. Quoted in Davis, "Philip Morris's Big Bite," p. 32.

16. Quoted in Taylor, *Smoke Ring*, p. 40.

17. Trachtenberg, "Here's One Tough Cowboy," p. 110.

18. Personal communication, Jan. 31, 1992.

19. Michael Schudson, *Advertising; The Uneasy Persuasion* (New York: Basic Books, 1984), p. 184.

20. This condition of the Philip Morris gift was confirmed by an employee of the Smithsonian's Center for Advertising History on July 8, 1993.

21. *New York Times*, Sept. 13, 1992.

22. Davis, "Philip Morris's Big Bite," p. 40.

23. Former Surgeon General, C. Everett Koop, wrote in his memoirs: "One night before I gave the banquet speech at the Congressional Country Club, my host introduced me to the two bartenders. At first they were astonished that the Surgeon General was a real person and not just a symbol like, as a cabbie once put it, Betty Crocker." C. Everett Koop, *Koop: The Memoirs of America's Family Doctor* (New York: Random House, 1991), p. 182.

24. Davis, "Philip Morris's Big Bite," p. 40.

25. Hal Kane, "Putting Out Cigarettes," *World Watch*, September/October 1991, p. 34.

26. Council on Scientific Affairs, "The Worldwide Smoking Epidemic," *JAMA*, June 27, 1990, p. 3317.

27. Koop, *Koop*, p. 184.

28. *Washington Post*, May 18, 1986.

29. Larry C. White, "Smoke Scream," *Business Month*, May 1988, p. 75.

30. *Wall Street Journal*, Feb. 20, 1990.

31. *Advertising Age*, Jan. 31, 1983, p. M-14.

32. The document was reprinted in the *Washington Post*, Feb. 17, 1990.

33. *Wall Street Journal*, Feb. 2, 1990.

34. Colin McCord and Harold P. Freeman, "Excess Mortality in Harlem," *New England Journal of Medicine*, Jan. 18, 1990, p. 173.

35. Michael Kamber, "Signs of Life, Signs of Death," *Z Magazine*, May 1990, p. 10.

36. Myron Levin, "The Tobacco Industry's Strange Bedfellows," *Business and Society Review*, Spring 1988, p. 16.

37. *Wall Street Journal*, Feb. 20, 1990.

38. The publication *Tobacco and Youth Reporter*, put out by Stop Teenage Addiction to Tobacco, reports regularly on tobacco-company promotions to young people.

39. White, "Smoke Scream," p. 75.

40. Walecia Conrad, "I'd Toddle a Mile for a Camel," *Business Week*, Dec. 23, 1991, p. 34.

41. *New York Times*, Jan. 12, 1990.

42. Amy Dunkin, "The Globe-Trotter Who Took Philip Morris Global," *Business Week*, Aug. 8, 1988.

43. *Philip Morris Annual Report 1988*, p. 8, and *Philip Morris Annual Report 1989*, pp. 7–8.

44. Taylor, *Smoke Ring*, p. 280.

45. The Tobacco Institute, Washington, D.C., *Time, Newsweek, U.S. News & World Report*, Autumn 1978.

46. U.S. Department of Agriculture, *Tobacco in the United States* (Washington, D.C.: Agricultural Marketing Service, Misc. Publication no. 867, February 1979), p. 1.

47. Kathy Kiely, "Tobacco's Road Is Nearing Its End," *Management Today*, May 1988, p. 23.

48. Kiely, "Tobacco Road," p. 23.

49. Taylor, *Smoke Ring*, p. 269. The U.S. figure is from Frank Adams, "Vegetable and Fruit Crops: Viable Alternative for Farmers," in William R. Finger, ed., *The Tobacco Industry in Transition: Policies for the 1980s* (Lexington: D. C. Heath, 1981), p. 95. The soybean figure is from Nelson A. Navarro, "Controversy in North Carolina," *New World Outlook*, July/August 1984, pp. 267–268.

50. *New York Times*, Apr. 13, 1980, and Alexander Cockburn, "The Real Drug Kingpins," *New Statesman*, Oct. 20, 1989, p. 22.

51. *New York Times*, Apr. 13, 1980.

52. Koop, *Koop*, pp. 171–172.

53. *Philip Morris Annual Report 1989*, p. 8.

54. Calculated from figures of the U.S. Department of Agriculture, Economic Research Service.

55. *Philip Morris Annual Report 1989*, p. 8.

56. *Washington Post*, Feb. 2, 1989.

57. Quoted in *Washington Post*, Apr. 6, 1990. Representative Henry Waxman, chairman of the House Subcommittee on Health and Environment, invited the official, Dr. James O. Mason, to testify before his committee. In Waxman's words: "Dr. Mason had accepted the subcommittee's invitation to appear. . . . But two days

before the hearing, we were informed that the administration would not allow the assistant secretary for health to testify." Henry A. Waxman, "Tobacco Exports: Why the Silence?" (*Washington Post*, June 26, 1990).

58. Mintz, "Pro-Corporate Tilt," May 1991, p. 28.

59. Interview.

60. Louise de Rosario, "Mild Seven, Move Over," *Far Eastern Economic Review*, Mar. 29, 1990, p. 63.

61. "Where There's Smoke There's Fire," *Business Japan*, April 1986, p. 55.

62. Gale Eisenstodt and Hiroko Katayama, "A Trade Threat That Worked," *Forbes*, Apr. 3, 1989, p. 38.

63. *Ibid.*

64. *Los Angeles Times*, June 20, 1989; Carl Goldstein, "No Smoke Without Ire," *Far Eastern Economic Review*, Mar. 29, 1990, p. 64.

65. Paul Ensor, "Tempers Up in Smoke," *Far Eastern Economic Review*, Feb. 21, 1985, p. 65.

66. Mark Clifford, "Foreigners Left Fuming," *Far Eastern Economic Review*, Mar. 29, 1990, p. 64; Ensor, "Tempers Up in Smoke," p. 66.

67. Clifford, "Foreigners Left Fuming," p. 64.

68. Louis Kraar, "Smoking U.S. Cigarettes Is Dangerous in Korea," *Fortune*, May 28, 1984, p. 89.

69. Cockburn, "Real Drug Kingpins," p. 22.

70. Ensor, "Tempers Up in Smoke," p. 66.

71. Jonathan Friedland, "When Eats Meet West," *Far Eastern Economic Review*, May 31, 1990, p. 44.

72. Richard McKerron, "Merchants of Death Target Third World," *Third World Resurgence*, October 1992, pp. 8–9.

73. Uma Ram Nath, "India's Shame," *New York State Journal of Medicine*, December 1983, p. 1320.

74. Chinese smoked 1.5 trillion of the world's estimated 5.3 trillion cigarettes in 1989 (*Philip Morris Annual Report 1989*, p. 7); Carl Goldstein, "Drags to Riches," *Far Eastern Economic Review*, Mar. 29, 1990, p. 62.

75. Andy Plattner and Sharon F. Golden, "Tough Times for Tobacco Lobby," *U.S. News & World Report*, Feb. 23, 1987, p. 17.

76. *Tobacco Observer*, November 1986, p. 1.

77. Koop, *Koop*, p. 178.

78. Verner Grise, *Tobacco: Background for 1990 Farm Legislation* (Washington, D.C.: U.S. Department of Agriculture, Economic Research Service, Commodity Economics Division, October 1989), p. iii, and U.S. Department of Agriculture, *Tobacco: Situation and Outlook Report*, Economic Research Service, TS-211, June 1990, p. 28.

79. Grise, *Tobacco*, p. 7 and U.S. Department of Agriculture, *Tobacco: Situation and Outlook Report*, p. 28.

80. U.S. Department of Agriculture, Foreign Agriculture Service, *World Tobacco Situation*, Circular Series FT 3-90, March 1990, p. 12.

81. Navarro, "Controversy in North Carolina," pp. 267–268.

82. Timothy Clark, "Tax and Price Support Issues Causing Tobacco Interests' Solidarity to Crack," *National Journal*, Oct. 26, 1985, p. 2424.

83. Grise, *Tobacco*, pp. 22–23.

84. *Ibid.*, p. 11.

85. U.S. exports of 142 billion cigarettes in 1989 brought in $3.37 billion in revenues. Over 76 billion of these cigarettes went to five Asian countries: Japan, Hong Kong, Singapore, Taiwan, and South Korea (*Tobacco: Situation and Outlook Report*, p. 5, and *World Tobacco Situation*, p. 13).

86. Fourteen of the top twenty tobacco exporters to the United States were developing countries: six from Latin America (Brazil, Mexico, Guatemala, Argentina, Chile, and the Dominican Republic), six from Asia and the Middle East (Turkey, Thailand, Indonesia, South Korea, the Philippines, and Lebanon), and two from Africa (Malawi and Cameroon). See *World Tobacco Situation*, pp. 102–104.

87. United Nations Center on Trade and Development, *Handbook of International Trade and Development Statistics* (New York: United Nations, 1988), p. 219. Figures for 1983–84.

88. Taylor, *Smoke Ring*, p. 277.

89. See Mike Muller, "Preventing Tomorrow's Epidemic," *New York State Journal of Medicine*, December 1983, pp. 1305–1306.

90. Sterling Seagrave, *The Marcos Dynasty* (New York: Harper & Row, 1988), p. 135.

91. John Madeley, "Tobacco: A Ruinous Crop," *Ecologist*, February/March 1986, p. 128.

92. *Ibid.*, p. 125.

93. *Ibid.*

94. See R. Goodland, C. Watson, and George Ledec, *Environmental Management in Tropical Agriculture* (Boulder, Colo.: Westview Press, 1984), ch. 8.

95. Mike Muller, *Tobacco and the Third World: Tomorrow's Epidemic* (London: War on Want, 1978), p. 61.

Chapter Three. The Global Grocer

1. Don Cohn, "Peppers sans Transports," *Far Eastern Economic Review*, Mar. 12, 1992, p. 28.

2. Council of Economic Advisers, *Economic Report of the President 1993* (Washington, D.C.: U.S. Government Printing Office, 1993), p. 464.

3. United Nations Food and Agriculture Organization report, cited in *Washington Post*, Sept. 29, 1992.

4. United Nations Development Program, *Human Development Report 1992* (New York: United Nations, 1992), p. 14; UNICEF, *The State of the World's Children 1992* (New York: United Nations, 1992).

5. Calculated from *New York Times*, Feb. 26, 1992.

6. Michael Reed and Mary Marchant, *Globalization of the U.S. Food Processing Sector*, Occasional Paper (Columbus: Ohio State University, August 1991), p. 2.

7. Ian Williams, "Marlboro Man Rides a New Range," *Business* (U.K.), January 1991, p. 41.

8. Subrata N. Chakravarty, "Philip Morris Is Still Hungry," *Forbes*, Apr. 2, 1990, p. 98.

9. *Ibid.*; Alan Farnham, "His Own Best Customer," *Fortune*, Aug. 3, 1987.

10. *Ibid.*

11. *Ibid.*

12. Williams, "Marlboro Man," p. 43.

13. Bryan Burrough and John Helyar, *Barbarians at the Gate: The Fall of RJR Nabisco* (New York: Harper & Row, 1990), pp. 117–118.

14. Stratford P. Sherman, "How Philip Morris Diversified Right," *Fortune*, Oct. 23, 1989, p. 82.

15. Amy Dunkin, "Hamish Maxwell's Big Hunger," *Business Week*, Oct. 31, 1988, p. 25.

16. L. J. Davis, "Philip Morris's Big Bite," *New York Times Magazine*, Apr. 9, 1989, p. 40.

17. *Ibid.*, p. 30.

18. Correspondence reprinted in Harvard Business School Case Study No. 9-289-045, "Philip Morris-Kraft," March 1990, pp. 19–20.

19. *Chicago Tribune*, Apr. 23, 1989.

20. Davis, "Philip Morris's Big Bite," p. 86.

21. Calculated from *Philip Morris Annual Report 1989*, pp. 4–5.

22. Dunkin, "Hamish Maxwell's Big Hunger," p. 24.

23. Lois Therrien, "A Cup of Jell-O, Velveeta to Taste . . . ," *Business Week*, May 8, 1989, p. 74.

24. James M. Kilts, "Adaptive Marketing," *Journal of Consumer Marketing*, Summer 1990, p. 40.

25. Chakravarty, "Philip Morris Is Still Hungry," p. 100.

26. *Chicago Tribune*, Apr. 23, 1989.

27. Chakravarty, "Philip Morris Is Still Hungry," p. 101.

28. *Washington Post*, Feb. 9, 1992.

29. William Drozdiak, "Merger Mania Goes Abroad," *Business* (U.K.), January 1991, p. 41.

30. *Washington Post*, May 24, 1992.

31. *Wall Street Journal*, Mar. 18, 1992.

32. John Marcom, Jr., "Feed the World," *Forbes*, Oct. 1, 1990, p. 111.

33. Kilts, "Adaptive Marketing," pp. 44–45.

34. *New York Times*, Oct. 19, 1988.

35. Laura Holland, "Kraft Cooks Up Plans to Boost Imports," *Japan Economic Journal*, Feb. 23, 1991, p. 6.

36. Sherman, "How Philip Morris Diversified Right," p. 121.

37. *Ibid.*

38. *Ibid.*

39. Marcom, "Feed the World," p. 118.

40. Sharon Reier, "New World Threat," *Financial World*, July 9, 1991, p. 22.

41. Bill Saporito, "Can Anyone Win the Coffee War?" *Fortune*, May 21, 1990.

42. Marcom, "Feed the World," p. 111.

43. *Ibid.*, p. 110.

44. Reier, "New World Threat," p. 22.

45. John M. Connor, "Research Puzzles Arising from the Internationalization of U.S. Food Processors," in *Transnational Structure in Food Processing and Marketing*, Project NC-194 (Columbus: Ohio State University, September 1989), p. 31.

46. John M. Connor and Frederick E. Geithman, "Mergers in the Food Industries: Trends, Motives, and Policies," *Agribusiness*, July 1988.

47. John Sutton, *Sunk Costs and Market Structure: Price Competition, Advertising, and the Evolution of Concentration* (Cambridge: MIT Press, 1991), p. 499;

Milton Moskowitz et al., *Everybody's Business* (New York: Doubleday, 1990), p. 18.

48. Moskowitz, *Everybody's Business*, p. 28.

49. Nathaniel Gilbert, "More Financing Goes Global," *Management Review*, June 1987, p. 26.

50. Lean J. Nathans, "The Money Magician at Philip Morris," *Business Week*, Apr. 10, 1989, p. 78.

51. Ellen Benoit, "Mine's Okay, Theirs Isn't," *Financial World*, Feb. 10, 1987, p. 36.

52. A. V. Krebs, *The Corporate Reapers: The Book of Agribusiness* (Washington, D.C.: Essential Books, 1992), p. 303.

53. Charles R. Handy, "The Globalization of Food Marketing," *National Food Review*, October/December 1990, p. 1.

54. Council of Economic Advisers, *Economic Report of the President 1993*, p. 459.

55. *Wall Street Journal*, Aug. 10, 1992.

56. John Connor et al., *The Food Manufacturing Industries* (Lexington: Lexington Books, 1985), pp. 296–297.

57. *Washington Post*, July 17, 1991.

Chapter Four. A Matter of Taste

1. Diane Ackerman, *A Natural History of the Senses* (New York: Random House, 1990), p. 127.

2. *Ibid.*

3. *Ibid.*, pp. 132–133.

4. *Wall Street Journal*, Feb. 22, 1991.

5. Peter Farb and George Armelagos, *Consuming Passions: The Anthropology of Eating* (New York: Houghton Mifflin, 1980), p. 3.

6. "Fresh Trends," *The Packer Focus*, 1991, quoted in unpublished manuscript by William H. Friedland, "The New Globalization: The Case of Fresh Produce," University of California, Santa Cruz, June 1991, p. 4.

7. *Eurofruit*, January 1991, p. 34, quoted in Friedland, "New Globalization," p. 8.

8. *Washington Post*, Feb. 21, 1992.

9. Friedland, "New Globalization," p. 4.

10. Lois Therrien, "Kraft Is Looking for Fat Growth From Fat-Free Foods," *Business Week*, Mar. 26, 1990, p. 100.

11. *Wall Street Journal*, Jan. 10, 1992.

12. *Wall Street Journal*, Oct. 10, 1990.

13. *New York Times*, May 12, 1991.

14. *Wall Street Journal*, Nov. 6, 1991.

15. *Ibid.*

16. William Mueller, "Are Americans Eating Better?" *American Demographics*, February 1989, p. 30.

17. *Washington Post*, Feb. 19, 1992.

18. *Ibid.*

19. Peter Tettweiler, "Snack Food Worldwide," *Food Technology*, February 1991, p. 60.

20. Ackerman, *Natural History of the Senses*, p. 142.

21. David Bodanis, *The Secret House*, cited in Ackerman, *Natural History of the Senses*, pp. 142–143.

22. Tettweiler, "Snack Food Worldwide," pp. 60, 62.

23. *Washington Post*, Apr. 29, 1991.

24. *Wall Street Journal*, Dec. 20, 1990.

25. *Ibid.*

26. Alan B. Durning, "Junk Food, Food Junk," *World Watch*, September/October 1991, p. 7; See also *Farmline*, October 1987, p. 8.

27. Durning, "Junk Food," pp. 7–8.

28. Fergus M. Clydesdale, "Present and Future of Food and Science Technology in Industrialized Countries: A Plenary Paper," *Food Technology*, September 1989, pp. 134–146.

29. Ricardo Bressani, "Food Science and Technology in Developing Countries During the Past 50 Years," *Food Technology*, September 1989, p. 109.

30. Third World Studies Center, University of the Philippines, "The Socio-Economic Impact of TNCs in Developing Countries: Case Studies in the Food and Beverage Industry in the Philippines with Specific References to Coca-Cola and McDonald's," paper prepared for the UN/ESCAP/CTC joint unit of TNCs, Bangkok, 1984, p. 1.

31. "Keeping Well On Their Way," *Economist*, July 7, 1990, p. 39.

32. Brad Miller, "Pass the Froot Loops, Por Favor," *Progressive*, February 1991, p. 30.

33. *Ibid.*, pp. 30, 32.

34. Mary J. Weismantel, *Food, Gender, and Poverty in the Ecuadorean Andes* (Philadelphia: University of Pennsylvania Press, 1988), p. 96.

35. *Washington Post*, Feb. 19, 1992.

36. Durning, "Junk Food," p. 7.

37. Margaret Visser, "A Meditation on the Microwave," *Psychology Today*, December 1989, pp. 39–40.

38. *Ibid.*, p. 10.

39. Susan Strange, "Cave! hic dragones: A Critique of Regime Analysis," *International Organization*, Spring 1982, p. 491.

40. *Wall Street Journal*, Feb. 24, 1992.

41. World Bank, *World Development Report 1991* (Washington, D.C.: World Bank, 1991), pp. 232–233.

42. Tom Barry, ed., *Mexico: A Country Guide* (Albuquerque, N. Mex.: Inter-Hemispheric Education Resource Center, 1992), p. 163.

43. Joshua Karliner, "A Report to Greenpeace on the Proposed North American Free Trade Agreement: A View From the US," Greenpeace internal memo, June 3, 1991, p. 47.

44. *Mexico Business Monthly*, July 1991, p. 4.

45. Richard Rothstein, "Free Trade Scam," *L.A. Weekly*, May 17–23, 1991.

46. S. Baker and S. L. Walker, "Mexico: The Salad Bowl of North America," *Business Week*, Feb. 25, 1991, p. 70.

47. Margaret Littman, "Border Bonanza," *Prepared Food*, September 1991, p. 15.

48. Inter-Hemispheric Education Resource Center, *Resource Center Bulletin*, Spring 1991, p. 3.

49. *Los Angeles Times*, Apr. 2, 1989.

50. *Wall Street Journal*, Feb. 25, 1992.

Part Three

Chapter One. Mass Production in Postmodern Times

1. James P. Womack et al., *The Machine That Changed the World* (New York: Rawson Associates, 1990), p. 27.

2. *Ibid.*, p. 28.

3. David Halberstam, *The Reckoning* (New York: Avon, 1986), p. 74.

4. *Ibid.*, p. 60.

5. *Ibid.*, p. 84.

6. Womack, *Machine That Changed the World*, p. 35.

7. *Ward's Auto World*, November 1985, pp. 81–83.

8. *New York Times*, Jan. 10, 1993.

9. Halberstam, *Reckoning*, pp. 83–101.

10. Milton Moskowitz et al., *Everybody's Business* (New York: Doubleday, 1990), p. 238.

11. Halberstam, *Reckoning*, p. 198.

12. Richard J. Barnet and Ronald E. Müller, *Global Reach: The Power of the Multinational Corporations* (New York: Simon & Schuster, 1974), p. 341.

13. Moskowitz, *Everybody's Business*, pp. 237–239.

14. Carl H. A. Dassbach, *Global Enterprises and the World Economy* (New York: Garland, 1988), p. 404.

15. Milton Moskowitz et al., *Everybody's Business* (San Francisco: Harper & Row, 1980), p. 270.

16. Halberstam, *Reckoning*, p. 659.

17. Womack, *Machine That Changed the World*, pp. 17–18.

18. *Ibid.*, pp. 51–53.

19. *Ibid.*, p. 57.

20. *Ibid.*, pp. 67–68.

21. *Ibid.*, p. 87.

22. Dassbach, *Global Enterprises*, p. 406.

23. Based on figures in *Automotive News Market Data Book* 1979, 1987; *Automotive Industries*, November 1987, quoted in Mike Parker and Jane Slaughter, *Choosing Sides: Unions and the Team Concept* (Boston: South End Press, 1988), p. 11.

24. Peter Dicken, *Global Shift: Industrial Change in a Turbulent World* (London: Harper & Row, 1986), p. 304, fig. 9.9.

25. Dassbach, *Global Enterprises*, pp. 407–408.

26. Richard A. Melcher, "Meet Ford's Brave New 'World Car' " *Business Week*, Jan. 18, 1993, p. 46.

27. *Ibid.*

28. Moskowitz, *Everybody's Business* (1990), p. 248.

29. Dassbach, *Global Enterprises*, pp. 408–409.

30. *Automotive News*, May 27, 1985, p. 2; Nov. 4, 1984, p. 45.

31. Business Higher Education Forum, "The Rational Revolution in U.S. Industry," report from the Summer 1983 meeting in Dearborn, Michigan, p. 16.

32. Robert Wrubel, "If You Can't Beat 'Em . . . ," *Financial World*, Apr. 3, 1990, p. 32.

33. James B. Treece and Karen Lowry Miller, "The Partners," *Business Week*, Feb. 10, 1992, p. 102.

34. Wrubel, "If You Can't Beat 'Em," p. 32.

35. *Ibid.*, p. 34.

36. Parker and Slaughter, *Choosing Sides*, p. 175.

37. James B. Treece, "How Ford and Mazda Shared the Driver's Seat," *Business Week*, Mar. 26, 1990, p. 95.

38. Wrubel, "If You Can't Beat 'Em," p. 34.

39. Barnet and Müller, *Global Reach*, notes, p. 420.

40. *Ibid.*, p. 305.

41. *Wall Street Journal*, July 5, 1991.

42. Joseph Grunwald and Kenneth Flamm, *Global Factory: Foreign Assembly and International Trade* (Washington, D.C.: Brookings Institution, 1985), p. 30n.

43. Stephen S. Cohen and John Zysman, *Manufacturing Matters* (New York: Basic Books, 1987), p. 4; Council of Economic Advisers, *Economic Report of the President 1992* (Washington, D.C.: U.S. Government Printing Office, 1992), p. 344.

44. Paul Knox and John Agnew, *The Geography of the World Economy* (London: Edward Arnold, 1989), p. 180.

45. *Ibid.*, pp. 182–184.

46. *Wall Street Journal*, July 30, 1991.

47. *New York Times*, Feb. 23, 1992.

48. *New York Times*, Mar. 8, 1992.

49. *Washington Post*, Jan. 21, 1992.

50. *Wall Street Journal*, Jan. 24, 1992.

51. *Wall Street Journal*, July 5, 1991.

52. William J. Holstein, "The Stateless Corporation," *Business Week*, May 14, 1990, p. 100.

53. Larry Reynolds, "Has Globalization Hurt America?" *Management Review*, September 1989, pp. 16–17.

54. Holstein, "Stateless Corporation," p. 99.

55. *Ibid.*, p. 98.

56. Robert B. Reich, *The Work of Nations* (New York: Knopf, 1991).

Chapter Two. The New Division of Labor and the Global Job Crisis

1. See UN Centre on Transnational Corporations, *World Investment Report 1991* (New York: United Nations, 1991), pp. 9, 11.

2. Robin Broad and John Cavanagh, "No More NIC's," *Foreign Policy*, Fall 1988, p. 81.

3. For more on this and the other groups, see Robin Broad, *Unequal Alliance: The World Bank, the International Monetary Fund, and the Philippines* (Berkeley: University of California Press, 1988). See also Walden Bello and Stephanie Rosenfeld, *Dragons in Distress: Asia's Miracle Economies in Crisis* (San Francisco: Food First, 1990).

4. *Washington Post*, May 5, 1992.

5. *New York Times*, June 21, 1992.

6. Belinda Coote, *The Trade Trap* (Oxford: Oxfam UK, 1992), pp. 6–7.

7. Walt W. Rostow, "The Stages of Economic Growth," *Economic History Review*, August 1959.

8. Bela Balassa, "The Process of Industrial Development and Alternative Development Strategies," *Essays in International Finance* (Princeton: Princeton University Press, 1980), pp. 25–26.

9. Jim Vallette and Heather Spaulding, eds., *International Trade in Wastes*, 5th ed. (Washington, D.C.: Greenpeace, 1990), pp. 20–23.

10. Louis S. Richman, "The Coming World Labor Shortage," *Fortune*, Apr. 9, 1990, p. 72; Lawrence Mishel and David M. Frankel, *The State of Working America* (Washington, D.C.: Economic Policy Institute, 1991), p. 268; and *New York Times*, June 13, 1993.

11. Barry Bluestone, "Deindustrialization and Unemployment in America," *Review of Black Political Economy*, Fall 1988, p. 29.

12. *Washington Post*, Apr. 4, 1992.

13. Bluestone, "Deindustrialization," p. 34.

14. *Washington Post*, April 18, 1992.

15. Bluestone, "Deindustrialization," p. 31.

16. Joseph F. Coates et al., "Future Work," *Futurist*, May/June 1991, p. 13.

17. Mishel and Frankel, *State of Working America*, p. 81.

18. Jeff Faux, testimony before the Labor Subcommittee, U.S. Senate, Apr. 7, 1992, p. 2.

19. Mishel and Frankel, *State of Working America*, p. 266.

20. United Nations Development Program, *Human Development Report 1992* (New York: United Nations, 1992), p. 6.

21. International Labor Organization figures for 1987 in Guy Standing, "Global Feminization Through Flexible Labor," *World Development*, vol. 17, no. 7, 1989, p. 1086.

22. *Ibid.*, p. 1077.

23. United Nations Development Program, *Human Development Report 1992* (New York: United Nations, 1992) p. 6.

24. *Los Angeles Times*, June 24, 1991.

25. *San Francisco Chronicle*, July 1, 1991.

26. Immigration and Naturalization figures in *The 1992 Information Please Almanac* (Boston: Houghton Mifflin, 1992), p. 804.

27. Richard Worthington, "Human Dimensions of Global Production," unpublished ms., June 1991, p. 30.

28. For a review of a range of other theories of international migration, see Aristide R. Zolberg, "The Next Waves: Migration Theory for a Changing World," *International Migration Review*, Fall 1989, pp. 403–430; Alejandro Portes and John Walton, *Labor, Class, and the International System* (New York: Academic Press, 1981), pp. 21–67.

29. Saskia Sassen, "America's Immigration 'Problem,' " *World Policy*, Fall 1989, p. 814.

30. Worthington, "Human Dimensions," p. 31.

31. World Bank, *Country Paper, Haiti* (review draft), May 20, 1983, p. 16.

32. Sassen, "America's Immigration 'Problem,' " p. 823.

33. *Wall Street Journal*, June 16, 1992.

34. Philip L. Martin and J. Edward Taylor, "The North American Free Trade Agreement and Rural Mexican Migration to the United States," paper prepared for the UC AIC Conference at Los Angeles, Mar. 5, 1992, p. 17.

35. *San Francisco Chronicle*, July 1, 1991.

36. Michael J. Mandel and Christopher Farrell, "The Immigrants: How They're Helping to Revitalize the U.S. Economy," *Business Week*, July 13, 1992, p. 118.

37. *Forbes*, May 27, 1991, p. 110.

38. Mandel and Farrell, "The Immigrants," pp. 114, 118.

39. Richman, "Coming World Labor Shortage," p. 74.

40. William R. Johnston, "Global Work Force 2000: The New World Labor Market," *Harvard Business Review*, March/April 1991, p. 125.

41. Richman, "Coming World Labor Shortage," p. 70.

42. *Ibid.*, p. 71.

43. Saskia Sassen, *The Global City: New York, London, Tokyo* (Princeton: Princeton University Press, 1991), p. 308.

44. See Robert Bellah et al., *Habits of the Heart* (Berkeley: University of California Press, 1985).

45. 1990 Census Bureau figures, reported in *Washington Post*, May 29, 1992.

Chapter Three. The Transformed Workplace

1. *Washington Post*, July 5, 1992.

2. Joyce Kolko, *Restructuring the World Economy* (New York: Pantheon, 1988), p. 327.

3. Lawrence Mishel and Jared Bernstein, *State of Working America* (Washington, D.C.: Economic Policy Institute, 1993), chapter 9.

4. Donald E. Petersen, *A Better Idea: Redefining the Way Americans Work* (Boston: Houghton Mifflin, 1991), p. 20.

5. Steve Babson, "Lean or Mean: The MIT Model and Lean Production at Mazda," manuscript, Wayne State University Labor Studies Center, June 1992, pp. 6, 16.

6. Mike Parker and Jane Slaughter, *Choosing Sides: Unions and the Team Concept* (Boston: South End Press, 1988), p. v.

7. *Washington Post*, Mar. 8, 1992.

8. Stephen Baker, "Detroit South," *Business Week*, Mar. 16, 1992, p. 100.

9. Harley Shaiken, "High Tech Goes Third World," *Technology Review*, January 1988, p. 41.

10. *Ibid.*, p. 43.

11. Baker, "Detroit South," p. 102.

12. Shaiken, "High Tech Goes Third World," p. 44.

13. Harley Shaiken, "Transferring High Tech Production to Mexico," *Columbia Journal of World Business*, Summer 1991, p. 130.

14. *Washington Post*, Dec. 26, 1992.

15. Ho Kwon Ping, "Birth of the Second Generation," *Far Eastern Economic Review*, May 18, 1979, p. 76.

16. Charles Kernaghan et al., *Paying to Lose Our Jobs* (New York: National

Labor Committee Education Fund in Support of Worker and Human Rights in Central America, 1992), p. 11.

17. Jim Naughton, "Marketing Michael," *Washington Post Magazine*, Feb. 9, 1992, p. 14.

18. Correspondence with Nike Public Relations, June 3, 1993.

19. Mark Clifford, "Spring in Their Step," *Far Eastern Economic Review*, Nov. 5, 1992, p. 56.

20. Interview with Dusty Kidd of Nike Public Relations, July 9, 1993.

21. Quoted in "What Ever Happened to the New World Order?" *24 Hours Supplement*, February 1992, p. 8.

22. *Boston Globe*, Dec. 30, 1991.

23. *24 Hours Supplement*, p. 8.

24. *Boston Globe*, Dec. 30, 1991.

25. Adam Schwarz, "Running a Business," *Far Eastern Economic Review*, June 20, 1991, p. 16.

26. *Boston Globe*, Dec. 30, 1991.

27. Schwarz, "Running a Business," p. 16; Donald Katz, "Triumph of the Swoosh," *Sports Illustrated*, Aug. 16, 1993, p. 54.

28. Ann Misch, "Lost in the Shadow Economy," *World Watch*, March/April 1992, p. 18.

29. Average wages and benefits in South Korea increased from $0.33 per hour in 1975 to $4.93 in 1992. By contrast, the average real wage of U.S. blue-collar workers fell from $12.91 an hour in 1987 to $11.93 in 1992. Mishel and Bernstein, *State of Working America*, p. 138; and conversation with U.S. Bureau of Labor Statistics in June 1993.

30. Sharon Begley, "The New Sweatshops," *Newsweek*, Sept. 10, 1990, pp. 51–52.

31. Misch, "Lost in the Shadow Economy," p. 21.

32. *Washington Post*, Feb. 10, 1992.

33. Aaron Bernstein, "The Global Economy: Who Gets Hurt?" *Business Week*, Aug. 10, 1992, p. 52.

34. Amy Borrus, "Stanching the Flow of China's Gulag Exports," *Business Week*, Apr. 13, 1992, p. 52.

35. Milton Moskowitz et al., *Everybody's Business* (New York: Doubleday, 1990), p. 91.

36. Borrus, "Stanching the Flow," p. 52.

37. National Labor Committee in Support of Democracy and Human Rights in El Salvador, "Worker Rights and the New World Order" (New York: National Labor Committee, 1991).

38. Cornelia H. Aldana, *A Contract for Underdevelopment: Subcontracting for Multinationals in the Philippine Semiconductor and Garment Industries*, IBON Databank, Philippines, 1989, pp. 98–101.

39. *Washington Post*, Mar. 6, 1991.

40. See the publications of the Washington-based International Labor Rights Education and Research Fund, including John Cavanagh et al., *Trade's Hidden Costs: Labor Rights in a Changing World Economy* (1988).

41. *Globe* (Philippines), May 17, 1989.

42. United Nations, *Directory of the World's Largest Service Companies* (New York: United Nations, 1990), pp. 331–332.

43. Herbert Schiller, *Culture Inc.* (Oxford: Oxford University Press, 1989), pp. 83ff.

44. *Wall Street Journal*, Mar. 11, 1992.

45. *Wall Street Journal*, May 10, 1991.

46. John Maxwell Hamilton, *Entangling Alliances* (Cabin John, Md.: Seven Locks Press, 1990), pp. 27, 40.

47. *Ibid.*, p. 52.

Chapter Four. Politics, Markets, and Jobs

1. Joyce Kolko, *Restructuring the World Economy* (New York: Pantheon, 1988), p. 313.

2. Quoted in *New York Times*, Jan. 25, 1987.

3. William Greider, *Who Will Tell the People?* (New York: Simon & Schuster, 1992), p. 52.

4. Steven Mufson, "The Privatization of Craig Fuller," *Washington Post Magazine*, Aug. 2, 1992, p. 30.

5. Donald L. Barlett and James B. Steele, *America: What Went Wrong?* (Kansas City: Andrews & McMeel, 1992), p. 47.

6. *Ibid.*, pp. 41–46.

7. See Gabriel Kolko, *Railroads and Regulation: 1877–1916* (Princeton: Princeton University Press, 1965), pp. 47–48.

8. Robert B. Reich, "Regulation by Confrontation or Negotiation," *Harvard Business Review*, May/June 1981, p. 84.

9. Barlett and Steele, *America: What Went Wrong?*, p. 92.

10. Larry Martz, "The Corporate Shell Game," *Newsweek*, Apr. 15, 1991, p. 48.

11. Pat Choate, *Agents of Influence* (New York: Knopf, 1990), p. 137.

12. Quoted in Greider, *Who Will Tell the People?*, p. 328.

13. *Ibid.*, p. 329.

14. *Washington Post*, Sept. 6, 1992.

15. Council of Economic Advisers, *Economic Report of the President* (Washington, D.C.: U.S. Government Printing Office, 1985), p. 114.

16. Robert Gilpin, *The Political Economy of International Relations* (Princeton: Princeton University Press, 1987), p. 173.

17. *Ibid.*, p. 180.

18. John Cavanagh et al., eds., *Trading Freedom: How Free Trade Affects Our Lives, Work and Environment* (San Francisco: Institute for Food and Development Policy, 1992), p. 30.

19. *Ibid.*, p. 28.

20. Tom Hilliard, "Trade Advisory Committee: Privileged Access for Polluters," *Public Citizen*, December 1991, p. 12.

21. Chakravarthi Raghavan, *Recolonization: GATT, the Uruguay Round and the Third World* (Penang, Malaysia: Third World Network, 1990), p. 123.

22. *Ibid.*, pp. 124–125.

23. Sandra Masur, "The North American Free Trade Agreement: Why It's in the Interest of U.S. Business," *Columbia Journal of World Business*, Summer 1991, p. 100.

24. Barlett and Steele, *America: What Went Wrong?*, p. 31.

25. U.S. International Trade Commission, *The Likely Impact on the United States of a FTA with Mexico*, USITC Publication 2353 (Washington, D.C.: U.S. Government Printing Office, 1991), p. viii.

26. Jeff Faux and Thea Lee, *The Effect of George Bush's NAFTA on American Workers: Ladder Up or Ladder Down?* (Washington, D.C.: Economic Policy Institute, 1992), p. 18.

27. Jonathan Schlefer, "What Price Economic Growth," *The Atlantic Monthly*, Dec. 1992, p. 115.

28. Quoted in *Philippine Daily Globe*, June 28, 1991.

29. Economic Policy Institute study, quoted in Aaron Bernstein, "The Global Economy: Who Gets Hurt?" *Business Week*, Aug. 10, 1992, p. 50.

Part Four

Chapter One. Bankers in a World of Debt

1. Geoffrey Jones, ed., *Banks as Multinationals* (London, New York: Routledge, 1990), p. 8.

2. Jonathan Friedland, "Streetwise Strategy," *Far Eastern Economic Review*, Mar. 8, 1990, p. 38; *Business Week*, May 16, 1993, p. 124.

3. Harold van B. Cleveland and Thomas F. Huertas, *Citibank 1812–1970* (Cambridge: Harvard University Press, 1985), p. 77. Also see chs. 2–3.

4. Noel Tichy and Ram Charan, "Citicorp Faces the World," *Harvard Business Review*, November/December 1990, p. 137.

5. Jones, *Banks as Multinationals*, p. 254.

6. Tichy and Charan, "Citicorp Faces the World," p. 135.

7. Sarah Bartlett, "John Reed's Citicorp," *Business Week*, Dec. 8, 1986, p. 90.

8. Lisa Gubernick, ed., "Bank to the Future," *Forbes*, July 13, 1987.

9. Edward Boyer, "Citicorp After Wriston," *Fortune*, July 9, 1984, p. 146.

10. Christopher Knowlton, "The Guys Who Gave Us Portfolio Insurance," *Fortune*, Jan. 4, 1988, pp. 28–29.

11. *Ibid.*

12. *Ibid.*

13. Boyer, "Citicorp After Wriston," p. 149.

14. John A. Byrne, "Think Like the Boss—and Take Chances," *Forbes*, July 16, 1984, p. 151.

15. Raul L. Madrid, *Overexposed: U.S. Banks Confront the Third World Debt Crisis* (Washington, D.C.: Investor Responsibility Research Center, 1990), pp. 42–45.

16. *Ibid.*, p. 7.

17. James S. Henry, "Where the Money Went," *New Republic*, Apr. 14, 1986, p. 22.

18. *Ibid.*, p. 21.

19. *Ibid.*

20. Madrid, *Overexposed*, p. 221.

21. *Ibid.*, p. 132.

22. *Ibid.*, p. 140.

23. *Ibid.*, p. 162.

24. Testimony of L. William Seidman to the Committee on Banking, Finance, and Urban Affairs, U.S. House of Representatives, Jan. 5, 1989.

25. Elizabeth Corcoran, "Banking Futures," *Scientific American*, February 1990, p. 65.

26. John Meehan, "All That Plastic Is Still Fantastic for Citibank," *Business Week*, May 28, 1990, p. 90.

27. Robert E. Norton, "Citibank," *Fortune*, June 8, 1987, p. 50.

28. Saul Hansell, "Will Rick Braddock's Retail Gamble Pay Off for Citi?" *Institutional Investor*, April 1990, p. 58.

29. David Lascelles, "Gaining Strength from a Long Global Reach," *Financial Times*, June 29, 1991; Karen Berney, "Citibank Goes for Broke," *International Management*, August 1990, p. 36.

30. Gary Hector, "Why U.S. Banks Are in Retreat," *Fortune*, May 7, 1990, p. 100.

31. Tichy and Charan, "Citicorp Faces the World," pp. 137–138.

32. *Ibid.*, p. 141.

33. Pete Engardio, "For Citibank, There's No Place Like Asia," *Business Week*, Mar. 30, 1992, p. 66; *Wall Street Journal*, Aug. 20, 1990.

34. Hansell, "Will Rick Braddock's Retail Gamble Pay Off," p. 61.

35. Interview with Stuart Pratt, Communications Dept., Association of Credit Businesses, Oct. 14, 1992.

36. "Citibank Taps Consumer Credit with New Card," *Manila Bulletin*, Oct. 25, 1990.

37. Bartlett, "John Reed's Citicorp," pp. 91–92.

38. John W. Milligan and Ida Picker, "The Collapse of Citibank's Credit Culture," *Institutional Investor*, December 1991, p. 53.

39. Bryan Burrough and John Helyar, *Barbarians at the Gate: The Fall of RJR Nabisco* (New York: Harper & Row, 1990), p. 208.

40. Reuters, Jan. 15, 1990; *Washington Post*, June 26, 1990; *Fortune*, Jan. 14, 1991, p. 97.

41. Milligan and Picker, "Collapse of Citibank's Credit Culture," p. 60.

42. Carol J. Loomis, "Citicorp's World of Troubles," *Fortune*, Jan. 14, 1991, p. 92.

43. *Wall Street Journal*, Apr. 3, 1991.

44. Loomis, "Citicorp's World of Troubles," p. 92.

45. William P. Barrett, "A Blank Check It Was Not," *Forbes*, Apr. 29, 1991, p. 40.

46. *Washington Post*, May 16, 1993.

47. *Wall Street Journal*, Aug. 20, 1990.

48. Interview of May 9, 1989, quoted in Anthony Sampson, *The Midas Touch: Money, People and Power From West to East* (London: Hodder & Stoughton, 1989), p. 179.

Chapter Two. Money Without a Home

1. Peter Passell, "Fast Money," *New York Times Magazine*, Oct. 18, 1992, pp. 43, 66.

2. *Ibid.*, p. 66.

3. Anthony Sampson, *The Midas Touch: Money, People and Power From West to East* (London: Hodder & Stoughton, 1989), p. 4.

4. Bernard Hoekman and Pierre Sauve, *Integration and Interdependence: Information Technology and the Transformation of Financial Markets* (Geneva: ATWATER Institute, 1991), p. 25.

5. Richard O'Brien, *Global Financial Integration: The End of Geography* (New York: Council on Foreign Relations Press, 1992), p. 14.

6. *Ibid.*

7. Passell, "Fast Money," p. 42.

8. James Ring Adams and Douglas Frantz, *A Full Service Bank: How BCCI Stole Billions Around the World* (New York: Pocket Books, 1992), p. 13.

9. R. T. Naylor, *Hot Money and the Politics of Debt* (New York: Linden Press/Simon & Schuster, 1987), p. 20.

10. Jonathan Beaty and Richard Hornik, "A Torrent of Dirty Dollars," *Time*, Dec. 18, 1989, p. 50.

11. *New York Times*, Sept. 29, 1992.

12. Adams and Frantz, *Full Service Bank*, p. 110.

13. *New York Times*, Aug. 11, 1992.

14. Passell, "Fast Money," p. 66.

15. *New York Times*, Sept. 13, 1982.

16. Penny Lernoux, *In Banks We Trust* (New York: Penguin, 1986), p. 37.

17. Remarks to American Bankers Association, Boston, Oct. 18, 1992, p. 9.

18. Clive Crook, "Fear of Finance," *Economist*, Sept. 19, 1992, p. 10.

19. Jeffry Frieden, *Banking on the World: The Politics of American International Finance* (New York: Harper and Row, 1987), p. 84.

20. O'Brien, *Global Financial Integration*, p. 33.

21. Richard Levich and Ingo Walter, "The Regulation of Global Financial Markets," in Thierry Noyelle, ed., *New York's Financial Markets: The Challenges of Globalization* (Boulder, Colo.: Westview Press, 1989), p. 55.

22. Barbara B. Diamond and Mark P. Kolar, *24-hour Trading: The Global Network of Futures and Options Markets* (New York: John Wiley & Sons, 1989), p. 14. We are grateful to Dr. Christopher Lind of St. Andrews College, Saskatoon, for calling our attention to these sources. See also Hoekman and Sauve, *Integration and Interdependence*.

23. Michael Lewis, *Liar's Poker* (New York: Norton, 1989), p. 35.

24. O'Brien, *Global Financial Integration*, p. 19.

25. Julien-Pierre Koszul, "Trends in Eurodollars," *Euromoney*, February 1970, p. 27.

26. *Washington Post*, Sept. 17, 1992.

27. *Wall Street Journal*, Sept. 18, 1992.

28. *Ibid.*

29. W. A. Thomas, *The Big Bang* (Oxford: Philip Allan, 1986), p. 159; Donald N. Thompson, "Big Bang: The City Revolution Begins," *Business Quarterly*, November 1986, p. 82.

30. "In Praise of Bunty Frobisher," *Economist*, Oct. 20, 1990, p. 16.

31. O'Brien, *Global Financial Integration*, ch. 5.

32. *Ibid.*, p. 46.

33. *Economist*, Dec. 16, 1989, p. S19.

Chapter Three. Global Finance and America's Banking Crisis

1. Daniel Burstein, *Yen! Japan's New Financial Empire and Its Threat to America* (New York: Simon & Schuster, 1988), p. 129.

2. Jeffrey A. Frankel, *The Yen/Dollar Agreement: Liberalizing Japanese Capital Markets* (Washington, D.C.: Institute for International Economics, 1984), p. 3.

3. *American Banker*, July 26, 1990; and Burnstein, *Yen!*

4. *New York Times*, May 20, 1987.

5. Burstein, *Yen!*, p. 79.

6. *Far Eastern Economic Review*, Sept. 24, 1992, p. 56.

7. Carla Rapaport, "Tough Times for Japan's Banks," *Fortune*, July 16, 1990, pp. 67–68.

8. *Wall Street Journal*, Nov. 6, 1992.

9. See Bryan Burrough and John Helyar, *Barbarians at the Gate: The Fall of RJR Nabisco* (New York: Harper & Row, 1990), and Michael Lewis, *Liar's Poker* (New York: Norton, 1989).

10. R. Taggart Murphy, "Power Without Purpose: The Crisis of Japan's Global Financial Dominance," *Harvard Business Review*, March/April 1989, p. 72.

11. Andrew Zimbalist et al., *Comparing Economic Systems: A Political-Economic Approach*, 2d ed. (New York: Harcourt Brace Jovanovich, 1989), p. 36.

12. James C. Abegglen and George Stalk, Jr., *Kaisha: The Japanese Corporation* (New York: Basic Books, 1985), p. 36.

13. William Kistler, investment banker and analyst, "Memo for President-Elect Clinton," Dec. 20, 1992, p. 1.

14. Memo from William Kistler, November 1992.

15. *Economist*, world banking survey, May 2, 1992, p. S35.

16. *Wall Street Journal*, June 8, 1990.

17. *New York Times*, Aug. 15, 1991.

18. Michael Thomas, *Lords of Misrule* (book in progress).

19. Craig McDonald and David Eppler, "The Road Back to Representation: The Case for Public Funding of Elections," in Jonathan Greenberg and William Kistler, eds., *Buying America Back* (Tulsa: Council Oak Books, 1992), p. 127.

20. Martin Mayer, "New Rules for Banking," in Greenberg and Kistler, *Buying America Back*, p. 146.

21. *New York Times*, Aug. 22, 1990.

22. Interview with William Kistler, Jan. 20, 1993.

23. William Greider, *The Trouble With Money* (Knoxville: Whittle Communications, 1989), reprinted in part in *Best of Business Quarterly*, Spring 1990, p. 59.

24. *Fortune*, Apr. 19, 1993, p. 176.

25. Jane W. D'Arista and Tom Schlesinger, *The Parallel Banking System* (Washington, D.C.: Economic Policy Institute, 1993).

26. *New York Times*, Oct. 11, 1992.

27. Howard Wachtel, *The Money Mandarins* (New York: Pantheon, 1986), p. 209.

Conclusion. Global Thinking in a Disorderly World

1. "A Survey of Multinationals," *Economist*, Mar. 27, 1993, pp. 5–6.

2. Robert Heilbroner, "Anti-Depression Economics," *The Atlantic Monthly*, April 1993, p. 103.

3. *Fortune*, Apr. 19, 1993, p. 244.

4. Paul Kennedy, *Preparing for the Twenty-First Century* (New York: Random House, 1993), p. 76.

5. Richard Falk, "The Making of Global Citizenship," in Jeremy Brecher, John Brown Childs, and Jill Cutler, eds., *Global Visions: Beyond the New World Order* (Boston: South End Press, 1993), p. 39.

SELECTED BIBLIOGRAPHY

Books

Abegglen, James C., and George Stalk, Jr. *Kaisha: The Japanese Corporation*. New York: Basic Books, 1985.

Ackerman, Diane. *A Natural History of the Senses*. New York: Random House, 1990.

Adams, James Ring, and Douglas Frantz. *A Full Service Bank: How BCCI Stole Billions Around the World*. New York: Pocket Books, 1992.

Aldana, Cornelia H. *A Contract for Underdevelopment: Subcontracting for Multinationals in the Philippine Semiconductor and Garment Industries*. IBON Databank, Philippines, 1989.

Aliber, Robert Z. *The International Money Game*. New York: Basic Books, 1987.

Barlett, Donald L., and James B. Steele. *America: What Went Wrong?* Kansas City: Andrews & McMeel, 1992.

Barnet, Richard J., and Ronald E. Müller. *Global Reach: The Power of the Multinational Corporations*. New York: Simon & Schuster, 1974.

Barry, Tom, ed. *Mexico: A Country Guide*. Albuquerque, N. Mex.: Inter-Hemispheric Education Resource Center, 1992.

Bello, Walden, and Stephanie Rosenfeld. *Dragons in Distress: Asia's Miracle Economies in Crisis*. San Francisco: Food First, 1990.

Benjamin, Curtis. *U.S. Books Abroad: Neglected Ambassadors*. Washington, D.C.: Library of Congress, 1984.

Bergsten, C. Fred, Thomas Horst, and Theodore H. Moran. *American Multinationals and American Interest*. Washington, D.C.: Brookings Institute, 1978.

Brecher, Jeremy, John Brown Childs, and Jill Cutler, eds. *Global Visions: Beyond the New World Order*. Boston: South End Press, 1993.

Broad, Robin. *Unequal Alliance: The World Bank, the International Monetary Fund, and the Philippines*. Berkeley: University of California Press, 1988.

Burrough, Bryan, and John Helyar. *Barbarians at the Gate: The Fall of RJR Nabisco*. New York: Harper & Row, 1990.

Burstein, Daniel. *Yen! Japan's New Financial Empire and Its Threat to America.* New York: Simon & Schuster, 1988.

Carnoy, Martin, Manuel Castells, Steve S. Cohen, and Fernando Enrique Cardoso. *The Global Economy in the Information Age: Reflections on Our Changing World.* University Park, PA: Pennsylvania State University Press, 1993.

Cavanagh, John, et al., eds. *Trading Freedom: How Free Trade Affects Our Lives, Work and Environment.* San Francisco: Institute for Food and Development Policy, 1992.

Choate, Pat. *Agents of Influence.* New York: Knopf, 1990.

Clairmonte, Frederick, and John Cavanagh. *Merchants of Drink: Transnational Control of World Beverages.* Penang, Malaysia: Third World Network, 1988.

Clark, Eric. *The Want Makers.* New York: Viking, 1988.

Cleveland, Harold van B., and Thomas F. Huertas. *Citibank 1812–1970.* Cambridge: Harvard University Press, 1985.

Cohen, Stephen S., and John Zysman. *Manufacturing Matters.* New York: Basic Books, 1987.

Cole, John Y., ed. *Books in Our Future.* Washington, D.C.: Library of Congress, 1987.

Cole, John Y. *Responsibilities of the American Book Community.* Washington, D.C.: Library of Congress, 1981.

Connor, John M. *Transnational Structure in Food Processing and Marketing.* Project NC-194. Columbus: Ohio State University, 1989.

Connor, John, et al. *The Food Manufacturing Industries.* New York: Lexington Books, 1985.

Coote, Belinda. *The Trade Trap.* Oxford: Oxfam UK, 1992.

Council of Economic Advisers. *Economic Report of the President.* Washington, D.C.: U.S. Government Printing Office, 1993.

Council of Economic Advisers. *Economic Report of the President.* Washington, D.C.: U.S. Government Printing Office, 1991.

Crawford, Richard D., and William W. Sihler. *The Troubled Money Business.* New York: HarperBusiness, 1991.

Dannen, Fredric. *Hit Men.* New York: Times Books, 1990.

Dassbach, Carl H. A. *Global Enterprises and the World Economy.* New York: Garland, 1988.

Davis, Suzanne. *Spectacular Nature.* Unpublished book manuscript, 1993.

Diamond, Barbara B., and Mark P. Kolar. *24-hour Trading: The Global Network of Futures and Options Markets.* New York: Wiley, 1989.

Dicken, Peter. *Global Shift: Industrial Change in a Turbulent World.* London: Harper & Row, 1986.

Drucker, Peter F. *Post-Capitalist Society.* New York: HarperCollins, 1993.

Durning, Alan. *How Much Is Enough? The Consumer Society and the Future of the Earth.* New York: Norton, 1992.

Farb, Peter, and George Armelagos. *Consuming Passions.* New York: Houghton Mifflin, 1980.

Finger, William R., ed. *The Tobacco Industry in Transition: Policies for the 1980s.* Lexington, Mass: D. C. Heath, 1981.

Frankel, Jeffrey A. *The Yen/Dollar Agreement: Liberalizing Japanese Capital Markets.* Washington, D.C.: Institute for International Economics, 1984.

Frieden, Jeffry. *Banking on the World: The Politics of American International Finance*. New York: Harper & Row, 1987.

Frith, Simon, ed. *Facing the Music*. New York: Pantheon, 1988.

Galbraith, John Kenneth. *A Short History of Financial Euphoria*. New York: Viking, 1993.

George, Susan. *The Debt Boomerang: How Third World Debt Harms Us All*. London: Pluto Press, 1992.

Gill, Stephen, and David Law. *The Global Political Economy: Perspectives, Problems and Policies*. Baltimore: Johns Hopkins University Press, 1988.

Gilpin, Robert. *The Political Economy of International Relations*. Princeton: Princeton University Press, 1987.

Goodland, R., C. Watson, and George Ledec. *Environmental Management in Tropical Agriculture*. Boulder, Colo.: Westview Press, 1984.

Goodman, Louis W. *Small Nations, Giant Firms*. New York: Holmes & Meier, 1987.

Greenberg, Jonathan, and William Kistler, eds. *Buying America Back*. Tulsa: Council Oak Books, 1992.

Greider, William. *The Trouble With Money*. Knoxville: Whittle Communications, 1990.

Greider, William. *Who Will Tell the People?* New York: Simon & Schuster, 1992.

Grunwald, Joseph, and Kenneth Flamm. *Global Factory: Foreign Assembly and International Trade*. Washington, D.C.: Brookings Institution, 1985.

Halberstam, David. *The Reckoning*. New York: Avon, 1986.

Hamilton, John Maxwell. *Entangling Alliances*. Cabin John, Md.: Seven Locks Press, 1990.

Heilbroner, Robert. *The Debt and the Deficit: False Alarms, Real Possibilities*. New York: Norton, 1989.

Herman, Edward S. *Corporate Control, Corporate Power*. Cambridge: Cambridge University Press, 1981.

Horowitz, Irving Louis. *Communicating Ideas*. Oxford: Oxford University Press, 1986.

Jones, Geoffrey, ed. *Banks as Multinationals*. London, New York: Routledge, 1990.

Kennedy, Paul. *Preparing for the Twenty-First Century*. New York: Random House, 1993.

Kernaghan, Charles, et al. *Paying to Lose Our Jobs*. New York: National Labor Committee Education Fund in Support of Worker and Human Rights in Central America, September 1992.

Knox, Paul, and John Agnew. *The Geography of the World Economy*. London: Edward Arnold, 1989.

Kolko, Joyce. *Restructuring the World Economy*. New York: Pantheon, 1988.

Koop, C. Everett. *Koop: The Memoirs of America's Family Doctor*. New York: Random House, 1991.

Krebs, A. V. *The Corporate Reapers: The Book of Agribusiness*. Washington, D.C.: Essential Books, 1992.

Kuttner, Robert. *The End of Laissez-Faire*. New York: Knopf, 1991.

Lernoux, Penny. *In Banks We Trust*. New York: Penguin, 1986.

Lewis, Michael. *Liar's Poker*. New York: Norton, 1989.

Lull, James, ed. *Popular Music and Communication*. Newbury Park, Calif: Sage, 1987.

Lyons, Nick. *The Sony Vision.* New York: Crown, 1976.

Madrid, Raul L. *Overexposed: U.S. Banks Confront the Third World Debt Crisis.* Washington, D.C.: Investor Responsibility Research Center, 1990.

Mishel, Lawrence, and David M. Frankel. *The State of Working America.* Washington, D.C.: Economic Policy Institute, 1991.

Mohn, Reinhard. *Success Through Partnership.* New York: Doubleday, 1988.

Morita, Akio. *Made in Japan: Akio Morita and Sony.* New York: NAL, 1988.

Moskowitz, Milton. *The Global Marketplace.* New York: Macmillan, 1987.

Moskowitz, Milton, et al. *Everybody's Business.* New York: Doubleday, 1990.

Moskowitz, Milton, et al. *Everybody's Business.* San Francisco: Harper & Row, 1980.

Muller, Mike. *Tobacco and the Third World: Tomorrow's Epidemic.* London: War on Want, 1978.

Naylor, R. T. *Hot Money and the Politics of Debt.* New York: Linden Press/Simon & Schuster, 1987.

Noyelle, Thierry, ed. *New York's Financial Markets: The Challenges of Globalization.* Boulder, Colo.: Westview Press, 1989.

O'Brien, Richard. *Global Financial Integration: The End of Geography.* New York: Council on Foreign Relations Press, 1992.

Ohmae, Kenichi. *The Borderless World: Power and Strategy in the Interlinked Economy.* New York: HarperBusiness, 1990.

Parker, Mike, and Jane Slaughter. *Choosing Sides: Unions and the Team Concept.* Boston: South End Press, 1988.

Petersen, Donald E. *A Better Idea: Redefining the Way Americans Work.* Boston: Houghton Mifflin, 1991.

Porter, Michael E. *The Competitive Advantage of Nations.* New York: The Free Press, 1990.

Postman, Neil. *Amusing Ourselves to Death: Public Discourse in the Age of Show Business.* New York: Viking, 1985.

Prestowitz, Clyde. *Trading Places.* New York: Basic Books, 1988.

Raghavan, Chakravarthi. *Recolonization: GATT, the Uruguay Round and the Third World.* Penang, Malaysia: Third World Network, 1990.

Reich, Robert. *The Work of Nations.* New York: Knopf, 1991.

Ross, Robert J. S., and Kent C. Trachte. *Global Capitalism: The New Leviathan.* New York: State University of New York Press, 1990.

Rydell, Robert W. *All the World's a Fair.* Chicago: University of Chicago Press, 1984.

Sampson, Anthony. *The Midas Touch: Money, People and Power From West to East.* London: Hodder & Stoughton, 1989.

Sassen, Saskia. *The Global City: New York, London, Tokyo.* Princeton: Princeton University Press, 1991.

Schiller, Herbert. *Culture Inc.* Oxford: Oxford University Press, 1989.

Schor, Juliet. *The Overworked American: The Unexpected Decline of Leisure.* New York: Basic Books, 1991.

Shaiken, Harley. *Work Transformed: Automation and Labor in the Computer Age.* New York: Holt, Rinehart & Winston, 1985.

Strange, Susan. *Casino Capitalism.* Oxford: Basil Blackwell, 1986.

Sutton, John. *Sunk Costs and Market Structure: Price Competition, Advertising, and the Evolution of Concentration.* Cambridge: MIT Press, 1991.

Taylor, Peter. *The Smoke Ring: Tobacco, Money, and Multinational Politics.* New York: NAL, 1985.

Thomas, W. A. *The Big Bang.* Oxford: Philip Allan, 1986.

Ungar, Sanford J. *Estrangement: America and the World.* Oxford: Oxford University Press, 1985.

UNICEF. *The State of the World's Children 1992.* New York: United Nations, 1992.

United Nations. *Directory of the World's Largest Service Companies.* New York: United Nations, 1990.

United Nations. *World Economic Survey, 1990.* New York: United Nations, 1990.

United Nations Center on Trade and Development. *Handbook of International Trade and Development Statistics.* New York: United Nations, 1988.

United Nations Development Program. *Human Development Report 1992.* New York: United Nations, 1992.

Vallette, Jim, and Heather Spaulding, eds. *International Trade in Wastes,* 5th ed. Washington, D.C.: Greenpeace, 1990.

Wachtel, Howard. *The Money Mandarins.* New York: Pantheon, 1986.

Weismantel, Mary J. *Food, Gender, and Poverty in the Ecuadorean Andes.* Philadelphia: University of Pennsylvania Press, 1988.

Womack, James P., et al. *The Machine That Changed the World.* New York: Rawson Associates, 1990.

World Bank. *World Development Report 1992.* Washington, D.C.: World Bank, 1992.

Wriston, Walter. *Twilight of Sovereignty.* New York: Macmillan, 1992.

Zimbalist, Andrew, et al. *Comparing Economic Systems: A Political-Economic Approach,* 2d ed. New York: Harcourt Brace Jovanovich, 1989.

Zysman, John, and Laura Tyson. *American Industry in International Competition: Government Policies and Corporate Strategies.* Ithaca: Cornell University Press, 1983.

Articles and Papers

Aufderheide, Pat. "Music Videos: The Look of Sound." *Journal of Communication,* Winter 1986.

Babson, Steve. "Lean or Mean: The MIT Model and Lean Production at Mazda." Manuscript, Wayne State University Labor Studies Center, June 1992.

Bagdikian, Ben H. "Assembly Line Publishing." *Tikkun,* May/June 1990, pp. 42–44, 102.

Baker, Will. "The Global Teenager." *Whole Earth Review,* Winter 1989.

Balassa, Bela. "The Process of Industrial Development and Alternative Development Strategies." In *Essays in International Finance.* Princeton: Princeton University Press, 1980.

Boyer, Peter J. "Sony and CBS Records: What a Romance!" *New York Times Magazine,* Sept. 18, 1988.

Bressani, Ricardo. "Food Science and Technology in Developing Countries During the Past 50 Years." *Food Technology,* 43 (September 1989).

Broad, Robin, and John Cavanagh. "No More NIC's." *Foreign Policy,* Fall 1988.

Brown, Jane D., and Kenneth Campbell. "Race and Gender in Music Videos: The Same Beat but a Different Drummer." *Journal of Communication*, Winter 1986.

Carlson, Peter. "It's an Ad Ad Ad Ad World." *Washington Post Magazine*, Nov. 3, 1991.

Carton, Paul. "Mass Media Culture and the Breakdown of Values Among Inner City Youth." *Future Choices*, 1991.

Coates, Joseph F., et al. "Future Work." *Futurist*, May/June 1991.

Davis, L. J. "Philip Morris's Big Bite." *New York Times Magazine*, Apr. 9, 1989.

Faux, Jeff, and Thea Lee. "The Effect of George Bush's NAFTA on American Workers: Ladder Up or Ladder Down?" Washington, D.C.: Economic Policy Institute, 1992.

Friedland, William H. "The New Globalization: The Case of Fresh Produce." University of California, Santa Cruz, June 1991.

Heilbroner, Robert. "Anti-Depression Economics." *The Atlantic Monthly*, April 1993.

Henry, James S. "Where the Money Went." *New Republic*, Apr. 14, 1986.

Hilliard, Tom. "Trade Advisory Committees: Privileged Access for Polluters." *Public Citizen's Congress Watch*, December 1991.

Hoekman, Bernard, and Pierre Sauve. "Integration and Interdependence: Information Technology and the Transformation of Financial Markets." Geneva: ATWATER Institute, 1991.

Holstein, William J. "The Stateless Corporation." *Business Week*, May 14, 1990.

Horowitz, David H. "The Record Rental Amendment of 1984: A Case Study in the Effort to Adapt Copyright Law to New Technology." *Columbia-VLA Journal of Law and the Arts*, March 1988.

Johnston, William R. "Global Work Force 2000: The New World Labor Market." *Harvard Business Review*, March/April 1991.

Kane, Hal. "Putting Out Cigarettes." *World Watch*, September/October 1991.

Levitt, Theodore. "The Globalization of Markets." *Harvard Business Review*, May 1983.

Madeley, John. "Tobacco: A Ruinous Crop." *Ecologist* 16 (1986).

Mandel, Michael J., and Christopher Farrell. "The Immigrants: How They're Helping to Revitalize the U.S. Economy." *Business Week*, July 13, 1992.

Masur, Sandra. "The North American Free Trade Agreement: Why It's in the Interest of U.S. Business." *Columbia Journal of World Business*, Summer 1991.

Milligan, John W., and Ida Picker. "The Collapse of Citibank's Credit Culture." *Institutional Investor*, December 1991.

Mintz, Morton. "Tobacco Roads." *Progressive*, May 1991.

Misch, Ann. "Lost in the Shadow Economy." *World Watch*, March/April 1992.

Murphy, R. Taggart. "Power Without Purpose: The Crisis of Japan's Global Financial Dominance." *Harvard Business Review*, March/April 1989.

Nath, Uma Ram. "India's Shame." *New York State Journal of Medicine*, December 1983.

Navarro, Nelson A. "Controversy in North Carolina." *New World Outlook*, July/August 1984.

Passell, Peter. "Fast Money." *New York Times Magazine*, Oct. 18, 1992.

Reich, Robert B. "Regulation by Confrontation or Negotiation." *Harvard Business Review*, May/June 1981.

Rostow, Walt W. "The Stages of Economic Growth." *Economic History Review*, August 1959.

Sassen, Saskia. "America's Immigration 'Problem.' " *World Policy*, Fall 1989.

Shaiken, Harley. "High Tech Goes Third World." *Technology Review*, January 1988.

Shaiken, Harley. "Transferring High Tech Production to Mexico." *Columbia Journal of World Business*, Summer 1991.

Standing, Guy. "Global Feminization Through Flexible Labor." *World Development* 17 (July 1989).

Tettweiler, Peter. "Snack Food Worldwide." *Food Technology*, February 1991.

Tichy, Noel, and Ram Charan. "Citicorp Faces the World." *Harvard Business Review*, November/December 1990.

INDEX

A & M Records, 122

accountability, 422, 427–28

Acheson, Dean, 421

acquisitions. *See* mergers and acquisitions

advertising. *See* marketing and promotion

African-Americans: cigarettes and, 196–97; dietary habits of, 244; recent immigrants and, 302, 304, 307; restructuring of labor market and, 292, 293

Agnelli family, 227, 401

agriculture, 208, 209, 284, 333; subsistence farming and, 210, 291, 299. *See also* food; food industry

Agriculture Department, U.S., 205, 244

alcohol, 182, 185, 186, 196–97

Algeria, 296

Allen, Richard, 203

American dream: migration patterns and, 300, 301

American Express, 370

American Psychological Association (APA), 156–57

American Tobacco Company, 188, 189

Angola, 252

antismoking movement, 187, 194–95, 198, 204

antitrust laws, 73, 231–32

apples, 238, 239–40

Argentina, 191, 284, 370, 372

Ariola Records, 116, 118

Arista, 26, 117, 118, 121, 123

Armstrong, C. Michael, 280

Asia: cigarette market in, 199, 200–201, 202–4, 206; Citicorp's expansion into, 376–77; consumer spending in, 64–65; as market for Occidental food, 220–21;

piracy in, 141–43; Sony's move into, 63–65. *See also specific countries*

Aspin, Les, 343

assembly line, 260–61, 315, 320–21. *See also* factories; manufacturing; mass production

AT&T, 46, 47, 53, 168

austerity measures, 353, 373

Australia, 171, 297

Australian Card Services, 376

autarchy, 349–50

authoritarian governments, 422–23

authors: as celebrities, 96; earnings of, 93–94; in marketing of their books, 99. *See also* books; publishing industry

automatic teller machines (ATMs), 367, 374, 375

automation, 268, 310, 324, 325, 420

automobile industry, 176, 182, 260–74, 314–20; "Buy American" policy and, 278–79; food companies acquired by, 227; Japanese, 261, 265–68, 271–74, 278–80, 281, 345, 355, 404; jobs transferred to Mexico by, 318–20; just-in-time production in, 267, 268, 315–16; labor movement and, 261, 262, 312–13, 316, 317–18, 319, 320; layoffs in, 268, 274, 278, 291, 312–13, 317–18; local content rules and, 279–80; marketing and promotion in, 267; mass production introduced in, 260–61; strategic alliances in, 271–274, 316; team production in, 266, 314–315, 316, 318; variety introduced in, 262; vehicle size and profit margins in, 269–70; wage levels in, 260–61, 262, 313. *See also* Ford Motor Company; *specific companies*

Bagdikian, Ben H., 346
Bailey, James, 374
Baker & McKenzie, 335
Balassa, Bela, 288
Bangladesh, 252, 417–18; migrant workers from, 296, 297
Bank America, 412
Bankers Trust, 371, 379, 380, 386, 410, 411
banking and financial services, 17–18, 361–418, 420; activities shifted offshore in, 394–95; circumvention of legal requirements in, 392, 394, 395; commercial loans and, 378–81, 393–94, 412; credit cards and, 367, 373, 374–75, 376, 377, 383–84, 411; crisis in, 381, 393–94, 409–10, 415; in developing countries, 401–2; electronic transfers and, 385–91; Euromarket and, 365, 395, 397, 400, 418; foreign-exchange trade and, 390–91, 395–96, 397–98; fraudulent or criminal operations in, 388–89; GATT and, 354; government regulation of, 364–65, 378, 380, 391–95, 397, 402, 412, 413, 415; history of, 361–63; information technology and, 386–87, 398–99; international loans and, 353, 368–73, 378, 380, 382, 394–395, 400; international supervision of, 418; investment, 399–402, 411, 412, 415; in Japan, 361–62, 364, 378, 391, 404, 405–6, 407–8, 410–11, 412, 415; mergers and consolidation of, 411–13; national differences in, 410–12; real-estate market and, 380–81, 393–94, 413; reform proposals for, 415–18; social role of, 413–16, 417–18; technology and, 398–99; Third World debt crisis and, 368–73, 378, 380. See also Citicorp; money; specific banks
Bank of America, 376
bankruptcy, 413, 414
Bankwire, 388
Bantam, 91, 92, 95, 101, 103
Barbados, 285
Basel Group, 418
Bayer, 182
BCCI, 418
Beatles, 37
Beatrice Foods, 227
Beech-Nut, 224
Belgium, 276, 361, 411
Belize, 285
Bell Labs, 230
Benetton, 176
Bennett, Harry, 262, 263
Benson & Hedges, 196
Benton, Philip, 268–69, 272
Bertelsmann, 16, 18, 68–89, 134, 381; as benevolent, paternalistic employer, 86–87; book and record clubs of, 69, 73, 81, 101, 102, 103, 117; businesses outside communications industry rejected by, 79; division of earnings at, 87–88; history of, 70–73; holdings of, 69–70; as international vs. global company, 79–81; magazines published by, 69, 74–77, 81–84, 86, 117; major competitor of, 83–84; management of, 77–79, 84–86; in music industry, 26, 73, 83, 116–23, 139, 140, 142, 143, 144–45, 150, 155, 158–59; U.S. publishing houses acquired by, 92, 94, 100–103
Bertelsmann, Carl, 71
Betamax, 56–55, 57, 125
Big Bang, 399, 400, 401
billboards, 174
biotechnology, 251, 426
Bissinger, Manfred, 77
Bluestone, Barry, 291, 292
BMG, 121, 122–23, 139, 140, 141, 159
BMW, 321
Bolivia, 286–87, 369
books: active collaboration of reader required by, 107–8; electronic, 107; global, 80–81, 94–95; shelf life of, 109. See also authors; publishing industry
bookstore chains, 98–99, 100
Borden, 224
Bosnia, 421
Bourdieu, Pierre, 110
Braddock, Richard, 373–74
Brady, Nicholas, 391–92
brand-name products, 174
Brazil, 182, 284, 307, 357, 366; bank loans to, 369, 370, 371, 372; cigarette market in, 191, 206; disparities of wealth in, 179; music market in, 149; as potential market, 181; television in, 159, 171; tobacco grown in, 205, 206–7
"bread and circus" strategy, 39
Bretton Woods system, 249–50, 349, 352
British American Tobacco (BAT), 182, 198, 204, 206–7
British Columbia, 351
Brown, Jerry, 346
Brown, Tina, 84
Bulova Watch Company, 50, 275
Bundesbank, 401
Burnett, Leo, 190, 191, 221
Burstein, Daniel, 406
Bush, George, 153, 201, 204, 221, 279, 293, 344, 350, 408–9, 410; NAFTA and, 355, 356
"Buy American" slogan, 278–79
Buziak, Bob, 122
Byrd, Robert, 307–8
Byrne, Bridget, 128

cable television, 27, 126, 138, 148, 172; MTV, 38–39, 126, 138, 153–54, 157, 171

California: Asian immigrants in, 298; food operations moved to Mexico from, 254–255; taxes on foreign-owned firms in, 345–46

Camel, 197

Campbell (company), 244

Campbell, Donald G., 106–7

Campeau, Robert, 379–80

Canada, 253; auto industry in, 313, 317; cigarettes in, 194, 195; fears of foreign cultural domination in, 106–7, 149; NAFTA and, 356–57

C&S/Sovran, 413

Cape Verde, 289

capital: global mobility of, 300, 310, 349, 351–52; removed from Third World, 370

capitalism, 260, 287, 288

Capitol Records, 119, 120

Carnation, 224

Carter, Jimmy, 367

Caterpillar, 355

Catholic Church, 336

CBS, 91

CBS Records, 58, 115, 118, 119, 122, 132, 145; history of, 124; Sony's acquisition of, 67, 124–29, 132. See also Sony Music

censorship, 105, 108–9, 155, 159

Census Bureau, 335

CHAPS, 388

Chase Manhattan, 400

Chase National Bank, 369

Chemical Bank, 398, 412–13

Chia, Pei-yuan, 374, 377

Chicago Board Options Exchange, 401

Chicago Mercantile Exchange, 395–96

child labor, 333–34

children: malnutrition among, 210; media's effects on, 156–59; product promotions geared to, 166, 241

Chile, 383; bank loans to, 368, 369, 372; fresh fruits exported by, 235, 238

China, 105, 178, 182, 220, 283–84, 285, 294, 326, 424; cigarettes in, 185, 201, 204; consumer spending in, 167, 181–83; entertainment industry and, 139–40, 142; Euromarket and, 365, 395; language barrier and, 170; migrant workers from, 297, 298, 304; as potential market, 181–182, 183; slavelike working conditions in, 332; special economic zones in, 321; U.S. banking interests in, 363

CHIPS (New York Clearing House Interbank Payment System), 387–88, 390

Chirac, Jacques, 33–34, 83

Christopher, Warren, 340

Chrysler, 317, 318

cigarettes, 16, 18, 182, 184–207, 222, 225, 228, 229, 286; African-American causes supported by makers of, 197; antismoking campaigns and, 187, 194–95, 198, 204; associations of, 186; cigarette companies' attitudes toward health risks of, 186–87, 192–93; dangers of secondhand smoke from, 186, 194; deaths caused by, 184, 186, 192–93, 194, 196, 202; excise taxes on, 193–94, 199; female market for, 189, 196; global market for, 184–85, 198–99, 200–204; government-industry partnership and, 199–202, 204; imported tobacco in, 205–7; laws restricting smoking of, 195, 197; marketing and promotion of, 189–192, 193, 195, 196–98; model changes in, 197–98; pharmacology of tobacco and, 185–86; potential new smokers of, 195–97; price of, 213; profitability of, 185; trade restrictions and, 201, 202, 204; warning labels on, 193; youth market for, 197. See also Marlboro; Philip Morris

Citicorp (Citibank), 15, 17–18, 362–84, 392, 405, 410, 411; commercial loans of, 378–81, 394; consumer-banking activities of, 367, 373–77, 380, 383–84; credit-card business of, 367, 373, 374–75, 376, 377, 383–84; crisis at (late 1980s), 381–383; early history of, 362–63; exodus of capital from Latin America facilitated by, 370; foreign-exchange operations of, 390–91, 398; information systems marketed by, 381; international loans of, 368–73, 378, 380, 382, 395; real-estate portfolio of, 380–81; securities operations of, 400

cities, 334; loss of manufacturing jobs in, 276–77, 291; migration to, 179, 210, 299–301

classical music, 113, 118–19

Clinton, Bill, 39, 180, 204, 408, 409, 416, 417

Clydesdale, Fergus M., 245

CNN, 171, 346

Coca-Cola, 15, 65, 79, 129, 169–70, 176, 181, 182, 189, 227, 246

coffee, 209, 220, 225, 250–51

Cold War, 105, 311, 420; end of, 20, 21, 125, 355, 372

Columbia Pictures, 55, 67; Sony's acquisition of, 125, 129, 134–36

Commodity Credit Corporation, 199–200

communications industry, 15–16, 68–111; consolidation of various media in, 92–93; controlled by handful of global giants, 346–47; technology and, 79. See also cultural products; entertainment industry;

publishing industry; television; *specific companies*
communism, 38, 137, 139, 288, 311, 420
community, 22; alternative notions of, 429–430; banking and needs of, 414–16, 417–418; decline of, 38, 39, 342
Community Reinvestment Act, 416, 417
compact discs (CDs), 144, 146
computers, 46, 57, 352; banking and, 385–390, 398–99; entering data into, 335, 336–37; music industry and, 143; pirated software for, 145; publishing industry and, 91, 109, 110
ConAgra, 227
Confederation of Mexican Workers (CTM), 318, 320
Congress, U.S., 64, 145, 205, 239, 317; banking and, 364–65, 380, 392, 393, 409; private interests's influence in, 343–44
Connor, John M., 226, 230–31
consumer confidence, 180
consumer electronics, 42–67, 182, 355; control over entertainment software for, 125, 130–31, 132–34; decline in profit margin of (1990s), 130–31; new technologies in, 143–46; prices and, 146–47. *See also* Sony
consumer spending, 163–256, 426; accumulation mentality and, 177–78; Americans' profligate consumption habits and, 177–78; in Asia, 64–65; in Communist nations, 167; cost-consciousness and, 174; credit cards and, 367, 373, 374–75, 376, 377, 383–84, 411; decline in (1990s), 180; marketing and promotion and, 168–83 (*see also* marketing and promotion); in 1980s, 166–68; segmentation by income level and, 178. *See also* global products; *specific products*
contracting-out: in garment industry, 331–334; in information industries, 337; in sport-shoe industry, 325–26, 327–28
copyright protection, 106
corporations: foreign-owned, in U.S., 345–346; global (*see* global corporations;) multinational (*see* multinational corporations); political influence of, 342–47, 348; social responsibility lacked by, 422, 427–28; tax burdens of, 344, 345–46
corruption, 347
Coser, Lewis, 109
Costa Rica, 285
CPC International, 227
credit, 17, 167–68, 387; social and political development related to, 414–16, 417
credit cards, 367, 373, 374–75, 411; global market for, 376, 377, 383–84
Cuba, 299, 369

Cullman, Joseph, III, 189–90, 193–94
cultural imperialism, 104–7, 149–50, 159–60
cultural products, 15–16, 18, 25–160, 419; American, worldwide interest in, 35–36; and backlash against global commercial cultures, 155–60; children affected by, 156–59; cultural domination and, 104–7, 149–50, 159–60; ethnicity of immigrants and, 307; migration patterns and, 300, 301; as opiates, 37, 40; tourism and, 29–35. *See also* books; entertainment industry; magazines; movies; music; music industry; publishing industry; television
currency trade, 390–91, 395–96, 397–98
Czechoslovakia, 286

Dannen, Fredric, 149
data banks, 335–36, 381
data-processing jobs, 335, 336
Davies, Alun, 104
Davis, Clive, 115, 118, 122, 123
Davis, Martin S., 342
Davis, Ron, 202
DDT, 350–51
Deaver, Michael, 203
debt crisis, 179, 368–73, 378, 380; austerity measures and, 353, 373; Citibank's loan policies and, 368–69; defusing of, 372–73; flight of capital and, 370; U.S. government and, 371–72
deficit spending, 341–42, 403, 406, 409
Dell, 92, 94, 101, 103
democracy, 343, 414, 421, 427
demographics, 28–29, 175, 176, 179
Denmark, 314, 351
Depression, Great, 369, 392, 414
Deregulation and Monetary Control Act (1980), 393
developing countries, 342, 396; austerity measures in, 353, 373; banking in, 401–2; cigarettes marketed in, 184, 198–207; debt crisis in, 179, 353, 368–73, 378, 380; development orthodoxy and, 250, 251, 287–88; educational levels in, 305; exploitation of workers in, 325–29, 331–34; export-processing zones in, 300–301, 321, 326–27; exposure to global products in, 165–66; factories relocated to, 53–54, 274–76, 318–20, 325, 326, 332, 356; as food exporters, 250–56; food in, 245–47; foreign cultural domination feared in, 105–6, 107; GATT and, 354–55; growth of labor pool in, 294; infant formula in, 223–24; informal economy in, 328–29; loss of self-sufficiency in, 252–53; mass-consumption product ladder in, 182; migration from, 296–309; multinationals courted by, 424;

developing countries (*cont.*)
music industry and, 141; Nestlé's strategy in, 225–26; as potential market, 179–80, 181–83; public enterprises in, 339; in seven tiers of global division of labor, 284–87; supranational institutions and, 352–53; telecommunications in, 337; tobacco grown in, 205–7; trade concessions offered to, 354; urban migration in, 179, 210
development aid, 299
development theory, 250, 251, 287–88
Diamandis Communications, 83
digital audiotape (DAT), 133, 143–45
Digital Equipment, 336
Dingell, John, 381–82
direct marketing, 172, 173, 381
Walt Disney, 29, 49, 92; theme parks and, 30, 31, 32–35
division of labor, global, 283–309, 420; development theory and, 287–88; in early 1950s, 283–84; environmental concerns and, 289–90; erosion of union power and, 310–11, 312–13, 316; mass migrations and, 296–309; relocation of factories to low-wage enclaves and, 53–54, 274–76, 318–20, 325, 326, 332, 356; seven tiers in, 284–87; unemployment and, 290–93; wage levels and, 313–14, 330–31. *See also* labor market; workplace
dollar (U.S.), 312, 321, 395–96; Eurodollars and, 365, 395, 397, 400, 418; offshore accumulation of, 394–95; U.S. trade balance and, 404–5
Dominican Republic, 332
Dornemann, Michael, 102, 116–23, 143, 158–59
Dothan, Ala.: foreign-owned firms in, 321–25
Doubleday, 83, 92, 101–3
Dow Chemical Company, 281
Drexel Burnham, 379
drug traffic, 389

Eastern Europe, 285–86, 305, 339, 340. *See also specific countries*
Eby, Jack, 270–71
economic growth, 340; development orthodoxy and, 250, 251, 287–88
economies, national: governmental control over, 20–21, 340, 408–9, 422–23, 428
economies of scale, 27–28
Ecuador, 246
education, 110, 282, 305, 417, 429; immigrants and, 308; media and, 157–58
Edwards, David, 390–91
Egypt, 297
Ehrlich, Paul and Anne, 177–78

electoral process, 343, 414
electronic books, 107
Electronic Industries of Japan, 346
El Salvador, 325; migration from, 299, 301
Elsevier, 97
EMI, 120, 132
employment: jobs crisis and, 425–27. *See also* division of labor, global; labor market; layoffs; unemployment; workplace
energy: used by food industry, 244–45
entertainment industry, 15–16, 25–29, 35–41, 112–60; demographics and, 28–29; earnings of, 25, 26; economies of scale in, 27–28; escapism and, 36–38; explanations for global expansion of, 26–29; foreign acquisition of U.S. corporations in, 67, 80, 104–5, 116–36; global market of, 35–38, 137–38; ideological barriers to, 139–40; lack of global consciousness and, 138–39; leisure time and, 40; messages of rebellion spread by, 36–37, 38–39, 40; multimedia conglomeration in, 116, 131; piracy and, 141–43, 144–45; state manipulation of, 39–40; synergy in, 131, 132–34; technology and, 26–27, 40; theme parks and, 30–35, 164, 398; youths as consumers of, 137–38. *See also* cultural products; movies; music; music industry; publishing industry; television; *specific companies*
environment: degraded by tourism, 30; industrial processes' effects on, 289–90, 352
environmental movement, 35, 150, 237, 290; food industry and, 242–43
environmental regulation, 270; GATT and, 351; in Mexico, 255–56
Equidata Philippines, Inc., 336
Esaki, Leo, 48
Ethiopia, 299, 302
ethnicity, 104, 340, 429
Euro Disneyland, 30, 33–34
Euromarket, 365, 395, 397, 400, 418
European Commission, 350, 351
European Community (EC), 106, 219, 349; banking in, 391; cigarette advertising in, 195; guest workers in, 296, 305–6, 308–9; integration of, 88, 104, 219, 355, 421; unemployment in, 291
exchange rates, 390–91, 395–96, 397–98
excise taxes, 193–94, 199
Export-Import Bank, 368
export-processing zones, 300–301, 321, 326–27

factories: environment damaged by, 289–290; foreign-owned, in U.S., 321–25; moved out of inner cities, 276–77, 291; relocated to low-wage enclaves, 53–54,

274–76, 318–20, 325, 326, 332, 356; women as workers in, 321, 325, 326–27, 328–29, 332–33. *See also* manufacturing; mass production; workplace

family, 334; decline of, 13, 37, 39, 110, 158; dinner rituals and, 248–49

"family values," 155

fast-food industry, 234–35, 238–39, 246

fats, 247; Americans' consumption of, 240–241; health concerns and, 237, 238–39; tropical oils, 251, 287

Federal Deposit Insurance Corporation (FDIC), 393, 412, 413, 415–16

Federal Reserve, 382, 385, 388, 392–93, 394, 396, 408, 411

Federal Reserve Act (1913), 362

Fedwire, 388

"feminization" of work, 294–96

fiber-optic technologies, 27

finance. *See* banking and financial services; money

Finland, 397

Fischer, Manfred, 78

fishing industry, 289–90

Fitzpatrick, Robert, 33

Fitzwater, Marlin, 344

food: American eating habits and, 240–41; developing countries as exporters of, 250–56; distribution problems and, 211, 252; entertainment value of, 241–42; exported by U.S., 210, 252–53, 254; in future, 245; GATT and global safety standards for, 350–51; local tastes in, 234, 241; malnutrition and, 210, 211, 212, 245–46, 247, 253, 353; microwave revolution and, 247, 248–49; in poor countries, 245–47; price of, 231; shifting tastes and, 236–37, 251; shopping for, 243–44 (*see also* supermarkets); social and cultural functions of, 233–34, 247, 248–49; spending on, 212; taboos and, 234; traditional, decline in consumption of, 246–47; world market system and, 249–56

Food and Drug Administration (FDA), 212, 239, 255, 350–51

Food for Peace, 200

food industry, 16, 208–56; consolidation in, 212–18, 219, 226–28, 229–32; "counterseasonal" fruits and vegetables and, 235–36; desire for freshness and, 237, 239–40; energy inefficiencies in, 244–45; environmental movement and, 242–43; fast-food and, 234–35, 238–39, 246; flavor enhancers and, 242, 287; globalization of taste and, 234–35, 245–47; grain market and, 229–30, 252–53, 254; health concerns and, 237–39, 240, 247, 251, 255–56; history of, 209–10; impov-

erished unable to buy products of, 211; local economies transformed by, 250–56; local tastes and, 225, 241; marketing and promotion in, 239, 241–42, 246; recession and, 219–20; snacks and, 240–42; technology and, 235, 251, 426; time-saving products and, 247–48; traditional diets affected by, 246–47; transportation methods and, 209. *See also* specific companies and products

Ford, Henry, 62, 259, 260–63, 313, 320

Ford, Henry, II, 263–64, 271–72

Ford Escort, 270–71, 272–74

Ford Fiesta, 270

Ford Mondeo, 271

Ford Motor Company, 14, 17, 18, 260–64, 265, 266, 267–74, 315–16, 317, 387, 416; as global company, 268–71; Japanese practices adapted by, 267–68; mass production introduced at, 260–61; Mexican plants of, 319–20; in strategic alliances with non-American automakers, 271–74; unions and, 261, 262, 312, 313; "world car" built by, 270–71, 272–74

foreign-exchange trade, 390–91, 395–96, 397–98

Forman, Milos, 37

Fortas, Abe, 193

France, 107, 296, 311, 314, 411; banking in, 361, 364, 401, 412; foreign cultural products restricted in, 149; foreign workers in, 306, 308; loss of manufacturing jobs in, 275, 276

Frankfurt Book Fair, 90–91

free trade, 348–52, 372; arguments for and against, 349–50; GATT and, 250, 350–352, 354–55, 402; as misleading term, 348–49; NAFTA and, 253–54, 350, 351, 355–57; world food market and, 250–56

Freston, Tom, 153, 154

Friedman, Milton, 395–96

Frith, Simon, 147–48

fruits, 245, 254–55; "counterseasonal," 235–36

Fuller, Craig, 344

fundamentalism, 37, 140, 155, 429

futures market, 395–96

Gap, 332

garment industry, 330–34; contracting-out in, 331–34; "gulag labor" in, 332; sweat shops in, 330–31, 333

Garn, Jake, 343

Garn-St. Germain Act (1982), 380, 393

Gassner, Rudi, 139–40, 142

Geffen, David, 128–29, 133

General Agreement on Tariffs and Trade (GATT), 250, 350–52; developing countries and, 354–55; financial services and,

(GATT) (cont.)
402; foreign investment and, 252–53; global safety standards and, 350–51
General Electric (GE), 53, 117–18, 276, 280, 285, 336, 347, 355, 387
General Foods, 203, 214, 218, 373; history of, 215–16; Philip Morris's acquisition of, 213, 215, 216, 229, 231
General Mills, 248
General Motors (GM), 172, 261, 262, 263, 267, 313, 316, 357, 393, 403, 411, 416, 423, 425; plants closed by, 317–18
Germany, 168, 182, 250, 313, 314, 321, 341, 361, 383, 394, 398, 408, 423; banking in, 391, 401, 410, 412; guest workers in, 296, 305, 306, 308–9; reunification of, 341, 420
Germany, East, 73, 81, 167, 285
Gerstacker, Carl A., 281
Ghana, 286, 287
Gilpin, Robert, 349
Ginn & Company, 96
Glasser, Joel M., 225
Glass-Steagall Act (1933), 364–65, 399, 415
global corporations, 15; hyperbole about, 423; influence of, 14; national economies and, 20–21; national governments undermined by, 19–20; power vacuum filled by, 342; statelessness of, 280–81, 342, 424. See also multinational corporations; specific corporations
globalization: not really global, 427; use of word, 13–14, 79–80. See also specific topics
global localization strategy, 65–66
global products, 163–256, 419; books as, 80–81, 94–95; local differences and, 173; marketing and promotion of, 168–83 (see also marketing and promotion); at shopping centers and malls, 164–66; in supermarkets, 166; supposed homogenization of tastes and, 176–77. See also cigarettes; consumer spending; food; food industry
Goizueta, Roberto C., 169, 170
Goldman, Elliott, 118, 120–21, 122
Gold Star, 56–57
Gore, Al, 155
Gore, Tipper, 155
government regulation, 348; of banking, 364–65, 378, 380, 391–95, 397, 402, 412, 413, 415; environmental laws, 255–256, 270, 351; GATT and, 350–51; of securities business, 399, 400, 401
governments. See national governments
grains, 229–30; U.S. export of, 252–53, 254
Grand Metropolitan, 230

grapes, 235
Great Britain, 20, 32, 209–10, 311, 354, 421, 423; banking in, 361, 362, 397, 398; books from, altered for U.S. market, 95; London Stock Exchange deregulated in, 399, 400, 401; loss of manufacturing jobs in, 275, 276; magazine publishing in U.S. vs., 84; migration to, 308
Greece, 295, 302
Greider, William, 343
Grolier Inc., 83, 92
Gross, Johannes, 77
Grüner & Jahr, 74, 82, 86, 87
Guatemala, 285, 299; garment facilities in, 332–33
Guber, Peter, 129, 134, 135, 136
Gulf & Western, 91

Hachette, 83–84, 92
Haiti, 285, 289; migration from, 299–300
Hamilton, Alexander, 349–50
Harnischfeger, Manfred, 78
Harper & Row, 92, 99
Harrison, Bennett, 291, 292
health care, 297, 357
Heilbroner, Robert, 426
Heineken, 168
H. J. Heinz, 227–28
Helms, Jesse, 200
Henry, James S., 370
high-definition TV (HDTV), 130
high-technology industries, 277–78, 304
Hispanic-Americans, 305
Hitler, Adolf, 70–71, 75, 77
Hoffmann-La Roche, 182, 354
holding companies, 392
Hollings, Ernest F., 278
Holt, Rinehart & Winston, 91
Hong Kong, 142, 191–92, 235, 275, 284, 285, 294, 300, 305, 376; migrant workers in, 296, 297
Houghton Mifflin, 104
housing: credit available for, 414–15, 416
Hungary, 285, 305
Huxley, Aldous, 39

IBM, 65, 168, 230, 336, 357, 395, 416, 423, 425; as stateless corporation, 280
Ibuka, Masaru, 43–44, 45, 46–48, 49, 50, 60, 62
immigration. See migration
Immigration Reform and Control Act (1986), 303
Imperial Tobacco Company, 188
India, 151, 182, 207, 220, 284, 294, 337; cigarettes in, 204, 328–29; Citibank's credit-card business in, 377; eating habits

in, 247; migrant workers from, 296, 298, 302, 304, 307, 308; piracy in, 141, 142; as potential market, 181; television in, 153

Indonesia, 142, 285; Citibank's credit-card business in, 377; as food exporter, 251–252; migrant workers from, 296, 297; Nestlé's operations in, 225–26; as potential market, 181; sport shoes manufactured in, 326, 327–28

infant formula, 182, 223–24

infant mortality, 210, 223

inflation, 340, 396, 408

informal-sector production, 328–29

information industries, 259, 334–38; banking and, 381; commercialization of information and, 335–36; exportation of menial jobs in, 336–37

information revolution, 334–35, 380, 399

information technology: banking and, 386–387, 398–99

intellectual property, 106; GATT and, 354

interest rates, 348, 367, 369, 396, 407, 408, 411; Regulation Q and, 392–93

International Labor Organization, 294–95, 307, 328

International Monetary Fund (IMF), 250, 254, 339, 352–53, 368, 371

International Trade Commission, 356

Iran, 140

Iraq, 297

Isgur, Lee, 92

Ishihara, Shintaro, 55

Islamic fundamentalism, 140

Italy, 295, 311, 314, 347, 354, 361, 397; financial services in, 401

It's a Wonderful Life, 413

Iwaka, Ken, 130

Jackson, Michael, 113, 114, 127–29, 131, 132, 137, 138, 140, 146

Jacobs Suchard, 213, 219, 226

Jamaica, 285

Janklow, Morton, 117

Japan, 107, 171, 182, 199, 235, 288, 289, 296, 298, 301, 355, 376, 394, 409, 420–421, 422, 423; Americans' animosity toward, 278–79; Asian market and, 181; auto industry of, 261, 265–68, 271–74, 278–80, 281, 345, 355, 404; banking in, 361–62, 364, 378, 391, 404, 405–6, 407–8, 410–11, 412, 415; business culture in, 61–62; capital accumulation in, 404, 405; cigarette market in, 200, 201, 202, 203–4; coffee sales in, 220; consumer spending in, 168; corruption in, 347; as dominant force in world economy, 403–4; eating habits in, 241, 246, 247, 248, 251–52; economic reverses in

(1990s), 407–8; export-based economy of, 250; factories in U.S. owned by companies in, 321–25; financial-services industry in, 404, 405–6; food imports in, 220–21, 225; government's relationship with large corporations in, 282; labor movement in, 266, 311–12; labor shortage in, 306–7; loss of manufacturing jobs in, 275; mass production modified in, 265–68; part-time workers in, 340; shopping centers and malls in, 164–65; stateless corporations and, 280–81; team production in, 266, 314; trade imbalance between U.S. and, 54–55, 58, 64, 221, 404–5; U.S. debt financed by, 406–7; U.S. occupation of, 265–66; wage levels in, 314

Japan Tobacco Inc., 202

job rotation, 315, 316

jobs: employment crisis and, 425–27; environmental security traded for, 290. See also division of labor, global; labor market; layoffs; unemployment; workplace

Johnson, Lyndon B., 394–95

Johnson & Johnson, 182

Jones, Thomas, 375

Jordan: migrant workers from, 296, 297

junk bonds, 378, 379

junk food, 240–42, 246

Jurgs, Michael, 77

just in time production, 267, 268, 312, 315–16, 332

JVC, 55–56

Kapur, Dee, 273

Keidanren, 59

keiretsu, 61–62, 410

Kellogg, 172, 220, 225, 231

Kennedy, John F., 394–95

Kentucky Fried Chicken, 222, 239

Kenya, 207, 294, 329

Keynes, John Maynard, 17, 163

Keynesianism, 20, 348

Khian Sea, 289

Kidder Peabody, 347

Kilts, James M., 220

Kmart, 98, 291, 332

Knopf, 104

Knox, George, 201

Koch, Peter, 75

Kohlberg Kravis Roberts, 227

Koop, C. Everett, 200, 202

Korea, South, 182, 205, 235, 284, 285, 288, 294, 296, 300, 321, 326, 355, 356, 376, 423; cigarettes in, 200, 201, 203–4; consumer electronics in, 56–57; migrant workers from, 298, 302, 304, 306–7; piracy in, 142–43; as potential market, 181

Kraft Foods, 213, 237, 241; history of, 216–17; Philip Morris's acquisition of, 216, 217–18, 229, 231
Kraft General Foods (KGF), 218–21, 225, 244; health concerns and, 238, 239
Krasnow, Bob, 114
Kulkarni, Mohan, 377
Kurr, Rainer, 66
Kutsukaka, Mitsuo, 65
Kuwait, 297, 396

labels, on food products, 239
labor market, 17; growth of labor pool and, 293–94; increased mobility of, 300 (see also migration); restructuring of, 291–93; women's entry into, 294–96. See also division of labor, global; unemployment; workplace
labor movement, 86, 87, 310–13; auto industry and, 261, 262, 312–13, 316, 317–318, 319, 320; erosion of power of, 310–311, 312–13, 316, 317–18, 343; in Japan, 266, 311–12; in Mexico, 318, 319, 320; migration and, 303–4
Lagardère, Jean-Luc, 83
L.A. Gear, 327
Latvia, 220
lawyers, corporate, 345, 352
layoffs, 416, 420; in auto industry, 268, 274, 278, 291, 312–13, 317–18
lean production, 265–68, 312, 315–16, 318, 331
least developed countries (LDCs), 287. See also developing countries
leisure time, 28, 40, 247, 334–35
Leninism, 20
leveraged buyouts, 378, 379–80, 411, 412
Levi Strauss, 171, 285, 331–32, 335
Levitt, Theodore, 168
Literary Guild, 101, 103
L.L. Bean, 173
lobbying, 345, 346
local content rules, 279–80
localism, 21–22
London Stock Exchange, 399, 400, 401

Maastricht Treaty, 351
MacArthur, Douglas, 265–66
MacBride, Seán, 106
McDonald's, 79, 167, 172, 235, 246, 291; health concerns and, 238–39
McKinsey & Co, 26, 27–28, 82
Macmillan, 99
McNamara, Robert, 353
Madonna, 148, 151, 154, 165
magazines: proliferation of, 173; published by Bertelsmann, 69, 74–77, 81–84, 86, 117
Malawi, tobacco grown in, 205, 206, 207

Malaysia, 142, 249, 285, 287, 325, 383
malls. See shopping centers and malls
malnutrition, 210, 211, 212, 245–46, 247, 253, 353
Mandai, Junshiro, 62
Manufacturers Hanover Trust Co., 379, 412–13
manufacturing, 310–34; child labor in, 333–34; contracting-out in, 325–26, 327–28, 331–34; in export-processing zones, 300–301, 321, 326–27; at foreign-owned factories in U.S., 321–25; global division of labor and, 283–86; informal economy and, 328–29; job rotation in, 315, 316; just in time production in, 267, 268, 312, 315–16, 332; lean production in, 265–68, 312, 315–16, 318, 331; loss of jobs in, 53–54, 259, 268, 274–76, 291–92, 310, 317–20, 325, 332, 356, 416–17; migration to cities and, 299–301; relocated to low-wage enclaves, 53–54, 274–76, 318–20, 325, 326, 332, 356; of sport shoes, 325–26, 327–28; in sweat shops, 330–31, 333; team production in, 266, 314–15, 316, 318; wage trends in, 313–14, 330–31. See also factories; mass production
maquiladoras, 64, 254–55
Mares, Peter, 326–27
Marine Mammal Protection Act, 351
marketing and promotion, 16, 168–83; aimed at children, 166, 241; alternatives to advertising in, 173; in auto industry, 267; of books, 98–100, 109, 110; of cigarettes, 189–92, 193, 195, 196–98; decline in effectiveness of, 174; developing countries' potential and, 179–80, 181–183; emphasis on, 168; focused on wealthiest countries, 176, 178; in food industry, 239, 241–42, 246; global ads in, 168–171, 174, 178; language problems and, 170–71; local sensibilities and, 171; in music industry, 114, 148–49; pop songs in, 147–48, 154; proliferation of ads and, 172–73; of Sony, 48–52, 61; worldwide expenditures on, 171–72
market niches, 173, 178
market research, 174–75
Marlboro, 16, 169, 185, 187, 188, 194, 196, 198, 200–201, 204; ad campaigns for, 189–92, 193, 195; history of, 189–90
Marlboro man, 188, 190–92, 193, 195, 196, 202, 204
Marshall Plan, 105
Marx, Karl, 288
Marxism, 155
Mason, James O., 201–2
mass production, 259, 312, 315; introduced

at Ford, 260–61; Japanese modification of, 265–68; variety introduced into, 262. *See also* factories; manufacturing
Matra, 83
Matsushita, 16, 26, 31, 44–45, 48, 55–56, 57, 61, 62, 92, 130, 133, 144, 147, 182
Mattel, 177
Maucher, Helmut, 226
Mauritius, 285
Maxwell, Hamish, 198, 199, 220, 221, 222; background of, 213–14; food companies acquired by, 212–13, 214–18, 219
Maxwell, Robert, 68, 76, 90, 92, 97, 99, 108
Mayer, Peter, 104
Mazda, 271–72, 315
MCA, 26, 31, 92, 133, 144, 146
merchandising, 146
Merck, 182
mergers and acquisitions: in banking, 411–413; capital needed for, 400; in entertainment industry, 67, 80, 104–5, 116–36; in food industry, 212–18, 219, 226–28, 229–32; history of, 231; leveraged buyouts and, 378, 379–80, 411, 412; in publishing industry, 91–92, 93
Mexico, 284, 294, 295, 351; auto plants relocated to, 318–20; bank loans to, 369, 370, 371, 372; cigarettes in, 191, 192; eating habits in, 246; as food exporter, 253–56; foreign cultural domination feared in, 106, 107; labor movement in, 318, 319, 320; *maquiladoras* in, 64, 254–55; migrant workers from, 298, 302–3, 307; NAFTA and, 253–54, 351, 355–57, 402
Michelin, 322
microwave cooking, 247, 248–49
Middle East: migrant labor in, 296, 297; oil-producing nations in, 286, 368, 396. *See also specific countries*
Middle East Credit Company (MECICO), 377
migration, 296–309; to cities, 179, 210, 299–301; of college and university graduates, 304, 309; cultural attitudes about work and, 296–97; historic perspective on, 297–99; illegal, 298, 303, 307; Japanese labor shortage and, 306–7; local labor-relations culture changed by, 303–4; loss of skilled workers and professionals due to, 309; neoclassical economic theory and, 303; preservation of cultural identity and, 304, 307, 308; racial and ethnic tensions resulting from, 298, 302, 304, 307–9; receiving countries affected by, 303–6, 307–9; transnational networks of poor people and, 302–3; to Western Europe, 296, 305–6, 308–9

Milan Stock Exchange, 401
Miles, Michael, 198, 214, 218, 219, 220, 221–22
Milken, Michael, 378
Milli Vanilli, 123
Minckwitz, Bernard von, 103
Mini Disc, 144
minimum wage, 327
Mitsubishi Bank, 410
Mitsubishi Electric, 61–62
Mitsui Bank, 62
Miyaoka, Senri, 57
Mobil, 243
Mohn, Reinhard, 68, 70–79, 83–89, 116. *See also* Bertelsmann
money, 17, 359–418; in American life, 413–14; currency devaluations and, 397; electronic transfers of, 385–91; Eurodollars and, 365, 395, 397, 400, 418; foreign-exchange trade and, 390–91, 395–96, 397–98; value of, 385, 395–96. *See also* banking and financial services; *specific currencies*
money laundering, 389
money-market funds, 393
Monsanto, 279
Montgomery Ward, 335
Moore, George, 364–65
J. P. Morgan, 382, 410, 411
Morita, Akio, 42–67, 136, 323, 346; Asia as viewed by, 64–65; music industry and, 125, 127, 128; U.S. as viewed by, 50, 51, 53–55. *See also* Sony
Morita, Masaaki, 62–63
Motorola, 57
Mottola, Tommy, 132
movies, 26, 27, 28, 36, 38, 55, 94, 104–5, 107, 132, 153; cultural imperialism and, 159–60; foreign acquisition of U.S. studios and, 80, 125, 128, 129, 134–36; violence in, 157
Mozambique, 252
MTV, 38–39, 126, 138, 153–54, 157, 171
multiculturalism, 308
multinational corporations, 14, 15, 168, 423–25; courted by developing countries, 424. *See also* global corporations; *specific corporations*
multiple-channel recording, 151–52
Murdoch, Rupert, 76, 84, 92, 99, 380
Murray, William, 213
music, 94; classical, 113, 118–19; expressions of discontent in, 36–37, 38–39; in workplace, 40–41
music industry, 26, 27–28, 112–36, 145–160; Bertelsmann in, 26, 73, 83, 116–23, 139, 140, 142, 143, 144–45, 150, 155, 158–59; cultural imperialism and, 149–150; demographics and, 29; distribution

music industry (*cont.*)
in, 113; downturn and resurgence of
(1980s), 126–27; foreign acquisition of
U.S. companies and, 67, 104–5, 116–36;
globalization of market and, 112–13,
137–41, 145–46, 151–52; local traditions and, 149–53; marketing and promotion in, 114, 148–49; merchandise
sales and, 146; non-retail markets of,
147–48; piracy and, 141–42, 143, 144–
145; prices and, 146–47; selection of talent in, 147; social critics and, 155;
superstars and, 113, 114; synergy in,
154; talent-raiding campaigns in, 122;
technology and, 27, 143–44, 152; uneasy
alliance of "creative types" and "suits"
in, 114–15, 120
music videos, 153–54, 155, 157

Nabisco, 168, 214, 229. *See also* RJR
Nabisco
Nader, Ralph, 352
Nannen, Henri, 74–75
National City Bank, 362–63, 369
national debt, 341–42, 403, 404, 406–7,
408
national governments: authority crisis of,
19–20, 340–41, 342, 348, 408–9, 422–
423, 428, 427; Bertelsmann's views on,
88; breakup of nations and, 20, 340–41;
control over national economies lost by,
20–21, 340, 408–9, 422–23, 428; corporations' political influence over, 342–47,
348; global economic integration and,
408–9, 415, 421–23; global financial
markets and, 397–98; large corporations'
relationships with, 281–82; public-service
jobs in, 339–40; reorganization of global
production and, 339–42, 357–58; socially
integrative role of, 340, 341; stateless corporations and, 280–81, 342, 424
nationalism, 20, 104, 427, 429
NBC, 91, 117, 347
Nescafé, 220, 225
Nestlé, 16, 172, 173, 182, 187, 206, 211,
219, 220, 222–26, 227, 275, 346
Netherlands, 295, 311, 314; banking in,
411, 412
New Deal, 341, 392
Newhouse, 91–92, 99
newly industrializing countries (NICs), 284,
285; aspiring, 284–85; GATT and, 352;
migrant workers from, 299. *See also* developing countries
New York Stock Exchange, 399, 400–401,
407
niche marketing, 173, 178
Niewiarra, Manfred, 79
Nigeria, 182

Nike, 15, 54, 325–26, 327–28
Nikko Securities, 405
Nippon Life, 406
Nissan, 355
Nixon, Richard M., 395, 396
Nomura Securities, 405
North American Free Trade Agreement
(NAFTA), 253–54, 350, 351, 355–57,
402
North Carolina National Bank (NCNB),
413
Norway, 171

O'Brien, Richard, 396–97
oceans: pollution of, 289–90
Ochno, Taiichi, 265, 266
Ohga, Norio, 45, 57–58, 63, 64, 125, 127,
134
oil, 286, 368, 396
O'Neill, Richard, 142–43
organic food, 238
Organization of Petroleum Exporting Countries (OPEC), 286
Orwell, George, 39–40

packaging, 242–43, 244–45, 289
Pakistan, 207, 226, 294; migrant workers
from, 296, 297, 302
Paley, William, 124, 127
Panama, 285, 357
Paraguay, 207
Pareles, John, 146, 154
Parents Music Resource Center, 155
part-time work, 310, 340
Passell, Peter, 387, 388, 390
patents, 354
Pepsico (Pepsi-Cola), 127, 128, 148, 167,
172, 182, 213, 241, 246, 254
Perot, Ross, 343
Persian Gulf War, 297
Peru, 369
Peters, Jon, 129, 135
Petersen, Donald E., 268, 271, 272, 314
petrodollars, 368, 396
pharmaceutical industry, 192, 230, 354
Philip Morris, 14, 16, 18, 172, 176, 182; in
cigarette industry, 184–85, 186–204,
206, 212–15, 218, 222, 225, 228, 229,
286; diversification of, 187–88, 212–13;
in food industry, 211, 212–22, 225, 226,
228–29, 231, 237–38, 239, 240; foreign
tobacco used by, 206; history of, 188–
192; overseas markets developed by, 187,
188, 198–204; political influence of, 344;
potential new smokers targeted by, 195–
197. *See also* Marlboro
Philippines, 142, 179–80, 182, 285; Citibank's credit-card business in, 377; Citibank's loans to, 368; data-processing

jobs in, 336–37; eating habits in, 246; as food exporter, 251–52; garment industry in, 333–34; migrant workers from, 296, 297, 298, 304, 306–7; shopping malls in, 165–66; tobacco grown in, 206, 207
Philips, 16, 26, 53, 113, 120, 122, 133, 144, 147, 275
Phillips-Van Heusen, 332
Pillsbury, 254
piracy, 141–43, 144–45
Pittman, Robert, 157
Poland, 171, 305, 331
politics: American pop culture and, 37–38; corporate interests and, 342–47, 348; electoral process and, 343, 414; as spectator sport, 41. See also national governments
pollution, 289–90, 352
PolyGram, 26, 120, 132
population growth, 179, 211, 294, 299
Portugal, 297
postindustrial age, 334
potato chips, 242
poverty, 179–80, 183, 288, 289, 293, 299
prawns, 251–52
Prentice Hall, 96
prison-made goods, 332
privatization, 339, 357, 424
Procter & Gamble, 171, 172, 182, 221, 225
production: environment damaged by, 289–290. See also factories; manufacturing; mass production; workplace
productivity, 312, 417; team concept and, 315, 316, 318
profit-sharing, 87–88
propaganda, 39–40
protectionism, 349, 350
Prudential, 393
public relations, 345, 346
public-service jobs, 339–40
publishing industry, 68–111; Americans as fashion setters in, 97–98; assembly-line approach in, 100; bottom line as driving force in, 108; commercialization of, 93, 109–11; consolidation of, 91–92, 93; cultural domination and, 104–7; educational, 91, 96, 105; European integration and, 104; executive censorship in, 108–9; foreign acquisition of U.S. houses and, 92, 94, 97, 100–103, 104–5; global products and, 80–81, 94–95; marketing and promotion in, 98–100, 109, 110; obstacles to globalization of, 104–7; retail distribution and, 98–100, 109, 110; scientific, 96–97; synergies in, 92–93; technology and, 109; trade-book, 93–96, 98–100, 109–11. See also authors; books; Bertelsmann; specific publishers

purchasing power, wage levels and, 314

quality control, 324–25
Quayle, Dan, 202, 279
Quotron, 381

radio, 48, 107, 143, 148–49
Random House, 91, 92, 99, 100, 102, 104
RCA, 26, 83, 91, 92, 116–23, 276, 280; Bertelsmann's acquisition of, 116–18; Bertelsmann's management of, 119–23
RC Cola, 154
Reagan, Ronald, 20, 55, 99, 153, 167, 202, 206, 231, 293, 339–40, 342, 351, 367, 375, 406, 410
real-estate market: banking and, 380–81, 393–94, 413; Japanese investors and, 405, 407, 408
recycling, 351
Redstone, Sumner, 138
Reebok, 49, 326, 327
Reed, John S., 363, 364, 366–67, 371, 372, 373, 375, 376, 378, 379, 380, 381, 382–384, 412
Regan, Donald, 404
Regulation Q, 392–93
Reich, Robert, 280, 281, 334, 345
religion, 40, 340; fundamentalism and, 37, 140, 155, 429
Reward America program, 381
Richman, John M., 217–18
Riesman, David, 155
R. J. Reynolds, 189, 203, 204, 214, 229
RJR Nabisco, 172, 182, 201, 227, 228; in cigarette industry, 195, 196, 197, 198, 206
Robinson's Galleria (Manila), 165–66
robots, 62–63, 268, 316, 324
rock 'n' roll, 38
Rohatyn, Felix, 55, 386
Ross, Ken, 128
Rostow, Walt, 288
Rubberworld, 333
Rubin, Stephen, 103
Russia, 305, 337, 421, 424; cigarettes in, 185, 195; entertainment industry and, 139–40; global products in, 167. See also Soviet Union

Saatchi, Charles and Maurice, 170
St. Lucia, 285
Samsung, 56–57
Sara Lee, 227
Sassen, Saskia, 299, 301
Saudi Arabia, 140, 396
savings-and-loan crisis, 381, 393–94, 415
Saztec, 336–37
Scandinavia, 311

Schiffrin, Andre, 108
Schmuckli, Jacob, 66
Scholl-Latour, Peter, 77
Schulhof, Michael P., 61, 66, 128, 130–31, 132–33, 134
Schulte-Hillen, Gerd, 74–76, 77, 78, 81, 82–83, 85–86
Schumpeter, Joseph, 278
Schwinn, 54, 285
Sears, 172, 332, 335, 393, 416
secessionary impulses, 20, 340–41
securities: banking and, 399–401, 411, 412; Japanese vs. U.S., 410–11; taxes on gains from, 416; U.S.-government, 386, 406, 408, 411
Securities and Exchange Commission (SEC), 391
Security Pacific, 400, 412
semiconductors, 46, 57, 63
Senegal, 289
Serbia, 421
Servan-Schreiber, Jean-Jacques, 423
service industries, 259–60, 293
Shaiken, Harley, 319–20
Shannon International Free Port, 300
shopping centers and malls, 164–66, 168, 178–79; decline of, 180; in developing countries, 165–66
Siemens, 275
Sierra Leone, 252
Simon & Schuster, 91, 96, 97, 109
Singapore, 142, 250, 284, 285, 294, 296, 300, 305, 376–77, 383
slave trade, 298
Sloan, Alfred P., 85, 262
Smith, Adam, 287–88
"smokers' rights" movement, 195
smoking. See cigarettes
snack industry, 240–42, 246
Snyder, Richard, 109, 110
socialism, 20, 106, 287, 424
software industry, 145, 337
Somalia, 252–53, 299
Sommer, Ron, 134
Sony, 16, 18, 42–67, 79, 138, 182, 306, 357, 410; Betamax and, 55–56, 57, 125; consumer electronics and, 42–67, 130–132, 133, 134, 141, 143–45, 146–47; diversification of, 57, 63, 67, 80; Dothan, Ala., plant of, 322–25; downturn of (1980s), 55–57, 61; early days of, 42–48; economic development in Asia and, 63–65; engineering talent of, concentrated in Japan, 63, 66; erosion of U.S. industry and, 53–55; four-part revitalization of (1990s), 63–67; "global localization" strategy of, 65–66; hardware and software combined by, 125, 130–31, 132–34; Japanese business culture and,
61–62; local sensibilities respected by, 59; marketing of, 48–52, 61; in movie industry, 125, 128, 129, 130–31, 132–33, 134–36; in music industry, 26, 58, 67, 113, 116, 124–35; overseas production facilities of, 52–53, 59, 63–65, 66; political influence of, 346; as quintessentially Japanese corporation, 60–61; as un-Japanese company, 59–60
Sony Music, 26, 130–35, 146, 155
Sony Pictures, 130–31, 132–33, 134–36
South Africa, 152
Soviet Union, 105, 283–84, 286, 339, 340, 355, 420. See also Russia
Spain, 291, 311, 397, 401, 411, 412
Spiegel, Der, 74, 81
Spielberg, Steven, 134, 135
sport-shoe industry, 325–26, 327–28
Springer, Axel, 74
Springsteen, Bruce, 114, 124, 128, 129
Sri Lanka, 151, 207, 285, 287, 289; textile factories in, 326–27
standard of living, 340, 375; migration and, 296, 299, 303
state taxes: on foreign-owned firms, 345–46
Steel, Danielle, 94
Stempel, Robert C., 317
Stern, 74–76, 77, 81
stock markets, 399, 400–401, 407, 410
Storr, Hans, 198, 228–29
strategic alliances, 424; in auto industry, 271–74, 316
strikes, 311, 320
subsistence farming, 210, 291, 299
suburbs, migration to, 276–77
sugar, 240, 247, 251, 287
Sumitomo Bank, 405–6
supermarkets, 175, 181, 218, 230; in affluent vs. poor neighborhoods, 243–44; in developing countries, 166
Supreme Court, U.S., 188, 193
sweat shops, 330–31, 333
Sweden, 314, 340; local music in, 150–51
SWIFT (Society of Worldwide Interbank Financial Telecommunications), 387–88
Switzerland, 171, 250, 296, 423; banking in, 389, 397, 412
synergy, 190, 215; entertainment industry and, 131, 132–34; music industry and, 154; publishing industry and, 92–93

Taiwan, 142, 284, 285, 288, 294, 300, 321, 326, 355, 376; cigarettes in, 200, 201, 202, 204; as food exporter, 251–52; migrant labor in, 296–97, 307; as potential market, 181
Tanzania, 150, 207
tape players: digital audiotape (DAT) and, 133, 143–45; Walkman, 49, 63, 131–32

tape recorders, 45–46, 58
taxes, 344, 345, 348, 409; capital gains and, 416; on corporate earnings, 344, 345–46; excise, 193–94, 199; global money-transfer system and evasion of, 388–89, 390–91; transfer pricing and, 345
Tax Reform Act (1986), 344
Taylor, Peter, 206–7
team production, 266, 314–15, 316, 318
technology, 398; banking and, 386–87, 398–99; bioengineering and, 251, 426; communications industry and, 79; competitiveness of largest firms and, 425; consumer electronics and, 42–67, 143–146; entertainment industry and, 26–27, 40; food industry and, 235, 251, 426; jobs crisis and, 426; music industry and, 27, 143–44, 152; publishing industry and, 109
telecommunications, 337
telemarketing, 172, 173
television, 15, 27, 36, 38, 80, 91, 107, 108, 167, 249; cable (see cable television); cigarette advertising banned from, 193, 195; cultural imperialism and, 159–60; global ads on, 168–71; in Mexico, 246; music videos on, 153–54, 157; proliferation of channels on, 172–73; psychological effects of, 156–59
temporary employment, 340
Texas Instruments, 337
textile factories, 326–27
Thailand, 142, 143, 285, 326; cigarettes in, 201, 204; Citibank's credit-card business in, 377; as food exporter, 251–52; tobacco grown in, 205, 206
Thatcher, Margaret, 20, 52–53, 339–40, 344
theme parks, 30–35, 164, 398
Third World. See developing countries; newly industrializing countries; specific countries
Thompson, Donald N., 400
Thoreau, Henry David, 108
Thorn-EMI, 26
Thurow, Lester, 55
Thyssen, 75, 76
Time Inc., 335
Time Warner, 16, 68, 80, 92, 97
Tisch, Laurence A., 126, 127
tobacco: growing of, 205–7; mood-altering properties of, 185–86. See also cigarettes
Tobacco Heritage Committee, 204
Tobacco Institute, 195, 199, 200
Togo, 252
Tokyo Stock Exchange, 401, 407
tourism, 29–35; degradation of natural environment and, 30; theme parks and, 30–35
toxins, exportation of, 289
Toyota, 265–67, 316, 320, 345, 411
Trade Act (1974), 201, 202
trade-advisory panels, 352
trade barriers, 176. See also free trade
trade deficit, 54–55, 58, 64, 200, 201, 221, 229, 403, 404–5
transfer pricing, 345
transistor technology, 46–48
translations, 94
travel, 29–35, 236. See also tourism
Treasury, U.S., 342, 356, 394, 406
Treasury bonds and bills, 386, 406, 408, 411
Trimmer, Rev. Thomas E., 332–33
Trinidad, 151
tropical oils, 251, 287
Truman, Harry S., 365
Trump, Donald, 378, 380, 414
Tsuda, Akihiko, 125
tuna, 351
Tunisia, 151, 207
Turkey, 295; migrant workers from, 296, 308

Uganda, 286
Ukraine, 337
unemployment, 178, 221, 290–93, 294, 329, 355, 416–17, 422; factory relocation and, 276; government policies and, 339–40, 348; human costs of, 292; wage levels and, 313
unemployment benefits, 317
Unilever, 16, 172, 182, 219, 336, 346
unitary taxation, 345–46
United Auto Workers (UAW), 313, 314, 315, 316, 317, 318
United Nations, 29, 284, 300
United Nations Educational, Scientific, and Cultural Organization (UNESCO), 106
Universal Pictures, 57
Uruguay, 369
U.S. Agency for International Development (USAID), 325
U.S. Information Agency, 105

Vale, Norman, 169
Valenti, Jack, 38
Vanity-Fair, 84
vegetables, 245, 254–55; "counter-seasonal," 235–36
Viacom, 138
video cassette recorders (VCRs), 55–56, 57, 63, 125
video home system (VHS), 55–56, 57
videos, 107, 140; music, 153–54, 155, 157; pirated, 142–43
Vietnam, migration from, 299, 301, 307

violence, media portrayals of, 155, 156–57, 158–59
Virginia Slims, 196
Virgin Music Group, 132
Visser, Margaret, 248–49
Vitale, Alberto, 98, 101, 102, 103
Voice of America, 38, 40
Volcker, Paul, 396, 406
Volkswagen, 320

Wada, Yoshihiro, 273
wages, 321, 340, 375; in auto industry, 260–61, 262, 313; downward pressure on, 313–14, 330–31, 349, 384, 420, 427; factory relocation and, 53–54, 274–276, 318–20, 325, 326, 332, 356; of skilled vs. unskilled workers, 357
Waldenbooks, 98
Wales, 151
Walkman, 49, 63, 131–32
Warner, 26, 113, 122, 129, 132, 142
Washington, D.C., immigrants in, 307–8
Wasserman, Lew, 133
wealth, disparities of, 179–80, 277, 278, 341–42
Weissman, George, 190, 193
Welch, John, 118
welfare, 305, 341, 357
Wenner, Jann, 38
Whirlpool, 53
Winston, 193
Woessner, Frank, 85
Woessner, Mark, 77–78, 79–80, 81, 85–86, 101, 116, 117, 119, 121, 141
Wolters Kluwer, 97

women: cigarettes marketed to, 189, 196; as factory workers, 321, 325, 326–27, 328–29, 332–33; "feminization" of work and, 294–96; migration of, 300–301, 304
work hours, 28, 40
workplace, 16–17, 259–358; automation of, 268, 310, 324, 325, 420; deregulation of, 294–95; establishing global standards for, 333–34; government policies and, 339–42, 357–58; music in, 40–41. See also automobile industry; division of labor, global; factories; labor market; manufacturing; mass production
World Bank, 207, 250, 250, 251, 288, 299–300, 352–53, 368, 371
"world beat," 152
world's fairs, 31, 34–35, 398
World Tourism Organization, 29
World War II, 70–71, 263, 265, 352, 394, 426
Wriston, Walter B., 364–66, 367–69, 370, 372, 378, 380, 391

Yasuda Mutual Life, 406
yen (Japan), 64, 314, 404–5, 407
Yetnikoff, Walter, 114–15, 125, 126, 127, 128–29
Yeutter, Clayton, 201, 202, 203
Yugoslavia, 289, 421
Yunich, Peter, 109

Zambia, 286
Zenith, 57
Zimbabwe, 206